CALIFORNIA
Property and Casualty

Insurance License Exam Prep
Updated Yearly

Study Guide Includes State Law Supplement and 3 Complete Practice Tests

Previously published under ISBN 9798632395540 as *2020 Edition California Property and Casualty Insurance Agent/Broker Exam Prep: Includes 3 Complete Practice Exams with Fully Explained Answers*

Leland Chant

This edition contains the most thorough and accurate information available at printing time. Due to the dynamic nature of insurance licensing, examination content outlines constantly change, and this edition may not feature this new or revised content.

This study guide provides complete and reliable information regarding the covered subject matter. The publisher is not engaged in providing accounting, legal, or other professional services. If such assistance is required, seek the services of a competent professional.

If you find errors or incorrect information in this publication or have any questions or comments, please email us at brightideapublishers@gmail.com.

© 2024 Leland Chant All rights reserved.
Published by Bright Idea Publishers.
Printed in the United States of America.
ISBN: 9798745959318

CONTENTS

INTRODUCTION

Thank you for choosing Bright Idea Publishers. You are preparing to pass the California Property and Casualty Examination using the content found in this book. We've developed our state-specific prep books based on the exam content outlines published by testing providers in each state (e.g., Pearson VUE, PSI Exams, Prometric). Leland Chant, who has over two decades of experience in the Insurance industry, provides the most up-to-date information that educates test-takers in a streamlined manner. Our number one goal is to prepare you for the actual exam and to help you pass the test on the first attempt.

Study Pointers

- The author presents the information in each chapter based on the exam subject matter outlines provided by the state of California. This material covers only the information you need to learn for the exam.
- Be sure to take notes. This best practice will help you be proactive and engage in the learning process to solidify these insurance concepts.
- Create an outline or "hint" sheet. This best practice will help you complete a full review at the end of each chapter or the end of the book.
- Review the Exam Index section later in this Introduction to identify how every chapter corresponds to the actual exam. Test questions are associated with each chapter to help focus your study efforts accordingly.
- Every so often, take a break from studying. If you have been hitting it hard, but feel like you're having trouble retaining the information, try taking a few days off to recharge your mind.
- Keep the information fresh by studying until the day of your exam. When you cannot take the exam immediately after finishing the book, you should begin the study and review process again. It is always better to delay taking the exam than to be unprepared while taking it.
- Practice exam answers include the page number to the corresponding section of the book. This feature will help streamline the studying process!

Test Taking Pointers

- Be sure to get a whole night's sleep, and don't study right before you take the exam. This best practice will allow you to be well-rested and alert when arriving at the testing center.
- Carefully read the test tutorial and be sure to follow the instructions. Depending on your state, test providers may divide the exam into multiple parts. In this case, you may not be able to go back to review your answers once you have completed the section.
- Be calm and feel at ease. Breathe deeply and remember it is just an exam. If you prepare, the correct answers will become clear if you put in the time.
- Read every question and all the answer choices carefully, but do so quickly. Try not to linger on any one question.
- If a particular question has you stumped, you can mark it for review and move on to the next question. Sometimes you may answer a question later in the exam, which may jog your memory.
- Answer every question!
- Try to understand what the question is asking. Don't allow unfamiliar terms to throw you off since test builders mostly use them as examples or distracters. Read the question multiple times if necessary.
- Rule out incorrect answers. Each answer you exclude increases your chance of selecting the correct one.
- Trust your first answer. If you studied thoroughly, you know the material. Listen to your gut instinct and try not to overthink the question.
- Keywords such as NEVER, ALWAYS, EVERY, EXCEPT, ALL, or NOT may change the meaning of a question. Be sure to pay extra attention to them.
- Every question is multiple choice, and they are commonly either direct questions, incomplete sentences, or "all of the following EXCEPT."
- Remember that being a little nervous is not a bad thing. Most people perform better when they know the heat is on.
- Most importantly, RELAX! If you put in the work and if you put in the time, the results will be there.

Setting Expectations

Before taking your state exam, you must know the material and be familiar with testing procedures and the testing center environment.

Each state provides a candidate handbook or bulletin containing important information about specific testing procedures:

- Scheduling or rescheduling exams;
- Required identification;
- Arriving at the testing center; and
- Items prohibited in the testing center.

Test-takers should read the Candidate Information Bulletin (CIB) in preparation for their exam. This handbook is on the California Department of Insurance (CDI) website and their state testing provider's (PSI Exams) website.

The Exam	<ul><li>It will test your knowledge and includes questions about various concepts and laws.</li><li>Test questions are designed to evaluate your basic understanding and retention of the material in this book.</li><li>Verify specific forms of identification required for your state exam by reviewing the candidate's handbook or bulletin or calling the testing center.</li></ul>
The Testing Center	<ul><li>Be sure to arrive at least 30 minutes before your scheduled exam.</li><li>You are not allowed to take personal items like cell phones or study materials into the testing center. Some testing centers will provide lockers.</li><li>Food, drinks, or gum are not allowed inside the testing center.</li><li>Have your identification ready when you check in at the front desk.</li><li>Adjust the seat height and computer monitor as needed to feel comfortable.</li><li>Before beginning a computer-based exam, you will have a chance to take a tutorial to help you learn how to mark and review answers.</li><li>Remain focused and do not get distracted by others around you. Other test-takers may enter and leave the room while taking your exam.</li></ul>
Taking the Exam	<ul><li>Most testing centers will provide scratch paper and a pencil to write down challenging questions during the exam.</li><li>When you review marked questions, go over the rest of the questions to ensure you didn't overlook any familiar concepts or terms that change what the question is asking.</li></ul>

Exam Index

The Exam Index will help you focus your studying. According to each chapter, all three practice tests include the number of questions. You will most certainly benefit when taking the actual exam by concentrating your efforts.

California Property and Casualty Insurance Examination
150 Questions (plus five to ten non-scored experimental questions)
Time Limit: 3 hours 15 minutes
Passing Score: 60%

CHAPTER	# OF QUESTIONS
Basic Insurance Concepts and Principles	7
Contract Law	6
The Insurance Marketplace	8
Basic Legal Concepts – Tort Law	6
Property and Casualty Basics	7
Property and Casualty Policies – General	7
Dwelling Policy	14
Homeowners Policy	12
Homeowners – Section I: Property Coverage	8
Homeowners – Section II: Liability Coverage	8
Personal Auto	14
Other Personal Lines Policies	13
Commercial Coverages	5
Commercial General Liability (CGL)	5
Commercial Auto	5
Other Commercial Coverages	4
Farm	5
Businessowners	4
Ocean Marine	4
Surety Bonds and General Bond Concepts	4
Workers Compensation – General Concepts	4
Total	**150**

ISO

The Insurance Services Office (ISO) is essential in property and casualty or personal lines insurance licensing exams. One of the ISO's many functions is to create standardized property and casualty insurance policies approved by individual states and utilized as a standard policy form for insurers. The basic ISO policy forms are modified to comply with each state's regulations. They may be modified to a degree by each insurance company to create its own policy form.

State insurance licensing exams will test over the standard ISO policies approved by the state to provide equal opportunities for a passing score to prospective licensees from different insurance companies.

CHAPTER 1:
Basic Insurance Concepts and Principles

Before you learn about specific policies and their provisions, you will first need to understand some basic concepts and terms associated with the insurance industry. This chapter discusses ideas that make it easier for you to learn the rest of the content in this book, so you need to master these concepts before moving on to the next chapter.

- Examples of Insurance
- Risk
- Peril
- Hazard
- Law of Large Numbers
- Loss and Loss Exposure
- Risk Management Techniques
- Ideally Insurable Risk
- Insurable Events
- Insurable Interest
- Underwriting
- Benefits and Costs of Insurance to Society
- Self-Funding
- Deductible
- Reinsurance
- Classes of Lines of Insurance

Examples of Insurance

Insurance is a transfer of loss or risk from a business entity or a person to an insurance provider, which then spreads the costs of unexpected losses to many people. If there were no insurance, the cost of a loss would have to be incurred solely by the person who suffered the loss.

In the eyes of the law, a person is a legal entity that acts on behalf of itself. People accept legal and civil responsibility for their actions and make contracts in their own name. Individual human beings, partnerships, corporations, associations, and trusts are included in the definition of a person.

Insurance is a contract in which one individual undertakes to indemnify another individual against damage, loss, or liability arising from an unknown event (Cal. Ins. Code Section 22).

In broader terms, insurance is the legal agreement, or contract, in which the two parties agree to the limits of the indemnification. The parties also agree to the contract's terms and conditions and the consideration (things of value) that will be exchanged.

Risk

Risk is the uncertainty or likelihood that a loss occurs. There are two types of risk – pure risk and speculative risk, only one of which can be insured.

- *Pure risk* applies to circumstances that can only result in no change or a loss. There is no chance for financial gain. Pure risk is the only kind of risk that insurance companies accept.
- *Speculative risk* includes the opportunity for either gain or loss. Gambling is an example of speculative risk, and insurance companies cannot insure these types of risk.

Peril

In an insurance policy, *perils* are the insured against *causes of loss* that insurance providers will cover.

- *Property insurance* insures against (covers) the loss of physical property or the loss of its ability to produce income;
- *Casualty insurance* insures against the resulting liabilities from the loss or damage of property;
- *Life insurance* insures against the financial loss caused by the untimely death of an insured; and
- *Health insurance* insures against the loss of income or medical expenses caused by the insured's accidental injury or sickness.

Hazard

Hazards are circumstances or settings that increase the likelihood of an insured loss. Conditions such as congested traffic or slippery floors are hazards and may increase the odds of a loss occurring. Insurers categorize hazards according to physical, moral, or morale hazards.

- *Physical hazards* arise from the risk's structural, material, or operational features, separate from those managing or owning it.
- *Moral hazards* deal with any applicant who lies on an insurance application or submits fraudulent claims against an insurer.
- *Morale hazards* refer to an increase in the danger presented by a risk, stemming from the insured's apathy towards loss because of the presence of insurance. (e.g., "I have no intention of fixing this. If it breaks, my insurance policy will pay to have it replaced.")

Legal hazards describe an array of legal or regulatory conditions that affect an insurer's ability to collect premiums comparable in value with the loss exposure the insurer must bear.

Law of Large Numbers

The foundation of insurance is sharing risk between a large pool of people (a homogenous group) with a similar exposure to loss. The *law of large numbers* states that the actual losses will be more predictable among a *larger* group of people having a similar loss exposure. This law forms the basis for the statistical prediction of loss which insurers use to calculate insurance rates.

Example 1.1 – When an insurance company issues a policy on a 35-year-old male, the company cannot know or accurately predict when he will die. However, the law of large numbers examines a large group of similar risks, which in this case are 35-year-old males of similar lifestyles and health conditions. It makes conclusions based on the statistics of past losses. The law of large numbers gives the insurer a general idea about the predicted time of death for these insureds and sets the premiums accordingly.

Loss and Loss Exposure

Loss is the disappearance, reduction, or decrease of the value of the property or person insured under a policy resulting from a named peril. Insurance provides a way to transfer loss.

A unit of measure used to determine insurance coverage rates is known as *exposure*. A large number of units with the same or similar loss exposure are known as *homogeneous*. Sharing risk between a sizeable homogeneous group with similar loss exposure constitutes the basis of insurance.

Depending on the subject, a *loss* is defined in different ways. The following are standard definitions of loss:

- In *property insurance*, a loss is defined as the amount of the reduction in the value of an insured property caused by a peril insured against;
- In *casualty insurance*, a loss is defined as the amount paid to a third party on behalf of an insured who was legally obligated to pay; and
- In *insurer operations*, a loss is defined as the basis of a claim for indemnification or damages against an insurance policy.

Loss exposure refers to the potential for loss which is the basis for setting insurance rates. Again, the definition can vary in the following ways:

- In *property insurance*, loss exposure is based on the location of the property, type of construction, occupancy, fire protection class, adjacent structures, etc.

- In *general casualty*, loss exposure is based upon area, gross receipts, payroll, and the insured's risk and location; and
- In *automobile liability*, loss exposure factors include a driver's age, the territory of a garage, etc.

Risk Situations Presenting the Possibility of Loss

When establishing an insurance program, insureds must first recognize their loss exposure. They must also acknowledge the probability of how likely a loss will occur and how "big" the loss might be. Because of the severity of the possible loss, certain risks will demand attention above others.

For example, a person who handles power tools when engaged in the hobby of carpentry is exposed to the possibility of injuring their hand. If the person is a heart surgeon, this would be considered a critical risk of financial loss because the injury may prevent them from performing their job. However, when the individual is a television announcer, the loss of hand function may be considered a less significant risk.

Exposures to potential losses should be classified into appropriate groups and ranked in the order of their importance:

- *Critical risks* include every exposure in which the potential losses are of the magnitude that would result in the financial ruination of the insured, their business, or their family;
- *Important risks* include loss exposures which would lead the person to major lifestyle changes or a change in profession; and
- *Unimportant risks* include those exposures in which the potential losses could be absorbed by current income or assets without imposing unnecessary lifestyle changes or financial strain.

In deciding to establish an insurance program, it would be prudent always to consider the following commonsense principles:

- Consider the odds;
- Never risk more than one can afford to lose; and
- Never risk a lot for a little.

Loss Costs – The ISO developed a rating method known as *loss costs*. This method provides insurers with a portion of a rate that does not include expense or profit provisions. It is based on actual cumulative loss and loss adjustment expenses projected through a future point in time. The insurer must add the expense and profit components to develop the final rate.

Risk Management Techniques

Sharing – *Sharing* is a way of dealing with risk for a group of individuals or businesses with the same or similar loss exposure to share the losses within that group. A reciprocal exchange of insurance is a formal arrangement for risk-sharing.

Transfer – The most effective approach to handling risk is to *transfer* it so that another party bears the loss. Insurance is the most accepted means of transferring risk from a person or group to an insurance company. Though buying insurance will not remove the risk of illness or death, it relieves the insured of the financial losses accompanying these risks.

There are numerous ways to transfer risk, including holding harmless agreements and other contractual agreements. Still, the most common and safest method is to buy insurance coverage.

Avoidance – *Avoidance* is one of the methods of dealing with risk, which means removing exposure to a loss. For instance, if a person wants to avoid the risk of dying in a motorcycle crash, they may choose never to ride a motorcycle. Risk avoidance can be effective, but it is hardly practical.

Retention – An insured's planned assumption of risk through self-insurance, co-payments, or deductibles is known as risk *retention*. Self-insurance is when the insured accepts responsibility for the loss before the insurance provider pays. The aim of retention is

1. To decrease expenses and improve cash flow;
2. To increase control of claim settlements and claim reserving; and
3. To finance losses that cannot be insured.

Reduction – Since risk usually cannot be avoided entirely, we often try to reduce the likelihood or severity of a loss. *Reduction* includes having an annual health exam to detect health problems early, installing smoke detectors in a home, or perhaps even changing one's lifestyle.

Ideally Insurable Risk

Even though insurance is one of the most effective ways to handle risks, insurers cannot cover every risk. As previously stated, insurance companies will only insure pure risks or those only involving a chance of loss without a chance of gain. However, not all pure risks are insurable. Certain elements or characteristics must exist before a pure risk can be insured:

- **The loss has to be due to chance (accidental)** – For a risk to be considered insurable, it must involve a possibility of loss that the insured cannot control.
- **The loss must be definite and measurable** – An insurable risk must involve losses with an exact time, place, cause, and amount. An insurance provider must determine the benefit amount and when it will pay the benefit.
- **The loss must be statistically predictable** – This characteristic allows insurance companies to estimate the severity and average frequency of future losses and to set appropriate premiums.
- **The loss cannot be catastrophic** – Insurance companies will not insure a risk that exposes them to catastrophic losses that would exceed certain limits. Usually, insurance policies exclude coverage for losses from wars or nuclear events. No statistical data exists that would allow for developing rates necessary to cover these events should they occur.
- **The loss exposure to be insured has to involve large homogenous units of exposure** – A sufficiently large pool of insureds with similar risks must be grouped into classes so the insurance company can predict losses using the law of large numbers. This large group allows insurers to accurately predict the average severity and frequency of future losses and set appropriate premiums. In life insurance policies, mortality tables allow insurers to estimate losses based on statistics.
- **The insurance must not be mandatory** – Insurers are not required to issue a policy to every applicant. An insurer must be able to require insureds to meet specific underwriting guidelines.

Insurable Events

If a likely future event could result in loss or liability to a person, it may be insurable (Cal. Ins. Code Section 250). These insurable events may never happen, but insurance can provide protection when those times do occur.

Losses become more *insurable* when they become more *predictable*. If a loss is *more unpredictable*, it becomes *less insurable*. For instance, a person cannot insure gambling losses or lottery outcomes because of unpredictability. The law does not address a limit as to the level of loss that may be insured against; it only clarifies the type of event that can be insured. The contract designates the level of loss to be indemnified (repaid).

Insurable Interest

The financial interest in any property that will be insured is known as *insurable interest*. In property and casualty insurance, insurable interest has to exist *at the time of loss*. The contract is void if the insured has no insurable interest. There are three requirements to prove insurable interest:

1. *Legitimate financial interest* in protecting the property that will be insured.
2. There has to be no potential for gain.
3. There has to be a potential for loss.

Underwriting

Underwriting is the process of reviewing insurance applications and the information on them. Specifically, it is a risk selection process.

Function – The underwriter's *function* refers to an insurer's operations where an employee, called an *underwriter*, classifies risks and evaluates applications submitted to the insurer. Underwriters determine whether or not to issue a policy and, if so, the policy's rates, terms, and conditions.

Loss Ratio – The *loss ratio* is a formula used by insurers to compare premium income to losses, including paid claims and expenses related to claims. The formula is as follows:

$$Loss\ ratio = (Loss\ adjusting\ expense + Incurred\ losses) \div Earned\ premium$$

Adverse Selection – Insurers strive to protect themselves from *adverse selection*, which refers to insuring risks more prone to losses than the average risk. Poorer risks seek insurance or file claims to a greater extent than better risks.

Insurance companies can refuse or restrict coverage for bad risks or charge them a higher rate for insurance coverage to protect themselves from adverse selection.

Spread of Risk – *Spread of risk*, or a profitable distribution of exposures, exists when poor risks are balanced with preferred risks, with "standard" or "average" risks in the middle. The reason for distributing risks is to protect the insurance company from adverse selection. This principle is the most fundamental in insurance.

Benefits and Costs of Insurance to Society

Reduction of Uncertainty – Individuals may significantly reduce uncertainty through insurance because insurance provides financial compensation for covered losses. Financial concerns, such as the breadwinner's death or a fire that destroys a home, are eliminated through the transfer of the uncertainty of loss to an insurer. While insurance cannot stop the stress and anxiety of losing a loved one or a valuable property, it can address the financial concern of such an event.

Society experiences a reduction in uncertainty because insurance providers use the law of large numbers to better predict losses for individuals or businesses.

Loss Control – Insured losses require insurers to pay claims. *Loss control* reduces the money insurance companies must pay in claim settlements. The result for the consumer is reflected in improved finances and reduced insurance costs.

Insurers employ loss control representatives to perform that task. These engineers and inspectors help insureds identify and evaluate their loss exposure and recommend ways to minimize the severity and frequency of potential losses. The experience and knowledge gained from one insured are shared with other insureds facing similar exposures to loss.

Securing Credit – Insurance can be used to provide security for a credit. Before lending money, a lender wants assurance that the borrower will repay the money. The lender generally acquires an interest in that property when it loans money to purchase the property. For instance, the lender can repossess a truck or foreclose on a house if the loan is not repaid. Insurance guarantees that the lender will be paid if the truck or house is destroyed or the borrower becomes disabled or dies.

Reduction of Social Burdens – Uncompensated accident victims impose a severe financial burden on society. Insurance helps reduce such burdens by compensating for medical expenses, lost wages, and death benefits to survivors.

Social Costs of Insurance – Insurance provides many benefits to society; however, these benefits come with a cost. Premium rates must be charged to collect the funds required to make loss payments. Because of the operating expenses incurred by insurers, the money collected for premiums will always be greater than the amount insurers pay for the losses.

For example, an insurer may use $0.80 of each insurance dollar to pay claim settlements, with $0.20 used for commissions, salaries, and operating expenses. In addition to these costs, society might bear other insurance costs, perhaps because it encourages dependence on insurance, creating moral and morale hazards.

Self-Funding

The employer pays all claims in the case of a *self-funded* plan. It is the responsibility of the employer to hire a claims administrator and handle all procedural issues. It is the employer's responsibility to hire a claims administrator and handle all procedural issues. The employer may contract with another insurance provider to administer the plan, called an *Administrative Service Only (ASO)* contract. In this way, self-funded benefits are tailored to the group. There is no provision for converting the coverage if the insured leaves the plan. If the insured dies, the beneficiary receives the proceeds as stated in the plan.

Deductible

In property and casualty insurance, a *deductible* is a dollar amount an insured must pay on a claim before the insurer provides coverage. Higher deductibles usually mean lower premiums.

Reinsurance

A *reinsurance* contract is one by which an insurance provider solicits a third party to insure it against loss or liability. A reinsurance contract is presumed to be for indemnifying a *liability*, not merely for indemnity against *damages*. Where an insurance provider acquires reinsurance, they must communicate all the representations of the original insured, in addition to all the information and knowledge they possess, which are material to the risk. The original insured has no insurable interest in a reinsurance contract (Cal. Ins. Code Section 620).

Purposes of Insurers Obtaining Reinsurance – A reinsurance contract prevents the insurance provider from paying for large or catastrophic losses. In other words, reinsurance is the spreading or sharing of a risk between insurers that is too large for one insurer to accept. The risk or a portion of the risk is shared with another insurance company called a reinsurer.

Classes of Lines of Insurance

Cal. Ins. Code Section 100 divides lines of insurance into the following classes for regulatory purposes:

- Life
- Property/Fire
- Disability
- Liability
- Automobile
- Marine
- Aircraft
- Credit
- Title
- Surety
- Workers compensation
- Plate glass
- Sprinkler
- Common carrier liability
- Team and vehicle
- Boiler and machinery
- Burglary
- Mortgage
- Mortgage guaranty
- Insolvency
- Legal, and
- Miscellaneous.

Under Cal. Ins. Code Sections 101 through 120, these classes of insurance are defined by the following:

Life insurance includes life insurance and annuity coverage upon the lives of individuals.

Fire insurance protects against losses in the following categories:

- By fire, lightning, tornado, windstorm, or earthquake;
- Loss or destruction of, or damage to different property types;
- All-risk policies against any loss or damage to personal property, excluding merchandise, commonly known as a *personal property floater*.

Disability insurance includes insurance incidental to injury, disability, or death due to an accident or sickness. It is worth noting that the term *health insurance* refers to individual or group disability insurance. However, it excludes disability insurance for hospital indemnity or accident only, accidental death and dismemberment, long-term care, credit disability, and other limited coverage policies.

Liability insurance involves insuring against a loss resulting from liability for a fatal or nonfatal injury suffered by a natural person or resulting from liability for property damage or damage to the property interests of others. It does not include common carrier liability, workers compensation, team and vehicle, or boiler and machinery insurance.

Automobile insurance involves insuring automobile owners, users, dealers, or other individuals with an insurable interest against hazards related to the ownership, operation, maintenance, and use of automobiles. Automobile insurance includes a contract of guarantee or warranty that assures maintenance, service, parts replacement, or any other indemnity in the event of loss or damage to a motor vehicle.

Marine insurance protects against losses to vessels, craft, or any other water or air vehicle and any individual or property in connection with these losses. Precious stones, jewelry, silver, and gold are also covered.

Aircraft insurance involves insuring aircraft owners, users, and dealers against loss through hazards related to ownership, operation, and maintenance of aircraft, other than against losses to any natural person resulting from a fatal or nonfatal accident or physical injury.

Credit insurance covers individuals engaged in business against loss resulting from the extension of credit to those dealing with them. It protects against loss from individuals who fail to meet current or anticipated financial obligations.

Title insurance ensures free and clear ownership of property. In other words, it insures, guarantees, and indemnifies owners of real or personal property or lien holders against loss or damage suffered because of any of the following:

- Liens or encumbrances on the title to said property;
- Invalid liens or encumbrances; or
- Incorrect searches involving the title to real or personal property.

Surety insurance involves the following types of coverage:

- Guaranty of a contract's performance other than an insurance policy;
- Loss resulting from the alteration or forgery of any signature or instrument;
- Protection against loss or destruction from any cause of evidence of debt or evidence of ownership of mortgages, deeds, bills of lading, etc.

Workers compensation insurance includes insuring against loss to an employer resulting from liability to compensate employees and their dependents for injury sustained during their employment. Compensation occurs regardless of either party's negligence or fault.

Plate glass insurance covers the breakage of glass.

Sprinkler insurance insures against losses caused by damage from water to goods or premises resulting from broken or leaky water pipes, pumps, or other equipment positioned for fire extinguishing, or loss resulting from broken or leaky sprinklers, or through accidental damage to such pumps, sprinklers, or other equipment.

Common carrier liability insurance protects against losses arising from the liability of a common carrier for fatal or nonfatal injury or accident incurred by any person. It does not include liability or workers compensation insurance.

Boiler and machinery insurance covers loss of property and liability for damage to individuals or property resulting from an explosion or accident involving pipes, boilers, pressure vessels, tanks, engines, electrical machinery, wheels, or connected equipment operating nearby.

Team and vehicle insurance will cover losses from damage or liability for damage to property caused by teams or vehicles other than boats, ships, or railroad rolling stock resulting from an explosion or accident involving pipes, tanks, engines, boilers, or tires of vehicles. This type of insurance also covers vehicle theft.

Burglary insurance involves covering loss resulting from burglary, theft, or both, as well as against loss or damage to any of the following property subsequent to any cause:

- Money, coins, bullion, and stamps;
- Notes, securities, drafts, and accounts;
- Manuscripts, books, indexes, maps, and other valuable papers; or
- Records and documents related to the profession, business, or activity in which the insured is involved.

This type of insurance does not include coverage of the property listed above while in the possession of, custody of, or being transported by any for-hire carrier or in the mail.

Mortgage insurance guarantees the principal payment, interest and other amounts agreed to be paid under the terms and conditions of any bond or note secured by a mortgage.

Mortgage guaranty insurance includes insurance against financial loss caused by the failure to pay the principal, interest and other amounts agreed to be paid under the terms and conditions of any bond or note or other evidence of any debt secured by a deed of trust, mortgage, or other instrument constituting a lien or charge on real estate.

Insolvency insurance protects against losses resulting from insolvent insurers' failure to dismiss their obligations under their insurance policies from responsibility.

Legal insurance involves the assumption of a contractual duty to reimburse the insured against fees, costs, and expenses related to or arising out of legal services performed by a practicing attorney within the jurisdiction of the United States.

Miscellaneous insurance includes:

- Coverage against loss resulting from damage caused by windstorms, lightning, earthquake, or tornado;
- An open policy that indemnifies the producer of any television, motion picture, sport, or similar event, production, or exhibition against loss caused by postponement, interruption, or cancellation due to death, accidental injury, or sickness preventing performers, directors, or others involved from beginning or continuing their performances or duties; and
- Any insurance which is a proper subject of insurance not included in any of the classes of insurance.

Chapter Review

This chapter explained the basic insurance concepts and principles you need to know. Let's review them:

BASIC INSURANCE PRINCIPLES	
Insurance	• Insurance transfers loss or risk from a business entity or a person to an insurance provider, which then spreads the costs of unexpected losses to many individuals

Types of Risk	• Uncertainty regarding financial loss
	• Two types of risks:
	   ○ *Pure* – insurable because it only involves the chance of loss
	   ○ *Speculative* – not insurable because it involves the chance of gain

Peris and Hazards	• Hazards give rise to a peril; there are three kinds of hazards:
	   ○ *Physical* – a physical condition
	   ○ *Moral* – a tendency toward increased risk
	   ○ *Morale* – an indifference to loss

Law of Large Numbers	• Larger numbers of individuals with a similar exposure to loss are more predictive of future losses

Loss Exposure	• A unit of measure used to calculate rates charged for insurance coverage
	• Factors considered in calculating rates:
	   ○ The insured's age
	   ○ Sex
	   ○ Occupation; and
	   ○ Medical history

Adverse Selection	• Insurers strive to protect themselves from adverse selection, which refers to the insuring of risks that are more prone to losses than the average risk
Risk Situations	• *Critical risks* – every exposure in which the potential losses are of the magnitude that would result in the financial ruination of the insured, their business or family; • *Important risks* – loss exposures which would lead the person to major lifestyle changes or a change in profession; and • *Unimportant risks* – those exposures in which the potential losses could be absorbed by current income or current assets without imposing unnecessary lifestyle changes or financial strain

Ideally Insurable Risks	• Certain elements or characteristics must exist before a pure risk can be insured:
	   ○ The loss must be due to chance (accidental)
	   ○ The loss must be definite and measurable
	   ○ The loss cannot be catastrophic
	   ○ The insured's loss exposure must involve large homogenous exposure units
	   ○ The insurance must not be mandatory

Risk Management Techniques	• *Sharing* – a way of dealing with risk for a group of individuals or businesses with the same or similar exposure to loss in order to share the losses that happen within that group • *Transfer* – the most effective approach to handling risk is to transfer it so that another party bears the loss • Avoidance – one of the methods of dealing with risk, which means removing exposure to a loss • *Retention* – the planned assumption of risk by an insured through the use of self-insurance, co-payments, or deductibles • *Reduction* – reducing the likelihood or severity of a loss (e.g., having an annual health exam to detect health problems early, or installing smoke detectors)

BASIC INSURANCE PRINCIPLES *(Continued)*	
Insurable Events	<ul><li>If a likely future event could result in loss or liability to an individual, it may be insurable</li><li>Losses become more insurable when they become more predictable</li><li>If a loss is more unpredictable, it becomes less insurable</li></ul>
Insurance Interest	<ul><li>A valid insurable interest can exist between the policy owner and the insured when the policy insures:<ul><li>The policy owner's life</li><li>The life of a family member like a spouse or a close blood relative; or</li></ul></li><li>The life of a key employee, business partner, or someone who has a financial obligation to the policy owner, like a debtor to a creditor</li></ul>
Indemnity	<ul><li>Often referred to as reimbursement</li><li>Insureds or beneficiaries are allowed to collect to the extent of financial loss</li><li>An insured cannot gain financially from a loss</li></ul>
Reinsurance	<ul><li>A reinsurance contract is one by which an insurance provider solicits a third party to insure it against loss or liability</li></ul>
Self-Funding	<ul><li>The employer pays all claims in the case of a *self-funded* plan.</li></ul>

CHAPTER 2:
Contract Law

This chapter will explain some essential concepts relevant to insurance contract law. First, you will learn about an insurance contract's special characteristics and the required elements to be included in all contracts. Next, you will focus on legal definitions and concepts for every insurance policy. This chapter contains several key insurance terms; be sure you understand them without referring to the text.

- Contract Law vs. Tort Law
- Elements of a Contract
- Special Characteristics of an Insurance Contract
- Legal Terms and Contracts
- Six Specifications for Insurance Policies
- Rescission
- Other Important Insurance Terms

Contract Law vs. Tort Law

A *contract* is a written agreement that is legally enforceable by law.

Insurance allows risk to be transferred from the insured to the insurer through a contractual arrangement where the insurer promises to pay an agreed-upon amount or indemnify the insured in the event of the specified loss. This promise is in consideration of premiums paid by the insured and their promise to abide by the contract provisions. The insurance policy is the instrument through which this risk transfer is achieved.

Much of the law that shaped the formal structure of insurance and influenced its content comes from the general *law of contracts*. However, because of the many unique facets of insurance transactions, the general law of contracts needed to be modified to fit the insurance requirements.

A *tort* is a civil, private, non-contractual wrong which can be remedied through legal action. A tort can either be unintentional or intentional. Insurance usually will only respond to unintentional torts (losses other than those deliberate acts by an insured intended to cause damage or loss).

An *intentional tort* involves deliberate acts that cause harm to another person irrespective of whether the offending party intended to hurt the injured party. Breach of contract is not considered an intentional tort.

An *unintentional tort* is a consequence of acting without care. This action is commonly referred to as negligence.

Elements of a Contract

Contracts are defined as legally enforceable agreements between two or more parties. A contract must contain certain essential elements to be enforceable by law or legally binding. The four elements of a contract are:

- Agreement (offer and acceptance);
- Consideration;
- Competent parties; and
- Legal purpose

Offer and Acceptance – There has to be a definite offer by one party. The other party must accept this offer in its exact terms. Concerning insurance, the applicant usually makes the *offer* when applying. *Acceptance* occurs when an insurance provider's underwriter approves the application and issues a policy.

Consideration – The binding force in any contract is known as *consideration*. Consideration is when each party gives something of value to the other. The consideration on the insured's part is the premium payment and the representations provided in the application. The consideration on the insurance provider's part is the promise to pay if a loss occurs.

Competent Parties – In the eyes of the law, the *parties to a contract* must be able to enter into a contract willfully. Usually, this requires that both parties be mentally competent to comprehend the contract, of legal age, and not under the influence of alcohol or drugs.

Legal Purpose – The contract must have a *legal* purpose and not be against public policy. To ensure the legal purpose of a life insurance policy, for example, it must have both consent and insurable interest. A contract without a legal purpose is void and is not enforceable by any party.

Special Characteristics of an Insurance Contract

Contract of Adhesion – One of the parties to the agreement (the insurer) drafts a *contract of adhesion*. It is either accepted or rejected by the other party (the insured). Insurance companies do not write policies through contract negotiations, and an insured has no input regarding its provisions. Insurers also offer contracts on a "take it or leave it" basis by an insurance provider.

Conditional Contract – Before each party fulfills its obligations, a *conditional contract* requires that the policy owner and insurance company meet certain conditions to execute the agreement. The insured must pay the premium and provide proof of loss for the insurer to cover a claim.

Aleatory Contract – Insurance contracts are *aleatory*. In other words, the parties to the agreement are involved in an unequal exchange of amounts or values. Premiums paid by the insured are small compared to the amount the insurance provider will pay in a loss.

Example of Property and Casualty Insurance – Chad purchases a homeowner's insurance policy for $50,000. His monthly premium is $50. If Chad only had the policy for two months, he only paid $100 in insurance premiums. If a covered peril unexpectedly destroyed the home, Chad would receive $50,000. A $100 contribution on the insured's part in exchange for a $50,000 benefit from the insurance provider demonstrates an aleatory contract.

Example of Life and Health Insurance – Chad purchases a life insurance policy for $50,000. His monthly premium is $50. If Chad only had the policy for two months, he only paid $100 in insurance premiums. If he unexpectedly dies, his beneficiary will receive $50,000. A $100 contribution on the insured's part in exchange for a $50,000 benefit from the insurance provider illustrates an aleatory contract.

Unilateral Contract – In a *unilateral contract*, only one of the parties to the agreement must do anything according to the law. The insured makes no lawfully binding promises. Regardless, an insurance carrier must legally pay for losses covered by an in-force policy.

Personal Contract – In general, insurance contracts are *personal* contracts because they are between individuals and insurers. Insurance companies have a right to decide with whom they will not do business. The insured cannot be changed to another person without the insurer's written consent, nor can the policy owner transfer the contract to anyone else without approval from the insurance provider. Life insurance is an exception to this rule. A policy owner can assign or transfer policy ownership to another person; however, the policy owner must still notify the insurance provider in writing.

Utmost Good Faith – An insurance contract is a personal contract between the insured and the insurer. Each party to the contract must be able to rely on the other for critical and valid information. *Utmost good faith* is the ability of the parties to rely on each other.

Indemnity – Sometimes referred to as reimbursement, *indemnity* is a provision in an insurance contract that states that in the event of loss, a beneficiary or an insured is allowed to collect only to the extent of the financial loss. The insured cannot be entitled to gain financially because of an insurance contract. Insurance aims to restore an insured following a loss but not let a beneficiary or insured profit from the loss.

Example of Property and Casualty Insurance – Karen has a $200,000 homeowners insurance policy. After the destruction of her house, her cost to rebuild the home totaled $150,000. The insurance policy will only reimburse Karen for the amount of the loss ($150,000) and not for the total amount of insurance ($200,000).

Example of Life and Health Insurance – Karen has a $20,000 health insurance policy. After being hospitalized, her medical expenses totaled $15,000. The insurance policy only will reimburse Karen for the amount of the loss ($15,000) and not for the total amount of insurance ($20,000).

Legal Terms and Contracts

Insurance Policy – The *insurance policy* is the written instrument that sets forth a contract of insurance (Cal. Ins. Code Section 380).

Representations and Misrepresentations – *Representations* are statements believed to be true to the best of one's knowledge; however, they are not guaranteed to be true (Cal. Ins. Code Sections 350 through 361). For insurance purposes, representations are the answers an insured provides to the questions on an insurance application.

Untrue statements on an insurance application are considered *misrepresentations* and can void the contract (Cal. Ins. Code Sections 780 through 784). A *material misrepresentation* is a statement that would alter the insurer's underwriting decision if discovered. Additionally, if material misrepresentations are intentional, they are considered fraudulent.

It is worth noting that representations may be *withdrawn* or *changed* before the policy implementation but not after. A misrepresentation relevant to underwriting the level of risk is grounds to void a contract. However, an insurer must conclude that the information was given under false pretenses with the intent to commit fraud and was material in deciding to enter into the contract.

Any individual violating this provision is guilty of a misdemeanor punishable by a maximum fine of $25,000, imprisonment in a county jail for no longer than one year, or by both a fine and imprisonment. If the loss to the victim exceeds $10,000, the penalty should not exceed three times the amount of the loss. In addition, the Commissioner can suspend the agent's license for a maximum period of three years.

Warranty – A *warranty* is a statement guaranteed to be true and becomes a part of the contract. A particular format of words is not necessary to create a warranty (Cal. Ins. Code Sections 440 through 445 and 447). Warranties can either be *implied* or *expressed*. An implied warranty is an unspoken or unwritten guarantee based on the circumstances of a transaction. Statements in a policy are express warranties. Every express warranty becomes part of the insurance contract.

The warranty is created at or before the execution of the policy and will be included in the policy. The warranty is not limited by time. Therefore, it can relate to the past, the present, the future, or any combination of these time frames. Violating a material warranty by either party entitles the other to *rescind* the policy.

Furthermore, the breach of an immaterial (unimportant) provision does not void the policy unless specified by the policy itself. Also, it will be taken as a warranty that such an act or omission will occur if the policy contains a statement implying an intention to affect the risk.

Materiality – The concept of *materiality* states that all parties to a contract are entitled to all necessary information to decide on the nature or quality of the contract (Cal. Ins. Code Section 334). Materiality is determined by the "reasonable and probable influence of the facts" on the party needing them to make an informed decision, whether they are the insured or the insurer. The "injured" party may be entitled to rescind the contract if a failure to disclose material information occurs.

The weight of *disadvantages* on either party is of paramount importance. Disadvantages are always material information. All contracts have disadvantages for both parties, but they may not be compelling when deciding whether to accept the contract. Insurance companies are allowed to know material information about prospective insureds, such as: Have they been diagnosed or treated for heart disease, cancer, or diabetes? Have they ever been hospitalized? Have they ever been convicted of a felony? Do they fly an aircraft?

The materiality of a concealment establishes the importance of a misrepresentation. For example, if an insured deliberately conceals information about a recent stroke, this would have a more significant impact than if the insured individual had misrepresented their age by five years.

Insureds, however, are allowed to know the contract's disadvantages, which include the following: cash value surrender charges, length of term, increase in premium at the end of the period, internal expenses and fees, a substandard rating, or principal exclusions like war, terrorism, aviation, and suicide, for example. Producers must share disadvantages with the prospect instead of only sharing the advantages of the contract.

Concealment – *Concealment* is the legal term for intentionally withholding information of a material fact that is crucial in the decision-making process (Cal. Ins. Code Sections 333 and 339). For insurance purposes, concealment occurs when the applicant intentionally withholds information that will result in an imprecise underwriting decision. Concealment may void a policy.

Concealment is the failure to disclose known facts. An injured party is entitled to void the policy regardless of whether the concealment was intentional or unintentional. Every party should reasonably expect the other party to act in good faith without attempting to conceal or deceive the other. Neither party of the contract is legally bound to provide any information regarding their judgment, opinions, or matters in question. The right to rescind the policy is allowable for either party's intentional and fraudulent omission.

The following information is not required to be communicated in a contract:

- Known information;
- Information that should be known;
- Information that the other party waives;
- Information that is not material to the risk and excluded by a warranty;
- Information that is not material to the risk and excepted from insurance; and
- Information based on personal judgment.

Waiver and Estoppel – *Waiver* is the voluntary act of surrendering a legal claim, right, or privilege.

Estoppel is a legal process that can be used to prohibit a party to a contract from re-asserting a privilege or right after that privilege or right has been waived. Estoppel is a legal consequence of a waiver.

Fraud – *Fraud* is the intentional concealment or misrepresentation of a material fact used to persuade another party to make or refrain from making a contract or convince them to cheat or deceive a party. Fraud is grounds for rescinding an insurance contract.

Six Specifications for Insurance Policies

Every contract of insurance must identify the following six specific elements (Cal. Ins. Code Section 381):

1. The parties involved in the contract;
2. The property or individuals being insured;
3. If the insured is not the owner, a statement of the insurable interest that exists;
4. The risks insured against;
5. The period during which the policy will continue or be in force; and
6. The stated monthly, quarterly, semi-annual, or annual premium. If it can only be determined at the expiration or termination of the contract, a statement of the method by which the insurer will calculate a premium rate and total premium.

It is worth noting that the financial rating of an insurer does not have to be specified in an insurance policy.

Rescission

Right of Rescission – Injured parties are *permitted to rescind the contract* if any of the following occurs:

- A false material representation in which rescission becomes effective from the time the representation turns out to be false;
- Concealment, irrespective of whether it is intentional;
- Negligence of a material warranty or other material provisions contained in a policy.

Other Important Insurance Terms

Application — A written request to an insurance company for coverage. It must honestly represent the facts regarding the property or person to be insured; otherwise, the policy will be voided.

Policy — A contract between the insured (policy owner) and an insurer that agrees to compensate for loss caused by specified covered events.

Riders and Endorsements — *Riders* are added to a policy to amend existing provisions (typically used in life and health insurance). *Endorsements* are additions to a contract that change a policy's original terms, conditions, or coverages (typically used in property and casualty insurance).

Cancellation — *Cancellation* is the act of terminating or revoking an insurance policy.

Lapse — *Lapse* refers to terminating an insurance policy due to the insured's failure to pay the premium. A policy terminated due to nonpayment of premiums is called a *lapsed* policy.

Renewal — *Renewal* is the continuation of an insurance policy beyond its original term.

Nonrenewal — *Nonrenewal* is the automatic termination of an insurance policy beyond its original term. The renewal or nonrenewal of a policy may occur on a date stated in the contract (typically on the premium due date or policy anniversary).

Grace Period — A *grace period* is a period after the due date of a premium in which policy owners can provide payment of a late premium without penalty or the policy lapsing.

Reinstatement — *Reinstatement* refers to a provision allowing the insured to put a lapsed insurance policy back in force under certain conditions.

Rate and Premium — The *rate* is the price of insurance for each exposure unit. The payment required by the insured to keep the policy in force is known as the *premium*. Premiums are determined by multiplying the number of units of insurance purchased by the rate. The formula is as follows:

$$Premium = Units\ of\ Insurance\ x\ Rate$$

Earned and Unearned Premium — An *earned premium* is the percentage of a premium belonging to the insurer for providing coverage for a specified period. The *unearned premium* is the percentage of the premium the insurer has collected but has yet to earn because it has not provided coverage for the insured. For example, if an insured pays an annual premium for life insurance and dies before that year is up, the insurer would have to return the portion of the premium that was unearned or unused.

Chapter Review

This chapter explained the concepts relevant to insurance contract law. Let's review some of the key points:

CONTRACT LAW	
Four Elements of a Legal Contract	• *Agreement* – offer and acceptance • *Consideration* – premiums and representations on the part of the policy owner; payment of claims on the part of the insurance provider • *Competent parties* – must be of legal age, have sound mental capacity, and not under the influence of alcohol or drugs • *Legal purpose* – the contract must be for a lawful reason, not against public policy
Special Characteristics of Insurance Contracts	• *Adhesion* – one party prepares the contract; the other party must accept it as is • *Aleatory* – an exchange of unequal amounts • *Conditional* – certain conditions must be met • *Unilateral* – only one of the parties to the contract is legally bound to do anything • *Personal* – insurance contracts are between individuals and insurers
Legal Terms	• *Insurance Policy* – the written instrument that sets forth a contract of insurance • *Concealment* – intentionally withholding information of a material fact that is crucial in the decision-making process • *Warranty* – a statement guaranteed to be true that becomes a part of the contract • *Representations* – statements believed to be true to the best of one's knowledge; however, they are not guaranteed to be true • *Misrepresentations* – untrue statements on an insurance application • *Materiality* – all parties to a contract are entitled to all necessary information to decide on the nature or quality of the contract

CONTRACT LAW *(Continued)*	

Six Specifications for Insurance Policies	• Every contract of insurance must identify these six specific elements:
	   o The parties involved in the contract;
	   o The property or individuals being insured;
	   o If the insured is not the owner, a statement of the insurable interest that exists;
	   o The risks insured against;
	   o The period during which the policy will continue or be in force; and
	   o The stated monthly, quarterly, semi-annual, or annual premium. If it can only be determined at the expiration or termination of the contract, a statement of the method by which the insurer will calculate a premium rate and total premium
	• The financial rating of an insurance company does not have to be specified in an insurance policy

Rescission	• Injured parties are permitted to rescind the contract if any of the following occurs:
	   o A false material representation in which rescission becomes effective from the time the representation turns out to be false;
	   o Concealment, irrespective of whether it is intentional;
	• Negligence of a material warranty or other material provisions contained in a policy

Other Important Insurance Terms	• *Application* – The application is a printed form of questions about a prospective policy owner and the desired insurance coverage and limits • *Contract* – A contract is a written agreement that puts the insurance into effect and is legally enforceable • *Rider* – Riders are written modifications attached to a policy that provide benefits not included in the original policy • *Cancellation* – Cancellation refers to terminating an insurance policy or bond before it expires by either the insurer or the insured • *Lapse* – Lapse refers to terminating an insurance policy due to the insured's failure to pay the premium • *Grace Period* – A grace period is a time after the premium due date that the policy owner has to pay the premium before the policy lapses (usually 30 or 31 days) • *Rate* – A rate is a unit of cost multiplied by an exposure base to calculate an insurance premium • *Premium* – Premiums are the amount of money an insurance company charges for providing the coverage described in the policy

CHAPTER 3:
The Insurance Marketplace

This chapter begins with an overview of marketing distribution systems. It then focuses on producers, describing their licensing and education requirements, duties and authorities, and code of ethics. This chapter also explores the different types and qualifications of insurance providers. Finally, you will learn about market regulations for rate making, sales, underwriting, and claims handling. Be sure to pay close attention to the regulations regarding unfair trade practices and fair claims settlement practices.

- Distributions Systems
- Producers
- Insurers
- Underwriting
- Market Regulation
- Excess and Surplus (E&S) Lines

Distribution Systems

Agency

A *producer* is a legal entity. Producers can be either a person or corporation that acts on behalf of, or in place of, its principal. In insurance, the producer is the agent, and the principal is the insurance provider.

An insurance agent must first establish a licensing relationship with the state or states where the agent wishes to conduct business. This requirement entails meeting educational standards and passing required tests for the type of insurance sold. This licensing relationship is separate from and can exist without any agent or insurance provider relationship being established.

The *independent agent* has contracts with more than one insurance provider, which puts them in an enhanced position to provide clients with a wide range of product options. When it comes time to renew a policy, the independent agent is said to *own the renewal or the expiration*. In other words, the independent agent can move the client to a different insurance provider for the renewal. These agents should only do this to the client's advantage. An ethical challenge facing the independent agent is to avoid moving clients to earn new or higher commissions.

The *exclusive* or *captive*, or *career agent* chooses to have a contract with one insurance company. An agent can choose this when they find the insurance provider's products to be of extraordinary quality and applicability and feel no need to have other insurer relationships. An agent may also make this choice because the insurance provider only allows its products to be sold through its exclusive agents.

Depending on the viewer, exclusivity can appear to be positive or negative. Positively, the agent can market a product that would otherwise be unavailable to the client. Negatively, the agent cannot search throughout the insurance industry to find a product that will benefit the client.

Direct Response

The mass marketing of insurance products through mail and print media advertisements, solicitations, or television and radio is known as direct response marketing. The policies provided are usually low in benefits and low in premiums. The term *direct response* means the necessity of the potential client to take the initiative and respond to the advertisement through a telephone or mail contact with the insurer as directed in the ad.

Producers

Relationship of Agent and Principal or Insured

By definition, an *agent* is an individual who acts for another person or entity, known as the principal, regarding contractual arrangements with third parties. In insurance, an agent is authorized by and on behalf of an insurance provider to transact insurance.

Legal Relationship – An agent or producer is a person licensed to solicit, negotiate, or sell insurance contracts on behalf of the *principal (insurer)*. The *law of agency* defines the relationship between the principal and the agent or producer. This relationship includes the acts of the agent or producer within the scope of authority deemed to be the acts of the insurer.

In this relationship between the principal and the agent or producer, it is a given that:

- An agent represents the insurance provider, not the insured;
- Any knowledge of the agent is assumed to be knowledge of the insurance provider;
- If the agent is working within the boundaries of their contract, the insurance provider is fully responsible; and
- When the insured provides payment to the agent, it is the same as submitting a payment to the insurance provider.

The agent is responsible for accurately completing an insurance application, submitting the application to the insurance provider for underwriting, and delivering the policy to the policyholder.

Insurer as Principal – When applying the law of agency, the insurance provider is the *principal*. The acts of agents or producers acting within the scope of their authority are the acts of the insurance provider.

Agent of Insurer – An agent or producer will always represent the insurance provider, not the insured. Concerning an insurance contract, any knowledge of the agent is presumed to be knowledge of the insurer. If the agent works within the boundaries of their contract, the insurance provider is fully responsible.

Responsibilities to the Applicant and to the Insured – The *agent* is responsible to the insurance provider when completing insurance applications, submitting the application to the insurance provider for underwriting, and when issued, delivering the policy to the policyholder and explaining the contract. In addition, if the insured submits a payment to the agent, it is the same as submitting a payment to the insurance provider.

Even though producers act on behalf of the insurance company, they are legally required to treat insureds and applicants ethically. Since an agent handles the funds of the insured and the insurance provider, they have a *fiduciary responsibility*. An individual in a position of trust is called a *fiduciary*. More specifically, it is illegal for insurance agents to commingle premiums collected from the applicants with their own personal funds.

Authority and Powers of Producers – The agency contract specifies a producer's authority within their insurance company. Contractually, only those actions for which the producer is authorized can bind the principal (insurance provider). In reality, an agent's authority is a lot broader. There are three agent authority types: express, implied, and apparent.

Express – *Express authority* is the authority that is written into the contract. It is the authority a principal intends to grant to a producer through the producer's contract.

Implied – *Implied authority* is the authority that is not expressed or written into the contract but which the producer is assumed to have to conduct insurance business for the principal. Implied authority is incidental to and derives from express authority because not every single authority of a producer can be listed in the written contract.

For example, suppose the agency contract does not explicitly authorize the producer to collect premiums and remit them to the insurance provider. However, the agent routinely does so during the solicitation and delivery of policies. In that situation, the producer has the implied authority to collect and remit premiums.

Apparent – *Apparent authority*, also called perceived authority, is the assumption or appearance of authority based on the principal's words, actions, or deeds or due to circumstances the principal created. For example, suppose a producer uses the insurance provider's stationery when soliciting coverage. In that case, an applicant could believe the producer is authorized to transact insurance on behalf of that insurer.

Transacting Insurance – When an individual performs any of the following actions, they are *transacting insurance* (Cal. Ins. Code Sections 35, 1631, and 1633). Transacting insurance includes:

- Solicitation of insurance;
- Negotiations before the execution of a contract;
- The actual execution of a contract; and
- Any later transactions that arise from the operation of the contract.

Except for individuals who receive non-commission compensation from their employer for these actions, any other individual who receives payment for "transacting insurance" must be licensed as an agent or broker. It is a misdemeanor to transact insurance without a license. This misdemeanor carries a maximum fine of $50,000 or imprisonment in a county jail for one year or both.

Types of Licensees

An individual cannot solicit, sell, or negotiate insurance in this state unless licensed for the appropriate line(s) of authority. The purpose of licensing is to ensure that a producer meets the educational and ethical standards required to fulfill the producer's responsibilities to the insurance provider and the public. Licensing regulations specify the requirements, procedures, and fees for insurance producers' qualifications, licensure, and appointment.

Insurance Agents and Insurance Brokers – An *insurance agent* in this state refers to a person authorized to transact all classes of insurance on behalf of an admitted insurance provider *other than life, health, or disability insurance.*

Insurance brokers are licensees who, for compensation and on behalf of an individual other than an insurance company, transact insurance other than life, accident and health or sickness, or disability. It is worth noting that there is *no such license* as a "life broker" or "health broker." However, an individual can be life licensed as an independent, acting in the capacity of a broker.

A *life licensee* is authorized to act as a life agent on behalf of a life insurance provider or a disability insurance provider. These individuals transact life insurance, accident and health or sickness insurance, or a combination of life and accident and health or sickness insurance.

Agents legally represent the insurer, not their clients. An agent's actions are considered to be made on behalf of the insurance company, not the insured. With brokers, however, this is reversed. *Brokers legally represent their clients*, not insurers. They negotiate contracts of insurance on behalf of their clients.

The broker represents and is expected to act in the client's best interests, not those of the insurance provider. Although a broker could receive compensation from an insurer for a transaction, typically, the broker gets a fee for their services directly from the client. It could be unethical for a broker to accept a commission from the insurance provider and a fee from the client.

Agent vs. Broker vs. Solicitor – A *limited lines automobile insurance agent* is authorized to transact automobile insurance as an agent, not as a broker. Consequently, broker fees cannot be charged. It is worth noting that limited lines automobile licensees cannot act as the agent of an insurance provider or business entity without being appointed or endorsed.

An insurance *solicitor* is a *natural person* employed to assist a property and casualty broker-agent acting as an insurance broker or insurance agent in transacting insurance *other than life, health, or disability* (Cal. Ins. Code Section 1624). In California, an insurance solicitor is not eligible to act simultaneously as an insurance broker or agent. An individual authorized to act as an insurance broker or agent is not eligible to work simultaneously as an insurance solicitor.

Solicitors can make prospecting telephone calls, set appointments, offer quotes, or even take applications for insurance other than life insurance. A solicitor can be employed by more than one broker-agent at a time. A notice of appointment can be filed by a second or subsequent property and casualty broker-agent to appoint a solicitor. To perform the duties of an insurance solicitor, the Insurance Code requires that an individual hold an insurance solicitor's license.

A "life solicitor" license does not exist (Cal. Ins. Code Section 1704(d)).

Property and Casualty Licensee – A *property and casualty* licensee (formerly known as a fire and casualty agent or broker), this license type is split into two separate lines: property and casualty.

A *property* licensee is an individual authorized to transact insurance for coverage on loss or damage to property of any kind.

A *casualty* licensee is authorized to provide coverage against legal liability, including damage to property, injury, disability, or death.

Personal Lines Licensee – A personal lines licensee is an individual authorized to transact any of the following insurance coverages:

- Automobile insurance (including recreational vehicles);
- Residential property insurance (including earthquake and flood);
- Personal watercraft insurance;
- Inland marine insurance; and
- Umbrella or excess liability insurance providing coverage when written on top of one or more underlying residential property or automobile insurance policies.

Life and Health Licenses – In California, *life-only* agents are authorized only to transact insurance on human lives, including the following benefits:

- Annuities;
- Endowments;
- Death or dismemberment by accident; and
- Disability income.

Accident and Health or Sickness Agent – *Accident and health* agents can transact the following types of insurance:

- Bodily injury;
- Sickness;
- Accidental death;
- Disability income; and
- 24-hour coverage.

Life and Disability Analysts – A *life and disability analyst* is any individual who accepts a fee or other compensation from any individual or source other than an insurer for the following: advising or offering to advise an insured, beneficiary, or another individual who has an interest in a life or disability insurance contract about their benefits, rights, or any other aspect of the contract. Under California law, a life and disability analyst must be appropriately licensed.

To be licensed as a life and disability insurance analyst, an individual must be a state resident, competent and knowledgeable on insurance, and have a good business and general reputation. The candidate must take a pre-licensing examination no more than *12 months* before applying for this type of license.

An organization can also hold a license to act as a life and disability insurance analyst if it has an eligible natural person named under an organizational license.

The following eligibility requirements for life and disability analysts include:

- Be a California state resident;
- Pass the license exam within 12 months of the license issue;
- Have a good business and general reputation;
- Have extensive knowledge of life and disability insurance;
- Not be associated with any business that has failed in its fiduciary duty toward any other individual;
- Not attempt to avoid or prevent the operation of insurance laws by being licensed; and
- Not be an employee of an insurer.

In addition to these requirements, before applying for a life and disability insurance analyst license, an individual must have been *licensed as a life and accident and health insurance agent for at least five years*.

Life and disability analysts are not allowed to charge a fee for any services unless they have a signed, written agreement with the party being charged. This agreement must include a statement of the charges or the basis on which charges will be made. They are not allowed to receive a fee from a client for any service generally associated with soliciting or transacting insurance. These individuals also cannot receive fees from clients for any service for which the analyst receives compensation from an insurer.

The written agreement must disclose the services that life and disability analysts will provide and that the same information and services can be available directly from the insurer for free. When the analyst is licensed as a life-only agent, the agreement must inform the client of this fact and that the analyst receives commissions from selling insurance products.

Life Settlement Brokers – A *life settlement* is a financial transaction where a life insurance policy owner sells a policy they no longer need to a third party for compensation, typically cash. While *viatical settlements* are still used for terminally ill individuals, most states regulate policies sold to a third party for compensation under the "Life Settlements" term.

In life settlements, the seller (the policy owner) could have a life expectancy of more than one year. They can sell their policies because they no longer need the coverage or the premium costs have become too high to justify continuing the policy.

The *business of life settlement* refers to any activity related to soliciting and selling life settlement contracts to third parties with no insurable interest in the insured.

The term *owner* refers to the policy owner who can seek to enter into a life settlement contract. The term does not include an insurer, a financing entity, a qualified institutional buyer, a special purpose entity, or a related provider trust.

The *insured* is the person covered under the policy that is considered for sale in a life settlement contract.

A *qualified institutional buyer* is a person that owns and invests at least $100 million in securities and is allowed by the SEC to trade in unregistered securities. A life settlement provider can sell or transfer ownership of a settled policy to a qualified institutional buyer or other investment entity approved by the Commissioner.

Life expectancy is an essential concept in life settlement contracts. It refers to a calculation based on the average number of months the insured is projected to live because of medical history and mortality factors (an arithmetic mean).

The *life settlement contract* establishes the terms under which the life settlement provider will compensate the policy owner in return for the absolute assignment, transfer, sale, or release of any portion of any of the following:

- Policy ownership;
- The death benefit;
- Any beneficial interest; or
- Interest in a trust or any other entity that owns the policy.

A life settlement contract also includes a premium finance loan that is made on or before the policy's issue date if one or more of the following conditions apply:

- The loan proceeds are not used exclusively to pay premiums for the policy;
- The owner receives a guarantee of the policy's future life settlement value; and
- The owner agrees to sell the policy in case of default.

The following *would not comprise* a life settlement contract:

- A policy loan issued by a life insurance provider;
- A loan made by a lender or a bank;
- A collateral assignment of a life insurance policy by the policy owner;
- An agreement between closely related parties (by law or by blood);
- A bona fide business succession agreement;
- Employer-owned life insurance for key employees;
- A contract or agreement between a service recipient and a service provider;
- Any other form identified by the Commissioner.

A *life settlement broker* is an individual who, for payment, solicits, negotiates, or offers to negotiate life settlement contracts. Life settlement brokers represent only the policy owners and have a fiduciary duty to the owners to act in their best interest and according to their instructions.

Life settlement brokers do not include licensed life settlement providers or their representatives, accountants, attorneys, or financial planners. These individuals would not receive a commission when completing a life settlement contract but charge a fee for their services, irrespective of whether or not ownership of the policy is transferred.

A *life settlement producer* is an individual licensed as a resident or nonresident insurance agent who is qualified to transact life settlements.

The *financing entity* includes any accredited investor who provides funds for purchasing one or more life settlement contracts and has an agreement in writing to do so.

A *financing transaction* occurs when a licensed settlement provider secures funds from the financing entity.

Before an individual can act as a life settlement broker in California, they must be appropriately licensed. The following qualifications are required for a licensee:

- Complete the required pre-licensing education (15-hour training course);
- Pass the licensing examination;
- Submit an application on the approved form to the Commissioner;
- Pay any required fees; and
- Be competent, determined, and trustworthy.

If an individual has been licensed as a *life agent for at least one year*, they can act as a life settlement broker. However, they must inform the California Department of Insurance (CDI) within ten days of transacting life settlements. Instead of a broker's license, life agents will be required to pay the notification fee and renew that notification biennially at the time of their life license renewal.

Licensed *viatical settlement brokers* or providers will be deemed to have met the licensing requirements for life settlement brokers or providers.

Insurance Adjuster – A public *insurance adjuster* is an individual who, for a fee, acts on behalf of an insured in negotiating the settlement of a claim or claims for damage or loss under any insurance policy covering real or personal property.

Surplus Lines and Special Surplus Lines Broker – Surplus lines, or special lines brokers, are intended to insure risks for which no market is available through the original broker or agency system. Such coverage is marketed through non-admitted insurance providers on an unregulated basis by *surplus lines brokers* according to state surplus lines provisions of the California Insurance Code.

Regardless of the type of license held, except for a surplus line broker, agents or brokers cannot advertise or transact insurance on behalf of a non-admitted insurer or aid a non-admitted insurer in any way to transact insurance in California.

Filing Notice of Appointment

An insurance producer or agent cannot legally act as an agent of an insurance provider unless they become an *appointed agent* of that insurance company. An insurance producer who does not act as an agent of an authorized insurance provider does not have to become appointed.

The insurance provider must submit a notice of appointment within *14 days* to the Commissioner to legitimize and validate the insurance contract and the agency relationship. The licensee will be legal to conduct business, and the insurance provider will become responsible for the acts of the licensee as of the date the insurance company signs the appointment.

An appointment will cease, and the licensee will become unable to conduct business for the insurance provider when any of the following conditions exist:

- The licensee loses their license; or
- The licensee resigns their appointment or is terminated.

Inactive License – A licensee does not lose their license when they have no active appointments. The insurance license is the result of the licensee's relationship with the Department of Insurance, and a lack of appointments does not change that relationship. A licensee with no appointments has a license that is designated as *inactive*. Upon being appointed by any insurance provider, the license becomes *active* again.

Surrender of a License – A licensee can surrender their license for cancellation at any time. If the license is in the licensee's possession, they can surrender the license by delivering it to the Commissioner. When the license is in the possession of the insurance provider or the licensee's employer, the licensee can still surrender the license by submitting a written notice of surrender to the Commissioner.

Continuing Education Requirements

Continuing education rules aim to protect the public by maintaining high standards of professional competence in the insurance industry and maintaining and improving licensed producers' insurance skills and knowledge. The State of California has implemented pre-licensing and continuing education requirements for initial applicants and license renewals that apply equally to the following: life-only agents, accident and health or sickness agents, property and casualty broker-agents (formerly fire and casualty broker-agents).

Any licensee must complete *24 hours* of continuing education (CE), including *three hours of ethics*, per each 2-year license renewal term for the particular license (Cal. Ins. Code Sections 1749.3(b) and 1749.33(a)). This regulation applies to the following licenses:

- Life-only agent;
- Accident and health or sickness agent;
- Life and accident and health or sickness agent
- Property and casualty broker-agent; and
- Personal lines broker-agent.

Licensees can complete these hours at any time before the license renewal date. The Commissioner must approve all continuing education programs and courses.

Suppose an agent holds two types of licenses (for example, a life agent and a property and casualty broker-agent license). In that case, the agent can satisfy the CE requirement by completing it for any license type.

It may not be practical to complete the minimum number of CE units during a license period. While it is not possible to renew a license without the required number of credits, any credits above the required number will be carried over into the next licensing period.

Licensees can carry over only those hours completed during the second year of the licensing period. The number of hours a licensee can carry over cannot exceed the hours required to renew the license.

Licensees can complete continuing education in a variety of settings. Courses are available with a live instructor, known as a "contact" setting. They are also available via mail-order as a "self-study" course and by computer over the Internet, which is also a "self-study" method. Before purchasing a continuing education course, producers should ensure that the California Department of Insurance has approved it. A licensee can gain valuable knowledge by taking any CE course, but only approved courses will meet license renewal requirements.

Miscellaneous Code Requirements and Specifications

Agency Name, Use of Name – California state law cannot limit a person's right to use their actual name to transact insurance business. Other than that, the insurance regulators are responsible for ensuring that California residents are not misled by the name or names attached to a licensed entity.

Every licensee, individual, and corporate entity must reveal to the Insurance Commissioner the actual name of the legal person and all Doing Business As (DBA) names intended for use. To prevent confusing the insurance consumer, the Commissioner can deny the use of a name for any of the following reasons:

- The name would interfere with another business or is too similar to the name of another;
- The name would mislead the consumer;
- The name gives the impression that the licensee is authorized to conduct a type of business that it cannot legally conduct;
- The terms "Chartered Life Underwriter" and "Chartered Property and Casualty Underwriter" are frequently used by those who earned those designations. It is not acceptable to use the term "underwriter" to give the impression that the licensee is authorized to act in such a capacity. The term "underwriter" can be used in the name of an organization of insurance agents who are individually licensed; or
- The licensee is already using two approved names. The exception is a licensee who acquires ownership of another licensee, where the use of two names for each entity is permitted.

There is room for negotiation with the Commissioner when there are extenuating circumstances concerning "fictitious" names like a DBA.

Suppose a broker or agent has a contract to provide service for a corporation that holds an insurance license in its own name, is a member of an incorporated agency, or is a stockholder in a licensed corporation. In that circumstance, the broker or agent can use the name of such organization in printed materials provided that the broker or agent identifies the relationship.

Licensed agents or brokers who advertise online must identify the following information, even if they are not responsible for maintaining their Internet presence:

- The licensee's name approved by the Commissioner;
- The state of the licensee's principal place of business; and
- The licensee's license number.

Anyone who conducts the following actions online is transacting insurance in this state:

- Provides insurance premium quotes to California residents;
- Accepts applications from California residents; or
- Communicates with California residents regarding the terms of an insurance agreement.

Change of Address – On their initial license application, every licensee has to provide their business, residence, and mailing addresses. The licensee's responsibility is to immediately notify the Commissioner of any changes in the principal business, mailing, residence, or e-mail addresses through an electronic service approved by the Commissioner (Cal. Ins. Code 1729).

Reporting Administrative Actions and Criminal Convictions – Every licensee and applicant for licenses must report any *background changes, administrative actions, or criminal convictions* to the California Department of Insurance Producer Licensing Bureau *within 30 days* of the matter's final disposition. Background information that needs to be reported includes the following:

- Filing of felony criminal charges against the licensee in federal or state court;
- Misdemeanor or felony convictions;
- Administrative actions regarding an occupational license;
- Personal or organizational bankruptcy filings; or breach
- Any financial misappropriation or.

Licensees and applicants must submit supporting documents, like certified court documents, a statement regarding the background change, administrative documents, or other related documents.

To report this information to the Department, licensees can use the background change disclosure form available at the California state insurance website, insurance.ca.gov.

Filing License Renewal Application – Insurance licenses in this state must be renewed every *two years*. Suppose a licensee delays completing the renewal requirements and finds themselves near the license expiration date. In that case, the licensee can continue transacting insurance for *60 days* past that expiration date, provided they complete all requirements and remit the license renewal fee no later than the expiration date (Cal. Ins. Code Section 1720).

Printing License Number on Documents – To facilitate a potential client's investigation of an agent, each agent must place their license number on all printed materials provided to the public in California, including proposals, business cards, and all print advertisements. (Cal. Ins. Code Section 1725.5).

The license number must be printed as large as the smallest telephone number or address on the same document. This requirement ensures the number is not minimized and would not be missed by a prospective insurance consumer. A single license number will be sufficient for licensees with more than one license. Solicitors are required to use the license number of their employer.

A first offense for being caught using illegal documents will be punished by a $200 fine, a second by a $500 fine, and a third by a $1,000 fine. A separate penalty, however, cannot be imposed for each piece of illegal material used. The Commissioner can consider extenuating circumstances and relieve the licensee of the penalty.

The one exception to the license number requirement is motor club (AAA, etc.) advertisements. These materials include insurance in a general list of services offered without providing details regarding the insurance products.

Record Maintenance – One of the challenges facing new brokers and agents is accepting the responsibility to obtain and maintain legible, accurate records. These records must be available within 30 days after a request to the insurance provider from the Department of Insurance. Each admitted insurance provider must maintain specific records regarding its life activities, life and disability, and disability agents for *five years*. Life, life and disability, and disability insurance agents must also maintain all applicable records at their primary place of business for a minimum of five years. The records need to be maintained in an orderly manner and be available for the Commissioner's review at all times (Cal. Ins. Code Sections 10508 through 10508.5).

The records can be in the form of copies, originals, or electronic data-processing records and must include the following:

- Policy number;
- Name of the insurance provider;
- Name of the insured;
- The date insurance becomes effective and any date it ceases to be in force;
- Renewals;
- All information regarding binders;
- Coverage changes;
- A copy of the application or other request for insurance;
- Proposals, including comparisons with existing coverage;

- All correspondence or other written records that describe the transaction, except printed materials in general usage;
- All correspondence regarding cessation of coverage; and
- Legally required disclosure statements or outlines of coverage.

Brokers and agents must keep the following records regarding policies, premium payments, and commissions:

- The original policy application;
- Amount of premiums received by the insurance provider;
- Production records that show policies sold by each agent;
- Itemization of the premiums received;
- All written communications sent by the insurance provider or its agents to a prospect, applicant, or insured;
- A copy of the disclosure statements or outlines of coverage.

Display of License – Every license to act as a property and casualty agent or broker has to be *prominently displayed* by the holder in their office. Producers must display their license so that anyone can readily inspect it and ascertain its currency and the capacity in which its holder is licensed to act.

Office Location – Every resident insurance property and casualty agent or broker has to maintain a *principal office* in this state for the transaction of business. The office's address needs to be specified on all license and renewal applications. All licensees and applicants for a license must immediately notify the Commissioner, in writing, of any change in their address.

Premium Finance Disclosures – If an individual is engaged in business as a broker or insurance agent, participates in the arrangement of a premium financing agreement, and accepts compensation, that individual must disclose to the insured the amount of compensation received from the premium financer. Brokers and agents must also maintain a list of accounts for *three years* for which they have accepted compensation for premium financing services. These lists must be made available to the Commissioner, showing the amount of compensation regarding each premium financing agreement and each financing schedule used by the broker or agent.

Fictitious Names – All licensees, from individuals to organizations, must file their true names and any fictitious names under which they are doing business with the Commissioner. They must also notify the Commissioner if any names are discontinued or changed. The Commissioner has the right to approve and disapprove names.

Licensees cannot use more than two names, real or fictitious. When licensees purchase or inherit a business, they can use two additional names for that business.

Internet Advertisements – A California broker or agent who advertises their services over the internet has to include all of the following information in the ad, regardless of whether the broker or agent created the ad or someone created it on their behalf:

- Their name as it appears on the insurance license, as well as any fictitious name approved by the Commissioner;
- The state of their domicile and principal place of business; and
- Their license number.

An individual is "transacting insurance" when they advertise on the Internet, regardless of whether the broker or agent maintains the Internet presence or if it is maintained on their behalf, and does any of the following:

- Provides an insurance premium quote to a California resident;
- Accepts an application for coverage from a California resident; or
- Communicates with a California resident regarding one or more terms of an agreement to provide insurance or an insurance policy.

Fiduciary Responsibility – The agent is legally required to perform ethically. An insurance agent who agrees to obtain coverage for a client must exercise the same degree of care as expected from a prudent, reasonable, and competent professional in the field. This responsibility is referred to as the producer's *fiduciary responsibility*. A *fiduciary* is a producer who handles insurance provider funds in a trust capacity. They do not commingle premiums collected with their personal funds. If failure to exercise this degree of care results in a loss to a client, the agent can be held liable for that loss. Agents have been held liable for breach of contract and negligence regarding clients in numerous areas.

All funds received by any individual acting as a broker, insurance agent, life agent, life analyst, solicitor, surplus line broker, special lines surplus line broker, motor club agent, bail agent, or permittee are received and held by that individual in their fiduciary capacity. Individuals who divert these funds to their own use are guilty of theft.

Upon receiving fiduciary funds, the person must do either of the following:

- Remit premiums, minus commissions, and return premiums received or held by the person to the insurance provider or the individual entitled to them; or
- Maintain fiduciary funds on California business in a trustee bank account or depository in California separate from any other account or depository, in an amount at least equal to the premiums and return premiums (net of commissions) received by them and unpaid to the people entitled to them. It is also acceptable to deposit this money directly into the account of these individuals at their direction or in accordance with a written contract.

A *trustee bank account* or *depository* includes (but is not limited to) a checking account, savings account, or demand account, each designated as a trust account. The individual can put money in this account for additional funds for advancing premiums, establishing reserves for the payment of return commissions, or for contingencies that might arise in receiving and transmitting premium or return premium funds.

Funds can also be maintained in the form of any of the following:

- U.S. government bonds and treasury certificates or other obligations for which the full faith and credit of the U.S. are pledged for the payment of principal and interest;
- Certificates of deposit of banks or savings and loan associations licensed by any state government;
- Repurchase agreements collateralized by securities issued by the U.S. government; or
- Other types of bonds specified by the Insurance Code.

The bonds, certificates of deposit, obligations, and repurchase agreements are valued based on their acquisition cost.

Investment losses to the principal of fiduciary funds are the responsibility of the individual licensed. Any obligation to insurance providers or other people entitled to the fiduciary funds will not be reduced because of any loss in the value to the principal of the fiduciary funds.

A property and casualty agent, broker, or surplus line broker can offset funds due an insured for return premiums on any policy against amounts due to them from the same insured for unpaid premiums on the same or any other policy. Any insurance provider can pay return premiums to any property and casualty agent or broker. The Insurance Code does not render null and void an assignment of return premium made concurrently with policy issuance as security for financing that premium, nor the right of the assignee to enforce the assignment as a previous claim.

Non-Admitted Insurer

A non-admitted insurer has not satisfied the requirements, either by failure or choice, to legally have its representatives physically present to transact insurance business in California. Such an insurer can be represented within California by specially licensed individuals, known as surplus lines brokers. These non-admitted insurers must obtain a valid Certificate of Authority from the California Department of Insurance before conducting business in the state.

Surplus lines brokers are of value to California residents because they help the residents purchase types of property and casualty insurance that are not available from admitted insurers.

Advertising Requirements – This is a relatively clear-cut portion of the Insurance Code. An individual is either a licensed surplus lines broker or not. If not licensed as a surplus lines broker, an individual cannot in any way represent, advertise or assist a non-admitted insurer.

Prohibited Acts (Unless a Surplus Lines Broker) – The following acts are *misdemeanors* except when committed by a surplus lines broker:

- Acting as an agent on behalf of a non-admitted insurer in an insurance transaction;
- Advertising for a non-admitted insurer;
- Aiding a non-admitted insurer to transact insurance.

Along with any penalty for committing a misdemeanor, individuals violating any provision will be fined $500 and $100 for each month the individual continues the violation.

New legislation was recently enacted to streamline the surplus lines broker licensing laws, and the following changes were included. All individuals are required to hold an individual surplus lines broker license. Applicants for such a license must already be licensed to transact property and casualty insurance.

Also, a surplus lines broker's application and renewal fee allow for a 2-year license term.

It is essential to note there is a fee for a licensed surplus lines broker organization to endorse a licensed individual lines broker. The California Department of Insurance must be advised when terminating such a broker.

Surplus lines brokers transacting insurance for a licensed surplus lines broker organization will not have to file a bond. However, all other surplus lines brokers must file a $50,000 surplus lines broker bond.

Basic Prohibitions

Any individual licensed to transact insurance business or who advertises themselves as qualified to offer advice on insurance is prohibited from

- Recommending or suggesting that an employer obtain aggregate excess or aggregate stop-loss workers compensation insurance; or
- Recommending a non-admitted insurer from whom aggregate excess or aggregate stop-loss workers compensation insurance might be purchased.

An individual found doing this is guilty of a *misdemeanor*. This regulation does not apply to the employer if it is a self-insured public entity or anyone issued a certificate by the Director of the Department of Industrial Relations to self-insure.

Prohibitions of Free Insurance

The state has adopted the philosophy that insurance is a product of sufficient importance. It should be paid for by the insured for its intrinsic value to preserve the integrity of the insurance industry in California. To this end, it is *illegal* for any insurance licensee to offer *free insurance* as an incentive to transact some other type of business.

Suppose any insurance provider, broker, agent or solicitor willfully violates this provision. In that situation, the Insurance Commissioner can revoke or suspend that individual's certificate, license, or other authority to conduct business for a period not exceeding one year.

The following *exceptions* to the free insurance prohibition include:

- Insurance provided in association with newspaper subscriptions;
- The purchase of credit union shares;
- Insurance to guarantee the performance of a product and reimburse a customer for losses caused by such a product's failure;
- Title, life, or disability insurance which will pay off a debt in case a debtor dies or becomes disabled;
- Services provided by an attorney; and
- The services of a motor club, like AAA, regarding emergency roadside service, towing, bail bond service, DMV transactions, or other services that are not considered transacting insurance.

Charges for Extra Services

Insurance providers might include an expense factor (typically a dollar amount) added to the premium charged for a class of policies, which would produce insufficient premium to cover the cost of issuing and servicing them.

A broker fee is an agreed-upon commission paid from an insurer to a person or entity that represents the consumer in servicing, negotiating, or obtaining coverage with insurers on behalf of an insured.

A broker is required to meet the following requirements to charge a broker fee:

- The consumer agrees to the fee in advance (following a full disclosure);
- The fee is not being charged on a FAIR Plan, CAARP, or "low-cost auto" policy;
- The broker is not an appointed agent of the insurance provider with which the coverage is or will be placed;
- The broker provides the consumer with a specific disclosure form;
- The broker and consumer sign a *broker fee agreement* including standard information;
- The broker has an in-force bond on file with the Department; and
- The broker discloses the broker fee during the initial premium quotation.

The *standard disclosure and agreement* must be printed in English and in any other language the broker uses to solicit, advertise, or negotiate the sale and purchase of insurance.

The disclosure and agreement, signed or initialed by the consumer, has to be kept for 18 months after policy expiration.

The following acts and practices are considered unfair or deceptive:

- Failing to give the consumer the *standard disclosure form*;
- Failing to complete all relevant portions of the broker fee agreement before giving the agreement to the consumer for review;
- Failing to provide the consumer a completed copy of the broker fee agreement, signed by the broker and the consumer, as soon as practicable;
- Failing to place a consumer with an insurance provider with which the broker is appointed as an agent exclusively to charge a broker fee;
- Charging (or attempting to charge) a broker fee for a renewal, endorsement, or another service without having disclosed those fees in the broker fee agreement; and
- Failing to refund an entire broker fee if the broker acted with dishonor or incompetence, resulting in financial loss to the consumer, or if the broker did any of the following, regardless of financial loss:
  - Intentionally or negligently misquoted the premium to the consumer, causing an uprate;
  - Permitted an unlicensed employee to transact insurance for, or on behalf of, the consumer paying the fee, where the Insurance Code required the employee to be licensed;
  - Failed to refund unearned premium as required by the Code;
  - Intentionally or negligently failed to remit a consumer's coverage within the period indicated to the consumer or within a timely manner;
  - Negligently or intentionally failed to remit a consumer's premium payment to an insurance provider or general agent, resulting in policy cancellation;
  - Failed to disclose the existence of the insurance provider's periodic payment plan if one was available;
  - Failed to refund unearned commission in the broker's possession to the individual to whom it is owed within 30 days of the unearned commission being generated due to amendment or cessation of coverage; and
  - Failed to remit or apply to another policy a premium finance company credit owed to the consumer within 15 days of receiving the credit from the premium finance company.

If an agent violates these rules, their license can be suspended. The Commissioner can also impose discipline for conduct or nonfeasance not explicitly addressed in the law.

The *standard broker fee agreement* does not have to be used verbatim. It can be modified, provided that the modified agreement includes all of the provisions of the standard agreement and nothing conflicts with the following provisions:

- The consumer appoints the broker as the consumer's insurance broker of record;
- The broker fee agreement continues until terminated by either party;
- The broker agrees to represent the consumer competently and honestly;
- The agreement needs to indicate the amount of the broker fee and whether it is refundable;
- The broker may, in the future, charge consumers. The consumer needs to agree to pay additional specified fees for services listed explicitly in the agreement;
- The agreement must list the nature and amount of all fees known to the broker that will be charged by individuals other than the broker or the insurer;
- The agreement has to provide the Department of Insurance consumer assistance telephone number; and
- The agreement requires the consumer and broker to sign and date the agreement.

Purpose, Duties, and Authority of an Agency

Applications – The agent must ensure that the application is filled out completely, correctly, and to the best of their knowledge. The agent must probe beyond the stated questions in the application if they believe the applicant is misrepresenting or concealing information or does not understand the questions asked. Any inaccurate, misleading, or illegible information can delay the policy's issuance. If the agent feels there could be some misrepresentation, they must notify the insurer. Some insurance companies require that the applicant complete the application under the watchful eye of the agent. In contrast, other insurance providers require the agent to complete the application to help avoid unanswered questions and mistakes.

Binders – A *binder* is a temporary agreement issued by a producer or insurance company providing temporary coverage until a policy can be issued. A binder is typically in writing, but it can also be oral. Binders *expire* when the policy is issued. However, the policy's effective date would remain the same as the date of the binder. When the insurance provider declines to issue the policy, the binder expires on the date following receipt of the notice of cancellation.

Binders are valid for the period specified in the binder. This period cannot exceed 90 days from the date of the binder's execution. No binder can remain valid on or after the insurance policy issue date. The expiration of coverage under a binder cannot be considered a cancellation or nonrenewal of an insurance policy.

Certificates of Liability Insurance and Evidence of Property Insurance – The Financial Responsibility Law requires individuals or organizations to provide evidence of their ability to respond to claims for harm from a specified activity. The most common financial responsibility requirement applies to motor vehicle operators, who must have evidence of their ability to pay for automobile-related damage or injuries. An auto liability policy is the main form of financial responsibility. A licensed producer is responsible for providing archival copies of such evidence to the client for the purposes directed by law. An insurer provides an information card required in some states to be carried by the insured or in the insured auto and produced on demand as proof of insurance.

Renewal Responsibilities – A policy renewal is a continuation of a policy about to expire with the same terms as the previous policy. This process can be accomplished by issuing a new policy, certificate, or renewal receipt, which takes effect upon the expiration of the old policy. Whenever any insurer has previously sent renewal premium notices to an insured and intends to discontinue that practice, it must inform the insured of its intention.

Suspense and Diary System – A *suspense and diary system* is a record-keeping system often maintained on a database by an agent and insurance provider. It tracks the inception and expiration dates of all policies they have written. These insurance records must be maintained for a certain period and be made available for examination upon the Insurance Commissioner's request.

Lost Policy Release – A *lost policy* release is a form signed by a policyholder who wishes to surrender a policy that has been lost. The signed and dated receipt becomes evidence that the policy is no longer in force. It releases the insurance provider from liability for coverage that would have been provided during the remaining term of the policy.

Personal Lines Requirement – Anytime an applicant or insured applies for insurance or pays the initial premium, a producer must *disclose the effective date of coverage* (if known). They must also disclose the circumstances under which coverage will be effective as soon as specific conditions are met. This regulation only applies to coverage for personal lines of insurance.

Insurance in Connection with Sales or Loans

Requirements – No individual engaged in the business of financing the purchase of real or personal property is allowed to require, as a condition of the sale of real property, that the individual buying that property negotiates any insurance covering such property through a particular insurance broker, insurance agent, or insurance solicitor.

Any borrower or purchaser has the *free choice of an insurance broker or agent* at any time. They can revoke any designation of an insurance agent or broker at any time, regardless of the provisions of any loan, purchase agreement or trust deed. However, the lender has the right to furnish the needed insurance or to renew that insurance. It can also charge the borrower or purchaser's account with the costs associated with this transaction if they fail to deliver to the lender proof of insurance at least 30 days before the policy's expiration.

Penalties – The Commissioner, after a hearing, can issue a *cease and desist order* to any individual if they find that such individual has, in more than one transaction, violated the legal provisions specified by California law which prohibits sellers and lenders from requiring the purchase of insurance from a particular insurance broker or agent. The violation of such a cease and desist order is a *misdemeanor*.

Return Premium Offsets – Funds due to an insured for return premiums can be used by a property and casualty agent or broker to pay off anything the insured owes to the agent. The insurance provider can pay the premiums directly to the agent.

This stipulation does not apply to a return premium made when the policy goes into effect as security for financing that premium. The law also will not interfere with the assignee's right to enforce the assignment as a prior claim.

Errors and Omissions

An insurance broker or agent might seek professional liability insurance to protect against financial losses that could happen because of the agent's negligent acts or actions. This coverage is known as *errors and omissions (E&O)* liability insurance.

Types of Coverage – E&O insurance is written for professionals (such as insurance agents) to provide protection resulting from actions charging that the professional failed to render reasonable services or duties. Some professional liability insurance coverage is written with a limit of liability on an occurrence basis. The insurer must obtain the insured's consent for any out-of-court settlement. The modern trend is to provide coverage on a claims-made basis and to remove previous requirements for the insured's consent for out-of-court settlements.

Errors and omissions liability contracts are renewable annually. They are typically written with "per claim" deductibles of at least $500 or $1,000. They have either a "limit for all claims during the policy period" or a "limit per claim" provision that specifies the contract's maximum benefit.

Types of Losses – The following examples of acts or omissions may lead to professional liability claims:

- An agent unintentionally records an answer incorrectly on an insurance application, concealing the client's actual response to a question concerning qualifying information. Upon investigating a claim, the insurance provider discovers the correct information, legally rejects the claim, and voids the contract based on the incorrect answers in the application, refunding the premiums paid. The E&O policy pays for the actual claim losses of the agent's client.
- The agent fails to disclose material information about a contract of insurance, such as coinsurance, deductibles, copayments, premium increases, surrender charges, or principal exclusions. The E&O policy could cover actual damages incurred by the agent's client.

- The agent tells a client, "I suppose I made a mistake" in calculating the original premium quotation when, in fact, the increased premium was because of the client's substandard rating. Suppose an insured later discovers the misrepresentation and elects to cancel the contract. In that situation, an E&O policy could pay the difference between the actual premiums paid and what the client was initially quoted as the periodic premium from the date the client discovered the error.
- The agent leads a client to believe that the sales illustration for a contract with non-guaranteed interest, or that projected investment results in a variable contract, are guaranteed elements of the contract. An E&O policy could pay for actual client losses.
- The agent collects a check from a client, representing an unscheduled deposit to the cash account in a variable or flexible premium policy, and fails to send it to the insurance provider promptly. An E&O policy could restore actual investment or interest losses.

Losses Not Covered – Errors and Omissions insurance does not protect against liabilities caused by a person's criminal acts. Such acts include unfair trade practices, fiduciary crimes, or material misrepresentations that cause damages or financial loss to a client.

It is worth noting that the E&O policy will not pay the claim if any of the previously named liability claims arise out of a criminal conviction or result in a criminal conviction. The broker or agent will remain personally liable for the client's damages.

Need for Coverage – E&O insurance is necessary because of the risk of injuring an individual due to the advice or services rendered (an error) or not rendered (an omission) to that individual.

At any time during the sales process, there can be a misrepresentation or misunderstanding that could lead to legal action being taken by the insured. Producers should document all requests for information, interviews, phone conversations, etc. The sales interview and the policy delivery are commonly the time for E&O situations.

Ethics

A producer should be able to *identify and apply* the meaning of the following:

- Put the customer's interest first;
- Know the job and continue to increase competence levels;
- Identify and recommend products and services that meet the customer's needs;
- Truthfully and accurately represent products and services;
- Use simple language that insurance consumers can understand;
- Stay in contact with customers and conduct periodic coverage reviews;
- Protect the confidential relationship with a client;
- Keep informed of and follow all insurance laws and regulations;
- Provide exemplary service to clients; and
- Avoid making inaccurate or unfair remarks about the competition.

It is worth noting that the California Code of Regulations and the California Insurance Code (Cal. Ins. Code) identify many unethical or illegal practices. It is impossible, however, to write legislation for each possible unethical act that could occur.

A producer's role in the insurance industry is a great responsibility toward others. The Insurance Code articulates the ethical and legal aspects of the client-agent relationship in many ways. Fiduciary responsibilities are very high on the list, including the contact a producer has with the insureds' premiums or the recommendations and advice given to others that have implications for their money or financial security.

An insurance agent must practice and demonstrate the highest integrity, ethics, and morals. Failures or lapses in any of these areas can cause significant financial harm to others. Misrepresentation, concealment, twisting, commingling client money with general business funds and other practices that lack integrity are unethical and prohibited by the Insurance Code. Failing to answer or providing an intentionally wrong answer to questions that prospects or insureds ask is also an ethical problem. It can lead a client to make a decision that might not be in their best interest. Unethical conduct can lead to the loss or suspension of a license, monetary penalties, and even time in jail or prison.

Producers must make recommendations to clients based on the clients' best interests. For a producer to recommend products or services to an individual that they would not recommend for themselves in the same situations is an ethical dilemma. This dilemma is regularly described as a conflict of interest. The normal conduct of business, especially in the insurance industry, can give producers many opportunities for conflicts of interest.

Agents are usually paid on a commission basis. Commissions are typically calculated based on an annual premium submitted, even though the client may have paid just the initial monthly installment with their application. For an agent, the higher the premium collected, the higher the commission. When the higher premium and the higher commission result from an inappropriate recommendation for the client, that is an unethical act and a conflict of interest.

An agent's opportunity to represent multiple insurance providers can be in the client's best interest. It can also lead to conflicts of interest, especially if a decision to book business with a particular insurer is made based on which insurer offers the best "perk" to its agents. Incentives like trips or cruises, commission bonuses, computers, or other sales-based contests present opportunities to do what is right for the agent. They do not offer opportunities to do what is right for the client.

Ethics demands that the other individual and their family are of primary importance. A producer with the highest respect for others will succeed the most. Producers who neglect this respect for others might have success initially, but they rarely achieve long-term success. The responsibility for ethical behavior is squarely on the producer.

Special Ethical Concerns Regarding Seniors – Senior citizens are the least likely to report abuses or financial crimes against them. They may feel embarrassed at being taken advantage of and do not want to appear to be losing the ability to manage their daily lives or personal finances.

Unethical agents have been caught selling multiple duplicative policies to senior citizens. Such agents propose one insurance policy or annuity contract but deliver another (bait and switch). They also mislead senior consumers into believing that an annuity product is a long-term care contract (or vice-versa).

California's Medicare supplement and LTC insurance regulations address unethical practices. Such practices include:

- Misleading or inaccurate comparisons of existing and proposed replacement contracts; and
- Selling an insured a third LTC policy within 12 months or a second Medicare supplement policy.

California passed the Financial Elder Abuse statutes in 2002, which, in part, explicitly addresses insurance agent abuses of individuals age 65 or older (Cal. Ins. Code Sections 785 through 789.10).

In most cases, insurance institutions, producers, and insurance-support organizations are not allowed to use pretext interviews to acquire information about an insurance transaction.

In an attempt to gain information about another natural person, a *pretext interview* is conducted when any individual does one or more of the following:

- Pretends to represent someone they do not actually represent;
- Pretends to be someone they are not;
- Misrepresents the purpose of the interview; or
- Refuses to identify themselves upon request.

Pretext interviews are prohibited during any phase of the insurance transaction process, including information gathering during underwriting. Using a pretext interview could reveal privileged information that would not usually be available to the insurance provider or producer. It could result in an *adverse underwriting decision*. As an investigative technique, pretext interviews are allowed when investigating a claim, particularly when fraud is presumed.

The purpose of the interview must be to investigate a claim where there is a reasonable basis for suspecting fraud, criminal activity, material misrepresentation, or material nondisclosure.

License Denial, Suspension or Termination

The Commissioner is obligated to the consumers of California to ensure that each insurance licensee is qualified regarding their character and knowledge. The Commissioner is authorized to require the provision of any documents or information necessary to make such a determination. After the investigation is complete, the applicant can be authorized to conduct business.

Denial of Applications – There are many possible causes listed in the Insurance Code for denying an insurance license. Remember that these causes apply to legal "persons," which include individuals and business entities such as corporations and agencies. The applicant can be denied licensure if the applicant is unqualified or if licensing the applicant would be against the public's best interest.

An applicant's license *can be denied* if the applicant:

- Has no intention of selling the type of insurance allowed by the license;
- Lacks integrity;
- Does not have a respectable business reputation;
- Was denied or lost another state license within the previous five years for a reason which would also result in an insurance license being denied;
- Wants the license to avoid insurance law consequences;
- Previously acted dishonestly in business;
- Has lied on their application;
- Lied about an insurance policy;
- Exposed the public to loss as a result of incompetence or lack of trustworthiness;
- Has either not done something required by or has done something forbidden by the Insurance Code;
- Has been convicted of (not charged with) any misdemeanor violation or a felony of insurance law;
- Has helped someone else commit a crime that would make that other individual lose or be denied a license;
- Has allowed an employee to violate the Insurance Code;
- Has acted as a licensed individual before the issuance of a license; or
- Has submitted a fraudulent educational certificate.

The applicant can be *denied a license* without the right to a hearing if they have a history of any of the following:

- Misdemeanor violations of insurance law;
- Felony convictions;
- Denial of an insurance license within the past five years; or
- Insurance license revocation or suspension within the past five years.

Anyone *caught cheating* on the licensing exam will be barred from taking any licensing examination and holding an active license for *five years*.

Regarding what could constitute a conviction, any applicant for licensure in California will be considered convicted of a misdemeanor or felony if they were found guilty or convicted after entering a "no contest" plea.

It is important to remember that *every conviction* has to be disclosed on the license application at *any time* in an applicant's past. This stipulation applies to convictions where the charges were later expunged or dismissed or where an individual was given probation or received a suspended sentence. If an applicant does not disclose all convictions, the application for a producer license will be denied.

Termination of a License Due to Dissolving Partnerships – A licensee can surrender their insurance license at any time, either by returning the license to the Commissioner or submitting a notice of resignation if not in possession of the license.

An insurance license automatically terminates upon the licensee's death. If the licensee is an organization, the license will terminate if its corporation, association, or partnership is dissolved. Also, a partnership will lose its license if it changes the individuals listed as partners. When a new partner joins, a partnership can continue its license if it files a notice with the Department within 30 days and the changes are approved.

Suppose any of the above organizations cease to exist. In that situation, they can continue conducting business under another name, provided the same individuals remain involved. The necessary paperwork must be filed within 30 days (Cal. Ins. Code Sections 1708 through 1712.5).

Suspension or Revocation of a License – A permanent license can be revoked for the same reason a license could be denied. Hearings will not be permitted if any of the four previously discussed conditions exist.

Insurers

Insurers can be classified based on ownership, location (domicile), authority to transact business, rating (financial strength), or marketing and distribution systems.

As you read about different classifications of insurance companies, remember that these categories are not mutually exclusive. The same company can be described based on who owns it, where it is located and allowed to transact insurance business, and what type of agents it appoints.

Admitted and Non-Admitted Insurers

Before insurers can transact business in a state, they must be granted a license or *certificate of authority* from the Department of Insurance and meet the state's financial capital and surplus requirements. Insurance providers who meet the state's financial requirements and are approved to do business in the state are considered *authorized or admitted* into the state as legal insurance companies. Insurance providers not approved to do business in California are deemed *unauthorized or non-admitted*. Many states do not allow unauthorized insurance companies to do business in the state, except through excess and surplus lines brokers (Cal. Ins. Code Sections 24 and 25).

Regulation of Admitted and Non-Admitted Insurers – The Insurance Code provisions limit the insurance that can be placed with non-admitted insurers to the following:

- Insurance against perils of navigation, transportation, transit, or other shipowner property, or marine insurance needs;
- Reinsurance of the liability of an admitted insurer;
- Aircraft or spacecraft insurance; and
- Insurance on property or railroad operations in interstate commerce.

These insurance types can only be placed with a non-admitted insurer through a licensed surplus lines broker.

Placing insurance in violation of these regulations is a *misdemeanor*.

Penalty for Acting as an Insurer without a Certificate of Authority – Transacting insurance business in California without a certificate of authority is a *public offense punishable* by:

- Fine up $100,000; or
- Imprisonment according to the Penal Code; or
- Imprisonment for up to one year in county jail; or
- Both the fine and imprisonment.

In California, except when performed by a surplus lines broker, the following acts are *misdemeanors*:

- Acting as an agent for a non-admitted insurance company;
- Advertising in any form of a non-admitted insurance company;
- In any other manner aiding a non-admitted insurance company to transact insurance business.

Individuals violating any provision of this section will be fined $500 and $100 for each month they continue the violation.

These rules are not applicable to sanctioned advertising.

Domestic, Foreign, and Alien Insurers

Insurance companies are classified according to where they are incorporated. An insurance company must obtain a certificate of authority before transacting insurance within the state, regardless of the location of incorporation (domicile) (Cal. Ins. Code Sections 26, 27, and 1580).

A *domestic insurer* is an insurance company that is incorporated in this state. In most cases, the company's home office is in the state where it was formed (the company's domicile). For instance, a company chartered in Colorado would be considered a Colorado domestic company.

Insurance companies incorporated in another state, the District of Columbia, or a territorial possession are known as *foreign insurers*. Presently, the United States has five major U.S. territories, including Puerto Rico, the Northern Mariana Islands, Guam, American Samoa, and the U.S. Virgin Islands.

An *alien insurer* is an insurance company incorporated outside the United States.

Mutual and Stock Insurers

The most common types of ownership include the following:

Mutual companies are owned by the policy owners and issue *participating policies*. Policy owners are entitled to dividends, which are a return of excess premiums that are *not taxable*. Dividends are generated when the combined earnings and premiums create a surplus that exceeds the coverage costs. *Dividends are not guaranteed.*

Stock companies are owned by the stockholders who supply the capital necessary to establish and operate the insurance company and share any profits or losses. Officers manage stock insurance companies and are elected by the stockholders. Stock companies generally issue *nonparticipating policies*, where policy owners do not share in losses or profits.

Policy owners of nonparticipating policies do not receive dividends; however, stockholders are paid taxable dividends.

Excess and Surplus Lines Insurers

Excess and surplus lines insurers will issue insurance coverages in states where an insurer is not licensed and there is no available market for admitted insurers. These coverages are marketed through non-admitted insurers who specialize in providing insurance to the high-risk market on an unregulated basis under each state's surplus lines laws. While surplus lines insurers are not admitted, most states mandate that they be on that state's "approved" list.

Standard Market Insurers

Standard market insurers offer insurance coverage rates to insureds with an average or better-than-average loss exposure.

Operating Divisions of Insurers

Insurers operate with many different divisions and departments. Among them are four principal departments responsible for the primary functions: Sales or Marketing, Underwriting, Claims, and Actuarial. These departments each have a specific purpose within the structure of an insurance company, and each can have an impact, positive or negative, on the company's profitability.

Sales and Marketing – The *marketing department* is responsible for promoting, advertising, and distributing an insurance provider's products to the public. This department also trains the producers, sells the products and develops any materials related to the marketing process. Agents are field representatives of the marketing department, responsible for putting the company's products and services into clients' hands. The marketing department can also handle monitoring compliance with the various laws regarding the conduct of producers and the transacting of contracts. It is also responsible for observing consumer trends and then researching and developing or modifying products and services to meet the demands or needs of the marketplace.

Underwriting – The *underwriting department* is responsible for accepting insurance applications and evaluating them according to established guidelines. Applications are either declined or approved. Declined applications do not meet the insurer's guidelines, but not all approved applicants are equal. The insurance company is willing to insure many applicants' risks that are more significant than the average risks the company expects to insure. These risks are classified as *substandard*. Certain applicants will also have risks more favorable than average, and those will be classified as *preferred*.

The underwriting department's primary objective is to prevent an imbalance of risks or the selection of poor risks, including too many substandard risks compared to preferred and standard risks. The prevention of selecting these poor risks is known as *adverse selection*. When the underwriting department approves too many poor risks, the statistical predictions of the actuaries may not hold up. Under these circumstances, the insurer will not attain the level of profit expected and could potentially suffer a loss.

Claims – The *claims department* is responsible for accepting claim requests, evaluating them in light of the actual contract, paying those claims which are covered by the terms of the contract, and rejecting those which are not. The claims department can employ or contract with adjusters or other investigators to assist in evaluating claims or to seek evidence of fraudulent or false claims. When the claims department does not settle claims fairly or promptly or makes payments for claims that are not covered by the contract, the insurance company's profitability can be affected.

Actuarial – The *actuarial department* is where the science of statistics is put into practice. Insurance company actuaries study morbidity and mortality statistics, the nature of claims, and actual claims experience. They even weigh the potential for fraudulent claims and the financial impact of those claims, including investigating fraudulent claims and payments. The actuaries must also account for the everyday expenses of doing business. These expenses include the payment of claims and making a conservative estimate of earnings from invested reserves (premiums received by the insurer but not currently needed to pay the expenses). After the analysis and calculations have been made, the actuaries publish the rates that must be charged for each line of business the company insures to achieve profitability.

Qualifications of an Insurer

Any individual capable of making a contract can be an insurance provider, subject to the Code restrictions. To become an admitted insurer (legally entitled to transact insurance business in this state), an insurer must meet many technical, financial, and legal qualifications. The Code regulation is intended to prevent unqualified individuals from offering insurance to the public (Cal. Ins. Code Section 150).

The term *person* is used in the law to refer to any entity which is lawfully capable of performing legal acts, like making contracts, on its own behalf. In California, a person can be either a natural person *at least age 18* who is legally competent or any of the following entities:

- Organization;
- Association;
- Partnership;
- Limited liability company;
- Corporation; or
- Business trust.

Any person can be an insurance provider by satisfying the following guidelines of the California Insurance Code:

- Using only licensed brokers and agents;
- Submitting all products, forms, premiums, and advertising for approval before use;
- Using acceptable Doing Business As (DBA) names; and
- Maintaining required financial reserves.

Reciprocal Exchanges and Risk Retention Groups

A *reciprocal* refers to insurance resulting from an interchange of reciprocal agreements of indemnity among individuals called subscribers, collectively referred to as a Reciprocal Insurance Company or Exchange. The company is implemented and administered through an attorney-in-fact common to all individuals. Subscribers agree to become liable for their share of losses and expenses incurred among all subscribers. They authorize the attorney-in-fact to operate and manage the exchange.

A *risk retention group* (RRG) is a liability insurer owned by its members. The members are exposed to similar liability risks by being in the same business or industry. The purpose of a risk retention group is to assume and spread all or part of its group members' liability. A risk retention group can reinsure another risk retention group's liability as long as the members of the second group are engaged in the same or similar business or industry.

Insurance Underwriting

Producer's Responsibilities

The business of insurance requires honesty and good faith. For this reason, the insurance industry is regulated to ensure that its responsibilities to the public are upheld. Engaging in any insurance marketing practice involving a deceptive act or unfair competition is illegal.

As *field underwriter*, the broker or agent is the first line of client selection. They are obligated not to attempt to provide insurance to an insured that will financially damage the insurance company. Therefore, client pre-selection is the field underwriter's responsibility, under guidelines provided by each insurer. There are legal limitations as to the types of information that can be gathered by field underwriters, which will be examined. The producer should realize they may be, depending on underwriting guidelines, the only one who will physically be in the presence of that client. This circumstance presents an opportunity to perform a "real world" visual analysis of a client's desirability.

Insurer's Requirements

Pre-selection – The broker or agent can achieve a good pre-selection by accurate, complete, and thorough completion of the insurance application. The application will ask for all the legally allowed information that an insurance provider can collect to perform effective post-selection underwriting.

During the application process, the producer is in a position to terminate at any time if they find that the client poses an untenable risk to the insurer. Producers must also explain to the client why their risk might be higher than usual. Notifying clients of a possible premium rating can help them overcome "sticker shock" later.

For example, suppose an applicant is morbidly obese. In that case, they could still submit the application to the insurance provider. Still, the producer should warn the applicant that since their height/weight ratio is out of the standard range, they can expect to pay a significantly higher premium rate. The same applies to extreme sports enthusiasts, smokers, skin divers, and individuals of similar risk.

The producer is not allowed to gather information not asked for on the application but can seek details for those items that do appear. This information can include the extent of involvement in hazardous activities, dosages and frequency of use of medications, specifics regarding employment duties, etc.

It is also necessary to emphasize the producer's responsibility to not withhold from the principal any information that could be harmful regarding the client's risk.

Post-selection – Once the agent has chosen to complete and submit an insurance application, the in-house underwriters begin the post-selection process.

Using the application as a foundation, the underwriter starts an investigation of the client's complete risk profile. Federal and state law delineates the types and extent of information that can be obtained and considered, which we will see below. After considering the legally available information, the underwriter will classify the client as *standard*, *substandard*, or *uninsurable*.

If the client is sub-standard, they will be offered the opportunity to obtain coverage under a higher-than-standard premium. The client can decline to be insured under the stated conditions.

After the producer receives a signed authorization for disclosure of information, the underwriter can begin an investigation using the following sources of information:

- **MIB** – The Medical Information Bureau (MIB) is a centralized information database into which insurance companies provide information from applications and claims. Subscribing insurance providers can then search the MIB database for information regarding an applicant for insurance.
- **Department of Motor Vehicles** – Statistically, half of all accidental deaths in the United States occur due to traffic collisions. Therefore, insurance providers are very interested in the driving records of their applicants. A poor driving record can cause a rating or even a declination.
- **Physician/medical facility records** – The APS (attending physician statement) enables the insurance provider to receive the complete medical treatment history of the client.
- **Additional medical testing/Current physical** – The insurance provider can request that the applicant be examined by a physician and the results submitted for consideration. It is also common to require examination by a paramedical company and the use of urine, blood, or saliva samples to check for nicotine or other drugs and the presence of HIV. Insurers could also require an EKG (electrocardiogram).
- **Financial reports** – Using financial inspection reports and information from major credit reporting agencies, the insurance company can detect whether the client has a history of financial wrongdoing.
- **Personal interviews** – The underwriter can contact individuals with information about the applicant by telephone. These individuals can include relatives, neighbors, coworkers, or other acquaintances.
- **Hazardous activity questionnaire** – The insurer can also ask the applicant to fill out a separate hazardous activity questionnaire to determine the risk classification of the applicant. The questionnaire can include questions regarding scuba diving, hobby aviation, and auto, boat, or motorcycle racing.

Market Regulation

Market conduct regulations are state laws that regulate insurer practices regarding sales, underwriting, rate-making, and claims handling. The role of the Commissioner and the Department of Insurance is to regulate the conduct of insurers and agents. The overriding concern of the Commissioner is that consumers are not abused or taken advantage of by the companies and agents with whom they do business. The insurance and financial services industries are the most highly regulated today. While insurers are free to set their own rates for insurance, in most cases, the Commissioner has the authority to disapprove those rates as unfair. However, the Commissioner does not have the power to set an insurer's rates.

Throughout the Code, some sections are designed to expand or limit the rights of agents, insurance providers, and insureds. All regulations aim to create a "level playing field" for each participant. The law does not unfairly limit the ability of an insurer to be profitable; it does not freely allow limitless profits. Agents have the freedom to transact insurance with anyone capable of contracting. Yet, they are prohibited from discriminating against individuals in most circumstances. Insureds are free to do business with any insurer of their choosing. The law does not protect them if they choose to be insured by a non-admitted insurer. All are subject to regulations regarding unfair or fraudulent practices.

Legislation

McCarran-Ferguson Act – In 1945, the National Association of Insurance Commissioners (NAIC) proposed a bill sponsored by U.S. Senators Pat McCarran and Homer Ferguson. This bill would ensure insurance regulation would remain in the hands of the states. The bill became law later that year and is known as the McCarran-Ferguson Act (the Act). This Act is still significant today. It includes the basic delegation of authority from Congress to the states concerning the taxation and regulation of the insurance industry.

The McCarran-Ferguson Act stated that the federal government would not regulate insurance as long as the states adequately regulated the industry. In effect, the law unequivocally grants the states the right to regulate insurance. The Act also limited the application of antitrust laws to the insurance industry to the extent of state law regulating the insurance industry. After the Act's passing, several states enacted rating laws, created standards for fair trade practices, and licensing and solvency requirements. Working through the NAIC, state insurance regulators established the model laws that introduced the frameworks for the current rating laws and a prohibition against offering rebates.

California Insurance Code

The *California Insurance Code (CIC)* is the main body of laws set up by the state legislature, which regulates the insurance industry in California. The present form of the Code was enacted in 1935 as a restatement and expansion of previously established law. It is a dynamic, fluid device, constantly being reviewed, added to, amended, and even having outdated sections repealed. The CIC remains consistent with current practices and issues in the marketplace.

How the Code May be Changed – Legislative action is required to change the Insurance Code in any way. A bill repealing or amending an existing section or adding something new is introduced into the Assembly or the Senate. Here, it undergoes a variety of committee hearings and revisions before the bill is presented to the entire body for a vote. If approved, it goes to the other house for the same process. If additional changes are made before the bill is approved, it must be returned to the first body for re-approval. Once approved by both houses, the bill goes to the Governor for approval or veto, or it can also become law without the Governor's action.

Definitions

Shall and May – Certain terms or concepts have particular relevance to insurance but do not have different legal interpretations in insurance law. For example, the words "shall" and "may" always have the same implications, whether they appear in the Insurance Code or any other law (Cal. Ins. Code Section 16).

Shall is a word that compels action; it usually indicates that a specific action or response is required. Where the Code states that a person "shall" or "shall not" do something, there is usually no room for misunderstanding. On the other hand, *may* is a word of options or permission; it leaves room to act or not to act and remains in compliance with the law. However, the Code opens the possibility that, in context, even the word "may" could be interpreted the same as the word "shall."

Person – Even the word "person" is expansive. A *person* does not simply refer to a living, breathing human being (a natural person). A person can also refer to organizations, associations, partnerships, limited liability companies, corporations, and even trusts (all non-natural persons). Whether natural or non-natural, all persons are distinguished by their ability to contract, sue, or be sued. Non-natural persons only have to designate a natural person to represent them or act as their agent.

California Code of Regulations

The *California Code of Regulations (CCR)*, also called the *California Administrative Code*, is the set of regulations issued by the Department of Insurance that identifies the standards for the Insurance Code, and how it is to be administered. The CCR includes the regulations that have been issued by the Insurance Commissioner for clarification and administration of the Code.

The Commissioner

Selection of the Commissioner – In California, the Commissioner of Insurance is an *elected official*. The Commissioner is elected to serve not more than *two consecutive 4-year terms*.

The Commissioner is expected to be an individual knowledgeable in the insurance industry but cannot be an active agent, director, officer, or employee of an insurance company. If a licensed person is elected Commissioner, they must surrender their license within ten days of taking office. At the end of their term, they can have their license reinstated for the balance of the license term without penalties or fees.

Responsibilities – The Commissioner of Insurance has no authority or power to write or change the law but has the authority to enforce the law. The Commissioner's responsibility is to issue regulations establishing how the Department of Insurance intends to interpret and enforce the law. The regulations proposed by the Commissioner have to undergo a public hearing to determine their fairness or applicability before they can go into effect (Cal. Ins. Code Sections 12900 and 12921).

The Commissioner must oversee the California Department of Insurance (CDI) and direct all of the CDI's affairs and staff.

The Commissioner can appoint individuals to act on their behalf. These representatives can negotiate settlements with insurers or agents who have violated the Code. However, it is the responsibility of the Commissioner to make the final approval of a sanction.

The Commissioner is responsible for responding to inquiries and investigating complaints. When warranted, the Commissioner can bring enforcement actions against insurance providers. The system for managing complaints needs to include the following:

- A toll-free number published in telephone books throughout the state of California, dedicated to handling inquiries and complaints;
- Public service announcements to update consumers on the toll-free telephone number and how to report a complaint or make an inquiry to the California Department of Insurance;
- A simple, standardized complaint form intended to assure that complaints are appropriately registered and tracked;
- Retention of records related to complaints for at least three years;
- Guidelines to disseminate complaint and enforcement information to the public. This information contains license status, the number and type of complaints filed within the previous calendar year, the violations found, and any enforcement actions. Also included is the ratio of complaints received to total policies in force, premium dollars paid in a particular line, or both.

The Commissioner is responsible for giving the insurance provider an explanation of any complaint against the company that the Commissioner received and considered to be justified. This information must be provided at least 30 days before the public release of a report summarizing the required information. The summary includes:

- The date it was filed;
- The complainant's name;
- A description of facts; and
- A statement of the CDI's reasoning for determining whether the complaint is valid.

The Commissioner must prepare a report made available by the Department to interested individuals upon written request that details complaint and enforcement information on individual insurance providers according to the CIC. This report has to be made available by telephone, mail, Internet, and email.

Every public record of the Department and the Commissioner must be available for inspection and copying.

The Commissioner receives inquiries and complaints, investigates complaints, prosecutes insurance companies according to guidelines determined by the California Insurance Code, and responds to complaints and questions regarding alleged misconduct. The Commissioner is required to notify the complainant of receipt within *ten working days*. Once a determination is made, the Commissioner will inform the complainant of the final order within 30 days of judgment.

The Commissioner can issue a *cease and desist order* against the following: any individual acting as a broker or agent without being licensed and any individual transacting insurance without a certificate of authority. The Commissioner can also issue a cease and desist order without holding a hearing before allocating the order. A fine of up to $5,000 can be issued for each day the individual violates the order. An individual to whom a cease and desist order is issued can request a hearing by filing a request with the Commissioner within seven days after receiving the order.

California Guarantee Association and Insolvent Insurers

In California, all insurance providers must be members of the California Insurance Guarantee Association to provide *insolvency insurance* for each insurer. The Association also allows for the *indemnification of insured claims* of policy owners of member companies. As a condition of its authority to transact insurance in this state, each insurer, including the State Compensation Insurance Fund, must be a member of the Association.

Member insurer means an insurance provider must be a member of the Association.

An *insolvent insurer* refers to a member insurer against which a court of competent jurisdiction has entered an order of liquidation or receivership with a finding of insolvency.

Covered claims are the obligations of an insolvent insurance company, including the obligation for unearned premiums. "Covered claims" have to meet the following criteria:

- Imposed by law and within the coverage of an insurance policy of the insolvent insurance company;
- Unpaid by the insolvent insurance company;
- Presented as a claim to the liquidator in California or the Association on or before the last date fixed for the filing of claims in the domiciliary liquidating proceedings;
- Incurred before the date that coverage under the policy terminated and before, on, or within 30 days following the date the liquidator was appointed;
- The assets of the insolvent insurance company are inadequate to cover the claim;
- Regarding other insurance classes, if the claimant or insured is a resident of California at the time of the insured occurrence or the property from which the claim arises is permanently located in California.
- The obligations assumed by an assuming insurer from a ceding insurer where the assuming insurer subsequently becomes an insolvent insurer if, at the time of the assuming insurer's insolvency, the ceding insurer is no longer admitted to conducting business in California. Both the assuming insurer and the ceding insurer must have been member insurers when the assumption was made.

The Association can recover any deposit, bond, or other assets that might have been required to be posted by the ceding company to the extent of covered claim payments. The Association will also be subrogated to any policy owners' rights against the ceding insurer.

Insolvent Insurers – *Insolvency* (Cal. Ins. Code Section 985) refers to either of the following:

- Any impairment of the minimum paid-in capital required of an insurance provider by the Insurance Code provisions for the class, or classes, of insurance that it transacts anywhere;
- An incapacity to reinsure any risk over and above the state's retention limits; or
- An inability of the insurance provider to meet its financial obligations when they are due.

When the insurer can provide reinsurance of all outstanding risks and liabilities, it cannot escape insolvency unless it has additional assets equal to the aggregate paid-in capital required by the state.

Paid-in Capital – *Paid-in capital* or *capital paid-in* (Cal. Ins. Code Section 36) refers to the following:

- In the circumstance of a *foreign mutual insurer* not issuing or having outstanding capital stock, the value of its assets over and above the sum of its liabilities for losses reported, taxes, expenses, and all other indebtedness and reinsurance of outstanding risks as provided by law. However, foreign mutual insurers cannot be admitted unless their paid-in capital consists of available cash assets amounting to at least $200,000.
- In the circumstance of a *foreign joint stock and mutual insurer*, its paid-in capital is calculated, according to its desire, based on the standards for subdivision (a) or subdivision (c). If paid-in capital is calculated according to subdivision (a), then its admission is subject to the same qualifications.
- In the case of *all other insurance providers*, its paid-in capital is the lesser of:
  - The value of its assets over and above the sum of its liabilities for losses reported, taxes, expenses, and all other debt and reinsurance of outstanding risks; or
  - The total par value of issued shares of stock, including treasury shares. Shares of stock are not considered liabilities to calculate paid-in capital or capital paid-in.

Refusal to Issue Information – Suppose the Commissioner learns that irreparable loss and injury to the property and business of an individual has occurred or could occur unless the Commissioner acts. In that case, before applying to the court for any order, the Commissioner can take possession of the business, property, records, books, and accounts of the individual and their office. The Commissioner can continue to retain possession after receiving a court order.

Anyone against whom a seizure order has been issued and who refuses to deliver pertinent records, books, or assets will be guilty of a *misdemeanor*. This violation may be punishable by a maximum fine of $1,000, imprisonment for no longer than one year, or both.

Conservation – Insurers are exempted explicitly under federal bankruptcy laws, which means that any *liquidation* of an insolvent insurance company is strictly a matter for the state to pursue. To accomplish this, California has adopted the *Uniform Insurers Rehabilitation Act*. This Act describes the steps the Commissioner must take when attempting to rehabilitate a *delinquent* or *insolvent* insurer to sound financial condition or liquidate an insurer that cannot be rehabilitated. The Code also describes the superior court's mandatory action when the Commissioner presents a petition for either a conservation or liquidation order (Cal. Ins. Code Sections 1011, 1013, and 1016).

Each year, on or before March 1, every insurer conducting business in California must report its financial condition to the Commissioner. When an insurance provider's legal reserve funds are less than the minimum required by law, the insurer is *impaired* in its ability to pay claims and is technically *insolvent*. The Commissioner has authority under the Code to take control of the insurance company, and the superior court must grant the Commissioner's petition for conservation. There is no long, drawn-out legal battle (the insurance provider has no power to prevent the act of conservation).

The court order gives the Commissioner absolute control over the operations and assets of the insurer. The Commissioner's first responsibility is to try to rehabilitate the insurer, if at all possible. Initially, every new business transaction is terminated. Existing and new claims are paid, and ways to return the insurer to solvency are explored. When there is no possibility of rehabilitating the insurer, the Commissioner's final move will be to liquidate the insurer and sell assets to continue to pay claims. If all claims have been satisfied, the insurer will use any remaining assets to satisfy the claims of other creditors.

If the insurer cannot pay its claims, the two Guarantee Associations in California are prepared to pay a portion of the claims, depending on the type of policy. Suppose one or both of the Guarantee Associations must pay claims because of the inability of the insurer to pay. In that situation, they become creditors of the insurer and can seek repayment through the liquidation process.

In a conservation or liquidation effort, the Commissioner also has the power to sue directors, officers, or others who might bear responsibility for the company's condition. These individuals include managing general agents, actuaries, auditors, and accountants to add to the "estate" of the insurer to pay the claims of insureds or creditors. Even industry rating companies have been held responsible for their published inaccuracies.

Additionally, in a liquidation, other parties not generally associated with the claims-paying responsibility of the insurer can have their assets seized. Suppose the insolvent insurance provider was a substantial owner of another business or partnership. In that circumstance, those assets can satisfy the insurer's obligations, regardless of whether that business was involved in the insurance industry.

When the Commissioner is involved in liquidating an insurer, there is a legal requirement to publish the notice of liquidation for four consecutive weeks. In most cases, the Commissioner must also mail notices to known potential claimants against the insurer's estate. Once the notices have been published or mailed, claimants have no more than six months to file their claims. The Insurance Code establishes the priority of claims. Only when the claims of a class or group have been fully satisfied will the next claimant in order be entitled to pursue their claims.

Privacy Protection

The Gramm-Leach-Bliley Act – The *Gramm-Leach-Bliley Act (GLBA)* mandates that an insurance provider cannot divulge nonpublic information to a nonaffiliated third party except for the following reasons:

- The insurance provider discloses to the consumer in writing that information may be disclosed to a third party;
- The consumer is given a chance, before the information is initially disclosed, to require that the information not be divulged to the third party; or
- The consumer receives an explanation of how the consumer can exercise a nondisclosure option.

The Gramm-Leach-Bliley Act requires two disclosures to a customer (a consumer who has an ongoing financial relationship with a financial institution):

1. When the customer relationship is established (e.g., a policy is purchased); and
2. Before disclosing protected information.

The customer must be given an annual privacy disclosure and the right to opt out or decide not to have their private information shared with other parties.

California Financial Information Privacy Act – The California Financial Information Privacy Act was enacted on July 1, 2004. It allows consumers to control how their nonpublic personal information is shared or sold to third-party financial institutions. The act provides greater privacy protections than the federal Gramm-Leach-Bliley Act (GLBA).

The act restricts the financial profiling of consumers. It makes consumers aware of their rights through a written and easy-to-understand notice, allowing them to opt in or out of sharing nonpublic personal information.

Nonpublic personal information refers to personally identifiable information collected by a financial institution through the consumer, a transaction between the institution and consumer, or some other means.

Examples of *personally-identifiable information* include:

- Information about an application obtaining credit cards, loans, or other financial services or products;
- Payment history, debit or credit card purchase information, and account balance information;
- Information from past and current financial institutions used by a consumer;
- Financial information gathered through web servers or internet cookies; and
- Information contained on a consumer report.

Authorized privacy notices must include the following:

- A form, statement, or writing that remains separate from other documents;
- A title that reads "Important Privacy Choices for Consumers;"
- The date and the consumer's signature;
- A disclosure stating the consumer consents to the release of personally identifiable information to a nonaffiliated third party;
- A disclosure confirming that consent will remain in effect unless revoked or modified by the consumer;
- A process for the consumer to revoke consent; and
- A statement confirming that the financial institution will maintain the notice, and the consumer can receive a copy upon request.

A financial institution is not required to obtain a consumer's consent if nonpublic personal information is shared with its wholly owned financial institution subsidiaries.

Suppose a financial institution violates the California Financial Information Privacy Act. In that circumstance, the institution may be fined up to $2,500 per violation of one consumer's information being released or $500,000 for multiple consumers.

Insurance Information and Privacy Protection Act – Cal. Ins. Code Section 791 is concerned with the collection and distribution of, or the access to, a person's private or privileged information, which can be necessary to obtain in connection with an insurance application. The law is sensitive to a consumer's desire to keep certain information private. However, it also acknowledges that an insurance provider might approve an individual for insurance without that information. The insurer could lawfully decline coverage if it knew that information.

Practices – Section 791 of the CIC balances fairness for applicants and insurance providers when gathering and using information. The law is designed to apply to natural persons who are residents of the state and are seeking life or disability insurance. It also applies to any individual seeking property or casualty insurance for policies issued or delivered in California.

The information necessary for proper underwriting can be personal and highly sensitive. Because of this, there is great potential for harm to an individual if their personal information is disclosed to others who have no legitimate reason for receiving it. How and from whom that information is collected, obtained, kept, and when or how it will be disseminated to others must be disclosed to insurance applicants.

In some cases, insurance providers can decide to conduct an investigative consumer report with an application. An investigative consumer report goes beyond simply gathering information from the Medical

Information Bureau (MIB) or the credit reporting bureaus. It can include interviews with applicants, employers, their relatives, neighbors, or any other individual with information about the person's general reputation, character, personal characteristics, and lifestyle. The Insurance Code allows individuals to request that they be interviewed personally. It also requires that the person be given a copy of the report upon request and provided with a mechanism to protest and request a correction of inaccurate information about them. The individual has a right to know to whom the information has been given and the source or sources.

If an adverse underwriting decision occurs, the individual must be given the reason for the decision. The reason can include being declined, rated, or considered less than a standard risk. It can also mean being issued coverage by an insurer other than the one to which the applicant initially intended to apply. Insurers must give this information to the individual in writing. An insurer can also advise these individuals that they may request the reason for the action to be furnished to them in writing.

Suppose the information is medically-related and supplied by a medical professional or medical care institution. In that situation, it must be disclosed (upon request) directly to the individual or a licensed medical professional to treat the person for the condition to which the information relates. When the information is related to an individual's mental health, it can only be disclosed with the consent of the medical professional who is responsible for the treatment related to that information.

Prohibitions – The Insurance Code also describes how information about an individual's previous adverse underwriting decisions cannot be used as the basis of a new underwriting decision. An exception is made if it is received directly from the agent or insurer who made the adverse decision. Being declined or rated for insurance in the past or having insurance provided by a residual insurer is insufficient for denying or rating an individual for new insurance. A residual insurer is one other than the original insurer to which the application for coverage was submitted.

Additionally, applications for insurance that include questions that are not intended to gather information about the applicant but are intended for marketing or other purposes need to be clearly identified. Marketing or research questions could include those designed to reveal an individual's shopping habits, for example. Still, they could disclose other *privileged information* that the agent or insurer has no reason to need or possess. These questions do not have to be answered, and a decision not to answer such questions may not be used as the basis for an adverse underwriting decision.

Penalties – Section 791 of the CIC details under what circumstances the Commissioner can examine insurance providers, agents, and others engaged in the information collecting processes. It also details how these individuals must maintain or distribute the information gathered. There are a variety of penalties that may be applied to the various violations that can be committed. Some of the penalties include:

- Suspension or loss of license; and
- Civil fines for violating cease and desist orders of up to $10,000 per violation; or
- Up to $50,000 if the violations are discovered to be committed with a frequency indicating they are a general business practice.

Agents or insurers can also be liable for civil damages and legal fees arising from the unlawful collection or distribution of private or privileged information about an individual that causes harm. Certain acts could also violate other criminal laws and subject an individual to prosecution, resulting in fines or imprisonment.

Cal-GLBA

The California Financial Information Privacy Act provides standards for financial institutions regarding sharing or selling nonpublic personal information about consumers. California legislation known as *Cal-GLBA* delivers greater privacy protection to consumers than the federal Gramm-Leach-Bliley Act. Cal-GLBA outlines consumer privacy choices and rights and allows California consumers to have greater control over disclosing nonpublic personal information.

As defined by the California Financial Code, *nonpublic personal information* refers to any financial information that is

- Provided to a financial institution by a consumer;
- Acquired as a result of a transaction with the consumer; or
- Acquired by a financial institution through any other means.

Health Insurance Portability and Accountability Act (HIPAA)

Under the Privacy Rule for HIPAA, protected information includes all "individually identifiable health information," including information held or transmitted by a covered entity or its business associate in any form or media, whether paper, electronic, or oral. This information is known as *protected health information (PHI)*.

Individually identifiable health information includes demographic data related to present, past, or future physical or mental health, condition, or payment information that could easily identify the person.

A covered entity has to obtain the person's written authorization to disclose information that is not for payment, treatment, or health care operations.

Rates

Requirements for Rates to be Approved or Remain in Effect – Insurance rates cannot be approved or remain in effect if they are inadequate, excessive, unfairly discriminatory, or in violation of the California Insurance Code. In considering whether a rate is inadequate, excessive, or unfairly discriminatory, no consideration can be given to the degree of competition. The Commissioner must consider whether the rate reflects the insurer's investment income mathematically.

Types of Rating Laws

Prior Approval – Under this plan, insurance providers must file proposed policy rate information with the state insurance department. Upon filing, the insurance provider must deliver supporting evidence that such rates are justified and do not charge inadequate, excessive, or unfairly discriminatory premiums. The Commissioner has a predetermined number of days, usually 30 to 60, to approve or reject the submitted rate plan. However, the Commissioner's failure to reject the plan is considered approval to adopt and market such a plan.

File and Use – *File-and-use* laws stipulate that the rate plan be filed *before marketing the plan*. However, such laws state that once the plan is filed, the insurance provider does not have to wait for the Commissioner's approval to begin marketing the plan.

Use and File – *Use-and-file* laws stipulate that rate plans be filed within a specified period, usually 15-30 days, *after being used* with the public.

Open Competition – The *open competition* rating method, also called no-file laws, allows insurance providers to compete with one another by quickly changing rates without review by the state regulators. Under such a plan, market forces, rather than administrative action, determine what rates will be charged for a given risk.

State Regulation of Rates – The Commissioner must notify the public of any application by an insurance provider for a rate change. The application will be considered approved 60 days after public notice unless:

- A consumer requests a hearing within 45 days of a public notice, and the Commissioner grants the hearing or determines not to grant the hearing and issues written findings in support of that decision;
- The Commissioner, on their own motion, determines to hold a hearing;
- The proposed rate adjustment exceeds 7% of the then-applicable rate for personal lines or 15% for commercial lines. The Commissioner must conduct a hearing upon a timely request.

A rate change application will be *deemed approved 180 days* after the Commissioner receives the rate application unless a final order from the Commissioner has disapproved that application.

Fair Claims Settlement Practice Regulations

Definitions – A *claimant* is any individual who maintains a right of recovery under a surety bond (10 Cal. Code Regs. Section 2695.2(c)). Claimants can also include an attorney, any individual authorized by law to represent the claimant, or any of the following individuals properly designated by the claimant:

- Insurance adjuster;
- Public adjuster; or
- Any member of the claimant's family.

A *notice of legal action* is a document confirming a legal action has been initiated against the insurer regarding a claim or notice of action against the insured (10 Cal. Code Regs. Section 2695.2(o)). A notice of action against the principal under a bond can also be initiated, including any arbitration proceeding.

A *proof of claim* is any documentation in the claimant's possession submitted to the insurer that provides evidence of the claim and supports the amount of the claimed loss (10 Cal. Code Regs. Section 2695.2(s)).

File and Record Documentation – The Commissioner reserves the right to examine every licensee's claim files, including all notes, documents, and work papers (including copies of all correspondence). The files should be detailed so the Commissioner can reconstruct all events and dates and determine the licensee's actions (10 Cal. Code Regs. Section 2695.3).

Insurance providers must do the following:

- Maintain claim records that are legible, accessible, and retrievable;
- Record the dates the licensee received, processed, and transmitted or mailed relevant documents in the file; and
- Maintain hard copy files. If the files are not hard copies, they have to be in a format that is legible, accessible, and capable of being duplicated into hard copies.

When the licensee cannot construct complete records, they must document the difficulty or inability to obtain data for the Commissioner because of catastrophic losses or other unusual circumstances.

In this case, the licensee needs to submit to the Commissioner a plan for file and record documentation to be utilized while the circumstances that keep the licensee from compiling a complete record persist.

Duties upon Receipt of Communications – Upon receiving any inquiry from the Department of Insurance regarding a claim, the licensee has to respond within *21 calendar days*. The response must address all issues the Department of Insurance raised in its inquiry.

Upon receiving any communication from a claimant (concerning a claim) that reasonably suggests that a response is expected, every licensee has to furnish the claimant with a complete response within *15 days*.

A designation of claimant needs to be in writing, signed and dated by the claimant, and must indicate that the designated individual is authorized to handle the claim. All designations must be given to the insurance provider and will be valid from the date of execution until the designation is revoked or the claim is settled. A designation can be revoked by a written communication given to the insurance provider, signed and dated by the claimant, indicating that the designation is to be revoked and the effective date of the revocation.

Upon receipt, every licensee must immediately communicate a notice of claim to the insurance company. The licensee's duty to convey the information will be met when the licensee complies with proper written instructions from the insurer.

Upon receiving a notice of claim, every insurance provider must do the following (unless the notice of claim is a notice of legal action) within *15 days*:

- Acknowledge receipt of the notice to the claimant unless payment is made within that period. If the acknowledgment is not in writing, a notation of acknowledgment has to be made in the insurance provider's claim file and dated. Failure of an insurance agent to promptly transmit a notice of claim to the insurance provider will be attributed to the insurer;
- Provide to the claimant instructions, reasonable assistance, and necessary forms. This information includes specifying that the claimant must provide proof of claim; and
- Begin any necessary investigation of the claim.

Standards for Prompt, Fair and Equitable Settlements – Insurance providers cannot discriminate in their claims settlement practices based on a claimant's age, gender, race, language, income, religion, sexual orientation, national origin, ancestry, physical disability, or the territory of the property or person insured (10 Cal. Code Regs. Sections 2695.7(a), (b), (c), (g), (h)).

Once the claim is received, insurers have to either accept or deny it within *40 calendar days*. The amounts accepted or denied must be documented unless the claim has been denied in its entirety. The time frame does not apply to claims arising from disability insurance and disability income insurance policies or to automobile repair bills arising from policies of automobile collision and comprehensive insurance.

If an insurance provider rejects a first-party claim, it must do so in writing and state the basis for the rejection. Insurers are protected from disclosing information that could alert a claimant that a claim is being investigated as a suspected fraudulent claim.

Written notification must include a statement confirming a claimant can have a claim reviewed by the California Department of Insurance. A claimant may request a review if they suspect the claim has been rejected or denied wrongfully. The notice will include the address and telephone number of the unit of the Department which reviews claims practices.

Suppose an insurer needs more time to determine if a claim should be accepted or denied. In that case, within the 40-day acceptance period, it must inform the claimant in writing of the need for more time, any additional information the insurer needs, and any continuing reasons for the insurer's inability to decide. Subsequently, the written notice has to be submitted every 30 calendar days until a determination is made or notice of legal action is served.

An insurer cannot try to settle a claim by making an unreasonably low settlement offer. Upon acceptance of the claim, insurers must provide payment within *30 days*.

Notice by Mail

There is always the possibility that a party to a policy could attempt to avoid responsibility under the policy. They may falsely claim they sent a notice or that the other party never sent the required notice. The law explains what is considered to be sufficient proof of mailing.

Suppose the notice had postage applied and was put in the hands of the U.S. Postal Service with the recipient's last known address on it. In that case, an affidavit by the sender stating such facts is proof of the mailing. Any notice provided by electronic transmission must be treated as if mailed or given for any provision of the Insurance Code. A valid electronic signature will be sufficient for any provision of law requiring a written signature (Cal. Ins. Code Sections 38 and 38.6).

A licensee must acquire an insured's consent to opt-in to receive records electronically. Additionally, a licensee must disclose to insureds that they may opt-out of electronic transmission at any time. Licensees must also disclose a description of the records the insured will receive, a process to change or correct an insured's email address, and the licensee's contact information.

The insurer must retain a copy of the confirmation and electronic signature with the policy information. The insurer must be able to retrieve them upon request by the Department of Insurance when the policy is effective and for five years after that.

Upon the insured's request, a licensee must provide at least one free printed copy of records annually.

When required to transmit a record by return receipt, a licensee may demonstrate actual delivery by:

- Having the recipient acknowledge the receipt;
- Have the record securely posted on the licensee's website; or
- Having the record transmitted to the named insured through a secure application.

A licensee must contact the insured to confirm their email address when a record is not delivered directly to the insured's email. Licensees can also resend the record by regular mail within five business days.

Unfair Trade Practices

After passing the McCarran-Ferguson Act in 1945, California adopted regulations concerning unfair practices, affirming the state's role in insurance regulation. This section of the CIC, together with its subparts, contains different practices that the Code has identified explicitly as unfair and the other regulations and penalties related to unfair practices. The Code is also clear regarding any other undefined act or practice that the Commissioner determines to be unfair to insurers or consumers. Even though they are not mentioned in particular, such acts or practices can still violate the Code. (Cal. Ins. Code Sections 790 through 790.15).

General Prohibitions – Many of the most prevalent practices which are problems include things like misrepresentations in sales illustrations or advertised policy terms, or in the financial condition of an insurance provider, including its reserves and policy titles which could mislead an individual into believing that the contract performs differently, or other misrepresentations which could lead a person to forfeit, surrender, or lapse a policy. Additionally, acts such as unfairly discriminating against classes of insureds, filing false financial documents, or simply making false statements that should be known as untrue by using reasonable care are identified as unfair practices.

Unfair claims settlement practices include the following:

- Failure to determine within a reasonable amount of time after the submission of proof of loss forms whether or not a claim is payable;

- Misrepresenting facts or provisions of policy coverage;
- Not making a fair settlement of a claim after the insurance company's liability has been made clear;
- Compelling insureds to sue the insurer to obtain a judgment to enforce a claim by offering substantially less than the insured receives following a trial, only to collect an amount the same or nearly the same as the insured hoped to receive;
- Advertising insurance that the insurer will not sell; and
- Providing untrue or deceptive information about an individual or entity engaged in insurance.

Also included in this subpart are other offenses, such as the following:

- An insurance provider attempting to appeal arbitration awards to get the insured to accept a compromise or settlement for less than the arbitration award;
- Requiring insureds to submit preliminary claim reports followed later by a request to submit essentially the same information to either deny or accept a claim;
- Advising an insured not to seek or retain an attorney;
- Delaying payment regarding hospital, medical, or surgical claims for individuals with HIV or AIDS for more than 60 days after filing a claim to attempt to invoke a pre-existing condition exclusion;
- Advertising membership in the state's Guarantee Association;
- Unfair discrimination;
- Filing false financial statements; and
- Intimidation, coercion, boycott.

Specific Unfair Trade Practices Defined

False Advertising – Advertising covers a wide range of communication, from publishing an ad in a magazine or newspaper to broadcasting a commercial on television or the Internet. Advertisements cannot include any deceptive, untrue, or misleading statements that apply to the business of insurance or anyone who conducts it. Violating this rule is called *false advertising*.

It is forbidden to advertise or circulate any materials that are deceptive, untrue, or misleading. Deceptive or false advertising specifically includes *misrepresenting* any of the following:

- Benefits, terms, conditions, or advantages of any insurance policy;
- The financial condition of any individual or the insurance carrier;
- Any dividends to be received from the policy or previously paid out; or
- The true intention of an assignment or loan against a policy.

Representing an insurance policy as a share of stock or utilizing names or titles that could misrepresent the true nature of a policy will be considered false advertising. Also, a person or an entity cannot use a name that deceptively suggests it is an insurance provider.

Misrepresentation – It is illegal to publish, issue, or circulate any illustration or sales material that is misleading, false, or deceptive as to the policy benefits or terms, the payment of dividends, etc. This illegal activity also refers to oral statements and is known as *misrepresentation*.

Rebating – *Rebating* is any inducement offered to the insured during the sale of insurance products not specified in the policy. Both the offer and the acceptance of a rebate are illegal. Rebates can include, but are not limited to, the following:

- Rebates of policy premiums;
- Special services or favors;

- Kickbacks for referrals;
- Advantages in dividends or other benefits; and
- Securities, stocks, bonds, and their profits or dividends.

Twisting – *Twisting* s a misrepresentation. It is also a fraudulent or incomplete comparison of insurance that persuades a policy owner, to their detriment, to lapse, cancel, switch policies, or take out a policy with another insurer. Twisting is prohibited.

Unfair Discrimination – *Discrimination* in premiums, rates, or policy benefits for individuals within the *same class* or with the same life expectancy is illegal. Insurers cannot discriminate based on a person's race, national origin, marital status, sexual orientation, gender identity, creed, or ancestry unless it is for business purposes or required by law.

Defamation – *Defamation* occurs when oral or written statements are intended to injure a person engaged in the insurance business. It also applies to statements that are maliciously critical of the financial condition of any individual or company.

Boycott, Coercion, and Intimidation – It is illegal to engage in any activity of *boycott, coercion, or intimidation* intended to create a monopoly or restrict fair trade. This activity also would include unfair behavior that influences clients, competing brokers, and agents.

Coercion is to require, as a condition of a loan, that the applicant purchase insurance from a specific insurance company.

Penalties – Whenever the Commissioner has reason to believe that an individual is engaging in or has engaged in any unfair trade practices, the Commissioner must issue a cease and desist order. The cease and desist order must show cause, in addition to the individual's liability, and it must accompany the notice of a hearing, which must be at least *30 days* from the date of the order. The Commissioner can issue a penalty if the charges are justified at the hearing.

The *civil penalties* that can be assessed for violations of unfair trade practices are $5,000 for each act in violation of the Code, whether intentional or not. However, suppose the act or practice is determined to be a willful violation or a general business practice. In that case, the penalty increases to a maximum of $10,000 for each violation. The Commissioner can also act against a licensee who engages in any unfair practice.

When the Commissioner believes an individual has violated a cease and desist order, after a hearing, the Commissioner can order that individual to pay a sum not to exceed $5,000. This amount may be recouped in a civil action. If the violation is willful, the amount of the penalty can be a sum not to exceed $55,000. These fines are in addition to civil penalties for violation of the Insurance Code ($5,000 per act) and intentional violation of the Insurance Code ($10,000 per act).

Unfairly Discriminatory Practices

Insurance has two types of discrimination: fair and unfair discrimination (Cal. Ins. Code Sections 10140 through10145). *Fair discrimination* occurs when an insurance provider's underwriting department finds information that indicates an increase in risk that can be verified through statistical (actuarial) proof. Suppose an insurer decides to limit coverage or other policy benefits, increase premiums, or refuse coverage for that type of client (discriminate). In that case, it is appropriate for them to do so since the law permits it.

Unfair discrimination is morally unacceptable and illegal. One step in enabling insurance providers to avoid unfair discrimination is to place applicants and insureds in classifications based on actuarially acceptable guidelines. Such classifications upon which risk and insurability can be based will inherently vary with the specific type of coverage. Generally, they can include the following:

- Gender;
- Age;
- Tobacco use;
- Height/weight ratio;
- Geographic location; or
- Profession and avocations (hobbies).

Insurers can use a combination of these, but only if statistics prove that the classification increases a claim's risk on the specific type of insurance being considered.

For example, it would be unacceptable for an insurer to charge life insurance clients a higher premium based on their ZIP code. Their geographic location does not increase their risk of death. However, it would be acceptable to charge these same clients a higher or lower premium for health insurance, provided the costs of care in their ZIP code are higher or lower than the average. For this reason, it is typical for insurers to apply a *rating factor* to raise or lower a health insurance premium based solely on the ZIP code.

Once a client's actuarial classifications have been determined, that client must be treated the same as every other client within the same classifications. The person cannot be provided with different policy benefits or charged a different premium than everyone else in those classifications.

The following are specific classifications that *cannot* exist:

- Race;
- Color;
- Religion;
- National origin;
- Ancestry;
- Sexual orientation; and
- Physical and mental impairments that do not increase risk or vision impairment, including blindness.

Classifying people according to these classifications would be unfair as these characteristics do not affect the client's risk. It is forbidden for insurance providers or their representatives to request, acquire, or share such information. It is acceptable to ask an applicant for their place of birth if that information is only used for identification purposes.

Regarding sexual orientation, it would be a blatant violation for an insurance provider to ask an applicant any question regarding the subject. While insurers won't ask a direct question, they can attempt to conclude sexual orientation by analyzing other factors in the applicant's life. Then, the insurer can adjust the benefits or the premium based on a presumption of an increased risk of AIDS. Insurance providers cannot use the following to attempt to make a judgment about sexual orientation:

- Gender;
- Marital status;
- Living arrangement;
- Jobs;
- Beneficiary;

- ZIP code or any other geographic classification; or
- Any combination of these.

Therefore, if an insurance provider is concerned about the risk of claims resulting from AIDS and wishes to test for HIV, it is necessary to test everyone under the same guidelines.

Suppose an insured with a condition expected to cause death within one year requests an experimental treatment and is refused by their insurance provider. In that case, the insurer has to provide the following:

- The specific medical and scientific reasons for the denial and specific references to related policy provisions upon which the denial is based;
- A description of the alternative treatments or medical procedures covered by the policy, if any; and
- A description of the appeal/review process within 30 days or five days if delaying treatment would be detrimental.

Insurance providers offering life or health insurance cannot affect the coverage or premium of anyone because the insurer suspects the individual may become a victim of *domestic violence*. Underwriters are, however, allowed to consider an actual medical condition that does exist, as long as they don't consider whether the condition was caused by domestic violence. Intentional acts of the insured can still result in the loss of benefits.

Section 6211 of the California Family Code defines *domestic violence* as abuse perpetrated against any of the following:

- A cohabitant or former cohabitant;
- A spouse or former spouse;
- An individual with whom the respondent is having or has had a dating or engagement relationship;
- An individual with whom the respondent has had a child, where it is presumed that the male parent is the child's father and the female parent is the mother under the Uniform Parentage Act;
- A child of a party or a child who is the subject of an action under the Uniform Parentage Act, where the male parent is the father of the child to be protected; or
- Any other individual related by blood or affinity within the second degree.

Medical policies must include coverage for diagnosing and treating severe mental illness for every insured and serious emotional disturbances in children. This coverage then excludes insurance providers from offering any specific-coverage policy, such as accident only, dental, etc.

Penalties – In addition to any other remedy permitted by law, the Commissioner has the administrative authority to assess penalties against life or disability insurance companies for violations of the Insurance Code section on discriminatory practices. The penalties for the insurance provider for *unfair discrimination* violations are as follows:

- 1st violation – $2,500;
- Subsequent violations – $5,000 each;
- Violations so frequent as to indicate they are a general business practice of that insurer – $15,000 - $100,000 per violation.

Any individual who *negligently discloses* the results of a genetic test for an unauthorized third party will be assessed a civil penalty of up to $1,000, plus court costs, payable to the test subject. Any willful violations will be subject to a civil penalty between $1,000 and $5,000, plus court costs.

When the subject suffers bodily, emotional, or economic harm, the violation becomes a misdemeanor punishable by a fine of up to $10,000. Each unauthorized disclosure is considered a separate violation. Suppose an individual decides to share that information with the public. In that case, the penalty and damages could be hundreds of thousands of dollars.

Fraud

Common Circumstances – Insurance fraud is a significant problem for insurers and insureds. Premiums for most forms of insurance have risen in recent years due to the increasing number of fraudulent claims being presented to insurance companies for payment. The most common forms of insurance fraud include:

- Fraudulent health care billings;
- Staged automobile accidents;
- False or inflated property loss claims;
- Phony workers compensation claims;
- Fraudulent denial of workers compensation benefits;
- Workers compensation premium fraud by employers;
- Fake life insurance claims; and
- Arson for profit.

In 2002, the California Department of Insurance estimated that up to 50% of all automobile insurance claims might be fraudulent. Many of them are being "staged" on paper instead of occurring. This automobile insurance fraud is estimated to cost California consumers as much as $500,000,000 annually. Due to the high cost of medical claims, California has the highest rates for workers compensation insurance, even though the actual compensation benefits are among the lowest in the country.

Efforts to Combat Fraud – Federal, state, and local law enforcement officials work together with insurers and industry support organizations to combat insurance fraud. The California Department of Insurance has created the *Fraud Division* to enforce the Penal Code's provisions and administer the fraud reporting provisions.

Among other agencies and systems to help combat fraud is the Arson Information Reporting System. It allows for cooperation between insurance providers, fire investigating agencies, law enforcement agencies, and district attorneys. This system permits all parties to deposit arson case information in a common database within the Department of Justice.

All insurance providers must report covered private passenger vehicles involved in theft to prevent auto insurance-related fraud. Insurers must include the vehicle identification number (VIN) and any other relevant information to the National Automobile Theft Bureau or a similar organization approved by the Commissioner. Before the payment of theft losses, insurance companies have to comply with verification procedures according to the regulations adopted by the Commissioner.

Insurers, brokers, and agents also have a legal responsibility to report suspected fraud. Suppose an insurer or licensed rating organization knows the identity of an individual or entity that has perpetrated fraud relating to a workers compensation insurance policy or claim. In that case, the insurer must notify the local district attorney's office and the Fraud Division of the Department of Insurance. It can inform any other authorized government agency of that suspected fraud and provide additional information.

The Commissioner can license an organization as an *Insurance Claims Analysis Bureau*, provided that it is a nonprofit corporation organized for fraud prevention with at least two years of relevant experience. An Insurance Claims Analysis Bureau must perform the following functions:

- Gather and compile information and data from members concerning the insurance claims;
- Disseminate claims-related information to members to suppress and prevent insurance fraud;
- Promote training and education related to suppression, investigation, and prosecution of insurance fraud; and
- Provide to the Commissioner (without fee or charge) all state data and information contained in the records of the Bureau to further prevent and prosecute insurance fraud.

Every insurance company admitted to conducting business in this state must allow for the continuous operation of a unit or division to investigate possible fraudulent claims for services or repairs against policies held by insureds.

Insurers, brokers, and agents have legal immunity from civil suits claiming libel or slander. These lawsuits could result from filing reports, giving statements, or furnishing any other information, provided the information is offered *in good faith and without malice*.

Fraudulent Claim Forms – If a claimant signs a fraudulent claim form, the claimant can be found guilty of perjury.

Insurance Fraud Prevention Act – Chapter 12 of the Insurance Code is devoted exclusively to the Insurance Fraud Prevention Act. The Insurance Code explains the primary responsibilities that the Commissioner, law enforcement agencies, insurers, brokers, agents, and others have when aggressively confronting the problem of insurance fraud in this state.

State insurance claim forms must carry a notice informing claimants of their liability in the event of a fraudulent claim.

Every individual who *commits insurance fraud* can be punished as follows:

- A fine up to $150,000 or twice the dollar amount of the fraud, whichever is greater;
- Imprisonment in county jail for one year, or in state prison for up to five years; or
- Both imprisonment and fine.

The court will determine the restitution amount and where the restitution needs to be paid. An individual convicted can be charged for the costs of the investigation at the court's discretion.

An individual who commits insurance fraud and has a prior felony conviction will receive a 2-year enhancement for each prior conviction in addition to the sentence provided.

Interstate Commerce

It is fraudulent for anyone engaged in the insurance business to deliberately make any oral or written statement with the intent to deceive. *Unlawful insurance fraud* includes false statements or omissions of material fact, false information and statements made on an insurance application, and malicious statements regarding the financial condition of an insurance company.

Anyone engaged in insurance whose activities affect interstate commerce and who intentionally makes false material statements can be imprisoned for up to ten years, fined, or both. If the activity jeopardized the security of the accompanied insurance provider, the sentence could be extended up to *15 years*. Anyone acting as an agent, officer, director, or another insurance employee caught embezzling funds will be subject to the imprisonment and fines previously described. However, if the embezzlement was in an amount that is *less than $5,000*, prison time could be reduced to one year.

Federal law makes it illegal for anyone convicted of a crime involving breach of trust, dishonesty, or a violation of the Violent Crime Control and Law Enforcement Act of 1994 to work in the insurance business affecting interstate commerce without written consent from an insurance regulatory official (Commissioner of Insurance, Director of Insurance, etc.) This requirement is known as a 1033 waiver. The consent from the official has to specify that it is granted for the purpose of 18 U.S.C. 1033. Anyone convicted of a felony involving breach of trust or dishonesty, who also transacts insurance, will be imprisoned for up to five years, fined, or both.

Anyone who engages in conduct that violates Section 1033 can be subject to a civil penalty of not more than $50,000 for each violation or the amount of payment received from the prohibited conduct, whichever is greater.

Section 1034: Civil Penalties and Injunctions – According to this section, the *Attorney General* can bring a civil action in the appropriate United States district court against any individual who engages in conduct constituting an offense under section 1033 and, upon evidence of such conduct, the individual will be subject to a civil penalty of not more than $50,000 for each violation, or the amount of payment which the individual offered or received for the prohibited conduct, whichever is greater.

Excess and Surplus (E&S) Lines

Surplus lines insurance is a type of coverage that is not readily available on the admitted market. Such coverages are marketed through non-admitted insurers who specialize in providing insurance to the high-risk market on an unregulated basis under the surplus lines laws of each state. While surplus lines insurers are not admitted, most states require that they be on that state's "approved" list.

All states require insurers to obtain a license or certificate of authority to conduct insurance business in the state. These insurance carriers are known as admitted or authorized insurers. The term *non-admitted insurance* means any property and casualty insurance allowed to be written directly or through a surplus lines broker with a non-admitted insurance carrier eligible to accept such insurance.

Each state makes certain exceptions to allow nonauthorized or non-admitted insurance carriers to transact business within the state. The permitted types of transactions are typically limited to insurance that is not easy to write or insurance that is not readily available through an authorized insurer in the state. These unauthorized insurance carriers are called *excess* or *surplus lines* insurers.

Although the insurance company is unregulated, only licensed excess and surplus lines brokers can sell this insurance. Each state defines its parameters for writing excess and surplus lines insurance business. The following are some of the general requirements:

- An authorized insurance carrier cannot write the insurance;
- The purpose of writing the insurance through an excess or surplus lines insurance carrier must not be to gain better terms or a better price; and
- The coverage has to be written through a state-licensed excess or surplus lines broker.

Because these insurance carriers are considered unauthorized, most states compile an approved listing of excess and surplus lines insurers. The National Association of Insurance Commissioners also publishes a list of excess and surplus lines insurance carriers it deems acceptable. Many states have come along to adopt this NAIC listing.

A surplus line broker's license applicant must, as part of the application and a condition of the license issuance, file a bond to the people of the State of California for $50,000.

Any natural person applying for a surplus lines broker license must prove competency. Licensees must show that they hold an existing license to act as a property and casualty agent or broker, which requires passing the qualifying exams for those licenses.

Absence of Binding Authority – Binding authority for excess risk coverage must contain verification by all individuals assuming any risk of loss. If there is more than one person, the binding authority and any document issued or certified by the placing broker must specify whether their obligation is joint or several. If the document specifies the latter, the proportion of the obligation is assumed by each individual.

The Nonstandard Nature of Coverage – Since surplus lines insurers are non-admitted, they do not need to obtain a Certificate of Authority from the Commissioner. They also do not need to file their rates and policy forms with the state of California. In other words, surplus lines insurers are usually unregulated. Admitted insurers must file their rates for approval with the Commissioner and usually only offer standardized coverage forms designed by the Insurance Services Office (ISO). In contrast, surplus lines insurers can charge any rates they want and often create nonstandard policy coverage forms customized to fit specific exposures.

Conditions of Obtaining Business – An individual within this state *cannot* transact any insurance on property located or operations conducted within California or on the lives of individuals or residents of California with non-admitted insurers, except by and through a licensed surplus line broker.

List of Approved Surplus Lines Insurers (LASLI) – The List of Eligible Surplus Line Insurers (LESLI) has been replaced by the List of Approved Surplus Line Insurers (LASLI). The LASLI is a voluntary list of non-admitted insurers that the California Department of Insurance (CDI) has approved for use by surplus line brokers in California. The list includes all insurance providers eligible to supply surplus lines of insurance and the date they became approved. This list is openly available for consumer use. All insurance providers on the LESLI were automatically transferred to LASLI and continue to be eligible for the benefit of surplus line brokers in this state.

Chapter Review

This chapter explained the concepts relevant to the insurance marketplace in the state of California. Let's review some of the key points:

PRODUCERS	
Authority and Powers of Producers	• *Law of agency* – agents or producers always represent the insurance provider • *Three agent authority types* – express, implied, and apparent
Transacting Insurance	• Solicitation of insurance • Negotiations before the execution of a contract • The actual execution of a contract • Any later transactions that arise from the operation of the contract
Types of Licenses	• Property and casualty broker-agent • Life-only agent (formerly life agent) • Accident and health or sickness agent (formerly life agent) • Life and accident and health or sickness agent • Personal lines agent • Surplus lines broker
Agents vs. Brokers	• Agents legally represent the insurer, not their clients • Brokers legally represent their clients, not insurers

Continuing Education Requirements	<ul><li>Any licensee must complete 24 hours of continuing education, including three hours of ethics, every two years</li><li>Agents holding two types of licenses can satisfy the CE requirement by completing it for any license type</li><li>Any credits above the required number will be carried over into the next licensing period</li></ul>
INSURERS	
Admitted vs. Non-Admitted	<ul><li>Insurers must be granted a license or certificate of authority from the Department and meet the state's financial capital and surplus requirement</li><li>*Authorized or admitted* – insurers who meet the state's financial requirements and are approved to do business in the state</li><li>*Unauthorized or non-admitted* – insurers not approved to do business in California</li></ul>
Domicile	<ul><li>*Domestic* – the home office is chartered or incorporated in the same state where policies are being sold</li><li>*Foreign* – the home office is located in a different state than the one where policies are being sold</li><li>*Alien* – the home office is chartered in any country other than the United States; considered an alien insurer in all U.S. states and territories</li></ul>
Ownership	<ul><li>*Stock* – owned and controlled by stockholders; participating and nonparticipating policies; dividends are a share of profits and are taxable</li><li>Mutual – owned and controlled by its policyholders; only participating policies; dividends are a return of premium and are not taxable</li><li>Fraternal Benefit Society – operates as a corporation, association, or society; is for the benefit of its members and beneficiaries; is a not for profit lodge system</li></ul>
MARKET REGULATION – GENERAL	
The Commissioner	<ul><li>In California, the Commissioner of Insurance is an elected official who will serve not more than two consecutive 4-year terms</li><li>The Commissioner's responsibility is to issue regulations and cease and desist orders, respond to inquiries, and investigate complaints</li></ul>
Consumer Privacy Regulations	<ul><li>Gramm-Leach Bliley Act (GLBA)</li><li>California Financial Information Privacy Act</li><li>Insurance Information and Privacy Protection Act</li><li>Cal-GLBA</li></ul>
CLHIGA	<ul><li>The California Life and Health Insurance Guarantee Association (CLHIGA) pays the claims of insureds or beneficiaries when an insurer is impaired or insolvent</li></ul>
Unfair Trade Practices	<ul><li>*Unfair trade practices* - false advertising, misrepresentation, rebating, twisting, unfair discrimination, defamation, boycott/coercion/intimidation, and fraud</li></ul>
Fair Claims Settlement	<ul><li>Insurers cannot discriminate in their claims settlement practices</li><li>Upon receiving a claim, insurers must accept or deny it within 40 calendar days</li><li>An insurer cannot try to settle a claim by making a low settlement offer</li></ul>

CHAPTER 4:
Basic Legal Concepts – Tort Law

Now that you have examined some basic concepts in the insurance industry, you'll focus on the specific terms related to property and casualty insurance. This chapter introduces the concepts of tort, negligence, and liability and their applications. It is essential to learn the terms and definitions presented in this chapter before discussing different types of policies.

- Intentional Torts
- Negligence
- Liability
- Damages
- Comparative vs. Contributory Negligence
- Pure No-Fault and Modified No-Fault Laws

Intentional Torts

An *intentional tort* is a deliberate act that harms another individual regardless of whether the offending party intends to injure the aggrieved party. Breach of contract is not considered an intentional tort for this definition.

Libel – Any *printed or written untrue statement* that injures the reputation of an individual or company is considered libel and provides grounds for litigation against the offending party.

Slander – Any *verbal or oral untrue statement* that injures the reputation of an individual or company is considered slander and provides grounds for litigation against the offending party.

False Arrest – The *unjustified physical restraint* of another person's freedom and the ensuing inconvenience such detention causes is considered false arrest and provides grounds for litigation against the offending party.

Negligence

Negligence is failing to use the care that a prudent, reasonable person would have taken under the same or similar circumstances to prevent injury to another individual or damage to their property.

Elements of Negligence

Most people behave in a manner that is prudent and reasonable – with exceptions for incompetent individuals and minors. Failure to act in this manner constitutes *negligence*. When this negligence causes damage to property belonging to another or injury to another, the negligent party may be held legally responsible for the damage. Generally, the burden of proof is on the injured party to prove that the other party was negligent. However, certain doctrines also shift the burden of evidence from the injured party to the defendant or impose liability by statute. There are four primary elements to be considered when negligence is established, and all four must be present to prove that another party is negligent:

1. Legal duty;
2. Standard of care;
3. Unbroken chain of events; and
4. Actual loss or damage.

Duty – It must be proven whether the defendant had a legal duty to act.

Breach – The defendant must have used a standard of care that breached their legal duty. Standard of care infers acting as a reasonable person would act.

Injury – The mere fact that carelessness existed is not adequate cause for legal liability. Actual damage or injury must have been suffered by the party seeking recovery.

Proximate Cause – *Proximate cause* is an event or act considered reasonably foreseeable and a natural cause of the event that occurs and damages property or injures a plaintiff. The negligence must have been the proximate cause of the damage if the injured party is to be compensated for the damage. This correlation signifies an unbroken chain of events, starting with negligence and leading to damage or injury. Also referred to as *direct liability*, this negligence must be the cause without which the accident would not have occurred.

Gross Negligence

Gross negligence is reckless behavior that demonstrates a disregard for the lives or safety of other individuals. Behavior classified as gross negligence is a decisive violation of another's right to safety. In terms of property, gross negligence is a failure to actively take care of another person's property like one would for their own property.

Legal Defenses

An individual's negligent behavior does not necessarily result in that person being held legally liable. Certain defenses may be interceded by the negligent party to defeat a claim.

Assumption of Risk – This defense of an action for compensation for injuries affirms that if a person understands and recognizes the danger involved in an activity and willingly chooses to encounter it, the *assumption of risk* may bar compensation for injury caused by negligence. Courts have held that in seeking admission to a PGA event, a spectator has chosen to undergo the risk of being struck by a golf ball. Another common example is a passenger in a car. In many jurisdictions, a passenger is considered to have assumed the risk of injury while riding in an automobile. Even if the vehicle is driven in a grossly negligent way, the passenger may be considered to have assumed the risk of injury if the passenger fails to protest the dangerous driving.

Liability

Absolute Liability – *Absolute liability* is imposed upon a company or person engaged in a dangerous or potentially hazardous business that results in injury or harm to another person or property by negligence or omission. Examples of absolute liability include harboring wild animals, owning a swimming pool, or selling explosives. The injured party does not have to prove negligence.

Strict Liability – *Strict liability* is usually applied in product liability cases. A business or person that manufactures or sells a product makes an implied warranty that the product is safe. The business is responsible for defective products, regardless of negligence or fault. Suppose the product causes injury, and the claimant can prove the defect. The defendant will be held strictly liable for the damage in that case.

Vicarious Liability – The doctrine of *vicarious liability* comes from the old English law "respondeat superior," in which the master was liable for their servants' negligent acts. This doctrine aims to transfer the liability from one person to another who would probably have a greater ability to pay. In some jurisdictions, employers may be held vicariously liable for negligent acts of their employees and parents liable for their children's actions.

Damages

A tort can result in two forms of injury to another, including property damage and bodily injury. In the case of *property damage*, the loss is typically easy to determine. Insurers measure the monetary loss the injured party suffered by calculating the destroyed or damaged property's value and the loss of use of that asset.

In the case of *bodily injury*, it is harder to determine the loss monetarily. Bodily injury can lead to claims by the injured party not only for lost wages and medical expenses but also for loss of consortium, mental anguish, pain and suffering, and disfigurement. The two classes of *compensatory damages* insurers can award are special and general damages. *Special damages* are specific out-of-pocket expenses for lost wages, miscellaneous expenses, and medical coverage. *General damages* compensate the injured person for disfigurement, mental anguish, pain and suffering, and other similar losses. Determining the general damages amount is highly subjective and can amount to whatever a judge or jury decides is suitable. *Punitive damages* are another class of damages; it is a form of punishment for gross negligence, outrageous extreme behavior, or willful intent.

Comparative vs. Contributory Negligence

Due to the harshness of contributory negligence, most states have adopted a somewhat more lenient doctrine, known as *comparative negligence*. Here, the other party's negligence or fault will not necessarily defeat the claim but will be used to mitigate the damages payable to the other party. Under this statutory defense, the fault is shared between the parties involved. The awards for damages are decreased by the percentage of negligence of each party.

Some states have adopted the rule of *pure comparative negligence*, which allows the party who brings the lawsuit (the plaintiff) to recover the damages, as long as they are not 100% negligent. In contrast, under the rule of *modified comparative negligence*, the injured party can only recover damages if their fault is less than that of the party being sued (the defendant). This rule is also known as the "equal to or greater than" rule.

Under *contributory negligence*, the injured party must be completely free of fault to collect. Any negligence that contributed to the injury on the part of the injured party, however slight, will usually defeat the claim. A variation of contributory negligence is called the last clear chance rule. It may be used as a defense by a negligent party who can prove the injured party had the last clear chance to avoid the loss but did not.

Pure No-Fault and Modified No-Fault Laws

Many states have adopted *no-fault* insurance laws that allow for the payment of loss claims from a policyholder's insurance company. These laws reduce the judicial impact of lawsuits in conjunction with car accidents. In these no-fault states, automobile owners purchase insurance to protect themselves and their passengers from auto accidents' medical and economic effects. Vehicle owners also purchase liability insurance at whatever limit the statute dictates. In such states, the judicial system is available for those who are the victims of gross negligence and whose losses exceed a threshold amount.

Modified no-fault laws are similar to pure no-fault laws in that the insured's insurance provider covers part of the claim. However, modification is made to the settlement amounts based on comparative negligence, which assigns a percentage of negligence to all parties involved.

Chapter Review

This chapter explained the topics relevant to basic legal concepts like tort law, negligence, and liability. Let's review some of the key points:

BASIC LEGAL CONCEPTS – TORT LAW	
Intentional Torts	• *Libel* – Any printed or written untrue statement that injures the reputation of an individual or company is considered libel • *Slander* – any verbal or oral untrue statement that injures the reputation of an individual or company is considered slander • *False Arrest* – the unjustified physical restraint of another person's freedom and the ensuing inconvenience such detention causes is considered false arrest
Negligence	• *Negligence* – failing to use the care that a prudent, reasonable person would have taken under the same or similar circumstances to prevent injury to another individual or damage to their property • *Gross negligence* – reckless behavior that demonstrates a disregard for the lives or safety of other individuals • *Comparative negligence* – the other party's negligence or fault will not necessarily defeat the claim but will be used to mitigate the damages payable to the other party • *Pure comparative negligence* – the party who brings the lawsuit (the plaintiff) to recover the damages, as long as they are not 100% negligent • *Contributory negligence*, the injured party must be completely free of fault to collect
Liability	• *Absolute liability* – imposed upon a company or person engaged in a dangerous or potentially hazardous business that results in injury or harm to another person or property by negligence or omission • *Strict liability* – usually applied in product liability cases • *Vicarious liability* – aims to transfer the liability from one person to another who would probably have a greater ability to pay

CHAPTER 5:
Property and Casualty Basics

This chapter continues an overview of the basics of property and liability coverage to help you build a solid foundation of related knowledge. You will learn about risk and managing it, different types of loss, and insurable interest requirements specific to property and casualty insurance. In general, this chapter contains essential information to help you understand the rest of the material in this book.

- Independent Rating Organizations
- Property vs. Casualty Insurance
- Property and Casualty Terms
- Loss Cost Rating
- Insurable Interest – Property Insurance Policies

Independent Rating Organizations

Financial Status Guides

An insurer's financial strength and stability are critically important factors to potential insureds. Its financial strength is based on investment earnings, prior claims experience, level of reserves, and management, to name a few. Reserves are an amount of money held in a separate account to cover debts to policyholders. Guides to the financial integrity of insurers are published regularly by the following independent rating services:

- Fitch
- AM Best
- Moody's
- Standard and Poor's
- Weiss

Insurance Services Office (ISO)

Part of the obligation of state government to the public is ensuring policies are understandable and quality products and rates are reasonable. This duty requires insurance companies to file any forms they use for the insurance regulatory authority to review them for compliance with minimum standards. The regulatory authority approves or declines the form and advises the insurance provider on necessary changes.

To avoid the costly duplication process across 50 states, the *Insurance Services Office (ISO)* creates forms acceptable to the state regulatory authority. In other words, the advisory organization develops forms for the standard market. Insurance companies pay a fee to ISO for the right to use their copyrighted material. Consequently, most insurers offering ISO homeowners policies provide the same policy as other insurers.

Another well-known organization is the *American Association of Insurance Services (AAIS)*, which provides programs similar to ISO's. AAIS is a national advisory and statistical organization that creates standardized rating information and policy forms used by personal, commercial, and inland marine insurers.

Some insurance companies may even create and file their own forms.

California Workers Compensation Inspection Rating Bureau

The *California Workers Comp Inspection Rating Bureau (WCIRB)* is an unincorporated, nonprofit association formed of all companies licensed to transact workers compensation insurance business in California and has over 400 member companies. The following are its main functions:

- Provide reliable statistics and rating information for workers compensation and employer's liability insurance;
- Collect and tabulate statistics and information to develop pure premium rates to be submitted to the Commissioner for issuance or approval; and
- Inspect risks for classification or rate purposes and provide this information to the insurance provider (and employer, upon request).

Association for Cooperative Operations Research and Development (ACORD)

The Association for Cooperative Operations Research and Development (ACORD) is an international nonprofit organization consisting of agents and insurers dedicated to building efficiencies in the property and casualty insurance industry.

The Association is most widely known for maintaining and publishing an extensive library of standardized forms for the insurance marketplace. Before ACORD, most property and casualty insurance companies used their proprietary forms for claims and new business. ACORD forms are currently the industry standard.

ACORD created electronic standards to complement its form standards. It also expanded its electronic data standards and forms beyond property and casualty insurance to include life, surety, and reinsurance markets.

Other national rating organizations include the National Council on Compensation Insurance (NCCI) and the National Association of Insurance Commissioners (NAIC).

Property vs. Casualty Insurance

Property insurance typically covers a building, the contents of a building, or both.

Casualty or liability insurance provides compensation or indemnity for harm or wrong that is done to others that the insured is legally required to pay. The obligation may be assumed by contract or imposed by law.

Property and Casualty Terms

Accident vs. Occurrence

An *accident* is a sudden, unexpected and unplanned event not under the insured's control, resulting in damage or injury that is neither intended nor expected.

An *occurrence* is a more expansive definition of loss than an *accident*. It includes those losses caused by repeated or continuous exposure to conditions resulting in damage to property or injury to individuals that is neither intended nor expected.

Direct and Indirect Loss

Direct and *indirect* losses are the two types of property losses a business or individual could experience. Property insurance only covers direct losses. However, indirect losses are related to the direct loss, and coverage to protect against these indirect losses is often added to property insurance policies. Direct losses mean direct physical damage to personal property (e.g., vehicle, furniture, or equipment) or real property, like a building.

Direct loss also involves other damage where the covered peril was the *proximate cause of loss*. For example, an insured building catches fire. When the local fire department uses water to put out the fire, the floor and wall coverings suffer water damage. While water damage is not an insured peril, the damage is covered under the peril of fire because the fire was the proximate cause.

Indirect losses, also called *consequential losses*, are losses resulting from a direct loss. Such losses typically result from the time it takes to replace or repair damaged property. The most prevalent indirect loss for individual homeowners is the extra living expense they may incur while the home is under repair. The primary type of indirect or consequential loss for commercial risks is the loss of profits a business may suffer because of having to close down until the repairs are complete.

Indirect Loss Exposures

The most common personal indirect loss exposures are the loss of rental value and the extra living expenses incurred by an insured after a direct loss caused by a covered peril, such as fire. For example, suppose the named insured bought a Dwelling Property Broad Form (DP-2) policy to insure a duplex where they live in one unit and rent out the other. In that situation, they could incur both losses in the event of a fire. Not only would the tenant have to relocate after a covered loss, but the insured would also have to stay at a hotel while the property is being repaired.

In commercial lines, the most common indirect loss exposures are the loss of business income or the additional expenses incurred by a business after a direct covered loss. In some cases, the monetary amount of the indirect loss may exceed the damage caused by the direct loss.

"All-Risk"

An old term still commonly used in the insurance industry is *all-risk*. However, in most of today's policies, all-risk has been replaced by the terms open peril or special form.

To be covered for loss or damage under a *basic contract*, the loss or damage must be caused by a listed or named peril. In an *all-risks contract*, listing or naming the insured perils is unnecessary since the intent is to cover every risk of loss or damage. The contract's exclusions need to be considered; however, the all-risks form of coverage provides a much broader level of coverage. It should be noted, however, that all-risks coverage does not mean that all losses are covered. Specific types of loss are definite and consequently not insurable. All-risks coverage can also be referred to as special coverage by many insurers.

Named Peril and Open Peril

Named peril is a term used in property insurance to describe the extent of coverage provided under an insurance policy form that lists covered perils. Insurance providers do not cover unlisted perils.

Open peril is a term in property insurance to describe the extent of coverage provided under an insurance policy form that insures against any risk of loss not explicitly excluded. The term open peril has replaced the term "all risks."

Concurrent Causation

In many circumstances, the action of more than one cause produces a particular harm or loss to an insured. The preeminent legal rule is that coverage is applied if a loss is caused by both an uninsured peril and an insured peril. This rule of law is referred to as *concurrent causation*.

Expense

Expense is an insurer's operations costs, including commissions, marketing, and overhead.

Vacancy and Unoccupancy

Vacancy refers to a covered structure in which no one has been working or living. Also, no property has been stored for the required period stated in the policy (generally 60 days).

Unoccupancy (non-occupancy) refers to a covered structure in which no one has been working or residing within the required period, but some property is stored there.

For instance, if the policy owner moves, the house is considered *vacant*. The house is considered *unoccupied* if the policy owner travels for two weeks.

Short Rate, Flat Rate, and Pro-Rata Cancellation

When a policy is canceled upon its effective date, it is called a *flat-rate cancellation*, and there is usually no premium penalty.

When the insurer cancels a policy mid-term, the insured will receive a *pro-rata refund*. This refund is determined by calculating how many days of coverage were paid minus how many days the policy was in force. The unearned (or unused) premium is fully returned to the insured.

Example 5.1 (pro-rata) – Chad has a homeowner's policy with ABC Insurers. His policy runs from Jan 1 through Dec 31 and pays the $730 premium annually. Chad receives notice that ABC Insurers is canceling his policy effective June 1. Because Chad's policy was in effect for 151 days, he will receive a refund of $428.

- 365 days/year - 151 days used = 214 days to refund.
- $730 annual premium / 365 days = $2/day cost of insurance.
- 214 days to refund × $2/day = $428 refunded to Chad.

Short-rate cancellation is applied when the insured cancels the policy before its renewal date. A short rate allows the insurer to impose a penalty (usually 10%) on the refund of unearned premiums.

Example 5.2 (short rate) – Chad has a homeowner's policy with ABC Insurers. His policy runs from Jan 1 through Dec 31 and pays the $730 premium annually. Chad notifies ABC Insurers he is canceling the policy effective June 1. ABC Insurers will refund Chad $385.20.

- 365 days/year - 151 days used = 214 days to refund.
- $730 annual premium / 365 days = $2/day cost of insurance.
- 214 days to refund × $2/day = $428 - 10% penalty of $42.80 = $385.20 refunded to Chad.

Earned and Unearned Premium

The cost of a unit of insurance is known as the *rate*. The *premium* is the payment required by the insured to keep the policy in force. The premium is calculated by multiplying the rate by the number of units of insurance purchased.

An *earned premium* is the portion of a premium that belongs to the insurer for providing coverage for a specified period. The *unearned premium* is the portion of the premium the insurer has collected but has yet to earn because it has not provided coverage for the insured. For instance, if an insured pays an annual life insurance premium and dies before that year concludes, the insurer would have to return the portion of the premium that was unearned or unused.

Types of Ratings

The method of setting rates is very similar in most cases. However, it is possible to distinguish between two different types of rates, including *class* and *individual*.

Class rating – *Class rating* (or *manual rating*) refers to calculating a price per unit of insurance that applies to every applicant possessing a given set of characteristics. For example, a class rate may apply to all drivers of a particular gender and age driving in the same geographic area or all types of dwellings of a given kind of construction in a specific city.

The advantage of the class-rating system is that it allows the insurance provider to apply a single rate to many insureds, simplifying the process of calculating their premiums. In creating the classes to which class rates apply, the rate maker has to compromise between a large class. This large class will include more exposures that increase the credibility of predictions and one sufficiently narrow to allow homogeneity.

Class rating is the most common approach used by the insurance industry. It is used in life insurance and most property and casualty fields.

In some areas of risk, the characteristics of the insured units are widely varied. It is considered desirable to depart from the class approach and calculate rates based on the attempt to measure an individual's loss-producing characteristics more precisely. There are five basic individual rate-making approaches:

1. Judgment rating
2. Schedule rating
3. Experience rating
4. Retrospective rating
5. Merit rating

Judgment rating – *Judgment rating* is used when credible actuarial data is lacking or when the exposure units are so diverse that it is impossible to build a class. Underwriters must use their skills and experience to develop judgment rates. This approach is used in Ocean Marine insurance, and it is also used in other lines where permitted by a state's rate laws. Risks that have been judgment-rated can also be referred to as "A" rated.

Schedule rating – In *schedule rating*, the rates are calculated by applying a schedule of credits and charges to some base rate to determine the appropriate rate for an individual exposure. Today, schedule rating is used less frequently due to the introduction of ISO's *class-rating program* for various types of commercial buildings previously schedule-rated. This reduction in use leaves only the largest and most complex risks to schedule-rated.

Experience rating – In *experience rating*, the insured's past loss experience becomes a factor in determining the final premium. Experience rating is overlaid on a class-rating system. It adjusts the insured's premium up or down, depending on whether the insured's experience deviates from the average experience of the class.

Retrospective rating – *Retrospective rating* is a *self-rating* plan under which the policy term's actual losses determine the final premium, subject to a minimum and maximum premium. A deposit premium is mandatory at the inception of the policy. That premium is adjusted at the end of the policy period based on the actual loss experience.

Merit rating – Another type of rating is *merit rating*, commonly used in personal auto insurance. In this rating method, the insured's premium is *not* based on the actual loss record but on other factors that signify the *probability* that a loss will occur. An example would be a bad driving record that does not include any accidents.

Combined Ratios

The *combined ratio* is the percentage of every dollar of premium a property/casualty insurer spends on expenses and claims. An increase in the combined ratio means financial profitability is not improving; a decrease means profitability is increasing. The insurer has an underwriting loss when the ratio is over 100.

Claims Terms

First Party – *First-party* risk protection is insurance coverage that applies to the insured or their property. In contrast, third-party coverage protection is insurance coverage that applies to the property or person of someone other than the insured.

Third Party – *Third-party* means someone other than the insured or insurer or a person or individuals who are not a party to the insurance contract. This individual is typically the injured party for which the insured is liable.

Subrogation – *Subrogation* is the legal right of an insurer to seek compensation for damages from third parties after it has reimbursed the insured for the loss. Subrogation is based on the indemnity principle. It prevents the insured from collecting on the loss twice, once from the insurance provider and a second time from the party that caused the damage.

Arbitration – *Arbitration* is a technique of *casualty* claim settlement used when the insured and insurance provider cannot agree on how to settle a claim. Depending on state law, the settlement is submitted to an arbitrator, or multiple arbitrators, whose decision may or may not be binding on both parties.

Loss Reserve

For individual claims, the *loss reserve* is the approximate amount that will ultimately be paid out on the claim to the insured by the insurance provider. For legal reserves, this is the amount designated by an insurance provider to settle claims that have occurred but have not been settled.

Loss Cost Rating

An insurer must collect enough premiums to cover the cost of operations, pay for the insured losses that occur, and allow for a reasonable profit. To determine the premiums to charge, the insurer predicts the expenses they will incur.

Since the insurance company understands that this prediction is uncertain, an extra charge will be added to cover the margin of error. Remember that this additional charge reflects any investment income earned on the funds held for future payment of claims.

Insurance companies use rate classification systems that rate insureds based on loss potential. All insureds possessing similar characteristics are placed in the same class and charged the same rate.

Insurable Interest – Property Insurance Policies

An interest in the property insured must exist when the insurance *becomes effective* and when the loss occurs, but it *need not exist*. In contrast, an interest in the life or health of an insured person must exist when the insurance becomes effective but need not exist when the loss occurs.

Requirement for an Insurable Interest to Exist

According to the California Insurance Code, *the contract is void* if the insured has no insurable interest.

Contingent or Expectant Interests

A simple conditional or expectant interest in anything, *not based on any actual claim or right* to that thing, nor upon any *valid contract for the possession or ownership* of it, is not considered an insurable interest.

Chapter Review

This chapter covered the basics of property and casualty insurance. Let's review some of the key points:

PROPERTY AND CASUALTY BASICS	
Independent Rating Organizations	<ul><li>Financial Status Guides</li><li>Insurance Services Office (ISO)</li><li>California Workers Compensation Inspection Rating Bureau</li><li>Association for Cooperative Operations Research and Development (ACORD)</li></ul>
Property and Casualty Terms	<ul><li>*Accident* – a sudden, unexpected, and unplanned event, not under the insured's control, resulting in damage or injury</li><li>*Occurrence* – includes losses resulting from repeated or continuous exposure to conditions that cause damage to property or injury</li><li>*Direct Loss* – direct physical damage to personal property and/or buildings</li><li>*Indirect Loss* – losses resulting from a direct loss</li><li>*"All-Risk"* – all-risk has been replaced by the terms open peril or special form</li><li>*Named Peril* – the extent of coverage provided under an insurance policy form that lists certain covered perils</li><li>*Open Peril* – the extent of coverage provided under an insurance policy form that insures against any risk of loss that is not specifically exclude</li><li>*Concurrent Causation* – if a loss is caused by both an uninsured peril and an insured peril, coverage is applied</li><li>*Expense* – an insurer's costs of operations including commissions, marketing, and overhead</li><li>*Vacancy* – a covered structure in which no one has been working or living, and no property has been stored for generally 60 days</li><li>*Unoccupancy* – a covered structure in which no one has been working or living within the required period of time, but in which some property is stored</li><li>Short Rate, Flat Rate, and Pro-Rata Cancellation</li><li>*Combined Ratios* – the percentage of every dollar of premium a property and casualty insurer spends on expenses and claims</li><li>*Loss Reserve* – the approximate amount of what will ultimately be paid out on the claim to the insured by the insurance provider</li><li>*Subrogation* – the legal right of an insurer to seek compensation for damages from third parties after it has reimbursed the insured for the loss</li><li>*Arbitration* – a technique of *casualty* claim settlement used when the insured and insurance provider cannot agree on how to settle a claim</li></ul>
Types of Ratings	<ul><li>Judgment rating</li><li>Schedule rating</li><li>Experience rating</li><li>Retrospective rating</li><li>Merit rating</li></ul>

CHAPTER 6:
Property and Casualty Policies – General

Now that you have learned some basic property and liability insurance concepts, you will focus on the specific provisions and components found in those policies. This chapter includes a lot of important general and state-specific information regarding policy cancellation, valuation, and other features. You will also learn about the California Standard Form Fire Insurance Policy and understand how it differs from the Standard Fire Policy.

- Insurance Policies
- Types of Valuation
- Valued Policy
- Standard Mortgage Clause
- Concurrent vs. Nonconcurrent Policy
- Policy Cancellation and Failure to Renew
- California Standard Fire Policy vs. the Standard Fire Policy
- Microbial-Matter Exclusions
- Casualty – Referral of Auto Insureds to Repair Facilities

Insurance Policies

Components

Each property or casualty policy includes the following major components:

- Declarations;
- Insuring agreement;
- Definitions;
- Conditions;
- Exclusions and policy limits;
- Endorsements; and
- Additional coverage.

Declarations – *Declarations* are the part of an insurance policy containing the basic underwriting information, such as the name and address of the insured, amount of coverage and premiums, and a description of insured locations. It also contains any additional representations by the insured. This section is generally the first page of the policy.

Insuring Agreement – An *insuring agreement* is the part of an insurance policy that establishes the obligation of the insurer to provide the insurance coverages stated in the policy. Among other things, the insuring agreement lists the perils, the description of the coverage delivered, effective and renewal dates, and the parties to the contract. It is generally placed after the policy Declarations but may come after the Definitions.

Definitions – The *definitions* section of an insurance policy clarifies the terms used in the policy. Usually, words printed in bold, italics, or quotations have a definition of their meaning in that contract.

Conditions – *Conditions* are the portion of an insurance policy that specifies the general procedures or rules that the insured and insurance provider agree to follow under the terms of the policy.

The following illustrates examples of conditions:

- *Inspections* can be made as needed by the insurer. The insurer maintains the right to examine or inspect the insured's books or location to determine the exact exposure for rating and underwriting purposes.
- *Changes to the policy* have to be made by the insurance provider and be in writing.
- The *liberalization clause* guarantees that if the insurer introduces new or free coverage, the insured will immediately receive these benefits and will not have to wait until policy renewal.
- *Return of premium* determines the method that the insurer will use to compute the return of premium when the policy is canceled before the expiration date.

In many cases, insureds are entitled to a return of premiums if a policy is rejected, canceled, or otherwise surrendered as follows:

- The entire premium if the insurance provider has not been exposed to a risk of loss; and
- A portion of the premium that corresponds with unexpired time if the coverage is made for some time and the insured surrenders their policy.

Policies for individual motor vehicle liability or homeowners insurance cannot include a provision mandating that the premium is fully earned upon the occurrence or any contingency except the policy's expiration.

When a personal lines policy ends (or there is a reduction in coverage), the insurance provider must return the unearned premium within *25 days*. If any policy other than a personal lines policy ends, the insurer must return the unearned premium within *80 days*. *Ten percent interest* will be applied when an insured does not return any unearned premium within these periods.

Exclusions – The exclusions section of an insurance policy describes the perils that are not insured against and the individuals who are not covered. Exclusions limit some of the broad terms used in the insuring agreement. This section can exclude perils, property, and people (except a spouse).

The following examples of exclusions are from coverage in a property policy, including *earth movement* and *water damage*.

- Earth movement is excluded if it resulted from an earthquake, volcanic eruption, or a mudflow; and
- The water damage exclusion does not cover the following perils: flood and subsurface water, water that backs up through drains and sewers, water that overflows from a sump pump, or water below ground that leaks through a basement's walls.

Endorsements – *Endorsements* are printed supplements to a contract that modify the policy's original coverages, conditions, or terms. Policy owners can include endorsements when the policy is issued or during the policy's term. Endorsements must be in writing, attached to the policy, and signed by an executive officer of the insurance provider to have any effect on the contract. They may be used to delete or add coverage or to correct items such as the insured's name, address, etc.

Provisions

Cancellation and nonrenewal – The *insured* can cancel the policy at any time by returning the policy to the insurance company or by providing the insurer with written notice.

If the insurer cancels coverage, it must give the insured *ten days' advanced written notice*. Cancellation can occur for nonpayment of premium or if the policy has been in force for less than 60 days. The insurance company must provide the insured with at least a *30-day* advanced written notice for all other cancellations or nonrenewals. The insurance provider can only cancel a policy after it has been in force for *60 days* for the following reasons:

- There has been a material misrepresentation of a fact which, if known, the insurance company would not have issued the policy; and
- There has been a considerable change in the risk since the policy was issued.

Assignment – *Assignment* refers to transferring a legal interest or right in an insurance policy. In property and casualty insurance, assignments of policies are valid only with the prior written consent of the insurance company.

Supplementary Payments – Business Auto and Commercial General Liability (CGL) policies provide supplemental payments to *protect an insured against financial hardships*. Such hardships include those required to defend themselves against a claim or lawsuit seeking damages that would be covered under the policy. These supplemental payments are in addition to the limits that apply to the policy itself.

Severability – The *severability clause* is a standard provision in a Business Auto policy. Under this clause, the coverage provided by the policy applies separately to every insured seeking coverage or against whom a claim is being made. The severability clause has been essential in interpreting the common exclusion for bodily injury to an insured's employee.

Liberalization – *Liberalization* is a property insurance clause that extends broader regulated or legislated coverage to current policies, provided it does not result in a higher premium. For instance, if the insurer introduces a new coverage or improves coverage, the insured will immediately acquire the benefit of that coverage. It won't have to wait for their policy to renew.

Coverage Extensions

Extensions of coverage is a provision in some property policies that permits the extension of a major coverage to apply to specific types of loss to property and not expressly to an insured. Examples of coverage extensions include lawns, trees, shrubs, plants, debris removal expenses, and fire department service charges.

Types of Valuation

When a property insurance policy is written, the policy owner has several options as to how the insurer will value a loss to the insured property at the time of a loss. *Loss valuation* is a factor in calculating the premium charged and the coverage amount required.

Actual Cash Value – The *actual cash value (ACV)* method of valuation reinforces the principle of indemnity because it recognizes the decline in value of a property as it ages and becomes subject to obsolescence and wear and tear. Generally, insurers calculate actual cash value as follows:

Actual Cash Value (ACV) = Current Replacement Cost – Depreciation

Replacement Cost – *Replacement cost* refers to replacing the damaged property with like kind and quality at today's price, without deducting depreciation. This loss valuation method opposes the basic concept of indemnity because it could give the insured a settlement that exceeds the property's actual cash value after a loss.

Another loss valuation method allows the insurance company to adjust the loss based on the *functional replacement cost* at the time of a loss. This cost is for replacing the damaged property with less expensive and more modern equipment or construction. For example, the insurer may replace a building with lath and plaster walls with drywall at a lower cost to repair but just as functional.

Market Value – *Market value* is a rarely used method of loss valuation based upon the amount a willing buyer would pay to a willing seller for the property before the loss occurs. This method considers the value of land and location rather than just the cost of rebuilding the structure itself.

Agreed Value – *Agreed value* is a property policy that includes a provision agreed upon by the insured and the insurance provider. Both parties agree to the amount of coverage that signifies a fair valuation for the property when the policy is written and suspends any other contribution clauses or coinsurance. Insurers use this valuation method for items whose value does not fluctuate much. When a loss occurs, the policy pays the agreed value as stated on the policy schedule, irrespective of the insured item's depreciation or appreciation.

Stated Amount – A *stated amount* is an amount of coverage scheduled in a property policy that is not subject to any coinsurance requirements if a covered loss occurs. This scheduled amount is the maximum amount the insurance provider will pay in the event of a loss.

Valued Policy

Valued policies are used when it is difficult to establish the value of the insured property after a loss or when it is appropriate to agree on a specific value in advance. A valued policy requires payment of the full policy amount if a total loss *without* regard to depreciation or actual value occurs.

Valued policies are frequently used in marine coverages because it is hard to establish the value of a ship's lost cargo after it sinks.

Standard Mortgage Clause

The *standard mortgage clause*, also called the loss payable clause, is a keystone provision of all property policies for real property. In insurance, non-movable property like a house and other structures is considered real property. Movable property like an auto, mobile home, furniture, and equipment is considered personal property. If a loss to real property occurs, insurers will pay the policy owner and the mortgagee as their insurable interest appears. In other words, the mortgagee's right to recover is limited to the amount of the outstanding debt. At no time will the mortgagee receive more than the insurable interest in the property. If an insurance policy is to be canceled, a mortgagee must receive prior written notice of such cancellation.

When a person is named in a mortgagee clause attached to a fire or other direct damage policy, the compensation for the loss will be paid to the mortgagee as their interest may appear. The mortgagee's rights of recovery will not be defeated by any act or neglect of the policy owner. The mortgagee is also given other rights, such as bringing a lawsuit in their own name to recover damages, paying policy premiums, and submitting proof of loss. There is nothing that *either the insured or the insurer* can do to defeat the mortgagee's position.

Concurrent vs. Nonconcurrent Policy

Concurrent policy coverage is provided by two or more policies, all of which are the same except that they may vary in policy period or amount. *Layering* is one way of structuring multiple policies to cover a risk so that each policy provides a layer of coverage. The benefit of layering is that the risk is spread among insurance companies and can result in a savings of premium that each insurer grants the insured. However, a lack of coordination between the insurers providing multiple policies could create coverage gaps.

Policy Cancellation and Failure to Renew

Auto Insurance – Notice of policy cancellation may be effective only if it is mailed or delivered by the insurer to the policy owner. It must be, accompanied by the reason for cancellation, at least *20 days before* the effective date of cancellation or *ten days'* notice when the cancellation is for *nonpayment of premium*.

When a policy of automobile liability insurance is canceled for a reason other than nonpayment of premium, the insurer must notify the named insured of their possible eligibility for coverage through the automobile liability assigned risk plan.

No admitted insurer licensed to issue motor vehicle liability policies can refuse to renew or cancel a motor vehicle liability policy covering drivers hired by a commercial business because those drivers have been convicted of Vehicle Code violations or any state traffic laws *while operating private passenger vehicles not leased or owned by their employer*. In addition, insurance companies may not renew a policy solely based on the insured's age.

Liability insurance policy – A liability insurance policy issued to a state agency or local public entity as a named insured cannot be canceled or have renewal declined for any reason except for nonpayment of premium. In these instances, notice is mailed to the policy owner *at least 45 days before* the effective date of nonrenewal or *at least 60 days before* the effective date of cancellation. A notice does not need to be sent if a renewal notice stating a premium for an additional coverage period has been sent to the named insured *at least 45 days before* the cancellation or expiration of an existing policy. This premium has yet to be tendered for the insurance company before such cancellation or expiration.

Homeowners policy – The arbitrary termination of the insured's homeowners policy solely on the basis that the insured has a license to operate a family home daycare at the insured location will subject the insurer to administrative penalties authorized by the Insurance Code unless any of the following is true:

- Nonpayment of premium
- The insurer no longer writes homeowners policies
- The risk has changed significantly since the policy was issued
- There has been a substantial misrepresentation of facts.

Financed insurance policy – Lenders cannot exercise the right to cancel a financed insurance policy due to the default of the policy owner under a premium payment loan agreement until the lender provides the insured *ten days' notice* of cancellation.

California Standard Fire Policy vs. the Standard Fire Policy

The California Standard Form Fire Insurance Policy was adopted in 1950. It is substantially similar to the 1943 New York Form. The principal deviations from the Standard Fire Policy lie in the wording. There are four main differences:

1. The policy form insures against *loss* rather than *direct loss;*
2. The right to waive provisions is further limited *by statute;*
3. Notice of loss is to be *without unnecessary delay* rather than *immediate;* and
4. Plans and specifications are required to be furnished *only if obtainable*.

Microbial-Matter Exclusions

Policies that include a *microbial-matter exclusion* will not cover mold-related damage to an otherwise insured property. These exclusions are sometimes seen when policies renew, and it is difficult to "buy back" coverage. Such an endorsement covers insured property from damage due to mold.

Casualty – Referral of Auto Insureds to Repair Facilities

Insurance companies are not allowed to require an automobile to be repaired at a particular repair shop or even recommend or suggest that a vehicle be repaired at a particular repair shop, except for the following circumstances:

- The claimant specifically requests the recommendation; or
- The claimant has been notified in writing of the right to choose the repair facility. The insurer that chooses to repair a vehicle causes the damaged vehicle to be restored to its previous condition before the loss at no additional cost to the claimant (unless stated in the policy.

Insurers are prohibited from requiring a claimant to travel an unreasonable distance to conduct an inspection of the vehicle, inspect a replacement automobile, obtain a repair estimate, or have the automobile repaired at a specific repair shop.

Insurance providers cannot require that a vehicle be repaired at a specific automotive repair dealer. Further, they are not allowed to recommend or suggest that a vehicle be repaired at a specific auto repair dealer unless the claimant explicitly requests a referral or has been notified in writing of the right to choose the auto repair dealer.

Suppose the claimant accepts the suggestion. In that case, the insurance provider will restore the damaged vehicle to its previous condition before the loss at no additional cost to the claimant. When the suggestion of a particular automotive repair dealer is made orally to the claimant, and if the oral suggestion is accepted, the insurer must provide a specific statement to the claimant. The insurance provider must send the written notice within five calendar days from the oral recommendation.

After the claimant has selected an automotive repair dealer, the insurance provider cannot recommend or suggest that the claimant choose a different automotive repair dealer.

Insurers that recommend or suggest that an automobile be repaired at a specific automotive repair dealer must also do both of the following:

- Prominently disclose the contractual provision in writing to the insured when the coverage is applied for and when the insurance provider acknowledges the claim; and
- If the claimant chooses to have the vehicle repaired at the shop of their choice, the insurance provider cannot limit or discount the reasonable repair costs based on charges that would have been incurred if the insurer's shop of choice had repaired the vehicle.

Part of the Commissioner's responsibilities is to ensure the enforcement of this section of the law.

Chapter Review

This chapter discussed general concepts commonly found in property and casualty policies. Let's review some of the key points:

POLICY STRUCTURE	
Policy Components	• *Declarations* – contains underwriting information such as the insured's name, address, amount of coverage, premiums, and a description of insured locations • *Definitions* – clarifies the terms used in the policy • *Insuring agreement* – establishes the obligation of the insurer to provide the insurance coverages as stated in the policy • *Additional coverage* – provides an additional amount of coverage for specific loss expenses at no additional premium • *Conditions* – indicates the general procedures or rules that the insured and insurer agree to follow under the terms of the policy • *Endorsements* – printed addendums to a contract that are used to revise the policy's original coverages, terms, or conditions • *Exclusions* – perils that are not insured against and individuals who are not insured • *Policy Limits* – the maximum amounts a policy owner can collect under the terms of the policy
COMMON POLICY PROVISIONS	
Property and Casualty Policy Provisions	• *Appraisal* – used during a disagreement between the insurer and the insured on the value of any property loss • *Arbitration* – utilized when the insurer and the insured do not agree on how to settle a claim; sent to one or more arbitrators • *Cancellation* – the termination of an in-force policy, by either the insurer or the insured, before the expiration date shown in the policy • *Loss Settlement* – under a professional liability policy, the insurance provider must gain the insured's consent before settling a claim • *Mortgagee clause* – attached to a policy to protect the interest of the mortgagee in the mortgaged property • *Nonrenewal* – the termination of an insurance policy at its expiration date by not offering a replacement policy or a continuation of the existing policy • *Notice of claim* – a statement or form from an insured to an insurer informing the insurer of events leading to a possible claim; the form includes when, how, and where the loss took place • *Other insurance* – defines how a policy will respond if there is other valid insurance written on the same risk • *Pro rata* – provides for the sharing of loss with other insurance • *Proof of loss* – a sworn statement that must typically be provided by the insured to an insurer before any loss under a policy can be paid
LOSS VALUATION	
Types of Loss Valuation	• Actual cash value (ACV) • Replacement cost • Market value • Agreed value • Stated value

CHAPTER 7:
Dwelling Policy

This chapter begins your introduction to specific policies available in Personal Lines insurance. First, you will focus on the purpose and coverage of a dwelling policy, which protects dwellings, other structures, personal property, and personal liability. You will learn about covered perils, policy conditions, and exclusions. Finally, you will read about selected endorsements available in dwelling policies.

- Characteristics and Purpose
- Coverage Forms – Perils Insured Against
- Property Coverages
- General Exclusions
- Conditions
- Selected Endorsements
- Personal Liability Supplement

Characteristics and Purpose

The ISO created the dwelling property policy to be used mainly as a property coverage form. Property owners can use the policy to insure the dwelling, its contents, or both. There are three separate coverage forms available under the dwelling program, which include *basic*, *broad*, and *special* form coverage. Endorsements exist to alter the coverage to tailor it to the applicant's particular needs. The policy does not include liability coverage, but it can be added. This form is a commonly used policy form to insure rental dwellings.

It is critical to note that the ISO classifies dwelling property policies as DP with a corresponding form number to indicate the policy type (DP-1, DP-2, or DP-3).

Property owners can purchase a dwelling property policy to cover properties used exclusively for residential purposes in the following situations:

- Up to four residential units;
- Up to five roomers or boarders;
- Properties in the course of construction;
- Owner occupied, tenant occupied, or both;
- Mobile homes on the basic form only, if they contain no more than one apartment and are located at a permanent site listed in the policy;
- Seasonal dwellings vacant for three or more months during a 12-month period; or
- Not intended as farm property.

Under the dwelling property program, business occupancies may impact eligibility. Insurers can accommodate business occupancies if they are incidental, conducted by the policy owner on the dwelling premises, and as long as no more than two workers are employed. Allowable incidental occupancies include small service operations where the sale of merchandise is not the primary function. Examples include tailors, beauty and barber shops, or shoe repair operations that use handwork only. Insurers may also consider studios such as music or photography, private schools, or professional offices.

Who is an Insured

Under the homeowners policy forms, which we will discuss in the next chapter, the words "you" and "your" refer to the named insured in the Declarations and the spouse if they reside in the same household. The terms "we," "us," and "our" refer to the insurer providing this coverage.

An *insured* means:

1. You and any household residents who are:
    - Your relatives (by blood or marriage); or
    - Other individuals under 21 years old and in your care or the care of a relative who is a resident of your household;
2. A full-time student enrolled in school who was a resident of your household before moving out to attend school, provided that the student is under the age of:
    - 24 and your relative; or
    - 21 and in your care or the care of a relative who is a resident of your household.

Coverage Forms – Perils Insured Against

The three coverage forms that apply to the dwelling property policy define the perils or causes of loss insured against, coverages, other coverages, exclusions, and conditions. All ISO forms have a specific flow to the information. The DP form structure is as follows:

1. **Agreement** – Insuring agreement (states that the insurer will provide coverage described in the policy in return for the premium paid and compliance with all applicable policy provisions);
2. **Definitions** – Limited in nature;
3. **Deductible** – Applies to every covered loss unless otherwise noted in the policy form;
4. **Coverages, including Other Coverages** – Defines direct and indirect property coverages and other coverages that are included with the premium;
5. **Perils Insured Against** – Perils vary by form and are a key differentiator in selecting a form;
6. **General Exclusions** – Perils that are not covered in all forms; and
7. **Conditions** – Specify when coverage applies.

The forms available in the dwelling program include:

Form Name	Form Number	Peril Type(s)
Basic	DP 00 01 or DP-1	Named Peril
Broad	DP 00 02 or DP-2	Named Peril
Special	DP 00 03 or DP-3	Open and Named Peril

Basic

The *basic* dwelling form DP-1 is a named peril coverage form that provides the most limited coverage of the three forms. Understanding the conditions in which a particular peril does not apply is essential. Unlike the broad and special forms, no minimum coverage is required for the basic form. The basic form covers the following perils or causes of loss:

Fire or Lightning and Internal Explosion – An explosion that occurs in a dwelling, other structure, or a structure containing insured personal property will be covered. Coverage does not include damage or loss caused by electric arcing, breakage or operation of pressure relief devices, breakage of water pipes, or explosion of steam pipes or steam boilers leased, owned, or operated by the policyholder. An explosion of a gas stove is an example of a covered loss.

For the peril of fire to be covered, the loss must result from a hostile fire. This type of fire is not intentional and not contained within its intended boundaries, unlike a friendly fire (e.g., a fireplace or firepit). If a friendly fire escapes these boundaries and causes damage to other property, the fire would then be considered a hostile fire and will be covered by the policy. However, a fire does not have to originate from a friendly fire to be considered hostile.

In addition to these causes of loss, the policy owner can add the *extended coverage perils* to the basic policy for an *added premium*. This coverage is included in the basic form. Still, it is only activated if it appears in the Declarations and with payment of the added premium.

Windstorm or hail – Damage to the covered property from windstorm or hail is insured subject to the following limitations:

- Antennas, signs, and awnings outside the dwelling are not covered.
- Damage by rain, sleet, snow, dust, or sand to the interior of a building or personal property located in the dwelling. Insurers will only cover this damage if the wind or hail damages a wall or the roof of the building first, which creates an opening to the interior of the building. For example, if interior damage resulted from wind or hail entering through an open window, there would be no coverage.
- No coverage applies to canoes and rowboats (outside of the building); and
- No coverage for lawns, plants, shrubs, or trees.

Explosion – The peril of *internal explosion* is broadened in the extended coverage perils. The explosion does not have to take place *inside* the dwelling. The same coverage limitations apply to explosions as in the internal explosion peril.

Riot or civil commotion;

Aircraft – Includes spacecraft and self-propelled missiles.

Vehicles – Coverage does not apply to damage resulting from vehicles operated or owned by a policyholder or a resident of the location listed in the policy. There is also no coverage for damage or loss to walks, driveways, or fences caused by a vehicle.

Smoke – Sudden and accidental damage caused by smoke is covered (including the puff back or emission of vapors, fumes, soot, or smoke from a boiler or furnace). Coverage does not include smoke from a fireplace (friendly fires), industrial operations, or agricultural smudging.

Volcanic eruption – There is no coverage for loss caused by earthquakes, tremors, or land shock waves.

It may be helpful to use the following acronyms to help remember the extended coverage perils:

WHARVES	W.C. SHAVER
• **W**indstorm;	• **W**indstorm;
• **H**ail;	• **C**ivil commotion;
• **A**ircraft/vehicles;	• **S**moke;
• **R**iot/civil commotion;	• **H**ail;
• **V**olcanic eruption;	• **A**ircraft;
• **E**xplosion;	• **V**ehicle and volcano;
• **S**moke.	• **E**xplosion;
	• **R**iots.

The policy owner could also add protection against vandalism and malicious mischief if the policy insures against extended coverage perils.

Vandalism or malicious mischief (VMM) – Covers damage or loss to property resulting from malicious and willful destruction of the insured property. Exceptions to coverage include:

- Glass breakage or safety glazing material that is part of the building (except glass building blocks) is not covered by this peril. For example, insurers would not cover a vandalized window, but they would cover decorative glass building blocks.
- Damage to the building resulting from burglary or theft is covered; however, the stolen property is not covered.
- There is no coverage if, immediately before the loss, the insured's location has been vacant for *more than 60 consecutive days.*

Dwelling Property 1 – Basic Form (DP-1)		
Included in Base Form	**Option 1 (Additional Charge)**	**Option 2 (Additional Charge)**
Fire Lightning Internal Explosion	Basic Perils + Extended Coverage Perils Windstorm or Hail Explosion Smoke Aircraft Vehicles Riot or Civil Commotion Volcanic Eruption	Basic Perils + Extended Coverage Perils + Vandalism or Malicious Mischief (must be purchased)

Broad

The *broad form* (DP-2) coverage expands the causes of loss insured under the basic form with extended coverage perils, and protection against vandalism or malicious mischief (must be purchased). The broad form further broadens coverage for the following perils:

- Breakage of glass and safety glazing material that is part of the building would be protected against vandalism or malicious mischief. Remember, under the DP-1 form, only glass building blocks are covered for this type of loss;
- The explosion peril no longer has the exceptions listed under the basic form.

Described below are the *seven additional broad form perils*:

Damage by burglars – The dwelling broad form includes burglary damage as a separate peril. The DP-1 form has this protection under vandalism or malicious mischief. Coverage is now provided for damage to any covered property (not just the building) if it resulted from burglary. There is no coverage for property theft if the dwelling has been unoccupied for *more than 60 consecutive days* immediately before the loss occurs.

Falling objects – Coverage for loss or damage caused by falling objects, except damage to towers, masts, outdoor radio and television antennas or aerials, outdoor equipment, fences, or awnings. Damage to a building's interior is covered only if an exterior wall or the roof was damaged first. There is no protection against the falling object itself.

Weight of snow, sleet, or ice – Loss or damage to the building or contents caused by the weight of snow, sleet, or ice is covered. There is no coverage for damage to patios, pavement, retaining walls, foundations, fences, awnings, swimming pools, docks, wharves, or piers.

Accidental discharge or overflow of water or steam – Damage from accidental discharge or leakage of water or steam from an automatic sprinkler system, heating, air conditioning, or plumbing is covered. The cost of tearing out and replacing part of the building is also covered if necessary to replace or repair the appliance. Tear-out coverage will apply to other structures only if actual damage occurs to these structures.

However, the policy will not pay for damage or loss resulting from repeated or continuous seepage over weeks, months, or years. It will also not cover the cost of replacing or repairing the appliance itself. Nor will it consider a downspout, gutter, roof drain, or sump pump as an appliance that triggers coverage. Damage caused by discharge from an off-premises storm drain, sewer, or steam pipe is not covered. When a dwelling is unoccupied for *more than 60 consecutive days* immediately before the loss, this peril will be excluded from coverage.

Sudden and accidental bulging, burning, cracking, or tearing apart – The sudden and accidental bulging, burning, cracking, or tearing apart of appliances from an automatic fire protection sprinkler system, an air-conditioning system, steam or hot water heating system, or an appliance for heating water is covered. Loss resulting from freezing is not covered, but it is covered in the freezing peril noted below.

Freezing – The freezing of automatic sprinkler systems, heating, air conditioning, or plumbing is covered only if the policy owner has shut off the water and drained the pipes and appliances or has taken appropriate steps to maintain heat in the building. Items that are not considered appliances will not be covered for freezing.

Sudden and accidental damage from artificially generated electrical current – There is no coverage for damage to transistors, tubes, circuitry, or electronic components of computers, appliances, fixtures, and home entertainment units.

The acronym **B.B. BICE-GOLF** can be utilized to memorize the broad form coverage perils:

- **B**ursting of heating systems;
- **B**urglary damage;
- **B**reaking of water heaters;
- **I**ce, snow, or sleet weight;
- **C**ollapse of a building;
- **E**lectrical damage (artificially generated);
- **G**lass breakage;
- **O**bjects falling from outside;
- **L**eakage of water or steam damage;
- **F**reezing of plumbing.

In addition, the following other coverages are included in the broad form:

Lawns, trees, shrubs, and plants – Plants, shrubs, trees, and lawns are covered if the damage or loss was caused by the following: lightning, fire, explosion, riot or civil commotion, vandalism, malicious mischief (excluding theft), non-owned or operated vehicles, or aircraft. This additional insurance is limited to $500 per plant, shrub, or tree and a maximum per loss of 5% of the dwelling's coverage.

Breakage of glass – Glass or safety glazing material that is a part of the insured building, including storm windows and storm doors, is covered. Also covered is damage or loss to other covered property resulting from the glass breakage. There is no protection for glass breakage if the building or structure has been unoccupied for a certain number of days (more than 60 consecutive days).

Collapse – The broad and special forms protect against the collapse of a building or a part of a building if the loss is caused by the following: the use of defective methods or materials in construction (if the collapse occurs during construction), the weight of personal property, or rain that collects on the roof, insect, vermin (only if the existence of such was unknown to the policyholder) or hidden decay, or one of the broad form perils. Collapse does not include expansion, bulging, shrinkage, cracking, or settling; it is not considered an additional amount of insurance.

Special

The special form (DP-3) is an open peril form, unlike the basic and broad forms, which are named peril forms. In other words, every peril is covered except those that are excluded. The special form only insures the dwelling and other structures on an *open peril basis*. The policy owner's personal property is covered for the *broad named perils* found in the DP-2 form, with a few exceptions that will be discussed.

The main differences between the special form DP-3 and broad form DP-2 coverages include the following:

- Theft of property that is a part of the dwelling or other structure is insured against in the special form.
- Coverage for *accidental discharge or overflow of water and steam* is broadened to cover loss caused by accidental discharge or overflow from steam or water pipes that occurs *off* the insured premises.
- Awnings, fences, outdoor equipment, or antennas are not excluded from the peril of *falling objects* in the special form.
- The special form policy will provide coverage for damage to a roof resulting from freezing or thawing of water under roof shingles (an ice dam).

BASIC FORM	BROAD FORM	SPECIAL FORM
Fire **Lightning** **Internal explosion** **Extended Coverage Perils:** Windstorm or hail Explosion Riot or civil commotion Aircraft Vehicles Smoke Volcanic eruption **Added coverage:** Vandalism and malicious mischief	**Basic perils + Extended coverage perils + VMM** Damage by burglars Falling objects Weight of ice, snow, or sleet Accidental discharge or overflow of water or steam Sudden and accidental damage from artificially generated electrical current Sudden and accidental tearing apart, cracking, burning, or bulging Freezing	All risks except those specifically excluded

Property Coverages

The dwelling policy has four core property coverages for policy owners. The broad and special forms add additional coverage, totaling five property coverages. The table on the following page breaks down these coverages:

	Damage Type	DP-1	DP-2	DP-3
A – Dwelling	Direct	x	x	x
B – Other Structures	Direct	x	x	x
C – Personal Property	Direct	x	x	x
D – Fair Rental Value	Indirect	x	x	x
E – Additional Living Expense	Indirect	Added by Endorsement	x	x

Coverage letters A through D are included in the basic, broad, or special policy forms. Additional living expense (Coverage E) is not included in the basic form but can be added by endorsement. Fair rental value (Coverage D) and additional living expense (Coverage E) are indirect coverages that can only be added to direct property coverage.

Coverage is indicated by showing a premium and limit of liability on the declarations page. A standard deductible will apply to all property coverages except for fair rental value (Coverage D) and additional living expense (Coverage E).

Coverage A – Dwelling

Coverage A – Dwelling defines what is covered as a dwelling. The owner must use the dwelling primarily for dwelling or residential purposes. The description of coverage is divided into two parts, including property covered and not covered.

PROPERTY COVERED

1. Dwelling on the listed premises described in the Declarations and all attached structures;
2. Any supplies or materials located on or next to the described premises used to repair, alter, or construct the dwelling or other structures on the premises;
3. Outdoor equipment and building equipment located on the premises and used to service the location unless insured elsewhere.

PROPERTY NOT COVERED

1. Land, including land on which the dwelling described on the declarations page is located.

Coverage B – Other Structures

Coverage B – Other Structures insures separate structures at the same location, such as a detached garage and other *outbuildings* (e.g., fences or sheds). The policy allows other structures to be used for business purposes within defined parameters.

PROPERTY COVERED

1. Other buildings or structures on the described premises that are separate from the dwelling by a clear space or connected only by a utility line, fence, or similar connection;
2. Other buildings or structures rented to anyone besides a tenant of the dwelling, but only when used as a private garage; and
3. Buildings or structures used in business (farming, manufacturing, and commercial) when storing property owned solely by a tenant of the dwelling or the policy owner. Property owners must store liquid or gaseous fuel in a tank that is part of a craft or vehicle in the building or structure.

PROPERTY NOT COVERED

1. Land, including the land where the other buildings or structures are located;
2. Buildings or structures rented or held for rental to anyone besides a tenant of the dwelling when not used as a private garage;
3. Other buildings or structures that are used in business (farming, manufacturing, and commercial), whether in part or whole, unless used as noted above;
4. Mausoleums and grave markers.

Coverage C – Personal Property

Coverage C – Personal Property can be purchased to cover personal property found in a residence. When no premium is charged, and no limit is shown, the coverage does not apply even though it may be referenced in the policy. Personal property coverage provided by the dwelling policy is primarily designed to protect private property located on the described premises. In actuality, personal property coverage is defined more by the property that is not covered. Be sure to carefully review the list of property covered and not covered below.

PROPERTY COVERED

1. Personal property found in a dwelling, located on the described premises for the policy owner and resident family members, as well as property of residence employees or guests (may be insured at the discretion of the policy owner);
2. Hobby or model aircraft (not designed or used to carry cargo or people), including any parts whether or not they are attached to the aircraft;
3. Motor vehicles and other conveyances but only while used to assist the disabled or designed to service the premises;
4. Canoes and rowboats;
5. Prepackaged computer software and blank storage media;
6. Property relocated to a newly acquired residence for 30 days. The limit shown on the declarations page will be applied proportionally to each residence. Insurers will not extend coverage beyond the expiration date of the policy.

PROPERTY NOT COVERED

1. Currency, coins, securities, accounts, bills, deeds, banknotes, passports, manuscripts, and evidence of debt;
2. Birds, fish, animals, and property that was damaged by domestic animals;
3. Aircraft designed or used for flight, including any parts, whether they are attached or not, other than hobby aircraft noted above;
4. Watercraft other than noted above;
5. Hovercraft and parts;
6. Motor vehicles and other motorized land conveyances, including electronic equipment powered by the vehicle, other than noted above. Also included are accessories, parts to the vehicle, and electronic equipment, but only while in or upon the vehicle;
7. The cost to recover data stored in various mediums;
8. Debit cards, credit cards, or any device used to transfer, withdraw or deposit funds;
9. Water or steam (e.g., a broken water pipe significantly increases an insured's water bill);
10. Mausoleums and grave markers.

Coverage D – Fair Rental Value

Coverage D – Fair Rental Value is applied if the property under Coverage A, B, or C is destroyed or damaged by a covered peril in the policy.

For example, Don owns a 2-family home that he rents to tenants. A fire damages the downstairs unit, rendering the property uninhabitable. Don cannot collect his standard rent while the property is under renovation. Insurers will cover this type of loss. However, when a flood damages Don's rental property, insurers will not cover this loss because the dwelling property form does not cover the flood.

Key points of this coverage include the following:

- The policy will pay the fair rental value of the described premises. It will deduct any expenses that discontinue while the premises are unfit for use (such as electricity and heat).
- Coverage continues until all repairs are complete, but only for the shortest time required. The insurance provider will pay only a proportional share of the total rental amount for every month the rented area of the insured location is unfit for its regular use.
- Policy expiration will not end the payment of an existing covered claim.
- If a civil authority prohibits the use of the insured property due to direct damage to a neighboring property, insurers will cover payment for the loss for up to two weeks.
- Coverage does not apply to any expense or loss associated with the cancellation of a lease.

Coverage E – Additional Living Expense

Coverage E – Additional Living Expense is only available if broad or special form dwelling coverage is issued. It can be added to the basic form by endorsement. It pays for the increase in the insured's usual living expenses while the described premises are unfit for regular use. This coverage is indirect, like fair rental value, so the policy is triggered only when the policy covers a direct damage claim (A, B, C). These increased expenses include things such as rent for alternative housing. The intention is to allow the family to maintain their usual standard of living.

The following are essential points for this type of coverage:

- Coverage will continue until all repairs are complete, but only for the shortest time required;
- Policy expiration will not end the payment of an existing covered claim;
- If a civil authority prohibits the use of the insured property due to direct damage to a neighboring property, payment for the loss will be covered for up to two weeks; and
- Coverage is not applied to any expense or loss associated with the cancellation of a lease.

Other Coverages

The DP-1, DP-2, and DP-3 coverage forms include other coverages that extend the major coverages (A, B, C, D, and E). These other coverages are included in the premium and are subject to the property deductible unless noted in the form. Every coverage form contains the following eight other coverages:

Other structures – The policy owner may elect to apply up to 10% of the dwelling insurance amount (Coverage A) to protect other structures on the insured premises. In the basic form, this is not an additional amount of insurance and will lower the available amount under Coverage A by 10% in the event of a concurrent loss. In the broad and special forms, coverage is automatically provided and considered an additional amount of insurance.

Debris removal – Debris removal coverage pays reasonable costs to remove debris after a covered loss occurs. Coverage includes the cost of removing dust or ash caused by a volcanic eruption. This coverage is not considered an additional amount of insurance.

Improvements, alterations, and additions – If the policy owner is a tenant, up to 10% of the personal property limit (Coverage C) will apply to damage or loss to additions, alterations, or improvements by the tenant.

In the DP-1 form, this is not considered an additional amount of insurance and will not increase the total amount of insurance payable in the event of a loss. In the DP-2 and DP-3 forms, this is considered an additional amount of insurance and will not lower the Coverage C limit for the same loss.

Worldwide coverage – The policy owner may apply up to 10% of the personal property limit (Coverage C) to pay for losses to personal property away from the premises anywhere in the world. Coverage is not applied to canoes or rowboats in any dwelling form. Property of servants and guests is not covered away from the insured premises in the DP-1 form; however, the broad and special forms allow for servant or guest property coverage. This coverage is not regarded as an additional amount of insurance.

Rental value and additional living expense – Up to 20% of the limit of liability (Coverage A) may be used for loss of both fair rental value (Coverage D) and additional living expense (Coverage E). The DP-1 form will only apply this coverage to fair rental value because additional living expense is not included. The 20% coverage extension is not considered additional insurance in the DP-1 form; it is additional insurance in the DP-2 (broad) and DP-3 (special) forms.

Reasonable repairs – Reasonable expenses incurred by the policy owner for repairs necessary to protect property from further damage at the time of a covered loss are also covered. This coverage is not considered an additional amount of insurance.

Property removed – The policy will protect against loss or damage to property removed from the insured premises when threatened by a covered peril. Perils insured against are converted to *open peril coverage* during the removal process. The basic form provides five days of coverage, while the broad and special forms provide coverage for 30 days.

Fire department service charge – Insurers will cover up to $500 for expenses incurred by the policy owner because of an agreement to pay the fire department if they respond to a fire at the described premises. This coverage is considered additional insurance, and no deductible applies to this coverage.

Other coverages that are only included in the *broad and special forms* are as follows:

Plants, shrubs, trees, and lawns – Loss or damage to plants, shrubs, trees, and lawns are covered on a named peril basis if the loss or damage resulted from the following: lightning, fire, explosion, riot or civil commotion, vehicles (if not owned or operated by a policy owner), aircraft, or vandalism and malicious mischief (excluding theft). This coverage is considered an additional amount of insurance and is limited to a maximum of:

- 5% of the amount of coverage on the dwelling per loss; or
- $500 per plant, shrub, or tree.

Breakage of glass – Glass or safety glazing material that is a part of the insured building or structure, including storm windows and storm doors, is covered in the policy from perils, including earth movement. Loss or damage to other covered property resulting from the breakage of glass is also covered. There is no coverage for the breakage of glass if the building or structure has been unoccupied for a stated number of days. This limitation does not apply to damage resulting from earth movement. If safety glazing materials are required by law or ordinance, the insurer will settle the loss on a replacement basis.

Collapse – Collapse refers to an abrupt falling down of the building or part of the building in which the building can no longer be used for its intended purpose. Suppose the building is in danger of collapse or shows signs of settling, leaning, bending, sagging, bulging, cracking, shrinkage, or expansion. In that case, it will not be considered in a state of collapse.

The covered perils include

- Damage from vermin or insects hidden from sight;
- Decay that is hidden from sight;
- The use of defective methods or materials in construction (if the collapse happens during construction);
- The weight of rain that collects on the roof or personal property; and
- Broad form perils for both the broad and special forms.

Ordinance or Law – This coverage provides a policy owner additional insurance for expenses associated with changes to building codes and ordinances after a covered loss. The broad and special form policies allow up to 10% of Coverage A (or B if there is no coverage limit for A) if the policy owner owns the premises. If the insured is a tenant, then 10% of the limit of liability associated with additions, alterations, and improvements will apply. Coverage is provided for the undamaged and damaged portions of the dwelling with limitations for cleanup of pollutants and loss of value.

General Exclusions

Several general exclusions in the dwelling policy forms define the extent of coverage provided. The exclusions contained in all three dwelling forms are explained below.

Ordinance or law – Coverage does not apply to costs incurred from any ordinance or law that regulates the use, construction, or repair of any property. Also, costs incurred from the required tear-down of any property are not covered. This general exclusion conveys the intent of the form. It narrows the focus of covered claims to only what is described in the Other Coverage section. Coverage is also excluded for requirements to test, monitor, clean up, or remove pollutants and a resulting loss in value of the structure.

Earth movement – Earthquakes and land shock waves associated with volcanic activity are not covered. Sinkholes, mudslides, rising, sinking, mudflow, shifting, and landslides (caused by or resulting from any act of nature or human or animal forces) also are not covered. However, any resulting damages caused by the ensuing fire or explosion are covered.

Water damage – Damage resulting from the following is not covered: surface water, flood, waves (including tsunami and tidal wave, tidal water, tides, the overflow of any body of water or spray from any of these), whether driven by wind or not, including storm surge. Water or waterborne material that backs up through drains or sewers or overflows from a sump or sump pump is also not covered. Below-surface water that seeps or exerts pressure on a building and other structures would be excluded from coverage.

Power failure – A failure of power or other utility services that occurs off the location listed in the policy. When a power failure occurring off-premises triggers a peril covered in the policy, the insurer will cover damage to property by that peril.

Neglect – If further damage occurs at the time of loss because the policy owner neglected to try to preserve or save the property, there is no coverage for the additional damage or loss.

War – Damage resulting from war, revolution, rebellion, or insurrection is not covered.

Nuclear hazard – This exclusion refers to a policy condition we will discuss later in the chapter. The policy will not respond to losses caused by nuclear reaction, radiation, or radioactive contamination.

Intentional loss – Coverage is not provided for an individual who commits or directs another to commit an act with the intent to cause a loss.

Governmental action – This refers to the seizure, confiscation, or destruction of property (Coverages A, B, and C) by order of governmental authority. This exclusion is not applied to action taken to prevent the spread of a fire if the policy covers fire losses.

Special Form (DP-3) Exclusions – Other than the general exclusions found in all dwelling forms, the special form contains the following additional exclusions that only apply to Coverages A and B. There is no coverage for damage or loss that results from:

- Weather conditions contributing to an excluded cause of loss;
- Decisions, acts, or the failure to act; and
- Faulty design, planning, or materials.

Conditions

All dwelling policy forms include the following conditions:

- Policy period;
- The limit of insurance and insurable interest;
- Fraud or concealment;
- Loss settlement;
- Duties after a loss;
- Appraisal;
- Pair or sets;
- Subrogation;
- Other insurance;
- Insurer's option to repair or replace;
- Suit against the insurer;
- Abandonment;
- Loss payment;
- No benefit to bailee;
- Mortgage holders;
- Liberalization;
- Cancellation and nonrenewal;
- Death;
- Assignment;
- Recovered property;
- Nuclear hazard;
- Volcanic eruption; and
- Loss payable clause.

Because some of these conditions are explained elsewhere in the book, the following only describes parts of any condition specific to the dwelling property forms.

Policy period – The policy will only apply to losses during the policy's effective dates.

Insurable interest and limit of insurance – Suppose more than one individual has an insurable interest in the property. In that scenario, the insurance provider will not be liable for more than the policy owner's interest under the coverage at the time of loss or more than the limit of liability.

The *loss settlement* condition varies depending on the dwelling policy form used.

Under the basic DP-1 form, insurers settle a loss on an actual cash value (ACV) basis, subject to the limit of insurance and the cost to replace or repair the damaged property.

The broad and special forms both contain the following loss settlement conditions:

- Outdoor equipment, household appliances, carpeting, awnings, structures that are not buildings, and personal property are all covered on an ACV basis at the time of the loss.
- Dwelling and other structures covered to at least 80% of the *replacement cost* when a loss occurs are insured on a replacement cost basis, with the policy owner receiving no more than the cost to repair or replace with like kind and quality, the limit of insurance, or the amount actually spent.

If the structure is rebuilt at a new location, the cost to rebuild will be no more than the cost to rebuild at the premises described in the policy. It is worth noting that claims covered under Coverage A (Dwelling) or Coverage B (Other Structures) will be settled at replacement cost without deducting any depreciation. When a loss occurs, the amount of coverage on the damaged building must be 80% or more of the building's total replacement cost before the loss, but not more than the limit of liability that applies.

When the loss occurs, if the property is covered for less than 80% of the replacement cost, the policy will pay the ACV or the amount determined by the coinsurance formula, whichever is greater.

Losses from replacement costs are first paid on an actual cash value basis. When the policy owner proves that the repair is complete, the insurance company pays the balance to the policy owner. However, small claims (both are less than 5% of the coverage and less than $2,500) will be settled whether or not the actual replacement or repair is complete. The 80% coinsurance requirement will still apply.

The policy describes the items not included in calculating the 80% value noted above.

The policy owner may disregard the replacement cost provisions and file a claim only for the actual cash value of the buildings. Policy owners must make this election within 180 days of the loss.

Duties After Loss — In the event of a loss to covered property, the insurer has no obligation to provide coverage under the policy unless the policy owner complies with the following duties:

1. Give prompt notice to the insurance provider or its agent;
2. Protect the property from additional damage; if repairs are needed, the policy owner must make necessary and reasonable repairs to protect the property and keep an accurate record of repair costs;
3. Cooperate with the insurance provider in the investigation of the claim;
4. Prepare an inventory of the damaged personal property, showing the amount, actual cash value, description, and quantity of the loss;
5. Show the damaged property, provide documents and records, and agree to an examination under oath while not in the presence of another policy owner; and
6. Send the insurance provider a signed, sworn proof of loss within 60 days.

Pair or Set – The insurance provider may elect how to insure losses to the property that was part of a pair or set. The insurance provider can elect to replace or repair the missing piece to restore the set to the value before the loss. The second option is to compare the actual cash value of the pair or set before the loss to the value after the loss and then pay the difference.

Other insurance and service agreement – When other fire insurance applies to the same loss, the insurance provider is only liable for the portion of the loss that the limit of insurance bears.

Suit against the insurer – No one may bring a lawsuit against the insurer unless the policy owner has complied with all policy conditions. Policy owners must bring legal action within *two tears* of the date of loss.

Insurer's option to repair or replace – The insurance company can repair or replace any part of the damaged property with like property. It must provide written notice to the policy owner within *30 days* of receiving a signed, sworn proof of loss.

Loss payment – Losses will be paid within *60 days* of receiving a signed, sworn proof of loss and reaching an agreement with the policy owner regarding the amount payable.

Cancellation and nonrenewal – Insurers can cancel a policy for nonpayment of premium or any other reason within the first 60 days of coverage. In that scenario, the insurer must give the insured *ten days'* advance notice. After 60 days, or if the insurance company plans not to renew coverage, it must provide at least *30 days'* notice of cancellation to the insured. The insurer could cancel the policy midterm only if the risk changed substantially from when it was first insured or due to the misrepresentation of a material fact.

Liberalization – There will be times when the insurance provider makes changes that broaden coverage in the policy during the policy period or 60 days before the effective date. In these cases, the revisions will apply automatically without needing to be endorsed by the policy. There are restrictions to this condition in case of general program changes from a form change or amendatory endorsement.

Death – In the event of a policy owner's death, the legal representatives of the deceased policy owner will be considered insured but only concerning the covered property at the time of death.

Nuclear hazard – Nuclear hazard refers to any nuclear reaction or radioactive or radiation contamination. Losses from nuclear hazards will not be considered caused by smoke, explosion, or fire. This condition also states that direct or indirect losses are not insured if related to a nuclear hazard unless a fire ensues. The insurer will cover the fire damage in this case.

Recovered property – There may be cases when the property is recovered, and the insurer has already made a loss payment. The policyholder can take the property and return the amount paid or give the property to the insurer.

Volcanic eruptions – All volcanic eruptions within 72 hours of the initial eruption will be regarded as a single occurrence, with only one deductible.

Selected Endorsements

Several optional endorsements are available to the policy owner to broaden their coverage. Listed below are the most commonly added optional dwelling policy endorsements.

Automatic Increase in Insurance – Policy owners may add this endorsement to a dwelling policy to increase the amount of coverage by an annual percentage to offset the effects of inflation. An automatic increase in insurance endorsement requires an additional premium.

Broad Theft Coverage – The only theft coverage provided in any dwelling policy forms is theft of property that is a part of the building listed under the special form.

There are no policy forms that insure the theft of personal property. However, policy owners can add broad theft coverage by endorsement to a dwelling policy if the insured is the owner-occupant of the dwelling.

The endorsement will cover loss or damage to personal property owned by the policy owner or a resident of the policy owner's household caused by the following: theft, attempted theft, malicious mischief, or vandalism. There is no coverage if the premises are unoccupied for more than *60 consecutive days* before the loss.

The broad theft endorsement can provide both on-premises and off-premises insurance coverage. Insurers can only insure off-premises coverage if on-premises coverage is written first. The Declarations will show a separate limit of liability for both coverages.

On-premises coverage insures loss of property used or owned by the policy owner or a resident employee at the premises listed in the policy. It also extends to property placed for safekeeping in a public warehouse, a bank, trust, or safe-deposit company, or a vacant dwelling not occupied, owned, or rented by the insured.

Off-premises coverage protects property either used or owned by the policy owner when it is away from the described premises. This coverage also protects a resident employee's property while in a dwelling occupied by a policy owner or employed by the policy owner.

No off-premises coverage for the property at a newly acquired primary residence exists. However, the on-premises limit will automatically apply for 30 days while the property is transported to the new location.

Insurers can cover certain types of property for specific amounts. Policy owners can purchase additional insurance if they require higher limits for these particular items. Listed below are the categories of property with these special sub-limits.

For a Dwelling Policy, the following coverage limits apply:

- $200 for banknotes, money, coins, bullion, gold, silver, platinum, and other metals;
- $1,500 for securities, deeds, accounts, letters of credit, evidence of debt, notes other than banknotes, passports, manuscripts, stamps, and tickets;
- $1,500 for watercraft and their outboard motors, equipment, furnishings, and trailers;
- $1,500 for other trailers;
- $1,500 for jewelry, furs, watches, and precious and semiprecious stones;
- $2,500 for firearms and related equipment; and
- $2,500 for gold and gold-plated ware, silver and silver-plated ware, and pewterware, including hollowware, flatware, trays, tea sets, and trophies.

In addition to the special limits of coverage, certain property types are *excluded*. The following are the types of property not insured by the broad theft endorsement:

- Fish, birds, or animals;
- Fund transfer cards and credit cards;
- Aircraft, hovercraft, and their parts (except hobby or model aircraft);
- Property while in the mail;
- Property held for sale or as a sample;
- Property specifically described and covered by any other insurance;
- Property of roomers, boarders, and tenants (other than relatives);
- Business property of the policy owner or resident employee;
- Property in the custody of a cleaner, laundry, tailor, dryer, or presser, except loss by burglary or robbery;
- Property at any other location occupied, rented, or owned by the policy owner, except if the policy owner is temporarily residing there;

- Motor vehicles (except motorized vehicles used to service the premises that are not subject to motor vehicle registration and vehicles designed to assist the disabled); and
- Motor vehicle accessories and equipment, including sound recording, transmitting, or receiving devices, while in the vehicle.

Dwelling Under Construction – Dwellings that are under construction are eligible for insurance. However, due to the distinctive nature of these risks, an endorsement is required to change the policy provisions. The limit of liability for a structure under construction is provisional and based on the finished value of the dwelling. When a loss occurs, the applicable limit is a percentage of the provisional limit, based on the proportion of the property's actual cash value at the time of loss. The premium is based on an average amount of coverage during construction.

Sinkhole Collapse – The earth movement exclusion found in the dwelling property policy also excludes coverage for earth sinking, otherwise called sinkhole collapse. Sinkhole collapse means the sudden collapse or settlement of the earth supporting the property resulting from an underground hole caused by water on limestone or other rock formations. This endorsement will provide coverage for such losses; however, there is no coverage if the underground hole is manufactured.

Condominium Unit-Owners – If the policyholder owns a residential condominium unit, they may need additional coverage to define the covered property clearly. Appliances, fixtures, alterations, and improvements that are part of the building but which the policyholder must insure because of the condominium association agreement can be covered with this endorsement.

Water Backup and Sump Pump Overflow – Water that overflows from a sump pump or backs up from sewers is not covered under the dwelling policy forms. This endorsement covers up to $5,000 in damage or loss, subject to a $250 deductible, for an additional premium.

Limited Theft – The *limited theft* endorsement is for landlords. The definition of covered property is more limited than the broad form. Covered property is limited to property used or owned by the named insured and, if a resident of the same household, the named insured's spouse. Since the limited theft endorsement is for a nonowner-occupied residence, there is no extension of coverage for the property of residence employees.

This endorsement excludes losses caused by roomers or boarders, tenants, members of their families, or their employees.

The exclusions in the limited theft endorsement are the same as the broad theft endorsement. In addition, it excludes coverage for the following types of property:

- Banknotes, money, gold, silver (including goldware and silverware), silver-plated ware, pewterware, platinum, bullion, coins, and other metals;
- Securities, deeds, accounts, evidence of debt, notes other than bank notes, letters of credit, passports, manuscripts, stamps, and tickets;
- Furs, jewelry, watches, precious and semiprecious stones; and
- Loss caused by a roomer or boarder, tenant, member of the tenant's household, or employee.

Only three special limits apply to certain types of property. The three sub-limits found in the limited theft coverage form are the following:

1. $1,500 for watercraft, including their outboard motors, trailers, equipment, and furnishings;
2. $1,500 for other trailers; and
3. $2,500 for firearms and related equipment.

Manufactured (Mobile) Home – The owner of a mobile home may be covered by either the HO-2 or HO-3 form when the *Mobile Home Endorsement* is attached to the policy. This endorsement changes particular Section I policy provisions to provide mobile home coverage. The liability coverage provided under Section II of the policy stays the same. The mobile home must be intended for year-round living and meet specific size requirements to be eligible for coverage.

Personal Liability Supplement

Unlike homeowners policies, dwelling policies do not include *personal liability* coverage. Policy owners can add the personal liability supplement to the dwelling policy, or it can be written as a separate stand-alone policy. Endorsements are added for comprehensive on-premises or off-premises personal liability or premises-only liability, provided the dwelling is rented to other individuals. The coverage form includes three coverage types: personal liability (Coverage L), medical payments to others (Coverage M), and additional coverages.

The additional coverages include claims expenses, first aid to other individuals, and damage to the property of others.

Liability insurance excludes a list of perils for Coverage L or Coverage M. Instead, coverage is subject to the definitions, conditions, and exclusions present in the policy.

A basic limit of $100,000 per occurrence applies to the personal liability coverage, and a limit of $1,000 per person is applied for medical payments to others. Policy owners can increase these limits for an additional premium.

Personal liability provides coverage for property damage or bodily injury to third parties that resulted from the policy owner's negligence or a condition of the policy owner's premises. Medical payments coverage pays for necessary medical expenses incurred by individuals other than an insured injured on the insured's premises or because of an insured's off-premises activities.

This coverage is included in the homeowners policy; we will discuss it in more detail later in the following chapters.

Chapter Review

This chapter explained the different types of property insurance policies. Let's review them:

DWELLING POLICY	
Form Structure	• Agreement
	• Definitions
	• Deductible
	• Coverages, including Other Coverages
	• Perils Insured Against
	• General Exclusions
	• Conditions

Coverage Forms	<ul><li>*Basic (DP1):*<ul><li>Named peril</li><li>Basic perils</li></ul></li><li>*Broad (DP2):*<ul><li>Named peril</li><li>Basic perils + extended coverage perils + VMM + broad form perils</li></ul></li><li>*Special (DP3):*<ul><li>Open Peril</li><li>Basic perils + extended coverage perils + VMM</li></ul></li></ul>
Property Coverages	<ul><li>*Coverage A - Dwelling* defines what is included for coverage as a dwelling and must be used primarily for residential or dwelling purposes</li><li>*Coverage B - Other Structures* covers other separate structures at the same location, like detached garages and other outbuildings (e.g., fences or sheds)</li><li>*Coverage C - Personal Property* can be purchased to insure personal property common to a residence</li><li>*Coverage D - Fair Rental Value* applies if property under Coverage A, B, or C becomes destroyed or damaged by a peril covered in the policy</li><li>*Coverage E - Additional Living Expenses* is only available if broad or special form dwelling coverage is written and pays for the increase in normal living expenses the policy owner sustains while the described premises are unfit for use</li></ul>
Conditions	<ul><li>Policy period</li><li>Insurable interest and limit of insurance</li><li>Concealment or fraud</li><li>Duties after a loss</li><li>Loss settlement</li><li>Pair or sets</li><li>Appraisal</li><li>Other insurance</li><li>Subrogation</li><li>Suit against the insurer</li><li>Insurer's option to repair or replace</li><li>Loss payment</li><li>Abandonment</li><li>Mortgage holders</li><li>No benefit to bailee</li><li>Cancellation and nonrenewal</li><li>Liberalization</li><li>Assignment</li><li>Death</li><li>Nuclear hazard</li><li>Recovered property</li><li>Volcanic eruption</li><li>Loss payable clause</li></ul>

DWELLING POLICY *(Continued)*
General Exclusions   • Ordinance or law   • Earth movement   • Water damage   • Power failure   • Neglect   • War   • Nuclear hazard   • Intentional loss   • Government action

CHAPTER 8:
Homeowners Policy

This chapter explains the homeowners policy, and you will learn about its features and the perils it insures. By the end of the chapter, you should be able to explain the purpose of the homeowners policy and the different parts of the policy, including coverage forms, conditions, exclusions, and endorsements.

- Overview
- Coverage Forms
- Definitions
- Perils Insured Against
- Exclusions
- Conditions
- Selected Endorsements
- Homeowners Insurance Valuation

Overview

A *homeowners* insurance policy is a comprehensive coverage form used to insure residential risks. The homeowners and dwelling property forms are very similar; however, the homeowners form includes coverage for personal liability protection and personal property of the insured.

The ISO specifies homeowners policies as HO with a corresponding form number to signify the policy type (HO-2, HO-3, HO-4, HO-5, HO-6, and HO-8).

Homeowners policies can be used in the following situations or for the following types of properties:

- Owner-occupied residences with *one to four families*;
- No more than two roomers or boarders or two families per unit;
- Various ownership types to include duplexes, townhomes, dwellings under construction, life estates, and sales installment contracts;
- Insuring a tenant of a non-owned dwelling (under a renter's form);
- A residential cooperative unit or condominium (under a condominium form); and
- Secondary residences and seasonal dwellings.

Business occupancies can have an impact on eligibility under the HO program. An insurer may accommodate business occupancies provided they are incidental and conducted by the policyholder on the dwelling's premises. Acceptable incidental occupancies include studios, schools, or offices.

Coverage for businesses is very limited in the property section of the homeowners policy. These limitations affect the coverage of personal property and other structures. Liability associated with a business is omitted from the policy; however, business owners can use endorsements to offer coverage.

Coverage Forms

The currently used six coverage forms applicable to HO policies define the coverages, perils, exclusions, conditions, and additional coverages. The homeowners form includes personal liability coverage. The form is separated into two sections. Section I explains the property coverage, and Section II describes the liability coverage. The insuring agreement, definitions, and common conditions unify the form.

1. Agreement;
2. Definitions;
3. Section I – Property Coverage;
4. Section I – Perils Insurance Against;
5. Section I – Exclusions;
6. Section I – Conditions;
7. Section II – Liability Coverages;
8. Section II – Exclusions;
9. Section II – Additional Coverages;
10. Section II – Conditions; and
11. Sections I and II – Conditions.

Unlike the dwelling property (DP) coverage form, the use of a homeowners form is first determined by the type of residential exposure. For example, a single-family residence owned and occupied by the policyholder will be eligible for certain HO forms. If the policyholder rents an apartment or a home, they will use a different form. After the appropriate form is selected, the ISO homeowners program offers other cause of loss forms based on the needs and budget of the insured.

Form Name and Number	Peril Type	Residential Dwelling Use
Broad Form HO 00 02 or HO-2	Named Peril	1-4 Unit Owner Occupied
Special Form HO 00 03 or HO-3	Open Peril and Named Peril	1-4 Unit Owner Occupied
Renters or Tenants Form HO 00 04 or HO-4	Named Peril	Occupied by Tenant
Comprehensive Form HO 00 05 or HO-5	Open Peril	1-4 Unit Owner Occupied
Condominium Form HO 00 06 or HO-6	Named Peril	Condominium Unit Owner Occupied
Modified Form HO 00 08 or HO-8	Named Peril	1-4 Unit Owner Occupied, Historic or Older Home

HO-2 through HO-5

Homeowners policies are designed to insure dwellings used primarily as private homes. Forms HO-2, HO-3, and HO-5 may be written only for the owner-occupant of a dwelling used solely for private residential purposes and not as a vacation home. In other words, the owner must reside in the dwelling. The homeowner rules allow professional occupancy (like a private school or a beauty shop) or incidental office. However, there can be no retail sales or more than two individuals working at any time. The dwelling may not contain more than two roomers or boarders, nor more than one additional family.

The HO-2, HO-3, and HO-5 forms provide building coverage on a replacement cost basis if the building is covered for 80% or more of its replacement cost. The HO-8 form provides coverage on an *actual cash value* basis.

The *HO-2 (broad form)* protects against losses caused by named perils. Agents should point out several apparent limitations to a client. The following are not covered:

- The inside of a building for damage caused by rain, sleet, snow, sand, or dust unless hail or wind damage first creates the opening;
- The inside of a building for loss caused by a falling object unless it first damages an outside wall or the roof;
- Walks, driveways, and fences for damage from a vehicle owned or operated by a resident; or
- Damage from steam or water if the dwelling is unoccupied for more than 60 days.

The *HO-3 (special form)* protects the dwelling and other structures on an open peril basis. Personal property is covered only for broad perils. Unlike coverage under the HO-2 (broad form), vehicle damage to walks, driveways, or fences is protected even if caused by a resident or the insured.

Exclusions of the HO-3 (special form) to the dwelling or other structures include the following:

- All perils, losses, and property not covered because of limitations of the insuring agreement and the general exclusions;
- Damage caused by freezing while the dwelling is unoccupied, vacant, or being constructed *unless* the policy owner takes reasonable care to shut off and drain the water supply or to maintain heat in the premises;
- Malicious mischief and vandalism if the dwelling has been unoccupied for a certain period (more than 60 consecutive days in most states);

- Theft in or to a structure or dwelling under construction;
- Expected, preventable, or gradual losses such as latent defect, contamination, wear and tear, bulging, or expansion of floors, walls, pavements, or foundations;
- Defective, inadequate, or faulty design, planning, zoning, surveying, etc.;
- Losses caused by weather conditions to the extent that they contribute to causes found in the general exclusions (e.g., power failure, flood); and
- Acts, decisions, or the failure to act.

The *HO-4 (contents broad form),* also known as a tenant broad form, covers personal property for broad perils. Insurance may not be issued to an owner-occupant. An insurer can write the HO-4 form for a tenant who resides in a mobile home, apartment, or rented dwelling; it does not provide coverage for the dwelling.

The *HO-5 (comprehensive form)* insures the dwelling and other structures on an open peril basis. It also insures personal property on an open peril basis, except landlord furnishings in an apartment rented or held for rental to others. Landlord furnishings are provided on a named peril basis and are limited to $2,500.

Another expansion of coverage stems from the definition of theft. In the HO-5 form, theft includes losing or misplacing insured property, also known as a *mysterious disappearance.*

HO-6

The *HO-6 (condominium unit-owners)* also expands coverage to include parts of the building, such as appliances and alterations that the policy owner must insure because of the condominium association agreement.

The HO-6 condominium unit-owners form is designed for the owner-occupant of a condo.

Under Coverage A (Dwelling), the HO-6 policy covers the following:

- The improvements, fixtures, appliances, and alterations that are a part of the building contained within the residence premises;
- Items of real property that only pertain to the residence premises;
- Property that is the insurance responsibility of an insured under a corporation or a property owners association agreement; and
- Other than the residence premises, structures that the policyholder exclusively owns at the location of the residence premises.

The HO-6 under Coverage A does not insure any of the following:

- Land, including land on which the structures, real property, or residence premises are located;
- Structures rented or held for rental to any individual that is not a tenant of the dwelling unless used exclusively as a private garage;
- Structures from which any business operates; or
- Structures used to store business property. It does cover a structure that contains business property exclusively owned by an insured or a tenant of the dwelling. However, the business property cannot include liquid or gaseous fuel other than fuel in a permanently installed fuel tank of a craft or vehicle stored or parked in the structure.

Under Coverage C (Personal Property), HO-6 covers the following:

- Personal property used or owned by an insured while it is anywhere in the world
- After a loss and at the insured's request, it will insure personal property owned by:

- Others while the property is on the part of the residence premises occupied by a policy owner; or
- A residence employee or a guest, while the property is in any residence occupied by a policy owner.

The HO-6 form under Coverage D (Loss of Use) is the total limit of liability for the coverages in:

- Fair rental value;
- Additional living expenses; and
- Civil authority prohibits use.

The HO-6 coverage form does not protect against loss or expense due to an agreement or lease cancellation.

HO-8

The *HO-8 (modified coverage form)* is a homeowners form used when replacement cost coverage is not practical. This form may be useful when the replacement cost is considerably higher than the structure's market value, such as in some older homes, elaborate homes, and those with detailed designs or decorative architecture. Some of the differences that apply to this form are listed below:

- **Theft coverage** — A $1,000 basic limit applies to theft losses, and coverage is not provided for theft of personal property off the premises.
- **Worldwide coverage** — Coverage for personal property away from the insured premises is limited to the larger of $1,000 or 10% of the personal property limit.
- **Debris removal** — This is not considered an additional coverage and is included in the total policy limit.
- **Shrubs, plants, or trees** — The maximum limit for any one shrub, plant, or tree is only $250.
- **Property of residence employees or guests** — Property may be covered only while on the insured premises.
- **Coverages A and B** — These coverages are written on a functional replacement cost basis.
- **Glass or safety glazing material** — These losses will have a limit of $100.

Definitions

Homeowners policy forms include a Definitions section that defines several important terms. Understanding the terms used throughout the policy is vital to comprehend the extent of coverage provided. Some of the essential terms described in the policy include the following:

Bodily Injury – *Bodily injury* includes bodily harm, sickness, or disease, including loss of services, required care, and death caused by the bodily injury.

Insured – The policy defines *an insured* as any of the following:

- The named insured;
- Family members of the named insured who reside with the named insured;
- Resident relatives under age 21 or nonrelative residents in the care of the named insured;
- Full-time students under the age of 24 who are relatives of the named insured and who were residents before attending school (the coverage is provided only until the age of 21 if the full-time student is a nonrelative); and
- In addition, for Section II – Liability, any individual who is legally liable for the insured's animals, watercraft, or certain motorized vehicles.

Insured Location – An *insured location* can be any of the following:

- The residence premises;
- Part of other premises used by the named insured as a residence and listed in the Declarations or newly acquired during the policy period;
- A location not owned by the insured but where the policy owner is living temporarily (a hotel room);
- Vacant land rented or owned by the insured, excluding farmland;
- Land owned or rented by the insured where a 1- to 4-family residential dwelling is being constructed;
- Individual or family burial vaults or cemetery plots of the insured; and
- Any part of the premises occasionally rented by an insured, except for business purposes (e.g., an insured rents a hall for a daughter's birthday party).

Residence Premises – *Residence premises* refers to:

- The single-family dwelling where the policy owner resides;
- The 2-, 3- or 4-family dwelling where the policy owner resides in at least one of the family units; or
- The part of any other building where the policy owner resides listed as the residence premises in the Declarations. Residence premises also include other grounds and structures at that location.

Property Damage – *Property damage* is the destruction of, the physical injury to, or the loss of use of any tangible property.

Residence Employee – *Residence employee* includes employees of the policy owner whose duties are related to the use or maintenance of the home, including performing similar responsibilities elsewhere.

Perils Insured Against

In the HO-2, HO-4, and HO-6 forms, the *broad form perils insured against* in the event of property damage, include:

- Windstorm or hail;
- Fire or lightning;
- Explosion;
- Riot or civil commotion;
- Vehicles;
- Aircraft;
- Smoke;
- Theft;
- Vandalism or malicious mischief;
- Falling objects;
- Sudden and accidental burning, cracking, tearing apart, or bulging;
- Weight of snow, ice, or sleet;
- Freezing;
- Accidental discharge or overflow of water or steam;
- Electrical damage; and
- Volcanic action.

The perils mentioned above were covered in depth in the dwelling policy section and have the same characteristics in the homeowners form. Broad form perils will apply to all applicable coverages (A, B, C, and D). These are the covered perils insured against under Coverage C in the HO-3, HO-4, and HO-6 forms.

The HO-3 form provides open or special coverage on Coverages A and B. Damage to the dwelling, and other structures will be covered unless excluded. The major exclusions are also listed in the section on dwelling policies. Losses under Coverage C in the HO-3 form are covered for broad form perils.

The HO-5 (Comprehensive) form is unique among the homeowners forms in that the entire policy is an open peril or special form. As a result, Coverage A, B, and C and the resulting indirect losses in coverage D will be covered unless excluded.

COVERED PERILS	
HO-2 **(Broad)**	Broad form perils on Coverages A, B, and C
HO-3 **(Special)**	Coverages A and B – open peril Coverage C – same perils as Form HO-2
HO-4 **(Contents Broad)**	Coverage C same perils as Form HO-2 (broad)
HO-5 **(Comprehensive)**	Building, other structures, and contents – open peril or special
HO-6 **(Condominium)**	Coverage A, B*, and C for the same perils as Form HO-2 (broad) *In this form, Coverage B is merged with Coverage A
HO-8 **(Modified Homeowners)**	Fire or lightning; windstorm or hail; explosion; riot or civil commotion; aircraft; vehicles; smoke; vandalism; theft; volcanic eruption

Exclusions

In any of the homeowners coverage forms, the following types of property are not insured:

- Structures used to conduct business;
- Structures rented to other individuals who are not the dwelling's tenants, other than a garage;
- Land;
- Specifically described items covered by other insurance;
- Birds, animals, or fish;
- Aircraft;
- Property rented or held for rental to other individuals away from the premises;
- Property of tenants;
- Property in an apartment rented to others, except as specified under the additional coverage for landlord furnishings;
- Motor vehicles and motorized land conveyances, including accessories and equipment, except motorized vehicles used to service the premises that are not subject to vehicle registration;
- The sound recording, transmitting, or receiving devices of a vehicle, including tapes or other media used with the equipment while in the vehicle; and
- Electronic data and paper records (coverage is provided for the cost of prerecorded computer programs or blank recording media).

Also, every policy excludes losses that result from any of the following:

- Ordinance or law, meaning a homeowners policy will not pay for loss of value of the insured property due to the requirements of an ordinance or law, but it will pay for the increased cost of repair due to the enforcement of such ordinance;
- Power failure;
- Intentional acts;
- The insured's neglect to preserve or save property; and
- Earth movement.

The homeowners policy also includes additional exclusions that apply to medical payments and personal liability. The policy does not cover property damage or bodily injury resulting from the following:

- War;
- Intended or expected losses;
- Rendering or failure to render professional services;
- Any business activity of the insured;
- Transmission of an infectious disease;
- Corporal punishment, sexual molestation, or physical or mental abuse;
- The possession, transfer, delivery, manufacture, sale, or use of illegal drugs by any person;
- Rental or holding for rental any part of the location resulting in a breach of use and occupancy rules;
- Premises rented to or owned by a policyholder who is not an insured location (this exclusion does not apply to bodily injury to a residence employee); or
- Ownership, use, maintenance, loading, or unloading of an excluded vehicle, aircraft, or watercraft, including consignment by a policy owner to any person or vicarious liability for a minor's actions (this exclusion does not apply to bodily injury to a residence employee).

Losses resulting from flooding and earth movement are excluded under homeowners policy forms. Insurers may cover losses if a *wildfire* is the *efficient proximate cause*, meaning flooding or earth movement was directly caused by a wildfire or wildfire mitigation efforts.

Conditions

The conditions found in the homeowners policy forms are separated into three sections:

1. Property conditions;
2. Liability conditions; and
3. Conditions that apply to both.

You already might be familiar with several of these conditions. The homeowners policy divides the conditions of the insured and insurer by section. The conditions that apply to *Section I – Property* are listed below. Since we have previously explained many of these conditions in the dwelling policy and property/casualty basics sections, we will only discuss the additions or differences.

Insured duties after a loss – If a loss occurs, the insured must do the following:

- Provide an agent or the insurer with prompt written notice of the loss;
- Notify law enforcement if a loss resulted from theft;

- Notify the fund transfer card or credit card company if the loss is covered under the fund transfer card and credit card coverage;
- Protect the property from additional damage, make necessary and reasonable repairs, and keep records of any repair expenses;
- Cooperate with the insurance provider during their investigation of a claim;
- Allow the insurance provider to inspect the property as often as reasonably necessary;
- If requested, agree to a medical examination under oath; and
- Send a signed, sworn proof of loss within 60 days of the insurer's request. This document must include an inventory, the time and events leading to the loss, any changes in occupancy or title, bills, receipts, other coverage on the property, interests of all insureds, and repair estimates.

Loss settlement – Insured property losses for the HO-2, HO-3, HO-4, and HO-5 policy forms will be settled as follows:

Actual cash value (ACV)

- Personal property;
- Carpeting, awnings, household appliances, outdoor antennas, and equipment;
- Structures that are not buildings;
- Mausoleums and grave markers; or
- If applicable, buildings or other structures at the time of loss are not covered to 80% of replacement value. The insurance provider can pay the greater of the ACV or the applied coinsurance formula.

Suppose the policy owner chooses not to file a claim on a replacement cost basis (e.g., the insured decides not to rebuild). In that situation, the policy owner may notify the insurer within 180 days after the date of loss.

Replacement cost

- Buildings and other structures if insured for at least 80% of their replacement cost. The insurer has the option of paying the *least* of the limit of liability, replacement with like kind and quality, or the amount necessary to replace or repair the damaged building;
- If the building is rebuilt at another location, the insurer will pay no more than the cost associated with building at the original premises; or
- The insurer will pay no more than ACV until actual replacement or repairs are complete. Suppose the cost to replace or repair the damaged property is less than 5% of the total amount of coverage, or less than $2,500. In that circumstance, the insurer will settle the loss without requiring the property to be replaced or repaired.

Appraisal – When handling claims, if the insurance company and the policy owner cannot agree on the value of the damaged property, either party may make a written request for appraisal.

Other insurance and service agreement – When other insurance applies to the same loss, the insurer is liable only for the portion of the loss that the coverage limit bears to the total amount of all insurance on the property. This condition is also known as proportionate share or pro rata. If a service agreement is in place for insured property (e.g., a home warranty), the policy will pay on an excess basis.

Loss payment – All losses will be covered within 60 days of receiving a signed, sworn proof of loss or after one of the following:

- An agreement as to the amount of loss has been reached;
- There is a final judgment; or
- An appraisal award has been filed with the insurance company.

Mortgage holders clause – When an insurer denies a claim, the denial will not apply to the mortgagee if they notify the insurer of any change in occupancy or ownership, pay any premiums due, and submit a signed proof of loss within 60 days. In addition, if the insurance provider decides to cancel or nonrenew coverage, it will provide the mortgage holder with *ten days'* advance written notice.

Volcanic eruption period – All volcanic eruptions that occur within *72 hours* will be considered *one event*.

Loss payable clause – If the Declarations show a loss payee for specific covered personal property, the loss payee will be considered an insured under the policy. If the policy is canceled or not renewed, the insurer must notify the loss payee in writing.

Other conditions that we previously discussed include:

- Insurable interest and limits of liability;
- Suit against the insurance provider;
- Pair or set clause;
- Insurer option to replace or repair;
- Recovered property;
- Nuclear hazard clause;
- The policy period; and
- Fraud or concealment.

The following common policy conditions apply to *Section II – Liability*:

Bankruptcy of an insured — Bankruptcy of the policyholder will not free the insurance provider of its obligations under the policy.

Limit of liability — The total limit shown on the declaration page is the insurer's total liability for any occurrence, regardless of the number of claimants involved or lawsuits filed. The insurer's responsibility to settle or defend a lawsuit ends when the limit of liability for the occurrence is exhausted by payment of a settlement or judgment.

Severability of insurance — The insurance applies separately to each policy owner. This condition does not increase the insurance company's liability for any occurrence.

Duties after an occurrence — In the event of a covered occurrence, when applicable, the policy owner is required to perform the following duties:

- Provide written notice to the agent or insurance provider as soon as possible that identifies the following:
    - The identity of the policy and named insured;
    - Reasonably available information on the place, time, and circumstances of the offense; and
    - Names and addresses of any claimants and witnesses;
- Cooperate with the insurer during the investigation, defense, or settlement of any claim or lawsuit;
- Promptly forward to the insurer every summons, demand, notice, or other process relating to the offense;
- At the request of the insurer, assistance with:
    - Making settlement;
    - Enforcing indemnity or any right of contribution against any individual who may be liable to an insured;
    - Conducting suits and attending trials and hearings;
    - Securing and presenting evidence and obtaining the attendance of witnesses;

- Except at their own cost, insureds may not voluntarily assume the obligation, make payment, or incur expenses other than for first aid to others at the time of the personal injury;
- Assist the insurance provider in any subrogation rights; or
- If the loss involves property damage to others, submit to the insurance provider a signed, sworn proof of loss within 60 days of their request.

When the insured does not comply with these requirements, the insurance provider has no obligation to provide coverage under the policy.

Duties of an injured person – Coverage F (Medical Payments to Others) — Injured parties or someone representing the injured party must provide the insurance company (or its agent) written authorization to obtain any medical records and proof of claim. The injured person also must agree to a physical examination by a doctor of the insurer's choosing, as often as requested.

Payment of claim – Coverage F (Medical Payments to Others) — Payment of any claim under this section is not considered an admission of liability by the policy owner or the insurer.

Suit against the insurer — No legal action can be brought against the insurance provider until all policy provisions have been satisfied. No one has a right to join the insurer in legal action against the insured.

Other insurance – Coverage E (Personal Liability) — The insurance will be considered excess over any other valid and collectible coverage unless the other insurance is intended to be excess coverage (e.g., umbrella liability policies).

Policy period — Coverage only applies to losses during the policy period.

The following conditions apply to both *property* and *liability* coverages:

Liberalization clause — Suppose the insurer adopts any revisions that broaden coverage in the policy. In that case, those revisions will automatically apply to the policy at no additional premium as of the date the insurer administers the revisions in the insured's state. This date must fall 60 days before or during the policy period listed in the Declarations.

Waiver or Change of Policy Provisions — Any waiver or change of policy provisions must be in writing by the insurance company.

Cancellation and Nonrenewal — The policy owner can cancel the policy at any time by returning it to the insurer or providing the insurer with a written notice. If the insurer cancels coverage, it must give the policy owner a *10-day* advanced written notice for cancellation due to nonpayment of premium. Insurers can also cancel a policy with a 10-day advanced notice if the policy has been effective for no more than 60 days. The insurer must provide the policy owner with at least a *30-day* advanced written notice for all other cancellations or nonrenewals. The insurer can only cancel a policy after it has been effective for 60 days for two reasons:

1. Material misrepresentation, which would have precluded the insurer from issuing the policy; or
2. Substantial change in the risk after the policy was issued.

Assignment — The insured may not assign the policy to any other individual without the insurance company's written consent.

Subrogation — The policy owner may waive all rights of recovery against any other person; however, that has to be done in writing and before a loss. If the rights are not waived, the insurer may require an assignment of the rights of recovery for a loss to the extent that the insurance provider makes payment. If an assignment is sought, an insured must sign and deliver all related papers and cooperate with the insurer. This condition does not apply to additional coverage damage to the property of others and *Coverage F – Medical Payments*.

Death — If a named insured or spouse dies, the deceased's legal representative will be considered an insured under the policy, but only regarding the deceased's property covered at the time of death. The definition of an insured is broadened to cover an insured who is a member of the deceased's household but only while residing at the residence location. It also extends to a person in the care of the insured's property, but only until a legal representative is appointed.

Selected Endorsements

Many endorsements available under the homeowners policy program broaden the coverage provided by the basic policy forms. The following optional endorsements are available on the homeowners policy. (Some also are available for the dwelling policy.)

Manufactured (Mobile) Homes

The *mobile home endorsement* modifies the homeowners policy to insure a mobile home and other structures on land leased or owned by the mobile home resident. The limit of liability for Coverage B (other structures) is $2,000 or 10% of the Coverage A limit, whichever is greater. This endorsement does not decrease the Coverage A limit.

The additional coverage of property removed is up to $500 for reasonable expenses incurred in the removal and return of the mobile home to avoid damage or being endangered by a covered peril. The additional coverage of ordinance or law is withdrawn.

The mobile home has to be designed for year-round living and must meet certain size requirements to be eligible.

Other Structures – Increased Limits Endorsement

The policy owner can choose to apply up to 10% of the dwelling insurance amount to cover *other structures* on the insured premises. In the basic form, this is not an additional amount of insurance and will lower the amount available under Coverage A in case of a concurrent loss. In the broad and special forms, coverage is automatically provided and considered an additional amount of insurance. Coverage is provided under Coverage B. Coverage B limits may be increased for an added premium if the amount is inadequate.

Scheduled Personal Property

Suppose the policy owner requires higher limits for certain types of property. In that circumstance, the *scheduled personal property endorsement* can be used to schedule specifically described items or classes of items on a blanket basis. This endorsement usually provides open peril or special form coverage on listed items. This endorsement allows for the scheduling of nine different classes of property:

1. Furs;
2. Jewelry;
3. Musical instruments;
4. Cameras;
5. Golfer's equipment;
6. Silverware;

7. Fine arts (including glassware and porcelains);
8. Rare and current coins; and
9. Postage stamps.

Newly acquired furs, jewelry, musical instruments, and cameras are insured up to the lesser of the following limits:

- $10,000; or
- 25% of the amount of coverage for that class of property.

The new property must be reported within 30 days of being acquired, and the policy owner may have to pay the additional premium from that date. For coverage to apply to fine arts, a policy owner must submit the acquisition report within 90 days.

Insured perils – This endorsement covers direct physical loss to property caused by any of the following perils:

- Nuclear hazard;
- War;
- Insects or vermin;
- Wear and tear;
- *If fine arts are covered* – breakage resulting from malicious damage or theft, explosions, earthquake or flood, windstorm, and fire or lightning; or
- *If postage stamps are covered* – disappearance, transfer of colors, denting or scratching, creasing, and fading.

The following are additional features and benefits of the scheduled personal property endorsement:

- The Coverage C limits do not apply to the scheduled property on this endorsement;
- Insured locations – scheduled personal property endorsement insures eligible property worldwide;
- Antiques and fine arts can be covered on a basis other than ACV;
- The special limits of liability do not apply to items or classes of scheduled property; and
- No deductible will be applied to a covered property loss.

When the scheduled personal property coverage is purchased as a stand-alone policy, it is called a *personal property floater*. Either way, it is extensive coverage and an attractive way of insuring valuable types of personal property against any risk of loss.

The following *examples* illustrate times when a policyholder would seek such endorsements:

- The policy owner is lucky enough to acquire a homerun baseball hit by Babe Ruth. If the baseball is stolen or destroyed by a covered peril, homeowners Coverage C will pay for a baseball. However, it will not be a baseball hit by Ruth. The insured could schedule the baseball (fine arts) and insure it for its value as a baseball "hit by the Babe." Such items typically require an appraisal to determine their value.
- A vase was given to the policy owner by her grandma. In addition to the fact that it was her grandmother's, the vase's age adds to its value.
- The policy owner lives in an area prone to earthquakes and has expensive glassware collections. This endorsement would cover the cost of the glassware if breakage resulted from an earthquake.

Inflation Guard

The *inflation guard endorsement* is utilized to assist in maintaining insurance-to-value requirements for replacement cost coverage. Under this endorsement, the limit of coverage on the dwelling automatically rises each year by a selected percentage. This endorsement is not required on actual cash value policies.

Personal Property – Replacement Cost

The *personal property replacement cost endorsement* adjusts the actual cash value settlement on personal property, carpeting, household appliances, awnings, and outdoor equipment to a replacement cost basis. Specific property types will not benefit from this coverage, including items that are stored and have become obsolete, items that are not in good working order, memorabilia, antiques, and fine arts.

No personal property is required to be insured to 80% of replacement cost at the time of loss. However, some insurance companies require that Coverage C be raised to 70% of the Coverage A amount when purchasing this endorsement.

Personal Injury

Personal injury coverage, including those that result from an invasion of privacy, defamation of character, libel, slander, and false arrest, may be added by endorsement.

Guaranteed and Extended Replacement Cost Options

Extended coverage is a standard extension of property insurance coverage that goes beyond the coverage for fire and lightning. This coverage extends insurance against losses caused by perils such as hail, windstorms, riots, strike-related civil unrest, vehicle damage, aircraft damage, and smoke damage. Previously, extended coverage was issued as an endorsement. In recent years it has been added to many forms as part of the minimum coverage provided by the policy or as optional coverage.

This endorsement is not intended to minimize the amount of insurance sold.

Additional Residence Rented to Others

The *additional residence rental provision* is an optional coverage endorsement to the homeowners policy that insures scheduled residential structures on the insured's premises that are being rented to others. It changes the liability exclusions to extend liability coverage to the rented residence.

Ordinance or Law Coverage

In many jurisdictions, once a structure or building has been substantially destroyed or damaged, even if a property insurance policy covers the cause of loss, the policy owner may incur significant additional expenses. Such expenses include the loss of value of an undamaged portion of the existing building, which has to be removed or demolished to conform with municipal law. An unendorsed property policy does not protect the policy owner from those additional costs required by ordinance. It also does not cover the policy owner from other expenses they have no option but to comply with if they want to remain in operation at that location. Insurance can be obtained for losses caused by the enforcement of ordinances or laws that do not allow restoring the property to the same condition that existed before the damage. This restriction is due to more strict building codes, environmental standards, or local ordinances.

Ordinance or Law Coverage is additional insurance coverage on all forms except the DP-1 for the increased cost of rebuilding or making repairs to conform to current building codes. It is 10% of Coverage A or Coverage B for policy owners if there is no Coverage A. It is 10% of the Improvement, Alterations, and Additions coverage for tenants. Coverage does not apply to a loss of value to the building due to an ordinance or law. Costs to comply with laws relating to pollution are also not covered.

Home Business Coverage

With the rise in home-based businesses over the last decade, insurers have developed a special endorsement to a standard homeowners policy called the *Home Business Insurance Coverage* endorsement. The home business endorsement offers a broader range of coverages than a standard homeowners policy that includes property and liability coverage typically found in a commercial insurance policy. Although the home business endorsement expands coverage, it provides a smaller coverage level than that found in a businessowners policy (BOP), which we will discuss in an upcoming chapter.

Limited Fungi, Wet or Dry Rot, or Bacteria Coverage

Limited Fungi, Wet or Dry Rot, Or Bacteria Coverage is an endorsement that can add special limits for losses caused by fungi, wet or dry rot, and bacteria. This endorsement applies to both property and liability losses.

Watercraft

For an additional premium, *Coverage E – Personal Liability* and *Coverage F – Medical Payments to Others* apply to "property damage" or "bodily injury" arising out of the following:

- The use, maintenance, ownership, loading, or unloading of certain types of watercraft;
- The entrustment by an "insured" of watercraft to any individual; or
- Vicarious liability for the actions of a minor or child using a watercraft (whether or not statutorily imposed).

The homeowners form provides automatic coverage for personal watercraft (sailing boats under 26 feet, inboard motor boats up to 50 horsepower, and outboard motor boats under 25 horsepower). However, the Section I coverage is limited to $1,500.

Section II – Liability of the homeowners form automatically applies to a boat (rented or owned) that meets specific size and horsepower limitations. By endorsement, Section II may apply to larger boats; however, there is no liability coverage if, at the time of an occurrence, the watercraft is any of the following:

- Operated in or used to practice for any organized or prearranged race;
- Rented to others;
- Used to carry cargo or individuals for hire; or
- Used for any "business" purpose.

Workers Compensation – Residence Employees

California law requires that an endorsement be available to provide workers compensation insurance under a homeowners policy for residence employees. Insurance carriers that offer the *Workers Compensation – Residence Employees* endorsement must provide the endorsement rating to the Department of Insurance for approval. The carrier may modify the endorsement and its coverage criteria.

Homeowners Insurance Valuation

Every property broker-agent, casualty broker-agent, and personal lines broker-agent must be trained to estimate the replacement value of structures and explain different levels of coverage under a homeowners policy.

Every property broker-agent, casualty broker-agent, and personal lines broker-agent must complete a *Homeowners Insurance Valuation* course as part of their continuing education (CE). This course does not add to the required CE hours. Based upon the recommended curriculum, each provider of CE courses must submit its course content to the Commissioner for approval.

Unlicensed individuals are *prohibited* from explaining insurance coverages or estimating dwelling replacement costs. Estimates of the replacement value of a structure should not be completed by individuals who are not agents, underwriters, contractors, or architects. Those individuals should also not explain coverage levels under a homeowners insurance policy.

Documentation of the Person Making an Estimate

Suppose a licensee submitted or communicated an estimate of the replacement cost to an applicant or insured regarding an application for or renewal of a homeowners policy that insures on a replacement cost basis. In that scenario, the licensee is responsible for documenting and maintaining in the file of an applicant or insured the following information:

- The status of the individual preparing the estimate of replacement value, as a broker-agent, the insurer, actuary or underwriter, or other individual specified by the insurer, a contractor, a real estate appraiser, an architect, or other person or entity allowed to prepare such an estimate by the Insurance Code;
- The name, address, telephone number, job title, and, if applicable, license number of the individual estimating the replacement value;
- The method by which or source from which the estimate of replacement cost was prepared, to include any real estate appraisal, architectural report, contractor's estimate, replacement cost calculator, or other source or method; and
- A copy of any reports or documents used to estimate the replacement value.

Suppose a licensee's estimate of replacement cost is provided to an applicant or insured regarding an application for or renewal of a homeowners insurance policy that insures on a replacement cost basis. In that situation, the licensee must maintain the specified records in the policy owner's file for the duration of coverage or the entire term of the insurance policy, whichever ends later, and for *five years* after that. In the event the estimate of replacement cost is provided by a licensee to an applicant to whom coverage is never issued, regulations will not apply.

Catastrophic Losses and Increased Cost of Construction

After a catastrophic event, such as a wildfire or earthquake, the demand for rebuilding materials and labor may create temporary shortages, which in turn causes claims costs to increase. Further, widespread catastrophic damage in areas of older homes only amplifies the problem because they cannot be repaired unless brought into compliance with current building codes. These repairs would significantly increase claim costs.

Since these increased construction costs are directly reflected in replacement cost calculations at the time of loss, insureds may find that their Homeowners policy limits are inadequate.

Some insurers offer Homeowners policies with residential dwelling coverage to solve this problem. This coverage will increase, often by 20%, over and above their standard replacement cost coverage to cover temporary increases in the cost of construction after a catastrophic event occurs.

Chapter Review

This chapter discussed the Homeowners insurance policy and the different parts of the policy, including coverage forms, conditions, exclusions, and endorsements. Let's review the key points:

HOMEOWNERS POLICY	
Types of Properties Covered	• 1-to-4 family-owner-occupied residences • No more than two families or two roomers/boarders per unit • Tenants in non-owned dwellings (HO-4) • Residential condominiums (HO-6) • Seasonal dwellings and secondary residences • Other types of ownership (e.g., dwellings under construction)

Coverage Forms	• *HO-2 (broad form)*
	  ○ Named peril basis
	• *HO-3 (special form)*
	  ○ Dwelling and other structures on an open peril basis
	  ○ Personal property only for broad perils
	• *HO-4 (contents)*
	  ○ Tenant broad form
	  ○ Insures personal property for broad perils
	• *HO-5 (comprehensive form)*
	  ○ Covers both dwelling and other structures on an open peril basis
	• *HO-6 (condominium owners)*
	  ○ Broadens coverage to include parts of the building
	• *HO-8 (modified coverage)*
	  ○ Used when replacement cost coverage is not practical

Property Coverages	• *Coverage A – Dwelling* – dwelling and premises; must be used primarily for residential or dwelling purposes • *Coverage B - Other Structures* – separate structures at the same location, such as detached garages and other outbuildings • *Coverage C - Personal Property* – can be purchased to insure personal property common to a residence • *Coverage D - Loss of Use (Fair Rental Value)* – applies if property under Coverage A, B, or C becomes damaged or is destroyed • *Coverage E - Additional Living Expenses* – only available if broad or special form dwelling coverage is written

CHAPTER 9:
Homeowners – Section I: Property Coverage

This chapter continues the discussion of homeowners policies. You will now concentrate specifically on Property Coverages A through D, as well as some additional coverages available in the homeowners policy.

- Overview
- Coverage A – Dwelling
- Coverage B – Other Structures
- Coverage C – Personal Property
- Coverage D – Loss of Use
- Additional Coverages
- California Residential Property Insurance Disclosure Statement

Overview

The homeowners policy form includes property coverage for the insured residence (Coverage A – Dwelling), other structures (Coverage B), and personal property (Coverage C – Contents), similar to the dwelling policy forms. The fourth coverage, loss of use (Coverage D), is similar to the additional living expense and fair rental value coverage described in the broad and special dwelling forms.

Every coverage form includes a basic deductible, which applies to all coverages unless otherwise noted in the policy.

Coverage Name	Damage Type	HO-2	HO-3	HO-4	HO-5	HO-6	HO-8
A Dwelling	Direct	X	X	None	X	X	X
B Other Structures	Direct	X	X	None	X	In A	X
C Personal Property	Direct	X	X	X	X	X	X
D Loss of Use	Indirect	X	X	X	X	X	X

Coverage A – Dwelling

Dwelling coverage is provided in every form except the HO-4. The coverage is defined similarly to the dwelling property form, except that outdoor equipment or building equipment used for servicing the residence is no longer in Coverage A. Because contents coverage is in every HO form, these items will be insured in Coverage C. The HO-6 condominium form combines Coverage A and Coverage B in this policy section.

PROPERTY COVERED

1. A dwelling on the described premises shown on the declarations page and all attached structures;
2. Supplies or materials located on or next to the residence used to construct, repair, or alter the dwelling or other structures on the premises;
3. HO-6 policies also include the following: appliances, alterations, items of real property, fixtures that are part of the building, property which is the policy owner's duty to insure as part of an agreement, and structures owned solely by the policy owner other than the residence.

PROPERTY NOT COVERED

1. Land, including land on which the residence or other tangible property is located;
2. The HO-6 form also includes items that typically are not insured under Coverage B. Such items include:

- Other structures for renting to an individual who is not a tenant of the dwelling unless it is a private garage;
- Structures used to conduct business operations; and
- Structures used to store business property unless the policy owner or a tenant of the dwelling owns the property.

Coverage B – Other Structures

Under *Coverage B – Other Structures*, a basic amount of insurance equal to 10% of the limit found in Coverage A is included for outbuildings and other structures. Still, a policy can be issued with higher limits. The definition of other structures is similar to that of the dwelling policy program, with several notable exceptions. The HO form substitutes the definition of a business with the coverage description. The homeowners forms add coverage for mausoleums and grave markers as they are no longer included in the list of property not covered.

PROPERTY COVERED

1. Other structures on the residence premises that are separated by a clear space from the dwelling or connected only by a utility line, fence, or similar connection;
2. Other structures rented to another person besides the dwelling's tenant, but only when used as a private garage;
3. Structures used to store the dwelling tenant's business property, as long as liquid or gaseous fuel is stored in a fuel tank of a craft or vehicle stored in the structure.

PROPERTY NOT COVERED

1. Land, including land on which the other structures are located;
2. Structures held for rental or rented to another person besides the dwelling's tenant when not being used as a private garage;
3. Other structures used to transact any business.

Coverage C – Personal Property

Personal property coverage is the most notable change from the dwelling property policy. Coverage C was optional in the dwelling policy but is now mandatory coverage in every homeowners form. The HO-2, HO-3, HO-5, and HO-8 will automatically include a limit of insurance equal to 50% of the Coverage A limit. This limit may be increased or decreased, but not below 40% for 1- and 2-family residences. Because the HO-3 policy form covers structures on an open peril basis, the insurance provider would pay $1,000 minus any deductible the policy owner must pay. In the HO-4 and HO-6 policy forms, the amount of insurance is chosen by the policy owner, with coverage minimums varying by state.

Special limits of liability in a homeowners policy are as follows:

- $200 for money, banknotes, coins, bullion, gold, silver (except goldware and silverware), platinum, and other metals;
- $1,500 for securities, accounts, notes other than bank notes, deeds, letters of credit, evidence of debt, tickets, passports, manuscripts, and stamps;
- $1,500 for watercraft and their outboard motors, equipment, furnishings, and trailers;

- $1,500 for other trailers;
- $1,500 for theft of jewelry, furs, watches, precious, and semiprecious stones;
- $2,500 for theft of firearms;
- $2,500 for theft of goldware and gold-plated ware, silverware and silver-plated ware, and pewterware, including hollowware, flatware, trays, tea sets, and trophies;
- $2,500 for business personal property on the premises;
- $1,500 for property away from the premises used to conduct business;
- $1,500 for loss of portable electronic equipment that produces, transmits, or receives audio, visual, or data signals while in a motor vehicle; and
- $250 for loss of wires, antennas, or any media used with the electronic equipment in a motor vehicle.

The limit of property at *other residences* includes the following:

- Personal property usually located at another residence of the policy owner is covered for 10% of the Coverage C limit, or $1,000, whichever is larger. This limitation does not apply if the property is moved because the residence premises is being rebuilt, renovated, or repaired.
- When the property is moved to a newly obtained residence for 30 days, the limit shown in the Declarations will apply proportionally to each residence. Coverage will not extend beyond the policy's expiration date.

PROPERTY COVERED

1. Personal property used or owned by the policyholder while it is anywhere in the world. At the named insured's discretion, guests, property of others, or residence employees may also be covered while on the residence premises. Residence employees may also have their personal belongings covered while in any residence a policyholder is occupying;
2. Property of roomers and boarders related to a policyholder;
3. Hobby aircraft and parts not used or designed to transport people;
4. Motor vehicles and other conveyances but only while in use to service the premises or designed to assist disabled individuals;
5. Prepackaged computer software and blank storage media.

PROPERTY NOT COVERED

1. Any items that are separately described and insured irrespective of the limit of insurance;
2. Fish, birds, and animals;
3. Aircraft and parts, whether attached or not, except hobby aircraft noted above;
4. Hovercraft and parts;
5. Motor vehicles and other motorized land conveyances, except those noted above. Included in this is electronic equipment powered exclusively by the vehicle. Also included are vehicle accessories and parts and electronic apparatus, but only while in or upon the vehicle;
6. Business data contained in paper records or books of accounts in computer equipment;
7. Property of tenants, roomers, and boarders (when not a relative of the policy owner);
8. Property in an apartment usually held for rental or rented by a policy owner;
9. Property held for rental or rented by the policy owner to others while off the residence premises;
10. Debit cards, credit cards, or any device used to withdraw, deposit, or transfer funds;
11. Water or steam (e.g., a broken water pipe considerably increases a policy owner's water bill).

Coverage C in homeowners forms is divided into four categories. Some of the notable *differences* between HO and DP property policy forms include

1. **Covered property** — HO policies extend coverage to anywhere in the world. The DP policy is predominantly used for personal property in the described location.

2. **Limit for the property at other residences** — Similar to the worldwide property coverage included in the DP policies. The sublimit only applies to other owned residences.
3. **Special limits of liability** — Sublimit amounts and property types are similar to those found in the Broad Theft Endorsement for DP forms; however, in HO forms, it is essential to note the categories that are only limited by the peril of theft.
4. **Property not covered** — Limitations are added to the HO policy for the property of tenants, roomers, and boarders.

Coverage D – Loss of Use

Every homeowners policy contains the *Loss of Use* coverage, which is a combination of Coverage D (Fair Rental Value) and Coverage E (Additional Living Expense) found in the dwelling property policy. When a covered loss makes part of the residence premises unfit to live in, the insurer will cover the loss of rent and additional living expenses for the shortest time required to replace or repair the damage. If the policy owner permanently relocates, the insurer will pay additional living expenses for the shortest time necessary to settle elsewhere.

Additional living expenses include any necessary increase in the cost of living the policy owner incurs for their household to maintain its usual living standard. Suppose loss of use results from the order of a civil authority. In that instance, the fair rental value payments and additional living expenses are limited to two weeks.

The policy expiration will not impact the payment of this indirect coverage.

Coverage Name	HO-2	HO-3	HO-4	HO-5	HO-6	HO-8
A Dwelling	$15,000 minimum	$20,000 minimum	Not Covered	$30,000 minimum	$1,000	$15,000 minimum
B Other Structures	10% of A	10% of A	Not Covered	10% of A	Part of A	10% of A
C Personal Property	50% of A	50% of A	Varies by State	50% of A	Varies by State	50% of A
D Loss of Use	30% of A	30% of A	30% of C	30% of A	50% of C	10% of A

Additional Coverages

The following additional coverages are available under HO policy forms:

1. Debris removal will cover all reasonable expenses for the debris removal of covered property for a covered cause of loss.

133

This coverage is not an additional amount of insurance. The HO policy will allow for additional debris removal expense coverage if the amount for the removal, plus the property damage amount, exceeds the limit of liability. This limit is an extra 5% of the applicable limit. Debris removal expenses can apply to Coverage A, B, or C.

A homeowners policy also will pay a policy owner's reasonable expense for the removal of trees from the residence premises:

- The policy owner's tree(s) felled by the peril of hail or windstorm or weight of snow, sleet, or ice; or
- A neighbor's tree(s) felled by a Coverage C peril (broad form perils), provided the tree:
    o Damages a covered structure;
    o Does not damage a covered structure but blocks a driveway that prevents a motor vehicle registered for use on public roads from leaving or entering the residence premises; or
    o Blocks a ramp or other fixture designed to assist a disabled individual in entering or leaving the dwelling.

The total amount of coverage included for tree removal is $1,000, with a $500 sublimit for the removal of any one tree.

2. Reasonable repairs coverage is provided to pay for the expenses incurred by the policy owner to make reasonable repairs to protect property from additional damage following a loss caused by a covered peril.

3. Trees, shrubs, and other plants are covered if damage or loss is caused by the following: lightning, fire, explosion, riot or civil commotion, a vehicle not operated or owned by a resident of the residence premises, aircraft, malicious mischief or vandalism, or theft. This additional insurance has a maximum limit of $500 per tree, shrub, or plant and a maximum per loss limit of 5% of the amount of coverage on the dwelling. In both the HO-4 and HO-6 forms, the maximum limit per loss is 10% of the Coverage C limit.

4. Fire department service charge will cover up to $500 for liability assumed by agreement for fire department service charges to protect covered property. The deductible is not applied, and the limit is considered an additional amount of insurance.

5. Property removed coverage is provided for any cause of loss (up to 30 days) while the covered property is removed due to endangerment by a covered peril.

6. Credit card, electronic funds transfer card or access device, counterfeit money, and forgery will cover up to $500 to insure the legal obligation of a policy owner to pay due to the unauthorized use or theft of a credit card or electronic funds transfer card. Loss resulting from the forgery of a check or loss through acceptance of counterfeit money replicating currency from the U.S. or Canada are also covered. No deductible applies, and the limit is an additional amount of insurance.

7. Loss assessment will cover up to $1,000 for the policy owner's share of a loss assessment during the policy period against the policyholder as a tenant or owner of the residence premises by an association of property owners or corporation. The assessment must be made due to direct loss to property owned collectively by all members. It must be of the type of property the insured's policy would cover if it were owned by the named insured. Damage to association property must result from a peril insured against and does not include land shock waves after a volcanic eruption or earthquake.

8. Collapse applies to covered property under Coverages A and B concerning this additional coverage. This additional coverage does not increase the limit of liability.

Collapse refers to the abrupt caving in or falling over of a building or any part of a building. The collapse must result in the building or part of the building being unable to be occupied for its current intended purpose. A building or any part of a building not at risk of caving in or falling over is not in a state of collapse.

Direct physical loss to covered property that involves the collapse of a building or any part of a building is insured if the collapse resulted from one or more of the following:

- The perils insured against;
- Decay that is hidden from view unless the presence of this decay is known to a policy owner before the collapse occurs;
- Vermin or insect damage that is hidden from view unless the presence of this damage is known to a policy owner before the collapse occurs;
- Weight of people, animals, equipment, or contents;
- Weight of any rain that collected on a roof; or
- The use of defective methods or materials in construction, renovation, or remodeling if the collapse occurs during the course of the work.

Unless the loss directly results from the collapse of a building or any part of a building, the following items are not included under the definition of collapse: loss to retaining walls, foundations, pavement, septic tanks, cesspools, underground pipes, drains, flues, swimming pools, decks, patios, fences, or awnings.

9. Glass or safety glazing material will cover breakage of glass or safety glazing material that is part of a covered building, storm window, or storm door. Coverage is provided for the same property if the loss results from earth movement. Covered property is protected from splinters or fragments of broken glass or safety glazing material. Insurers will not provide coverage if the dwelling has been unoccupied for more than 60 consecutive days immediately before the loss. This limitation does not apply to loss resulting from earth movement.

10a. (Except in the HO-4 form) Landlord's furnishings will cover up to $2,500 for a policy owner's carpeting, appliances, and other household furnishings in each apartment on the residence premises typically rented or held for rental to others. Covered causes of loss are limited to Coverage C perils, except theft. This coverage is not regarded as an additional amount of insurance.

10b. (In the HO-4 form only) Building additions and alterations — If the policyholder acquires or makes improvements to the residence premises at their expense, the policy will provide an additional limit of insurance equal to 10% of Coverage C.

11. Law or ordinance allows policy owners to use up to 10% of the limit of liability that applies to Coverage A (or the limit for buildings, additions, and alterations in the HO-4 form) for the additional cost incurred due to the enforcement of any ordinance or law that requires one of the following:

- The demolition, construction, or renovation of part of a covered building damaged by a covered peril; or
- The demolition and reconstruction of a covered building's undamaged part if it must be demolished because of damage to another part of the covered building resulting from a covered peril.

Law or ordinance *does not cover*:

- The loss in value to a covered building or structure because of the requirements of any law or ordinance. For example, although the Americans with Disabilities Act (ADA) establishes specific requirements for minimum clear floor space dimensions in restrooms, law or ordinance coverage does not include any costs necessary to ensure the restroom's compliance with the ADA; or

- The costs to comply with any law or ordinance that requires any policy owner to clean up, test for, or respond to pollutants on any covered building.

12. Grave markers will cover up to $5,000 for grave markers, including mausoleums, for loss resulting from a peril insured against, on, or off the residence premises. This coverage does not increase the limits of liability that apply to the damaged covered property.

California Residential Property Insurance Disclosure Statement

For every policy written or renewed on residential property in California, the named insured is given a copy of the California Residential Property Insurance Disclosure Statement. The producer or insurance provider must obtain the applicant's signature confirming receipt of the form within 60 days of the application date, beginning at the time of the original application.

The Disclosure Statement explains the principal forms of coverage for residential dwellings in California. It also identifies the form of dwelling coverage that was obtained or selected. This disclosure form includes only a general description of coverages. It is not part of the actual residential property insurance policy.

Coverage provided for building code upgrades by residential property insurance will apply to building codes and laws. This application is only to the extent that those codes and laws do not set stricter standards on the property based on the level of insurance coverage that applies to the property.

Chapter Review

This chapter discussed Section I – Property Damage of the Homeowners insurance policy. Let's review the key points:

HOMEOWNERS – SECTION I: PROPERTY COVERAGE	
Coverage A – Dwelling	• Dwelling coverage is provided in every form except the HO-4 • The coverage is defined similarly to the dwelling property form, except that outdoor equipment or building equipment used for servicing the residence is no longer in Coverage A • The HO-6 condominium form combines Coverage A and Coverage B in this policy section
Coverage B – Other Structures	• A basic amount of insurance equal to 10% of the limit found in Coverage A is included for other structures • The HO form substitutes the definition of a business with the coverage description
Coverage C – Personal Property	• Coverage C was optional in the dwelling policy but is now mandatory coverage in every homeowners form • The HO-2, HO-3, HO-5, and HO-8 will automatically include a limit of insurance equal to 50% of the Coverage A limit
Coverage D – Loss of Use	• A combination of Coverage D (Fair Rental Value) and Coverage E (Additional Living Expense) found in the dwelling property policy

CHAPTER 10:
Homeowners – Section II: Liability Coverage

This chapter will focus on liability coverages available in homeowners policies, including Coverage E – Personal Liability and Coverage F – Medical Payments to Others. You will also review some additional coverages in this homeowners policy section.

- Liability Coverages
- Additional Coverages
- Exclusions

Liability Coverages

Unlike the dwelling policy, liability coverage is included in every HO policy form. The liability section of all HO policies includes two liability coverages:

1. Coverage E – Personal Liability; and
2. Coverage F – Medical Payments to Others.

Coverage E – Personal Liability

Personal Liability (Coverage E) will respond if a claim is made or a lawsuit is brought against a policy owner for damages resulting from property damage (PD) or bodily injury (BI). Damages must have resulted from an occurrence to which the coverage applies. This coverage will do the following:

- Pay up to the policy's limit of liability for the damages for which a policyholder is legally liable. Damages include prejudgment interest awarded against a policyholder.
- Provide a defense at the insurance carrier's expense by counsel of the insurer's choice, even if the lawsuit is false, groundless, or fraudulent. The insurance company may investigate and settle any claim or suit that it decides is appropriate. The insurer's responsibility to defend and settle ends when the policy's limit of liability for the occurrence has been exhausted by payment of a settlement or judgment.

Under Coverage E, a $100,000 basic limit of liability is standard. However, the policy owner can purchase higher limits for an additional premium.

Coverage F – Medical Payments to Others

Medical Payments to Others (Coverage F) will cover necessary medical expenses incurred within *three years* of an accident causing bodily injury. Necessary medical expenses include medical, surgical, ambulance x-ray, dental, and funeral services.

Coverage applies if an individual is injured on the residence premises with the policy owner's permission to be there (e.g., a guest or visitor). Coverage will also apply if a policy owner injures a person off the residence premises, and the injury:

- Arises from the residence premises or ways adjoining the premises;
- Is caused by the activities of a policy owner;
- Is caused by a residence employee of a policy owner during their employment; or
- Is caused by an animal in the care of or owned by the policy owner.

This coverage *does not apply* to the policy owner or residents of the policy owner's household, except for residence employees.

Additional Coverages

As with the personal liability supplement, the liability section of the HO policy includes several additional coverages that are *paid in addition* to the limit of liability:

- **Claims expense** — The policy will cover the following: expenses incurred and costs taxed against the policy owner in any lawsuit the insurer defends, premiums on bonds required in a suit, valid expenses incurred by the policy owner, including up to $250 per day for loss of income, and interest on the entire judgment that accumulates after judgment has been entered and before the insurance company pays it.
- **First aid to others** — The policy will cover expenses the policy owner incurs to render first aid for bodily injury to third parties. The insurer, however, will not pay for first aid to a policy owner.
- **Damage to the property of others** — The policy will cover up to $1,000 per occurrence on a replacement cost basis for damage the policy owner causes to the property of others. This coverage does not apply to the extent a loss is covered for intentional damage under Section I. Coverage will apply if the damage results from a minor under age 13 to property owned by a policy owner or resident of the household, to property rented to or owned by the insured's tenant, or arising out of the policy owner's business.
- **Loss assessment coverage** — The policy will cover up to $1,000 per occurrence for the policy owner's share of loss assessment charged against them as tenant or owner of the residence premises, during the policy period, by an association of property owners or corporation.

Exclusions

The exclusions section of the HO policy contains exclusions specific to both Coverage E and Coverage F, as well as exclusions that apply to both coverages. Exclusions that apply to *both Coverages E and F* include:

Motor Vehicle Liability – Coverages E and F do not apply to motor vehicle liability arising from the following:

- Unregistered motor vehicles that should have been registered;
- Vehicles registered for public roads;
- Motor vehicles used in a competition or race;
- vehicles rented to others;
- Motor vehicles used to carry individuals or cargo for a fee; or
- Vehicles used in a business unless it is a motorized golf cart.

The exclusion further clarifies coverage by stating that if the above situations are not applicable, the motor vehicle is still not covered unless it meets the following conditions:

- Is on an insured location in dead storage;
- Solely used to service the residence premises;
- Designed to assist the disabled and parked at the insured location;
- Designed for use off public roads and not owned by the policyholder or owned by the policyholder, but at the time of the occurrence, the vehicle is located on the insured premises that meet specific criteria; or
- A motorized golf cart not altered from factory specifications meeting specific speed criteria and used for golf and leisure activities in a private residential community.

Watercraft Liability – Liability arising from the use of watercraft is not insured in the following instances:

- While the watercraft is operated in a speed contest or race. Coverage is allowed for a sailboat and if a vessel is used in a predicted log race;
- Rented to others;

- Used to carry cargo or individuals for a fee; or
- Used for any business purposes.

However, this exclusion does not apply to watercraft meeting the following criteria:

- Is stored;
- Is a sailing vessel under 26 feet long, or 26 feet or longer if not rented to or owned by an insured;
- Is a watercraft powered by an inboard-outboard engine, including those that power a water jet pump, and if it is 50 horsepower (hp) or less but only when borrowed or rented by an insured. If the watercraft is over 50 hp, coverage applies if borrowed by the policy owner; or
- If one or more outboard engines or motors are 25 hp or less, but if more than 25 hp, coverage is applied if borrowed or rented by the policy owner. Coverage for over 25 hp will also apply when newly acquired by the policy owner within specific timeframes and if the insurance carrier is notified.

Expected or Intended injury – Property damage or bodily injury expected or intended by the policyholder, even if it is of a different kind or degree than initially expected or is sustained by a separate entity, individual, or property than initially expected or intended.

Business liability – Coverage does not apply to business exposures of a policy owner. Coverage is arranged for the occasional rental of an insured location, but only if it is used as a residence. The policy also provides coverage for the partial rental of the home, but only if the portion rented is intended to house no more than two roomers or boarders. Coverage is also provided for specific business exposures such as schools, offices, private garages, or studios.

Other *exclusions that apply to both coverages*:

- Hovercraft liability;
- Aircraft liability;
- War;
- Professional Services;
- Controlled substances;
- Corporal punishment, sexual molestation, or physical or mental abuse; and
- Communicable disease.

The following exclusions only apply to *Coverage E – Personal Liability*:

- Damage to property owned by the policy owner;
- Damage to property of others in the control, custody, or care of the policy owner (damage caused by an explosion, smoke, or fire is covered);
- Bodily injury to any individual eligible for workers compensation or similar benefits;
- Bodily injury to the named insured or any minor or relative living in the household;
- Liability for any assessment charged against the policy owner as a member of a corporation, association, or community of property owners; and
- Contractual liability (excluding contracts related to the use, maintenance, or ownership of the insured premises).

The following exclusions only apply to *Coverage F – Medical Payments*:

- Bodily injury caused by any nuclear hazard;
- Bodily injury to a residence employee if it does not occur during employment;

- Bodily injury to anyone, not including a resident employee, who regularly lives on the premises; and
- Bodily injury to anyone eligible to receive workers compensation or benefits under another similar law.

Chapter Review

This chapter discussed Section II – Liability Coverage of the homeowners insurance policy. Let's review the key points:

HOMEOWNERS – SECTION II: LIABILITY COVERAGE	
Coverage E – Personal Liability	• Will respond if a claim is made or a lawsuit is brought against a policy owner for damages resulting from property damage (PD) or bodily injury (BI) • Pay up to the policy's limit of liability for the damages for which a policyholder is legally liable • Provide a defense at the insurance carrier's expense by counsel of the insurer's choice, even if the lawsuit is false, groundless, or fraudulent
Coverage F – Medical Payments to Others	• Will cover necessary medical expenses incurred within three years of an accident causing bodily injury • Necessary medical expenses include medical, surgical, ambulance x-ray, dental, and funeral services • Coverage applies if an individual is injured on the residence premises with the policy owner's permission to be there (e.g., a guest)
Additional Coverages	• Claims expense • First aid to others • Damage to the property of others • Loss assessment coverage
Exclusions	• The exclusions section of the HO policy contains exclusions specific to both Coverage E and Coverage F, as well as exclusions that apply to both coverages

CHAPTER 11:
Personal Auto

Although the Personal Auto Policy is mostly liability insurance, it also contains some property coverage for vehicle owners. This chapter begins with general definitions of auto policies. It continues with an explanation of policy components, eligibility requirements, and coverage forms. You will also learn about specific conditions and types of coverage available for motorcycles and recreational vehicles and state programs available to the policyholder. This chapter contains several terms and definitions, time limits, and dollar amounts for different types of coverage. Please pay close attention to any numbers because they may appear on your state exam.

- Personal Auto – General Concepts
- Personal Auto Coverages
- Other Types of Vehicles
- California Automobile Assigned Risk Plan (CAARP)
- Low-Cost Automobile Insurance

Personal Auto – General Concepts

The *personal auto policy (PAP)* is insurance for anyone who owns a private passenger vehicle. The policy combines insurance for physical damage to the automobile with liability insurance for claims from operating the auto. The PAP includes several parts, each describing a specific area of coverage:

- Part A – Liability Coverage;
- Part B – Medical Payments Coverage;
- Part C – Uninsured Motorist Coverage;
- Part D – Coverage for Damage to Your Auto;
- Part E – Duties After an Accident or Loss; and
- Part F – General Provisions.

Most of the PAP parts include the insuring agreement, exclusions, and limits of liability sections.

The operation or ownership of an auto involves three types of potential loss, and the PAP is required to protect these losses under diverse circumstances:

1. Legal liability (for property damage or injuries to others);
2. Injury to the policyholder or family members of the policyholder; and
3. Loss of or damage to the auto.

Definitions

The Definitions section of the personal auto policy is on the first page of the policy. It defines various terms used throughout the policy. Several of the more important terms are listed below.

Bodily Injury – *Bodily injury* refers to sickness or disease, bodily harm, and death resulting from the injury.

Property Damage – *Property damage* refers to destruction, physical injury, or the loss of use of tangible property.

You and Your – The terms *"you"* and *"your"* used throughout the PAP refer to:

- The named insured listed on the declarations page; and
- The named insured's spouse, if they are a resident of the same household. Suppose the spouse ceases to be a resident of the same household before the policy's inception or during the policy period. In that case, the spouse falls under the terms *you* and *your* until the earlier of:
    - The end of 90 days after the spouse changes residency;
    - The effective date of another insurance policy listing the spouse as a named insured; or
    - The end of the policy period.

Family Member – A *family member* is an individual who is related by blood, adoption, or marriage and who is a resident of the household. This term also includes a ward or foster children.

Your Covered Auto – The term *"your covered auto"* includes:

- Any vehicle listed in the Declarations;
- A newly acquired auto;

- Any owned trailer; or
- Any auto or trailer not owned by the policyholder but used as a temporary substitute for a vehicle listed above which is out of regular use because of its destruction, loss, service, repair, or breakdown.

Trailer – A *trailer* refers to a vehicle designed to be pulled by a private passenger auto, van, pickup, or farm wagons and implements while towed by any of the above vehicle types.

Newly Acquired Auto – A *newly acquired auto* refers to any of the following vehicle types that the policy owner acquires during the policy period:

- A private passenger auto;
- A van or pickup, for which no other insurance policy provides coverage, that:
  - o Has a gross vehicle weight (GVW) of less than 10,000 lbs. (GVW is the maximum recommended weight including the vehicle, passengers, fuel and fluids, and all cargo);
  - o Is not used for the transportation or delivery of goods and materials unless such use is incidental to a business of maintaining, installing, or repairing equipment or furnishings; or
  - o Is not used for ranching or farming.

Insurers will provide coverage for a newly acquired auto with several notification requirements. The requirements will depend on the new vehicle's coverage type and if the vehicle is replacing an existing auto listed in the Declarations or is in addition to the listed vehicles.

Uninsured motorist coverage, medical payments, and liability will be extended to a newly acquired auto for replacement vehicles as follows:

- The coverage will be the broadest offered on any existing vehicle on the declarations page, and there is no stipulation that the insurance carrier be notified; and
- If the vehicle is in addition to the listed vehicles, the policy will offer coverage but only if the insurance provider is notified within *14 days* of the policyholder becoming the owner.

Collision – *Collision* refers to the upset or impact of a covered vehicle or non-owned auto with an object or another vehicle.

Other-than-collision – *Other-than-collision* (previously called comprehensive) includes losses that result from the following:

- Fire;
- Falling objects or missiles;
- Explosion or earthquake;
- Theft or larceny;
- Windstorm;
- Water, flood, or hail;
- Malicious mischief or vandalism;
- Civil commotion or riot;
- Contact with animals or birds; and
- Breakage of glass.

Collision Coverage and Other Than Collision Coverage – This coverage for a newly acquired auto starts on the date the policyholder becomes the owner:

- The policy owner must ask the company to insure the vehicle within 14 days of taking ownership when the Declarations section indicates that this coverage applies to at least one vehicle.
- In this case, the newly acquired auto will have the broadest coverage currently provided for any auto listed in the Declarations.
- If no such indication is made and the policy owner incurs a loss within the first *four days* of ownership, coverage can still be requested (within the first four days). A $500 deductible will apply.

Occupying – *Occupying* means in, upon, getting in, out of, on, or off a vehicle.

Types of Auto

Owned Autos – *Owned autos* are eligible vehicles titled by the policyholder or acquired during the policy period.

Non-owned Autos – *Non-owned autos* include private passenger autos, vans, pickups, or trailers operated by or in the custody of the named insured or a family member but not titled by or provided for the regular use of the policy owner.

Hired Autos – *Hired autos* are rented, leased, hired, or borrowed from someone other than an employee or partner.

The classes *non-owned automobile* and *hired automobile* are mutually exclusive, and the distinction between the two is often misunderstood. Hired autos include automobiles rented, leased, hired, or borrowed, excluding those owned by employees. Autos rented, leased, hired, or borrowed from employees are considered non-owned automobiles. The distinction between non-owned and hired autos does not depend on whether payment is made for using the auto but on whether an employee owns it. This somewhat artificial distinction exists mainly for rating and premium determination.

Temporary Substitute – The PAP covers any auto or trailer not owned by a policy owner while used as a *temporary substitute* for a listed vehicle that is out of everyday use due to servicing, breakdown, repair, destruction, or loss.

Shared Rides – A shared ride or share-the-expense carpool is when the carpool members share the expenses of the commute to and from work, not to be confused with hired autos. Unlike a hired auto, in which one individual pays another for services, each individual in a share-the-expense carpool pays for their share of the transportation costs. The exclusion of private passenger vehicles used to transport individuals for hire usually does not apply to shared rides.

Auto Policies vs. ISO

As you have previously learned, ISO forms were established by the Insurance Services Office to standardize property and casualty insurance policies. However, individual states and insurance carriers can modify those forms to meet the specific insurance needs of each state.

Any personal auto insurance carrier can use the ISO program entirely, modify it as needed, or use an independent program. The primary differences between ISO forms and forms used by auto policies in this state would be the different order of coverage provisions, specific definitions of covered losses, and dollar amount limits. Agents must be aware that a PAP sold to a consumer will differ from the ISO Personal Auto Policy.

Primary vs. Excess Coverage

Usually, the auto policy covering the auto involved in an accident acts as the primary coverage. When an insured auto is in an accident while in the custody and care of a facility such as a parking lot, garage, or valet, the PAP covering the vehicle is excess coverage over any coverage belonging to the facility.

Generally, when a person rents a private passenger vehicle while on a short vacation, the owner's insurance coverage is *primary*, meaning that it pays first if the driver negligently injures another person or damages their property while driving a rented vehicle. In this instance, the driver's auto insurance policy is excess coverage. The primary and excess coverage concept applies when a driver damages a rented vehicle. Most car rental companies carry a very high deductible that will apply when a customer damages one of their vehicles. In other words, the car rental company is the primary, and the customer's Collision and Other Than Collision coverage is excess coverage.

Named Insured

The *Named Insureds* extends the liability coverage provided in the policy for individuals named explicitly on the endorsement. It covers non-owned autos available for the policy owner's regular use, the use of covered vehicles to transport property or individuals for a fee, or the use of covered vehicles in other businesses except the automobile business.

Good Driver Discount

Eligibility Requirements – An individual is qualified to buy a Good Driver Discount policy if they meet all of the following criteria:

- Has had a motor vehicle driver's license for the *previous three years*.
- Has NOT done any of the following during the *previous three years*:
  o Had more than one violation point count of the Vehicle Code. Being involved in an accident for which the driver was at fault and that resulted in damage only to the property will induce one violation point count;
  o Had more than one dismissal of charges under the Vehicle Code in three years for violations that would have resulted in the assessment of more than one violation point count; or
  o Was the driver of a motor vehicle involved in an accident and was mainly at fault for causing bodily injury or the death of any person.

Anyone who claims they have met the criteria based partially or entirely on a driver's license and driving experience acquired anywhere other than in the U.S. or Canada is considered qualified to buy a Good Driver Discount policy. They must be licensed to drive in the U.S. or Canada for at least the *previous 18 months* and have met the criteria for that period.

Discount Percentage – The rate charged for a Good Driver Discount policy must be *at least 20% lower* than the rate the policy owner would have been charged for the same coverage.

Principal Rating Factors for PAPs – Premiums and rates for an auto insurance policy have to be determined by application of the following factors in *decreasing* order of importance:

- The policy owner's driving safety record;
- The number of miles they drive yearly; and
- The number of years of driving experience the policy owner has had.

The Commissioner can adopt other premium and rate regulations that substantially relate to the risk of loss. The weight to be given to each deciding factor is determined by law.

Limits of Liability

Limits of liability – *Limits of liability* are the insurance carrier's liability for payment as stated in an insurance policy. Limits of liability are the maximum amount of money the insurer will pay for a particular loss or pay for a loss during a specific period.

Per Occurrence (Accident) – *Per occurrence* is a liability policy sublimit that puts a cap on the payment for all claims that result from a single occurrence or accident, regardless of how many insureds are involved.

Per Person – *Per person* is the maximum medical expenses payment amount available for bodily injury to a single person in an accident, regardless of the stated policy limit for bodily injury claims.

Aggregate Limit – *Aggregate limit* is the maximum limit of available coverage provided under a liability policy during a policy year. This coverage is provided regardless of the number of accidents that occur or how many claims are made. Losses paid under coverages subject to aggregate limits lower the available amount for future losses. Aggregate limits are restored on the policy's anniversary date.

Split Limit – *Split limits* are separate limits of liability for different coverages. The limits can be stated per occurrence, per person, per policy period, or split between property damage and bodily injury. Many auto liability policies are issued with split limits. For example, 25/50/25 indicates that the policy will pay the following:

- Up to $25,000 for the injury of a single individual;
- Up to $50,000 for bodily injury to two or more individuals (but not more than $25,000 to any one individual); and
- Up to $25,000 for damage to the property of others.

Combined Single – *Combined single* is a single dollar limit of liability that applies to the total damages for property damage and bodily injury combined, resulting from one occurrence or accident. The limit can be used in any combination of amounts, but it may not exceed the single limit.

Personal Auto Coverages

Part A – Liability Coverage

Insuring Agreement – Liability coverage protects the policy owner against loss arising from legal liability when an automobile that the policy owner operates, owns, or maintains is involved in an accident. Under liability coverage, the policy pays for the following:

- Property damage and bodily injury because of an accident for which the policy owner is legally responsible;
- Defense expenses as long as the policy covers a particular loss (these expenses are paid over and above the policy limits); and
- Expenses for defending or settling the policy owner as deemed appropriate (these expenses end when the limits of insurance are expended).

Who is an Insured – An *insured* is the individual named in an insurance policy protected under the contract and to whom the insurance carrier provides services or pays benefits.

Under *Part A – Liability*, an insured is defined as:

- The policy owner or any family member for the use, ownership, or maintenance of any auto or trailer;
- Any individual using an insured's covered auto with permission;
- For a policy owner's covered auto, any individual, or organization (this is only concerning legal responsibility for acts or omissions of an individual for whom coverage is afforded under liability); and

- For any auto or trailer other than the policy owner's covered auto, any other individual, or organization, but only concerning legal liability for acts or omissions of the policy owner or a family member for whom coverage is afforded under liability. This provision will apply if the individual or organization does not own or hire the auto or trailer.

Supplementary Payments – Under the supplementary payments provision, the insurance carrier promises to pay certain costs on behalf of a policy owner:

- Bail bonds required of the policy owner due to a covered loss are paid up to $250;
- Premiums on appeal bonds and bonds to release attachments in lawsuits covered under the policy are paid in full;
- Insurers pay interest on a judgment after it has been entered; and
- Other reasonable expenses incurred at the request of the insurance provider are covered, including up to $200 per day for loss of earnings to assist in legal proceedings.

Amounts payable under the supplementary payments provision are paid *in addition to the liability limit.*

Exclusions – The following *exclusions* apply to the liability coverage provided for specific vehicles and individuals in the personal auto policy:

- Intentional damage or injury;
- Damage to property being transported or owned by a covered person;
- Damage to property used, rented, or in the care of a covered person, except a home or private garage;
- Bodily injury to an employee during employment, except for domestic employees who are not required to be covered by workers compensation;
- Use of a vehicle as a livery or public conveyance, except carpools;
- Damage caused by any person while engaged in the business of parking, storing, repairing, servicing, or selling vehicles designed for use mainly on public highways (this exclusion does not apply to the use, maintenance, or ownership of your covered auto by the policy owner, any family member, or any employee, agent or partner of the policy owner or any family member);
- Use of commercial-type vehicles in any business operation;
- Individuals using a covered auto without permission;
- Individuals covered under a nuclear energy policy, including individuals that would have been covered except for the exhaustion of the policy limits;
- The use, maintenance, or ownership of:
  - A motorized vehicle with fewer than four wheels;
  - A vehicle designed mainly for use off public roads;
  - A vehicle owned or available for everyday use by the policyholder, other than a covered auto;
  - A vehicle owned by or furnished for regular use by a family member, other than a covered auto; the named insured is covered while occupying or maintaining such a vehicle; and
  - A vehicle located inside a racing facility for racing.

Limits of Liability – Under a PAP, the policy owner may choose between two types of liability limits, including split and combined single.

Split limit coverage uses three specific dollar amounts. If an auto accident occurs, these numbers specify the maximum amount the policy will cover:

- Bodily injury for each individual involved;
- Bodily injury for the entire accident (irrespective of the total number of individuals involved); and
- Property damage.

It is worth noting that split limits are always expressed in this order.

For example, policy limits expressed as 25/50/25 will provide $25,000 of coverage for bodily injury per person, a maximum of $50,000 for all bodily injuries, and $25,000 of property damage coverage per accident.

By contrast, *combined single* coverage uses only one specific dollar amount. This coverage indicates the maximum coverage for all losses regardless of the number of people involved or the amount of property damaged.

When the policy is used to satisfy *financial responsibility* requirements, the policy complies with the law to the extent required.

Out-of-State Coverage – This coverage applies if a covered auto is involved in an automobile accident in any state or Canadian province other than the one in which the automobile is principally garaged. The insurance carrier will interpret the policy for that accident as follows:

- The insured's policy will provide the *higher specified limits* if the state or province has a financial responsibility law that specifies limits of liability that are higher than the limits shown in the Declarations; or
- The insured's policy will provide the required minimum coverage if the state or province has a compulsory insurance law requiring nonresidents to maintain insurance whenever the vehicle is used in that state.

It is also worth noting that no individual is entitled to duplicate payments for the same loss.

Each state establishes the minimum liability limits for its policies. The limits *do not change* when a vehicle travels from state to state and remain the same regardless of the vehicle's location. However, suppose the policy owner is in an accident to be covered at the required minimum limits for the state where the accident occurs. In that scenario, the limits *adjust* to the minimum limits for that state and add other coverage where necessary.

Other Insurance – The liability section also includes the other insurance clause. This clause states that the insurer will only pay its share of the loss when other insurance is available to pay for a covered loss. The insurance carrier's share is the proportion that the limit of insurance bears to the total of all available limits. For non-owned vehicles, the coverage will be considered excess over any other collectible insurance.

Part B – Medical Payments

Insuring Agreement – *Medical payments* coverage pays reasonable expenses associated with necessary medical and funeral expenses resulting from an accident sustained by a policyholder. They must use these services and costs within *three years* of the accident.

Who is an Insured – An insured is defined under *Part B – Medical Payments* as:

- The named insured *"you"* or a family member while occupying a motor vehicle designed for use on public roads or any trailer;
- The named insured or family member as a pedestrian if struck by a motor vehicle or trailer intended for use on public roads; and
- Any other individual while occupying a covered auto.

Exclusions – The following *exclusions* apply to the medical payments coverage. The insurance company will not provide coverage for any policy owner for bodily injury sustained in the following situations:

- While occupying any vehicle that meets the following characteristics:
  - With fewer than four wheels;
  - Used as a residence or premises;
  - Used as a public livery (excluding carpools);
  - Used without permission;
  - A commercial-type vehicle when it is being used for an insured's business; or
  - Located inside a racing facility and to prepare for or compete in any organized or prearranged speed or racing contest.
- While occupying or when struck by a vehicle that is
  - Owned or regularly used by the policy owner; or
  - Owned or used by a policy owner's family, other than a covered vehicle (this exclusion does not apply to the named insured).
- During employment, if workers compensation benefits are required; and
- While occupying a vehicle inside a racing facility when used for competition or practicing for a prearranged or organized speed contest.

In addition, insurers will exclude losses caused by war, a nuclear weapon, rebellion, insurrection or revolution, nuclear radiation, reaction, or radioactive contamination.

Limits of Liability and Other Insurance – The coverage amount depends on the policy. It will apply on a per-person basis for bodily injury sustained in an accident covered by the policy, irrespective of fault. Medical payments coverage is similar to personal injury protection (PIP) coverage. For example, the policy has a medical payment coverage limit of $10,000. The policy owner and the passenger were injured in an accident; one person had $12,000 in injuries, and the other had $10,000. Part B will pay each person $10,000, up to the coverage limit.

Any payments available under uninsured motorist or liability coverage will reduce the amount payable under this coverage.

The *other insurance* clause is explained in the medical payments section of the policy, which is the same as the provision found in the liability coverage section.

Part C – Uninsured and Underinsured Motorists

Insuring Agreement – *Uninsured Motorist (UM)* coverage provides the policy owner with money for bodily injuries that they would be legally entitled to recover from the operator or owner of a vehicle without the required liability coverage. A vehicle not carrying the required insurance is defined as an *uninsured vehicle* in this section of the personal auto policy.

Although some definitions can vary by state law, uninsured motorist coverage usually defines four categories of uninsured motor vehicles, including a land motor vehicle or trailer. At the time of the accident:

1. There is no insurance or liability bond for the vehicle;
2. The insurance or bond is less than that required by the financial responsibility laws of the state in which the accident occurred;
3. The accident was a hit-and-run accident, and the driver is unable to be identified; and
4. The insurance provider or bonding company denies coverage or is insolvent.

Uninsured motor vehicle coverage does not include any vehicle or equipment:

- Owned or available for regular use by the policy owner or a family member;
- Owned by a government agency;
- Owned by a self-insurer unless it becomes insolvent;
- Designed primarily for use off public roads;
- Operated on crawler treads or rails; or
- Used as a residence or premises.

The current limit for property damage in an uninsured motorist property damage endorsement in this state is *$3,500* if there is no additional collision coverage. If the policy owner has collision coverage, the uninsured motorist property damage endorsement will waive the collision deductible and repair the damaged vehicle. The cost of repairs cannot exceed the vehicle's *actual cash value*.

Who is an Insured – Insured is defined under *Part C – Uninsured/Underinsured Motorist* as:

- The named insured and any family members;
- Any other individual while occupying a covered vehicle; and
- Any person eligible to recover damages because of injuries to one of the above.

Underinsured Motorist – *Underinsured Motorist (UIM)* coverage helps a policy owner with bodily injury damage caused by another motorist when that motorist lacks sufficient insurance coverage. UIM coverage will pay the difference between the policy owner's UIM limits and the at-fault driver's bodily injury limits.

For example, Chad has bodily injury limits of 25/50. Chad causes an auto accident in which Karen is injured. Karen's bodily injury damages come to $65,000. Chad's bodily injury coverage will only pay for $25,000 of Karen's damages, leaving her with $40,000 to pay. Here are two ways underinsured motorist coverage may respond:

1. If Karen's underinsured motorist limits are 100/150, her UIM coverage will pay the remaining $40,000 of BI damages.
2. If Karen's limits are 50/100, her UIM coverage would only pay another $25,000 of the $40,000 in BI damages. The remaining $15,000 will not be covered. $50,000 (Karen's UIM limit) − $25,000 (Chad's per person limit) = $25,000 (what the UIM pays)

Property Damage – *Uninsured motorist property damage* coverage protects against damage to the policy owner or the covered auto when involved in an accident caused by an uninsured motorist. The limits for uninsured motorist coverage are established at the time of auto policy purchase. Some states require a deductible every time an auto insurance claim is filed.

Underinsured motorist coverage protects against damage to the policy owner or the covered auto when in an accident caused by a driver with insufficient auto insurance. This property damage coverage typically pays the difference between the policy owner's underinsured motorist property damage limit and the other driver's property damage coverage limit. The limits for underinsured motorist coverage are established at the purchase of the auto policy.

Collision Deductible Waiver – The *Collision Deductible Waiver*, when acquired in conjunction with collision coverage, waives the collision deductible when the insured auto is damaged due to an accident caused by an uninsured motorist.

Part D – Coverage for Damage to Your Auto

Coverage for Damage to Your Auto, also called physical damage coverage, includes both Collision and Other Than Collision coverage (previously known as comprehensive). Coverage only applies when a premium is listed in the Declarations next to these coverages.

Insuring Agreement – The insuring agreement states that the insurer will pay for direct and accidental loss to a non-owned or covered auto minus any deductible listed on the declarations page. Only the highest deductible will apply when a loss to more than one non-owned or covered auto results from the same accident.

The PAP defines *non-owned autos* as any private passenger auto, van, pickup, or trailer in the custody of or operated by but is not owned or furnished for the regular use of the named insured or a relative.

Exclusions – The *exclusions* shown below apply to the physical damage coverage section of a personal auto policy for losses or damages caused by any of the following:

- While the vehicle is used as a public livery, except for car pools;
- Mechanical or electrical breakdown, wear and tear, freezing, and road damage to tires (*excluding* damage resulting from vandalism or the total theft of the covered vehicle);
- War, nuclear weapons, radioactive contamination, insurrection, revolution, or rebellion;
- To electronic equipment intended for reproduction of sound, including stereos, radios, compact disc players, and tape decks and accessories (unless permanently installed in the vehicle by the manufacturer);
- To any other electronic equipment that transmits or receives audio, visual, or data signals, including telephones, two-way mobile radios, citizen band radios, radar detection equipment, scanning monitor receivers, audio cassette recorders, video cassette recorders, television monitor receivers, and personal computers and accessories (does not include permanently installed equipment in the vehicle);
- Destruction or confiscation by civil or governmental authorities;
- To a trailer or camper body not listed in the Declarations (does not apply to newly acquired camper bodies or trailers obtained during the policy period or insured within 14 days of ownership);
- To any custom equipment or furnishings in or on any van or pickup, including special carpeting and insulation, bars, furniture, facilities for sleeping or cooking, height-extending roofs, paintings, custom murals, or other decals;
- To any non-owned vehicles under the following situations:
  - Used without permission;
  - Being used or maintained by any individual while engaged in the business of parking, storing, servicing, repairing, or selling vehicles;
  - Rented by any policyholder if the rental company is prevented from recovering loss or loss of use from the policyholder because of the rental agreement or state law; or
- To any auto located in a racing facility to practice, prepare for, or compete in any organized speed or racing contest; and
- Loss of personal effects.

Limits of Liability – The limit of liability is the *lesser* of:

- The vehicle's ACV at the time of the loss (including an adjustment for depreciation and physical condition); or
- The amount necessary to replace or repair the vehicle.

Losses to non-owned autos are covered the same as the coverage available for any covered auto, except non-owned trailers, which have a limit of $1,500. Permanently installed electronic equipment in a location not usually used by the auto manufacturer is covered up to $1,000.

Other Provisions – The physical damage section of the personal auto policy also includes four other provisions. These provisions are similar to the conditions discussed for other property coverages and include:

1. **Payment of Loss** — The insurance carrier can pay money, replace, or repair the damaged or stolen property. In addition, if the stolen property is recovered, the insurance provider can return the property to the policy owner, paying for any damage. The insurer can also take all or part of the property at an appraised or agreed-upon amount.

2. **No Benefit to Bailee** — The insurance will not directly or indirectly benefit any bailee or carrier. For example, suppose a vehicle is in the care of a service station for repairs or a garage, and it is damaged. In that case, the policy owner will need to seek recovery for the damages from the service station or garage.

3. **Other Sources of Recovery** — If other insurance can be applied, the insurer will pay proportionally. Coverage for any covered non-owned auto is over and above any other collectible source, including insurance and any other source of recovery available to the non-owned auto's owner.

4. **Appraisal** — If the policy owner and the insurance carrier cannot agree on a settlement, either party can request an appraisal. Each party will then choose and pay for its own appraiser. The appraiser will jointly select a third appraiser, known as an umpire. The decision reached by at least two appraisers will bind both parties.

For various reasons, an insurer may not want to insure an individual for full comprehensive physical damage coverage on their auto policy. In this circumstance, *nonstandard physical damage* can be written. Nonstandard physical damage coverage is issued on a named peril basis instead of open peril, like comprehensive coverage.

Selected Endorsements – Optional endorsements can be used to amend the PAP to fit the needs of individual policy owners. We will discuss some of the more commonly used endorsements next.

Miscellaneous Type Vehicles – The *miscellaneous type vehicle* endorsement is used to broaden the definition of covered autos to include motorized vehicles such as motor homes, motorcycles, dune buggies, golf carts, and other recreational vehicles. The liability and medical payments exclusions on vehicles with less than four wheels do not apply when this endorsement is attached to the policy. Coverage is not provided for vehicles rented or borrowed unless it is a temporary substitute for a miscellaneous vehicle listed in the endorsement.

Named Nonowner – The *named nonowner* endorsement provides coverage for individuals who do not own a car but rent or borrow vehicles as needed. Coverage is considered excess over and above any other valid and collectible insurance on the rented or borrowed vehicle and is only for the person named on the endorsement. Spouses and their family members are not provided automatic coverage and must also be listed on the endorsement. The exclusion for vehicles furnished and available for regular use of the policyholder will apply unless deleted in the Declarations. Physical damage coverage is typically not provided.

Extended Non-owned Coverage for Named Individuals – The *extended non-owned coverage for named individuals* endorsement will expand the liability only or liability and medical payments coverage provided in the policy for specifically named individuals on the endorsement. It covers non-owned autos available for the regular use of the policy owner, the use of covered vehicles to transport property or individuals for a fee, or the use of covered vehicles in other business operations (excluding the automobile business).

Optional Limits – Transportation Expenses – *Transportation expenses* will be covered if the loss results from collision or other-than-collision, provided that the corresponding coverage is indicated on the declarations page. Coverage will apply to a non-owned auto and a covered auto.

The policy will typically pay up to $20 per day up to a maximum of $600 (can vary by state) for transportation costs incurred by the policy owner due to a covered loss.

Expense payments will begin after a 24-hour waiting period for causes other than theft. Expenses are covered 48 hours after the robbery if a covered vehicle is stolen.

Transportation expenses are not subject to a deductible. They are limited to the period reasonably required to replace or repair the covered auto.

Customizing Equipment Coverage – Part D of a PAP does not include many items that are easily damaged or removed or considered customized accessories. A separate *Damage to Your Auto (Customized Equipment)* endorsement may be used to provide coverage for an auto's customized equipment.

Mexico Coverage – Since the coverage territory excludes Mexico, the policy owner must purchase separate *Mexico Coverage* if they plan on driving in Mexico. This coverage is limited and will only apply to accidents within 25 miles of the U.S. border and only if the policy owner is in Mexico for ten days or less. The policy owner must also purchase liability coverage through a Mexican insurance carrier, and coverage only applies as excess over and above other collectible insurance. Lawsuits must be brought within the U.S., but only by a United States citizen. Cases brought by Mexican citizens are not covered.

Towing and Labor Costs – The *towing and labor costs* endorsement includes a basic limit of $25 for towing and labor costs incurred at the location where a vehicle is disabled. Higher limits of coverage are available for an additional premium. Coverage will apply to a covered auto or a non-owned auto but only applies to costs incurred at the location of disablement.

Joint Ownership Coverage – The *joint ownership coverage* endorsement is used when multiple individuals own a vehicle together (insurable interest), but do not fit the traditional definition of an insured in the PAP. Coverage applies to individuals other than a husband and wife who reside in the same household and are nonresident family members. The vehicle owned must be shown in the endorsement, and coverage will not extend to any vehicle owned by a party not listed or included in the definition of a covered auto.

Trust Endorsement – A *trust endorsement* can be attached to the PAP. The term "trust" refers to a legal instrument that allows the transfer of ownership of titled property from a person to a trust. Upon transfer of the property from the individual, the trust becomes the legal owner of that property.

The primary function of the trust endorsement is that it allows private passenger autos, vans, and pickups owned by a trust to be legally "owned" by a single individual. This endorsement is sometimes recommended because the ownership of an automobile is considered a liability exposure to trust assets.

Auto Loan and Lease Endorsement (GAP Coverage) – A *GAP coverage* endorsement will pay the difference between the amount an insurance carrier pays for a totaled car and the amount owed on a loan or lease.

Rental Reimbursement Expense – The *Rental Reimbursement* endorsement is only available if Other Than Collision coverage is included in the policy. This endorsement reimburses the policy owner for rental costs incurred because the covered auto is out of use due to a covered loss.

Special Physical Damage – Through a rider or endorsement, *special physical damage* coverage protects a customized or specialized vehicle that would not qualify for normal physical damage coverage. Examples of such vehicles include big rigs, performance vehicles, antique or classic cars, and others.

Part E – Duties after an Accident or Loss

Part E – Duties after an Accident or Loss outlines the required duties of anyone seeking damages under the policy after a loss or accident. This part of the personal auto policy's coverage does not include subsections.

When the policy owner does not comply with this policy section, harming the insurance company, the insurer is relieved of its duty to provide coverage. These duties are similar to those previously discussed for other types of insurance and include:

- Prompt notification of loss;
- Cooperating with the insurance company;
- Forwarding any received legal papers;
- When requested, agreeing to a physical exam or an examination under oath;
- Providing the insurance company access to medical records;
- Submitting proof of loss;
- Notifying the police if a vehicle is stolen or when a hit-and-run accident occurs;
- Preventing the property from incurring additional loss; and
- Allowing the insurance company to appraise and inspect the damaged property.

Part F – General Provisions

Part F – General Provisions in the personal auto policy form describe the conditions applied to all coverage parts and the conditions applied to the individual coverages. These conditions, which are similar to some previously discussed, are as follows:

- **Bankruptcy** —A policy owner's bankruptcy does not relieve insurers of their obligations under the policy.
- **Policy changes** — The terms and conditions may not be waived or changed except by endorsement.
- **Fraud** — The insurance company will not provide coverage for any policy owner who has made a fraudulent statement or engaged in fraudulent conduct regarding any accident or loss.
- **Legal action against the insurer** — No individual can bring any legal action against the insurance provider until they comply with all policy provisions.
- **Subrogation (insurer right to recover payment)** — Subrogation rights apply to all coverages except physical damage coverage if it resulted from a person using the auto with a reasonable belief they were allowed to do so.
- **Policy period and territory** — The policy territory consists of the United States, its territories and possessions, Puerto Rico, or Canada.
- **Termination** — This provision specifies the duties and rights of the policy owner and insurance provider not to renew or cancel coverage. If a law where the policy was issued mandates a different notice period or any special procedures other than those listed below, the policy will comply with the state provisions. In most states, the insurance company must provide ten days' notice for nonpayment of premium or if the policy is canceled within the first 60 days of initial coverage. Insurers must provide 20 days' notice for any other reason. When the policy has been in force for more than 60 days, the insurer can only cancel due to nonpayment of premium. It can also cancel a policy for a revoked or suspended driver's license or if the policy was obtained through material misrepresentation. If the insurer decides not to renew coverage, they must provide at least 20 days' notice before the renewal date. When the policy owner obtains other insurance on a covered auto, the policy will terminate on the new policy's effective date.
- **Assignment (transfer of the insured's interest in the policy)** — The policyholder may not transfer their rights or interest in the policy without the *written consent* of the insurance carrier. If the named insured dies, coverage will be provided for the surviving spouse or legal representative of the policyholder, but only until the end of the policy period.
- **Two or more auto policies** — If the insurance provider has issued two or more policies that will respond to the same loss, the insurance provider's liability will be the highest applicable limit of insurance under one policy.

Individual Insured and Drive Other Car (DOC)

Individual Named Insured and Drive Other Car (DOC) insurance expands the definition of a covered auto to include non-owned vehicles operated by the insured individual. The Individual Named Insured endorsement extends physical damage and liability insurance on any non-owned vehicle driven by the insured. This endorsement also protects the insured when using a different vehicle not listed in a personal or commercial auto policy.

Drive Other Car insurance is frequently used in commercial auto policies. Since personal auto insurance provides coverage for individuals, a commercial auto insurance policy protects the vehicle listed in a commercial policy. DOC coverage is applied when an individual has a company car but not a personal auto and therefore does not have a PAP.

The company can add the DOC endorsement to the commercial auto policy to provide protection when the named individual or family member is driving a vehicle supplied by the company. Coverage can be obtained through DOC insurance if someone borrows, leases, or rents a vehicle.

This coverage is also known as non-owned vehicle coverage.

California Law

Financial Responsibility Law – California's Compulsory Financial Responsibility Law mandates all drivers and all owners of motor vehicles to maintain liability coverage (financial responsibility) at all times. The four forms of financial responsibility include:

1. A motor vehicle liability insurance policy;
2. A deposit of $35,000 with DMV;
3. A $35,000 surety bond obtained from a company licensed to conduct business in California; or
4. A DMV-issued self-insurance certificate.

Drivers must carry written evidence of financial responsibility whenever they drive and show it to a peace officer following a citation stop or accident. Drivers might have to pay a fine or have their vehicles impounded if they do not.

When a driver does not have acceptable proof of financial responsibility and has an accident, they could lose their driver's license for up to four years.

Policy Limits – Compliance with Financial Responsibility Law – Auto insurance policies issued in California cannot be considered effective unless:

- Issued by an insurer admitted to conducting business in this state by the Insurance Commissioner; and
- Have at least the following limits:
  - $15,000 for bodily injury or death for one individual;
  - $30,000 for bodily injury or death for two or more individuals in any one accident;
  - $5,000 if the accident resulted in injury or the destruction of the property of others in any one accident.

No policy or bond can be effective regarding any vehicle that was not registered in California or was registered in a state other than California at the policy's effective date or the most recent renewal. Also, no policy or bond can be effective regarding any vehicle unless the insurer issuing the policy is admitted to conducting business in this state. Suppose an insurer is not admitted to conducting business in this state. In that situation, it must execute a power of attorney authorizing the Department to accept service of notice or process on its behalf in any action upon the policy resulting from an accident.

Any nonresident driver whose driving privilege was revoked or suspended based on an action requiring proof of financial responsibility can provide written proof that is satisfactory to the Department instead of providing a certificate of insurance from an insurer admitted to conducting business in California. This written proof of financial responsibility must cover the operation of a vehicle in this state, meet the liability requirements, and is from an insurer admitted to conducting business in that individual's state of residence.

Uninsured Motorist Coverage – The insurance provider or any named insured can, before or after the issue or renewal of a personal automobile policy, make a *written request* to delete the *uninsured motorist provision* from their policy, reduce the amount of coverage, or exclude named drivers from the coverage provided by the policy.

Newly-Acquired Auto – The following information is important to remember about newly-acquired autos:

- **Broadest coverage** — A newly-acquired auto will have the broadest coverage provided for any vehicle listed in the Declarations, except for collision coverage;
- **Collision coverage** — When the insured has collision coverage on at least one vehicle listed on the Declarations page, collision coverage on a newly-acquired auto starts when the insured becomes the owner. The insured has to notify the insurance provider within *14 days*;
- **No collision coverage** — If the insured does not have collision coverage on at least one vehicle listed on the Declarations page, collision coverage on a newly-acquired auto starts when the insured becomes the owner, but the insured has to request collision coverage within four days, and a $500 deductible; and
- **Additional vehicles** — If a newly-acquired auto is in addition to any vehicle listed in the Declarations, the insured has to notify the insurance provider within *14 days*.

Cancellation and Nonrenewal – A policy's cancellation and nonrenewal conditions explain the circumstances under which a policy can be terminated. However, the *California Amendatory Endorsement* should also be consulted. Here, insureds will find that essential parts of their policy conditions have been deleted or expanded to be brought in line with the Code.

Cancellation – A notice of cancellation for an auto insurance policy will only be effective if it is based on any of the following reasons:

- Nonpayment of premium;
- Any insured's driver's license or motor vehicle registration has been revoked or suspended during the policy period or renewal in the 180 days before its effective date;
- Discovery of fraud in pursuing a claim;
- Discovery of material misrepresentation of any of the following information:
  - Number of years of driving experience;
  - Annual miles driven in previous years;
  - Safety record;
  - Record of prior automobile insurance claims; and
  - Any other factor that can substantially relate to the risk of loss.
- Substantial increase in the covered hazard.

An insured that makes a misrepresentation can avoid cancellation by providing corrected information within *20 days* of receiving notice of cancellation. In these cases, the insured must pay the difference in premiums for the period during which this information went undisclosed.

No notice of cancellation will be effective unless it is delivered to the insurer at least *20 days* before the effective cancellation date. If this cancellation is for nonpayment of premium, the insurer must provide just *ten days'* notice. Upon written request of the insured, the reasons for cancellation have to be delivered within *15 days*.

Nonrenewal – A notice of nonrenewal for an automobile policy will only be effective if it is based on any of the following reasons:

- Nonpayment of premium;
- Fraud or material misrepresentation impacting the policy; or
- A substantial increase in the covered hazard.

Before policy expiration, an insurance provider must deliver to the insured:

- At least *20 days* before the policy's expiration, an offer of renewal; or
- At least *30 days* before expiration, a written notice of nonrenewal.

When an insurance provider fails to provide adequate notice of renewal, the policy will remain effective for *30 days* from when the notice is delivered.

Driving History Report (MVR) – A *driving history report,* sometimes called a motor vehicle report (MVR), checks an individual's driving record. It can also provide information regarding substance abuse, irresponsible behavior, failures to appear, and unpaid fines. Under the Fair Credit Reporting Act, a copy of any MVR must be provided to the applicable person and a written description of their rights under the law.

Other Types of Vehicles

Motorcycles – *Motorcycles* do not meet the eligibility requirements for a personal auto policy. Usually, they cannot be added as an endorsement; therefore, specialty motorcycle coverage can be offered in California as a separate policy. Many insurance carriers only offer motorcycle coverage to customers with existing auto policies.

Motorcycle policies include the following unique characteristics:

- **Seasonal usage**;
- **Driving experience** — the number of years licensed to drive a motorcycle, not an automobile;
- **Liability coverage** — can only apply to a specified driver;
- **Extra payments coverage** — more limited transportation expenses than on a standard personal auto policy.

Coverage for uninsured motorists and medical payments will be similar to that in a personal auto policy. However, additional limitations may still be in place.

Recreational Vehicles – There are several types of recreational vehicles recognized by the California DMV, including:

- Conventional;
- Motor home;
- Folding camping trailer;
- Fifth-wheel;
- Van camper (or conversion); and
- Truck camper.

Coverage for these vehicles can differ, but policy owners may add endorsements covering them to a PAP. For example, since RVs are designed and used as private passenger vehicles, a 6-wheel RV would be considered a personal, not commercial, passenger vehicle.

Coverages specific to motor homes include, but are not limited to, the following:

- Coverage for attached accessories, such as awnings, TV antennas, or satellite dishes;
- Total loss replacement coverage to protect the motor home from depreciation effects;
- Campsite/vacation liability coverage to protect the RV when used as a residence;
- Replacement cost coverage for personal belongings after destruction or theft;
- Roadside assistance and towing.

Transportation Network Companies (TNC) – Transporting passengers for hire, also called "livery," has long been excluded from PAPs. However, the popularity of various *Transportation Network Companies (TNC)* such as Lyft and Uber has forced the California Department of Insurance, the California Public Utilities Commission, and the state legislature to consider ways to close the insurance gaps in ride-sharing coverage. This measure ensures that passengers, pedestrians, and other drivers are protected.

The services of these TNCs usually fall into three periods of time:

1. Waiting for a match (or pre-match);
2. Match accepted (driver is on the way to pick up the passenger); and
3. The passenger inside the vehicle and until they exit the vehicle.

The Commissioner has encouraged insurance companies to create new products to fill identified coverage gaps. The Department of Insurance has approved several new insurance products to cover ride-share drivers during the pre-match period. A current list of insurance companies that offer such coverage is available from the Department.

California Assembly Bill 2293 became effective on July 1, 2015. The new law requires that:

- Regular Personal Auto Policies provide no coverage for TNC activities;
- The TNC maintains $1 million in liability coverage from the time a match is accepted until the passenger exits the vehicle (periods two and three);
- The TNC or the driver maintains primary liability insurance in the pre-match period (period one) as follows:
  - $50,000 minimum for bodily injury to a single person;
  - $100,000 minimum for bodily injury to multiple individuals; and
  - $30,000 minimum for property damage;
- The TNC must also maintain $200,000 in excess liability insurance during the pre-match period.

California Automobile Assigned Risk Plan (CAARP)

Purpose – The *California Automobile Assigned Risk Plan (CAARP)* oversees the state's assigned risk insurance plan for drivers unable to secure insurance. It is designated by state law as the California Low-Cost Auto Insurance Program administrator. The Department of Insurance maintains regulatory oversight over the plan.

CAARP was established to provide automobile insurance for motorists who cannot obtain coverage in the conventional market because of their driving records or other extraordinary circumstances. The Plan assigns drivers to private insurance providers based on each insurer's share of the auto insurance market in the state.

Eligible to Place Business – Only CAARP-certified brokers or CAARP-certified agents are authorized to accept applications for the low-cost auto insurance policy. The program was introduced as a pilot program only in San Francisco and Los Angeles counties but is now available statewide.

Eligible Applicants – Any California resident with a valid driver's license and a good driving record can qualify for CAARP insurance. The following are the good driver requirements:

- Be at least 19 years old and have been continuously licensed to drive for the previous three years;
- Have no misdemeanor or felony convictions on the driving record;
- Have no at-fault accidents involving bodily injuries or death in the previous three years;
- Have no more than one property damage-only accident or a moving violation in the past three years;
- Not be a college student claimed as a dependent for state/federal income tax purposes.

Anyone is eligible for participation in the program, provided they:

- Have a valid driver's license;
- Do not owe money on any auto insurance policy within the previous *12 months*; and
- Can state (via the Eligibility Certification Statement on the back of the application) that they attempted to obtain insurance through the voluntary market and were denied coverage.

The vehicle to be insured *must be registered* in the state of California.

How Business is Placed – Individuals or companies having difficulty purchasing automobile liability insurance will contact any insurance agent and ask if they are a Certified Producer with CAARP. When the insurer is certified, it can assist the individual or company in applying for automobile liability insurance through the plan. Certified Producers with CAARP can estimate the premium costs and premium payment plans.

Coverages and Limits Available and Required – The program provides coverage based on the California Financial Responsibility Liability Limits of $15,000 for liability for bodily injury or death to one individual, subject to a cumulative limit of $30,000 for all individuals, and $5,000 for liability for damage to property unless higher limits are required by law.

Medical Payments and Uninsured Motorist Coverage are optional; however, physical damage coverage is not available.

Coverage May be Bound – Only Certified Producers can submit applications to the California Automobile Assigned Risk Plan and obtain immediate coverage through CAARP's *Electronic Effective Date Procedure (EEDP)*. This procedure lets producers use their telephones to input coverage data and is available for private passenger and commercial risks. Proposed effective dates will only be honored if the producer adheres to all of the Electronic Effective Date Procedure rules.

Applications submitted without using the Electronic Effective Date Procedure will become effective at 12:01 A.M. the day after receipt in the Plan office. Future effective dates are also available via the EEDP. To receive a future effective date, the Plan must receive the application before that requested date.

Commercial Risks – CAARP established the Commercial Automobile Insurance Procedure (CAIP) to provide for risks common to commercial operations. It is a pooling arrangement operated by CAARP, under which most large commercial risks (buses, taxis, truckers, etc.) are assigned to a servicing carrier (insurer) for handling. All the insurers share the losses and expenses. Therefore, risks requiring higher limits are less of a drain on the assets of any one insurer.

Low-Cost Automobile Insurance

The *California Low-Cost Auto Insurance Program (CLCA)* offers basic coverage for low-income California residents with good driving records. These new policies result from landmark legislation enacted in 1999 to provide low-cost automobile insurance to uninsured drivers. Initially, the program was only available in San Francisco and Los Angeles counties as a pilot program; it is now available *statewide*.

CAARP administers the CLCA, and licensed domestic insurers write these policies. Taxpayers do not subsidize the program.

Costs – The annual premium costs per car will vary by county, ranging from $241 to $556. Rates are set and adjusted annually in every county to ensure that the premiums collected are sufficient to cover losses and expenses. There is a 25% surcharge if the individual named on the insurance policy is an unmarried male between 19 and 24 years of age. This surcharge also applies if an unmarried male between 19 and 24 years of age lives in the policy owner's household and will be a driver of the insured automobile. However, insurance providers or producers are prohibited from charging fees (like paperwork fees, broker fees, etc.) when submitting an application through the CLCA program.

All qualified consumers are allowed up to two low-cost policies under the program guidelines. If the household contains two qualified consumers, each can have up to two policies for a total of up to four per household.

Eligibility – The insured drivers are required to meet the following qualifications:

- Be at least 19 years of age and a continuously licensed driver for the previous three years.
- **Qualify as a good driver** – Drivers cannot have more than one at-fault property damage-only accident or more than one moving violation in the previous three years. They also must have no misdemeanor or felony convictions for violating the Vehicle Code.
- Have an insured vehicle currently valued at $25,000 or less;
- **Meet income eligibility requirements** – The eligibility income level to qualify for the program is set at 250% of the Federal Poverty Level (FPL). Based on current data, a single individual earning less than the FPL would be eligible. The threshold income increases for each additional person in an insured family.

Cancellation or Renewal – Every low-cost auto policy is issued for a one-year term. It is renewable annually as long as the insured policyholder meets the program's eligibility requirements. Insurers can cancel the policy for fraud, nonpayment of premiums, or material misrepresentation affecting eligibility requirements if an insured obtains duplicate coverage from another insurance provider outside the program.

Insurers are not allowed to renew low-cost policies if there is a substantial increase in the covered hazard. They also cannot renew these policies if the insured no longer meets the program's eligibility requirements.

Coverages and Limits – The low-cost policy would provide the following basic liability coverage:

- $10,000 for bodily injury per person or death to one person;
- $20,000 for bodily injury per accident; and
- $3,000 for property damage per accident.

Optional Medical Payments and Uninsured Motorist Bodily Injury Coverages are also available for an additional premium. CLCA, however, does not provide coverage for Physical Damage (Comprehensive and Collision). That type of coverage has to be purchased separately.

The policy meets California's financial responsibility laws, which require drivers to carry minimum amounts of third-party liability coverage.

Chapter Review

This chapter explained personal automobile insurance policies and California's compulsory financial responsibility law. Let's review the key points:

PERSONAL AUTO	
Policy Parts	• Part A – Liability • Part B – Medical Payments • Part C – Uninsured Motorist • Part D – Coverage for Damage to Your Auto • Part E – Duties after an Accident or Loss • Part F – General Provisions
Types of Auto	• *Owned* - a vehicle titled to the policyholder or acquired during the policy period • *Non-owned* - private vehicles operated or in the custody of the named insured, not titled to the policyholder • *Hired* - leased, borrowed, or rented autos • *Temporary substitute* - an auto or trailer not owned by the policyholder used while the insured vehicle is out of service due to repair, loss, or destruction

Part A – Liability Coverage	• Pays for property damage and bodily injury, defense costs, and costs resulting from settlement or defense of the policy owner
	• *Limits of liability* - the maximum amount the policy will pay:
	  ○ *Split limit* - broken into bodily injury for each person involved, bodily injury for the entire accident, and property damage
	  ○ *Combined single limit* - A dollar amount indicating the maximum coverage for all losses
	• Common exclusions:
	  ○ Intentional injury or damage
	  ○ Use of an auto without permission
	  ○ Use of commercial-type vehicles in the business
	  ○ Damage to property in transit

Part B – Medical Payments	• Pays for necessary medical and funeral expenses resulting from an accident • Must be rendered within three years of the accident • Payments available from liability or uninsured motorist coverage reduce the amount of medical payments coverage
Part C – UM and UIM Motorist Coverage	• *Uninsured motorist (UM)* - for bodily injuries caused by another motorist who does not have the required liability insurance coverage • *Underinsured motorists (UIM)* - for bodily injuries caused by another motorist with insufficient insurance coverage • UIM coverage = the insured's UIM limits minus the driver's BI limits

PERSONAL AUTO *(Continued)*	
Part D – Coverage for Damage to Your Auto	<ul><li>Includes Collision and Other Than Collision coverages</li><li>Pays for direct and accidental loss to a covered or non-owned auto</li><li>Transportation expenses:<ul><li>Paid if the loss is a result of a collision or caused by something other-than-collision</li><li>Applies to owned autos</li><li>A 24-hour waiting period applies for losses other than theft</li><li>A 48-hour waiting period applies for expense payments from theft</li></ul></li></ul>
Part E – Duties After an Accident or Loss	<ul><li>Prompt notification of loss</li><li>Cooperation with the insurance provider</li><li>Forwarding legal papers</li><li>Submitting to a physical or other examination under oath</li><li>Allowing the insurance provider to access medical records</li><li>Notification of a hit-and-run or theft</li><li>Protection of property from an additional loss</li><li>Allowing the insurance provider to inspect and appraise the damaged property</li></ul>
Part F – General Provisions	<ul><li>*Bankruptcy* - does not relieve the insurer of their obligation to pay</li><li>*Policy changes* - terms and conditions cannot be waived except by endorsement</li><li>*Fraud* - coverage is not provided to an insured making fraudulent statements</li><li>*Legal action against the insurer* - legal action cannot be made against the insurer until there is full compliance with all policy provisions</li><li>*Subrogation rights* - the insurer has the right to recover payments</li><li>*Policy period and territory* - the United States, U.S. territories, and Canada</li><li>*Termination* - includes the rights and duties of the insured and the insurer to cancel or not renew coverage</li><li>*Assignment* - the insured cannot transfer their right or interest in the policy without the written consent of the insurer</li><li>*Two or more policies* - the insurer's liability is the highest limit of insurance if multiple policies cover the same loss</li></ul>
Common Endorsements	<ul><li>*Towing and labor costs* - includes a basic limit of $25</li><li>*Extended non-owned coverage for named individual* - provides coverage for non-owned autos, autos carrying individuals or property for a fee, or covered vehicles in other businesses</li><li>*Miscellaneous types of vehicles* - expands the definition of a covered auto to include motorized vehicles (e.g., golf carts, motorcycles, motor homes)</li><li>*Joint ownership coverage* - coverage for individuals who own a vehicle together</li></ul>
Financial Responsibility Law	<ul><li>Drivers in California must have at least the following limits: - $15,000 for bodily injury or death for one individual - $30,000 for bodily injury or death for two or more individuals in any one accident - $5,000 if the accident resulted in injury or the destruction of property</li></ul>
CAARP	<ul><li>The California Automobile Assigned Risk Plan (CAARP) oversees the state's assigned risk insurance plan for drivers unable to secure insurance</li></ul>

CHAPTER 12:
Other Personal Lines Policies

This chapter summarizes several types of personal lines insurance, from the standard fire policy to earthquake coverage and umbrella and excess liability insurance. You will continue learning about personal auto insurance and the California Low-Cost Auto Insurance Program.

- Standard Fire Policy
- Inland Marine
- Catastrophe Property Insurance
- Umbrella and Excess Liability Insurance
- Pet Insurance

Standard Fire Policy

In 1918 the *Standard Fire Policy (SFP)* was initially written by the insurance industry. It was designed to indemnify the policy owner from loss of or damage to the insured building, fixtures, furniture, or other personal property listed in the policy as a result of the fire.

The policy was standardized into the New York Standard Fire policy in 1943. It was adopted by 46 of the then 48 states as the "standard" fire policy form. (Texas adopted its own form, and Massachusetts adopted the New England Fire Policy.)

The Standard Fire Policy listed the applicable conditions and required the attachment of additional forms which address essential aspects of coverage.

The policy was used in most states as the foundation for providing property coverage on both personal and commercial insurance policies. With the introduction of the ISO simplified language policies in the 1980s, the Standard Fire Policy itself was phased out of day-to-day use by most insurers. However, its conditions and policy provisions are still incorporated into most property policies. Some states mandate that every property policy issued in the state contains language which, at a minimum, equals the policy language of the Standard Fire Policy.

Property Covered and Excluded

With the 1943 standardization, the Standard Fire Policy provided coverage for not only fire but also lightning and the removal of the property after a fire to prevent the undamaged insured property from incurring additional damage. Today's policy also provides coverage for insured property removed due to endangerment by an insured peril, even though a loss has not yet occurred.

Property covered for loss by a peril insured against is limited to the property listed in the policy.

However, suppose the described property is removed from the original location to protect it from the insured perils. In that case, the policy automatically covers the property for five days at the other location for virtually every type of peril.

Even though the Standard Fire Policy identifies covered property, an additional coverage form that describes the type of protected property must be attached. Bullion or manuscripts are only covered if they are specifically named in the policy.

For example, Jane's building and contents are insured. The building catches on fire, so Jane starts removing the contents and puts them in a warehouse so they will not burn. That night the contents that were removed are stolen. Even though theft is not a covered peril under the policy, Jane would collect for the loss under the removal provision.

The standard fire policy *excludes* coverage for the following:

- Currency;
- Accounts;
- Bills;
- Deeds; and
- Evidence of debt, securities, or money.

Perils Covered and Excluded

The Standard Fire Policy is a named perils contract; therefore, it only covers those specified in the policy. The insuring agreement states that the policy covers direct loss resulting from any of the following three perils:

1. Fire (only hostile fires);
2. Lightning; and
3. Removal of property from the premises endangered by the perils covered (fire and lightning). Removal coverage automatically applies for *five days*.

Since the Standard Fire Policy is a named perils contract, it does not insure any other perils not listed in the insuring agreement. However, numerous endorsements are available to add or increase the perils covered.

Losses Covered and Excluded

Without endorsement, the 165-line New York Standard Fire Policy of 1943 sets forth coverage in the Insurance Agreement on an actual cash value basis for loss or damage by the following perils:

- **Fire** – While the peril of fire is not defined in the Standard Fire Policy, its meaning is recognized by the courts as oxidation sufficiently rapid to cause a flame or glow. This knowledge is vital in settling losses denied for such occurrences as charring and scorching. Fires have also been defined into the following two classes:
    - Friendly fire, which is a deliberately ignited flame or glow that stays within its intended confines; and
    - Hostile fire, a fire that escapes its intended confines. Although not explicitly stated in the Standard Fire Policy, coverage is provided only for losses caused by hostile fires.
- **Lightning** – Damage caused by natural electricity is covered, but damage resulting from artificially generated electricity is not covered unless it results in a hostile fire, in which case, only damage from the fire will be covered.
- **Removal** – Coverage is provided for five days at another location for the insured property that is removed to protect the property from an insured peril. While the property is insured at another location, it is protected against all perils (all-risk) on a pro-rata basis.

The only type of loss insured by the Standard Fire Policy is a direct loss caused by named perils. Direct loss refers to actual physical damage to, or destruction of, the insured property.

All of the following are specifically excluded losses that are caused either directly or indirectly:

- An act of war;
- Ordinances of the civil authority;
- A policyholder's neglect to reasonably preserve or save the property;
- Theft;
- Loss occurring while the hazard is increased within the control or knowledge of the policyholder; and
- Loss that occurs when the building is vacant or unoccupied for *60 days or more*.

Limitations on Amount Payable

To prevent *over-insurance*, the insuring agreement of the standard fire policy has identified limitations on the maximum amount that the policy owner can collect for a loss. The amounts payable cannot exceed the *smallest* of the following amounts:

- **Policy limit** — the specified amount in the policy;
- **Actual cash value (ACV) at the time of loss** — replacement cost minus depreciation;
- **Cost to repair or replace** — replacing property of like kind and quality within a reasonable time;
- **Interest of the insured** — the amount equal to the policyholder's interest in the property at the time of loss; and
- **Pro rata liability** — limits the insurer's liability to a portion of the loss, which is no greater than the amount the policy owner bears to the whole insurance that covers the property, whether collected or not. Pro rata prevents a policy owner from collecting over-insurance from multiple policies. For instance, if a $100,000 building were insured under two separate standard fire policies, each insurance carrier would only have to pay one-half of any loss. Without this clause, the policy owner could attempt to collect $200,000 for the total loss of the $100,000 building.

California Regulations

All fire policies issued in California must be written on the standard form and cannot contain any additions. No part of the standard form can be changed or omitted except for a policy that only provides coverage against the peril of fire or in combination with coverage against other perils. Coverage for the peril of fire must be substantially equal to or more favorable to the policy owner than that contained in a standard form fire insurance policy.

Inland Marine

General Concepts

Inland Marine coverage is either filed or unfiled with state regulatory authorities. Filed coverages have standardized coverage forms. Unfiled Inland Marine classes provide a unique exposure to loss, in which standardized forms have yet to be created.

The *Nationwide Marine Definition* defines the coverage types written on Ocean Marine and Inland Marine insurance forms. In 1953 the National Association of Insurance Commissioners (NAIC) implemented a Nationwide Marine Insurance Definition and revised it in 1976. This definition is used mainly for classification purposes rather than as a definition of underwriting powers.

Inland Marine coverage can be written on almost any type of property that is considered to be *portable*. In addition, instruments of communication and transportation, such as docks, piers, and bridges, are also covered on Inland Marine coverage forms. Personal inland marine policies are often referred to as *floaters* because the coverage *floats* with the insured property anywhere in the world. Inland Marine must be differentiated from Ocean Marine, which insures property being transported over water. Inland Marine exposures pertain to property that is located on land.

The Nationwide Marine Definition defines four general classes of risks that can be the subject of Inland Marine coverage. These risks are as follows:

1. Domestic shipments and transportation risks;
2. Tunnels, bridges, and other instrumentalities of communication and transportation;
3. Personal property floater risks; and
4. Commercial property floater risks.

Inland Marine coverage is written on either filed or unfiled forms.

Filed forms are filed with state insurance departments by insurance carriers or on their behalf by bureaus.

Unfiled (or non-filed) forms are not standardized by a rating bureau but are developed by individual insurance companies.

Most personal lines Inland Marine coverage is written on filed forms.

Insurers can write the coverage of these forms on either an *open-peril* or a *named-peril* basis. Under a named-peril policy, the exclusions are common to most named-peril contracts. That is, losses from perils not insured against are excluded. Under the open-peril contracts, the following are common *exclusions*:

- **Inherent vice** — There is no coverage for loss or damage to the insured property that is caused naturally to the property or its material. For example, produce cannot be insured against spoiling. Metal cannot be insured against rusting. Colors cannot be insured against fading, etc.
- **Intentional damage by an insured** — Losses caused by the intentional acts of a policy owner or deliberate neglect of the policy owner are not covered.

All Inland Marine policies contain exclusions for loss by *war* or *nuclear events*. For both named-peril and open-peril forms, the actual insuring agreement and the exclusions must be examined to determine the scope of coverage.

Most personal lines Inland Marine insurance is issued on an *open peril basis*.

In an Inland Marine policy's conditions, "valuation" specifies 3 limits for the insured property:

1. The actual cash value of the property;
2. The cost to restore the property;
3. The cost of replacement with virtually identical property.

A special valuation can be applied using stated value or agreed-upon endorsements.

An *annual transit policy* is an unfiled coverage form used to insure the property interest of the consignee or the shipper. This policy is used by businesses that ship goods regularly. Insurers can write coverage for all incoming or outgoing shipments (or both) during the policy period. In addition, different coverage forms are used according to how the goods are shipped, whether by air, rail, or truck. Coverage is provided for the owner of the goods for any loss or damage, even if the common carrier is legally liable. These policies are written on a named peril form.

Personal Insurance

Personal Articles Floater (PAF) – A personal floater is an inland marine policy designed to insure movable personal property, wherever it may be located. Personal floaters can be written on an all-risk, open peril, or named peril basis.

The *Personal Property Floater* provides coverage to personal property on an all-risk basis anywhere in the world, provided that the policy does not exclude the property. Property is typically written on an unscheduled basis. Specific categories of property will be subject to special limits.

The *Personal Articles Floater* is used to cover certain types of personal property on a scheduled basis. The types of property that insurers can cover are typically pre-printed on the form, including furs, jewelry, cameras, fine arts, musical instruments, etc. Policy owners can also add other types of property to the coverage form.

The *Personal Effects Floater* covers personal effects worn or carried by travelers anywhere in the world, but not while the property is at home. Coverage is typically limited to $100 for watches, jewelry, and furs. There is no coverage for currency, travel tickets, vehicles, or bicycles.

Scheduled Personal Property Endorsement – The *Scheduled Personal Property Endorsement* covers items that would not be insured in a property policy or require more coverage than a property policy usually provides. Adding this endorsement to a homeowners policy offers open-peril coverage for scheduled items of personal property. Coverage C on an unendorsed homeowners policy contains special limits on certain property types, such as $1,500 for jewelry theft. Policy owners can raise the limit by adding this endorsement.

The HO-3 policy form includes open-peril coverage on the dwelling under Coverage A and the other structures under Coverage B. It only insures personal property under Coverage C for specific perils. Adding the scheduled personal property endorsement to the HO-3 policy for other perils would benefit the policy owner.

For example, the policyholder drops and breaks their expensive camera while on a camping trip. The HO-3 will not provide any protection since breakage is not a named Coverage C peril. However, the floater's open-peril coverage will apply if the policyholder has listed the camera on a Scheduled Personal Property Endorsement added to the HO-3 policy.

Personal Watercraft – Personal Insurance

Boatowners Coverage – HO policies limit the property and liability coverage available for watercraft. Only $1,500 of coverage is included in the HO policy for damage to watercraft, accessories, trailers, and equipment, and liability for watercraft is limited by the size of the boat.

Additional protection is available by endorsement or through the purchase of Boatowners coverage. The policy stipulates that the watercraft has to be used solely for private, pleasure use and that coverage is excluded if the boat is chartered, hired out, used in an official race or speed contest, or used to transport property or people for a fee.

The policy consists of two sections. Section I contains the Physical Damage Coverages. This section includes the insured perils, conditions, and exclusions that apply only to Section I. Section II contains the insuring agreements for watercraft liability, uninsured boaters, and medical payments. There is a set of Section II conditions and a set of general conditions that apply to both Section I and Section II.

Section I — Coverage A in the Boatowners Policy is designated for physical damage coverage on the boat. It includes coverage for the ACV (actual cash value) of:

- The motor(s) listed in the Declarations, including batteries and remote controls;
- The boat listed in the Declarations, including any permanently attached equipment;
- The trailer listed in the Declarations if it is specifically designed for transporting the boat; and
- When covered property includes a boat, any accessories, and equipment manufactured for marine use.

As indicated by the previous item, the physical damage coverage generally extends to cover equipment regarding the use of the vessel and is subject to a dollar limit.

Perils Insured Against — The Boatowners Policy insuring agreement is typical of the open-peril type, provided the insurer will pay for accidental and direct loss to the insured property.

In addition to an exclusion for loss by nuclear hazard and war, policies usually include the following physical damage exclusions:

- Damage due and confined to gradual deterioration, wear and tear, latent defect, inherent vice, faulty manufacture, mechanical breakdown, damage caused by any repairing or restoration process, and maintenance or service operation unless fire results and then for loss caused by the resulting fire;
- Damage while transporting property or individuals for a fee or while the covered property is rented to others; and
- Damage while the covered property, other than sailboats, is being operated in any official race or speed test.

Additional coverages for Physical Damage include the following:

- **Reasonable Repairs** — Coverage applies for the necessary costs to protect or to repair the covered property from additional damage from an insured peril. Payment for the loss under the Reasonable Repairs provision does not raise the policy limit.
- **Recovery** — Coverage applies for the reasonable expense incurred by the policy owner to recover the insured property in the event of sinking or stranding. This coverage is extrapolated from an Ocean Marine provision entitled Salvage. Unlike Ocean Marine Salvage charges, which are paid in addition to the limits of coverage on the hull, the Recovery coverage of the Boatowners policy does not raise the policy's limits of liability.
- **Automatic Coverage** — Automatic coverage is included on replacements for the boat, motor, or trailer described in the Declarations. The policy owner must notify the insurer within 45 days of acquisition and pay any additional premium.

Section II — The liability coverages of the Boatowners Policy match the coverages of the Personal Auto Policy. They include the following:

- Operations liability;
- Passenger liability;
- Uninsured boaters liability; and
- Flotilla (small fleet) liability.

Watercraft liability protection provides coverage up to the specified limits for claims or lawsuits against a covered individual for damages due to property damage or bodily injury caused by a watercraft occurrence. Along with the promise to pay judgments resulting from such lawsuits, the insurer also agrees to defend the policyholder. However, the insurance provider reserves the right to make a settlement if it deems it expedient. As in the case of other liability policies, coverage for defense costs is payable in addition to the policy's limits.

Exclusions under the Boatowners Policy include property damage or bodily injury intended or expected by the policy owner. The liability of any individual using a watercraft without permission is also excluded. Other exclusions are damage to rented or owned property in the policy owner's control, custody, and care, bodily injury to individuals eligible for workers compensation, and liability of an individual engaged in moving, storing, repairing, or selling watercraft. The policy excludes liability from speed tests, racing, nuclear hazards, and war.

Claim-related expenses will be paid as additional coverage, similar to the Personal Auto policy.

Medical payments coverage pays for accidents while the injured party is in, upon, getting into, or out of the insured boat. Some policies provide medical payment coverage for individuals who are injured while water-skiing.

Uninsured Boaters coverage generally includes a stipulated amount of coverage (e.g., $10,000) which can be applied for accidents with uninsured watercraft. Increased limits are available for an additional premium.

Navigation and Territorial Definitions — A policyholder should know about an essential part of the contract. The broadest policies cover the watercraft while being operated on any inland body of water within the continental United States, Canada, and coastal waters in the same region up to a limit of 10 to 25 miles (depending on the insurance company). The most restrictive policies only cover a specific body of water within a narrow parameter around that particular region. Many policies do not cover offshore waters, such as the Gulf of Mexico.

Ocean Marine Coverage – *Ocean Marine* coverage was one of the earliest forms of insurance ever to be written. It includes coverage for the property while it is in transit over water. The following are some common types of Ocean Marine coverage:

- **Yacht Policies** — This policy provides property and liability coverage on larger boats and some small sailboats and runabouts. Coverage is provided for losses occurring within defined navigational waters.
- **Hull Insurance** — This is a type of physical damage coverage. Replacement cost coverage is included for partial losses, and total losses are insured for an amount stated in the policy form. Hull coverage also consists of a collision clause that covers damage to other boats for which the policy owner is legally liable. This coverage is considered an additional amount equal to the limit of insurance written on the hull.
- **Protection and Indemnity** — This coverage, commonly called P&I, includes bodily injury and property damage liability coverage. Protection and Indemnity covers potential legal fees if a third party sues a boatowner. It will also insure wreck removal or salvaging costs and may even cover environmental charges if boat damage causes pollution. A common exclusion, called the water-skiing clause, excludes bodily injury to any individual water skiing or being towed by the insured boat.
- **Cargo Insurance** — This coverage is written separately from the insurance on the ship. It protects the cargo's owner from financial loss if it is destroyed or lost.
- **Freight Insurance** — This coverage is written to protect the vessel's owner from the loss of the charges assessed for carrying the goods. If the ship is lost, the income that would have been earned upon completing the voyage is also lost. Under freight insurance coverage, the ship's owner is reimbursed for the loss of these charges.

Catastrophe Property Insurance

Earthquake Coverage

An *earthquake* is a shaking or trembling of the earth that is seismic or volcanic, often resulting in severe damage. It is a peril that is excluded by most standard property forms. Coverage for the peril of an earthquake can be *added by endorsement* to most HO policies, or coverage can be written in a Difference in Conditions Policy.

Requirements for Insurers to Offer Earth Movement Coverage – Coverage can be provided in the policy of homeowners insurance, either by specific policy provision or endorsement. It can also be written in a separate stand-alone policy or certificate of insurance, specifically covering damage or loss resulting from the peril of an earthquake by itself or in combination with other perils.

Insurance providers writing residential property insurance in this state must comply with this provision in any of the following ways:

- By offering to underwrite the risk of damage or loss caused directly by the peril of earthquake;
- By arranging for earthquake coverage to be offered by an affiliated insurance carrier; or
- By arranging for earthquake coverage to be offered through an insurance broker or agent under a policy or certificate of insurance issued by a nonaffiliated insurance carrier.

State or Federal Facilities that Provide Coverage – The state has established the California Earthquake Authority (CEA). It is a publicly managed, not-for-profit organization that must be administered under the authority of the Commissioner. The authority is authorized to conduct insurance business in this state as necessary to sell *basic residential earthquake insurance policies.* However, it is not allowed to sell policies for any other line of insurance coverage. The participating insurer writing the underlying policy of residential property insurance can market the authority policies and be compensated reasonably for the claims and policy owner services they provide on behalf of the authority.

As stated in the California Insurance Code, earthquake loss assessment coverage can be issued in the following minimum amounts:

- $50,000 for individual condominium units valued at more than $135,000;
- $25,000 for individual condominium units valued at $135,000 or less.

The value of the land is excluded when determining the value of the condominium, as it pertains to the earthquake loss assessment coverage offered by the authority.

Insurers can offer a condominium earthquake loss assessment policy for different amounts of coverage other than those provided by the authority.

Whenever the authority issues or renews a residential earthquake insurance policy, they must provide the California Earthquake Authority Policy Disclosure, in 14-point boldface type, to the insured.

Endorsement vs. Separate Policy – Generally speaking, a *disadvantage* of buying a *separate earthquake insurance* policy is its high deductible. Rates for earthquake insurance depend on location, the probability of an earthquake, and the type of structure. While extremely useful when the entire home is destroyed, this type of policy may be too expensive when a home is merely damaged.

The disadvantage of offering earthquake coverage by *endorsement* is that endorsements affect the premium paid for the entire homeowners policy. The earthquake endorsement will most likely require an adjustment of the base premium.

As you have previously learned, in California, applicants can apply for Earthquake coverage from the California Earthquake Authority, a state-sponsored private-public partnership, through participating insurers. Earthquake policies obtained through CEA can be offered to qualifying applicants with a deductible applied as a percentage of the insured value, ranging from 10% to 15% of the policy limits.

Earthquake coverage obtained through sources other than those sponsored by the CEA range from 2% to 20% of the policy limits. However, given California has experienced more earthquake activity than any other state in the U.S., most Earthquake insurance is written through the CEA. The reason is that any insurer offering Homeowners insurance in California must also offer Earthquake insurance, known as the "mandatory offer law."

Single Limit Coverage vs. Multiple Limit – Single Limit coverage for earthquake damage is where all component coverages within the HO policy can be applied toward a single occurrence, like an earthquake. Multiple Limit coverage would include particular limits for specific parts of a dwelling property, such as a chimney, land, debris removal, emergency repairs, building code upgrades, loss of rent, additional living expenses, etc. Multiple Limits can also be expressed in terms of coverages available with Coverage A, B, C, and D.

Both have advantages and disadvantages. A combined single limit (CSL) can simplify the available coverage amount for an earthquake, regardless of how the damage may have occurred. A Multiple Limit restricts coverage to each of its components.

Earthquake Coverage Deductible – Any deductible on property insurance coverage is defined as the amount of loss the insured is responsible for paying before covered benefits from the insurance company are payable, typically expressed as a specific dollar amount. The higher a deductible is on a policy, the less the premium will be because the insurance company will not pay as much on a policy claim in case of a covered loss. The reverse is true for a lower deductible, where the premium will be higher because the insurer is subject to paying more on a policy claim in case of a covered loss. The insurer sets the deductible options for property insurance, from which the insured can select and typically start as low as $250 and can scale higher in various increments from $500 to $5,000 or more.

The main difference between earthquake deductibles and common property deductibles is the percentages used to calculate earthquake deductibles, as opposed to set dollar amounts used with other property deductibles. For example, the average deductible for HO Part A on a $100,000 property could be from $250 to $2,500. In contrast, a 10-15% earthquake deductible on the same property could be $10,000 to $15,000.

National Flood Insurance

Floods cause more property damage in the U.S. than any other type of natural disaster. The federal government established the *National Flood Insurance Program (NFIP)* to mitigate the coverage gap left by the private insurance industry. The NFIP was implemented by the Federal Insurance and Mitigation Administration (FIMA) through the Federal Emergency Management Agency (FEMA).

Congress created the NFIP in 1968 to respond to the increasing cost of disaster relief for flood victims and the rising damage resulting from floods. The program consists of three primary components:

1. Insurance;
2. Floodplain management; and
3. Floodplain mapping.

Nearly 20,000 communities across the U.S. and its territories participate in the NFIP by adopting and enforcing floodplain management laws to reduce potential flood damage. In exchange for participation, the NFIP makes flood insurance backed by the federal government available to renters, homeowners, and business owners in these communities.

Since the adoption of flood insurance was slow to take effect, in 1973, the federal government passed the Flood Disaster Protection Act, which required flood insurance in the following situations:

1. Flood insurance is a requirement in certain flood-prone regions as a condition for receiving loans through, or backed by, the federal government; and
2. Property owners who do not purchase flood insurance within 12 months after it becomes available will not qualify for full disaster relief funding. The amount of disaster relief will be decreased by the insurance amount that property owners could have purchased.

These participating communities are in the regular or standard flood program. They are eligible for coverage under the three policy forms that will be discussed later, to the full limits of insurance available through the program. The NFIP offers limits of insurance up to maximum amounts that may or may not be sufficient to cover an insured's loss. Insurance markets exist to provide flood coverage above the amounts of the NFIP.

For communities in the process of fulfilling floodplain management requirements, the full benefits of an NFIP policy are not available until their community is in full compliance with these requirements. In this interim stage, an emergency program offers reduced benefits until the requirements are met.

"Write Your Own" vs. Government – National Flood Insurance is written and serviced *directly through the NFIP* or a *write your own (WYO)* insurance program. The private insurance carriers participating in a WYO program sell and service policies on a no-risk-bearing basis through a special arrangement with the Federal Insurance Administration (FIA). They retain a portion of the flood insurance premium to pay administrative costs and commissions. The remaining premiums, plus any investment, are used to pay for losses. The NFIP reimburses the insurance carriers for the excess costs if the premium is insufficient to cover losses. The coverage purchased through the NFIP and the WYO insurance plan is the same. All licensed property and casualty producers can write business with the NFIP.

Eligibility – To be eligible for the flood program, a policy owner must reside in a community that has met the minimum floodplain management requirements. An eligible structure must have a roof and two solid walls, be mainly above ground, and not entirely over water.

FIMA can deny coverage through a provision in the 1968 Act for any property that violates state or local laws, ordinances, or regulations.

Certain restrictions also apply to any property located within areas determined by the federal government as part of the Coastal Barrier Resource System or as an Otherwise Protected Area.

Upon purchasing a flood policy, a *30-day waiting period* begins from the time of application and premium payment. This waiting period can sometimes be waived surrounding new or revised loans or map revisions. It can also be waived if a loan exists on a property that should have acquired flood insurance but did not.

Flood Definition – As defined by the NFIP, the key to triggering a flood policy is the damage caused by a flood. Water damage not meeting this definition will not be considered a flood.

According to the NFIP, a flood is a temporary and general condition of complete or partial inundation of two or more acres of normally dry land or two or more properties (at least one owned by the insured).

Floods can be caused by:

- Tidal waters or overflow inland;
- Rapid and unusual runoff or accumulation of surface waters from any source;
- Mudflow (a river of liquid and flowing mud on surfaces of normally dry land) and collapse; or
- Subsidence or collapse of land along a lake shore or similar body of water due to undermining or erosion caused by currents or waves of water exceeding projected cyclical levels that result in a flood.

The following losses are excluded from coverage or do not meet the definition of a flood: backup of sewers unrelated to a flood, landslides, windblown rain, snow, or sleet. Flooding that is within the policyholder's control is not covered.

Limits of Coverage – The following table shows the maximum coverage that is available under the regular National Flood Insurance Program for homes, small businesses, and other non-residential properties:

	BUILDING	CONTENTS
Single Family	$250,000	$100,000
Other Residential	$250,000	$100,000
Small Business	$500,000	$500,000
Other Nonresidential	$500,000	$500,000

The federal emergency flood insurance program takes effect when a community applies for the program. It ends when all NFIP criteria are met, and the regular program can start. A limited amount of coverage is provided with subsidized rates. The table below includes these coverage limits:

	BUILDING	CONTENTS
Single Family	$35,000	$10,000
Other Residential	$100,000	$100,000
Small Business	$100,000	$100,000
Other Nonresidential	$100,000	$100,000

Deductibles – Single-family dwellings are automatically provided with replacement cost coverage if they are insured to at least 80% of the replacement value or the maximum allowed under the regular flood insurance program. Every other building and its contents are insured on an ACV basis. Standard deductibles apply separately to building and contents losses, with higher deductibles available. Many of the exclusions in homeowners or dwelling policies for certain types of property are also excluded from the flood insurance policy. Such property can include bills, accounts, trees, lawns, motor vehicles, aircraft, retaining walls, fences, etc. In addition, other types of property that are especially prone to flood damage are also excluded. These include newly constructed buildings in, on, or over water, underground equipment and structures, and structures that are mainly considered containers.

There is a 30-day waiting period after the insurer accepts the application (binders are not issued during the waiting period) and before coverage becomes effective except in the following conditions:

- During the first 30 days after a community enters the normal or emergency programs, then coverage begins at 12:01 a.m. the following day after the application and premium are mailed;
- The assignment of an existing policy to a property purchaser; and
- At 12:01 a.m. on the 5th day after an endorsement request and premium payment are mailed for an existing policy.

No binders are issued during the waiting period.

NFIP Policy Forms – The NFIP offers three different standard flood insurance policy forms:

1. **Dwelling Policy Form** – covers residential structures and their contents;
2. **General Property Policy Form** – covers other residential and non-residential buildings or structures and their contents; and
3. **Residential Condominium Building Association Policy Form** – covers the entire condominium building under a single policy.

The *General Property Policy* Form covers commercial structures such as apartment buildings, office buildings, and schools. The General form includes four coverages:

1. *Coverage A – Building Property* insures the building, building property, extensions and additions attached to and in contact with the building, equipment and machinery (e.g., fire sprinkler system, light fixtures, awnings), certain fixtures, construction supplies and materials to be used on the building, travel trailers or manufactured homes, and certain property items in a basement;
2. *Coverage B – Personal Property* insures personal property owned by the policyholder against direct physical loss by or from a flood;

3. *Coverage C – Other Coverages* insures loss avoidance measures, debris removal, pollution damage, and removal of property for safety; and

4. *Coverage D – Increased Cost of Compliance* covers the extra costs necessary to comply with any ordinance or law during the reconstruction or repair of a building damaged by flood.

The National Flood Insurance Program does not provide business income or extra expense coverage. Also, *producers have no binding authority with the NFIP.*

A *3-hour training course* must be completed per Section 207 of the Flood Insurance Reform Act of 2004 to write flood insurance through the NFIP.

California Fair Access to Insurance Requirements (FAIR) Plan

Marketplace Needs Met by FAIR Plan – The Fair Access To Insurance Requirements (FAIR) Plan, an industry placement facility, and a joint reinsurance association were created to allow the equitable distribution among admitted insurers of the duty for insuring any qualified property that cannot be covered by basic property insurance through the normal marketplace.

Although the state created the Plan, it is not a state agency. It is an association of all California property insurers. Each insurance provider participates according to the amount of business they write in the state. When a company writes 10% of the property insurance in California, it underwrites 10% of every policy issued by the California FAIR Plan.

Types of Areas Served by FAIR Plan – FAIR plans provide property insurance to accept risks in the specifically designated inner city, urban areas, or brush fire-prone areas for which coverage is unavailable in the regular market due to the area's geographic location. In these areas, insureds are subject to losses from flooding and wave wash, high winds, and other perils for which coverage is generally written.

Applicants Eligible for FAIR Plan – Any individual having an insurable interest in real or tangible property who cannot secure basic property insurance through standard channels from an admitted provider or a licensed surplus line broker is eligible upon applying to the FAIR plan facility to an inspection of the property by inspection bureau representatives. The inability to purchase such insurance after diligent effort through normal channels can be demonstrated by a signed general statement to that effect on a form prescribed by the association.

Who Is Eligible to Submit Applications and Extent of Binding Authority – Broker-agents and agents who want to participate in the FAIR plan program *must be admitted by the Association.* The FAIR association is formed by insurance providers licensed to write basic property insurance within this state to help individuals obtain basic property insurance. However, all brokers or agents transacting basic property insurance must help individuals apply for insurance through the plan or provide those who desire that insurance with the toll-free number established by the Association.

The FAIR Plan does not have any internal insurance agents; all business submitted to the FAIR Plan is on a brokerage basis. A licensed insurance broker or agent is the representative of the insured, not the FAIR Plan, and places business with the FAIR Plan on behalf of their client. Insurance brokers and agents cannot bind or commit the FAIR Plan in any way.

Basic Property Insurance – According to the California Insurance Code, basic property insurance refers to insurance against direct loss to real or tangible personal property at a fixed location from perils insured under the standard fire policy. Basic property insurance can include the extended coverage endorsement for malicious mischief and vandalism. It can also include other insurance coverages that the industry placement facility can add with the Commissioner's approval. Basic property insurance does not include insurance on automobile or farm risks.

Fire Mitigation and How It Affects Insurance Costs

Fire Problem in the Wildland Urban Interface – In recent years, California has been under the serious threat of wildfires that destroy thousands of acres of land and thousands of residential and business structures, causing millions of dollars in property damage. The state spends hundreds of millions of dollars annually on suppressing and disaster recovery efforts required due to natural and human-caused fires. Property damages to residential homes and businesses amount to over $200 million annually. Wildfires also cause injuries and death to members of the public who live in the affected areas and to the state's fire department and law enforcement personnel.

According to a report issued by the California Department of Insurance, more than 5 million homes are currently located in California's wildland urban interface.

The California Department of Insurance initiated an effort to create economic incentives for insurance providers to mitigate fire risks and increase disaster preparedness among consumers and insurers. Together, the state Fire Director and the Commissioner of Insurance have signed the Memorandum of Understanding to mutually promote awareness and collaboration among the insurance industry, fire officials, and the public. This partnership prevents and mitigates losses resulting from wildfires.

Areas that Affect the Risks and Hazards – The factors increasing the threat of fires include the following:

- Location's topography (relative position, elevations, elements);
- Dry weather and frequent droughts;
- Increased fuel production and consumption;
- Greater urban interface and increases in population.

Another important consideration is a home's ignition potential during an extreme wildfire. This potential is determined by the characteristics of the home's exterior materials (masonry, wood, or fire-resistive) and their response to burning objects and embers within 100 feet. This region is known as the "ignition zone."

FEMA's Local Multi-Hazard Mitigation Planning Guidance helps local governments to create and adopt effective mitigation plans. Part of the plan is to conduct a risk assessment to define and clearly describe the conditions in the area that contribute to risks and hazards.

Current State Laws and Regulation – The initial memorandum issued by the Fire Director and the Commissioner of Insurance proposed the following measures:

- Initiate a public awareness campaign in the wildland-urban interface;
- Make insurance provider education programs available to all personal and commercial lines property insurers in this state;
- Create a statewide emergency services database for hazardous areas;
- Develop strategies to share fire activity information before, during, and after wildfires to ensure faster deployment of fire-fighting resources to affected communities;
- Re-evaluate inspection procedures of the California FAIR Plans Association for currency and appropriateness; and
- Increase incentives (like lower premiums) for homeowners, businesses, and insurers to prevent and mitigate fire risks actively.

California recently updated its State Hazard Mitigation Plan (SHMP), approved by FEMA. It serves as the primary guidance document and provides current hazard analysis, mitigation strategies, goals, and objectives.

The California Fire Plan was established by the State Board of Forestry and Fire Protection and the California Department of Forestry and Fire Protection. The Plan serves as the state's blueprint for reducing the risk of wildfires and sets goals and objectives for the collaboration of government and community to enhance the protection of lives, property, and natural resources.

Additional statutory strategies for reducing the chance of building damage or loss in a wildland urban interface area are as follows:

- **Defensible Space** – This law requires property owners to reduce flammable material around homes to keep direct flames and heat away from the building by establishing 100 feet of defensible space:
  o Proper clearance to 100 feet dramatically increases the likelihood of a home surviving a wildfire while also providing for firefighter safety when protecting a home during a wildland fire.
- **Exterior Wildfire Exposure Protection** – This law requires property owners to construct buildings so that they have less chance of catching fire from burning embers:
  o Recently adopted building codes and standards reduce the risk of burning embers igniting buildings by placing standards on roofing construction, siding, attic venting, decking, exterior doors, windows, wall vents, eaves, and enclosed overhanging decks.
  o The new California Building and Fire Code requires that ignition-resistant construction standards and methods be used for all new buildings in fire-prone wildland urban interface areas.

Umbrella and Excess Liability Insurance

Some personal and commercial insurance policies are not designed to insure first-party property exposures. A policy owner uses *umbrella policies or excess policies* when required or when they choose to purchase limits higher than what is offered through the primary policy. Here are a few essential terms related to these types of policies:

Underlying policy (primary liability policy) – The underlying policy is a policy that is covered by the excess or umbrella policy. For example, suppose a policy owner has a homeowners policy, automobile policy, and watercraft policy. In that case, these policies are underlying insurance for a personal umbrella policy. The limits of insurance for liability coverage (not property) of the underlying policies are used first, and then the limits available in the excess or umbrella coverage.

Umbrella (stand-alone) – Umbrella policies differ from excess policies because the coverage can be greater or less than the underlying policies.

Excess (follow form) – Excess policies do not restrict or expand coverage concerning the underlying insurance. The coverage parallels the underlying policy but increases the limit of liability based on the amounts chosen by the policy owner.

An excess or umbrella policy, also known as catastrophe insurance, provides coverage over the underlying policy. These policies are commonly issued to give a minimum of $1,000,000 worth of additional coverage. There is generally a minimum limit of liability the insured must carry and maintain on the basic policies.

When an underlying policy provides primary coverage, in a covered loss, no deductible has to be satisfied to access the excess or umbrella policy limits. However, in the case of true umbrella policies, the potential exists for coverage on a primary basis within the umbrella. In other words, the underlying or primary policy does not cover the loss, but the umbrella does.

In these cases, the insured must pay the *self-insured retention (SIR)* deductible.

The personal umbrella policy will cover damages exceeding the underlying or primary insurance for property damage or bodily injury due to a covered occurrence. It also covers personal injury for which a policy owner becomes legally liable because of one or more offenses listed under the definition of personal injury.

The personal umbrella policy defines an *insured* as any of the following:

- The named insured;
- A family member;
- Any individual using an auto or recreational motor vehicle (golf cart, dune buggy, all-terrain vehicle, snowmobile, or any other motorized land vehicle designed for recreational use off public roads) owned by the policy owner and covered under the policy;
- Any individual using a temporary substitute for such an auto or recreational vehicle is also an insured;
- Any other individual or organization, but only regarding the legal responsibility for acts or omissions of the policy owner or any family member while using an auto or recreational vehicle. However, the owner or lessor of an auto or recreational vehicle loaned or hired for use by a policy owner is not considered an insured); or
- Any individual or organization legally responsible for animals owned by the policy owner or any family member. However, an individual or organization using or having custody of such animals during any business or without the owner's consent is not considered an insured.

The umbrella policy mirrors the underlying policies' coverage for recreational vehicles and watercraft. However, optional endorsements to exclude coverage for designated recreational vehicles are available to the insurance company.

When a claim made or lawsuit brought against a policy owner is caused by an offense to which coverage applies, the umbrella insurer can participate in the investigation and settlement of a claim. However, the umbrella insurer will not contribute to any expenses incurred by the underlying insurer.

If underlying coverage is not effective, the umbrella insurer will provide defense at the insurer's expense by the counsel of the insurer's choice. The insurer can settle any claim without the consent of the policy owner.

Coverage provided by the umbrella policy *will not apply* to the following:

- Intentional damage or injury;
- Personal injury stemming from the published material, if done by or at a policy owner's direction with knowledge of its falsity;
- Property damage or bodily injury from the ownership, use, maintenance, loading, or unloading of any recreational vehicle owned by any policy owner;
- Loss from the use of any motor vehicle without the belief that the individual is entitled to do so;
- Loss from the use of any motor vehicle or watercraft while in operation or preparing for a prearranged speed contest or race; or
- Property damage or bodily injury from an act or omission of a policy owner as an officer or board member of a corporation.

The umbrella policy also excludes uninsured motorist/underinsured motorist coverage. Still, it can be reinstated through an endorsement in states that require such coverage.

A policy owner must maintain the underlying insurance at the full limits stated on the declarations page with no change to more restrictive conditions during the policy term. When any underlying insurance is canceled or not renewed or replaced, the policy owner must notify the insurance provider immediately.

When the insured does not maintain underlying insurance, the insurer will not be liable for more than it would have been if the underlying insurance was effective.

The policy's general provisions and other conditions are in line with the ISO personal lines format.

The ISO has filed approved umbrella policies for both personal and commercial lines. While the form is standardized, there is still flexibility that permits insurance companies to tailor a policy to meet their requirements regarding eligibility and underlying limits.

UM and UIM Extension under Umbrella or Excess Liability Policies

A personal umbrella or excess liability policy may or may not provide excess liability coverage for an Uninsured/Underinsured Motorist (UM/UIM) claim, depending on the language used in the policy form.

Policy owners can increase their UM/UIM limits to extend excess UM/UIM limits of liability. They cannot raise their UM/UIM limits above the Bodily Injury liability limits they carry on their policy.

Since umbrella policies are often written as *non-standardized forms*, some do not provide excess coverage for UM/UIM. Some may offer a limited amount of excess coverage for UM/UIM, such as $25,000, for no additional premium charge. Some may insure up to $1,000,000 or more by adding an excess UM/UIM endorsement to the umbrella for an additional premium charge.

If covered, claims will only be paid for UM bodily injury that exceeds the underlying primary UM/UIM coverage as listed in the Umbrella Declarations. Property damage liability is not covered.

Pet Insurance

Definitions

Key definitions in pet insurance policies include, but are not limited to, the following terms:

- **Chronic condition** — A treatable but incurable physical condition;
- **Congenital anomaly or disorder** — A physical condition present at birth due to environmental or inherited factors that contributes to disease or illness;
- **Hereditary disorder** — A disease or illness caused by a genetically transmitted abnormality from a parent to their offspring;
- **Pet insurance** — Individual or group insurance providing coverage for veterinary expenses;
- **Pre-existing condition** — Any condition for which a veterinarian provided medical advice, a pet received medical treatment, or a pet displayed symptoms or signs of a medical condition before the effective day of the policy or during the waiting period;
- **Veterinarian** — Anyone licensed by the Veterinary Medical Board to practice veterinary medicine;
- **Veterinary expenses** — All costs arising from advice, diagnosis, care, or drug treatment from a veterinarian; and
- **Waiting or affiliation period** — A period specified in a pet insurance policy that must pass before coverage begins.

Pet Insurance Basics

Pet insurance covers veterinary expenses and costs associated with medical advice, diagnosis, care, and treatment provided by a veterinarian, including prescription drug costs. Pet insurance is similar to human health insurance, as policy owners must meet a deductible before coverage can begin.

Disclosure Requirements

When transacting pet insurance in California, insurance providers must *disclose* all of the following to consumers:

- Policy exclusions (including pre-existing conditions, congenital anomalies or disorders, hereditary disorders, and chronic conditions);
- A statement for additional exclusions that reads: "Other exclusions may apply. For more information, please refer to the policy's exclusions section."
- Provisions that limit coverage through waiting or affiliation periods, coinsurances, deductibles, or annual or lifetime policy limits;
- Reductions in coverage or premium increases based on an insured's claim history;
- A summary description of the formula or basis used to determine claim payments, customary fee limitations, and benefit schedules within the policy or through a link on the main page of an insurance company's website;
- A benefit schedule for insurance providers that use a benefit schedule to calculate claim payments;
- A provision for usual and customary fee limitation that insurance providers use to determine claim payments through usual and customary fees or any other reimbursement limitation;
- A free-look provision allowing an insured to return a policy within *30 days* of delivery for a full refund of premiums, unless a claim has or will be paid before cancellation; and
- A summary of policy provisions in a separate document, titled "Insurer Disclosure of Important Policy Provisions:"
  - The "Insurer Disclosure of Important Policy Provisions" must be provided to a policy owner of new pet insurance upon the delivery of the policy and must be shown on the main page of the insurance company's website.

A pet insurer that utilizes a benefit schedule to determine the policy's claim payment must do the following:

- Disclose the policy's applicable benefit schedule; and
- Disclose all benefit schedules used by the insurance company under its pet insurance policies through a link on the main page of the insurance provider's website.

Pet insurers that determine a pet insurance policy's claim payment based on usual and customary fees or another reimbursement limitation based on current veterinary service provider charges must do the following:

- Include a provision for usual and customary fee limitation in the policy that describes the insurance provider's basis for determining the fees and how that basis applies to calculating claim payments; and
- Disclose the insurance provider's basis for determining usual and customary fees through a link on the main page of the insurance company's website.

Upon issuing or delivering a pet insurance policy, an insurance company must provide policy owners with a written disclosure in 12-point boldface type, which includes the following:

- The Department's mailing address, website address, and toll-free telephone number;
- The insurer's or the agent's address and customer service telephone number;

- A statement explaining that an insured should contact the Department only after speaking with an insurance provider and not being able to reach a reasonable solution to the problem; and
- A statement advising the insured to contact the agent responsible for delivering the policy if the insured requires further assistance.

Administrative Proceedings

Suppose the Commissioner suspects an individual is violating the Insurance Code concerning the sale or solicitation of pet insurance. In that case, the Commissioner could issue and serve an order containing a statement of the charges, a statement of that individual's potential liability, and a notice of a hearing. The hearing cannot be less than 30 days after the notice is served. If any of the charges are found to be justified, the Commissioner will issue a *cease and desist order*. Anyone who violates the Code can be liable for a civil penalty of up to *$5,000* for each violation and *$10,000* for each intentional violation.

Chapter Review

This chapter explained several types of personal lines insurance, from the standard fire policy to earthquake coverage and umbrella and excess liability insurance. Let's review the key points:

STANDARD FIRE POLICY	
Property Covered and Excluded	• The Standard Fire Policy is a named perils contract; it only covers those perils specified in the policy • The policy covers fire but also lightning and the removal of property after a fire to prevent the undamaged insured property from incurring additional damage • The standard fire policy excludes coverage for currency, accounts, bills, deeds, and evidence of debt, securities, or money
INLAND MARINE	
Features	• Filed (standardized) or unfiled (unique exposure) with state regulatory authorities • Coverage on any property that is portable • Policies are called floaters, because the coverage floats with the insured property, anywhere in the world

Nationwide Marine Definition	• Coverage is written on Inland Marine forms
	• *Defines four classes of risk:*
	   ○ Domestic shipments and transportation risks
	   ○ Tunnels, bridges, and other means of transportation and communication
	   ○ Commercial property floater risks
	   ○ Personal property floater risks

NATIONAL FLOOD INSURANCE PROGRAM (NFIP)	
Components	• Insurance • Floodplain management • Floodplain mapping
Types of Coverage	• Direct through the NFIP • *Write your own insurance program (WYO)* – through private insurance providers • Identical coverage through both

NATIONAL FLOOD INSURANCE PROGRAM (NFIP) *(Continued)*	
Eligibility	<ul><li>Community must meet the minimum floodplain management guidelines</li><li>Eligible structures: A roof, two solid walls, and mostly above ground</li><li>30-day waiting period</li><li>Damage must be a result of a flood as defined by the NFIP</li></ul>
Flood Definitions	<ul><li>Overflow of inland or tidal waters</li><li>Rapid and unusual accumulation or runoff of surface waters from any source</li><li>Mudflow (a river of flowing mud and liquid on surfaces of typically dry land) and collapse</li><li>Collapse of land along a lake's shore or similar body of water exceeding anticipated cyclical levels that result in flood</li></ul>

OTHER POLICIES	
Mobile Home	<ul><li>Similar structure to homeowners policy</li><li>Provides 40% of Coverage A</li><li>Pays $500 if the mobile home is moved to a safer area to prevent loss</li><li>Transportation/Permission to Move Endorsement:<ul><li>Must be obtained to move to a covered mobile home location</li><li>Includes perils of collision, upset, standing, and sinking</li></ul></li><li>Applied anywhere in continental U.S. and Canada, up to 30 days</li></ul>
Watercraft	<ul><li>Part A - Liability Coverage</li><li>Part B - Medical Payments Coverage</li><li>Part C *(not currently used)*</li><li>Part D - Coverage for Damage to Your Watercraft</li><li>Part E - Your Duties after Accident or Loss</li><li>Part F - General Provisions</li></ul>
Earthquake	<ul><li>Applies to seismic or volcanic earthquake triggers</li><li>Usually excluded from standard property forms</li><li>Added by endorsement or written in a Difference in Conditions (DIC) policy</li></ul>
Pet Insurance	<ul><li>Pet insurance is designed to cover veterinary expenses, which include costs associated with diagnosis, care, and treatment provided by a veterinarian</li></ul>

UMBRELLA AND EXCESS LIABILITY	
Types of Policies	<ul><li>*Underlying policy* – the primary liability policy</li><li>*Umbrella (stand-alone)* – coverage can be greater or less than the underlying policy</li><li>*Excess (follow form)* – mirrors the underlying policy and increases the limits of liability</li></ul>
Personal Umbrella	<ul><li>Also referred to as catastrophe insurance</li><li>Protects the insured from large claims and lawsuits</li><li>Offers a minimum of $1,000,000 in additional coverage</li><li>*Self-insured retention (SIR)* – retained limits that the policy owner must pay before the umbrella policy responds to certain losses</li><li>The policy owner must maintain underlying insurance</li><li>The insurance provider is not liable beyond what it would pay if underlying insurance were in effect</li></ul>

CHAPTER 13:
Commercial Coverages

In this chapter, you will learn about commercial lines policies. First, you will begin with the ISO standards for these policies. Then you will study the different causes of loss forms, read about indirect damage insurance, and review various endorsements and clauses available in commercial lines policies.

- ISO Modulized Commercial Lines Program
- Commercial Package Policy (CPP)
- Commercial Property
- Coinsurance
- Causes of Loss Forms
- Other Coverages and Endorsements
- New Developments – Commercial Lines

ISO Modulized Commercial Lines Program

Modular Concept

Modular policies effectively combine coverage forms and other customized documents based on the policyholder's specific needs. Any single form that makes up a part of the modular policy does not constitute a complete contract. Because modular policies include a combination of coverages, the policy owner elects which coverage forms they want to use and the limits of such coverage. This selection results in a premium for that component. The modular policy lists coverages in the Declarations with limits and premiums beside those selections and blanks beside those that were not.

Package Policies

Minimum Requirements – Each Commercial Packages Policy (CPP) *must contain four modules*. These modules include the common policy declarations, common policy conditions, interline endorsements (as needed), and one other coverage part, which we will discuss later in the chapter.

None of the coverage parts that can be included are required, meaning any two coverage parts that are included, such as commercial general liability and commercial property, make the policy a commercial package. If only one coverage part is included, the policy is considered monoline. Also, remember that although a CPP has a common declarations page that applies to the whole policy, every coverage part also has its own declarations page.

Monoline Basis – When a policy owner does not need multiple coverage parts, any commercial lines coverage can be written as a stand-alone monoline policy. Although the same common declarations and conditions would still be included, only a single coverage part, such as commercial general liability (CGL), would be attached. Other coverage parts, such as commercial property, could be added later if needed.

Advantages – The principal advantage of a modular (packaged) policy over a self-contained one is the *flexibility* with which the agent or broker and the insured can build a policy that meets the insured's needs while allowing them to retain the level of risk appropriate for each situation.

Another benefit for the policy owner is that the CPP minimizes possible gaps in coverage because multiple coverage parts can be included in the same policy. Policy owners also receive package premium discounts when multiple coverage parts are included in one policy.

First Named Insured

The *first named insured* is the individual or organization whose name appears first as the named insured in a commercial insurance policy. The first named insured is generally responsible for paying premiums and has the right to cancel the policy, receive any returned premiums, and receive the notification of nonrenewal or cancellation.

"You," "Your," and "We"

In a commercial policy, the words *"you"* and *"your"* refer to the named insured listed on the declarations page and the spouse if they reside in the same household.

The word *we*, *us*, and *our* refers to the insurance company providing the coverage for the policy owner.

Commercial Package Policy (CPP)

The coverages available under the *commercial package policy (CPP)* can all be *written together in a single contract (package)* or *written separately as single coverage (monoline)*. A package policy does not necessarily include all the available policies; it can be personalized to meet the insured's needs.

The following scenario illustrates the commercial package policy's flexibility and how the insured may use it in pieces based on their needs:

Marty and his wife, Sandra, decided to open a food manufacturing business. After years of planning and fine-tuning their fudge brownie recipe, they locate a commercial kitchen to begin processing their brownies. Using a commercial kitchen makes sense to Marty and Sandra because they can rent space and equipment instead of spending the money on a building and equipment during the early stages of the business.

The commercial kitchen uses a standard contract for every tenant. It requires at least liability insurance to be in place before the tenant can begin using the space. Marty and Sandra start their business with a monoline Commercial General Liability policy. This policy will provide the necessary coverage to meet the commercial kitchen's requirements. It will also protect them in case of a lawsuit for their business's operation and their product's consumption.

As the business grows, so does the need for additional space that the commercial kitchen cannot provide. Marty and Sandra find a small commercial building for sale in another part of town. They decide to buy the space and purchase equipment to run their business. Since they already have a General Liability policy, they add a Building and Business Personal Property form to their program. Both policies have a common policy number but cover different hazards associated with the business.

Because Marty and Sandra both work full-time in the business, they become concerned with the ramifications of their business being unable to operate because of a loss to the building. They purchase Business Income and Extra Expense coverage to protect against indirect losses associated with a covered direct damage loss.

The business continues to grow, and they later add Inland Marine, Equipment Breakdown, and Crime coverage to their package policy.

Components of a Commercial Policy

The following are *seven coverage components* that can be included in the commercial package policy:

1. General Liability;
2. Commercial Property (direct and indirect coverages);
3. Inland Marine;
4. Commercial Auto;
5. Equipment Breakdown (also called Boiler and Machinery);
6. Crime; and
7. Farm.

In every case, the policy contains *modular parts* combined to create the contract. A commercial policy written in this format includes the following parts:

- Policy cover;
- Common policy declarations;

- Interline endorsements applying to more than one component to eliminate redundancy);
- Line(s) of insurance declaration page(s);
- Line(s) of insurance coverage form(s);
- Common policy conditions;
- Line(s) of insurance conditions;
- Causes of loss forms; and
- Endorsements.

Common Policy Declarations – The Declarations page includes information about who, what, where, when, and how much. This information is consistent in every policy. It is important to note that *when* (when the policy takes effect) is 12:01 AM at the mailing address of the *who* (first named insured).

The Declarations page also lists the seven coverage components that can be made a part of the policy. When a premium amount is listed for these coverage parts, the insurer will include that coverage in the policy. If no premium amount is listed, that component has no coverage (shown in the sample Declarations on the following page).

COMMON POLICY DECLARATIONS	
Named Insured(s): <u>Marty and Sandra Jones.</u>	
Policy Period: <u>01/01/08 to 01/01/09 Time: 12:01a.m.</u>	
The policy consists of the following coverage parts for which a premium is indicated:	
Commercial General Liability	$ <u>10,000</u>
Commercial Property	$ <u>10,000</u>
Inland Marine	$ _____
Commercial Auto	$ _____
Equipment Breakdown	$ <u>10,000</u>
Crime	$ _____
Farm	$ _____

Common Policy Conditions – This interline form contains provisions applicable to each line of coverage that can be included in the policy. The conditions are as follows:

- **Cancellation** — The first named insured can cancel the policy at any time by providing written notice to the insurance company. The insurer can cancel for an allowable reason by giving the proper notice to the first named insured, based on state regulations.
- **Changes** — Changes in the terms can be made only by endorsement issued by the insurance company. Request for change in the policy must be made by the first named insured.
- **Examination of books and records** — The insurer has the right to audit the insured's records and books relating to the policy for up to three years after the end of the policy.
- **Inspections and surveys** — The insurer is given the right but is not responsible for making inspections, surveys, reports, and recommendations relating to the insurance. An insurance company does not warrant that conditions are safe and comply with laws, regulations, standards, or codes.
- **Premiums** — Responsibility for payment of the premium rests solely with the first named insured. All refunds will also be returned to the first named insured.

- **Transfer of rights and duties** — The insured's rights and duties under the policy can be transferred to another only with the written consent of the insurance carrier. However, in the event of the insured's death, rights and duties are automatically transferred to the insured's legal representative.

Interline Endorsements – *Interline endorsements* apply, or could apply, to more than one coverage part. They seek to eliminate redundancy and reduce the number of endorsements in the policy.

Commercial Property

Several commercial property coverage forms are available to meet the needs of commercial property owners. We will discuss each of these different commercial property coverage forms separately.

Building and Personal Property Form

The *Building and Personal Property Coverage Form* is the main commercial package form used to insure buildings, business personal property, and the property of others. This *direct damage form* grants the insured an option to choose a Cause of Loss form. These forms include the same names as the dwelling property and homeowners policies (basic, broad, and special).

The policyholder must elect the limits needed for coverage. Unlike the HO and DP policies, no percentage of building coverages, such as personal property or other structures, are automatically included. Suppose the policyholder wants a particular building covered. In that case, it needs to be listed on the declarations page with an appropriate limit of insurance. The same applies to business personal property; if there are no limits in the Declarations, no coverage exists.

Property Covered and Not Covered – *Building Coverage* insures the following: the building described in the Declarations, furniture and outdoor fixtures, items used to maintain the property, permanently installed equipment and machinery, and additions under construction including the supplies, materials, and equipment.

Business Personal Property (BPP) Coverage insures business personal property located in or on the structure or building described on the declarations page or in the open, within 100 feet of the structure or building, or within 100 feet of the premises, whichever is greater. BPP insures the following:

- Fixtures and furniture (that are not considered building items);
- Equipment and machinery (not permanently installed);
- Stock;
- All other personal property owned by the policyholder and used in their business;
- Materials, labor, or services provided or arranged on the personal property of others;
- The interest of tenant betterments or improvements; and
- Leased personal property for which the policy owner is contractually responsible unless otherwise specified in the personal property of others section of the policy.

Personal Property of Others covers items in the insured's control, custody, or care. The property must be located in the building described in the Declarations, within 100 feet of the building, or within 100 feet of the premises, whichever is greater.

The following types of property and costs are *not covered* in the Building and Personal Property Coverage Form:

- Money, currency, bills, accounts, or securities;
- Animals (unless boarded and owned by others or owned by the policyholder as "stock" while inside a building);
- Autos held for sale;
- Sidewalks, bridges, and other paved surfaces;
- Contraband or illegal property;
- Excavation costs;
- Foundations of structures, buildings, boilers, or machinery if their foundations are below the lowest basement floor or the surface of the ground if no basement exists;
- Land;
- Personal property while waterborne or airborne;
- Wharves, piers, or docks;
- Property insured under another coverage form;
- Retaining walls that are not a part of the described building;
- Underground drains or pipes;
- The cost to research or replace valuable records or papers (a minimal amount of coverage is provided in the coverage extensions);
- Electronic data, except as insured under the Electronic Data additional coverage;
- Self-propelled machinery or vehicles registered for use on the public highway or used primarily away from the described premises; and
- Plants, trees, shrubs, crops, and fences.

Additional Coverages – The Building and Personal Property Coverage Form will provide the following additional coverages:

- **Debris removal** — Debris removal is limited to no more than 25% of the loss. Debris removal covers the expense of removing debris following a covered loss. These costs must be reported to the insurance carrier within 180 days of the loss for coverage to apply. A separate section of the policy provides an additional $10,000 in coverage if the 25% limit is insufficient.
- **Preservation of property** — The policy will also cover any damage to property that is moved to protect it from additional damage. Coverage will only be for 30 days after the property is moved.
- **Fire department service charge** — If the policy owner is required to pay for fire department service calls, the policy will reimburse the insured for up to $1,000 for this charge. The policy owner can purchase a higher amount, as shown on the declarations page. A deductible does not apply to this additional coverage.
- **Pollutant cleanup and removal** — The policy will cover up to $10,000 for expenses incurred to remove pollutants if the discharge resulted from a covered cause of loss and is reported in writing within 180 days of the occurrence. This amount is the maximum the insurance provider will pay in 12 months.
- **Increased cost of construction** — The policy will pay the lesser of $10,000 or 5% of the limit of insurance that applies to the building for the added cost of construction resulting from building law enforcement.
- **Electronic data** — The policy will cover up to $2,500 for the cost to restore or replace electronic data that has been corrupted or destroyed by a covered cause of loss.

Coverage Extensions – The form also includes several *coverage extensions*. The following types of property can be insured if the policy has a value reporting period or an 80% or more coinsurance percentage:

- **Newly acquired or constructed property** — Coverage lasts 30 days for newly acquired buildings and personal property similar to the insured property. This extension will cover up to $250,000 for newly acquired buildings and up to $100,000 for business personal property.
- **Personal effects and property of others** — Coverage is for up to $2,500 for personal effects of the policyholder or their employees (coverage does not apply to theft). This coverage can also apply to the personal property of others in the control, custody, and care of the insured.
- **Valuable papers and records** — $2,500 for the cost to research, restore, or replace lost information from valuable papers and records, except electronic data.
- **Property off-premises** — Up to $10,000 for property, excluding stock, temporarily at the premises the policyholder does not lease, own, or operate. This coverage is not applied to personal property in a vehicle or a salesperson's possession.
- **Outdoor property** — Up to $1,000 for television and radio antennas (including satellite dishes) and fences, or $250 for plants, shrubs, and trees destroyed or damaged by lightning, fire, explosion, civil commotion or riot, or aircraft.
- **Non-owned detached trailers** — $5,000 of coverage applies only if the loss occurs when the trailer is in the insured's custody and only if they are contractually obligated to cover the loss or damage. Higher limits may be shown on the declarations page, and this coverage is considered excess coverage over other insurance.

The most the insurance provider is obligated to pay is the limit of insurance specified in the policy declarations, minus any applicable deductible. The deductible will apply only once per occurrence, irrespective of the number of different properties involved.

Loss Conditions – The Building and Personal Property Coverage Form includes several conditions in addition to the common policy conditions and the commercial property conditions. These additional conditions include the following:

- **Abandonment** — The policy owner cannot abandon property to the insurance provider.
- **Appraisal** — If the insured and insurer cannot agree on the property's value, both parties can make a written demand for an appraisal of the loss. The decision agreed upon during the appraisal process will bind both parties.
- **Duties in the event of loss or damage** — In the event of loss or damage, the following duties are required of the policy owner:
    - Inform the police if a law has been broken;
    - Provide the insurer with prompt notice of the loss and a description of when, how, and where it occurred;
    - Take every reasonable step to protect the property from additional damage;
    - Provide an inventory of both damaged and undamaged property at the insurer's request;
    - Allow the insurance provider to inspect the property as often as necessary;
    - Send the insurer a signed, sworn proof of loss within 60 days of its request; and
    - Cooperate with the insurance provider in the investigation;
- **Loss payment** — In the event of damage or loss, the insurer has the option to do the following:
    - Pay the value of the damaged or lost property;
    - Pay the cost of replacing or repairing the damaged or lost property;
    - Take all or any part of the property at an appraised value or agreed value;
    - Replace, rebuild, or repair the property with other property of like kind and quality; or
    - The insurer must provide notice of their intentions within 30 days after receiving the sworn proof of loss and then pay the covered loss within 30 days after they resolve to pay the claim;

- **Recovered property** — If the property is recovered after the insurer has already made the claim payment, the policy owner can keep the property and return the amount paid.
- **Vacancy** — When a building has been unoccupied for more than 60 consecutive days before the loss, the insurance provider will not cover the damage caused by glass breakage, sprinkler leakage, water damage, vandalism, theft, or attempted theft. If any other peril causes the loss, the insurance provider will decrease the amount it would have paid by 15%. When a vacancy permit endorsement is attached to a Building and Personal Property Coverage Form, under the basic policy, the vacancy condition is waived during this period.
- **Valuation** — The insurance carrier will settle the loss on an ACV basis *except* under the following conditions:
  - If the limit of insurance satisfies the coinsurance clause and the amount of the loss is less than $2,500, the insurance carrier will pay the cost of replacing or repairing the property.
  - Stock sold but not delivered will be valued based on the selling price. Stock means merchandise held in storage or for sale, raw materials, and in-process or finished goods, including supplies used for shipping and packing.
  - If required by law, the glass will be valued at the cost of replacement with safety glazing material.
  - Tenant's betterments and improvements will be valued at ACV if repairs are made promptly or a percentage of the original cost if the repairs are not made promptly.
  - Valuable records and papers will be valued on the cost of blank material and the labor necessary to transcribe the records.

The following *additional conditions* apply as well as the common policy conditions and the commercial property conditions:

- **Coinsurance** — The coinsurance clause determines how much will be paid if the limits of insurance do not meet the policy's coinsurance requirement.
- **Mortgage holders** — Insurance providers can deny coverage because the policy owner failed to comply with the policy provisions. A mortgage holder can still receive a payment if they pay any premium due under the policy, submit a signed proof of loss within 60 days, and notify the insurer of any changes in occupancy or ownership. When the insurer cancels coverage due to nonpayment of premium, it must provide the mortgage holder a written notice of cancellation (*10 days* if for nonpayment of premium, and *30 days* for all other reasons).

The perils in the *vacancy permit endorsement* include attempted theft and vandalism, building glass breakage, and sprinkler leakage. Losses from these perils are not covered if the insured building has been unoccupied for more than 60 consecutive days. A building is considered vacant when there is insufficient business personal property to conduct normal operations. It is also considered vacant when 70% of the total square footage is not rented or used to conduct normal operations.

Optional Coverages – The Building and Personal Property Coverage Form contains the following optional coverages, which must be listed on the declarations page and applied separately to each item:

- **Agreed value** — The insured and insurer will determine a value for the property. The carrier will pay no more for loss or damage to that property than the percentage the insurance limit for this coverage bears to the agreed value shown. Coinsurance will not apply to property with an agreed value.
- **Inflation guard** — Limits of insurance to which this coverage applies are automatically raised by an annual percentage shown in the Declarations and prorated over the policy term.
- **Replacement cost** — The actual cash value (ACV) in the valuation condition is replaced with replacement cost valuation. This coverage is not applied to the personal property of others, antiques or rare articles, works of art, contents of a residence, or stock unless stock is shown in the Declarations.

- **Extension of the replacement cost to personal property of others** — If the replacement cost option is selected, the policy owner can also purchase this option. Suppose a written contract outlines the policy owner's liability for third-party property. In that case, the policy will pay no more than what is specified in that contract. It will not exceed the replacement cost of the policy limit or the item.

Exclusions – The following types of property and costs are *not covered* in the Building and Personal Property Coverage Form:

- Money, currency, bills, accounts, or securities;
- Animals (unless boarded and owned by others or owned by the policyholder as "stock" while inside a building);
- Autos held for sale;
- Sidewalks, bridges, and other paved surfaces;
- Contraband or illegal property;
- Excavation costs;
- Foundations of structures, buildings, boilers, or machinery if their foundations are below the lowest basement floor or the surface of the ground if no basement exists;
- Land;
- Personal property while waterborne or airborne;
- Wharves, piers, or docks;
- Property insured under another coverage form;
- Retaining walls that are not a part of the described building;
- Underground drains or pipes;
- The cost to research or replace valuable records or papers (a minimal amount of coverage is provided in the coverage extensions);
- Electronic data, except as insured under the Electronic Data additional coverage;
- Self-propelled machinery or vehicles registered for use on the public highway or used primarily away from the described premises; and
- Plants, trees, shrubs, crops, and fences.

Builders Risk

The *Builders Risk Coverage Form* is utilized to insure buildings or structures while under construction. It provides coverage similar to the building and personal property coverage form. This coverage is mainly written on a completed value form. Still, it may also be written on a reporting form basis.

Property Covered and Not Covered – Property covered under a Builder's Risk Coverage Form includes the building and any temporary structures. Also covered are foundations, fixtures, equipment, machinery, supplies, and materials within 100 feet of the premises if they intend on becoming a permanent part of the building.

Property *not covered* includes:

- Land or water;
- Trees;
- Outdoor lawns;
- Plants or shrubs;
- Satellite dishes;
- Television and radio antennas; or
- Signs (unless attached to the building, the coverage limit is $2,500 per sign in any one event).

The covered causes of loss forms used with the Building and Personal Property Coverage Form also apply to the Builders Risk Coverage Form.

The required coinsurance on a Builder's Risk form is 100% of the building's completed value.

Coverage Period – Coverage *starts* on the date construction begins and *ends* when one of the following occurs:

- The policy on the construction is canceled or expires;
- Construction is abandoned without any intentions to complete it;
- Whenever the purchaser accepts the property;
- 90 days after construction is complete;
- 60 days after the constructed building is put to its intended use or is occupied; or
- When the policy owner's interest in the property ceases.

Additional Coverages – There are *four additional coverages* under the Builders Risk Coverage Form:

1. **Debris removal** — Applies if reported within 180 days of the damage or loss or the end of the policy period. The policy covers up to 25% of the direct physical loss and any applicable deductible. Suppose a covered property has not sustained direct physical damage or loss. In that scenario, the most the insurance company will pay is $5,000 at each location. However, when the direct loss and the debris removal expenses exceed the limit of insurance, the policy will cover an additional sum for debris removal over and above the amount of insurance.
2. **Preservation of property** — Property that is moved to a temporary location to protect it from damage or loss is covered as it is transferred or stored at another location. Damage or loss must occur within 30 days after the property is moved. This coverage is not viewed as an additional amount of insurance.
3. **Fire department service charge** — Up to $1,000 in coverage is included. The deductible does not apply to this additional coverage.
4. **Pollutant cleanup and removal** — The policy will cover up to $10,000 for expenses incurred to remove pollutants if the discharge results from a covered cause of loss and is reported to the insurer in writing within 180 days of occurrence. This amount is the maximum the insurer will pay in any 12 months.

Coverage Extensions – The policy also contains two coverage extensions:

1. **Building materials and supplies of others** — The policy owner may extend coverage to include construction materials that will become a permanent part of the building for up to $5,000. This extension is an additional amount of insurance.
2. **Sod, plants, shrubs, and trees** — The insured can also extend coverage to a loss outside the building. The damage or loss must have resulted from lightning, fire, explosion, civil commotion or riot, or aircraft. The most the insurer will pay for this extension is $1,000, but not more than $250 per plant, shrub, or tree.

Business Income

Coverage for indirect losses is not automatic in the Commercial Package Policy. The insured must purchase the coverage and choose an appropriate limit of insurance. There are three forms from which the policy owner can select coverage:

1. Business Income with Extra Expense;
2. Business Income without Extra Expense; and
3. Extra Expense.

An explanation of a few important concepts is essential for understanding these forms:

An indirect loss is only payable after a covered direct damage loss occurs. Because the Commercial Package Policy includes three Cause of Loss forms, the perils that trigger indirect coverage will vary.

Business income is also known as *business interruption coverage* or *time element coverage*. Coverage is triggered by a covered loss that leads to a required suspension of operations during the restoration period at the premises listed in the Declarations.

Extra expenses – *Extra expenses* are expenses incurred by the policy owner, above their regular operating costs, during the restoration period and to minimize the suspension.

To better comprehend the concepts previously discussed, you need to know the following terms and definitions:

Suspension — The cessation or slowdown of the insured's business activities.

Operations — Refers to any business activity at the premises described in the Declarations.

Period of restoration — Begins 72 hours after the direct physical loss of *business income*. It begins immediately for *extra expense* coverage.

Resumption of operations — A condition exists that allows the insurance provider to reduce the amount of the loss if the policyholder does not resume operations as quickly as possible.

Civil Authority — Coverage will be extended if the policy owner suffers a business income or extra expense loss at a neighboring property less than one mile from the premises. Damage from a loss covered in the insured's policy must require them to suspend business operations, or a civil authority needs unimpeded access to the damaged property. Coverage is limited to four weeks, and a *72-hour waiting period* will apply.

Extended business income — If a business income loss is paid, the policy provides time for the insured to resume their normal income levels. This additional coverage has a beginning and ending period as follows:

- Begins on the date the property is repaired (except finished stock) and operations are resumed; and
- Ends on the date the policyholder could restore operations with reasonable diligence and speed or 60 consecutive days following the date on which operations are resumed, whichever is earlier.

A policy owner can activate an option to extend this time frame by entering a new date in the policy's Declarations.

Coinsurance applies to business income coverage (it does not apply to extra expense coverage). The policy owner has three optional coverages to choose from that will waive the coinsurance; these coverages must be active on the declarations page to apply:

- **Maximum period of indemnity** — If the policy owner chooses this optional coverage, the coinsurance clause is replaced. The most the insurance provider will pay for loss of business income is the lesser of either of the following:
  - The amount of loss incurred during the 120 days immediately after the loss; or
  - The limit of insurance.
- **Monthly limit of indemnity** — When a policy owner chooses this optional coverage, the coinsurance clause is replaced. The most the insurance provider will pay every 30 days after a direct physical loss is the limit of insurance multiplied by a specified percentage listed on the declarations page.

- **Business income agreed value** — To activate this coverage, the policy owner must complete a business income report showing the business financial data for the previous 12 months. The policy owner must also provide an estimate for the next 12 months. This report becomes a part of the policy. The selected limit on the worksheet should be at least the percentage of coinsurance shown in the Declarations multiplied by the extra expenses and net income for the following 12 months. Coinsurance is suspended on the date the policy owner selected this optional coverage or when the policy expires, whichever is earlier.

Extra Expense

The *Extra Expense Coverage Form* covers consequential losses. It can be used by a business that will likely not have a business income loss. For instance, insurance agents earning most of their income from outside sales away from their office may not be concerned about a loss to the office. The agent may be more concerned with extra expenses needed to open a temporary office while the original office is undergoing renovation.

The key points to note in this form are as follows:

- Damage must be to property described in the Declarations. If damage is to property that is out in the open or a vehicle, it must be within 100 feet of the premises;
- Direct loss needs to be from a covered cause of loss (this will vary depending on the cause of loss form);
- Extra expenses include any necessary costs incurred during the restoration period. The policy owner would not have incurred these costs if no direct damage to the covered property occurred. Extra expenses also include those associated with minimizing the suspension of operations;
- The period of restoration does not have a waiting period so that insurers can pay extra expenses immediately;
- Civil authority coverage begins immediately and is applied upon an authority prohibiting access to the premises and lasting for four consecutive weeks;
- Expenses to replace or repair property are not included;
- $2,500 can be extended for losses associated with the interruption of computer operations; and
- The insured must resume operations as quickly as possible, or the insurance carrier will have the option to limit the loss payment.

Coinsurance does not apply in the extra expense form. A limit of insurance is chosen by the policy owner to be used per loss. The method of paying the policy owner for extra expense losses is governed by the limit selected and percentages noted on the declarations page for the following periods:

- 1st percentage – 30 days or less;
- 2nd percentage – 31 days to 60 days; and
- 3rd percentage – More than 60 days.

Each period will have a percentage. For example, a policy owner chooses $200,000 as a limit of insurance, and the following percentages – 30%, 60%, and 100%. In this scenario, the limit of insurance would be as follows:

- 30 days or less = $60,000
- 31 days to 60 days = $120,000
- More than 60 days = $200,000

If a covered direct damage loss were to result in an extra expense loss for this policy owner and the loss lasted for 30 days, the most that could be collected is $60,000. If the policy owner incurred $75,000 in extra expenses, the insurer would only pay $60,000. If the policy owner incurs $50,000 in losses, the insurer would only pay this amount.

Commercial Property Conditions

Commercial property coverage contains numerous conditions that are in addition to the conditions found in the common policy conditions form. Some of these conditions are included directly in the individual coverage forms, and others can be attached by a separate endorsement, known as the commercial property conditions.

The following common conditions are in Commercial Property Conditions Forms:

- **Concealment, misrepresentation, or fraud coverage** — Insurers will cancel coverage if the policy owner commits fraud as it relates to the policy at any time.
- **Control of property** — This condition states that any negligence or act by individuals not under the direction of the policy owner will not void coverage.
- **Insurance under two or more coverages** — If the same loss triggers more than one coverage under the policy, the insurer will pay no more than the actual loss.
- **Legal action against the insurer** — No one may bring legal action against the insurer until they fully comply with all the policy terms. Policy owners must bring legal action within two years of the loss (this time can vary from state to state).
- **Liberalization** — If the insurance carrier adopts any provisions that would broaden coverage during the policy period or 45 days before the effective date, the broadened coverage will automatically apply without an endorsement.
- **No benefit to bailee** — No individual other than the policy owner who has custody of covered property can benefit from the insurance.
- **Other insurance** — If the policy owner has other insurance with identical terms, conditions, and provisions, the policy will respond by limits. Suppose the other insurance is different than that described above. In that case, the policy will contribute on an excess basis, paying only for the amount of any loss exceeding the other insurance.
- **Policy period, coverage territory** — The coverage territory includes the U.S., its possessions and territories, and Canada.
- **Subrogation (transfer of rights of recovery against others)** — To recover damages, the policy owner must transfer any rights to the insurance carrier after they make payment for the loss.

Value Reporting Endorsement

A *Value Reporting Form* is a typical method of calculating premiums and amounts of coverage on those properties insured for fluctuating values. During the reporting period, the policyholder reports the values at risk and pays premiums for that period based on the report. Reporting periods are daily, weekly, monthly, or quarterly, whichever is indicated in the contract.

It would be neither cost-effective nor appropriate for a business with fluctuating inventory values during the year to buy a fixed amount of insurance. The Value Reporting Form lets the amount of coverage float with the changing values. Premiums are adjusted based on the average values reported when the policy period ends. This endorsement can be attached to any commercial property form as appropriate. The Value Reporting Form can be used to modify the insurance provided by the Building and Personal Property Coverage Form.

The policy limit must be the maximum value expected during the policy period. When the policy period begins, a provisional (or advance premium) is paid, typically based on 75% of the policy limit. During the policy period, the insured must file reports on the actual values for specified periods. When the policy period ends, the premium is adjusted as if the average value was held every day of the policy period.

The reports need to be kept current as required. Should a loss occur on a day when the reports are not current, the maximum payable amount will be whatever the last report indicated. If the reports are current, the policy will pay what the insured can prove they lost, up to the policy limit. If a loss occurs before the first report is due, up to the full amount of insurance is applied. If the first report is not submitted when a loss occurs, the insurer will pay *no more than 75%* of the amount it would otherwise pay.

If values are underreported, the insurance carrier will not pay a greater portion of a loss than the amount reported divided by the actual value shown on the report. For example, if the insured reported $50,000 when the actual value is $75,000, only two-thirds (approximately 67%) of any loss would be covered.

Coinsurance

The *coinsurance* clause states that the insured agrees to maintain a minimum amount of insurance on the insured property in consideration of a reduced rate. This clause encourages the policy owner to insure the property closer to its total value. In cases of partial loss, the insurer will pay for the partial loss in full, provided that the insured has maintained the minimum amount of insurance in relation to the property's value. Suppose the amount of insurance carried is less than the requirement in the coinsurance clause. In that case, the insurer will only cover the percent of the loss the insurance bears in relation to the needed insurance. In the event of a total loss, the coinsurance clause is not activated, and the insurer pays the face amount of the policy.

Example 13.1 – The formula for calculating *coinsurance penalties* is the amount of insurance carried over the amount the policy owner should have had, multiplied by the loss, which equals the reduced payment for the loss. For a $100,000 building insured with an 80% coinsurance percentage, the policy owner must carry at least $80,000 of coverage ($100,000 x .80) to meet the coinsurance requirement. If the insured only maintained $40,000 of coverage and had a $10,000 loss, they would have to bear 50% of the loss due to the deficiency, or $5,000, plus any deductible.

The *insurance to value* provision, typically found in homeowners (HO) policies, provides a replacement cost settlement to the policy owner with adequate coverage. This provision means that the property is insured to the exact dollar amount or percentage of value. Suppose the amount of insurance is less than the assumed value in the premium rate calculation. In that situation, the insurer would still indemnify the policy owner at least to the amount of the actual cash value of the loss.

Coinsurance is used in the area of commercial property; the Coinsurance Clause and rates are not usually applicable in the fields of Dwelling and Homeowners insurance. Although some individuals incorrectly refer to the Replacement Cost Provision of the HO form as a coinsurance provision, it is not. It is an extension of coverage that partially or entirely eliminates any deduction for depreciation in a loss settlement. Under the Coinsurance Clause, the policyholder could collect less than the actual cash value of the loss. Under the Homeowners Replacement Cost Provision, the policyholder will never collect less than the actual cash value of the loss.

To understand the reasoning behind the coinsurance concept, recognize that most fire losses are partial. The ISO's loss statistics show that about 85% of all losses are for less than 20% of the property's value. In comparison, only approximately 5% result in damage over 50% of the property's value. Fire insurance rates are based on the ratio of losses to the total values insured. The rate will be higher if the owners insure a lower percentage of their property values than if they insure it to a higher percentage.

Coinsurance allows insureds to obtain commercial property insurance at affordable rates and protects insurers from the possibility of paying the policy limits every time there is a partial loss to the insured property.

For example, assume that an insurance company insures 10,000 structures worth $10,000 each for 100% of their value (a total of $100,000,000). Based on prior experience, the insurer projects the following losses:

- 30 partial losses at $1,000 each = $30,000
- Two total losses at $10,000 each = $20,000

Taking the total losses ($50,000) over the total amount of insurance ($100,000,000) produces a loss of $0.05 per $100 of insurance.

Now consider the same structures insured for 50% of their value:

- 30 partial losses at $1,000 each = $30,000
- Two total losses at $5,000 each = $10,000

The insurance provider would need to double the insurance premium rate per $100 of insurance to pay for the losses when structures are insured for lesser values.

Under the provisions of the Coinsurance Clause, the policy owner agrees to maintain insurance equal to some specified percentage of the property's value (80% is generally the requirement) in return for a reduced rate.

Suppose the insured does not maintain insurance to the value as agreed. In that case, the insured will be penalized at the time of loss to an amount equal to the insurance amount carried, divided by the insurance amount required, multiplied by the loss amount.

Most commercial property insurance policies provide coverage on an ACV basis. The amount of insurance required is based on the building's Actual Cash Value at the time of the loss. When the policy provides coverage on a replacement cost basis, the required insurance amount will be that percentage of the replacement cost of the building.

In California, ACV is determined by the property's *fair market value* at the time of loss.

When "coinsurance" is used in connection with a health insurance policy, it has nothing to do with "insurance to value." It refers to a participation requirement where the policyholder is required to pay a certain percentage of covered expenses after the application of the deductible (if any). For instance, the insurance carrier pays 80%, and the policyholder pays 20%.

Causes of Loss Forms

Insurance providers can write commercial property coverage with one of three causes of loss forms that tell which perils are being protected against – *basic*, *broad*, or *special*. These are the same as the coverage forms discussed for the DP and HO policies; each form protects against a wider range of perils than the previous form.

Basic

The *basic* form is a named peril form that insures against 11 causes of loss. These causes of loss are similar to those previously discussed in the Dwelling and Homeowners sections:

1. **Lightning**;
2. **Fire**;
3. **Explosion** — Does not include an explosion of pressure relief vessels or if caused by the swelling of contents or accumulations from water;

4. **Windstorm or hail** — Loss to the interior of the building is not covered unless there is initial damage to the exterior of the building; signs, outdoor crops, television and radio antennas, shrubs, and plants are excluded;

5. **Smoke**, but not from industrial operations or agricultural smudging;

6. **Aircraft or vehicles** — Damage or loss caused by a vehicle operated or owned by the policy owner during business operations is not covered;

7. **Riot or civil commotion** — This cause of loss includes acts of employees striking while on the described premises and looting;

8. **Vandalism** — Damage caused by theft (except the damage resulting from breaking in or exiting the premises) is not covered;

9. **Sprinkler leakage** — Covers leakage or discharge from an automatic fire protective sprinkler system, including the collapse of a tank;

10. **Sinkhole collapse** — Covers direct loss resulting from the sudden sinking or collapse of land created by the action of water on dolomite or limestone. There is no coverage if the collapse is into an artificial hole. Also, coverage does not include filling the sinkhole; and

11. **Volcanic action** — Covers direct loss from volcanic eruptions if caused by dust, ash, lava, or airborne shockwaves. The cost to remove dust or ash that does not cause a direct loss is not covered. All volcanic eruptions occurring within 168 hours are considered one event.

The basic form contains the following *exclusions*:

- Ordinance or law;
- Governmental actions;
- War and military action;
- Nuclear hazard;
- Earth movement;
- Water;
- Wet rot, dry rot, fungus, and bacteria;
- Artificially generated electrical current;
- Bursting or rupture of water pipes, unless it resulted from another covered cause of loss;
- Discharge or leakage of water or steam;
- Explosion of steam pipes, steam boilers, or steam engines operated or owned by the insured;
- Mechanical breakdown;
- Neglect; and
- Utility services.

Special additional exclusions exist for certain forms attached to the package's property section. Exclusions exist for the legal liability, extra expense, and business income forms.

One additional coverage is added for limited coverage for wet rot, dry rot, fungus, and bacteria. Loss caused by these items has to be the result of a covered cause of loss other than fire. Coverage does not apply to plants, shrubs, trees, or lawns which are part of a vegetated roof. Coverage may also apply if the flood coverage endorsement is attached. There is a $15,000 sublimit for these losses to include testing, removal and tearing out, and replacing parts of the property to gain access. This coverage is not considered additional insurance.

Broad

The *broad* form includes the same 11 causes of loss as the basic form. In addition, the broad form contains three additional perils:

1. **Falling objects** — The insurer will not cover loss or damage to personal property in the open or the interior of a structure or building unless a falling object first damages an outside wall or the roof.
2. **Weight of snow, ice, or sleet** — Except for the loss or damage to personal property located outside of structures or buildings or for loss or damage to plants, shrubs, trees, or lawns that are part of a vegetated roof.
3. **Water damage** — Includes accidental leakage or discharge of water or steam as the direct result of the breaking apart of a heating, air conditioning, plumbing, or other system or appliance. Water damage *does not apply* to any of the following:
   o Leakage or discharge from a sump or related equipment, including overflow because of sump pump failure; an automatic sprinkler system; gutters, roof drains, downspouts, or similar fixtures;
   o The cost to repair defects that caused the water damage;
   o Loss or damage as a result of repeated or continuous leakage or seepage that occurs for at least 14 days; or
   o Loss or damage caused by freezing unless the policy owners do their best to maintain the heat or turn off the water supply and drain the system.

The *exclusions* in the broad form are the same as those in the basic form. There are also special exclusions regarding the extra expense, business income, leasehold interest, and legal liability coverage forms.

The broad causes of loss form will include the following additional coverages:

- **Collapse** — The policy will insure the collapse of the building if the loss is the result of a covered cause of loss. Such causes include insects or vermin, hidden decay, rain that collects on the roof, the weight of people, or the use of defective construction methods or materials if the collapse occurs during construction. Collapse does not include expansion, bulging, shrinkage, cracking, or settling.
- **Limited coverage for wet rot, dry rot, fungus, and bacteria** — Loss caused by these conditions must result from a covered cause of loss other than fire. Coverage does not apply to plants, shrubs, trees, or lawns which are part of a vegetated roof. If the flood coverage endorsement is attached, coverage may also apply. There is a $15,000 sublimit for these losses, including testing, removal, and tearing out and replacing any parts of the property to gain access. This coverage is not additional insurance.

Special

The *special* form does not list the covered causes of loss and is referred to as *open perils*. Instead, all causes of loss are insured against except for the exclusions.

The following *exclusions* apply if the damage is directly or indirectly a result of the following:

- Ordinance or law;
- War and military action;
- Governmental action;
- Nuclear hazard;
- Earth movement;
- Utility services;
- Water damage, including sewer backup; or
- Wet rot, dry rot, fungus, and bacteria.

The policy will not pay for damage or loss resulting from any of the following:

- Loss of market, loss of use, or delay;
- Artificially generated electrical current;

- Expansion, shrinking, cracking, smog, decay, settling, corrosion, or wear and tear;
- Gas, vapor, or smoke from industrial operations or agricultural smudging;
- Changes, extremes of temperature, dryness or dampness to personal property;
- Infestation or nesting or discharge of waste products from birds, insects, rodents, or other animals;
- Scratching or marring;
- Explosion of steam pipes, steam boilers, or steam engines;
- Mechanical breakdown;
- Water or other liquids that leak from plumbing equipment caused by freezing (unless the policy owner maintains the heat or turns off the water supply and drains the system);
- Repeated or continuous leakage or seepage of water for 14 days or more;
- Voluntary parting with any property;
- Criminal or dishonest acts of the insured or their employees;
- Rain, sleet, ice, or snow that damages personal property in the open;
- Collapse unless specified in an additional coverage;
- Dispersal, discharge, or release of pollutants unless a loss from a specified cause of loss results; or
- Neglect of a policy owner to preserve or save property from additional damage at the time of the loss.

The following perils are not insured against unless they result in a covered cause of loss:

- Weather conditions, but only if they contribute to further damage from an excluded cause of loss;
- Decisions or acts, including the failure to decide or act; and
- Defective, inadequate, or faulty planning, zoning, design, development, specifications, quality of work, and materials used for repair, maintenance, or construction.

Special exclusions are also in the extra expense, business income, leasehold interest, and legal liability forms. Product loss or damage is another exclusion that applies only to the specific property. Losses caused by an error or omission in testing, planning, packaging, and processing are not covered.

In addition to the exclusions, the special form also contains several limitations. Certain types of property will only be covered for a specific amount or are only covered for certain causes of loss. The insurer will not pay for damage or loss to the following types of property unless the damage or loss is caused by one of the following specified causes of loss:

- Animals, but only if they are killed, or their destruction is necessary;
- Fragile articles, if broken; or
- Builder's tools, machinery, and equipment while away from the described premises.

Specified causes of loss include the following:

- Lightning;
- Fire;
- Explosion;
- Windstorm or hail;
- Aircraft or vehicles;
- Vandalism;
- Riot or civil commotion;
- Leakage from fire-extinguishing equipment;
- Falling objects (unless the outside is damaged and there is no coverage to items in the open)

- Sinkhole collapse;
- Volcanic action;
- Weight of snow, ice, or sleet; and
- Water damage (accidental leakage or discharge of steam or water from an appliance).

For any damage or loss caused by theft, the following types of property are insured only for the following limits that are not in addition to the limits of insurance:

- $2,500 for furs and fur garments;
- $2,500 for jewelry (unless worth less than $100), watches, precious and semiprecious stones, gold, silver, other precious metals, and bullion;
- $2,500 for dies and patterns; and
- $250 for tickets, including lottery tickets held for sale, stamps, and letters of credit.

Additional Coverages and Extensions – The additional coverage of collapse and limited coverage for wet rot, dry rot, fungus, and bacteria are applied and subject to the limitations previously discussed.

Coverage extensions include:

- Property in transit for specific perils up to a limit of $5,000;
- Cost to tear out and replace part of the structure or building resulting from a loss due to water damage or other liquid discharge from an appliance or system; and
- Expenses incurred to install temporary glass plates or board-up openings while glass is waiting to be replaced.

Earthquake

The *Earthquake and Volcanic Eruption Endorsement* has to be used with one of the Causes of Loss forms (Basic, Broad, or Special). It adds two perils for coverage:

- Earthquake; and
- Volcanic eruption (explosion, eruption, or pouring forth of a volcano).

This coverage provided by the other causes of loss forms is limited to above-ground volcanic eruptions, excluding ground shock waves. All volcanic eruptions or earthquake shocks occurring within 168 hours (7 days) are considered one earthquake or explosion. The deductible is a percentage of the loss listed in the property Declarations.

The Exclusions and Limitations sections of the Causes of Loss Form apply to coverage provided under this endorsement.

The following are *exclusions* that apply to all coverage forms, which include basic, broad, and special:

- Ordinance or law – this exclusion applies to any ordinance or law that
    - o Regulates the construction, use, or repair of a property;
    - o Requires destruction of a property
- Government actions – this exclusion applies if an order of a governmental authority destroys a property
- Earth movement is excluded if it is a result of any of the following:
    - o Earthquake, including any earth sinking, rising, or shifting;
    - o Landslide, including any earth sinking, rising, or shifting;

- o Mine subsidence (artificial mines, whether active or not);
- o Earth sinking, other than sinkhole collapse;
- o Volcanic eruption, explosion, or effusion (All volcanic eruptions that occur within 168 hours from the original action are considered a single occurrence)
- Water exclusion applies to losses caused by the following:
  - o Flood, surface water, waves, tides, tidal waves, or overflow of any body of water;
  - o Mudslides or mudflows;
  - o Sewer backup, drain, or sump;
  - o Underground water that is flowing or seeping through foundations, walls, basements, etc.
- Nuclear hazard exclusion applies to nuclear reaction, radiation, and radioactive contamination.
  - o War and military service exclusion apply to the following:
  - o War, including undeclared or civil war;
  - o Warlike military action;
  - o Rebellion, revolution, usurped power, or any action taken by governmental authority associated with these or similar events.

When any of the above perils result in fire, explosion, or sprinkler leakage, the insurance provider will pay for the loss caused by that fire, explosion, or leakage.

CAUSES OF LOSS: DP, HO, AND COMMERCIAL PROPERTY FORMS

BASIC FORM	BROAD FORM	SPECIAL FORM
COMMON PERILS		
Fire Lightning Explosion Windstorm or hail Riot or civil commotion Aircraft Vehicles Smoke Vandalism and malicious mischief Volcanic eruption	**Basic Perils +** Damage by burglars Falling objects Weight of ice, snow or sleet Accidental discharge or overflow of water or steam Sudden and accidental damage from artificially generated electrical current Sudden and accidental tearing apart, cracking, burning, or bulging Freezing	All risks except those specifically excluded (Open Peril)
DWELLING POLICY		
(DP-1) Only fire, lightning, and *internal* explosion (the rest of the common basic perils are available for additional premium)	**(DP-2) Common Broad Perils +** Windstorm or Hail Riot or civil commotion Aircraft Vehicles Smoke Vandalism and malicious mischief Volcanic eruption	(DP-3) Common Open Perils
HOMEOWNERS POLICY		
(HO-8) Common Basic Perils + Theft	**(HO-2) Common Broad Perils +** Theft	(HO-3) Common Open Perils

BASIC FORM	BROAD FORM	SPECIAL FORM
COMMERCIAL PROPERTY POLICY		
<u>Common Basic Perils +</u> Sprinkler leakage Sinkhole collapse	<u>Common Broad Perils +</u> Sprinkler leakage Sinkhole collapse Water Damage	Common Open Perils

Other Coverages and Endorsements

Leasehold Interest

A *Leasehold Interest Coverage Form* is a third consequential loss form that insures tenants for any financial loss caused by the cancellation of a favorable lease following direct damage to the leased premises.

With the Leasehold Interest Coverage Form, the insurance provider agrees to pay for loss the insured sustains due to the cancellation of a favorable lease because of direct physical damage to the leased premises.

A leasehold interest is defined as the following:

- **Tenants lease interest** – The difference between the rent the policy owner currently pays and the rental value of the premises.
  - **EXAMPLE 13.2** – The insured has a long-term lease and pays $1,000 monthly at the listed premises. However, the current rental value for the premises is $1,500. The tenants lease interest is $500 per month.
- **Bonus Payments** – The unamortized portion of cash bonuses that will not be refunded to the policy owner. In addition to the rent and security deposit, a cash bonus is paid to secure a favorable lease.
  - **EXAMPLE 13.3** – If the insured paid $10,000 to acquire a favorable 20-year lease, and ten years had elapsed before the loss, the insured would receive half, or $5,000.
- **Improvements and Betterments** – The unamortized portion of payments the policy owner made for improvements and betterments. Improvements or betterments are alterations, fixtures, additions, or installations made part of the building and obtained at the policy owner's expense but cannot be legally removed. Improvements and betterments become the property of the building owner. In case of a loss, the policy owner has a "use interest" in them for the remaining lease term.
- **Prepaid rent** – The unamortized portion of any advance rent the policy owner paid that will not be refunded.

The Leasehold Interest Coverage Form contains the exact causes of loss and exclusions that apply to the Building and Business Personal Property Coverage Form.

The limits of insurance section of the Leasehold Interest Coverage Form is organized according to the four types of covered leasehold interest previously discussed.

For *tenants lease interest* the most the insurer will pay because of the cancellation of any one lease is the insured's net leasehold interest at the time of the loss (subject to the applicable limit of insurance). The insured's net leasehold interest decreases each month automatically. The amount of net leasehold interest at any time is the gross leasehold interest multiplied by the factor of the leasehold interest for the remaining months of the lease.

A net leasehold interest is the present value of the policyholder's gross leasehold interest for each remaining month of the lease's term at a specified interest rate listed in the policy schedule.

A gross leasehold interest is defined in the policy as the difference between the monthly value of the leased premises and the actual rent the policy owner pays. This amount includes insurance, taxes, janitorial or other services.

EXAMPLE 13.4 – The rental value at the leased premises is $5,000. The actual monthly rent the policy owner pays is $4,000. The gross leasehold interest is $1,000.

For prepaid rent, improvements and betterments, and bonus payments, the most the insurer will pay due to the cancellation of any one lease is the insured's net leasehold interest at the time of the loss. Net leasehold interest, as it applies to prepaid rent, improvements and betterments, and bonus payments, is the unamortized amount listed in the policy schedule. The net leasehold interest is the monthly leasehold interest multiplied by the number of months left in the lease.

Suppose the policy owner's landlord allows the policy owner to continue to use the premises under a new lease agreement. In that circumstance, the most the insurer will pay is the difference between the old and the new lease. The net leasehold interest automatically decreases each month by the amount of monthly leasehold interest.

A monthly leasehold interest is calculated by dividing the original cost of prepaid rent, improvements and betterments, or bonus payments by the number of months left in the lease at the time of the expenditure.

In addition to the Commercial Property Conditions and the Common Policy Conditions, the following conditions apply to the Leasehold Interest Coverage Form.

- **Appraisal** – The appraisal condition is identical to other property coverage forms.
- **Duties in the Event of a Loss** – This condition is similar to other conditions regarding the insured's duties in the event of a loss.
- **Loss Payment** – The policy owner will pay the covered loss within 30 days after the sworn statement is received, provided they comply with all applicable policy conditions and agree on a proper settlement.
- **Vacancy** – Suppose the premises had been vacant for more than 60 days before the damage or loss, and the policyholder had entered an agreement to sublease the premises. In that scenario, the insurer will not pay for any loss caused by sprinkler leakage, water damage, building glass breakage, vandalism, theft, or attempted theft. Insurers would cover the loss if the policy owner took precautions to protect the system from freezing. In addition, for any other covered cause of loss, the insurer will decrease the amount of the actual loss by 15%.
- **Cancellation** – The following condition supersedes the cancellation condition found in the Common Policy Conditions. If coverage is canceled, the insurer will calculate the earned premium by averaging the net leasehold interest at the inception date and the cancellation date and multiplying the rate for the coverage period by the average net leasehold interest.

Blanket, Specific, Schedule Insurance

Blanket insurance is a single property policy that offers coverage for more than one class of property at one location or multiple classes of property at more than one location. Every insured property is issued one total amount of coverage, and no single insured item is assigned a specific amount of coverage. However, different amounts may be listed for buildings, equipment, and other items.

Specific insurance is a property policy that insures a particular kind or unit of property for an exact amount of coverage.

One method of analyzing risk in commercial insurance is the *schedule rating* method. Under this approach, the underwriter can give credits and debits for specific actions that a policy owner takes in the ordinary course of business, increasing the probability of loss or decreasing the probability of loss. The schedule list adjustments are performed as a percentage increase or decrease from the standard rating class.

Ordinance or Law Coverage

Ordinance or law is a coverage endorsement that can be added to the property policy. It covers a building if the enforcement of any zoning, building, or land use law results in damage or loss, increased cost of reconstruction or repairs, or demolition and removal costs.

The endorsement is divided into three coverages, which the policy owner activates by purchasing each coverage. They can buy all or some of the coverages included. Policy owners can add the ordinance or law endorsement only to a property policy written on a replacement cost basis, and coinsurance does not apply.

The building listed in the endorsement must sustain covered direct damage to at least part of the structure. Only the part of the structure covered by a peril in the policy and subject to the ordinance or law will take advantage of this endorsement.

Coverage is for completing minimum requirements as specified by the ordinance or law. Insurers will provide no coverage for ordinances or laws the policy owner was required to comply with before the loss.

This endorsement can offer the following coverages when selected:

- **Coverage A** — Loss to the undamaged portion of the building-loss in value to the building's or structure's undamaged portion;
- **Coverage B** — Demolition cost of the undamaged portion of the covered building or structure; and
- **Coverage C** — Increased construction cost for the damaged and undamaged portions of the building or structure.

Glass Coverage

The *Glass Coverage Form* insures types of glass, including ornamentation and lettering.

Glass coverage in the Building and Personal Property Coverage Form is minimal. There is no coverage on the basic form, and the broad and special forms only offer coverage for $100 per pane and $500 per occurrence. The Glass Coverage Form covers commercial plate glass, frames, ornamentation, and lettering. Coverage may be written as a stand-alone policy or as part of a Commercial Package Policy (CPP).

When the Glass Coverage Form is used, all insured glass will be listed on a schedule, including its location and any ornamentation or lettering. The size and number of plates insured. Glass coverage is written on an actual cash value (ACV) basis, typically without a limit of insurance.

The Causes of Loss Forms will not apply to glass coverage. Instead, the Glass Coverage Form includes only two covered causes of loss. It insures against direct loss or damage to covered glass resulting from breakage and chemicals accidentally or maliciously applied.

The exclusions in the Glass Coverage Form do not cover damage or loss from fire, war and military action, and nuclear hazards. Fire is covered under the Building and Personal Property Coverage Form.

The form includes four additional coverages which apply over and above the limit of insurance:

1. Debris removal;
2. Expenses incurred to install temporary plates if repair is delayed;
3. Necessary replacement or repair of frames; and
4. Expenses to replace or remove obstructions when making repairs.

The Glass Coverage Form also includes one extension of coverage for newly acquired glass. The policy will insure additional glass of the same type at the described premises or a new location. Coverage will last for either 30 days, until policy expiration, or until the policy owner reports the new glass to the insurer, whichever comes first.

The conditions listed in the Glass Coverage Form are similar to other property conditions, including the following:

- Duties in the Event of Damage or Loss;
- Loss Payment includes giving the insurer the option to pay for the damage or loss or repair the damaged property. The insurer also has the option to take the property at an appraised or agreed-upon value or replace the damaged property with like kind and quality. This condition also requires the insurer to pay for the damage or loss within 30 days after an agreement has been reached between the insured and insurer;
- Vacancy for more than 60 consecutive days will suspend coverage unless the policy owner has purchased the optional coverage for vacant buildings; and
- Valuation will be based on the minimum cost to replace the glass with safety glazing material or the actual cash value at the time of loss.

There is also one optional coverage built into the Glass Coverage Form. If shown on the declarations page, coverage for Loss Payment for Large Plates will apply to each separate item. In case of loss to glass with a surface area of 100 square feet or more, the insurer has the option to settle the loss by replacing the glass with two or more plates or paying the policy owner the value of two smaller plates with a combined surface area equal to the larger glass, plus any alteration expenses to install the smaller plates.

Extended Period of Indemnity

The *Extended Period of Indemnity* endorsement, available only for business income insurance coverage, can be purchased to provide additional income protection. In contrast, a business re-establishes itself in the period between when it closed because of a covered loss and when it re-opened but is still not earning the income it had attained before the loss.

Terrorism Exclusions

One of the more recent and significant changes in commercial property policies is the exclusion of acts of terrorism as a result of the Terrorism Risk Insurance Act (TRIA), which Congress passed in 2002.

Terrorism Risk Insurance Act (TRIA) – The *Terrorism Risk Insurance Act (TRIA)* established a temporary federal program to share the risk of loss from future terrorist attacks with the insurance industry. The act mandates that all commercial insurers offer coverage for acts of terrorism. The federal government will reimburse the insurance carriers for a portion of paid losses resulting from terrorism.

TRIA defines *terrorism* as an act certified by the Secretary of the Treasury, in agreement with the United States Attorney General and the Secretary of State, with the following attributes:

- The act must be violent or dangerous to infrastructure, property, or human life;
- The act must have caused damage within the U.S., to a United States air carrier, to a U.S. flag vessel or another vessel that is based primarily in the United States and insured under U.S. regulation, or on the premises of any mission conducted by the United States;
- An individual must have carried out the act as part of a coordinated effort to intimidate the civilian population of the U.S., influence U.S. policy, or affect the conduct of the United States government by coercion; or
- The act must cause property and casualty insurance losses exceeding a specified amount.

Terrorism Risk Insurance Program Reauthorization Act of 2015 – The Terrorism Risk Insurance Act of 2002 has been revised several times. The final amendment is the Terrorism Risk Insurance Program Reauthorization Act of 2015, which has further amended and extended the Terrorism Insurance Program and revised several provisions as follows:

- The insurance deductible was set at 20% of an insurer's direct earned premium from the previous calendar year. The federal share of compensation was set at 85% of insured losses that exceed insurer deductibles. After that, the federal share will be reduced by one percentage point per calendar year until it reaches 80%;
- The certification process was amended to require the Secretary of the Treasury to authenticate terrorist acts with the Secretary of Homeland Security rather than the Secretary of State;
- The aggregate of industry insured losses caused by certified acts of terrorism will activate the federal share of compensation under the Program, which is now $200 million;
- The required indemnification of the federal share through policy owner surcharges increased to 140% (from 133%);
- Revised requirements for mandatory recoupment from insurers of federal financial assistance provided in connection with all acts of terrorism.

National Association of Registered Agents and Brokers (NARAB) Reform Act — The *National Association of Registered Agents and Brokers (NARAB) Reform Act* amends the Gramm-Leach-Bliley Act to revoke the incidental conditions under which the NARAB may not be established. NARAB is also prohibited from merging with or into any other public or private entity.

In addition, without affecting state regulatory authority, the NARAB must provide a mechanism for the adoption and multi-state application of conditions and requirements concerning:

- Licensing, continuing education, and other credentials of non-NARAB insurance producers;
- Appointments of resident or nonresident insurance producers;
- The supervision and disciplining of such producers; and
- Assessing licensing fees for insurance producers.

Also, the Property and Casualty Insurance Committee of the NAIC and its Terrorism Insurance Implementation Working Group (TIIWG) recently implemented a *Model Bulletin*.

This enforcement measure includes an expedited filing form to help state regulators advise insurance companies about regulatory requirements related to terrorism coverage under the modified program.

New Developments – Commercial Lines

Agents and insurance providers should be aware of new or evolving developments in Commercial Lines legislation and laws.

They should also be aware of the following categories and the coverage that is available for each:

- **Cyberattacks** – When individuals hack into a computer system and pillage it for confidential information about customers or clients. Such acts can expose a company (a financial business or a hospital, for example) to privacy-related lawsuits. Standard technology coverage should cover professional liability exposures, extortion threats, and network security liability.
- **Identity theft** – When an individual uses the personal identification information of another individual (a name, credit card number, or Social Security number) to commit fraud. In medical identity theft, an individual's name and health insurance are used to obtain medical services. Identity theft can be covered by homeowner and auto policies at no additional cost. Coverage will reimburse the customer for the expenses associated with the credit and identity restoration process.
- **Intellectual property** – A term that refers to items of a creative nature, such as literary, musical, and artistic works, inventions, designs, and symbols. The creator retains rights to the creative work, invention, or commercial symbol. Insurance covering intellectual property can protect an artist from lawsuits claiming their work infringes on a work used by someone else. It can also protect a company from claims that an artist's work has been stolen.

Example 13.5 – Sarah used to work for a company that creates computer software for airplane control systems. She left that company several years ago and formed her own company doing the same thing. Sarah's former employer suspects that her products incorporate software she designed while working for them years ago. They file a lawsuit against Sarah for theft of intellectual property. Sarah should have purchased liability insurance for the theft of intellectual property to protect herself. If she is found guilty of knowingly using that material, Sarah would not be covered by the insurance and could face criminal charges.

Chapter Review

This chapter explained the different types of commercial coverages. Let's review them:

COMMERCIAL PACKAGE POLICY (CPP)	
Policy Types	• Packaged (single contract) or monoline (separate single coverages)
Common Policy Declarations	• Lists who, what, where, when, and how much coverage exists • Policies take effect at 12:01 a.m. at the mailing address of the insured
Coverage Parts	• General Liability • Commercial Property • Inland Marine • Commercial Auto • Equipment Breakdown (also known as boiler and machinery) • Crime • Farm

Modular Parts	• Policy coverage • Common policy declarations and conditions • Interline endorsements (endorsements that apply to more than one coverage part to eliminate redundancy) • Line(s) of insurance declarations page(s) and coverage form(s) and conditions • Causes of loss forms • Endorsements
Common Policy Conditions	• *Cancellation* - the first named insured can cancel a policy with written notice • *Changes* - term changes have to be made by endorsement • *Examination of books and records* - insurers can audit an insured's records and books for a period of three years after the end of policy • *Inspection and surveys* - insurance provider may make surveys, inspections, reports, and recommendations • *Premiums* - the first named insured is responsible for making premium payments • *Transfer of rights and duties* - a policy owner's rights and duties may be transferred to another with written consent
COMMERCIAL PROPERTY	
Coverage Forms	• *Building and Personal Property* – covers buildings, business personal property and the property of others • *Builders Risk* – covers buildings under construction • *Business Income and Extra Expense* – combined or separate coverage for losses
Common Conditions	• *Concealment, misrepresentation, or fraud coverage* – coverage will be voided in the event the policyholder committed fraud at any time as it relates to the policy • *Control of property* – this condition states that any act or negligence by individuals not under the direction of the policyholder will not void coverage • *Insurance under two or more coverages* – if more than one coverage under the policy can respond to the same loss, the insurance provider will pay no more than the actual loss • *Legal action against the insurer* – no individual can bring legal action against the insurance provider until all policy terms have been complied with, and then only if the legal action is brought within 24 months of the loss • *Liberalization* – if the insurer adopts any provisions that expand coverage during the policy period or within 45 days before the effective date, the expanded coverage is applicable without having to be endorsed on the policy • *No benefit to bailee* – no individual who has custody of covered property, other than the policy owner, can benefit from the insurance • *Other insurance* – if the insured has other insurance with identical terms, conditions, and provisions, the policy will contribute by limits; if the other insurance is different, the policy will respond on an excess basis, paying only for the amount of a loss in excess of the other insurance • *Policy period, coverage territory* – the policy territory includes the United States, its possessions/territories, and Canada • *Subrogation (transfer of rights of recovery against others)* – the policy owner must transfer any rights they have to recover damages from another person to the insurance provider after the insurer makes payment for the loss

CHAPTER 14:
Commercial General Liability (CGL)

This chapter focuses on liability insurance, which pays for damages for which the policy owner is legally responsible. You will start by learning the basics of Commercial General Liability (CGL) contracts, including their coverage forms and components. You will also learn about the unique types of coverage available for the principles of occurrences and claims, professional liability, coverage triggers, and other essential concepts. At the end of this chapter, take a moment to review the major similarities and differences between liability insurance and property insurance.

- CGL – General Concepts
- CGL Coverage Form (Occurrence)
- Occurrence vs. Claims Made
- Professional Liability
- Products and Completed Operations
- Umbrella and Excess Liability

CGL – General Concepts

General liability encompasses any business liability hazards not covered by specialized coverages, such as professional liability, automobile, or marine.

General liability loss exposures include any claims associated with damage to property of third parties or injuries to individuals arising out of the course of doing business. The most common general liability exposures are the following types of liability: premises, operations, products, independent contractors, completed operations, and personal and advertising injury.

Businesses require general liability insurance to cover their exposure to liability losses that may occur from their business operations. *Commercial General Liability (CGL)* policies come in two forms: *occurrence* and *claims-made*. The essential difference between these two forms is how the coverage is triggered, which will be explained later in this chapter.

The latest ISO CGL Coverage Form is split into six sections as follows:

1. Section I coverages:
    - Coverage A – Bodily Injury and Property Damage;
    - Coverage B – Personal Injury and Advertising Injury; and
    - Coverage C – Medical Payments;
2. Section II – Who is an Insured;
3. Section III – Limits of Insurance;
4. Section IV – Commercial General Liability Conditions;
5. Section V – Extended Reporting Periods; and
6. Section VI – Definitions.

The earlier iterations of the ISO forms distinguish between occurrence and claims-made forms. The Extended Reporting Period section is available only in claims-made forms.

CGL Coverage Form (Occurrence)

Definitions

The *definitions* section appears last in the CGL form. However, you must understand these terms as you are learning about CGL coverages, so the definitions are presented next. The following are terms and definitions that apply to commercial general liability insurance:

Occurrence – An *occurrence* refers to an accident, including repeated or continuous exposure to the same dangerous conditions. Coverage exists for covered occurrences *during and after* the policy period if they are due to the same circumstances that took place during the policy period. An occurrence must also occur *within the coverage territory*, as defined in the policy.

Bodily Injury – *Bodily injury* refers to any bodily injury, disease, or sickness sustained by an individual, including death from any of these at any time.

Property Damage – *Property damage* is any physical injury to and the loss of use of tangible property. Also included is the loss of use of property that is not physically injured. Electronic data is not considered tangible property.

Personal and advertising injury refers to an injury, including bodily injury, arising from these offenses:

- Trade secret, copyright, or slogan infringement used in a policy owner's advertisement;
- Imprisonment, detention, or false arrest;
- Unlawful or wrongful eviction, entry, or invasion of privacy by an owner, landlord, lessor, or someone on their behalf;
- Malicious prosecution;
- Use of another's advertising idea;
- Slander or libel in oral or written publication; or
- Oral or written publication that invades or violates the privacy of another.

Coverage Territory – The coverage territory in which the policy applies includes the following:

- The U.S. and its territories/possessions, Puerto Rico, and Canada;
- International airspace and waters if the damage or injury occurs during travel to or from the defined coverage territories; and
- Anywhere in the world if damage or injury results from products or goods manufactured or sold in a coverage territory.

Premises and Operations – *Premises and operations* include the use, maintenance, or ownership of the insured's premises and all business operations.

Products and Completed Operations – This term refers to property damage or bodily injury away from the policy owner's premise and arising out of their work (your work) or product (your product). This definition includes several exceptions. Products still in the policy owner's physical possession do not meet the meaning of products and completed operations. Work not yet completed and products while being transported by the policy owner are also exceptions:

- **Your Work** — Work or operations performed by the policy owner or on their behalf. This term includes materials, equipment, or parts furnished in connection with the work;
- **Your Product** — Any products or goods, other than real property, manufactured, handled, sold, distributed, or disposed of by the policy owner, others trading in the policy owner's name, and acquired business assets. This term includes materials, containers, equipment, or parts used in connection with the products.

Employee – The term *employee* includes a leased worker but not a temporary worker. A *leased worker* in the policy refers to an individual who performs duties for the policy owner related to their business and is leased from a labor leasing firm. A *temporary worker* refers to a person who is a substitute for a permanent employee on leave or to meet short-term or seasonal workload conditions.

Mobile equipment – The following are included in the definition of mobile equipment:

- Farm machinery, bulldozers, forklifts, and other vehicles, including attached equipment, intended for use off public roads;
- Vehicles provided for use solely on or next to the insured premises;
- Vehicles used mainly to provide mobility to drills, diggers, loaders, shovels, and power cranes;

- Vehicles that travel on crawler treads; and
- Any other road resurfacing or construction equipment.

Vehicles falling under a compulsory financial responsibility law, insurance law, or motor vehicle insurance law will not be considered mobile equipment, even if it fits the definition.

Auto – A land motor vehicle, trailer, or semi-trailer used for traveling on public roads, including attached equipment or machinery. It also includes any other land vehicle that requires compulsory financial responsibility or insurance other than where it is licensed or primarily garaged.

Insured Contract – The CGL Coverage Form excludes property damage or bodily injury that the policy owner has assumed under any agreement or contract. The exclusion does not apply to specific contracts, provided the damage or injury occurs after the contract's execution. These insured contracts are in the definitions section of the coverage form as the following:

- Sidetrack agreements;
- Contracts for the leasing of premises;
- License or easement agreements, except in connection with demolition or construction within 50 feet of a railroad;
- Obligations to indemnify a municipality, except concerning work performed for a municipality;
- Elevator maintenance agreements; and
- Liability the policy owner assumes under any contract that would have been imposed by law even if the contract did not exist. Any agreement or contract indemnifying a surveyor, architect, engineer, or railroad under specified circumstances is not included.

Contractual Liability Insurance – This insurance provides coverage for liability that the policy owner has assumed under a written contract. Contractual liability coverage is included automatically in the Commercial General Liability form. Contractual liability appears as an exclusion in the CGL policy. Still, it will cover liability the policy owner would have without the contract and liability assumed under an insured contract.

Section I – Coverages

Coverage A — Bodily Injury and Property Damage Liability – This coverage protects bodily injury and property damage sustained by third parties because of the negligence of the policy owner. The bodily injury or property damage must emanate from the policy owner's premises, operations, products, or completed operations within the coverage territory and a time frame described by the policy.

The *insuring agreement* is summarized as follows: The insurer will pay those sums the insured is legally required to pay as damages from bodily injury or property damage under the policy. The insurer also has the right and responsibility to defend the insured in a lawsuit against them. This right and responsibility do not apply if the policy does not cover the nature of the suit. The insurer, at their discretion, can investigate any occurrence or lawsuit but will pay no more than the policy limits, and the right and duty to defend ends when the limits of insurance have been exhausted.

Exclusions – Causes of loss or perils do not determine coverage in liability policies; coverage is subject to exclusion. The policy cannot respond to settlements or pay for defense costs if one or more exclusions are applicable.

The *Coverage A – Bodily Injury and Property Damage* exclusions are as follows:

- **Expected or intentional injury** — Intentional losses caused by the insured are excluded, except if they result from using reasonable force to protect the property or individuals.

- **Contractual liability** — Assumptions of liability due to contractual agreements are excluded. This exclusion will not apply unless, in the absence of the agreement, the policy owner would be liable or it was assumed in an insured contract as noted below:
    - Sidetrack agreement;
    - Contracts for the leasing of premises;
    - License or easement agreements, except in connection with demolition or construction within 50 feet of a railroad;
    - Obligation to indemnify a municipality, except concerning work performed for a municipality;
    - Elevator maintenance agreements; and
    - Liability the policy owner assumes under any contract that would have been imposed by law even if no contract exists.
- **Liquor liability** — This exclusion applies to liability arising from contributing to or causing the intoxication of any individual, furnishing alcoholic beverages to individuals under the legal drinking age or individuals under the influence of alcohol, and any regulation, ordinance, or statute. However, this exclusion only applies to policyholders in the business of manufacturing, selling, or serving alcohol, in which case, there is no liability for alcohol-related injuries.
- **Workers compensation and employers liability** — The policy excludes coverage for bodily injury, disease, sickness, or death of any employee while employed by the policy owner. Insurers cover these types of losses more appropriately under workers compensation and employers liability policies.
- **Pollution** — A catastrophic exposure and one that is excluded for almost any cause under the general liability policy.
- **Aircraft, auto, or watercraft** — Insurers will not cover property damage or bodily injury caused by the use or ownership of any auto, aircraft, or watercraft under the general liability policy. The exclusion, however, does not apply to:
    - Non-owned watercraft less than 26 feet in length and not being used to transport property or individuals for a fee;
    - Watercraft while ashore on premises the policy owner rents or owns;
    - Parking a non-owned auto on or next to property rented or owned by an insured;
    - Liability assumed in an insured contract for the use, maintenance, or ownership of watercraft or aircraft; or
    - Operation of mobile equipment.
- **Mobile equipment** — There is no coverage for the transportation of mobile equipment by an auto operated or owned by the insured or while in a contest or race.
- **War** — Whether or not war is declared, it is excluded.
- **Damage to property** — Insurers will not cover damage to property rented by, owned, or loaned to the insured or property in the insured's control, custody, or care.
- **The insured's product** — Damage to the insured's products is not covered.
- **The insured's work** — Damage to the insured's work is not covered. This exclusion is not applicable if a subcontractor did the job for the insured.
- **Impaired property or property not physically injured** — Property damage to impaired property or property that has not sustained damage resulting from a deficiency or defect in the insured's product or work is not covered. There is no coverage for any damage caused by a delay or failure of the policy owner to perform under an agreement or contract.
- **Recall of products, work, or impaired property** — The policy excludes any loss sustained by the insured or others for withdrawal, loss of use, or recall of the insured's work or product.
- **Personal and advertising injury** — Bodily injury due to personal and advertising injury is not covered.
- **Electronic data** — There is no coverage for damages arising from the loss of, damage to, loss of use, inability to access, corruption of, or inability to manipulate electronic data.

- **Recording and distribution of material in violation of communications laws** — Property damage and bodily injuries are excluded if arising directly or indirectly out of any omission or action that violates the following: CAN-SPAM Act, the Telephone Consumer Protection Act, the Fair Credit Reporting Act, or any other local, state, or federal statute or regulation.

Coverage B — Personal Injury and Advertising Injury – This coverage insures against specific acts resulting in a non-physical injury to a third party due to offenses defined as personal and advertising injuries.

The *insuring agreement* for this coverage is similar to the bodily injury and property damage insuring agreement. However, third-party injuries must result from personal and advertising injury. The offense must be committed within the policy period and the coverage territory described on the declarations page.

Exclusions – The *Coverage B – Personal and Advertising Injury* exclusions are as follows:

- **Knowing violation of rights of another** — Personal or advertising injury if it is intentional and with the knowledge that the act would violate another's rights is not covered.
- **Material published with knowledge of falsity** — There is no coverage for personal and advertising injury resulting from the publication of oral or written material known to be false.
- **Material published prior to the policy period** — Injuries arising from oral or written material published before the policy's inception are not covered.
- **Criminal acts** — If the policy owner or someone at the policy owner's direction commits a criminal act, there is no coverage for any resulting damage.
- **Contractual liability** — There is no coverage for any liability the policy owner assumes through an agreement or contract. This exclusion will be the case unless, if no agreement exists, the insured would have been liable for the damages.
- **Breach of contract** — Breach of contract is not covered unless it is an implied contract to use another's advertising idea.
- **Quality or performance of goods – failure to conform to statements** — If the goods, product, or services fail to conform to the advertised performance or quality, there is no coverage.
- **Wrong description of prices** — There is no coverage for the resulting damage if the advertising material states the wrong price.
- **Infringement of copyright, patent, trademark, or trade secret** — There is no coverage for damage arising from the infringement of trademark, copyright, patent, trade secret, or other such intellectual property rights (excluding the use of another's advertising idea).
- **Insureds in media and Internet-type businesses** — There is no coverage for the business of broadcasting, telecasting, or advertising. Determining or designing the content of websites for others or an Internet search, content, access, or service provider is also not covered.
- **Electronic chatrooms or bulletin boards** — There is no coverage for damage caused by electronic chat rooms or bulletin boards controlled, owned, or hosted by the insured.
- **Unauthorized use of another person's name or product** — Insurers will not cover personal and advertising injury arising from the unauthorized use of another individual's or entity's name or product to mislead their potential customers.
- **Recording and distribution of material in violation of law** — Property damage and bodily injuries are excluded if arising directly or indirectly out of any omission or action that violates the CAN-SPAM Act, the Telephone Consumer Protection Act, the FCRA, or any other local, state, or federal statute or regulation;
- **Pollution or pollution-related losses**; and
- **War**.

Coverage C — Medical Payments – This coverage provides medical, hospital, surgical, ambulance, professional nursing, or funeral expenses for injuries to third parties. This coverage is viewed as goodwill coverage because insurers will make payments without regard to the negligence or fault of the insured. Medical expenses must be incurred and reported within *12 months* of the date of the accident to be covered.

A bodily injury must result from an accident and occur on premises rented or owned by the insured, on ways next to the rented or owned premises, or due to the insured's operations. The injury must occur within the coverage territory and during the policy period.

The table below summarizes all three coverages included in Section I of the Commercial General Liability policy:

COVERAGE	DESCRIPTION
Coverage A Bodily Injury (BI) and Property Damage (PD)	**BI** provides coverage for any injury, sickness, disease, or death third parties suffer because of the insured's business activities. **PD** provides coverage for injury to, destruction of, or loss of use of the property of others due to the insured's business activities.
Coverage B Personal Injury (PI) and Advertising Injury (AI)	**PI** covers injuries caused to third parties that result from mental anguish, false arrest or imprisonment, wrongful eviction or detention, malicious prosecution, defamation of character, slander or libel, and invasion of privacy. **AI** covers injuries that occur if, in the course of advertising, the policy owner inadvertently slanders, libels, defames, or violates the privacy of another.
Coverage C Medical Payments	Medical payments coverage provides for necessary medical, surgical, ambulance, hospital, professional nursing, or funeral expenses for third parties injured because of the insured's business operations, without regard to fault.

Exclusions – *Coverage C – Medical Payments* will not pay for bodily injury to or resulting from:

- Any policy owner except volunteer workers;
- Employees or anyone hired by the policy owner;
- The insured's tenants;
- If benefits have to be provided under workers compensation or similar law;
- Individuals injured while instructing, practicing, or participating in sports, physical games or exercises, or athletic contests;
- War, revolution, rebelling, or insurrection; or
- If excluded under Coverage A.

Supplementary Payments – Supplementary payments are provided for *Coverage A – Bodily Injury and Property Damage*, and *Coverage B – Personal and Advertising Injury*. These are the amounts the insurance provider will pay in addition to the stated policy limits. However, the insurer's duty to defend ends when the total of all claims paid reaches the aggregate limit. The following are similar to the supplementary payments provided in other liability insurance policies:

- Any expenses incurred by the insurance provider;
- Up to $250 for the cost of bonds to release attachments and bail bonds;
- Reasonable costs incurred by the policy owner, including up to $250 a day for loss of income;
- Court costs taxed against the policy owner (except attorney's fees or expenses);
- Prejudgment interest; and
- Interest that accrues on any judgment.

Section II – Who is an Insured

The ISO form describes *who is an insured* based on the following designations found in the Declarations:

Individual (sole proprietor) — An individual insured and their spouse, but only regarding the conduct of a business in which the insured is the sole owner.

Partnership or joint venture — A partnership, including joint ventures, is a legal entity in which two or more individuals agree to share the profits and losses of the business. Under this arrangement, the policy owners are the named insured, partners, members, and their spouses, but only regarding the business.

Limited Liability Company (LLC) — Named insured and members for business activities. Managers are considered insureds for their roles and duties as managers.

An organization other than a partnership, joint venture, or LLC — Named insured, directors, executive officers, and stockholders but only for their duties or liabilities as such.

Trust — The named insured and trustees but only concerning their duties as trustees.

Each of the following is also considered an insured under the policy, regardless of legal entity:

- The policy owner's volunteers and employees for acts within the scope of their employment;
- Any person or agent while acting as the insured's real estate agent (except volunteers and employees);
- Any person or legal representatives, or organization, having temporary custody of the insured's property if the insured dies; and
- Newly formed or acquired organizations (other than a limited liability company, joint venture, or partnership) for which no other insurance applies for up to 90 days after the policy expiration or ownership is acquired, whichever is earlier.

Section III – Limits of Liability

This section describes how each limit shown in the Declarations works in case of a covered claim. Before this is explained, it will be helpful to visualize the components of a typical CGL policy declarations page.

CGL POLICY DECLARATIONS	
Occurrence Limit	$1,000,000
Damage to Property Rented to You	$100,000
Medical Expense Limit	$10,000
Personal and Advertising Injury Limit	$1,000,000
General Aggregate	$2,000,000
Products and Completed Operations Aggregate	$2,000,000

It is vital to understand the concepts of the aggregate limits to know how the limits of liability work together. Each of these limits is the maximum available during the policy period. Once these aggregates are drawn down, the policy's limits are depleted, and any supplementary payments will cease.

There is a limit per occurrence for property damage and bodily injury and per occurrence for personal and advertising injury. Depending on the type of claim, each limit will be the maximum the policy will pay. Products and completed operations claims are also subject to the occurrence limit but exhaust a different aggregate. Medical expense payments are subject to a limit per person but have an occurrence limit for one event.

The general liability policy also includes a specific amount of coverage for fire damage legal liability, which can be increased.

Section IV – Conditions

A commercial general liability policy commonly includes the following conditions:

- **Bankruptcy** — Bankruptcy of the policy owner will not relieve the insurance provider of its obligation under the policy.
- **Insured duties in the event of an offense, occurrence, claim, or lawsuit** — The following duties are required of the insured in the event of a loss:
  - Inform the insurer as soon as possible of an occurrence or the possibility of a claim;
  - Immediately record the specifics of any claim or lawsuit brought, and notify the insurer;
  - Immediately provide the insurer any notices, demands, or summons relating to a suit or claim;
  - Authorize the insurance provider to obtain any records or other pertinent information, and assist the insurer in its investigation;
  - Don't assume any obligations, make any voluntary payments, or incur any costs without the insurer's consent, or it will be at the policyholder's own expense.
- **Legal action against the insurance provider** — No party can join the insurer as a party in any lawsuit asking for damages against the policy owner. In addition, no party may sue the insurance company until all policy provisions have been met.
- **Other insurance** — If other valid and collectible insurance is available to cover a loss under Coverages A and B, the general liability policy will pay as follows:
  - **Primary basis** — Except as noted in the excess section below, if other insurance is the primary coverage, the policy will share liability depending on how the other insurance shares liability. It will be shared pro rata up to the policy limit or in equal shares.
  - **Excess basis** — Certain insurance contracts regardless of the other insurance clause in those policies; any other primary insurance in which the policy owner has been added as an additional insured.
- **Premium audits** — The insurer is permitted to audit the policy owner's records or books at the end of the policy term to ensure sufficient premium has been collected for the exposure.
- **Representations** — By accepting the policy, the insured agrees that the statements listed on the declarations page are true and complete and that the policy was issued based on the representations made by the policy owner.
- **Separation of insureds** — This condition demonstrates how the coverage will apply to each individual insured. The insurance will apply as if the policy owner named in the lawsuit were the only named insured and separately to each policy owner against whom a claim or suit is brought. This clause, however, does not increase the limit of insurance listed in the Declarations.
- **Subrogation (transferring the rights of recovery against others to the insurer)** — The policy owner must transfer any rights they possess to recover damages from a negligent third party. The insured may not do anything to obstruct these rights after the loss.
- **Nonrenewal** — The minimum number of days' notice the insurance company will provide to the insured if the insurer decides not to renew the coverage is usually 30 days. This period can differ according to each state's regulations.
- **Insured's right to claim and occurrence information** — The insurer will provide the first named insured with information about the claim and occurrence. It will also give the insured information regarding any previous general liability claims-made coverage issued in the past three years.

Pollution

Pollution is considered a potentially catastrophic exposure, and many insurance carriers are unwilling to assume liability for the exposure. Some insurers will even attach a Total Pollution Exclusion to the General Liability policy to remove the limited pollution coverage provided in the policy. Nearly all pollution losses, including clean-up costs, are excluded from the General Liability policy. The General Liability policy, however, covers pollution from fumes or smoke from a covered fire. It also covers emissions away from the insured premises under products and completed operations coverage when others use the work or product.

Many businesses require this insurance and can typically purchase the following pollution coverage forms.

This coverage is written only on a *claims-made* basis. It can be written as an endorsement attached to the General Liability policy or as a separate policy. It offers two types of coverage:

1. Property damage or bodily injury liability caused by a pollution accident; and
2. Clean-up expenses mandated by a government entity. (Coverage can be purchased for voluntary clean-up expenses necessary to curtail or prevent a pollution accident and in which the insurance company provides written consent for an additional premium).

The common exclusions listed in the coverage form are:

*   Emissions from an abandoned or closed site;
*   Acid rain; and
*   Escape of fluids from a geothermal, water, mineral, oil, or gas well.

All claims must occur after the retroactive date and be reported during the policy period. The policy provides an optional one-year extended reporting period if the insurer cancels or nonrenews coverage, replaces it with another type of policy, or renews it with a new retroactive date. The policy owner must request this extended reporting period within 30 days following the end of the policy period and pay any additional premium due.

This endorsement can be used to provide *limited* pollution coverage. It provides a separate aggregate limit of liability for pollution coverage. However, discharges from underground storage tanks are excluded.

This endorsement only provides coverage for third-party damage or injury caused by pollution. Insurers will not cover clean-up expenses.

Occurrence vs. Claims Made

As you have previously learned, general liability policies come in two forms. The most common is the *occurrence* form. The other form is called the *claims-made* form. It is used for special situations such as product, professional, employment, and environmental liability.

The claims-made policy is often used when the occurrence could take a long time to manifest itself or spread over several years. The ISO developed this form because of how the legal system interpreted an occurrence. The ISO also developed the claims-made form because of how complex claims triggered occurrence forms.

The claims-made form has several unique features that include the following:

Retroactive Date — A date is entered on the declarations page to inform the policy owner that the policy will not cover any claim before this date.

Extended Reporting Period (ERP) — The policy allows the insured a period to report a claim and provide coverage even though the policy was canceled by the insurance provider or the insured. For example, an attorney decides to retire and no longer wants the insurance policy. It would provide the policy owner time to report any claim they become aware of even though the policy is no longer in force.

The combination of these two timeframes allows the insurer to predict better when the policy will respond. The insured's ability to report a claim, and the amount of time the policy responds to an occurrence, are now contingent upon defined periods.

Insurers do not include an extended reporting period in the occurrence form that pays for property damage and bodily injury *during the policy period*. Even if the loss is not identified or reported until months or years after the policy expiration, an occurrence form will pay for property damage and bodily injury.

Trigger

The *coverage trigger* causes a policy to respond to a claim. The policy in force when the claim is initially made will respond to a claims-made trigger, and the policy in force when the event took place responds to an occurrence trigger.

Example 14.1 – To help you better understand the concept, let's go back to Marty and Sandra Jones and apply the idea to their brownie operation.

First, let's assume that Marty and Sandra have an occurrence form CGL policy. The coverage trigger is, therefore, the occurrence of property damage or bodily injury. If a person were to claim an injury that occurred in 2008 but did not bring a lawsuit until 2010, the policy Marty and Sandra had in 2008 would pay any settlement and defend them. The limits that Marty and Sandra had at the time would also apply.

What if Marty and Sandra had a claims-made policy in the same situation? We need to know more information about the policy before we can decide. The policy in effect in 2010 has a retroactive date of 1/1/2006. Since the injury occurred after that date, the policy in force in 2010 would cover the defense costs and any settlement with the carried limits. If the injury had occurred in 2005, the claims-made policy would not respond.

Retroactive Date

A *retroactive date* is used to avoid paying for losses occurring before the effective date of a claims-made policy. Coverage does not apply for any loss arising before this retroactive date.

A retroactive date in a claims-made liability policy is a coverage limitation. It stipulates that coverage only applies to claims reported during the policy period and which are the result of events occurring on or after the specified retroactive date.

Although insurers can write claims-made forms without a retroactive date, insurers will write most of these policies with a retroactive date. Initially, the retroactive date will be the same as the inception of the first policy written by an insurance provider under the claims-made form. This stipulation eliminates duplicate coverage when a claims-made form replaces an occurrence form. Subsequent renewals of the first claims-made policy with the same insurance provider will usually have the same retroactive date as the renewed policy. This condition allows coverage to be provided uninterruptedly from the last occurrence form to the latest claims-made form.

Insurers will cover losses before the retroactive date under the occurrence forms that preceded the change to a claims-made basis. The claims-made form in effect when the claim was made will provide coverage for losses occurring after the retroactive date. Unless the retroactive date is advanced, it will usually be the same as the date on which the last occurrence policy expired. If the retroactive date is advanced, a coverage gap is created.

Extended Reporting Periods

At the termination of a claims-made liability coverage form, there are three extended reporting periods, known as *tail coverage*, that afford different degrees of protection to policy owners that may have an action for damages brought against them for occurrences that took place during the policy period, but were not identified, or not reported, until after the policy was terminated.

The *Basic Extended Reporting Period* includes the following two provisions:

1. Mini-tail; and
2. Midi-tail.

With the *Mini-tail* provision, the reporting period of a claims-made policy is extended for 60 days following the policy expiration. Claims arising from occurrences after the policy's retroactive date but before the policy expiration are covered if reported during these 60 days. Claims reported during these 60 days are treated like they had been reported during the policy period.

If the potential third-party claimant delays providing notice of a claim for damages, but the policyholder is aware of the event that could give rise to a claim, under the *Midi-tail* provision, the insured can report the event to the insurance provider, and that would provide the policyholder protection for that event, should it result in a claim within the next five years.

The Midi-tail provision only applies to events identified to the insurance company. Any unidentified events resulting in a claim after the policy expiration would still not be covered.

The *Supplemental Extended Reporting Period (SERP)*, also called *maxi-tail* coverage, differs from the mini-tail and midi-tail in two critical aspects:

- The added endorsement's reporting period is indefinite, meaning there is no time limit within which claims must be reported.
- When the SERP coverage is purchased, the policy's aggregate limits are reinstated. Both known and unknown events are covered.

The policyholder must request the Supplemental Reporting Period Coverage within 60 days after the policy period ends. Once the endorsement is effective, the expired policy provides coverage for "an unlimited time beginning with the end of the policy period."

The premium charge for this endorsement is usually 200% of the policy's annual premium. It is subject to a single policy aggregate limit for the length of the coverage.

Claim Information

An additional condition on the claims-made form is the policy owner's rights to *claim and occurrence information*. The insurance company will provide information on any current claims-made policy and any claims-made coverage it has issued for the prior three years. The report will show each occurrence with the date and a brief description. It will also summarize, by policy year, all amounts paid and any amounts held in reserve as they apply to the policy's aggregate limits.

When the insurer cancels the policy or opts not to renew it, the insurer will provide the occurrence and claim information at least 30 days before the last day of coverage. The first named insured can request the report in writing at any time up to 60 days after the policy ends. The insurance company will provide the report within 45 days of the request.

The claims information is seen as quantitative because the amounts claimed are known. The occurrence information is viewed as nonquantitative since claims have yet to be filed, and insurers cannot know future claim amounts.

Prior Acts Coverage

Uninsured individuals or those who have canceled a claims-made policy with an insufficient discovery period may obtain *prior acts coverage* from their new insurer or a separate insurer. Prior acts coverage will cover claims arising from acts before the policy period begins.

Professional Liability

Professional liability losses are not covered on a CGL form because they do not meet the definitions found in the policy. As you have previously learned, under a CGL policy, bodily injury means bodily harm, disease, or sickness sustained by any individual, including death.

Property damage is physical injury to tangible property, including the loss of use of that property.

Personal and advertising injury includes consequential bodily injury arising from offenses such as libel or slander, false arrest, invasion of privacy, etc. Because professional liability is excluded from coverage under a CGL policy, these exposures must be covered under professional liability policies.

Professional liability coverage protects the policy owner against legal liability caused by errors and omissions, negligence, and other aspects of rendering or failing to render professional services.

When the exposure is bodily injury, professional liability coverage is called *malpractice insurance*. When the exposure is primarily that of damage to the property of others, the professional liability coverage is called *errors and omissions insurance*.

Medical professionals purchase medical malpractice insurance, while professionals in other fields of exposure purchase errors and omissions insurance. There is an extensive range of professions having a possibility of property damage caused by the rendering or failure to render professional services:

- Insurance brokers and agents;
- Insurance adjusters;
- Abstracters;
- Attorneys;
- Accountants;
- Architects; and
- Many more.

Coverage is tailored to the needs of the particular profession. A common trait of professional liability insurance is that it is written on a claims-made basis. It requires that policy owners assume a retention for losses (professional liability insurance written on an occurrence basis is extremely rare).

Errors and Omissions

Errors and omissions coverage protects insurance brokers and agents from financial losses if a policy owner sues to recover their losses. Policy owners can take legal action against a broker or agent because they did not place requested coverage, gave incorrect advice, or hid potential issues. Insurers typically write coverage on a claims-made basis. States will vary in how they interpret mistakes made by brokers and agents. The coverage provided is very similar to professional liability.

Management Liability

Any profit and nonprofit organization may become exposed to management liability lawsuits, which could result in high claims costs and awards for damage. Directors and Officers Liability or Management Liability Insurance is related to the duties and performance of management and can help cover claims made during the policy period.

Directors and Officers (D&O) Liability – *Directors and Officers (D&O)* liability coverage will protect the directors and officers of an organization from any claims for losses resulting from a wrongful act made while acting in an official capacity.

Wrongful acts will trigger coverage instead of being triggered on an occurrence or accident basis. Wrongful acts include neglect, breach of duty, and misstatements by directors and officers.

Directors and Officers liability policies will only pay damages that the corporation would, under the law, be required to reimburse the individual director or officer. The policy usually will not cover penalties, fines, or punitive damages.

There are three common insuring agreements used in Directors and Officers Liability insurance:

1. **Insuring Agreement A, or A-Side Coverage** – Provides direct coverage to the directors and officers for losses resulting from claims made against them.
2. **Insuring Agreement B, or B-Side Coverage** – Reimburses a corporation for its losses. The corporation then indemnifies its directors and officers for claims made against them. This coverage does not apply to the corporation's liability.
3. **Insuring Agreement C, or C-Side Coverage** – Protects the corporation against securities claims (the corporation's liability).

The term "insured" includes directors, officers, executives, department heads, faculty and committee members, volunteers, and employees. All covered insureds are listed in the policy Declarations.

The Directors and Officers Liability policies will not cover the following: claims concerning dishonesty or willful violations, fraud, claims made by one policy owner against another, professional services claims, or claims related to pending or prior litigation.

Employment Practices Liability (EPLI) – *Employment Practices Liability (EPL)* refers to the exposures employers face in their role. Commercial general liability or the employers liability portion of workers compensation will not cover these claims. This coverage offers protection for liability resulting from the following:

- Refusal to employ, demotion or failure to promote, termination of the individual's employment, negative evaluation, discipline, reassignment, humiliation, or defamation of the individual based on discrimination;
- Work-related sexual harassment; or
- Other work-related physical, verbal, emotional, or mental abuse directed at the individual relating to color, race, gender, national origin, age, marital status, sexual orientation, mental or physical condition, or any other protected characteristic or class established by any local, state, or federal law.

The following insureds can be excluded from employment practices liability coverage:

- Any insured that operates a unit, commission, or board that is not covered; and
- Individuals on retainer as consultants or under contract for services for an insured.

There is *no exclusion for intentional or fraudulent acts.*

Employment practices liability coverage cannot extend to claims made against the policy owner:

- That may cause advantage or profit;
- Resulting from the deliberate violation of any law;
- Brought about by fraud or other dishonesty;
- For bodily injury (including mental anguish, emotional distress, invasion of privacy, defamation, or humiliation);
- For false imprisonment, false arrest, or other abuse of process;
- Alleging violation of civil rights (other than those that are related to employment);
- Arising out of:
  - Wrongful employment practices taking place before the policy period;
  - A loss of which the insured is entitled to payment under another policy;
  - Circumstances in which the policyholder acts in a fiduciary capacity;
  - Activity regarding any employee benefit plan;
  - Relief in any form other than monetary damages;
  - Any liability assumed by the policyholder under a contract;
  - By the named insured on their behalf; and
  - For overtime, back wages, or similar claims.

An *employment claim* refers to any of the following:

- A civil proceeding as a result of a complaint;
- A written request for monetary damages or non-monetary relief;
- A criminal proceeding as a result of filed charges;
- A formal regulatory or administrative proceeding;
- A mediation, arbitration, or similar alternative dispute resolution proceeding; or
- A written request to waive a statute of limitation regarding a potential administrative or civil proceeding against an insured.

Claims can include several different types of settlement between the injured party and the insurance provider. A claim process is initiated to recover a loss for which there is a claim against the policy owner by an injured party. The insurance policy's provisions will be accounted for by the insurer based on the extent of the loss covered by the policy and limited by the policy limits. A liability claim will often include a judgment by a court that will assign responsibility for a loss to the injured party, against which the insurer will defend the insured up to the limits payable by the policy.

Commercial entities facing a liability associated with employment practices can be subject to various types of settlement, like cash paid directly to the injured party (monetary damages). Settlement can also take the form of regulatory or administrative investigations of other responsible parties, including Equal Employment Opportunity Commission (EEOC) charges (non-monetary relief). The process can involve numerous parties and attachments of responsibility for a loss, including other entities or individuals. The coverage for employment practices intends to allow payment to the injured party up to the policy limits and minimize financial exposure to the insured.

The type of damages covered can be extensive, involving occurrences before and even following a judgment. Damages applicable to commercial insurance on employment practices can include several possible circumstances. For example, liability coverage minimizes business exposure to former or current employee's allegations and consequent rulings involving harassment, discrimination, or wrongful termination. Since employment-related litigation continues to rise, claims on the business entity can result from state and federal laws. Some examples of these laws include the Civil Rights Act, the Americans with Disabilities Act, the Age Discrimination in Employment Act, and other anti-discrimination laws.

The forms of damage caused by successful rulings on employment practice cases can include the following:

- Actual or direct damages, such as lost wages and other cash compensation due through the course of employment;
- Punitive damages, such as additional awards granted by a court in addition to lost wages and other compensation, intended to represent a "punishment" to the liable employer;
- Exemplary damages, a variation of punitive, where the plaintiff is awarded well above the value of loss sustained to "punish" the employer and deter other employers;
- Liquidated damages, where there is an employment agreement involved, and represents damages paid to fulfill a breach of contract, which can be defined by the court as well as the contract itself; and
- Multiplied damages, another variation of punitive, permitting a court to triple the amount of actual or compensatory damages, which would then be the total damage amount, not in addition to, where if an individual was initially awarded $1,000, a "treble" damage ruling would increase the award to $3,000, not $4,000.

Medical Malpractice

Today there are several types of *medical malpractice* insurance for hospitals, doctors, and other medical practitioners. It indemnifies the policy owner for injuries to third parties due to legal liability for bodily injury or death.

In the insurance field, "professional liability" has replaced the use of the terms "errors and omissions insurance" and "malpractice insurance" to describe the coverage of specialists in the various professional fields. Professional liability policies are tailored to cover the exposures of almost every professional. The policies that protect those medical professionals respond to actions caused by injurious acts resulting from claims that the policy owner was derelict in a professional duty. They also respond to harmful acts resulting from the failure of professional skill or learning, negligence, misconduct, or incompetence in the performance of a professional act.

Nearly every policy written provides coverage on a claims-made basis.

One of the significant differences in professional liability coverage compared to personal and general liability coverage is that the former insures against losses resulting from an insured's negligence. Personal and general liability policies *exclude coverage for intentional acts* committed by an insured.

A professional liability policy will also cover some intentional acts. Recently we have heard of doctors performing the wrong surgery or amputating the wrong leg. There have been some cases in the dental field where the wrong tooth was extracted. These are the kinds of intentional acts insured against; however, insurers typically exclude criminal acts from coverage.

Another difference in coverage is when a claim is made under a personal or general liability policy. The insurance provider will decide whether to defend the claim or pay the loss. They will generally decide on the option that is the least expensive.

In professional liability coverage, an insurance carrier cannot settle a claim without the consent of the insured. When the insured has not given up this right for a premium reduction, they may want to defend their reputation as a professional in their field. They can require the insurance carrier to defend the claim and prove in court that they are not liable.

Other medical malpractice coverages – Other types of medical professionals who require liability coverage for potential bodily injury that can result from providing or failure to provide professional services include nurses, hospitals, optometrists, opticians, chiropractors, and veterinarians.

Fiduciary Liability

Fiduciary liability covers individuals who administer employee benefit plans or pensions and have a fiduciary responsibility to manage the funds in the best interests of the plan's participants. Professional liability can cover losses associated with negligence, errors or omissions, or poor management of these plans. By law, if *the fund pays the premiums* for fiduciary liability insurance, the policy has to allow for subrogation against the individual trustees involved in the loss.

Products and Completed Operations

The *products and completed operations* hazard includes damage or injuries occurring after the policy owner completed their job, left the site, or gave over control of a product they manufactured or sold. Coverage to protect against this hazard is optional, although the coverage is included for specific business risks.

Umbrella and Excess Liability

The primary function of a *commercial umbrella* policy is to provide excess protection through higher limits of liability over general liability policies, business automobile liability policies, and many other types of liability programs. There is typically a minimum limit of liability the policy owner must carry and maintain on the basic policies, such as $1,000,000 for commercial risks. Also, there are retained limits known as a self-insured retention (SIR) that the policy owner must satisfy before the umbrella policy responds to certain losses. The SIR applies only for losses not covered by any underlying insurance.

The difference between a commercial umbrella policy and an excess policy is determined the same way as with personal umbrella policies. Once a liability claim is filed for recovery of damage or injury, the primary policy pays up to the policy limits, after which the umbrella policy will apply. If there is no primary underlying insurance, the excess policy will apply after the insured paid the self-insured retention.

Currently, no standard umbrella policies exist. The ISO has developed an umbrella and excess liability form; however, most insurance providers have their own forms with unique coverages.

Chapter Review

This chapter explained liability insurance, including commercial general liability (CGL) contracts. Let's review the key points:

COMMERCIAL GENERAL LIABILITY	
Who is an Insured	• Individual (sole proprietor) • Partnership/Joint venture • Limited liability company (LLC) or trust • An organization other than a partnership, joint venture, or LLC
Exposures	• *Premises and operations* - includes the use, maintenance, or ownership of an insured's premises; includes business operations; subject to limits and exclusions • *Product and completed operations* - includes injuries or damage taking place after the insured has completed their job and left the site or relinquishes control of the product

CGL Coverage Form	• *Coverage A – Bodily Injury and Property Damage* - Covers the bodily injury and property damage of a third party
	• *Coverage B – Personal and Advertising Injury Protection* - Covers non-physical injury (libel and slander)
	• *Coverage C – Medical Payments* - covers medical, surgical, ambulance, hospital, professional nursing, and funeral expenses of the third party
	• *Supplementary payments* - additional amounts up to the stated policy limits
	• Limits of liability:
	   ○ *Per occurrence* - maximum amount payable per occurrence or accident
	   ○ *Aggregate limit* - the most insurers will pay for losses in a policy period

PROFESSIONAL LIABILITY	
Purpose and Characteristics	• Protects against legal liability • Usually written on a claims-made basis
Errors and Omissions	• Protects brokers and agents from financial loss due to a lawsuit with the insured • Financial loss resulting from not placing correct coverage, incorrect advice, not informing the policy owner of potential issues • Written on a claims-made basis
Medical Malpractice	• Written for hospitals, doctors, or other medical practitioners • Indemnifies a policy owner for injuries
Directors and Offers (D&O)	• Protects directors and officers from losses stemming from wrongful acts while in an official capacity • Triggered by a wrongful act • Does not pay for penalties, fines, or punitive damages

Employment Practice Liability (EPL)	• Protects an employer for liability resulting from:
	   ○ Refusal to employment, termination, failure to promote, demotion, negative evaluation, discipline, reassignment, humiliation, or defamation based on discrimination
	   ○ Sexual harassment
	• Physical, verbal, emotional, or mental abuse relating to color, race, nationality, age, gender, sexual orientation, marital status, and mental or physical condition

CHAPTER 15:
Commercial Auto

Commercial auto insurance differs from personal auto insurance, as you might expect. This chapter will teach you about the different forms available for commercial auto insurance, including business auto, garage, truckers, and motor carriers. As you are reading, comparing and contrasting the different forms will help you better understand commercial auto insurance.

- Commercial Auto – Overview
- Commercial Auto – General Form Structure
- Garage Coverage Form – Garagekeepers Insurance
- Truckers Coverage
- Commercial Carrier Regulations

Commercial Auto – Overview

The *business auto coverage form* is split into the following sections:

1. Section I – Covered Auto;
2. Section II – Liability Coverage;
3. Section III – Physical Damage Coverage;
4. Section IV – Business Auto Conditions; and
5. Section V – Definitions.

Each section is further divided to describe specific perils that are covered and excluded from coverages and limits of insurance as they apply to the different types of coverage.

Types of Auto

Owned Autos – *Owned autos* are eligible vehicles titled by the policyholder or acquired during the policy period.

Non-owned Autos – *Non-owned autos* include private passenger autos, vans, pickups, or trailers operated by or in the custody of the named insured or a family member but not titled by or provided for the regular use of the policy owner.

Definitions

The Commercial Auto (CA) coverage form includes some essential definitions at the end of the policy. The following are key terms and definitions used in explaining the coverages provided by commercial auto insurance.

Auto — A land motor vehicle, trailer, or semitrailer intended for use on public roads and any other land vehicle must adhere to compulsory financial responsibility laws where it is licensed or principally garaged. However, *auto* does not include mobile equipment.

The term *trailer* also includes a semitrailer.

Mobile equipment – Includes any of the following types of land vehicles, including any equipment or attached machinery:

*   Forklifts, farm machinery, bulldozers, and other vehicles primarily used off public roads;
*   Vehicles that travel on crawler treads;
*   Vehicles that provide mobility to road construction equipment, loaders, shovels, or cranes; and
*   Vehicles that are not self-propelled that provide mobility to spraying or welding equipment, pumps, compressors, cherry pickers, and similar devices used to raise and lower workers.

This definition does not include self-propelled vehicles used in street cleaning, road construction, snow removal, or cherry pickers mounted on vehicles or autos subject to compulsory financial responsibility laws. Those will be considered autos.

Insured Contract — Coverage for contracts is excluded unless the contract falls within the following parameters:

- A contract for a lease of premises;
- A sidetrack agreement (made with a railroad when a policy owner uses a track);
- License or easement agreement (except within 50 feet of a railroad);
- Indemnification of a municipality unless work is being performed for a municipality;
- Part of a contract, including work for a municipality, in which the tort liability of another is assumed (would be imposed in the absence of a contract); or
- Rental agreements for "autos" but not for any damage to the auto.

An insured contract does not include agreements for autos rented with a driver, demolition near railroads, or certain agreements made by carriers for hire.

Commercial Auto – General Form Structure

Coverage Form Sections

Section I – Covered Autos

Section I of the business auto coverage form explains the auto designation symbols that define the vehicle types insured for specific coverages. The symbols are listed next to the appropriate coverage on the declarations page.

The following auto symbols are used with the business auto coverage form:

AUTO SYMBOLS USED WITH THE BUSINESS AUTO COVERAGE FORM	
1=	Any auto, including owned, leased, hired, or borrowed autos (used only for liability coverage)
2=	Owned autos only
3=	Owned private passenger autos only
4=	Owned autos, other than private passenger autos only
5=	Owned autos subject to no-fault
6=	Owned autos subject to a compulsory uninsured motorists law
7=	Specifically described autos only
8=	Hired autos only (rented, leased, hired, or borrowed other than from partners, employees, or members of an LLC)
9=	Non-owned autos only (autos that are not rented, leased, hired, or borrowed. Coverage is included for autos owned by partners, employees, and members of an LLC)
10=	Mobile equipment subject to financial responsibility or other motor vehicle insurance laws

It is worth noting that the commercial auto policy does not use the definition of covered auto like the personal auto policy. The covered auto symbols are a vital component of the form as they describe the vehicles granted coverage.

For example, Symbol 7, specifically described autos, corresponds to an attached Vehicle Schedule that lists the make, model, year, and other specifics about a particular vehicle.

Newly Acquired Autos – If symbols 1, 2, 3, 4, 5, or 6 are listed for any of the coverages, the policy will apply to any additional autos of the same type that the policy owner acquires during the policy period.

However, if Symbol 7 is used, newly acquired auto coverage applies if the insurer already covers all vehicles owned by the policy owner or if the newly acquired vehicle is replacing a previously owned auto. The insured must notify the insurer that coverage is requested within 30 days of obtaining the vehicle.

Certain Mobile Equipment, Trailers, and Temporary Substitutes – If liability coverage is provided, specific types of other vehicles are also covered for liability. These other vehicles include

- Mobile equipment that is being carried or towed by a covered vehicle;
- Trailers possessing a load capacity of 2,000 pounds or less; and
- Temporary substitute vehicles used while a covered auto is out of service because of loss, destruction, breakdown, servicing, or repair.

Section II – Liability Coverage

Section II – Liability Coverage states that the policy will pay for property damage or bodily injury to third parties resulting from an accident caused by the insured's use, maintenance, or ownership of any covered auto. The liability section also covers pollution expenses caused by an accident resulting from the use, maintenance, or ownership of a covered auto that results in property damage or bodily injury.

Who is an Insured – Under Section II of the business auto coverage form, an insured is any of the following:

- The organization or person named in the Declarations for any covered auto;
- Anyone else while using a covered auto with the policy owner's permission, *except* the following:
  - Owners of the auto (from whom a policy owner hires or borrows an auto other than a trailer);
  - Someone using a covered auto in the business of storing, parking, servicing, repairing, or selling autos unless the business is owned by the insured;
  - Anyone, other than partners, employees, lessees, or borrowers, while moving property from a covered auto;
  - Partners and employees for autos they own; and
- Anyone liable for a policy owner's conduct is an insured, but only to the extent of their liability.

Coverage Extensions – In addition, the liability section provides certain coverage extensions. The insurance company will pay the following *supplementary payments* in addition to the limit of insurance for property damage or bodily injury:

- All expenses the insurance provider incurs;
- The cost of bonds to release attachments;
- Up to $2,000 for bail bonds;
- Reasonable expenses sustained by the policy owner at the insurer's request, including up to $250 per day for time off work;
- Expenses taxed against the policy owner in any suit; and
- Accrued interest on any judgment.

A second coverage extension offers *out-of-state coverage* when a vehicle is driven in a state in which it is not registered. This extension provides increased liability protection to meet another state's financial responsibility requirements. It does not apply to carriers of property or people. If required, this extension also provides minimum amounts of other coverage, such as no-fault.

Exclusions – The liability coverage exclusions are shown in this section of the policy form. The coverage does not apply to:

- Intended or expected injury or damage;
- Contractual liability besides an insured contract;
- Duties under any disability benefits, workers compensation, unemployment, or similar law;
- Employer's liability and employee indemnification;
- Bodily injury to any fellow employee of the policy owner caused by a fellow employee's employment;
- Covered pollution expense or cost of property damage involving property that is transported or owned by an insured or in the insured's control, custody, or care;
- Property damage or bodily injury resulting from the operation of machinery or mobile equipment or equipment attached to or part of a vehicle that would be defined as mobile equipment if it were not subject to financial responsibility laws or other compulsory laws;
- Property moved by mechanical device unless the device is a hand truck or is attached to the covered vehicle;
- Losses resulting from work after it has been completed and is no longer in the hands of the policyholder (completed operations);
- Property damage or bodily injury caused by the handling of the property before or after it was moved;
- Losses because of pollution from operating a covered auto while pollutants are being loaded, unloaded, or transported from a covered auto. There is coverage when the pollution is from an object other than a covered auto, where the loss is caused by a covered auto;
- Stunts, demolition, or racing, including preparing for such activities; and
- War.

Limits of Insurance – The last section under *Section II – Liability Coverage* describes the limits of insurance. The limit of liability for property damage and bodily injury can be expressed as a single limit or split limit. A single limit defines the total amount the insurer will pay for all property damage or bodily injury, including any covered pollution expenses caused by a single accident.

Section III – Physical Damage Coverage

Coverage – Physical damage coverages available to the policy owner include the following:

- *Comprehensive coverage* pays for loss or damage to a covered auto by any cause other than overturn or collision;
- *Specified causes of loss coverage* will pay for loss to a covered auto if it resulted from lightning, fire, explosion, mischief or vandalism, theft, hail, windstorm, earthquake, or the burning, sinking, derailment, or collision of any conveyance transporting the covered auto;
- *Collision coverage* pays for losses to a covered auto caused by a collision with another object or overturn;
- *Towing coverage*, where the insurance provider will pay for labor costs incurred due to a disabled auto at the place of the disablement up to the towing limit of insurance listed in the Declarations. Coverage is provided only for passenger-type autos; and
- *Glass breakage (hitting an animal or bird, falling objects, or missiles)* is coverage for glass breakage, a loss caused by hitting an animal or bird or falling objects or missiles. Policy owners can collect for glass damage if the loss results from overturning the vehicle or a collision with an object.

The physical damage section provides *coverage extensions* for the following:

- *Transportation expenses* that would pay for substitute transportation, up to $20 per day for a maximum of $600, after the theft of a covered auto (private passenger type). The covered auto must be insured for comprehensive or specified causes of loss for this extension to be applied. This coverage included a 48-hour waiting period that lasts until the vehicle is returned or the insurance provider pays for the loss; and

- *Loss of use expenses* the insurer will pay for which a policy owner becomes legally liable for the loss of use of a vehicle hired or rented without a driver under a written rental contract. When coverage is purchased, this coverage extension pays for the damaged auto's loss of use up to $20 per day to a maximum of $600.

Exclusions – The exclusions found in the physical damage section of the business auto coverage form are as follows:

- War and military action;
- Nuclear hazard;
- Stunt, demolition, or racing activities;
- Freezing, wear and tear, mechanical breakdown, or tire damage (unless another covered loss caused it); and
- Loss to sound devices, such as audio-visual equipment, radar detection equipment, and other electronic equipment and accessories. However, permanently installed equipment intended solely for the reproduction of sound (e.g., a tape deck) is covered.

Limits of Insurance – The physical damage limit of insurance is the *lesser* of:

- The actual cash value of the covered vehicle at the time of the loss; or
- The cost of replacing or repairing the stolen or damaged property with other similar property.

The maximum paid for loss of electronic, audio, and video equipment is $1,000 for equipment permanently installed in the vehicle or removable from a permanently installed housing unit.

The *deductible* provision states that any loss will be decreased by the amount of the deductible listed in the Declarations. Any comprehensive deductible shown will not apply to losses caused by lightning or fire.

Section IV – Conditions

The following *conditions* apply:

- **Appraisal for physical damage coverage**;
- **Duties in the event of a loss, accident claim, or lawsuit**;
- **Legal action against the insurance company**;
- **Loss payment – physical damage coverage** — The insurance provider has the option to:
  - Pay for the replacement or repair of damaged property;
  - Return the stolen property and pay for any essential repairs; or
  - Take all or any part of the damaged property at an appraised or agreed value.
- **Subrogation** — The transfer of rights of recovery against others to the insurance company;
- **Fraud, misrepresentation, or concealment**;
- **Bankruptcy**;
- **No benefit to bailee – physical damage coverage**;
- **Liberalization**;
- **Other insurance** — If more than one policy applies to a loss, the policy will respond in the following ways:
  - **Primary insurance** — Owned auto, a trailer attached to an owned auto, when Hired Auto Physical Damage is selected and if liability is assumed in an insured contract;
  - **Excess insurance** — For the use of non-owned autos and when an owned trailer is attached to a non-owned auto;
- **Premium audit**;

- **Policy period, coverage territory** — The United States, its territories and possessions, Puerto Rico and Canada, or anywhere in the world if the covered auto is a private passenger auto rented, leased, hired, or borrowed without a driver for no more than 30 days. Any lawsuit must be based on the merits of the legal system within the United States and its territories and possessions, Puerto Rico, and Canada. Coverage also exists when a covered auto is in transit between locations); and
- **Two or more coverage forms or policies** — If more than one policy applies to a loss and is issued by the same insurer or affiliate, only the highest limit of liability will apply unless the policy is excess coverage.

Trailer Interchange Coverage

Trailer interchange coverage has no equivalent in either the business auto coverage form or the garage coverage form. Motor carriers regularly borrow or hire trailers from others with a written trailer interchange agreement. They require coverage for the trailer in their possession to cover the liability imposed upon them due to the contract. Coverage for loss or damage to property in the policyholder's control, custody, or care is usually excluded under liability coverage forms, including the business auto form. The trailer interchange coverage will cover loss or damage to a non-owned trailer in the policyholder's control, custody, or care if the insured is legally liable for the damage. Coverage can be provided for comprehensive or specified causes of loss and collision.

Exclusions – The trailer interchange coverage provides identical supplemental payments as the business auto policy, except for *costs related to bail bonds*. In addition, three types of exclusions apply to the trailer interchange coverage:

1. War or military action;
2. Nuclear hazard; and
3. Freezing, wear and tear, mechanical breakdown, or road damage to tires.

Limits of Insurance – The most the insurance provider will pay for any one trailer is the *least* of the following, minus any deductible that applies:

- The actual cash value;
- The cost to repair the damage or replace with like kind and quality; or
- The limit of insurance listed on the declarations page.

Selected Endorsements

Several optional endorsements are available to revise the coverage in the commercial auto coverage part.

Additional Insured – When a policy owner has leased autos, they may use the *Lessor – Additional Insured and Loss Payee* endorsement to provide liability and physical damage coverage for the lessor's interests as an additional insured. This endorsement was previously called Additional Insured-Lessor.

Auto Medical Payments Coverage – Commercial auto coverage forms do not automatically include coverage for medical payments. Typically, any individual who occupies the vehicle would be covered under workers compensation. Policy owners can add this coverage to a commercial auto policy through the *auto medical payments coverage* endorsement.

Hired Autos Specified as Covered Autos You Own – Policyholders can add this endorsement to Commercial Auto policies to add coverage for specified hired autos. Any hired automobile scheduled in the endorsement will be treated as if they were covered autos owned by the policyholder.

Individual Named Insured – The *Individual Named Insured* endorsement is used with the Business Auto and Motor Carrier coverage forms to insure a sole proprietor. Any owned private passenger vehicle (auto, van, or pickup not used in business) covered by the policy will include family members as insureds by adding this endorsement. Coverage is also granted to the policy owner and family members for the use of a non-owned auto subject to the similar exclusions found in the personal auto policy.

Physical damage coverage is also provided to the policy owner's family members for owned private passenger vehicles and non-owned autos. However, physical damage coverage for non-owned trailers will have a limit of up to $500. The endorsement also eliminates the fellow employee exclusion from the liability section of the Commercial Auto Coverage Form.

Mobile Equipment – In the Business Auto Coverage Form, mobile equipment is insured for liability when being carried or towed by a covered auto. Suppose a land vehicle meets the mobile equipment definition. However, because of where or how it is used, it becomes subject to compulsory insurance like it were an auto. In that scenario, a policy owner could have a coverage problem. For example, an excavator must have mandatory insurance. It must be driven on a public road to get from one part of a work site to another. When the policy owner has a Symbol 7 (Specified Auto) listed in the Declarations, that excavator would need to be included on the policy owner's vehicle schedule to be covered for liability. If it is not listed on the declarations page, a solution would be to use this endorsement for an added premium. The excavator would be described explicitly in the endorsement and granted coverage.

Covered autos liability coverage does not apply to property damage, bodily injury, or covered pollution expense or cost from operating equipment or machinery that is on, attached to, or part of any of the covered autos.

Broadened Coverage (Garage) – This optional coverage can be attached to a Garage Policy to add a package of additional coverages. The additional coverages include the following:

- Fire Legal liability;
- Personal and Advertising Injury;
- Incidental Medical malpractice;
- Limited Non-owned Watercraft liability; and
- Broader Host Liquor Liability.

Deductibles Liability – *Deductibles liability* is an optional endorsement that can be used to add a deductible to the commercial auto liability coverage. Deductibles can be applied for bodily injury or property damage. The bodily injury deductible can apply on a per-accident or per-person basis. In contrast, insurers can only write the property damage liability deductible on a per-accident basis.

Employees as Insureds – The *employees as insureds* endorsement will provide the policy owner's employees additional protection while using a vehicle not owned, borrowed, or hired for the insured business. For instance, an employee uses a personal auto to run an errand on behalf of the insured business owner. Employees are not covered under the commercial auto coverage section while using their own vehicles during the course of business because of one of the exceptions listed in the permission clause in the Who is an Insured portion of the policy.

Drive Other Car – This endorsement extends coverage from Business Auto, Business Auto Physical Damage, Motor Carrier, and Garage coverage forms to vehicles not owned, borrowed, or hired by the named insured and puts no stipulation that use must take place during the course of business. Because a corporate entity could have many people, only those listed (and their spouses while a resident of the same household) are provided coverage.

Garage Coverage Form – Garagekeepers Insurance

Businesses that store, park, repair, service, or sell vehicles do not qualify for coverage under the other Insurance Services Office forms. Therefore, specialized coverage is required. Similar to the Business Auto Coverage Form, the *Garage Coverage Form* provides the same basic coverage, and special coverages developed to meet these unique needs. Types of risks that qualify for coverage under the Garage Coverage Form include the following:

- Franchised and nonfranchised auto dealers;
- Commercial trailer, truck, and truck-tractor dealers;
- Mobile home, recreational vehicle, and motorcycle dealers;
- Service stations;
- Automotive repair shops;
- Car washes; and
- Public parking facilities and storage garages.

Section I – Covered Autos

This section of the Garage Coverage Form defines the covered auto designation symbols. Although some descriptions are similar to the Business Auto Coverage Form, the numerical symbols vary. Some additional descriptions are added that apply specifically to garage operations.

The table on the following page includes the auto designation symbols used in *Section I – Covered Autos* of the Garage Coverage Form.

AUTO DESIGNATION SYMBOLS FOUND IN THE GARAGE COVERAGE FORM	
21=	Any auto
22=	Owned autos only
23=	Owned private passenger autos only
24=	Owned autos other than private passenger autos only
25=	Owned autos subject to no-fault
26=	Owned autos subject to a compulsory uninsured motorists law
27=	Specifically described autos
28=	Hired autos only (rented, leased, borrowed or hired by the policyowner, but not autos owned by partners, employees, or members of an LLC)
29=	Non-owned autos used in your garage business (for vehicles not owned, rented, leased, borrowed, or hired by the policyowner also applies to vehicles owned by partners, employees and members of an LLC)
30=	Autos left for safekeeping, storage, repair, or service (used to provide garagekeepers coverage for employees or customers and members of their household who pay for services)
31=	Dealer's autos (physical damage coverage)

Newly Acquired Autos – When symbols *21, 22, 23, 24, 25, or 26* are listed for any of the coverages on the declarations page, the coverage applies to any additional vehicles of the same type the insured acquires for the rest of the policy period.

However, if *Symbol 27* appears in the Declarations, coverage for newly acquired vehicles will be limited to 30 days if every owned auto is covered unless the vehicle is a replacement.

Certain Trailers and Temporary Substitutes – If liability coverage is provided, insurers will also cover certain types of other autos for liability. These other vehicles include:

- Trailers possessing a load capacity of 2,000 pounds or less; and
- Substitute vehicles used temporarily while a covered auto is out of service due to destruction, loss, servicing, repair, or breakdown.

Section II – Liability Coverage

Section II — Liability Coverage is split into two parts:

1. Garage Operations — Other than Covered Autos; and
2. Garage Operations — Covered Autos.

As with other liability coverages, an accident must result from property damage or bodily injury. The policy owner must be legally liable for the loss of coverage to apply. Also, the *Garage Operations — Other than Covered Autos* form requires that the damage or loss directly results from the policy owner's garage operations. The *Garage Operations — Covered Autos* form protects the policy owner from losses resulting from the use, maintenance, or ownership of covered autos. Pollution costs or expenses are also covered under the liability coverage section.

The definition of an insured is also in the liability section of the Garage Coverage Form. The insured individuals differ according to whether the loss results from garage operations or covered auto exposure. For covered auto exposures, insured means:

1. The organization or individual named in the Declarations;
2. Individuals operating a covered auto with the policy owner's permission;
3. Any individual liable for the conduct of the policy owner; or
4. The insured's employee using a non-owned covered auto in the insured's personal or business affairs.

Owners (including employees and their families) of vehicles the policy owner borrows are not covered under the policy.

When the insured business is an auto dealership, customers are only insured for liability up to any mandatory financial responsibility law. Suppose the customer has primary coverage that is less than the financial responsibility law. In that case, the policy will cover the excess of any loss up to the required limit. Otherwise, their primary insurance will process the claim. Dealerships who provide full liability coverage to their customers, despite any other insurance, do so by paying an additional premium.

For garage operations (excluding covered autos), an insured refers to:

- The organization or individual named in the Declarations; or
- Partners, employees, officers, directors, and shareholders while acting within the scope of their duties.

The coverage extensions provide the same supplemental payments and out-of-state coverage extension included in the Business Auto Coverage Form.

The exclusions found in the Business Auto Coverage Form are the same as the liability exclusions found in the Garage Coverage Form. The exclusions for completed operations, handling of property, operations, and movement of property by a mechanical device are not found in the Garage Coverage Form. However, several liability exclusions in the Garage Coverage Form differ from those in the Business Auto Coverage Form. There are also other exclusions only in the Garage Coverage Form. We will discuss these differences below:

- **Expected or Intended Injury** — There is an exception to this exclusion when the property damage or bodily injury results from using reasonable force to protect property or individuals.
- **Employee Indemnification and Employer's Liability** — This exclusion is broader in that it excludes bodily injury resulting from employment-related practices, such as harassment, discrimination, termination, etc.
- **Care, Custody, or Control** — This exclusion is broadened to exclude property occupied, rented, loaned, or held for sale by the policy owner.
- **Leased Autos** — This exclusion is not in the Business Auto Coverage Form. It excludes autos rented or leased to others. However, autos rented to customers while their vehicles are serviced will be covered.
- **Pollution Exclusion Applicable to Garage Operations (Other than Covered Autos)** — There is no coverage for loss or expenses incurred because of dispersal, discharge, seepage, or escape of pollutants at locations used or owned by the insured or for contaminants handled, transported, stored, disposed of, or processed as waste by the insured or the insured's contractor. However, there is coverage for fumes, smoke, or heat that result from a hostile fire.
- **Pollution Exclusion Applicable to Garage Operations (Covered Autos)** — The pollution exclusion found in the Garage Coverage Form is similar to the one in the Business Auto Coverage Form.
- **Aircraft or Watercraft** — There is no liability coverage for aircraft or watercraft, except watercraft ashore on the policy owner's garage premises.
- **Defective Products** — There is no liability coverage for property damage to the policy owner's products resulting from an existing defect in the product. The policy defines a product as goods or services the insured manufactured or sold in the garage business, including providing or failing to provide instructions or warnings.
- **Work Performed** — No liability coverage is provided for property damage to work performed by the policy owner if the damage results from the work or the materials or parts used. Work performed is defined as work that someone performs for the policy owner, including providing or failing to provide instructions or warnings.
- **Loss of Use** — Property damage under the Garage Coverage Form includes loss of use. However, there are situations in which loss of use is not covered. Loss of use does not cover property that is not physically damaged because of delays or failure to perform according to the terms of an agreement or contract. It also does not cover any deficiency, defect, inadequacy, or dangerous condition in the product or work performed. Loss of use from sudden and accidental damage from a deficiency or defect is covered.
- **Products Recall** — Insurers will not cover any loss or expense incurred due to a recall or withdrawal of the policy owner's product.

The liability coverage limit includes an aggregate insurance limit that applies to Garage Operations (Other than Covered Autos). This coverage is the total amount the insurer will pay for all covered losses during the policy term. Also, there is a per accident limit that is the most the insurer will pay for a single loss. There is no distinction between property damage or bodily injury losses. The limit of liability insurance that applies to Garage Operations (Covered Autos) is also stated as a per accident limit; it is not subject to an annual aggregate.

Garage Liability Coverage has a deductible provision that is not included in the Business Auto Coverage Form. This deductible applies to completed operations. A $100 deductible applies for property damage to vehicles resulting from work performed by the insured business.

Section III – Garagekeepers

Garagekeepers coverage insures against damage for which the policy owner is liable to a customer's auto left in the policy owner's control, custody, and care for storage, parking, repairs, or service. This coverage is typically excluded unless this coverage is purchased). This section is triggered by the auto designation *Symbol 30*.

A *customer's auto* refers to a land motor vehicle, trailer, or semi-trailer lawfully in the policy owner's possession with or without the owner's consent. The vehicle must be held in the policy owner's custody for safekeeping, storage, repair, or service. It also includes autos owned by the policy owner's employees, or their family members, if they are paying for services performed.

The causes of loss that insurers may cover include:

- **Comprehensive** — All loss to a customer's auto except overturn or collision;
- **Specified Causes of Loss** — Loss to a customer's auto due to lightning, fire, explosion, theft, vandalism, or mischief; and
- **Collision** — A customer's auto loss caused by overturning or hitting an object.

The insurance provider has a right and duty to defend the policy owner against those seeking damages unless the insurance does not apply. The insurer can investigate and settle any claims as they deem appropriate. The duty to defend ceases when the limits of insurance are exhausted.

Unless noted otherwise in the Declarations, the garagekeepers coverage is triggered only when the policy owner is legally liable for the damages. This option is known as the *Legal Liability (or Standard) Coverage* option. Suppose the policy owner would prefer the coverage to be triggered without regard to liability. In that case, a *Direct Coverage* option must be activated on the declarations page and the additional premium paid.

Coverage Extensions for Garagekeepers insurance are identical to those in the Business Auto Policy:

- All expenses incurred by the insurance provider;
- Cost of bonds to release attachments in lawsuits against the policy owner defended by the insurer;
- Reasonable expenses sustained by the insured at the insurance provider's request, including $250 per day for time off from work;
- Costs taxed against the insured in lawsuits against the insured defended by the insurance provider; and
- Interest on the total amount of a judgment accrued after entry of a judgment in lawsuits against the policy owner defended by the insurer.

Garagekeepers insurance has the following *exclusions*:

- **Contractual obligations** — Liability resulting from an agreement in which the policy owner accepted responsibility for loss;
- **Theft** — Theft or conversion by the policy owner, shareholders, or employees;
- **Defective parts** — Defective materials or parts;
- **Faulty work** — Faulty work done by or for the policy owner; and
- **Loss to any of the following**:
  - Tape decks or other sound reproducing devices unless permanently installed;
  - Records, tapes, or other sound reproducing equipment;
  - Telephone, sound receiving equipment, 2-way mobile radios, citizens' band radios, scanning monitor receivers, and accessories for such equipment, including antennas, unless permanently installed where the manufacturer would typically install a radio; and
  - Equipment used for radar detection.

Section IV – Physical Damage

Section IV — Physical Damage Coverage for non-dealers is the same as the Business Auto Physical Damage coverage. However, the Garage Coverage Form also includes coverage for auto dealerships, which covers autos in transit or held for sale.

Like other Commercial Auto coverage forms, the Garage Coverage policy has a unique set of its own Declarations.

Based on the type of risk insured, one of the following supplemental schedules is required to be attached to the policy:

- *The Auto Dealers Supplemental Schedule* includes specific information regarding coverage for a customer's liability or damage to a customer's vehicles, the classes of vehicle operators, and physical damage coverage on insured vehicles. The supplemental schedule also designates whether liability coverage for pick-up and delivery of automobiles is insured and whether coverage is written on a reporting form basis.
- *The Non-Dealers and Trailer Dealers Supplemental Schedule* contains information on the garagekeepers coverage (damage to a customer's vehicles), policyholder's payroll, owned vehicle coverage, hired and non-owned vehicle coverage, and reporting form information.

Physical damage coverage applies to the policyholder's vehicles, such as tow trucks or vehicles held for sale. Autos held for sale are covered when auto designation *Symbol 31* is shown in the Declarations. The physical damage coverage for comprehensive, specified causes of loss and collision is identical to that found in the Business Auto Coverage Form. The specified causes of loss are not as limited as the coverage provided under a Garagekeepers policy.

The glass breakage provision contained in the Garage Coverage Form is identical to that found in the Business Auto Coverage Form. Also, the loss of use coverage extension is the same as the provision contained in the Business Auto Coverage Form. However, this provision applies only to vehicles rented or hired without a driver.

Under the limits of insurance provision of the physical damage coverage, the insurance provider will pay the cost to repair or replace a covered auto or the actual cash value, whichever is less. This provision is identical to the one in the Business Auto Coverage Form. However, an additional provision, unique to the Garage Coverage Form, applies only to auto dealerships. When the business shown on the declarations page is an auto dealership, a maximum limit of insurance is listed for each covered location. This maximum limit only applies to comprehensive and specified causes of loss coverage. There is also a maximum limit if the insurance for loss was in transit, irrespective of the number of vehicles involved.

Because a dealer's inventory of autos varies, the Garage Coverage Form also contains a reporting form provision that allows the amount insured at each location to fluctuate. The policy owner must make monthly or quarterly reports itemizing the values at each location. The policy owner's premium is based on these itemized amounts. Suppose, at the time of loss, the insurer identifies that the actual values are more than those reported by the policy owner in their last report. In that scenario, the policy owner will pay part of the loss based on the amount that the previously reported values bear to the actual values at the time of loss.

For example, the policyholder's last report indicated a value of $300,000. The actual value at the time of the loss was $400,000. Additionally, a loss of $24,000 takes place. In this scenario, the policyholder would have to pay $6,000 of the loss, while the insurer would only pay $18,000 of the loss ($300,000/$400,000 = 3/4 x $24,000 = $18,000).

A reporting form may not be necessary when the dealer's inventory is relatively stable throughout the year. Dealers can use the non-reporting form to list a stated coverage limit per location. When the actual values exceed the values listed in the policy at the time of a loss, the insurer will only pay the proportion of the loss the policy limits bear to the actual values.

Under the deductible provision in the physical damage coverage section of the Garage Coverage Form, the amount of any loss or damage will decrease by the deductible amount listed on the declarations page. The deductible for comprehensive or specified causes of loss only applies to losses caused by vandalism, mischief, or theft. There is also a per loss deductible for comprehensive or specified causes of loss. When the business is a non-dealer, the deductible for a comprehensive cause of loss does not apply to losses resulting from fire or lightning.

Some of the exclusions for Garage Physical Damage coverage are identical to those found in the Business Auto Physical Damage coverage section. These exclusions include damage or loss resulting from war or military action; nuclear hazard; freezing; wear and tear; mechanical or electrical breakdown; and blowout, punctures, or other road damage to tires. In addition, the following exclusions are either slightly different from those found in the Business Auto Coverage Form or are only applicable to the Garage Coverage Form:

- **Auto Leased or Rented to Others** — There is no coverage for autos leased to others, except for the policy owner's customers who have left their vehicle with the policy owner for repair or service.
- **False Pretense** — No coverage is provided if the policy owner voluntarily parts with a covered auto because of someone's scheme, trick, or false pretense, or for any loss the policy owner may suffer from acquiring an auto from a seller who did not have legal title. This exclusion is commonly called the Trick and Device exclusion. False Pretense Coverage can be added by endorsement.
- **Expected Profits** — This exclusion applies only to auto dealer risks and excludes expected profits. Insurers will only reimburse a dealership on a wholesale basis for loss or damage to an auto they expected to sell. Reimbursement would not be based on the dealer's expected profit if the dealer sold the auto.
- **Other Locations** — This exclusion applies only to auto dealers. It would exclude coverage for loss or damage to a covered auto at a location not in the Declarations. The loss or damage must have occurred more than 45 days after the policy owner started using the new location.
- **Transporting Autos** — This exclusion applies only to auto dealers. It excludes coverage for loss to autos while being transported or driven from the point of purchase to the final destination if the distance exceeds 50 miles. In addition, there is no coverage for loss or damage to a covered auto if caused by collision or upset of the vehicle transporting it. Auto dealers can purchase coverage for this exclusion for an additional premium.

Section V – Garage Conditions

The *Garage Conditions* are the same as those found in the Business Auto Coverage Form, except for the policy period and the coverage territory condition. The Business Auto Coverage Form states that accidents and losses occurring during the policy period and within the coverage territory are covered. However, in the Garage Coverage Form, the wording is slightly different. It refers to property damage and bodily injury within the coverage territory. This distinction is to clarify liability associated with *Garage Operations – Other Than Covered Autos* coverage. The garage form refers to covered pollution costs or expenses resulting from accidents.

Because the garage form offers product liability coverage, the language is revised to afford the policy owner coverage for losses associated with their products sold in the coverage territory. Policy owners must also file the original lawsuit in one of the places located in the coverage territory.

Section VI – Definitions

The *Definitions* section is technically the last section of the Garage Coverage Form. Still, it is helpful to understand these terms before reviewing each section below. The definitions are presented first in this book.

Most of the definitions used in the garage form are similar to the Business Auto Coverage Form, so be sure to review the definitions as needed. Some of the definitions unique to the garage form include the following:

Garage Operations – *Garage operations* refer to the use, maintenance, or ownership of locations for garage business, including adjoining roads and other accesses. It also includes the use, maintenance, or ownership of covered autos and all necessary or incidental operations.

Products – *Products* are goods manufactured or sold by the policyholder in the garage business. It also includes the failure to provide instructions or warnings.

Work performed by the insured – *Work performed by the insured* includes work that someone performed on the insured's behalf and the provision of or failure to provide instructions or warnings.

Truckers Coverage

A *trucker* is an individual who drives a truck as an occupation. These drivers have several special insurance needs that other drivers may not have.

Businesses that use their vehicles to transport goods for others require specialized insurance coverage that is not available through the business auto or garage coverage forms. Some of these additional coverages are required due to the very nature of the job. Others are necessary because of governmental regulations. The *truckers coverage form* was created to address the unique insurance needs of these businesses.

Businesses that haul goods for others are called *truckers* or *carriers for hire*. There are two classes of carriers for hire, both of which qualify for coverage under the truckers coverage form:

1. Common carriers who haul goods for anyone; and
2. Contract carriers who have written contracts with other companies to transport their merchandise

Businesses that use their vehicles to carry their own goods are known as *private carriers* and cannot be issued coverage under the truckers coverage form. Private carriers can be insured under the motor carrier coverage form or the business auto coverage form.

The truckers coverage form is identical to the business auto coverage and garage coverage forms. This coverage requires a separate declarations page and the nuclear energy liability exclusion (broad form). The truckers coverage form has one expanded definition and two new definitions not contained in the business auto coverage form:

Private passenger type — Includes a private passenger or station wagon type of auto, including a van or pickup if not used for business.

Trailer — This expanded definition from the business auto coverage form includes a semi-trailer or a dolly used to convert a semi-trailer into a trailer. The trailer also includes a container regarding trailer interchange coverage.

Section I

Section I – Covered Autos of the truckers form includes specific auto designation symbols that define the type of vehicles that insurers can cover under the policy. These symbols' descriptions are similar to those in the business auto coverage form. However, the designation numbers are different. The designation for owned private passenger vehicles is not included in the truckers coverage form.

Section II

Section II — Liability Coverage includes the same coverage, exclusions, extensions, and limit of insurance as the business auto coverage form. However, the definition of an insured is slightly different. The truckers coverage form includes liability coverage for partners and employees if they lend the insured a vehicle, *other than a private passenger vehicle*. Under the business auto coverage form, there is no liability coverage for any vehicle borrowed from partners or employees.

As in the business auto coverage form, any borrowed or hired trailers do not have to be attached to a covered auto owned for the owner of the trailer to be considered an insured for liability. The trailer can be attached to any vehicle considered a power unit, including hired and non-owned vehicles, if designated in the Declarations.

Section III

Section III — Physical Damage includes the same coverage as discussed for the business auto coverage form. However, one additional exclusion in the truckers physical damage coverage is not included in the business auto physical damage coverage section. This additional exclusion states that there will not be any coverage for a covered auto while in the possession of anyone else under a trailer interchange contract. This coverage has to be selected explicitly by the policy owner.

Designation Symbols

The following provisions in Section I are the same as those in the business auto coverage form (except the numerical symbols). If symbol 41, 42, 43, 44, 45, or 59 is listed for any coverages in the Declarations, coverage applies to any additional vehicles of the same type the insured acquires throughout the policy period.

DESIGNATION SYMBOLS FOUND IN THE TRUCKERS COVERAGE FORM	
41=	Any auto (used only for liability coverage)
42=	Owned autos only
43=	Owned commercial autos only
44=	Owned autos subject to no-fault
45=	Owned autos subject to a compulsory uninsured motorists law
46=	Specifically described autos
47=	Hired autos only
48=	Trailers in your possession under a written trailer or equipment interchange agreement
49=	Your trailers in the possession of anyone else under a written trailer interchange agreement
50=	Non-owned autos only
59=	Mobile equipment subject to compulsory, financial responsibility, or other motor vehicle insurance laws only

However, if designation symbol 46 is used, coverage for newly obtained vehicles is limited to 30 days and only if every owned vehicle is covered or the auto is a replacement. When symbol 42 or 43 is used to cover liability, coverage is also provided for non-owned trailers, including semitrailers connected to an owned power unit.

Liability Coverage

If liability coverage is provided, certain types of other vehicles are covered automatically for liability. This coverage includes mobile equipment while being transported by a covered auto and trailers possessing a load capacity of 2,000 pounds or less. Temporary substitute non-owned vehicles used in place of an out-of-service auto are also covered.

The difference between a semi-trailer and a trailer is that a semi-trailer must be attached to a fifth-wheel coupling device (dolly) that becomes the semi-trailer's front wheels. In contrast, a trailer has both front and rear wheels. A service or utility trailer can be either a trailer or a semi-trailer but is limited to a load capacity of 2,000 pounds or less.

This form also provides liability coverage to the owner of a borrowed vehicle (other than a trailer). It also covers a non-owned trailer not attached to a power unit if used exclusively in the policy owner's business or according to the operating rights awarded by a public authority.

The truckers coverage form's *conditions* are identical to those in the business auto coverage form. However, the truckers form includes an additional condition. The *Other Insurance – Primary and Excess Insurance Provision* specifies that the truckers liability coverage will be considered primary insurance when:

- A covered auto is an owned auto, not hired or loaned out to another;
- A covered auto is hired or borrowed by the policy owner for use in business as a trucker and used according to operating rights awarded by a public authority;
- A covered trailer is attached to a covered auto for which this coverage is primary;
- A non-owned trailer is not connected to a power unit and is being used by the policy owner in the business as a trucker; or
- If liability for damage has been assumed under an insured contract or agreement.

The truckers liability coverage will be considered *excess* when

- A covered auto (not borrowed or hired) is not owned by the named insured;
- An owned covered auto is borrowed or hired by the policy owner from another trucker;
- A covered trailer is attached to a covered auto for which this coverage is excess; or
- A covered trailer is attached to an auto that is not covered.

Under the liability coverage section of the truckers coverage form, the following are *not* defined explicitly as an insured:

- Other truckers subject to motor carrier insurance laws that meet these requirements through other than auto insurance;
- Other truckers whose coverage is not considered primary insurance for owners of borrowed vehicles; or
- Any water, rail, or air carrier for a detached trailer loaded, unloaded, or transported by the carrier.

Commercial Carrier Regulations

The state and the federal government have implemented regulations specific to trucking risks for truckers who travel within the boundaries of a single state and across state lines. The *Federal Motor Carrier Safety Administration (FMCSA)* is the federal body that regulates interstate truckers. Federal regulation also applies to interstate or intrastate truckers that transport hazardous materials.

The Motor Carrier Act of 1980

The *Motor Carrier Act of 1980* established the federal regulations that apply to common carriers hauling goods for a fee, contract carriers transporting goods of others under contract, and freight forwarders. The act establishes the minimum financial responsibility requirements for carriers of hazardous property and all for-hire interstate carriers.

These minimum requirements for haulers of property are:

- $1 million for the transportation of oil and specific categories of hazardous material or waste by private (haul their own goods) or for-hire carriers in interstate commerce;
- $750,000 for the transportation of nonhazardous property by for-hire carriers in interstate commerce; and
- $5 million for transporting other specifically defined hazardous materials and waste, gas, explosives, or radioactive material hauled by private or for-hire carriers. This amount applies to both interstate and intrastate carriers.

Endorsement for Motor Carrier Policies of Insurance for Public Liability

The FMCSA has developed an endorsement, MCS-90, that has to be attached to every motor carrier's policy under its jurisdiction. This endorsement ensures that motor carriers comply with the federally mandated public liability coverage, including property damage, bodily injury, and environmental restoration. This endorsement allows the insurance provider to seek reimbursement from the policyholder to pay a claim for public liability if the insurer would not cover the claim under the policy without the MCS-90 endorsement.

Environmental restoration is not usually covered in commercial auto policies unless it meets specific parameters defined in the policy. The environmental restoration definition in the MCS-90 endorsement is broad and includes coverage for damage done by commodities transported by a motor carrier. The endorsement uses the word commodity instead of pollutants, so the mitigation and cleanup expenses could be incurred for any commodity hauled by a carrier that is introduced into the environment.

Chapter Review

This chapter explained the different forms available for commercial auto insurance, including business auto, garage, truckers, and motor carriers. Let's review them:

COMMERCIAL AUTO	
Commercial Auto Coverage Form	• Covers commercial auto exposures except for garages, truckers, and motor carriers • *Section I – Covered Autos* - auto designation symbols that define the types of vehicles insured • *Section II – Liability Coverage* - designates how much a policy will pay for property damage or bodily injury to third parties • *Section III – Physical Damage Coverage* • *Section IV – Conditions* • *Section V – Definitions*

Garage Coverage Form	<ul><li>Covers businesses that regularly have autos of others in their care, custody, or control</li><li>*Section I – Covered Autos* - auto designation symbols that define the types of vehicles insured</li><li>*Section II – Liability:*<ul><li>Garage Operations – Other than Covered Autos</li><li>Garage Operations – Covered Autos</li></ul></li><li>*Section III – Garagekeepers* - covers damage to a customer's auto left in the insured's care:<ul><li>Comprehensive</li><li>Specified cause of loss</li><li>Collision</li></ul></li><li>*Section IV – Physical Damage* - similar to the Business Auto Coverage Form with additional exclusions</li><li>*Section V – Garage Conditions* - similar to the Business Auto Coverage Form</li><li>*Section VI – Definitions*</li></ul>
Truckers Coverage	<ul><li>Covers truckers or carriers for hire</li><li>Carriers for hire include:<ul><li>Common carriers who haul goods for anyone; and</li><li>Contract carriers who have written contracts with other companies to transport their merchandise</li></ul></li><li>*Section I – Covered Autos* - auto designation symbols that define the types of vehicles insured under the policy</li><li>*Section II – Liability*</li><li>*Section III – Physical Damage* - covers damage to a customer's auto left in the insured's care</li></ul>

CHAPTER 16:
Other Commercial Coverages

This chapter continues our discussion of commercial insurance by introducing the concepts of commercial crime, equipment breakdown protection coverage, and commercial inland marine policies. You will learn about coverage forms for each policy type and applicable terms and definitions.

- Commercial Crime
- Equipment Breakdown Protection Coverage
- Commercial Inland Marine

Commercial Crime

Insurers can add crime insurance to a commercial package policy or write it on a monoline basis. The crime program fills in some of the gaps in the building and business personal property form as they pertain to crime losses. Crime insurance is written on an all-risk or open peril basis. Both the basic and broad causes of loss forms do not cover the peril of theft. The special cause of loss form contains exclusions for dishonest acts of workers and sublimits for theft of patents, dies, molds, stamps, jewelry, and furs.

The crime program presents policies in two major sections: commercial and government entities. The insured can choose a discovery or loss sustained form for each section. Each form has different coverage triggers, and these trigger differences (occurrence and claims-made) are similar to the general liability form.

The crime policy consists of separate coverages that can be selected by the insured, regardless of the form chosen. Each coverage has its own insuring agreement, conditions, and exclusions. The declarations page of a crime policy activates the applicable coverages within the policy. As an example, a crime declarations page will illustrate the following coverage choices:

CRIME DECLARATIONS PAGE	
Employee Theft (Employee Dishonesty)	$_____
Alteration and Forgery	$_____
Inside-Theft of Money and Securities	$_____
Inside-Robbery or Safe Burglary of Other Property	$_____
Outside the Premises	$_____
Computer Fraud	$_____
Fund Transfer Fraud	$_____
Counterfeit Paper Currency and Money Order	$_____

Definitions

Employee — *Employee* can mean any of the following:

- A natural person in the insured's service for 30 days after termination;
- A temporary worker hired from an employment contractor;
- Managers, directors, or trustees performing acts within the usual duties of an employee; or
- Former managers, employees, partners, directors, or trustees performing consulting services for the insured.

Discover or discovered — The time when an insured first becomes aware of the facts that would lead a sensible person to assume that a loss occurred.

Banking premises — The inside of a premises occupied by a banking institution or similar establishment.

Occurrence — A single act or a series of acts that may or may not involve individuals.

Premises — The inside of a premises in which the insured conducts business

Money — *Money* denotes currency, coins, banknotes with a face value, register checks, travelers' checks, and money orders sold to the public.

Funds — *Funds* include money and securities.

Other property — *Other property* means property aside from money or securities.

Tangible property — *Tangible property* denotes any other property that has built-in value.

Securities — *Securities* are negotiable and non-negotiable contracts or instruments representing either money or other property such as revenue, tickets, tokens, other stamps, and evidence of debt issued in relation to credit cards or charge cards that are not issued by the insured.

Leased employee — The term *leased employee* may also be helpful to know in this context. Employee leasing is a contractual arrangement in which a professional employer organization (PEO), also referred to as a leasing company, is the official employer. While the leaser manages the work, the leasing company assumes additional responsibilities, including reporting employment taxes and wages. Sometimes, a PEO provides leasers with more competitive health care and workers compensation coverage rates.

Theft — *Theft* refers to any act of stealing, including burglary and robbery.

Burglary — *Burglary* is the crime of forced entry into or out of another person's premises by an individual or individuals with criminal intent. Insurance policies covering the peril of burglary require that, after a loss, there are observable signs of forced entry or exit from the premises.

Robbery — *Robbery* is the taking of property from the custody and care of an individual by someone who caused or threatened to cause that person bodily harm.

Crime Coverages

Common policy provisions that apply to crime coverage forms (both discovery and loss sustained) include the following *general exclusions*:

- **Acts carried out by the insured, the insured's partners or members** — Loss resulting from acts carried out by the insured or partners, or members of the insured, as well as the actions of employees, representatives, managers, or directors identified by the insured before the policy period;
- **Acts of managers, trustees, employees, or representatives**;
- **Acts of employees identified by the insured before the policy period**;
- **Confidential information** — Loss resulting from illicit disclosure of the insured's or other person's confidential information (e.g., customer lists, trade secrets, or patents);
- **Government action** — Loss from seizure or destruction of property due to a governmental authority;
- **Indirect losses** — Expenses incurred while determining the amount of loss;
- **Legal fees, expenses, and costs** — Legal expenses associated with legal action;
- **Nuclear hazards**;
- **Pollution** — Loss or damage resulting from or caused by pollution, including seepage, dispersal, discharge, release, or escape of any solid, liquid, gaseous or thermal pollutant (such as waste, chemicals, acids, fumes, vapor, or smoke); and
- **Military action and war** — Losses or damage caused by military action, war, revolution, rebellion, and similar actions.

Specific individuals not covered under commercial crime policies include employees, independent contractors, and officers.

Employee Theft – *Employee Theft* covers losses caused by the theft of covered property by employees. Covered property under this form includes money, securities, and property aside from money or securities.

The policy contains an extension of coverage that applies for up to 90 days to employees who are temporarily outside the coverage area. One additional condition articulates that coverage on any employee is immediately canceled when the insured finds out the employee is involved in a dishonest act, whether or not the action occurred before employment.

The following exclusions apply:

- Loss caused by a worker whose coverage was previously canceled under similar coverage and never reinstated;
- Losses that can only be proven through an accounting of profit and loss or a shortage in inventory;
- Losses caused by trading; and
- Losses caused by the fraudulent issuing, signing, canceling, or failing to cancel a warehouse receipt.

Inside the Premises (Theft of Money and Securities) – *Inside the Premises (Theft of Money and Securities)* covers the loss of money and securities from inside the premises or banking premises caused directly by theft, disappearance, or destruction. Coverage also applies to damage to the premises or its exterior and damage or loss to a locked cash box, cash drawer, cash register, vault, or safe inside the premises caused by actual or attempted theft.

In addition to those in the general provisions, several additional *exclusions* also apply to this coverage. This insuring agreement does not cover losses caused by:

- Fire;
- Errors in accounting or arithmetic or omissions;
- Surrendering of property in any purchase or exchange;
- Loss of money from a money-operated device, unless the machine is equipped with a continuous deposit recording mechanism;
- Loss or damage to motor vehicles, semi-trailers, or trailers, or accessories and equipment attached to them;
- Voluntarily parting with any property or inducement;
- Loss of property resulting from unauthorized instructions or the threat of bodily injury after it is transferred to another individual or place outside the premises or banking facility (this exclusion does not apply to covered property in a messenger's care or custody);
- Malicious mischief or vandalism; or
- Voluntarily parting with a title to possess property.

Inside the premises (Robbery or Safe Burglary of Other Property) covers loss or damage to other property inside the premises caused by an actual or attempted robbery of a custodian or from a vault or safe inside the premises.

Outside the Premises (Theft of Money and Securities) – *Outside the Premises (Theft of Money and Securities)* insuring agreements cover loss caused directly by theft, disappearance, or destruction of money, securities, and other property outside the premises in the custody and care of an armored motor vehicle company a or messenger. Exclusions are comparable to the inside the premises insuring agreements. The special limitation of $5,000 per occurrence to the same kinds of property is applied.

Conditions

The following conditions are found in the Crime General Provisions Form:

- **Consolidation – Merger** — If the insured acquires additional premises or employees because of a consolidation or merger, the policy will automatically cover them, provided the insured notifies the company in writing within 30 days and pays the added premium.
- **Coverage Extensions** — Coverage extensions are considered part of the limits of insurance, not additional limits unless otherwise noted.
- **Discovery Period for Loss** — Losses will only be paid if identified no later than one year following the end of the policy period.
- **Duties in Cases of Loss** — The insured must:
  1. Notify the insurance provider as soon as possible following a loss.
  2. Agree to an examination under oath if requested by the insurer.
  3. Provide a sworn detailed proof of loss to the insurance provider within 120 days.
  4. Cooperate with the insurance provider in any investigation of settlement.
  5. In addition to the other requirements, the insured must file a crime report with the proper law enforcement agency if a loss occurs.
- **Joint Insured** — The first named insured in the declarations will act on behalf of every insured. Any knowledge of other insureds will be considered the knowledge of the first person named.
- **Legal Action Against the Insurer** — The insured may not bring any legal action against the insurer until all conditions have been met. The suit must be within two years of when the loss was discovered and not before 90 days after the claim was filed.
- **Loss Covered Under More than One Coverage** — The most the insurance provider will pay is the *lesser* of the actual loss or the sum of all limits available under every coverage (if a loss can be covered under more than one coverage provided by the insurer).
- **Loss Sustained During Prior Insurance** — The policy will cover a loss that occurred under a previous policy that the insured cannot collect from due to the expiration of the discovery period. However, this coverage must be effective when the other policy is canceled, and the type of loss must be insured in both policies. The most the insurance provider will pay is the *lesser* of the limit of insurance in the previous policy or the limit available on this policy as of its effective date.
- **Loss Covered Under Previous Insurance and this Insurance** — For a loss partially covered under this insurance and partially covered under previous insurance issued by the same insurer or any affiliate, the most the insurer will pay is the *larger* of the recoverable amount under either policy.
- **Non-accumulation of the Limit of Insurance** — The limit of insurance does not accumulate from year to year.
- **Other Insurance** — The coverage over any other collectible and valid insurance is considered excess, but not for more than the limit of insurance.
- **Ownership of Covered Property Interest** — The Insurance to bailees or other individuals is of no benefit. The coverage only applies to the insured's property interest, for which the insured is legally liable.
- **Policy Period** — Only losses during the policy period are covered.
- **Records** — The insured must keep records of all covered property so that the insurance company can verify the amount of any loss.
- **Recoveries** — Any recovery made after a settlement has been paid will be allocated as follows:
  1. To the insured for any loss that exceeds the deductible and limit of insurance,
  2. Then to the insurance provider until they are reimbursed for the settlement made,
  3. The remaining settlement goes to the insured for reimbursement of any paid deductible.
     Example 16.1 – The insured's store had a $40,000 burglary loss. The crime policy has a limit of $35,000 with a $1,000 deductible; it pays $35,000 for the loss. The company later recovers

$10,000 of the stolen property and incurs $1,000 in recovery costs. Of the $10,000 recovered, the insured will collect $4,000 (the amount of loss over the deductible and the limit); the insurer will receive $6,000.

- **Territory** — Only acts committed in the United States, Canada, Puerto Rico, the U.S. Virgin Islands, or the Canal Zone are covered.
- **Transfer of Your Rights of Recovery** — The insured must transfer all subrogation rights to the insurer for losses they have already paid.
- **Valuation (Settlement)** — Money will only be insured up to its face value. Securities will be valued according to their value on the close of business the day the loss was identified. Other property will be valued based on the actual cash value, the cost of repairs, or the cost of replacing the property with like kind and quality.

Discovery and Loss Sustained Forms

Discovery — A covered occurrence happening at any time and identified during the policy period or extended reporting period. The extended reporting period to identify a loss in the discovery form is as follows:

- The loss has to be reported within 60 days of policy cancellation;
- The loss has to be reported within one year of policy cancellation regarding any employee benefit plan; and
- The extended reporting period ends upon replacement of coverage.

Loss Sustained — The policy will cover a loss discovered during the policy period and an extended reporting period. Coverage also applies if the loss took place under a prior policy, in whole or in part, based on the coverage and limits selected and the insurance company providing the coverage.

For a loss to be paid from a prior policy period, it must be insured in both policies. The insurance policy in place at the time of the loss has to be effective and with no lapse in coverage when the current policy is canceled. The most the insurance provider will pay is the limit available on this policy as of its effective date or the lesser of the limit of insurance in the prior policy.

The extended reporting period to identify a loss in a loss-sustained coverage form has the following features:

- The loss has to be reported within one year of cancellation; and
- The extended reporting period ends upon replacement of coverage in whole or in part.

Equipment Breakdown Protection Coverage

The *Equipment Breakdown Coverage Form,* formerly known as the Boiler and Machinery Coverage Form, is used to insure many types of business risks and all industrial risks. Coverage will pay for direct loss to covered property from the breakdown of covered equipment.

An equipment breakdown form is a one-peril form. That peril is the breakdown of covered equipment. Insurers will pay property damage as long as that property *sustains direct damage* to covered property at the premises listed in the Declarations.

Additional coverages provided by this form include:

- Expediting expenses up to $25,000 for expediting permanent repairs or temporary repairs or replacement of property. This coverage is not an additional amount of insurance;

- Spoilage damage to raw materials, finished products, or property in transit;
- Utility interruption if a breakdown directly causes the interruption. The covered equipment supplies electric power, air conditioning, heating, communication services, water, sewer, or gas to the premises. The interruption must last at least the consecutive period presented in the Declarations.
- Automatic coverage for newly acquired locations if the coverage is equal to the coverage at the currently insured location.
- Ordinance or law coverage is applied despite the law or exclusion ordinance. The enforcement of any law or ordinance in force when the breakdown occurs will require the increases in loss.
- Errors and omissions
- Brands and labels if branded or labeled merchandise that is covered property is damaged due to a breakdown. The insurance provider may accept an agreed or appraised value for all or any part of the property.
- Contingent business income and extra expense, or extra expense only coverage subject to the same terms and conditions. This coverage will pay for a loss to covered equipment caused by a breakdown.

This form includes a loss condition that affects the appraisal of covered property. Property is insured on a *replacement cost basis*. However, suppose damaged property is not replaced or repaired within *two years* after the accident. In that case, the insurance provider will pay the cost to replace or repair the property or the actual cash value, whichever is less.

The equipment breakdown form does not insure bodily injury liability or consequential losses, such as an interruption in business and extra expense. However, the insured may obtain optional coverage for business interruptions.

The form defines an *accident* as the accidental and sudden breakdown of an object, resulting in physical damage to the object. Accident does not include:

- Deterioration, depletion, corrosion, or erosion;
- Wear and tear;
- Leakage at joints, fittings, or valves;
- Breakdown of brushes, gas tubes, or vacuum tubes;
- Breakdown of a foundation supporting the object
- Breakdown of electronic data processing equipment or computers; or
- The performance of protective or safety devices.

Unless a higher limit appears in the Declarations, equipment breakdown coverage will pay for direct damage directly resulting from a breakdown to covered equipment up to *$25,000* for each of the following:

- Consequential loss;
- Data and media (the cost to replace, research, or restore the damaged data);
- Expediting expenses;
- Hazardous substance cleanup, or the replacement or repair of contaminated property;
- Ammonia contamination; and
- Water damage.

Following a covered breakdown, coverage for fungus, wet rot, or dry rot is usually limited to *one year* and *$15,000* for testing, removal, and restoration, regardless of the number of claims.

The insured generally can buy optional higher limits for each of these coverages. In addition, the losses are subject to a deductible presented in the Declarations. The highest deductible will be applied if more than one object is involved in an accident.

Equipment breakdown coverage *excludes* losses resulting from any of the following:

- Earth movement;
- Ordinance or law except for the operation and use of electrical supply and emergency generating equipment located on the premises of a hospital;
- Nuclear hazard;
- Water (surface water, flood, tidal waves and tsunami, overflow or spray of any body of water, mudflow and mudslides, drain or sewer backups, or water damage caused by the leakage or discharge of a sprinkler system);
- Military action or war;
- Fire or combustion explosion, including those resulting in or ensuing from a breakdown;
- Explosion of covered electric steam generators, steam boilers, steam piping, steam engines, steam turbines, or gas turbines, if not otherwise excluded. Rotating or moving machinery is covered if the explosion results from mechanical breakdown or centrifugal force;
- Explosion within the furnace of a chemical boiler or the path from the furnace to the atmosphere;
- Bacterium, virus, or other microorganisms (except if caused by a breakdown);
- Wet rot, dry rot, and fungus (unless a breakdown causes these conditions);
- Damage to covered machinery undergoing electrical or pressure tests;
- Deterioration, depletion, erosion, corrosion, or wear and tear. If a breakdown results from these causes, the insurer will pay for the resulting loss or damage;
- Water or other methods used to extinguish a fire, even when the attempt is unsuccessful;
- A mechanical breakdown caused by vehicles or aircraft, freezing caused by cold weather, sinkhole collapse, lightning, smoke, civil commotion or vandalism, riot, or weight of snow, sleet, or ice;
- An interruption of or a delay in any business, processing, or manufacturing activity except for coverage provided by the business income and extra expense, extra expense only, and utility interruption coverages;
- A breakdown resulting from hail or windstorm;
- Lack of or excess power, light, refrigeration, heat, or steam except for any coverage provided by the business income and extra expense, extra expense only, utility interruption, and spoilage damage coverages;
- Any indirect result of a breakdown to covered machinery except for any coverage provided by the business income and extra expense, extra expense only, utility interruption, and spoilage damage coverages; or
- The insured's negligence to use all reasonable means to preserve and save covered property from further damage during and after the loss.

No coverage is provided for the following circumstances under the business income and extra expense, extra expense only, and utility interruption coverages:

- Business that could not have been conducted if the breakdown had not taken place;
- The insured's failure to use due diligence and all reasonable means to operate the business at the premises presented in the Declarations;
- The lapse, suspension, or cancellation of a contract after a breakdown extending beyond the time business could have continued if the contract had not lapsed, been suspended, or canceled.

Utility interruption coverage *does not cover* the following:

- Lightning;
- Smoke;
- Collapse;
- Sinkhole collapse;
- Acts of sabotage;
- Intentional acts of load shedding by the supplying utility;
- Freezing caused by cold weather;
- The impact of objects falling from an aircraft or missile;
- The impact of a vehicle, aircraft, or missile;
- Civil commotion, vandalism, or riot; and
- The weight of snow, sleet, or ice.

Commercial property forms can cover many of these perils.

Since most of the premium pays for examinations and inspections, equipment breakdown insurance places a lot of emphasis on inspections and loss control. The policy contains a unique condition that allows the insurance company to immediately suspend coverage whenever an object is exposed to or found in a dangerous condition. The suspension will take effect when the insured is notified in writing, and no advance notice is required. The suspension only applies to losses resulting from a particular object, not to the entire policy (if more than one object is insured).

In the equipment breakdown form, covered objects are defined as covered equipment. They include electrical equipment, mechanical equipment, refrigeration equipment, high-pressure equipment, turbines, and production machinery.

If an accident causes other accidents, all related events will be considered a single accident. All accidents simultaneously at the same location and by the same cause will be treated as a *single accident*.

Although the *Causes of Loss – Special Form* for commercial property provides all-risk (open-peril) coverage for the property covered, mechanical breakdowns are excluded. A manufacturing company's owner may purchase a stand-alone Equipment Breakdown Protection policy to provide the desired coverage. The owner can also add it as optional coverage to their Commercial Package Policy (CPP).

Selected Endorsements

Equipment breakdown coverage forms can also be endorsed to add coverage for consequential damage, business interruption, and extra expense.

Actual Cash Value – The insurance provider will assess the property damage for covered equipment and will pay the lesser of the cost to repair or replace the damaged property with property of the same kind and quality or the actual cash value of the damaged property at the time the breakdown occurred. Damage to property that is obsolete or no longer used by the insured is not covered.

Commercial Inland Marine

Inland Marine insurance covers property in transit and property belonging to others while in the insured's custody or care.

Inland Marine Coverage Forms

Insurers can write commercial inland marine coverage as either a part of a commercial package policy (CPP) or a standalone policy. Forms are referred to as *filed* or *unfiled*. A *filed form* is a form that may require an insurance provider to file for rate and form approval. An *unfiled form* may not require an approved filing to the state insurance department. Regulations may vary from state to state.

A different inland marine declaration is used with each type of coverage written. Therefore, depending on written coverages, more than one inland marine declaration may be attached to a policy. Besides the endorsements, policy period, and general information concerning the insured's name, the commercial inland marine Declarations specifically describe the covered property.

Most filed forms include a $250 deductible for a single loss. In addition, the filed coverage forms are typically written on an open peril basis. The causes of loss forms for commercial property do not apply to these coverages. The following *exclusions* are commonly found in these forms:

- Governmental action;
- Military action and war;
- Nuclear hazard;
- Delay, loss of market (customer base or customer demand), or loss of use;
- Voluntarily parting with property by scheme, device, or fraudulent trick;
- Dishonest acts by the insured or the insured's representatives or employees;
- Unauthorized instruction to transfer property;
- An insured's failure to use all reasonable means to preserve and protect property from further loss or damage;
- Damage or loss caused by any of the following, but if loss by a covered cause of loss takes place, insurers will cover the additional loss in the following situations:
    o Acts or decisions, or the failure to act or decide;
    o Weather conditions;
    o Inadequate or defective planning, zoning, construction, or quality of work;
    o Collapse, other than that provided as an additional coverage; or
    o Wear and tear, gradual deterioration, or inherent device.

The table below includes a list of filed and unfiled forms used to write commercial inland marine coverage.

FILED FORMS		UNFILED FORMS
Accounts Receivable	Air Transit	Bailee's Customer
Equipment Dealers	Trip Transit	Warehouseman's
Camera and Musical Instruments Dealers	Annual Transit	Pattern and Die
Film	Parcel Post	Salespersons Samples
Floor Plans	Air Cargo	Processing Risk
Fine Arts	Motor Truck Cargo	Exhibition Floater
Jewelers Block	Bridges and Tunnels	Garment Contractors
Physicians and Surgeons Equipment	Radio and TV Towers	Installations
Mail Coverage	Furriers Block	Builder's Risk — Installation
Signs	Laundries and Dry Cleaners	Electronic Data Processing
Theatrical Property	Cold Storage Locker	Stamp and Coin Dealers
Commercial Articles	Processors Legal Liability	Fine Arts Dealers
Valuable Papers and Records	Contractors Equipment	

We will now describe only some of the forms listed above.

Accounts Receivable – *Accounts Receivable* coverage is one of the most popular and important inland marine coverage forms. Unlike most inland marine coverages, the coverage protects property located at a fixed location rather than mobile property. The Accounts Receivable Coverage Form is a filed form. It provides coverage for losses of due accounts from customers that become uncollectible because of a loss to the insured's accounts receivable records.

Coverage is written on an all-risk basis. Additional exclusions not including those already discussed include the following:

- Concealment, alteration, falsification, or destruction of records to hide a wrongful act;
- Accounting, bookkeeping, or billing records; or
- Electrical or magnetic disturbance, injury, or erasure.

The following totals will be deducted from the total:

- The total of accounts that the insured can re-establish and collect;
- The total of accounts in which there is no loss;
- A total for likely "bad debt" that the insured is ordinarily unable to collect; and
- All unearned service charges and interest on necessary loans.

In addition, the insured must store their accounts receivable records in a receptacle described in the Declarations when they are not in use.

Bailee's Customer – *Bailee's Customer* coverage forms protect against customer property losses in the insured's custody, care, or control. Each of these coverage forms is unfiled.

- **Bailee's Customer Policy** — This coverage form insures customer property loss without regard to the insured's legal liability for the loss. It insures the interest of both the bailee and the bailor.
- **Furriers Block** — This coverage is written for insureds engaged in the fur business. It insures merchandise held for sale and customers' property that the insured has temporary custody of for storage, repair, or cleaning.
- **Cleaners, Dryers, and Laundries** — This coverage form covers insureds in the dry cleaning or laundry business from damage or loss to customers' property while in their possession.
- **Warehouseman's** — This coverage form protects customers' property while stored at a warehouse. It is typically written as excess coverage over the property owner's other valid and collectible insurance.

Commercial Articles – The *Commercial Articles* form is a filed form that protects the owners' interest, as opposed to the dealers of musical instruments, commercial cameras, and similar property. This form also includes the same property of others in the insured's custody, care, or control. Property not covered includes property in illegal transportation or trade and contraband. Like every inland marine coverage form, coverage is provided on an all-risk basis. The form consists of each of the common exclusions previously discussed.

The coinsurance clause in this coverage form differs somewhat from other coinsurance clauses. It states that all items insured but not explicitly listed or described must be covered for their total value when the loss occurs to avoid a coinsurance penalty. Another condition exclusive to this coverage form relates to additional acquired property, which is automatically insured for up to 30 days if it is of the same type of property already covered. The insurer will pay 25% of the limit of insurance for the same property, up to a maximum of $10,000.

Contractors Equipment Floater – The *Contractors Equipment Floater* is an unfiled commercial inland marine coverage form that generates the most premium within the insurance industry. It insures mobile equipment and contractor's equipment rented, owned, or borrowed by other contractors, as opposed to dealers. It covers the equipment while it is located on the job site and temporarily stored between jobs or during transportation to and from the job site. Insurers can write coverage on either an open peril basis or a named peril basis.

Additionally (newly) acquired property – This form provides an added coverage that allows for a newly acquired property during the policy period to be covered for 60 days (but not beyond the policy period). This coverage extension is typically limited to 25% of the limit of insurance, or $50,000, whichever is less.

Equipment shipped by air within the United States, its territories and possessions, Puerto Rico, and Canada is considered to be in the form's coverage territory.

Coinsurance might apply and will be listed on the declarations page.

Electronic Data Processing – *Electronic Data Processing* coverage has grown in importance recently. Businesses that lease, own, or rent data processing equipment are eligible for coverage. These unfiled forms generally cover the following four coverages:

1. Data processing media, including paper tapes or magnetic tapes, discs, and punch cards;
2. Computer hardware that is purposely scheduled;
3. Extra expense incurred by the insured to continue business operations following a loss; and
4. Business interruption can also cover the loss of income when the business is interrupted due to damage to equipment media.

Equipment Dealers – The stock of construction equipment and mobile equipment dealers, including the similar property of others in the insured's custody, care, or control, may be covered under the filed *Equipment Dealers* coverage form. Property that is not protected includes the following:

- Automobiles, motorcycles, and motor trucks;
- Watercraft and aircraft;
- Currency, money, notes, bills, accounts, and deeds;
- Property during manufacturing;
- Property rented, leased, or sold;
- Fixtures, furniture, and office supplies;
- Improvements and betterments;
- Tools, machinery, fittings, molds, patterns, etc.; and
- Property in illegal transportation or trade, or contraband.

Insurers write this coverage on an all-risk basis, and the following additional *exclusions* apply:

- Flood, water, surface water;
- Unexplained disappearance;
- Damage related to processing or work performed on the property; and
- Artificially produced electrical current.

This coverage form provides the following *extensions of coverage*:

- Removal of debris;
- Pollution removal and cleanup; and
- Theft damage to a building.

There are several additional conditions listed in this coverage form:

- **Valuation** — This condition replaces the standard inland marine valuation clause. It states that the insurer will determine the value of the unsold property based on either the cost to reasonably restore the property, the actual cash value, or the cost of replacing the damaged property with the same property, whichever is less.
  - The value of sold yet undelivered property will be valued at the net selling price minus any discounts and allowances.
  - The value of the property of others will be the lesser of the following: the actual cash value of the property, including the cost of materials and labor the insured has added, or the amount for which the insured is liable, including the cost of materials and labor the insured has added.
- **Coinsurance** — Property must be covered up to *80%* of its replacement cost.
- **Records and Inventory** — The insured must maintain accurate records and inventory for three years after the end of the policy period. These records include a detailed list of all purchases and sales, stock in trade, and property of others. Also, a physical stock inventory must be sent to the insurance provider at least once each year.
- **Protective Safeguards** — If the insurer requires protective safeguards (e.g., automatic sprinkler, fire alarm), coverage will be suspended if the insured does not keep them in operation or in good working condition while the business is closed.

Installations Floater – The *Installations Floater* coverage form is unfiled and often purchased by contractors to insure items such as the heating and air-conditioning equipment in a building. The property is insured while in transit, during the unloading and equipment installation, and until the building owner takes control. Insurers can write coverage on either a named peril or open peril basis. Coverage ends when the work is finished and is accepted by the ultimate owner or user of the property.

Jewelers Block – The *Jewelers Block* coverage form is a filed dealer's form that insures merchandise held for sale by the insured and the property of others in the insured's custody, care, or control.

Usually, once the property leaves the premises, there is no additional coverage. Certain types of property *not covered* include the following:

- Property purchased under a deferred sales arrangement after it leaves the insured's premises;
- Property displayed in showcases away from the insured's premises;
- Property while it is at trade exhibitions;
- Property while being worn by any insured, representative, employee, or member of their family, friends, or relatives (an exception is made for watches being worn for the sole purpose of adjustments);
- Property in transit by:
  - Mail (excluding registered mail);
  - Express carriers;
  - Air carriers, railroad, or waterborne; or
  - Motor carrier;
- Other property in illegal transportation or trade, or contraband.

This coverage form provides several optional types of transit coverage, which will insure property in transit if one of the following is listed on the declarations page:

- Carriers operating solely as a merchant's parcel delivery;
- Armored car services;

- The baggage service or passenger parcel of railroads, passenger bus lines, airborne or waterborne carriers; or
- Registered mail.

One other condition not found in the other coverage forms is the Changes in the Premises condition. It states the policy does not insure the property if the risk has been substantially increased by changes in the premises unless agreed to in writing by the insurance company.

Signs – For attached outdoor signs, limited coverage for signs is provided in the commercial property coverage form, usually limiting coverage to $2,500. Protection under the filed *Signs* coverage form includes the insured's signs, including fluorescent, neon, automatic, or mechanical signs, and similar property of others in the insured's custody, care, or control. The form includes a 100% coinsurance requirement.

Valuable Papers and Records – One of the most popular and most important of the commercial inland marine coverages is the filed *Valuable Papers and Records* form.

Valuable papers and records are printed, written, or inscribed documents, manuscripts or records, books, abstracts, deeds, films, drawings, maps, or mortgages.

Valuable papers and records *do not include* any of the following:

- Money or securities;
- Converted data;
- Instructions or programs used in data processing; or
- Material on which such data is recorded.

Insured property under this form *does not include* the following:

- Any property not explicitly listed in the Declarations if the insurer cannot easily replace the property with other property;
- Property held as samples or for delivery after a sale;
- Property in storage away from the listed premises; or
- Other property in illegal transportation or trade and contraband.

Insurers will cover the property on an all-risk basis, subject to the following additional exclusions:

- Errors or omissions by the insured, the insured's representatives or employees (except for-hire carriers); and
- Electrical or magnetic disturbance, injury, or erasure.

The valuable papers and records coverage form does not have a coinsurance provision. However, a special condition requires the insured to keep all valuable records and papers, when not in use, in a receptacle described in the Declarations.

Commercial Inland Marine Conditions Forms

The commercial inland marine conditions are *added* to the common policy conditions and any conditions that apply to a specific coverage form. They are similar to other common conditions previously discussed and include the following:

- **Obligations of the insured following a loss;**
- **Insurance under two or more policies;**

- **Other insurance covering the same loss**;
- **Appraisal**;
- **Abandonment**;
- **Loss payment**;
- **Pair, set, or parts**;
- **Salvage (recovered property)**;
- **Subrogation (transfer of rights of recovery)**;
- **Privilege to adjust with the owner** — Since inland marine coverages can insure the property of others in the insured's custody, care, or control, this condition states that the insurer will settle with the actual property owners in the event of loss;
- **Reinstatement of limit** — This condition says that payment of any claim will not reduce the limit of insurance, except in the case of a total loss on a scheduled item. In this case, the insurance provider will cancel the specific coverage and refund any unearned premium for the insurance on that item;
- **Misrepresentation, concealment, or fraud**;
- **Legal action against the insurance provider**;
- **No benefit to the bailee**;
- **The policy period**; and
- **Valuation** — This condition states that the insurance provider will determine the value of an item following a loss based on the *lesser* of
  - The reasonable costs to restore the property;
  - The actual cash value of the item; or
  - The cost of replacing the property with like kind and quality.

A commercial floater refers to any inland marine policy designed to insure movable commercial property, wherever it may be located worldwide.

Transportation Coverages

The oldest form of inland marine coverage is *property in transit*. Transportation coverage is available to cover the exposure of the carrier, shipper, or consignee of goods.

Carriers of property can be separated into three categories:

1. *Common carriers* transporting the property of anyone who hires them;
2. *Private carriers* transporting their property; and
3. *Contract carriers* transporting the property of others for which they have a written contract.

In addition to the three types of carriers, three different parties can have a financial interest in the transported property:

1. **Shipper** — The company or person that is sending the goods;
2. **Consignee** — The company or person that will receive the goods; and
3. **Carrier** — The company that transports the goods.

The consignee and shipper have an ownership interest in the shipped property, the extent of which is determined by the sales agreement's terms. *Free on board (F.O.B.)* can be used with this coverage.

For example, when the agreement is written *F.O.B. – Shipper's Location*, the shipper owns the property until it is transferred to the carrier. When the carrier takes possession, the consignee owns the property and will incur any loss if the property is damaged during shipment. On the other hand, if the property is shipped *F.O.B. – Consignee's Location*, the shipper owns the property until it is delivered to the consignee.

Common Carrier Cargo Liability – The carrier is considered liable for safe delivery of the property. This additional coverage insures the carrier's legal liability for loss or damage to property in the insured's custody and care during transit.

The law recognizes instances where the carrier will not be liable for loss or damage. These defenses include:

- **Acts of God (nature) or acts of a public enemy**;
- **Exercise of public authority**;
- **Negligence of the shipper** — If damage results from negligence in the packing or shipping of items highly vulnerable to damage from ordinary handling; or
- **Inherent vice or nature of the property**.

Bills of Lading – A *Bill of Lading* is a contract for transporting goods between the shipper and the carrier. This document stipulates the carrier's responsibilities and duties for the property. Common carriers must issue a uniform bill of lading to each person (the shipper) for whom it transports goods. When a regular bill of lading is issued, the carrier is liable for the invoice cost of any damaged property, and the shipper is not required to declare a value. However, the carrier may issue a released bill of lading in which the shipper must declare the values of the shipped property. With the released bill of lading, the shipper is charged a lower fee because the carrier is only responsible for the damage up to the stated amount.

Legal Liability – The carrier has an interest in the property in their custody for any legal liability that may be imposed on them for damage or loss to the property during shipment. However, the extent of responsibility for damage to property in transit depends on whether the carrier is a contract carrier or a common carrier.

Common carriers that offer their services to the public are legally responsible for damage to property they are transporting with *exceptions* applying to loss caused by any of the following:

- Acts of God (floods, earthquakes, etc.) or acts of a public enemy (e.g., wars);
- Confiscated cargo by law enforcement (exercise of public authority);
- Shipper's fault (negligent or faulty packaging); or
- Perishable goods (inherent vice).

A common carrier provides a document called a bill of lading showing receipt of goods for shipment. A common carrier will issue a released bill of lading to limit its liability to a specified maximum dollar amount.

Contract carriers that agree to serve specific clients based upon a prearranged contract are responsible only for damage to cargo when they are negligent. The standard of care on a contract carrier is much lower than a common carrier requires.

Motor Truck Cargo Forms – The Motor Truck Cargo Policy - Carriers Form is unfiled and used by common carriers that transport the goods of others for a fee. This legal liability coverage insures the carrier against liability for damage to the goods. The property of others is insured on an open peril basis.

The property is insured until delivery to the final destination; coverage will last for 72 hours at a facility not listed in the Declarations. Carriers can purchase insurance to provide coverage at unspecified terminals.

Owners, or private carriers who ship their goods using their vehicles, are insured on the Motor Truck Cargo Policy Owners Coverage Form. Coverage is provided for direct damage to the owner's property. Similar to the Motor Truck Cargo Carriers Form, liability is not a factor in these forms. Insurers write coverage on an open peril basis. The form only covers goods in transit from where the shipment begins to the final destination.

Transit Coverage Forms

Annual transit – This policy is used by businesses that regularly ship goods. Insurers can write coverage for all incoming and outgoing shipments during the policy period.

Trip transit – This policy form is a variation of the annual transit policy. It is used to insure a specific trip or shipment. The policy period is when the goods leave the shipper until they reach their destination. Damage or loss to covered goods is provided without regard to the carrier's legal liability.

Insurers can issue coverage on a named peril or all-risk basis. The all-risk coverage can be issued only for goods shipped by a common carrier. Also, insurers can provide continuous coverage for goods shipped by several carriers while in transit until they reach their final destination.

Chapter Review

This chapter discussed other commercial coverages, like commercial crime, equipment breakdown protection coverage, and commercial inland marine policies. Let's review them:

CRIME	
Program Breakdown	• For commercial and government entities • Coverage triggers: ○ *Discovery form* – a covered occurrence taking place at any time and discovered during the policy period or extended reporting period ○ *Loss-sustained form* – the policy will pay for a loss that the policy owner discovered during the policy period and an extended reporting period
Crime Coverages	• Employee Theft • Inside and Outside the Premises (Theft of Money and Securities)
EQUIPMENT BREAKDOWN PROTECTION	
Coverage	• The equipment breakdown coverage form is used to insure many types of business risks and all industrial risks • Coverage will pay for direct loss to covered property resulting from the breakdown of covered equipment
COMMERCIAL INLAND MARINE	
Features	• Filed (standardized) or unfiled (unique exposure) with state regulatory authorities • Coverage is available on any property that is portable • Policies are called floaters because the coverage floats with the insured property anywhere in the world
Nationwide Marine Definition	• The coverage written on Inland Marine and Ocean Marine forms • Defines four classes of risk: ○ Domestic shipments and transportation risks ○ Tunnels, bridges, and other instrumentalities of transportation and communication ○ Commercial property floater risks • Personal property floater risks

CHAPTER 17:
Farm

Farmers face some unique property and liability risks. The farm coverage forms and endorsements provide property and liability protection to insure their particular needs. This chapter explains conditions, causes of loss, selected forms, and endorsements. As you learn, pay attention to what is covered and excluded from farm policy coverage.

- Farm Coverage
- Crop Insurance
- Federal Multi-Peril Crop Insurance

Farm Coverage

Farm coverage is unique because it insures the property and liability exposures of the business operation of a farm. It also may include the personal residential property and liability exposures of a family living on the farm premises. As in any commercial package policy, farm coverage may be written together in a package or separately as a monoline policy.

In addition to the common policy conditions and common policy declarations, farm coverage must include a Farm Conditions and a Farm Declarations form and one or more farm coverage forms. There are four farm coverage forms:

1. Farm property;
2. Farm liability;
3. Mobile agricultural machinery and equipment; and
4. Livestock.

Farm Property Coverage Form

Farm property coverage forms are subject to the causes of loss described on the declarations page. Like the commercial package policy, the cause of loss form will dictate coverage and exclusions for each property form. Farm property can be insured in a basic, broad, or special form.

Coverage A – Dwellings – *Coverage A – Dwellings* is similar to Coverage A of the Homeowners policy. Towers, antennas, and satellite dishes attached to the dwelling are covered under Coverage A but have a special limit of insurance of $1,000 in any one event. This limit of insurance is a part of the Coverage A limit.

The limits of insurance in Coverage A provide coverage for the dwelling, including structures attached to the dwelling at the described location. Supplies and materials located on or next to the described premises used to repair, alter, or construct the dwelling and its attached structures are insured, along with outdoor and building equipment used to service the dwelling. The extension of building coverage to equipment removes the need for a landlord to schedule a small amount of contents coverage to protect items like ladders, lawnmowers, and similar property used for maintenance.

Coverage B – Other Private Structures – *Coverage B – Other Private Structures* is similar to homeowners coverage. However, Coverage B does not include coverage for any detached structure used primarily for farming purposes. Coverage B provides a special limitation of $1,000 for loss to satellite dishes or antennas. The policy provides an automatic limit of 10% of Coverage A as an additional limit of insurance for other private structures.

Coverage C – Household Personal Property – *Coverage C – Household Personal Property* applies to personal property owned by an insured when the property is located on the covered premises. The following special limits of insurance for Coverage C include:

- $200 for money, gold, silver, and platinum;
- $1,500 for securities, letters of credit, manuscripts, and passports;
- $1,500 for watercraft and their equipment, outboard engines, furnishings, and trailers;
- $1,500 for trailers not used for farming operations or watercraft;
- $2,500 for business property located on the insured premises;

- $500 for business property located away from the insured premises;
- In the event of loss by theft:
    - $2,500 for jewelry, furs, precious and semiprecious stones, and watches
    - $2,500 for silverware, goldware, platinum ware, and pewterware
    - $3,000 for firearms and related equipment;
- $1,500 for electronic equipment and accessories in or on a motor vehicle only if equipped to be operated from the vehicle's electrical system and other power sources;
- $1,500 for electronic equipment and accessories used mainly for business operations or farming while off the insured premises and not in or on a motor vehicle.

Coverage D – Loss of Use – *Coverage D – Loss of Use* provides coverage for extra living expenses if the principal living quarters of the insured become uninhabitable. This coverage also includes the fair rental value if the dwelling the owner rents to others at the described premises becomes uninhabitable because of a loss from an insured peril.

Coverage E – Scheduled Farm Personal Property – *Coverage E – Scheduled Farm Personal Property* pays for direct physical damage to or loss of insured property. The insured property includes farm personal property covered on a scheduled basis and may consist of the following property:

- Grain and grain in stacks;
- Straw, hay, and fodder;
- Supplies, materials, and farm products;
- Livestock (excluding livestock at a stockyard or in transit);
- Fish, worms, bees, or other animals (except for the Basic or Broad Covered Causes of Loss);
- Poultry in any building designated for poultry under the Declarations or while in the open (excluding turkeys, unless specified);
- Computers used for farm management;
- Miscellaneous equipment; and
- Portable structures and buildings.

Coverage E does not provide coverage for trees, growing crops, or household personal property, and has *special limits of liability* that apply to the following:

- Straw, hay, or fodder in the open — $10,000 per stack;
- Miscellaneous farm machinery or equipment with a maximum limit of $3,000 per item;
- Poultry with a market value; and
- Livestock not specifically covered is limited to the least of ACV — 120% of the amount obtained by dividing the limit of insurance on the type and class of animal by the number of heads of that kind of animal owned at the time of loss, or $2,000. Each head of cattle, mule, or horse one year of age will be counted as 1/2 head when the loss occurs.

Coverage F – Unscheduled Farm Personal Property – Under *Coverage F – Unscheduled Farm Personal Property*, a single limit of liability applies to all farm personal property on the insured premises unless specifically excluded. Off-premises coverage is provided for ground feed, grain, and other items while being processed, stored, or in the custody of a common carrier. Farm machinery, equipment, and livestock can also be covered off-premises.

Some excluded properties from this broad definition include automobiles, crops, racehorses, and household property.

Coverage F is subject to an 80% coinsurance clause to discourage underinsurance. This clause has a provision to provide for an insufficient amount of insurance carried due to the replacement or purchase of additional equipment. In the event of damage or loss to the replacement or additional equipment within 30 days of purchase, up to $75,000 of the replacement equipment value and $100,000 of the new equipment value will not be used to determine the required limit of insurance.

Coverage G – Other Farm Structures – *Coverage G – Barns, Outbuildings, and Other Farm Structures* will protect farming structures such as:

- Farm structures or buildings;
- Silos;
- Portable structures and buildings;
- Fences (other than the field and pasture fences), pens, corrals, chutes, and feed racks;
- Outdoor television and radio equipment, towers, antennas, and masts;
- Betterments and improvements; and
- Building supplies and materials.

Coverage is subject to an 80% coinsurance clause.

Farm Liability Coverage Form

The *farm liability* coverage form is identical to the commercial general liability form. Coverages H, I, and J protect against bodily injury and property damage, personal and advertising injury, and medical payments.

Coverage H – Bodily Injury and Property Damage Liability – *Coverage H – Bodily Injury and Property Damage Liability* covers bodily injury and property damage claims from liability arising out of personal acts of the insured and the farming business. Although it protects the farming business, it excludes coverage for businesses other than farming. It contains the business pursuits and professional services exclusions similar to personal liability coverage.

Coverage I – Personal and Advertising Injury Liability – *Coverage I – Personal and Advertising Injury Liability* is similar to the coverage provided in the general liability coverage form. However, advertising injury is covered only if the offense is committed when advertising the insured's farm-related products, goods, or services.

Exclusions under this coverage include breach of contract, intentional acts, contractual liability, failure of goods to perform, and any offense committed by an insured in the business of broadcasting.

The personal injury coverage is similar to the coverage provided in the general liability coverage form.

Coverage J – Medical Payments – *Coverage J – Medical Payments* agrees to pay reasonable medical expenses resulting from an accident, regardless of fault, if the expenses are incurred and reported to the insurance provider within three years of the accident date. Coverage applies only to an individual who is not an insured. This means that farm workers are excluded from this coverage. However, resident workers are included.

Livestock Coverage Form

Livestock refers to cattle, horses, donkeys, mules, sheep, goats, and swine.

Loss refers to the death or destruction of livestock.

The covered property does not include livestock in sales yards, sales barns, public stockyards, slaughterhouses, or packing plants. Insurance companies will not cover livestock while in the custody of a contract or common carrier. However, that coverage may be extended for up to $1,000.

The *livestock coverage* form is a named peril coverage insuring losses that result in livestock's death or necessary destruction by the primary causes of loss. Covered causes of loss, not including theft, include the following:

- Windstorm or hail;
- Fire or lightning;
- Riot or civil commotion;
- Explosion;
- Aircraft (including objects falling from aircraft or contact with the aircraft);
- Smoke;
- Volcanic action;
- Sinkhole collapse;
- Collision causing the death of insured livestock except for the vehicles operated or owned by an insured. Death may occur from overturning, the collision of a vehicle on which the livestock is being transported, or livestock being struck by or running into a vehicle while crossing, moving along, or standing on a public road;
- Earthquake;
- Flood; and
- Vandalism.

The following exclusions apply:

- Intentional loss;
- Government actions;
- War and military action;
- Utility services;
- Nuclear hazard;
- Earth movement, including landslides and mine subsidence;
- Water (other than flood); and
- Neglect.

Mobile Agricultural Machinery and Equipment Coverage Form

Mobile agricultural machinery and equipment includes mobile devices used in the everyday operation of a farm. Such mobile devices include tools, accessories (whether attached or not attached), and spare parts specifically designed for operating and maintaining the mobile devices. The *mobile agriculture machinery and equipment coverage* form insures eligible equipment for open perils subject to policy exclusions and limitations. This coverage may also be written as a separate stand-alone policy.

Definitions

The definitions section provides definitions of terms used in the farm policy. Terms such as *advertising injury* and *bodily injury* are identical to those found in other types of property and casualty insurance. Some of the unique terms and definitions of farm coverage are:

- *Custom farming*, which refers to the implementation of specific planting, cultivating, harvesting, or similar specific farming operations by an insured at a farm that is not a covered location; and
- *Livestock*, meaning cattle, horses, donkeys, mules, sheep, and goats, but not poultry.

The terms found in the definitions section for farm *liability coverage* are identical to those found in the commercial general liability coverage and farm property coverage forms.

Causes of Loss (Basic, Broad and Special)

The causes of loss forms for farm coverage follow the same common perils in other types of property policies, with the following additions unique to farm coverage forms:

Basic causes of loss include collision coverage for Coverages E and F in the event of a collision causing only the following:

- Death of covered livestock;
- Damage to machinery; and
- Damage to other farm personal property.

The *Broad* form also includes the following perils:

- Electrocution of covered livestock;
- Accidental shooting of covered livestock;
- Attacks on livestock by wild animals or dogs (except attacks on the insured's sheep or goats by wild animals or dogs);
- Drowning of covered livestock (except swine under 30 days old); and
- Accidental death of livestock due to loading or unloading.

The *Special* form includes the common open peril exclusions. It adds an exclusion for fire if it results from curing tobacco.

The table below lists the causes of loss (common perils) found in the Basic, Broad, and Special forms.

When reviewing the table below, pay close attention to the common perils in other property policies, including the Dwelling Policy, Homeowners Policy, Commercial Property Policy, and Farm Coverage Policy.

BASIC FORM	BROAD FORM	SPECIAL FORM
COMMON PERILS		
Fire	**Basic Perils +**	All risks except those
Lightning	Damage by burglars	specifically excluded
Explosion	Falling objects	
Windstorm or hail	Weight of ice, snow or sleet	
Riot or civil	Accidental discharge or overflow of water or steam	
commotion	Sudden and accidental damage from artificially	
Aircraft	generated electrical current	
Vehicles	Sudden and accidental tearing apart, cracking, burning,	
Smoke	or bulging	
Vandalism and	Freezing	
malicious mischief		
Volcanic eruption		

BASIC FORM	BROAD FORM	SPECIAL FORM
DWELLING POLICY		
(DP-1) Only Fire, Lightning, and *Internal* explosion (the rest of the common basic perils are available for additional premium)	**(DP-2) Common Broad Perils +** Windstorm or Hail Riot or civil commotion Aircraft Vehicles Smoke Vandalism and malicious mischief Volcanic eruption	(DP-3) Common Special Perils
HOMEOWNERS POLICY		
(HO-8) Common Basic Perils + Theft	**(HO-2) Common Broad Perils +** Theft	(HO-3) Common Special Perils
COMMERCIAL PROPERTY POLICY		
Common Basic Perils + Sprinkler leakage Sinkhole collapse	**Common Broad Perils +** Sprinkler leakage Sinkhole collapse Water Damage	Common Special Perils
FARM COVERAGE POLICY		
Common Basic Perils + Sprinkler leakage Sinkhole Collapse Collision	**Common Broad Perils +** Sprinkler leakage Sinkhole Collapse Collision Water Damage Electrocution of livestock Attacks on livestock by dogs or wild animals Accidental shooting of livestock Drowning of livestock Accidental death due to loading or unloading of livestock	Common Special Perils

Conditions

The conditions under the farm coverage part are the standard commercial conditions, with one exception. When a structure or building is unoccupied or vacant for more than 120 consecutive days, the limits of insurance applicable to the building and its contents are decreased by 50%.

As well as the common policy conditions, the farm liability coverage form contains several conditions:

- Duties in the event of a suit, claim, or occurrence;
- Bankruptcy of the insured will not relieve the insurance company of its obligations;
- Insurance under two or more policies;
- Other insurance;
- Legal action against the insurance provider;
- No admission of liability with medical payments;
- Subrogation (transfer of rights of recovery);
- Liberalization;

- Representations; and
- Separation of insureds.

These conditions have already been talked about in our discussion of previous forms.

Exclusions

Regarding *property coverage*, the following exclusions apply to farm insurance:

- Intentional loss;
- Ordinance or law;
- Governmental actions;
- War and military action;
- Utility services;
- Nuclear hazard;
- Earth movement;
- Water (meaning flood and surface water); and
- Neglect.

These exclusions have already been talked about in our discussion of previous forms.

For farm liability coverage, other than the exclusions that are comparable to those in the general liability coverage and homeowners forms, several specific exclusions are unique to the nature of farm operations:

- Use of any animal, with or without an accessory vehicle, to provide rides for a fee or in connection with a charitable event, fair, or similar function;
- Use of any animal in a strength, speed, or racing contest or a prearranged stunt activity at the site chosen for the contest or activity;
- Rental of an insured location;
- Losses on the premises where a building or structure is being built, other than a dwelling that will be occupied by the insured or a farm structure for the insured's use; or
- Bodily injury to any insured.

Limits

Limits state that the most the insurance provider will pay due to a judgment against an insured will be the limit stated in the policy. The insurance provider will pay any cost it incurs for the investigation or defense of a lawsuit or claim above the limits shown in the policy.

Additional Coverages

The farm coverage policy provides the following *additional coverages*:

- Reasonable repairs;
- Debris removal;
- Water damage;
- Removal of trees;
- Grave markers;
- Fire department service charges;
- Restoration of farm records up to $2,000;
- Coverage for credit card and transfer funds up to $500; and
- Extra expense and collapse.

The farm liability coverage form provides the following additional coverages:

- Additional payments for Coverages H and I, including loss of earnings up to $250 per day due to time off from work while assisting the insurer in defense of a suit or claim; and
- Damage to the property of others, which is similar to personal liability, except it will not apply to borrowed farm equipment.

Crop Insurance

Crop insurance meets the needs of farmers and other crop growers who need protection against loss to their planted crops resulting from damage by the elements and other perils. The original crop insurance coverage protected against loss by hail only, and although this is still a major peril, coverage is now written to cover loss against fire and lightning. Specialty crop-hail insurers sell insurance on crop growing. In addition, coverage against loss from almost any peril (multi-peril) is available from the Federal Crop Insurance Corporation (FCIC) through a federally subsidized multi-peril crop insurance program. Private insurance companies, which the FCIC reinsures, also offer multi-peril crop insurance.

Eligibility

There are over 200 different crops that can be covered under crop insurance policies; however, the eligibility list varies geographically. Crops eligible for coverage are categorized into various classifications, with additional provisions applying to different classes. Some classifications include large grain crops, such as soybean, maize, and corn; small grain crops, including cereal grains such as wheat, oats, barley, etc.; tobacco; cotton; fruits and vegetables. Only the sellable portion of the crop is insured.

Application

In the crop-hail field, the applicant and the agent must sign the completed application alongside the time and date of signing. The application is a binder when adequately completed and accompanied by the premium or a promissory note.

In addition to the applicant's name and address, the crop-hail application requires information regarding the type of crop to be covered, the crop's location by section, township, range, and county, as well as the number of acres to be insured, and the amount of coverage per acre, the applicant's percentage interest in the crop, the total amount of coverage and finally the rate and premium.

When coverage is being written on crops where the applicant's interest is less than 100%, the applicant must provide information as to whether they are the tenant or landlord and the name of any other such party. A tenant farmer and a farm owner may have an insurable interest in a crop, and each may insure its interest separately.

If the applicant has any additional acres of the kinds of crops included in the application but intends not to specify them under the policy, the location of such crops must be provided.

The applicant must also specify whether additional coverage has been purchased on the crops (except FCIC insurance).

The insured must also specify whether any of the crops have been hailed upon prior to the signing of the application. If so, no insurance will be provided.

Finally, the application provides that the insurance company may reject the application within ten days of the effective date of the application upon giving five days' notice of its intent.

Term of Coverage

Most crop-hail applications contain a binder provision stating that coverage becomes effective at 12:01 AM on the day after the application is signed. There is no coverage if a covered peril damages any acres of crops listed in the schedule during this waiting period between the time the application is signed and 12:01 AM the next day. When the crops are damaged by hail during this waiting period, the applicant must give the insurer notice of such damage within 72 hours after the damage occurred. Once the notice is given in a timely fashion, the applicant receives a return of premium for coverage on any damaged acre of crop. When the applicant fails to notify the insurer within 72 hours, the right to a return of premium is automatically forfeited.

The insurance coverage expires at 12:01 AM on a specified date set by the insured crop and the state. The specific expiration dates are printed in the form and correspond with the particular harvest period of the crop. The expiration dates are decided based on typical growth and harvest patterns of individual crops, reflecting the climate of the county and state where the crop is grown. The purpose of scheduling different expiration dates for various crops is to exclude coverage from crops left out long past the harvest and have been subject to loss exposure not anticipated in the rates.

Crop-hail policies allow the insured to cancel the policy before the start of the insurance period and receive a refund of the paid premium for the amount of canceled insurance. Since the insurance does not become effective until a regular stand of the crop is visible above the ground, there is a period between the contract's inception (12:01 AM on the day after the application is signed) and when the insurance becomes effective (when a stand of the crop is visible).

In the event of "known crop failure," the policy can be returned for flat cancellation up to a date specified in the policy.

Covered Perils

The perils covered under the standard crop-hail policy are fire, hail, and lightning. Coverage against fire and lightning is applied before the crop's harvest and while it is still in the field or being transported to first storage. The policy does not protect against damage or losses resulting from rain, wind, flood, or frost.

Limits of Coverage

Crop-hail insurance can be obtained in any amount up to the full value of the expected crop. On early pre-season contracts, the coverage is typically for an average crop yield but adjusted for the individual insured's expectation. Some insureds purchase coverage for a potential value of the expected crop, while others may only insure for production costs.

Most crop-hail insurance is written on a "percentage plan." The insurance provider allows the insured to place a valuation on the crop, which is the amount of coverage purchased. If a loss occurs, the indemnity is based on the percentage of the crop damaged by fire, hail, or lightning.

Federal Multi-Peril Crop Insurance

The Federal Crop Insurance Act of 1938 established the Federal Crop Insurance Corporation (FCIC). This organization is managed and operated by the Risk Management Agency (RMA) as an agency of the Department of Agriculture to implement a federal crop insurance program. The FCIC undertook to insure wheat yields against loss by hail, flood, drought, frost, insects, diseases, and all-natural hazards for a premium based on the past loss history of the particular region. Over the years, this program has had many revisions and amendments. The current program dates from the Federal Crop Insurance Act of 1980, which created a new federal "all-risk" crop insurance program.

Basic and Catastrophic Crop Insurance

The current federal program was intended to replace all other forms of disaster protection for farmers. The all-risk coverage of the FCIC insures all losses caused by natural conditions beyond the farmer's control. Farmers can purchase crop insurance from private insurance companies against named perils or on an all risk basis and receive a premium credit when they purchase a federal policy.

The 1980 Act authorized the FCIC to subsidize farmer premium payments and to expand its coverage to include all commercial crops in every agricultural county.

The delivery system was expanded to include private insurers and licensed producers. Private insurers are allowed to sell federal crop insurance. They have now become the primary marketing arm for multi-peril crop insurance policies.

Private insurers conduct all aspects of the business, including marketing, data and information services, loss adjustment, and claim payments. These companies receive compensation for operating and administrative expenses, and the FCIC reinsures them.

Eligibility – Nearly every crop is eligible for insurance, provided it has been approved as a viable crop for the particular site. The farmer must have used approved farming techniques for such a crop.

Coverage Level – The FCIC's multi-peril policies indemnify insureds through a "yield guarantee plan." The FCIC guarantees a specific yield at the approximate cost of production and pays the farmer for every pound or bushel their yield falls below the guarantee. The maximum guarantee allowed by the FCIC is 75% of the mean yield. Indemnity is limited to 75% of the historical yield to reduce morale hazard. Under the current federal program for most crops, yield coverage options are 50, 65, and 75% of average yields.

Covered Causes of Loss – Nearly every unavoidable cause of loss for most field crops is insured. Insurers may cover only the most frequent and catastrophic loss cases for certain crops, such as fruit, vegetables, and specialty crops.

Losses due to poor market conditions, theft, mismanagement, or neglect, are not covered.

Application – The application deadline for crop insurance and renewal of crop insurance is set forth by the FCIC and differs by crop and region. It is usually about one month before the regular planting date for the crop.

Life of Policy – The policy provides coverage on an annual basis; however, the insured may continue it by paying a renewal premium and making the necessary reports.

Multiple Peril Policy Options

Levels of Coverage – The FCIC must offer two levels of yield coverage (one at 50% and the other at 75%) and can provide other coverages at any level below 75% of average yields. However, under the current federal program for most crops, yield coverage options are 50, 65, and 75% of average yields. Premium costs increase with the coverage level. The mechanics are similar to the deductible on any insurance policy.

Price Election – Price election coverage differs from crop to crop. It is determined several months before the application deadline based on a percentage of the projected market price of the crop during the policy term.

The 1980 Act mandates the FCIC to offer a single price election that is not less than 90% of the estimated market price for the commodity. Premium costs increase in tandem with rises in price protection.

Optional Units – Generally, the insured must insure their interest in all acreage of a specific crop planted in the county. The main exception to this rule stems from the "Unit" insurance rule.

"Unit" insurance allows separate coverage to be written for separate acreage. If one qualifies, the advantage of having unit insurance for indemnity payment purposes is that production on each unit is considered without regard to the insured's total production of the insured crop or production on other units.

The two types of units are:

1. **Units based on crop interest** – Unit insurance coverage, at no additional cost, is automatic when different ownership interests exist.
2. **Optional units** – When certain farming practices, locations, and recordkeeping criteria are met, insurers can write coverage on a unit basis. For optional units, an additional 10% premium charge will be applied.

Other Provisions

Individual Crop – Suppose the farmer chooses to insure some crops and not others for which coverage is available. In that circumstance, any loss on noninsured crops will not be considered in calculating the individual FMHA emergency loan eligibility.

Small Grain – Provisions that apply to small grains refer to cereal grains, including wheat, oats, barley, etc

Coarse Grain – Provisions that apply to coarse grains refer to soybean, corn, maize, etc.

Chapter Review

This chapter explained farm coverage forms and endorsements. Let's review them:

FARM	

Farm Property Coverage Form	• There are four farm coverage forms:
	  ○ Farm property;
	  ○ Farm liability;
	  ○ Mobile agricultural machinery and equipment; and
	  ○ Livestock

Crop Insurance	• Crop insurance meets the needs of farmers and other crop growers who need protection against loss to their planted crops resulting from damage by the elements and other perils
Federal Multi-Peril Crop Insurance	• Private insurers conduct all aspects of the business, including marketing, data and information services, loss adjustment, and claim payments • Nearly every crop is eligible for insurance, provided it has been approved as a viable crop for the particular site • These insurers receive compensation for their operating and administrative expenses and these companies are reinsured by the FCIC

CHAPTER 18:
Businessowners

Businesses need insurance just as much as individuals but usually require higher coverage limits. In this chapter, you will learn the Businessowners Policy's purpose, characteristics, and requirements for underwriting. You will also examine businessowners property and liability coverage forms in great detail, including conditions and limits for each.

- Businessowners – General Concepts
- BOP Section I – Property
- BOP Section II – Liability
- BOP Section III – Common Policy Conditions

Businessowners – General Concepts

The *businessowners policy (BOP)* is a combination policy that provides several different coverages for businesses that meet the eligibility requirements. The program was established in 1976 and has been revised extensively.

The BOP is a stand-alone policy with its own forms. Like the homeowners policy, the businessowners policy delivers property and liability coverage in a single contract. Also, like the homeowners policy, there is a single premium with no itemization or division of premium charged for property or liability.

The businessowners policy rules require that all buildings and personal property under one owner be covered in the same policy.

Characteristics and Purpose

The businessowners policy is a package policy designed to meet the needs of small to medium-sized businesses. Instead of choosing the individual's coverages to be insured, the insurer offers a package of coverage, which includes property and liability coverage. The policy owner usually cannot exclude coverage automatically provided in the package.

The following are several advantages of prepackaged policies:

- Property and liability coverage comes in one predesigned package;
- The options most frequently needed by small business owners are included or available for an additional premium; and
- The rates for the entire package are very favorable because the eligible types of risks typically have a lower potential for loss.

The businessowners policy premium is indivisible, meaning there are no separate premiums for property and liability coverage. A special package rate applies to all mandatory coverages. The final premium will depend on the deductibles, selected limits, and optional coverages.

Insurers cannot insure every business under a businessowners policy. These businesses predominantly conduct business on their premises and generally do not have an extensive product or completed operations exposure. Under the businessowners policy, specific businesses that are eligible include the following:

- Office buildings;
- Residential or commercial condominiums and apartments;
- Service, processing, and mercantile establishments;
- Contractors (such as plumbers, painters, electricians, or carpenters);
- Fast-food or limited cooking restaurants; or
- Convenience stores.

Besides general eligibility rules regarding the type of business, there are typically additional underwriting criteria imposed by insurance companies, such as income or size limitations:

- *Office buildings* up to 100,000 square feet and no more than six stories high;
- *Retail or service businesses* up to 25,000 square feet in floor space and up to $3,000,000 in annual gross sales;

- *Convenience stores with gas pumps*, no auto service or auto washing services, and no more than 50% of gross sales may come from gasoline sales; and
- *Fast-food restaurants* up to 7,500 square feet (beer and wine sales are allowed up to 25% of gross sales).

Businesses that are usually *ineligible* include the following:

- Automobile sales and servicing operations;
- Manufacturing operations;
- Bars and grills;
- Places of amusement;
- Financial institutions; and
- Self-storage facilities and certain types of contractors.

BOP Section I – Property

Covered Property

Businessowners property coverage must be activated in the Declarations and is available for buildings, business personal property, or both. Building and personal property definitions are similar to those in the Building and Personal Property Coverage Form. A separate limit of insurance for the property of others is not used in the businessowners form as it is included in the business personal property (BPP) limit. The exact radius of 100 feet in the commercial package section applies to the BPP of the policy owner in the businessowners form.

PROPERTY COVERED

1. Business personal property, buildings, or both

PROPERTY NOT COVERED

1. Money and securities;
2. Bills, accounts, and other evidence of debt;
3. Watercraft while afloat;
4. Aircraft and vehicles;
5. Computers permanently installed in any vehicle, watercraft, or aircraft (unless being held as stock);
6. Property or contraband in the course of transportation or illegal trade;
7. Lawns, crops, water, or land;
8. Plants and shrubs, trees, detached signs, satellite dishes, radio and television antennas, outdoor fences;
9. Electronic data, except as covered under the Electronic Data additional coverage and except for the policy owner's stock of prepackaged software; or
10. Animals (unless owned by others and boarded with the policy owner).

Causes of Loss, Limitations and Exclusions

The Businessowners Property Coverage Form insures risks of direct physical loss to covered property, contingent upon certain limitations and exclusions.

This form contains several limitations in coverage, so the policy will not pay for loss or damage to the following:

- Hot water boilers and other water heating equipment for occurrences inside the equipment, not including an explosion;

- Hot water boilers, steam pipes, steam boilers, or other water heating equipment caused by any condition inside the equipment; however, loss to the equipment caused by an explosion of fuel or gases in the device is covered;
- Missing property with no physical evidence to demonstrate what happened to the property or if only an inventory shortage is detected (mysterious disappearance);
- Property transferred to a place or person outside the premises listed in the Declarations based on unauthorized instructions;
- Loss to the interior of any structure or building caused by dust, sand, ice, sleet, snow, or rain unless the outside of the structure or building is damaged first. Coverage also applies if the loss results from the melting of sleet, ice, or snow on the structure or building;
- Restrictions on coverage for porcelain, marble, glassware, and animals unless loss or damage is caused by a list of named perils known as specified causes of loss. These perils are described in the Definitions section of the property portion of the policy and include water damage, sleet, ice, the weight of snow, falling objects, volcanic action, sinkhole collapse, sprinkler leakage, vandalism, riot or civil commotion, aircraft or vehicles, smoke, windstorm or hail, explosion, lightning, fire; or
- Special limits of liability exist for losses resulting from theft. The $2,500 sublimit applies to dies, molds, patterns, precious stones, gold, silver, platinum, watches, furs, and jewelry. Watches and jewelry worth $100 or less are not subject to the limitation.

The *exclusions* in the businessowners property coverage are similar to those previously discussed:

- Earth movement;
- Ordinance or law;
- Governmental action;
- Utility service (power failure);
- Nuclear hazard;
- War and military action;
- Water (waterborne material, mudflow, waves, and flood);
- Certain computer-related losses (malfunction, failure, or inadequacy of software, hardware, networks, etc.);
- Virus or bacteria;
- Wet rot, dry rot, and fungi except as covered in the additional coverage for wet or dry rot and fungi;
- Electrical apparatus (artificially generated electrical current);
- Consequential losses (delay, loss of market, or loss of use);
- Smoke, gas, vapor (smoke from industrial operations or agricultural smudging);
- Explosion of a steam apparatus;
- Frozen plumbing;
- Dishonesty;
- False pretense (voluntarily parting with the property if induced by device, scheme, or trick);
- Collapse (except as specified in the additional coverage);
- Exposed property damaged by sleet, ice, snow, or rain;
- Neglect;
- Pollution;
- Expected losses (gradual deterioration, wear and tear, mechanical breakdown, etc.);
- Errors or omissions;
- Electrical disturbance;
- Installation, testing, repair;

- Constant or continual seepage or leakage of water;
- Weather conditions that only contribute to an otherwise excluded cause of loss;
- Negligent work;
- Decisions or acts, including failure to decide or act;
- Loss or damage to products caused by an error or omission;
- Business income and additional expense resulting from delays or cancellation of a lease; and
- Accounts receivable — Loss or damage resulting from bookkeeping, accounting, or billing errors or omission; and falsification, alteration, destruction, or concealment of records of accounts receivable done to conceal the wrongful taking, giving, or withholding of money, securities, or other property.

Additional Coverages

The businessowners property coverage includes several *additional coverages* explained below. Be sure to pay close attention to the numbers associated with each coverage:

Debris removal: 25% / 180 days / $10,000 — Up to 25% of the direct loss is covered, plus the deductible if reported within the end of the policy period or 180 days of the loss, whichever is earlier. If the direct loss and debris removal amounts exceed the limit of insurance, or if the debris removal cost exceeds the 25% limitation, the policy will pay an additional $10,000 under the coverage for debris removal.

Preservation of property: 30 days — Commonly called removal coverage, this coverage provides 30 days of coverage for property that is removed temporarily to protect it from damage.

Fire department service charge: $2,500 — The limit of $2,500 is included as an additional amount of coverage unless a different limit is shown in the Declarations.

Collapse — The collapse of a building is covered if it is caused by one of the specified causes of loss. These include the weight of people or property, insects or vermin, hidden decay, or the use of defective materials if the collapse happens during construction. This additional coverage is provided only in the special form.

Water damage, other liquids, powder, or molten material damage — If damage or loss results from any of these causes of loss, the insurer will pay to tear out and replace any part of the structure or building. It will also repair the appliance or system from which the water or other substance leaked. This additional coverage is provided only in the special form.

Business income: Actual loss sustained / 12 months / Ordinary payroll / 60 days / 72-hour waiting period — Loss of business income is covered during the restoration period following a direct loss to covered property. Coverage is limited to one year following the loss of business income and 60 days following the immediate loss of ordinary payroll. The limit of insurance does not apply to this additional coverage.

Extended business income: 30 days — The policy will pay for the necessary postponement of business operations from the time property is rebuilt, repaired or replaced, and operations are resumed to the date operations are re-established to the level that would have existed without the loss, or 30 days after the property is rebuilt, repaired, or replaced, and operations are resumed, whichever is earlier.

Extra expense: Actual loss sustained / 12 months / No waiting period — Extra expense coverage in the businessowners policy is provided for up to 12 months after a direct loss to covered property. The limit of insurance does not apply to this additional coverage.

Pollutant cleanup and removal: $10,000 / 12 months / 180 days — The policy will cover up to $10,000 for expenses incurred in 12 months. These expenses are to remove pollutants from water or land at the described premises if the pollution is caused by a covered cause of loss and is reported to the insurance provider within 180 days. This coverage is an additional amount of insurance. This coverage does not apply to the cost of testing for the existence or effects of pollutants.

Civil authority: 72 hours / 4 weeks — Loss of business income or extra expense caused by an act of civil authority is also covered. This act must prevent access to the premises due to a direct loss elsewhere. Coverage for business income will start 72 hours after the action and continues for up to four consecutive weeks.

Money orders and counterfeit paper currency: $1,000 — The policy also will cover up to $1,000 for losses that result from the good faith acceptance of unpaid money orders or counterfeit currency. The limitation for money and securities does not apply to this coverage.

Forgery and alteration — Up to $2,500 for losses resulting from forged or altered checks or drafts is also covered, including defense coverage.

Increased cost of construction: $10,000 — Structures or buildings insured on a replacement cost basis are covered for increased costs incurred to comply with a law or ordinance. The enforcement of such regulations must occur while repairing, rebuilding, or replacing damaged parts of the property if the damage resulted from a covered cause of loss. This coverage is not subject to the law or ordinance exclusion and is subject to a $10,000 sublimit.

Glass expenses — The policy will pay for expenses incurred to install temporary plates or board-up openings in the damaged glass. It will also cover the cost of replacing or removing obstructions when repairing or replacing glass that is not part of a building.

Business income from dependent properties: $5,000 — Loss of business income due to physical damage or loss at the premises of a dependent property resulting from a covered cause of loss is covered up to a limit of $5,000. This coverage does not apply to loss or damage to electronic data.

Fire extinguisher systems recharge expense: $5,000 — The policy will cover up to $5,000 for replacing or recharging fire extinguishers if discharged on or within 100 feet of the premises. Loss from an accidental discharge of chemicals from extinguishers is also covered.

Electronic data: $10,000 — The policy will pay up to $10,000 (or more if a higher limit is listed in the Declarations) for the cost to restore or replace electronic data damaged by a covered cause of loss. Losses are valued at the replacement cost of the media on which the data is stored. Viruses are a covered cause of loss for this particular coverage.

Interruption of computer operations: $10,000 — The coverage provided under business income and extra expense may be broadened to apply to the suspension of business resulting from an interruption in computer operations due to damage of electronic data caused by a covered cause of loss, including a computer virus. The policy will pay up to $10,000 for this coverage unless a higher limit is indicated in the Declarations.

Limited coverage for wet rot, dry rot, and fungi: $15,000 — The policy will cover up to $15,000 for loss or damage by wet rot, dry rot, or fungi. The loss must result from a specified cause of loss other than lightning or fire.

Coverage Extensions

Coverage can be broadened from the business personal property or building coverage section when the applicable limit of insurance is specified on the declarations page. The policy contains several coverage extensions that are in addition to the limit of insurance:

Newly acquired or constructed property: $250,000 for buildings / $100,000 for BPP — The policy owner may extend coverage up to $250,000 to buildings being built on the premises and buildings acquired at a new location. Up to $100,000 is available for newly obtained business personal property. Coverage will only apply for 30 days after the policy owner acquires the property or the end of the policy period, whichever comes first.

Personal property off premises: $10,000 — Coverage up to $10,000 is available for business personal property. This coverage does not include securities and money during transportation or temporarily at the premises the policy owner does not operate, lease, use, or own.

Outdoor property: $2,500 total / $1,000 per tree, shrub, or plant — The policyholder may extend the coverage to apply to detached signs and trees, outdoor radio and television antennas, shrubs, and plants if the loss results from an explosion, lightning, fire, riot or civil commotion, or aircraft. The insurance provider will pay up to $2,500 for this coverage extension but not more than $1,000 for any shrub, plant, or tree.

Personal effects: $2,500 — Business personal property coverage may be broadened to apply to personal belongings owned by the policy owner, officers, partners, and employees. The insurance provider will pay up to $2,500 at each described premises.

Valuable papers and records: $10,000 on-premises / $5,000 off-premises — Coverage up to $10,000 is available for the cost to research, restore, or replace lost information for which copies are not available on the premises. It will also cover $5,000 for valuable papers and records not at the described premises. Insurers will value losses at the cost of replacement or restoration.

Accounts receivable: $10,000 on-premises / $5,000 off-premises — The policyholder may extend business personal property coverage to apply to *accounts receivable*. The policy will pay the following:

- All amounts due from the policy owner's customers that the policy owner is unable to collect;
- Interest charges on any loan required to offset uncollectible amounts pending the insurance provider's payment of these amounts;
- Collections expenses exceeding standard collection costs that are made necessary by damage or loss; and
- Other reasonable expenses that the policy owner incurs to restore records of account receivables. Such expenses result from direct physical damage or loss by a covered cause of loss to the policy owner's accounts receivable records.

The most the policy will cover under this extension for damage or loss in any one occurrence is $10,000 unless a higher limit of insurance for accounts receivable is described in the Declarations. For accounts receivable that are not at the indicated premises, the most the extension will pay is $5,000.

Limits of Insurance

The policy will cover up to the *limits of insurance* shown in the Declarations. The following specific limits apply:

- In any one occurrence, outdoor signs attached to the building are covered for $1,000 per sign;
- The following additional coverage extensions are paid in addition to the limits of insurance:
  - Pollutant cleanup and removal;
  - Fire department service charge;
  - Business income from dependent properties;
  - Increased cost of construction;

      o   Interruption of computer operations; and
      o   Electronic data.

The Business Property Coverage Form includes two provisions that pertain to automatic coverage increases:

1. **Building Limit (Automatic Increase)** — The building's limit of insurance will automatically increase annually by *8%* or the percentage amount listed in the Declarations; and
2. **Business Personal Property Limit (Seasonal Increase)** — The business personal property limit will automatically increase by *25%* for seasonal fluctuations unless stated in the Declarations. This increase is only applicable if the policyholder carries insurance equal to 100% of the average monthly values for the past 12 months.

Deductibles

The most the insurance provider will pay for any loss is the limit of insurance after the policy owner pays the deductible. The deductible *does not apply* to any of the following:

- Fire extinguisher systems recharge expense;
- Fire department service charge;
- Extra expense;
- Business income;
- Optional coverage selections; or
- Civil authority coverages.

Property Loss and General Conditions

The following *conditions* found in the Business Property Coverage Form apply in addition to the common policy conditions:

- **Appraisal**;
- **Abandonment**;
- **Duties in the event of loss or damage** — The following are the policy owner's duties in the event of loss or damage:
  - Inform the police if a law has been broken;
  - Give the insurance provider prompt notice of loss and a description of when, how, and where it took place, including a description of damaged property;
  - Take all reasonable steps to protect covered property from additional damage and keep a record of every expense;
  - Provide an inventory of the damaged and undamaged property at the insurer's request;
  - Allow the insurer to examine the property and inspect the insured's records and books;
  - Send the insurance provider a signed, sworn proof of loss within 60 days of the request;
  - Cooperate with the insurance provider in the investigation and settlement;
  - Resume business operations as soon as possible; and
  - The insurance provider has a right to examine any policyholder under oath;
- **Legal action against the insurer** — The policy owner must be in full compliance with all policy provisions before bringing legal action against the insurer, and the action must be brought within 24 months of the date of loss;
- **Loss payment** — In the event of damage or loss, the insurance company has the option to do the following:
  - Pay the value of the damaged or lost property;
  - Pay the cost to replace or repair the damaged or lost property;

- ○ Take all or any part of the damaged or lost property at an appraised or agreed upon price;
- ○ Replace, rebuild, or repair the damaged or lost property with like kind and quality;
- ○ The insurer will provide notice of intentions within 30 days of receiving the sworn proof of loss;
- ○ At the time of the loss, the policy will pay on a replacement cost basis if the property is insured for 80% or more of the full replacement value;
- ○ The policy will pay the greater of ACV or the coinsurance formula if the property is not insured to 80% of the full replacement value; and
- ○ Replacement cost payment will not occur until all repairs are made in a timely fashion. The policy owner can choose to settle the loss on an ACV basis. If the cost to replace or repair is less than $2,500, then the insurance company will not require replacement or repair of the property;

- **Recovered property** — If the property is recovered after loss settlement, the policy owner may either keep the property and return any loss settlement payment or surrender the property to the insurance provider;
- **Resumption of operations** — The insurer will decrease the amount of business income and extra expense losses to the extent the policyholder can resume operations by using damaged and undamaged property;
- **Vacancy** — If a building is vacant for more than 60 consecutive days, insurers will not cover losses caused by the following: theft or attempted theft, vandalism, building glass breakage, sprinkler leakage (unless the insured takes protective measures), and water damage. Insurers will cover losses in a building unoccupied for more than 60 days caused by any other covered perils for an amount that is 15% less than normal coverage under the policy. It is worth noting that buildings under renovation or construction are not considered unoccupied. When a policy is issued to a tenant, a vacancy occurs when the building does not contain sufficient business personal property to conduct normal operations. When the policy is issued to the general lessee or owner of a building, a vacancy occurs when at least 65% of the square footage is not rented or is unused.

General Conditions

The *four general conditions* in *Section I – Property* of the businessowners policy include:

1. **Control of property** — Any act of neglect of any person other than the policy owner beyond the policy owner's control or direction will not affect this coverage. The breach of any condition of this insurance form at any location will not affect coverage where the breach of condition does not exist at the time of loss or damage.
2. **Mortgage holders** — Protection for a mortgage holder exists in the policy as long as the mortgage holder meets certain conditions. We covered these conditions earlier, so be sure to review them.
3. **No benefit to bailee** — No organization or person (other than the policy owner) having custody of covered property will benefit from this coverage.
4. **Policy period, coverage territory** — The insurance provider will cover damages or losses during the policy period and within the coverage territory. Insurers will also cover property in transit between ports in the coverage territory. The U.S. (including its territories and possessions), Puerto Rico, and Canada are included in the coverage territory.

Optional Coverages

The businessowners property coverage form has several optional coverages built into it. For coverage to apply, a policy must indicate a limit and premium on the declarations page. The optional coverages include the following:

- **Outdoor signs** — All outdoor signs owned or in the policy owner's control, custody, or care can be insured. The signs are usually insured on an open peril basis for an amount of coverage specified in the

Declarations. Common exclusions include mechanical breakdown, corrosion, rust, hidden or latent defects, and wear and tear. Without additional coverage, the businessowners policy will pay $1,000 per sign in any one occurrence for loss or damage to outdoor signs *affixed to the building*. However, this additional coverage allows the policy owner to purchase more insurance for outdoor signs.

- **Money and securities** — Loss of money and securities resulting from destruction, disappearance, or theft can be covered. The policy owner must maintain records of the money and securities so that the insurance provider can verify the amount of loss or damage. For coverage to apply, the money or securities must have been located at a financial institution, the insured premises, the policy owner's or employee's home, or in transit from one of these locations. Separate limits are specified for losses inside and outside the premises.
- **Employee dishonesty** — Loss to money and securities or business personal property caused by dishonest acts of employees is covered. Under this additional coverage, employees refer to anyone currently employed or terminated within the past *30 days*. Acts committed by the policyholder or partners are excluded. The policy Declarations will indicate the applicable limit of insurance. In addition, coverage on any employee automatically ends once the policyholder learns of previous acts of dishonesty.
- **Equipment breakdown protection** — This additional coverage protects against a direct loss or damage to covered property, including mechanical or electrical equipment and machinery, resulting from a mechanical breakdown or electrical failure to pressure.

Definitions

Definitions found in the BOP coverage form include, but are not limited to, the following:

- *Money* means currency, bank notes, coins, and traveler's checks or money orders held for sale;
- *Period of restoration* for business income coverage will start immediately for extra expense coverage or 72 hours after the direct loss. The period of restoration ends on the date business has resumed or the property has been repaired;
- *Pollutants* include any thermal, gaseous, liquid, or solid contaminant or irritant;
- *Specified causes of loss* refers to water damage, snow or sleet, the weight of ice, falling objects, volcanic action, sinkhole collapse, leakage from fire-extinguishing equipment, vandalism, riot or civil commotion, aircraft or vehicles, smoke, windstorm or hail, explosion, lightning, and fire; and
- *Valuable papers and records* inscribed, manuscripts, written or printed documents, and records (including mortgages, deeds, maps, films, drawings, books, or abstracts). Money or securities are included in the term valuable papers and records.

BOP Section II – Liability

Coverages

Business liability – The liability coverage contained in the businessowners policy is similar to the CGL policy. One significant difference is that this section is included in every policy and cannot be written on a monoline basis. The businessowners policy liability section has the following features:

- Usually issued with an occurrence coverage trigger;
- Supplemental payment features are covered in addition to the limit of insurance in the Declarations;
- Includes coverage for property damage, bodily injury, and personal and advertising injury for an occurrence within the coverage territory and coverage period;

- The limit of liability is the most the insurance company will pay contingent upon an aggregate amount for the policy term; and
- The insurer's responsibility to defend terminates when the limits of insurance are depleted.

Medical expenses – Medical payments coverage will pay for hospital, medical, dental, and funeral services sustained within *one year* from the date of an accident. It covers an individual who suffers bodily injury from an accident on or near the policy owner's premises or because of the policy owner's operations.

Exclusions

The business liability and medical payments coverages contain the following *exclusions*:

- **Expected or intended injury** — This exclusion does not apply to bodily injury that is caused by the use of reasonable force to protect the property or an individual;
- **Contractual liability** — This exclusion does not apply to the insured contracts;
- **Liquor liability** — There is no coverage for liability arising out of the following: causing or contributing to a person's intoxication, providing alcohol to a minor or a person who is already intoxicated, or any ordinance or regulation relating to the distribution, sale, or gift of alcoholic beverages. This exclusion applies only to policy owners involved in any business that manufactures, distributes, sells, serves, or furnishes alcohol (host liquor);
- **Workers compensation and similar laws** — There is no coverage for any duty the policy owner has under workers compensation or similar laws;
- **Employer's liability** — Bodily injury to an employee during employment, including the employee's spouse, children, or siblings, is not covered. Any liability assumed under an insured contract does not apply to this exclusion;
- **Pollution** — Property damage or bodily injury resulting from alleged or actual pollution is excluded. The exclusion does not apply to fumes, smoke, or heat from a hostile fire;
- **Aircraft, auto, or watercraft** — Property damage or bodily injury resulting from the use, maintenance, ownership, or entrustment to others of any auto, aircraft, or watercraft is not covered. This exclusion does not apply to the following perils and property that insurers will cover:
  - Watercraft while on shore at the premises owned by the policy owner;
  - Non-owned watercraft *less than 51 feet long* and not being used to transport property or individuals for a fee;
  - Parking an auto on or next to the premises rented or owned by the policy owner. The auto cannot be rented, owned, or loaned to the policyholder;
  - Liability assumed under an insured contract;
  - If not subject to a compulsory or financial responsibility law, property damage or bodily injury arising out of the operation of equipment or machinery attached to or part of a vehicle that meets the definition of mobile equipment; and
  - Property damage or bodily injury that results from the operation of a cherry picker or similar equipment mounted on trucks, pumps, air compressors, and generators.
- **Mobile equipment** — The transportation of mobile equipment by an auto or the use of mobile equipment in any speed, demolition, or racing contest is not covered;
- **War** — War, including undeclared civil war, insurrections, warlike actions, revolutions, rebellions, or actions taken by government authority are not covered;
- **Professional services** — There is no coverage for property damage, bodily injury, or personal or advertising injury due to the rendering or failure to render professional services described in the exclusion;
- **Property damage to property the policy owner owns or is in their control, custody, or care;**

- **Damage to the policy owner's product or work**;
- **Damage to tangible property or property not physically injured**;
- **Recall of work, products, or tangible property**;
- **Personal and advertising injury exclusions** — These are the same as the exclusions discussed in the CGL coverage form;
- **Electronic data** — Damages arising out of damage to electronic data or its loss of use are not covered;
- **Criminal acts of the policy owner**;
- **Recording and distribution of information which violates the law** — Property damage, bodily injury, or personal and advertising injury caused by a violation of laws such as the CAN-SPAM Act, the Telephone Consumer Protection Act, the FCRA, and any federal, state, or local regulation, ordinance, or statute is not covered;
- **Medical expense exclusions** — These are the same exclusions previously discussed for medical payments in the CGL coverage form; and
- **Nuclear energy liability exclusion** — This applies to all liability coverages.

Who is an Insured

When the named insured is listed on the declarations page as *an individual or sole proprietor*, that individual and their spouse are insureds, but only regarding the business.

When the named insured is specified as a *partnership or joint venture*, the named insured, their spouse, and partners also are insureds, but only concerning the business.

When the named insured is listed as a *limited liability company (LLC)*, the named insured and members are also insureds, but only regarding the conduct of the business. Managers are also insureds, but only regarding their duties as managers.

The named insured and trustees are covered when the insured is designated as *a trust*.

When the named insured is listed as an organization other than a joint venture, partnership (corporations), or LLC, the named insured is covered. Directors and executive officers are insureds, but only concerning their duties as directors and officers. Stockholders are also insureds, but only regarding their liability as stockholders.

Each of the following can also be considered an insured:

- A volunteer while executing the duties related to the insured business or its employees;
- An employee during employment;
- Any individual (other than a volunteer or employee) of any organization acting as the policy owner's real estate manager;
- Any organization or individual having temporary custody of the property if the named insured dies; and
- The legal representative if the named insured dies, but only regarding their obligations as such.

No organization or person is considered an insured regarding the conduct of any past or current partnership, joint venture, or LLC that is not listed as a named insured on the declarations page.

Limits of Insurance

The amount of insurance listed in the Declarations is the most the policy will cover regardless of the number of insureds, organizations, individuals bringing suit, or claims filed or lawsuits brought.

Medical expenses are paid per person and are also contingent upon the limit in the Declarations.

Similar *aggregate limits* exist in the businessowners policy as in the CGL policy. The policy includes an aggregate for completed operations exposures and products, which is double the occurrence limit. Another aggregate similar to the general aggregate in the CGL policy applies to all property damage, bodily injury, personal and advertising injury, and medical expense claims not associated with completed operations or products. This aggregate is also double the occurrence limit shown in the Declarations.

In addition, the policy includes a *separate limit* of insurance for fire damage liability which can be incorporated in aggregate based on the nature of the claim.

The limits of insurance under the liability section apply separately to every successive yearly period and any remaining period of less than one year, beginning with the start of the policy period listed on the declarations page.

General Conditions

In addition to the common policy conditions, the following conditions apply to the liability coverage:

- **Bankruptcy** — Insolvency or bankruptcy of the policyholder does not relieve the insurer of any obligation.
- **Duties in the event of an occurrence, claim, or suit** — In the event of a loss, the policyholder's responsibilities include the following:
  - Promptly informing the insurance provider of the occurrence (when, how, where, names, and addresses of any injured individuals);
  - Prompt written notice of a claim;
  - Promptly informing the insurance provider of any legal papers received related to the loss; and
  - Assisting and cooperating in the investigation of a claim.
- **Legal action against the insurance provider** — No party can join or bring the insurer into legal action against the policy owner. Also, no party can sue the insurer unless full compliance with policy terms exists. A party can sue the insurer to recover an agreed-upon settlement; however, the payment cannot surpass the policy limits nor include items not insured by the policy.
- **Separation of insured** — The limit of insurance is only paid once per occurrence, irrespective of the number of insureds or the number of claimants covered by the policy.

Definitions

The Business Liability Coverage Form includes the definitions of bodily injury, personal injury, advertising injury, coverage territory, mobile equipment, insured contract, insured product, products/completed operations hazard, and other terms relevant to liability and medical expense forms.

BOP Section III — Common Policy Conditions

The businessowners policy contains the *common policy conditions* applicable to *Section I – Property* and *Section II – Liability*, in addition to the conditions included in those separate coverage sections. These conditions are similar to the previously discussed commercial property conditions, commercial liability conditions, and common policy conditions. The businessowners common policy conditions are listed below:

Cancellation — The policy owner can cancel the policy at any time by mailing a written notice to the insurer. Only the first named insured may request the cancellation in a policy listing two or more insureds in the Declarations. The insurance provider can cancel the policy by mailing the first named insured a written notice of cancellation.

The insurer requires advance written notice of policy cancellation so the policy owner can obtain other insurance. Additional requirements for *notice by mail* include the following:

- Delivered or mailed to the policy owner *five days* before the date of cancellation, provided that any of the following conditions exist at the insured building:
    - The building is vacant for 60 or more consecutive days (buildings with 65% or more of the floor area or rental units vacant are considered unoccupied);
    - Permanent repairs for damage caused by a covered loss have not been arranged for within 30 days of the initial payment of loss;
    - The building has a demolition order, outstanding order to vacate, or has been declared unsafe by a government authority;
    - Salvageable and fixed items have been removed from the building and are not being replaced;
    - The policy owner fails to furnish necessary utilities (water, heat, sewer) for 30 or more consecutive days (except during seasonal vacancy); or
    - The policy owner fails to pay property taxes owed or outstanding for more than one year;
- Must be delivered or mailed to the policy owner *ten days before* the date of cancellation if nonpayment of premium is the reason for cancellation;
- Must be delivered or mailed to the policy owner *30 days before* the date of cancellation for any other reason (may vary by state);
- The insurer only has to verify that the notice was mailed to the first named insured at the mailing address on file with the insurance provider, not that the notice was actually delivered; and
- When cancellation results in a return of premium, the refund is forwarded to the first named insured.

Changes — This condition states that the policy makes up the entire contract between the policy owner and the insurer. The policy can be revised only by a written request from the first named insured and with approval from the insurer.

Concealment, misrepresentation, or fraud — The policy will be voided if any policy owner commits fraud relating to the policy or intentionally misrepresents or conceals a material fact regarding the policy, covered property, the policy owner's interest in the covered property, or a claim under the policy.

Examination of books and records — The insurer can audit and examine the policy owner's records and books at any reasonable time during the policy period. Such audits can occur up to *three years* after a policy is no longer in force.

Inspections and surveys — The insurer has the right to inspect the policyholder's premises and operations at any time during the policy period. These inspections aim to determine the insurability of the property and operations, set proper insurance premiums, and make loss control recommendations. Such inspections do not guarantee that the property or operations are safe and in compliance with state laws.

Insurance under multiple coverages — If two or more coverages in the policy apply to the same loss, the insurance provider will not pay more than the actual amount of the loss.

Liberalization — If the insurer adopts any change that extends coverage without an additional premium within 45 days before or during the policy period, that coverage will immediately apply to the policy.

Other insurance — When a loss is covered by other insurance, the insurer will pay only the amount exceeding the other coverage, regardless of whether or not the policy owner can collect from the other insurance.

Premiums — The first named insured must pay the premium under the policy. In addition, if the insurance company ever gives any refund, it will be sent to the first named insured.

Premium audit — The policy is subject to an audit if a premium is designated as an advanced premium in the Declarations. The final premium due will be calculated when actual exposures are determined. The first named insured must maintain records of information necessary for premium calculation and send copies to the insurer at the insurer's request.

Subrogation (transfer of rights of recovery against others to the insurance provider) — The insurer has the right to recoup its claim payment from a negligent third party.

Transfer of rights and duties under the policy — The policy owner may not transfer any rights or duties under the policy to any other entity or individual without the insurer's written consent. Also, the policy owner's rights and duties are automatically transferred to the policy owner's legal representative upon death.

Chapter Review

This chapter explained the different types of property insurance policies. Let's review them:

BUSINESSOWNERS	
Purpose	<ul><li>For small to medium-sized businesses</li><li>A prepackaged policy that contains both property and liability coverages</li><li>Coverage is included in a package policy that cannot be excluded by the insured</li></ul>
Eligible Businesses	<ul><li>Apartments</li><li>Office buildings</li><li>Mercantile/processing/service establishments</li><li>Contractors (certain types)</li><li>Convenience stores</li><li>Fast-food restaurants</li></ul>
BOP Section I – Property	<ul><li>Businessowners property coverage must be activated in the Declarations and is available for buildings, business personal property, or both</li><li>This form insures risks of direct physical loss to covered property, contingent upon certain limitations and exclusions</li><li>The businessowners property coverage includes several additional coverages</li><li>Coverage can be broadened from the business personal property or building coverage section when the applicable limit of insurance is specified in the Declarations</li><li>The policy will cover up to the limits of insurance shown in the Declarations</li><li>The most the insurance provider will pay for any one loss is the limit of insurance after the deductible is paid</li><li>The four *general conditions* found in Section I of the businessowners policy include:<ul><li>Control of property</li><li>Mortgage holders</li><li>No benefit to bailee</li><li>Policy period, coverage territory</li></ul></li></ul>

BUSINESSOWNERS *(Continued)*	
BOP Section II – Liability	• *Business liability* – The liability coverage contained in the businessowners policy is very similar to the CGL policy • One major difference is that this section is included in every policy, and cannot be written on a monoline basis

BOP Section III – Common Policy Conditions	• These conditions are similar to the commercial property conditions, commercial liability conditions and common policy conditions previously discussed
	   o Cancellation
	   o Changes
	   o Concealment, misrepresentation, or fraud
	   o Examination of books and records
	   o Inspections and surveys
	   o Insurance under multiple coverages
	   o Liberalization
	   o Other insurance
	   o Premiums
	   o Premium audit
	   o Subrogation
	   o Transfer of rights and duties under the policy

Optional Coverages	• *Outdoor signs* – all outdoor signs owned or in the control, custody, or care of the insured can be covered • *Money and securities* – loss of money and securities resulting from disappearance, theft, or destruction can be covered • *Employee dishonesty* – loss to money and securities or business personal property that results from the dishonest acts of employees is covered • *Equipment breakdown protection* – this coverage protects against a direct loss or damage to covered property resulting from a mechanical breakdown or electrical failure to mechanical, pressure, or electrical equipment and machinery

CHAPTER 19:
Ocean Marine

You will now learn about the oldest type of insurance policy – ocean marine. This chapter explains the types of losses this insurance covers and typical policy provisions and exclusions. There are a lot of terms that you will need to know to understand the language of these policies. By the end of this chapter, you should know the differences between hull and cargo coverage and be able to explain the major provisions and exclusions that apply to ocean marine policies.

- Hull Coverage
- Cargo Coverage
- Freight Insurance
- Protection and Indemnity Insurance

Overview

The oldest type of insurance in the world is *Ocean Marine*. Edward Lloyd opened a coffeehouse in London in 1689 that became a meeting place for individuals to buy and sell insurance. Today's Lloyd's of London grew out of these beginnings. Lloyd's list provides the name, position, destination, and other essential data of all merchant ships operating in the free world.

Most ocean marine policy forms were implemented by Lloyd's around 1780 with little change since. The forms contain archaic terms but have proved reliable in courts, and Lloyd's is reluctant to make changes. They are kept up to date by adding printed institute clauses to them.

OCEAN MARINE TERMS

- *Adventure* is a trip or voyage
- *Assured* refers to the insured
- *Average* means loss
- *Constructive total loss* refers to the cost to repair or recover over and above the value or policy limit.
- *Demurrage* is a vessel delay beyond the usual time to on-load or off-load or a charge for the delay.
- *Laid up* refers to a vessel in port or at anchor.
- *Loss of specie* means the insured item is no longer what it was after severe damage.
- *Misfortune* is an accident or occurrence.
- *Particular* means partial.
- *Touching* means applying to something.

Hull Coverage

A hull policy is a type of ocean marine coverage that provides physical damage insurance for the ship while it is in transit.

If an insured vessel's *ownership changes*, the hull policy is terminated:

- At the time of a change in ownership;
- If at sea, when arriving at the final port; or
- If the termination is involuntary, 15 days following the transfer of ownership.

After a loss, a hull policy will pay maintenance and wages to the master, officers, and crew while removing the vessel from one port to another for repairs or a trial trip to test repairs.

The insurance provider will not pay maintenance and wages for the master and crew when the ship is undergoing repairs. The insurance provider has the right to pick the port of repair and has the right to veto any proposed repair facility.

The hull policy covers sighting the bottom after stranding, regardless of whether or not damage is detected. The hull policy never covers scraping and painting the bottom of the ship.

American Institute Hull Clauses (AIHC)

American Institute Hull Clauses were created to establish wording to be used in marine policies in order to minimize confusion. Although hull policies could be issued for a voyage, for a specific period of time, or for a voyage plus a stated amount of time in port after the voyage, most AIHC policies are written for a 1-year term. Explained below are clauses found in the American institute form.

Assured – The *assured* is listed in the policy. If payment is made to anyone other than the vessel's owner, it will be made to the extent the owner would have collected. It also includes a waiver of subrogation to related entities of the assured.

Loss Payee – The *loss payee* is the party to be paid by the insurance provider in the event of a loss. The loss payee could be a lien holder or mortgagee.

Vessel – The *vessel* is the ship itself and is insured for physical damage or loss by the hull policy. Insurers will also cover equipment owned by others and installed on the ship. No coverage exists for barges, cargo containers, or lighters (flat-bottom ships used to unload cargo ships).

Duration of Risk – The *duration of the risk* on hull policies could be for a stated period for a voyage. In other words, from one place to another and typically for an additional 24 hours after moored at anchor safely at the port of destination. The duration of the risk could also be for a stated period for a mixed voyage plus a specified period in port after arrival. Most AIHC policies are written with a 1-year coverage term.

Agreed Value – Most hull policies are written on an *agreed value* basis. The insured and insurance provider agree upon the ship's value when the contract is made. This amount is paid in the event of a total loss.

Amount Insured Hereunder – The limit of insurance is also known as the *amount insured hereunder*.

Deductible (or Deductible Average Clause) – Any *deductibles* will be expressed as a dollar amount in the policy. For total losses, a deductible does not apply.

Premium, Return of Premium, and Nonpayment of Premium – The *premium* is specified in the policy. It is fully earned in the event of a total loss.

Insurers will apply a *return of premium* on a pro rata basis upon a change of ownership of the vessel. Premiums will also be returned on a pro rata basis for every 30 consecutive days laid up in port, not under repair and not being used for lighting or storage. A pro rata refund is due if the insurance provider cancels the policy. If the assured cancels the policy, a short-rate refund is due.

The underwriter can cancel an in-force policy after 30 days for *nonpayment of premium* with ten days' notice to the assured or broker who negotiated the contract. The full annual premium will be earned if a total loss takes place before the cancellation.

Adventure – The *adventure* describes when the vessel is insured and not insured. Generally, it will be insured during the policy period while at sea, in docks, towing other ships in distress, on trial trips, and sailing with or without pilots. The vessel cannot be towed by other ships in other than a customary manner.

Causes of Loss – Hull policies cover losses caused by the perils of lighting, fire, earthquake, jettison, assailing thieves, and the barratry of the master and mariners. They also cover all other similar perils that may damage, detriment, or hurt the vessel.

Additional perils are also insured if such damage or loss has not arisen from want of due diligence by the vessel's assured, owners, or managers. This clause is commonly referred to as the *Inchmaree Clause* and covers the following perils:

- Accidents in loading, handling, or discharging cargo or in bunkering;
- Accidents in going on or off the vessel while on dry docks, graving docks, ways, pontoons, or gridirons;
- Explosions on shipboard or elsewhere;
- Breakdown of motor generators or other electrical equipment, breaking of shafts, bursting of boilers, or any latent defect in the hull or machinery;
- Accidents to or the breakdown of reactors or nuclear installations not on board the insured vessel;
- Contact with any land conveyance or with aircraft, rockets, or similar missiles;
- Negligence of charterers or repairers; or
- Negligence of masters, officers, pilots, or crew.

Deliberate damage to property resulting from government authorities acting on behalf of the public to prevent or mitigate a pollution hazard is covered under the hull policy. The event that created the situation leading to the governmental interaction must have caused a recoverable claim if the deliberate damage had not occurred.

Claims (General Provisions) – In any accident or occurrence that could lead to a claim, prompt notice needs to be given to the underwriters. The underwriters can appoint their own surveyor to determine the extent of the damage. The underwriters can decide where the vessel will proceed for repairs and veto any proposed repair firm.

When the underwriters direct the vessel to a particular port for repair, the insurance provider will pay the expenses, including maintenance and wages for the master, officers, and crew. Wages and maintenance also will be paid for the master, officers, and crew during any trial trip to test the repairs. Insurers will only pay wages and maintenance while the vessel is underway.

The costs of sighting the bottom after stranding will be covered new for old without deduction even when no damage is detected. In no case does the policy cover scraping or painting the bottom.

The insurance provider also will cover loss or damage to equipment installed for use on board the vessel and for which the assured has assumed responsibility but does not own.

General Average and Salvage – *Average* in ocean marine language means loss or damage. A general average is some sort of loss that everyone associated with the voyage helps to pay. A particular average is damage or loss that only the particular people involved in the loss help pay.

General average is a clause contained within ocean marine policies. It stipulates that when there is a sacrifice of property to save the ship, crew, and other cargo, all who benefit from this sacrifice have to share in the payment for the sacrificed property.

Insurers will pay the agreed value in the event of a total loss. A total loss could take place in two ways:

1. Actual total loss where all property is destroyed or the insured is deprived of all property even though it is not destroyed; or
2. Constructive total loss in which the cost to repair or replace exceeds the policy limit.

If a total loss is paid, the insured will unconditionally abandon their interest to the insurance provider. The insurer has the salvage rights.

Sue and Labor – In the event of a loss or misfortune, the master and crew must sue and labor to prevent further loss and keep the loss as slight as possible. The insurance provider will pay reasonable expenses in doing so. The insurance provider may refuse to pay the claim if the master and crew do not sue and labor to prevent further loss.

Collision Liability – The hull policy's collision clause is a type of liability coverage because it pays for damage to another's ship with which the assured's ship has collided. The assured must have been at fault for payment to apply.

The *sister ship clause* specifies that in the event the assured collides with a ship also owned by the same assured, each vessel has the same rights as if the collision was with a ship owned by someone other than the assured. If a question of liability arises, an arbitrator will determine the outcome.

When both vessels are at fault for a collision, the indemnity is determined on the principle of cross liabilities. Each vessel owner would pay the other vessel owner the amount of damage based on the percentage of fault, subject to its limit of collision liability. The exception is if one of the vessel's ability to collect damages is restricted by law.

Example 19.1 – A vessel owned by Buccaneer Shipping collided with a vessel owned by Nautical Shipping, and both were determined to be at fault. Buccaneer incurred $50,000 in damage and was judged 75% at fault. Nautical incurred $100,000 and was deemed 25% at fault. The principle of cross liability will apply as follows: Buccaneer owes Nautical 75% of $100,000, or $75,000. Nautical owes Buccaneer 25% of $50,000, or $12,500. The net settlement will be a payment of $75,000 minus $12,500 or $62,500 by Buccaneer to Nautical.

Limitations of Liability – Although most ocean marine insurance is issued on an all-risk basis, it intends to cover the perils of the sea. Losses because of war, civil commotion, riots, strikes, deterioration, decay, and inherent vice are not covered.

Pilotage and Towage – In some areas of the world, narrow waters exist (straits, ports, etc.). In these areas, vessels must use pilotage and towing services to complete the voyage promptly and safely. The insurance coverage remains in effect while the ship is under tow or the control of the specially qualified pilot in areas where towage and pilotage are common practices. If the towing or pilotage firm is responsible for the damage, the firm would be liable for paying for it.

Change of Ownership – In the event of a *change of ownership* (voluntary or otherwise, like new management changing from one entity to another), the coverage automatically terminates unless the following conditions apply:

- At that time, or if the ship is at sea with cargo, coverage terminates upon arrival at the final port.
- In case of an involuntary temporary transfer by requisition or otherwise, without the assured's prior written consent, the automatic termination will be 15 days after such transfer.

The insurance does not benefit the new owner.

Additional Insurances – Other insurance is not allowed except to cover perils excluded by the policy or the difference between the amount insured hereunder and the agreed value.

War, Strikes, and Related Exclusions – The hull policy does not cover losses caused by war, strikes, and related actions.

Other Hull Coverages

Taylor Hull Form – In addition to the AIHC, there are other frequently used hull clauses, like the Taylor Hull form, that are very similar to the AIHC. These different forms use the same terms, and the coverage works similarly.

Coastwise and Inland Hull Clause (CIHC) – Ocean marine hull policies insure ships on the high seas, coastwise vessels, and vessels on inland waterways. All the same terms, conditions, and provisions apply.

Increases Value and Excess Liability (IVEL) Clauses – Increased value and excess liability (IVEL) clauses work like umbrella policies. They offer excess coverage for the same losses covered by an underlining policy they are written to accompany. The underlining policy has to pay up to its limit before the IVEL pays anything.

The IVEL clause can offer excess coverage for the following: protection and indemnity, towers liability, collision, sue and labor, general average and salvage, sue and labor, charterers liability, ship repairers liability, wharfingers/or safe berth liability, and others as specified.

Cargo Coverage

Cargo policies are issued to insure loss or damage to the cargo. The owner of the cargo confirms that the cargo is suitable for shipment. The premium amount will be partly determined by the type of ship providing the transportation and partly by the packing method used.

Methods of Packing Cargo

Bulk Commodities – Bulk carriers are used to carry grain, coal, phosphates, and other loose cargo. The ship itself is the cargo's container. Tankers are used to carry liquid cargo like oil.

Break-bulk Cargo – *General cargo ships* carry break-bulk cargo. Things like rolls of wire, steel, and boxed goods are hauled in general cargo ships. Loading and offloading are slow because each piece of cargo must be handled individually. The cargo is not as well protected using this method, which results in higher premiums.

Containerization – Container ships carry cargo packed in 20- and 40-foot containers that also can be moved by railcars or trucks. This method is more efficient in cargo handling than break-bulk, resulting in shorter port times. Containers provide better protection for the cargo, which results in lower premiums than break-bulk.

Types of Cargo Losses

Total Loss – Actual Total Loss vs. Constructive Total Loss – An ocean marine total loss can occur by *actual total loss* or *constructive total loss*. *Actual total loss* is damage to the entire property. *Constructive total loss* is when the cost to repair or recover exceeds the policy limit, and the insurance provider pays the policy's agreed value. An actual total loss can occur when there is a loss of specie or if an insured is irretrievably deprived of all property, even if it is not destroyed. A loss of specie occurs when all property is damaged where it is no longer what it was and can no longer be insured. A loss of specie is payable as a total loss.

Sue and Labor Expenses – If a loss occurs, the master and crew must sue and labor to protect the insured property from additional loss. The policy will cover the cost of doing so. When the crew does not sue and labor to keep losses as minimal as possible, the insurance provider could refuse to pay for the loss.

Partial Loss – Particular vs. General Average – Partial loss could be a particular average where only the individuals involved in the loss are affected. It could also be a general average, in which everyone involved in the voyage shares in the loss.

Salvage Charges and Awards – When the cargo is damaged short of the destination port, an agent of the insurance provider at an intermediate port can agree to sell it at the best price. The settlement will be based on the difference between the net proceeds of the sale and the insured value, known as a salvage loss.

Open Cargo Policy

Designed for Frequent Shipper – Cargo policies can be written on a voyage or trip basis, or for a frequent shipper, like an importer or exporter, on an open cargo basis. The open cargo policy covers all insured cargo for a specified number of shipments or for a specified time.

Cargo Clauses of the American Institute of Marine Underwriters – No standardized open cargo policy form exists. The American Institute of Marine Underwriters' cargo clause is attached to cargo policies for cargo transported on U.S. ships.

Cargo policies are typically issued on a warehouse-to-warehouse basis, insuring the cargo from origin to destination even though parts of the trip might be over land. The coverage is in effect until the cargo reaches its destination or 60 days after discharge at the destination port. The American Institute warehouse-to-warehouse clause stipulates the coverage will expire 15 days following discharge at the destination port (30 days if the cargo's destination is outside the port's limits).

Provisions – The *warehouse to warehouse* or *transit* clause designates the points of the voyage. Insurance coverage applies from the time the goods leave a warehouse until:

- The goods are delivered to the final warehouse or place of storage listed in the Declarations;
- The goods are delivered to any other storage or warehouse which the assured chooses for storage other than the ordinary course of transit;
- For distribution or allocation;
- Sixty days following discharge (30 days for air shipments) from the vessel; or
- Fifteen days following discharge at the final destination port.

Insurers will still cover termination at a port other than the listed final destination at the port where the goods were unloaded and during shipping to the destination or another selected port. If the goods will not be forwarded, the insurance remains in place until the goods are sold.

The *craft* clause covers the cargo while being transported to or from the vessel in another craft, raft, or lighter.

The *change of voyage* clause provides continuous coverage in the event of a change of voyage or an error or omission in the description of the vessel, subject to payment of an additional premium.

The *constructive total loss* clause gives the insurer the right to pay the assured for a total loss when goods are so damaged that the cost of recovering and reconditioning them would exceed their original value.

The *general average* clause establishes the rules to be followed to settle general average claims and the salvage charges.

The *seaworthiness admitted* clause specifies that the assured and the underwriters agree that the vessel is seaworthy. If a loss occurs, the assured can still collect even though the loss might have been caused by the misconduct or a wrongful act of the crew or ship owner.

The *bailee* clause obligates the assured to file a claim against third parties who might be liable for the loss.

The *not to insure* clause prohibits the assured from assigning any right of recovery in the policy to the carrier or any other bailee.

The *theft, pilferage, and nondelivery* clause will cover these types of losses even if the crew is responsible.

The *malicious damage* clause covers deliberate damage to or destruction of the insured property because of the wrongful act of any individual(s).

The *dangerous drug* clause states that insurers will pay no claim in connection with drugs regarding international conventions relating to opium and other hazardous drugs apply. Exceptions are made if the drugs are expressly declared in the policy, the importing and exporting countries are stated, and the route by which the drugs are conveyed is usual and customary. Proof of loss must be accompanied by a certificate, license, or authorization issued by the government of the importing or exporting country.

Principal Average Clauses – Principal average clauses define how partial losses are covered. The insured will choose one of the five principal average clauses below to determine the method of calculating the claim payment.

- **Free of Particular Average American Conditions (FPAAC)** – This method is the most limited because it insures only partial direct losses to the vessel for fire, collision, stranding, or sinking.
- **Free of Particular Average English Conditions (FPAEC)** – This method insures partial losses to the vessel directly or indirectly caused by fire, collision, stranding, or sinking. The difference between the American and the English conditions is the requirement for the American condition that the peril must directly cause the vessel damage. The English condition broadens this coverage by not requiring that the damage be caused by fire, collision, stranding, or sinking.
- **With Average if Amounting to 3%** – This method insures partial losses from the perils of the seas (natural and inevitable forces like storms due to the uniqueness of the seas). It does not apply to particular average losses. The minimum amount of the claim is 3% of the insured amount.
- **Average Irrespective of Percentage** – All partial losses from the perils of the seas are fully insured. No minimum percentage limits the insurance amount. There is an optional named peril extension with this method that might cover nondelivery, breakage, leakage, fresh water, pilferage, theft, and others.
- **All Risk Conditions** – This insures all physical loss or damage from any external cause except the excluded losses. The following are excluded perils:
  - Delay;
  - Inherent vice;
  - Willful misconduct of the insured;
  - War, strikes, civil commotion, and riots;
  - Use of any nuclear or atomic weapon;
  - Ordinary leakage, ordinary loss in volume or weight, or ordinary wear and tear;
  - Insufficiency or unsuitability of packing;
  - The assured's knowledge of the vessel's or container's unseaworthiness at the time of loading; and
  - Insolvency or financial default of the owners or operators of the vessel.

The policy can be endorsed for an additional premium to cover losses caused by war, strikes, civil commotion, and riots.

Freight Insurance

Freight and cargo, although synonymous, are two separate things. The term *cargo* describes the physical goods being shipped from one place to another. The term *freight* describes the charges made to ship cargo from location to location.

The term *freight insurance* describes the indirect loss that an insured would sustain if insured cargo is damaged or lost. Such losses include the charges paid to transport such cargo or the income that would be generated. Freight charges can be prepaid, in which case coverage would be attached to the cargo policy obtained by the cargo owner. Freight charges also can be paid on delivery, in which case the ship owner could obtain coverage to be attached to the hull policy.

Protection and Indemnity Insurance

Under ocean marine contracts, *protection and indemnity* coverage is liability insurance that protects the ship's owner from the consequences of their negligent acts or the negligent acts of their agents. Suppose the owner is held legally liable for damages to a third party. In that situation, the P&I coverage would cover financial losses by paying those sums that the insured became legally liable to pay as damages. The P&I coverage can be issued with other marine coverages or as a stand-alone insurance policy.

Insuring Agreements

Indemnity principle – P&I policies are indemnity policies. In insurance, *indemnity* attempts to return an injured party to "whole" by paying the injured party for the economic loss. The amount of money required to indemnify the injured party can be up to the policy limit. Under a liability policy, the injury to the third party results from the insured's negligence or perceived negligence. Negligence is not demonstrating the same extent of care that a normal individual would exhibit under the same or similar circumstances.

Liability of Vessel Owner – The vessel owner's liability is limited to losses that happen while the vessel operates on behalf of the vessel owner. Liability coverage will be provided unless a stipulation in maritime law limits the vessel owner's liability.

Common Covered Losses – P&I covers the ship owner against liability:

- To seaman for injuries caused by the vessel's unseaworthiness and other negligent acts;
- To longshoremen, harbor workers, and stevedores (laborers who load and unload vessels in a port);
- For cargo lost or damaged by negligence;
- For damage to other vessels not resulting from collision; or
- For damage to other property, including fixed objects.

Exclusions

Insurers will not cover losses caused by intentional acts of the insured. The P&I policy includes *no right of recovery* regarding damage, loss, or expense, either directly or indirectly.

Conditions Regarding Claims

P&I coverage provides marine legal liability insurance for the ship owner in the event that the owner is sued for negligence.

Under the Jones Act, for example, seamen are insured for their injuries while working on a ship. The law allows the seaman to sue the ship owner for negligence and general damages resulting from such injuries resulting from negligence.

Also, the coverage would apply to lawsuits against the ship owner from a loss of cargo caused by negligence, injuries to harbor workers and longshoremen, and damage to other vessels caused by collision if the insured's ship was negligent.

Unlike other ocean marine coverage on boats, P&I protects against bodily injuries.

The Longshore and Harbor Workers Compensation Act (USL&H) was originally implemented to compensate workers primarily engaged in loading and unloading vessels from docks or piers if an injury or death occurred in navigable waters of the United States.

The law now covers several operations in or near navigable water, including repairers, shipbuilders, marine and diving contractors, and employers with "incidental" exposures. Generally, state workers compensation plans do not cover these activities.

An extension of the Longshore and Harbor Workers Compensation Act, the *Defense Base Act*, was established in 1941 to insure workers on military bases outside the United States.

The Defense Base Act provides workers compensation coverage to civilians employed outside the United States on U.S. military bases or under a contract with the U.S. government for national defense or public works. The Act provides disability and medical benefits to covered employees injured during employment and death benefits to eligible survivors of employees killed during employment.

Other Provisions

The protection and indemnity coverage can be issued with other marine coverages or as a stand-alone insurance policy.

Chapter Review

This chapter discussed ocean marine insurance and the typical policy provisions and exclusions found in this coverage. Let's review them:

OCEAN MARINE	
Hull Coverage	• A hull policy is a type of ocean marine insurance that provides physical damage coverage for the ship while it is in transit • The collisions clause pays for damage to another's vessel with which the assured's vessel has collided • Hull policies cover losses caused by the perils of lighting, fire, earthquake, jettison, assailing thieves, and barratry of the master and mariners
Cargo Coverage	• Cargo policies are issued to insure loss or damage to the vessel's cargo • Cargo policies can be written on a trip or voyage basis • The amount of premium will be partly determined by the type of ship providing the transportation and partly by the packing method used • An ocean marine loss can occur by actual total loss or constructive total loss

Chapter 20:
Surety Bonds and General Bond Concepts

This chapter presents the concept of surety bonds, their features, and participating parties, as well as the essential difference between insurance and a surety bond. You will also learn about the functions and conditions for issuing other types of bonds, like contract bonds, public official bonds, and fiduciary bonds.

- Surety Bonds vs. Insurance
- Parties of Surety Bonds
- Contract Bonds
- Judicial Bonds
- Public Official Bonds
- Fiduciary Bonds
- Guaranties

Surety Bonds vs. Insurance

A *surety* refers to someone who guarantees someone else's performance. The surety issues a bond on one party who must perform as required and financially compensates the other party when contractual obligations are not met.

In the traditional sense, *surety bonds* are not insurance and differ in several ways. At the outset, insurance is a 2-party agreement between the insured and the insurer. A surety is involved in a two-party contract between a principal, obligee, and surety.

When it comes to compensation for losses, insurance covers insureds without recourse for recovery against the insured. Unlike insurance, surety bonds do not pay for losses. Instead, they guarantee the individual(s) will fulfill specific responsibilities or obligations. If the duty is not performed as promised, the surety pays the bond amount to the individual to whom the promise had been made and broken. A bond is written for a fixed limit, and the surety will be liable only for this amount. This limit is known as the *bond penalty*.

Parties of Surety Bonds

The three parties to a bond include the principal, obligee, and surety.

Principal – The *principal* or *obligor* is the individual who purchases the bond and who promises to fulfill the obligation. This person or entity goes through the underwriting process. The underwriting for surety bonds considers the credibility and financial stability of the principal or obligor. The underwriting process can be as simple as an application or as complex as a thorough financial review.

Obligee – The *obligee or insured* is the person to whom the bond is payable and to whom the promise has been made as a result of the principal defaulting on its obligation. This party requires a bond for entering into a contract with the principal. For example, an entity that enters into an agreement with a construction firm to build an office building may require the contractor to be bonded to the amount of the project to ensure its completion. The building owner would be the obligee or insured.

Surety – The *guarantor or surety* (the bonding company) provides the financial backing for the guarantee, known as a bond penalty. If the principal or obligor defaults on its obligation, the surety will pay damages to the obligee or insured in the amount specified in the bond.

Example 20.1 – A business owner (obligee) may require a contractor (principal) to complete a specified job by a particular date. The contractor would purchase a bond from a surety company (guarantor) for a specified amount, which would be payable to the business owner if the contractor cannot meet the deadline. The bond guarantees that if the principal defaults on the agreement, the surety bond will pay the obligee. The surety bond acts like an insurance policy between the insurer and the insured; the surety guarantees that a particular outcome will occur as agreed. If it doesn't, the bond will pay the financial consequences to the obligee or claimant. However, unlike insurance, the obligor or principal is accountable for reimbursing the guarantor or surety the amount paid under the bond.

Contract Bonds

Contract bonds are used to guarantee the performance of written contracts. They are mainly used in contracts involving construction projects. The most common types of contract bonds include the following:

- **Bid bonds** — The obligee usually requires a bid bond when construction projects are granted based on the lowest bid. The bid bond promises that if the contractor is awarded the contract, the contractor will accept the contract, and a performance bond will be issued.
- **Completion bonds** — If a contractor must borrow money to finish a construction project, the lender will usually require a completion bond. This bond guarantees that the borrowed money will be used to fund the construction project that will be finished free of any other obligations.
- **Labor and materials bonds** — These bonds guarantee that work and materials will be delivered free and clear of any liens or other financial burdens. They are sometimes called payment bonds.
- **Performance bonds** — These bonds guarantee that the principal will fulfill the contract as agreed.
- **Supply bonds** — These bonds guarantee that a supplier will provide the materials, supplies, products, and equipment specified in the contract.

Judicial Bonds

Judicial bonds are required because of the following fiduciary or legal obligations:

- **Appeal bond** — If a person appeals to a higher court after an entered judgment, this bond might be required to guarantee that the judgment and the appeal costs will be paid.
- **Attachment bond** — When a court order requires the attachment of another party's assets, this bond may be used to guarantee that any damages suffered will be paid.
- **Release of attachment bond** — When a court order requires the attachment of another party's assets, the defendant uses this bond to have the property returned. A release of attachment bond serves as security for the plaintiff's claim instead of the property.
- **Bail bond** — This bond guarantees that the individual (plaintiff) who brings legal action against another (defendant) can cover the court costs and any resulting damages if the plaintiff loses the case.
- **Cost bond** — This bond guarantees that the individual (plaintiff) who brings legal action against another (defendant) will be able to cover the court costs and any resulting damages if the plaintiff loses the case.
- **Injunction bond** — The courts require this bond when anyone seeks an injunction against another party. It guarantees damages will be paid to the plaintiff caused by the defendant's wrongful injunction.

Public Official Bonds

Public officials hold office through selection, employment, election, or appointment. They are held accountable to the public to fulfill their responsibilities faithfully according to governing regulations and laws. Public officials can be government managers, court clerks or judges, sheriffs or the mayor, or even tax collectors. A public official is frequently required to obtain a *public official bond*. These bonds are issued in compliance with a statute requiring the bond, cover whatever liability the law imposes, and are written for the length of the elected public official's term.

Fiduciary Bonds

Fiduciary bonds, which can be issued for administrators or executors of an estate, trustees, or guardians, guarantee that the fiduciary will act and perform in the best interest of the party they represent. A fiduciary is someone that handles money or property for another and must do so in a responsible manner.

Guaranties

A *guaranty* is very similar to a surety. Both issue a bond to a principal or contractor who must meet the contractual obligations. However, if the principal defaults on the contract, the surety bond will pay the obligee. In contrast, the guarantor will pay after the obligee unsuccessfully tries to collect from the principal.

Good Faith

The intention of parties in a contract to deal fairly and honestly with each other is called good faith. A *good faith guaranty* is given to one party who relies on a third party's good faith intention. If the third party defaults on that promise of good faith, the guaranty will pay the obligation.

Financial

When the principal or its beneficiary fails to meet its contractual obligations to the obligee, the *financial guaranty* will pay a certain amount of money on behalf of the obligee. The surety may either pay the money or mitigate the loss by fulfilling the obligation.

Chapter Review

This chapter explained surety bonds and other bond concepts. Let's review them:

BONDS	
Definitions	• *Principal (or obligor)* – the person who promises to fulfill an obligation and purchases the bond; goes through the underwriting process • *Obligee (or insured)* – the person to whom the promise is made and to whom the bond is paid when the principal defaults on the obligation • *Guarantor (or surety)* – the surety or bonding company providing financial backing; only pays if the principal defaults on the obligation
Surety	• *Surety* – someone who guarantees the performance of another • *Surety bond* – the 3-party contract between a principal, obligee, and surety • *Penalty* – a set limit for which the surety is liable
Other Bonds	• *Contract bond* – used to guarantee the performance of written contracts • *Judicial bond* – fiduciary or legal obligations • *Public official bond* – required for public officials • *Fiduciary bond* – guarantees fiduciary performance • *Guaranty* – very similar to a surety

CHAPTER 21:
Workers Compensation – General Concepts

This chapter describes workers compensation insurance and the state and federal laws related to it. You will learn about the parts of a policy, the calculation of premiums, and selected endorsements. You will also learn about alternative sources of workers compensation insurance available in this state.

- Workers Compensation Laws
- Workers Compensation and Employers Liability Insurance
- Premium Computation
- Sources of Coverage
- 24-Hour Coverage

Workers Compensation Laws

Before states enacted workers compensation laws, employees injured on the job had to prove that an employer's negligence resulted in the injury. Even if the employer is negligent, generally, it could invoke the following *common law defenses*:

1. **Fellow servant rule** — The employer is not negligent if the negligence of a fellow employee caused the injury.
2. **Contributory negligence** — The employee is barred from any right to collect damages if the injured employee was partially responsible for the injury.
3. **Assumption of risk** — This affirmed that the employee knew in advance the risks associated with the job and received a salary for these risks.

Eventually, states enacted employer's liability laws, which diluted some of the common law defenses.

By the early 1900s, states enacted workers compensation laws. These laws were mainly elective, allowing the employee or employer to pursue the case outside of workers compensation laws or to use the fixed-benefit remedies provided under the law. States later enacted compulsory laws requiring that the exclusive remedy for injuries be provided under the workers compensation law. This law created a form of absolute liability that mandated compensation for injured workers *regardless of negligence or fault*. Today, workers compensation laws are in effect in all fifty states.

The federal government passed the Occupational Safety and Health Act (OSHA) in 1970, which set minimum standards for workplace safety. Under OSHA, individual states could keep jurisdiction over workplace safety, provided that their standards met the minimum standards created by OSHA. In addition to state workers compensation laws, the federal government enacted federal workers compensation laws for jobs falling under federal jurisdiction. These programs include the following:

1. The Federal Employees Compensation Act protects civil employees.
2. The United States Longshoremen's and Harbor Workers Compensation Act covers crews of vessels, including employees engaged in building or repairing ships.
3. The Defense Base Act provides benefits to nonmilitary personnel who work on a military base.
4. The Federal Black Lung Compensation insurance program provides coverage to coal miners.
5. In many states, railroad employees are exempt from compensation laws. However, in 1908 the Federal Employers Liability Act (FELA) was passed. This Act removed the common law defenses of assumption of risk and contributory negligence that allowed injured workers to sue their employer for negligence.

Today, all employers subject to workers compensation laws must purchase workers compensation insurance or set up a formal self-insurance program. Workers compensation insurance is generally purchased through a private insurance company.

Types of Laws

Monopolistic vs. Competitive – In some states, employers must purchase workers compensation insurance from an entity operated by the state. These are called *monopolistic state funds*. Private insurers may not write workers compensation insurance in competition with these state funds.

In other states, employers purchase workers compensation from those insurance companies authorized to write casualty insurance. State regulations mandate the benefits and coverage, known as a *competitive market*.

Compulsory vs. Elective – From state to state, the workers compensation laws vary. Most states have *compulsory laws* requiring every employer to provide workers compensation coverage for anyone meeting the definition of an employee. These laws do not apply to employers that are excluded due to employment type or staff size.

The remaining few states have *elective laws*, which means the employer does not have to be subject to the state's workers compensation laws. When an employer elects not to be subject to the state's laws, it loses its common law defenses against liability suits.

California Workers Compensation Law

Exclusive Remedy – Under a mandatory workers compensation law, injured employees are prohibited from seeking damages outside the workers compensation law. This stipulation is called the *exclusive remedy* doctrine. However, there are some instances when an employer needs insurance for claims not covered by workers compensation. Employers liability coverage is for such cases. The most common types of circumstances that insurers would cover under an employers liability policy include the following:

- Illegal or exempt employment;
- Third-party-over claims in which an employee brings a lawsuit against a third party, and then the third party sues the employer;
- Circumstances involving another relationship between the employer and employee are referred to as dual capacity. For instance, if an employer instructs an employee to make repairs using tools manufactured by the employer, and the employee is injured because of the tools, the employee can collect both workers compensation benefits and additional compensation due to being injured by a tool manufactured by the employer;
- Family loss of consortium or the loss of companionship resulting from the death or disability of an employee;
- Consequential bodily injury to any family member of an employee resulting from the employee's injury; and
- Employees who seek benefits from the employer's parent-subsidiary relationships. For example, suppose an employee is injured by a subsidiary company that another parent company owns. In that case, the employee might be able to collect workers compensation from the subsidiary company and seek additional benefits from the parent company.

Legal Relationship – Before workers compensation laws were enacted, employees were often forced to sue their employer for reimbursement of their direct or consequential losses when they were injured or became ill at work. Under workers compensation laws, employees are prohibited from suing their employers for their injuries, even if the employer is negligent. Nevertheless, lawsuits over workers compensation losses continue to rise, primarily due to disputes over the severity of an employee's disability, as opposed to who caused the injury.

Workers compensation regulations are *no-fault* laws. Provided an employee's illness or injury is not intentionally self-inflicted and resulted from their employment, the employer must cover the expense without remedy to the employee (except in cases of proven fraud). The employer is now legally responsible for medical treatment or first aid, lost wages resulting from a temporary disability, vocational rehabilitation costs, and compensation for the effects of a permanent disability (including lost wages and retraining for other employment). Additionally, in the event of a worker's work-related death, death benefits and survivor benefits are paid to the spouse and dependent children of the deceased employee.

Coverage Provided – Workers compensation law in California is *compulsory*. Employers must provide workers compensation benefits even if only one employee is on the payroll. Every employer must obtain a workers compensation insurance policy unless it is large enough to demonstrate stable cash flow. If this is the case, it can apply to the state Department of Industrial Relations (DIR) and, if qualified, be certified as *self-insured* for workers compensation. Most employers are also required to post *securities* with the state for the privilege of being self-insured. Securities include a surety bond or other cash deposit that could be used to pay claims if the employer fails to do so. As with any health insurance, employers can finance their liability for workers compensation benefits through the state, private insurers, or self-insurance.

An employer who does not obtain the required insurance can have their business temporarily closed by a stop order from the Department of Industrial Relations. Additionally, the employer can be fined up to $10,000 for violating the stop order and $1,000 per employee and the possibility of being charged with insurance fraud due to failure to obtain workers compensation insurance. California has an *uninsured employee fund* to handle uninsured workers' claims.

Temporary total *disability benefit* payments are typically *two-thirds* (66.67%) of the insured's wages before the injury. However, the insured cannot receive more than a maximum weekly amount established by law. For example, suppose that two-thirds of an employee's wages exceed the annual limit. In that circumstance, the employee may receive less than two-thirds of their wages in workers compensation disability benefits. On the other hand, low-wage workers are entitled to at least the minimum weekly benefit limit if two-thirds of their wages add up to a smaller amount.

Medical claims are not limited in either duration or dollar amount up to the worker's lifetime. Workers compensation benefits are not subject to state or federal income taxes or social security withholding. Retirement fund contributions and union dues deducted from workers compensation income benefits are also exempt.

benefit is also called the supplemental job displacement benefit (SJDB). It includes any expenses related to providing the necessary treatment to return the worker to full employment. The SJDB is paid as a non-transferable voucher that can be used to pay for skill enhancement or educational retraining at state-approved or state-accredited schools. The voucher covers tuition, books, fees, and expenses. Up to 10% of the voucher's value can be used for vocational and return-to-work counseling. The voucher amount may vary from $4,000 to $10,000, depending on the level of permanent disability.

Due in large part to rising fraud and medical claims, workers compensation insurance premiums are escalating rapidly. Premiums are based on actual payroll, occupational classifications, and actual claims experience. Employers pay the premiums and can be eligible for premium discounts if they offer regular safety training programs in the workplace. Due to the dramatic rise in premiums in the past few years, the Department of Insurance, insurance providers, and the state legislature are looking at ways to limit claims or benefits to stabilize premiums without adversely affecting claimants with legitimate illnesses or injuries.

Time and Dollar Limit – Current workers compensation law stipulates that insurers must pay the cost of medical care or treatments necessary to return the worker to the workforce without limitation. The time for treatment or services or the actual dollar amounts paid will not limit medical care. Only when the worker's injuries have been described as stationary and permanent might the employee waive further medical payments.

An injured worker can continue working under a doctor's restrictions and return to their former duties with accommodations in the type or amount of work to be performed. When a doctor determines that a worker cannot return to their former occupation, offering the employee *alternative work* that will last at least 12 months may be necessary. The employee will be compensated at least 85% of their former wage and will not require an unreasonable commute to or from the workplace.

Under workers compensation, medical expenses related to physical therapy and chiropractic services are limited to *24 visits* each.

Open Rating System – Before 1989, the Insurance Commissioner regulated California's workers compensation insurance rates.

The Workers Compensation Reform Act was passed in 1989. It created an academic commission to analyze California's workers compensation insurance market and insurance rate-making process. It also examined the relative effectiveness of rate-making systems in other states. In 1992 the Rate Study Commission recommended the current system that the Legislature adopted in 1993. This system is known as *open rating* or competitive rate making. Under the open rating plan, the Commissioner establishes recommended, nonmandatory pure premium rates expected to cover the costs of benefits and loss adjustment expenses. Other administrative overhead and expenses are to be added by individual insurers, resulting in a final rate plan that uses market competition to keep premium rates low.

Federal Workers Compensation Laws

Federal Employers Liability Act (FELA) – The *Federal Employers Liability Act (FELA)* is an employers liability law rather than a workers compensation law. It preceded workers compensation and made an interstate railroad liable for bodily injury sustained by employees. Unless directly excluded, liability coverage under FELA is covered under Section II of the workers compensation and employers liability policy.

Although most state workers compensation laws limit recovery only to economic losses, the FELA usually permits railroad employees to recover the following damages:

- Lost earnings (past and future);
- Medical expenses if the injured employee paid out of pocket;
- Compensation for the reduced ability of an employee to earn a wage because of the injuries suffered; and
- Payment for pain and suffering.

All actions of the FELA must begin within *three years* from the day the cause of action commenced.

U.S. Longshore and Harbor Workers Compensation Act – Individuals (other than seamen) engaged in maritime employment are covered under a federal workers compensation statute, the *U.S. Longshore and Harbor Workers Compensation Act (LHWCA)*. A worker is protected under the LHWCA only if they meet a situs and a status test. The injury must occur on navigable waters or on an adjoining pier, wharf, dock, or similar facility used in loading, unloading, building, or repairing vessels. In addition, the individual must have been engaged in maritime employment when an injury occurred. When coverage is required for LHWCA, it can be added by endorsement to a workers compensation policy.

The LHWCA, and its extensions, provide compensation for lost wages, medical benefits, and rehabilitation services to employees injured during employment or who contracted a work-related disease due to work. Survivor benefits also are provided if the occupational injury causes the death of an employee.

The Jones Act – The *Jones Act* is a federal act that covers ships' crews with the same remedy available to railroad workers. Usually, anyone spending more than 30% of their time on a vessel that is in navigation will qualify as a seaman under the Jones Act. Seamen may sue their employer for injuries sustained through the negligence or fault of the employer. The act applies to navigable waters used for interstate or international trade.

Any employee who does not qualify as a Jones Act seaman will typically be covered under longshore or maritime law and not under the Jones Act. An example would be an individual working as a contract employee who moves back and forth between multiple ships not under common ownership.

Workers Compensation and Employers Liability Insurance

Employer's liability is another aspect of workers compensation insurance. The basic statutory claims include the following: disability income, medical expenses, rehabilitation expenses, and death and survivor's benefits, all of which are covered by the contract's Workers Compensation (Part One) section. Employer's Liability (Part Two) pays for the tort claims (injuries or damages) of third parties claiming to have suffered losses due to the employee's injuries.

Particularly, the employer's liability coverage provides a legal defense against and protection from four common types of financial claims:

1. Loss of consortium lawsuits;
2. Third-party-over lawsuits;
3. Consequential bodily injury lawsuits; and
4. Dual capacity lawsuits.

Loss of consortium lawsuits could be brought by the children, spouse, or parents of an injured employee for the loss of services of this person. Under the common law, "services" could include companionship, sexual relations, household maintenance, chores, or other physical or psychological support an injured worker could not provide.

Third-party-over lawsuits would be brought against an employer by a third party held liable for the employee's disability. An example of this could be a driver who caused a traffic accident that injured a delivery driver (as an employee of a delivery company). The argument is that the employer was somehow responsible for the delivery driver being at the place where the crash occurred and is liable for damages.

Consequential bodily injury lawsuits could be brought by a child, spouse, parent, or any other family member whose own illness or injury directly results from the employee's work-related injury. An example of this could be a nurse or doctor exposed to an infectious disease while working at the hospital who infects their children or spouse.

Dual capacity lawsuits can result from situations where the employer is also responsible for damages to the employee caused by a product it manufactured which is required by or supplied to the employee during employment. Usually, statutory coverage under workers compensation is the exclusive remedy for an employee who suffered a work-related illness, injury, or death. However, when the employer has a dual role leading to the illness or injury of an employee, this goes beyond the common law assumptions.

These are not the only examples of claims which could be brought against an employer's liability policy, but they are the most common. All employers' liability contracts include a limit of liability provision, stating the insurer will not be liable for amounts over the amount of coverage purchased by the insured.

General Section

The different types of workers compensation benefits provided are

- Medical;
- Disability;
- Death; and
- Supplemental job benefits.

Every workers compensation and employers liability policy is based on the National Council on Compensation Insurance's (NCCI) standard policy. However, they might contain slight variations by different insurance companies.

The general section of a workers compensation policy is split into five subsections as follows:

1. **The Policy** — This subsection summarizes every component of the policy. The information page, which is a substitute for the declarations page in other liability insurance policies, all endorsements, and any schedules constitute the policy. Policy terms cannot be altered unless there is an endorsement. The contract is between the employer stated on the information page and the insurance provider.
2. **Who is Insured** — The insured is the employer named on the information page. In the case of a partnership, a partner is only insured as an employer of the partnership's employees.
3. **Workers Compensation Law** — This is an essential policy subsection because the language refers to the workers compensation laws for states listed on the information page (3A). Employers in "3A states" have employees. Workers compensation policies are very different from other policies discussed in this book. No coverage amounts for statutory benefits are listed in the policy or on the information page. The policy will pay the amount in the applicable state where a covered injury occurs. Employers must list every state in which they have employees in section 3A.
4. **State** — This subsection defines a state which is any state in the United States, including the District of Columbia (Washington, D.C.).
5. **Locations** — Coverage applies to every location listed on the information page and in section 3A unless states listed in section 3A have self-insurance or other insurance.

In every state, *medical payments are unlimited*. Except for certain types of care, no dollar or time limits will pay for necessary medical and surgical expenses.

Benefits provide *disability income payments* for an injured worker's *loss of wages*. Benefits start after an initial waiting period, but insurers will pay benefits retroactively to the beginning of the disability if it lasts for more than the period defined in the policy. Benefits are typically expressed as a percentage of the injured employee's wages, subject to certain weekly minimums and maximums for temporary total disability and permanent total disability. Total disability means a person's complete inability to work.

Temporary partial disabilities refer to an individual's capacity to do some work or the need to do alternative work. Benefits are expressed as a percentage of lost wages equal to wages earned before and after the injury. Some states also provide a schedule of benefits for specific permanent partial disabilities, such as losing a limb, eyesight, or hearing. These benefits are generally in addition to any other benefits paid.

Death benefits typically pay weekly income benefits to the surviving spouse and children and a small amount for burial and funeral expenses. The weekly benefit usually equals a certain percentage of the deceased employee's income. Benefits may continue for the surviving spouse's remaining life or until remarriage.

Rehabilitation expenses include occupational training and essential medical expenses for physical and mental therapy. Board, lodging, and travel expenses are also included benefits. States may levy weekly or maximum benefits or limit benefits for specific types of rehabilitation.

Every state has enacted a *second (or subsequent) injury fund*. These funds are designed to pay additional benefits that may be needed when a worker with a prior disability or injury (whether work-related or not) suffers a second injury that causes the disability to be more severe than if there had been no previous disability.

Example 21.1 – When a worker with only one arm loses the use of the second arm, the subsequent disability would be much worse, usually resulting in a permanent total disability. Without the second injury fund, employers would be subject to the additional liability imposed by such injuries. They would not have an incentive to hire disabled workers.

Part One – Workers Compensation Insurance

Workers compensation coverage applies to work-related disease, accidental bodily injury, or death. It covers the lawful benefits required under the state's workers compensation regulations. The policy also states that the workers compensation insurance provider will not pay benefits for intentional self-injury, willful misconduct, or a violation of safety.

Supplemental payments are also included and comparable to those found in other insurance policies. They consist of the following:

- Defense expenses;
- Costs incurred at the insurance provider's request;
- Premiums for specific bonds;
- Litigation expenses;
- Interest on judgments required by law until a settlement is offered by the insurance provider; and
- All expenses incurred by the insurance provider.

The *other insurance* clause is also contained in the workers compensation section. It states that the insurance company will pay equal shares when other insurance, including self-insurance, can also respond to the loss.

Part Two – Employers Liability Insurance

Employers liability insurance coverage defends the insured from circumstances not covered under a state's workers compensation law. Unlike the workers compensation coverage section, which does not explicitly show the statutory limits provided, the employer's liability limits are shown on the information page. The basic limits provided are:

- $100,000 per worker for disease;
- $100,000 for bodily injury per accident; and
- $500,000 policy limit for each disease claim within the policy term.

Most insurance companies allow the insured to buy higher employers liability limits for an added premium. In some states, these limits do not apply. In addition to the basic coverage, this section also provides supplemental coverage, similar to other policies.

Coverage is provided for the employers liability associated with bodily injury by work-related disease or accident. It includes resulting death and is initiated if:

- Injury results from employment by the insured;
- Takes place in a state or territory noted in section 3A of the information page;
- Takes place during the policy period; and
- If a lawsuit is brought in the United States, its territories, possessions, or Canada.

Several *exclusions* apply to employers liability coverage:

- Assumed liability under a contract;
- Exemplary or punitive damages;
- Workers intentionally employed in violation of the law;

- Injury knowingly caused by the insured;
- Injuries that take place outside the United States, its possessions, or Canada;
- Damages caused by the policies or employment practices of the insured, including harassment, defamation, humiliation, discrimination, or termination of any worker;
- Although coverage is typically available by endorsement, workers who are subject to federal workers compensation or employer's liability laws;
- Penalties or fines levied because of a violation of state or federal laws; and
- Damages payable under laws that protect migrant and seasonal agricultural workers.

The *other insurance* clause explains that insurers will pay losses based on a contribution by equal shares. The limit of liability provision states that the limits for bodily injury by accident on the information page apply per accident, and bodily injury by disease applies per person subject to the bodily injury by disease policy limit for any losses during the policy term. The final two provisions refer to actions against the insurer and the insurer's subrogation rights.

Part Three – Other States Insurance

Other states' insurance coverage extends a policy owner's coverage for incidental or new operations in other states (excluding the monopolistic states) on a temporary and automatic basis, subject to certain conditions and time limits.

The state where a temporary or new operation exists must be listed in the 3C section of the information page. It is common for this section to list or describe all states other than monopolistic states. This section also provides the insured with the greatest protection for incidental or new exposures. If the state is not listed, no coverage will apply.

A critical component of this coverage is when the work was started. Suppose it is after the policy's effective date and the insured has made no other arrangements for coverage (self-insurance). In that case, coverage will apply as if the state were listed in 3A – mandatory coverage. However, coverage will only apply when work gets underway on the effective date if the insurance provider is notified within 30 days.

Example 21.2 – An insured has a calendar year policy and starts work in June in a new state. The state in which work is conducted is not listed in 3A of the information page. Provided this state is listed in 3C, coverage will apply as if it were listed in 3A. The insured's work continues in policy period two of the following year. An injury takes place in March of the second policy term. To have coverage, the insured had to notify the insurance provider by the end of January of policy period two. If this is the case, the state would be listed in 3A, and coverage would apply. If the insured did not notify the insurance provider, there would be no coverage even if the state continued to be listed in 3C.

Injuries that take place in states in which the employer and employee do not reside can get complicated. It is easier to think of work performed when completed by employees who live and work in a particular state, even if the headquarters of the employer is not in that state.

Part Four – Your Duties if Injury Occurs

The *Your Duties if Injury Occurs* section explains the insured's responsibilities in case of an injury to an employee. These duties include the following:

- Notifying the insurer at once;
- Providing immediate medical care mandated by the law;
- Providing the names and addresses of the injured employee and any witnesses to the injury;

- Promptly sending any legal papers or other notices;
- Cooperating with the insurance provider; and
- Not making any voluntary payments or assuming any responsibilities.

Part Five – Premium

The premium section describes how premiums are determined, what the requirements are for the insured's record retention, and what rights the insurance company has in auditing the books and records of the insured.

Premiums are determined *by classification*. In most cases, classifications are not specific to any industry. Instead, they are for job types, such as clerical, executive, inside sales, outside sales, and many others. Each classification will have a corresponding premium associated with it. The higher the hazard, the higher the premium. These rates are determined by the insurer and often require approval by state insurance departments.

Remuneration is another component in determining rates and includes payroll and other compensation methods. The insured must keep records on all remuneration to workers so the final premium can be determined. The rate per job classification is charged per *each $100 of the annual payroll* of every job-related classification.

Because the insured does not know the final payroll until the end of the policy period, the initial premium is considered a deposit. It is subject to being adjusted at the end of the term. This adjustment occurs during the premium audit, which can be conducted during regular business hours during the policy period and up to three years following the policy's expiration.

Part Six – Conditions

The conditions found in workers compensation and employers liability policies include

- **Inspection** — At any time, the insurer has the right to inspect the workplace.
- **Long-term policy** — All policy provisions will apply as though a new policy was issued on each anniversary date if the policy period is longer than one year and 16 days.
- **Assignment (transfer of your rights and duties)** — The rights and duties of the insured may not be transferred to anyone without the insurer's written consent.
- **Cancellation** — The insurer must provide the insured with at least ten days' advanced written notice for any cancellation. The insured may cancel the policy with a written notice to the insurer.
- **Sole representative** — The first named insured will act on behalf of every insured under the policy.

Selected Endorsements

Voluntary Compensation – The *voluntary compensation* endorsement added to workers compensation policies will cover workers who do not fall under a state's workers compensation law. Such workers include some types of domestic employees and farmworkers working fewer than 40 hours per week for one employer. This endorsement stipulates that the insurance provider will pay statutory benefits to the insured person in exchange for the injured employee releasing the insurance provider and the employer from further liability. Any additional compensation under the endorsement ends if the worker does not sign the release.

Premium Computation

Job Classification – Payroll and Rates

A workers compensation rating is established by applying a rating bureau job classification to every $100 of an employer's payroll. Estimated payroll amounts are used when a policy is issued, and an audit decides the final premium. Payroll refers to remuneration. It includes wages, salaries, bonuses, commissions, vacation and sick leave pay, and noncash compensation.

Experience Modification Factor

A rating bureau determines the *experience modification factor*. These calculations relate to an employer's losses, payroll, and premiums. They are separated according to the classification of operations and reported to the bureau by the employer's insurer.

Premium Discounts

A *premium discount* is applied when an insured owes more than $5,000 in total standard premium.

Participation (Dividend) Plans

In some states, insurers or state workers compensation funds are permitted to write participating policies, also known as safety groups. The insured is eligible for a *partial premium refund* (dividends) if the experience during the policy term falls within parameters established by the insurance provider at the beginning of the policy term. Dividends are not guaranteed. To be eligible to participate, the insured is required to meet the associated underwriting participation requirements.

In the case of a group policy, the group has to qualify for the dividend. In the event the loss experience of the group is low, participating members may receive a dividend. No penalties are imposed for a high loss experience.

Sources of Coverage

California State Compensation Insurance Fund

California operates the *State Compensation Insurance Fund (State Fund or SCIF)*. However, many commercial insurance providers still have open competition for workers compensation insurance. The SCIF is expected to be the insurer of last resort. Large employers with the financial ability to pay premiums are being turned away or even asked to withdraw from the State Fund unless they can demonstrate their inability to obtain coverage through the commercial marketplace. Smaller employers with more limited payrolls are now being given priority, regardless of whether they previously sought coverage in the open market.

The SCIF's Board of Directors establishes the rates charged for the insurance it issues. These premiums have to be fixed within each class of business, taking into consideration work-related hazards and the following elements:

- Premises or work hazard and bodily risk or safety for each insured employer;
- How the work is carried out;
- A sensible regard for the accident experience of each insured;
- A sensible regard for the methods and means of caring for injured individuals.

The rates will not consider the extent to which the workers have or do not have individuals dependent upon them for support.

Smaller employers no longer have to prove that they have been declined for coverage by at least three insurers. Additionally, certain employers are regulated under the U.S. Longshoremens and Harbor Workers Compensation Act rather than under state workers compensation laws. They may also obtain that coverage from the SCIF and commercial insurance companies.

Employers that are not qualified to be self-insured are required to obtain the insurance. Any employer who fails to get the insurance is subject to having its operation closed under a cease and desist order issued by the Department of Industrial Relations. This order will remain effective until the insurance is obtained. The California Insurance Guarantee Association is equipped to pay claims of insolvent insurers. However, only limited resources are available to workers who should have been covered by the insurance and were not. An employer will be held personally responsible for such claims.

Self-Insured Employers

Almost every state permits employers to retain the risk of workers compensation losses. Employers who are authorized may self-insure their workers compensation obligation.

However, state requirements warrant a surety bond being pledged to the state. If the state deems it necessary, larger bond amounts may be required. Consequently, such a program is usually only feasible for larger employers.

An employer that provides a self-insured workers compensation plan may wish to limit liability by purchasing excess insurance coverage to cover catastrophic losses. Excess workers compensation coverage usually is one of two types, *aggregate excess* or *specific excess*.

A form of stop loss coverage, aggregate excess, requires the employer to pay the initial portion of all monetary claims up to a retained limit. Once a claim exceeds the plan's limit, the excess coverage pays all additional monetary claims to the stated limit of the aggregate excess policy. Specific excess coverage also requires a retention limit. However, the limit is for a single loss or all losses resulting from one occurrence. If covered losses exceed the retention limit, the insurance provider will pay additional losses up to the policy limits.

Voluntary Market

Usually, employers who require workers compensation coverage may buy it in the voluntary open market through private insurance carriers. However, every state has implemented a residual market mechanism for employers who cannot obtain coverage in the voluntary market.

24-Hour Coverage

The concept of *24-hour coverage* means an employee is provided with a workers compensation plan and some form of medical insurance coverage, like a disability insurance plan or health insurance policy for illnesses or injuries that occur outside work. The worker is covered *24 hours a day* (under the workers compensation plan while at work and under the medical insurance policy outside of work). This coverage cannot be distributed using a life insurance policy.

This coverage is different than other policies. It attempts to cover workers for every injury or illness using a combination of workers compensation and employer-sponsored individual or group health insurance. When a worker is injured or becomes ill under the 24-hour coverage plan, the time and place of the illness or injury do not matter. The worker will be covered 24 hours a day.

There are several disadvantages of 24-hour coverage plans, however. Some of the issues that result from 24-hour coverage include the following:

- Difficulty coordinating the workers compensation benefits and the benefits provided by the individual or group health insurance;

- Government regulation;
- The possibility of both plans overlapping in coverage; and
- Difficulties in determining coinsurance, deductibles, and copayments.

Chapter Review

This chapter discussed the general concepts of workers compensation insurance. Let's review the key points:

WORKERS COMPENSATION	
Workers Compensation Laws	• *Compulsory laws* – require employers, except those that are excluded, to provide workers compensation coverage for employees • *Elective laws* – the employer does not have to be subject to the state's workers compensation laws, but if an employer elects not to be subject to the laws of the state, it loses its common law defenses against liability suits
Exclusive Remedy	• Employees cannot seek damages outside of the workers compensation law unless as a result of claims not covered
Federal Workers Compensation Laws	• Federal Employer's Liability Act (FELA) • U.S. Longshore and Harbor Workers Compensation Act • The Jones Act

Employers Liability Insurance	• The employer's liability coverage provides legal defense against, and protection from, four common types of financial claims:
	    o Loss of consortium lawsuits;
	    o Third-party-over lawsuits;
	    o Consequential bodily injury lawsuits; and
	    o Dual capacity lawsuits

General Section	• The general section of a workers compensation policy is split into five different subsections:
	    o The Policy
	    o Who is an insured
	    o Workers Compensation Law
	    o State
	    o Locations

Premium Computation	• Established by applying a rating bureau classification to each $100 of payroll • *Expense modification factor* – calculated from an employer's payroll, losses, and premiums • *Premium discounts* – occurs when a policy owner owes more than $5,000 of the total standard premium • *Participating policies* – eligible dividends for a policy owner, dependent on associated underwriting requirements
Sources of Coverage	• California State Compensation Insurance Fund • Self-Insured Employers • Voluntary Market

KEY FACTS

Knowing the key facts can be the difference between passing and failing your exam. Read through each fact for a quick review of essential terms and concepts presented in this book.

General Insurance

Key Concepts

- Insurance is defined as the transfer of pure risk to the insurer in consideration for a premium.
- The chance of loss without any chance of gain is known as pure risk.
- Speculative risk is not insurable and has the possibility for gain or loss.
- Risk is defined as the probability of loss.
- A condition that could result in a loss is called exposure.
- A hazard increases the probability of loss.
- The presence of a physical hazard increases the probability of a loss.
- A peril is a cause of loss, like fire.
- To be insurable, losses have to be calculable.
- The law of large numbers lets insurance providers predict claims more accurately.
- The law of large numbers applies to groups of people, not to individuals. The more people in a group, the more accurate the predictions will be.
- Most insurance providers purchase reinsurance to protect themselves from a catastrophic loss.
- Insurance laws are not required to be uniform from one state to another.

Insurers

- Insurance providers cannot enforce a contract they enter into with a minor. However, the minor can enforce the agreement against the insurance provider.
- A stock insurer can pay dividends to its shareholders (stockholders), but they cannot be guaranteed.
- An attorney-in-fact manages a reciprocal insurer.
- An unincorporated association of individuals who insure each other is called a reciprocal insurer.
- The government offers insurance primarily based on social needs, like flood insurance and workers compensation, but does not offer insurance to prevent fraud.
- A foreign company has its home office in another state.
- An insurance provider incorporated outside of the U.S. who sells in the U.S. is an alien company.

Producers and General Rules of Agency

- A producer can be personally liable when violating the producer's contract.
- Producers represent the insurer, not the insured.
- Independent producers own their accounts and are not employees of an insurance company.
- Producers have express, implied, and apparent authority.
- The authority a producer has written into their contract is called express authority.
- A producer's binding authority is expressed (written down) in the producer's contract with the insurance provider the producer represents.
- The authority not expressly granted (written) but the actual authority the producer has to transact ordinary business activities is called implied authority.

Contracts

- A requirement for a valid contract is a mutual agreement or offer and acceptance.
- The elements of a legal contract can be remembered by the acronym C-O-A-L (consideration, offer, acceptance, legal purpose and legal capacity).

- Advertising the availability of insurance is not considered to be an offer.
- A specific proposal to enter into a contract is called an offer.
- The consideration of a policy does not need to be equal.
- A policy cannot be voided because of unequal consideration.
- Under the consideration clause, something of value has to be exchanged.
- Since insurance contracts are contracts of adhesion, policy ambiguities always favor the insured.
- Insurance policies are considered unilateral contracts in that only one party makes an enforceable promise to the insurance provider.
- The principle of indemnity stipulates the purpose of insurance is to restore the insured to the same position as before the loss occurred.
- The principle of utmost good faith stipulates that all parties to an insurance transaction are honest.
- A representation is the truth to the best of one's knowledge.
- A warranty is a sworn statement of truth, guaranteed to be true.
- A breach of warranty can void a property or casualty contract.
- Concealment refers to the failure to disclose a material fact.
- When an insurance provider voluntarily gives up the right to obtain information that they are entitled to, they have made a waiver.

The Insurance Marketplace

Producers

- An individual cannot transact insurance without a valid license.
- Transacting insurance includes the solicitation, negotiation, or execution of a contract and the business of matters arising out of the contract.
- An individual who transacts insurance without a license is guilty of a misdemeanor.
- Transacting insurance without a license is a misdemeanor punishable by a fine not to exceed $50,000 or up to one year in jail, or both.
- Under federal law, a prohibited person is anyone whose activities affect interstate commerce. These individuals deliberately, with the intent to deceive, make a false material statement or financial report to any insurance regulator to influence that regulator.
- Under federal law, a prohibited person cannot engage in insurance activities in this state without the prior written consent of the Commissioner.
- Under federal law, a convicted prohibited person can be imprisoned for 10 to 15 years and fined up to $50,000 for each violation.
- Insurance agents are authorized by and on behalf of insurance companies to transact all types of insurance other than life, disability, or health insurance.
- Life licensees are authorized to act on behalf of a life or disability insurance provider to transact life, accident and health, or life and accident and health insurance.
- Insurance brokers transact insurance other than life insurance. They do so for compensation and on behalf of another person but not on behalf of an insurance company.
- A licensed life or health agent can submit a life or health insurance application to an insurance company that has not appointed them. If the insurance provider issues the policy, they must appoint the agent within 14 days. This process is known as brokerage.
- An insurer does not appoint an insurance broker.
- A life or health insurance broker license does not exist.

- Property and casualty agents or brokers can offset funds due to an insured for return premiums against amounts due from the same insured for unpaid premiums due on the same or any other policy.
- A life settlement broker is an individual who, on behalf of a policyholder, offers to negotiate the sale of the owner's life insurance policy to a life settlement provider.
- Life settlement brokers only represent the owner. They owe a fiduciary duty to the owner to act according to their instructions.
- Viatical settlements are affected through the use of absolute assignment.
- An insurance solicitor is employed to assist a broker or agent in transacting insurance other than life or health insurance.
- An insurance solicitor can represent more than one broker or agent.
- Errors & omissions insurance protects producers against legal liability resulting from negligence or errors and omissions. It does not cover dishonest, fraudulent, or criminal acts.
- Except when performed by a surplus lines broker, it is a misdemeanor for an individual to act as an agent for a non-admitted insurer.
- A surplus lines broker can place insurance with a non-admitted insurer only if insurance cannot be obtained from admitted insurers in this state.
- Surplus lines coverage cannot be written to obtain a rate lower than the lowest rate an admitted insurer will charge.
- Surplus line brokers must conduct a diligent search among admitted insurers before placing the coverage with a non-admitted insurer.
- Offering free insurance coverage in connection with the sale of services as an inducement to complete the transaction is illegal.
- Agents do not need the Commissioner's approval to use their actual names.
- Licensees have to file with the Commissioner their true names and any fictitious names (DBAs) under which they do business.
- Fictitious names cannot be too similar to a name already on file, cannot mislead the public, or imply the licensee is an insurance provider.
- Licensees must immediately inform the Commissioner of any change in their residence, mailing, principal business, or email address.
- If an agent engages in Internet advertising, they must include their name, license number, and business address, but not their phone number.
- Licensees are required to inform the Commissioner in writing within 30 days of the date they identify a change in their background information.
- Life insurance agents do not have to keep records of printed material that the insurance provider has distributed in general.
- The rules regarding life insurance policy illustrations are not designed to ensure that the illustration states that nonguaranteed elements will continue unchanged for each year shown.
- Life insurance illustrations demonstrating nonguaranteed elements display values, premiums, charges, or credits that are not determined at issue.
- Life insurance illustrations do not have to include a statement that the benefits in the illustration are guaranteed. Benefits can be guaranteed or nonguaranteed.
- If an insurance provider indicates that an illustration will be used, they must submit a summary status report to the policy owner annually.
- The Commissioner can, without a hearing, deny a license application if the applicant has committed a felony as shown by a plea of guilty, no contest (nolo contendere), or by conviction.
- If an applicant has had a professional license revoked in the previous five years, the insurance Commissioner can deny their licensing application without a prior hearing.

- Suppose an insurer knowingly permits one of its agents to mislead a member of the public to induce the individual to change their existing insurance. In that circumstance, the Commissioner can suspend the insurer's certificate of authority for the class of business involved.
- Insurers cannot offer insurance as an inducement to purchase or rent any real or personal property or services without any separate charge to the insured for such insurance.
- Insurance providers must file a notice of appointment with the Commissioner appointing a licensee as the insurer's agent.
- Appointments are effective as of the date they are signed and will continue until the appointee's license expires or until the insurer cancels them.
- To transact insurance, agents must hold at least one insurer appointment.
- If a producer no longer holds any insurer appointments, their license is considered inactive.
- An inactive license can be reactivated before expiration by filing a new appointment.
- A licensee can surrender their license to the Commissioner for cancellation at any time.
- If an employer holds an agent's license and wishes to cancel it, the employer must send a written notice to the Commissioner.
- Upon termination of all appointments, the licensee's permanent license will become inactive.
- Every license issued to a natural person terminates upon that person's death.
- When a corporation ceases to exist, its insurance license is terminated.
- Any licensee who diverts fiduciary funds for personal use is guilty of theft.
- Insurance producers act as fiduciaries when they handle their customers' premiums.
- MGAs (managing general agents) can be any person, partnership, firm, corporation, or association. They handle all or part of an insurance company's business (including a separate department, division, or underwriting office).
- Producers have a fiduciary responsibility when they deal with, handle, supervise, or hold in trust and confidence the affairs of another person, mainly regarding financial matters.
- Licensees who receive fiduciary funds must remit them to the person so entitled or maintain such funds in a trustee bank account in California separate from any other account.
- Licensees can commingle fiduciary funds in their trustee bank account with other funds to establish reserves or advance premiums for the paying of return commissions.
- A written agreement must be obtained from every insurance provider or individual entitled to such funds authorizing the maintenance and retention of any earnings accruing on funds in a trustee bank account.
- Life-only agents or accident and health agents must complete 24 hours of continuing education every 2-year renewal period.
- Agents licensed for all lines of insurance life, health, and property and casualty must complete 24 hours of continuing education every 2-year renewal period, not 48 hours.
- Property and casualty broker-agents must complete 24 hours of continuing education every 2-year renewal period.
- In addition to completing the pre-licensing requirement, life agents, personal lines agents, and property and casualty broker-agents must also complete a 12-hour ethics and code course.
- Third-party administrators often assist employers with administering their self-funded plans.
- The Code of Ethics requires agents to place their customer's interests first.
- When an insurer is guilty of unfair trade practices while issuing, renewing, and servicing a policy, the insurer could be prosecuted for three violations, one for each act.
- When a producer engages in unfair methods of competition, the agent is subject to penalties of no more than $5,000 for each act. If the action is considered willful, the agent is subject to fines of no more than $10,000 for each activity.

- The California Insurance Code (Cal. Ins. Code) and the California Code of Regulations (CCR) identify many unethical or illegal practices. Still, they are not a complete guide to ethical behavior.
- The Cal. Ins. Code includes senior code protections. Individuals aged 60 or older who buy life insurance in California must receive a minimum 30-day free look. Individuals under age 60 who purchase life insurance must receive a minimum 10-day free look period.
- Every insurer offering individual life insurance or annuities to senior citizens using nonguaranteed elements in illustrations must provide a confirmation statement in bold print.
- The free look notice for seniors needs to be printed in no less than 10-point uppercase font on the policy's cover page or certificate and the outline of coverage.
- Agents cannot use or authorize pretext interviews to acquire information about an insurance transaction.

Insurers

- An insurer organized and selling in California is considered to be a domestic insurer in California.
- An insurance company based in another state selling in California is a foreign insurer in California.
- An insurance company based in another country (e.g., Mexico) and doing business in California is an alien insurer.
- A diligent search among admitted insurers is considered to have been made if three admitted insurers have declined the risk.
- In a reinsurance transaction, a primary insurer is the insurance provider who transfers its loss exposure to another insurance provider.
- The insurer that purchases reinsurance is referred to as the primary insurer (a.k.a. ceding insurer).
- The Cal. Ins. Code broadly defines a person to include individuals, partnerships, associations, organizations, corporations, limited liability companies, or business trusts.
- An insurer can be a person, partnership, association, organization, corporation, limited liability company, or business trust.
- Policies issued by mutual insurers pay dividends to policy owners. The dividend option is chosen by the policy owner on the insurance application.
- Policyholders own mutual insurers.
- A stock insurer is an insurance provider owned by individuals who purchase shares of stock in the company. They share the profits in proportion to the number of shares held and vote for a board of directors.
- Dividends received by policy owners of a mutual insurer are not taxable.

General Market Regulation

- The CIC can only be changed when the California state legislature passes a new statute modifying, amending, or repealing an existing one.
- Only the Commissioner can change the CCR according to the State Administrative Procedures Act.
- The Insurance Commissioner is elected by the people in the same manner as the Governor, not to exceed two 4-year terms.
- Under Cal. Ins. Code Section 770, the Commissioner will issue a cease and desist order for a violation of more than one transaction if the violation pertains to loans on the security of real or personal property.
- Pretext interviews can be used to investigate a claim with a reasonable basis for suspecting fraud, material misrepresentation, or criminal activity.
- When new insurance is being sought, the Gramm-Leach-Bliley Act (GLBA) requires a privacy protection notice be provided no later than at the time of policy delivery.
- The California Financial Information Privacy Act gives individuals greater privacy protections than the federal GLBA.

- The purpose of the CA Insurance Information and Privacy Protection Act is to establish standards for collecting, using, and disclosing information gathered during insurance transactions.
- An insurance company is considered insolvent when it cannot meet its financial obligations.
- An insurer cannot escape insolvency by being able to pay for all liabilities and reinsurance of all outstanding risks.
- An insurer with enough reserves to cover all liabilities is considered solvent.
- To remain financially solvent under the CIC, an insurance company must have enough assets to pay for its liabilities, reinsurance of all outstanding risks, and meet minimum requirements equal to their paid-in capital (value of the company if liquidated).
- The State Insurance Guarantee Fund protects policy owners whose insurer becomes insolvent (financially impaired). This fund only covers licensed insurance companies (member insurers).
- The paid-in capital of an insurance provider refers to the amount by which the value of assets exceeds the sum of liabilities.
- Producer records must be made available to the Commissioner at any time.
- It is a misdemeanor to refuse to deliver assets, records, or books to the Commissioner once a seizure order has been executed in an insolvency proceeding.
- Agents who receive a premium financing commission must keep their records for three years.
- If the Insurance Commissioner issues a notice of seizure for documents and the agent fails to produce the documents, the agent would be subject to a $1,000 fine or up to one year in jail.
- The Commissioner can undertake conservation proceedings when an insurance company is in such poor financial condition that its business transactions will be hazardous to policy owners.
- Employer self-funded plans are not covered by the California Life and Health Insurance Guarantee Association (CLHIGA).
- Group stop-loss plans are not covered by the California Life and Health Insurance Guarantee Association (CLHIGA).
- Fraud is an intentional and fraudulent omission on the part of an insured that allows the insurance provider to rescind the contract.
- Each authorized insurer must establish a division to investigate fraudulent claims.
- When an insured is guilty of turning in a fraudulent claim, they can face imprisonment or a $150,000 fine or double the amount of the fraudulent claim, whichever is greater. For example, if an insured turned in a fraudulent claim totaling $55,000, the insured would be fined $110,000.
- If an insured signs a fraudulent claim form, the insured could be guilty of perjury.
- Claims forms must include a statement related to fraudulent claims alerting anyone who knowingly presents a fraudulent or false claim for the payment of a loss is guilty of a crime. It can be subject to fines and imprisonment.
- As used in the CIC, the word "shall" means "mandatory," and the word "may" means "permissive."
- The affidavit of the individual who mails a notice, affirming the facts, is prima facie evidence that the notice was mailed.

Property and Casualty Basics

Terms and Concepts

- A direct cause of loss is also referred to as a proximate cause of loss.
- A deductible represents a form of risk retention.
- The higher the deductible, the lower the premium, and vice versa.

- Rates are a factor when calculating the premium.
- All-risk property policies are also known as open peril policies.
- To see what is covered on an all-risk or open-peril policy, an applicant must read the exclusions.
- Strict or absolute liability is liability without negligence.
- Strict liability is not a defense against a negligence lawsuit.
- Under the principle of comparative negligence, benefits payable to an injured party are reduced according to their own negligence, preventing an injured party from collecting damages related to their own negligence.
- Under contributory negligence, the injured party cannot recover if they are partly at fault.
- The purpose of subrogation is to prevent the insured from collecting twice.
- A binder of coverage can be either oral or in writing.

Policy Structure

- The four parts of a policy can be remembered by the acronym D-I-C-E (declarations, insuring agreement, conditions, and exclusions).
- The declarations list the named insured, policy limits, and the premium and policy periods.
- The limits of liability are found on the policy's declarations page.
- The insuring agreement lists the covered perils and describes the coverages provided.
- The conditions list the obligations of both parties, the insured and the insurance provider.
- The exclusions list the perils that are not covered.
- Exclusions exist in an insurance policy to clarify coverage.
- Supplementary payments included in the liability section of a policy are paid in addition to the liability limits.
- An endorsement modifies the terms of the policy, not policy conditions.

Provisions and Clauses

- The policy period is defined as the time the policy is effective.
- When an insured transfers their right of ownership to another party, it is called an assignment.
- Appraisal is used on property policies to determine the amount payable.
- Arbitration is used on liability policies to determine if coverage applies.
- If the insurance provider and the insured disagree that the liability policy does or does not provide coverage, the claim will go to arbitration.
- In arbitration, there are three arbitrators.
- The cancellation provisions are found in the conditions section of the policy.
- The insured must promptly notify the insurance provider about a claim.
- The maximum amount an insurance provider will pay is specified in the limits of liability.
- The purpose of coinsurance is to ensure the client carries adequate limits.
- The other insurance (or pro-rata liability) clause on a property policy allows two or more policies insuring the same property to pay claims proportionately.
- Pro-rata means proportionate; it does not mean equal.
- On property policies, abandonment of the property to the insurance provider is prohibited.
- The liberalization clause allows the insurance provider to increase coverage immediately at no charge.
- Insurance providers can sell the salvage to offset the claims expenses.
- Vacancy means a person has moved out of their home and taken their furniture.
- Unoccupied means a person is on an extended vacation. However, their furniture is still in their home, and they will return.

Dwelling Policy

- The primary difference among the various dwelling policy (DP) forms is the insured against property perils.
- DP policies do not cover personal liability; however, it can be added as a Personal Liability Supplement for an additional premium.
- DP policies include general exclusions for damage due to nuclear hazards, war, and floods but not wind.
- On a dwelling policy, Other Structures coverage applies to a structure rented as a private garage.
- DP policies will not cover the breakage of glass after 60 days of a vacancy.
- DP policies will not cover frozen plumbing unless the heat is on when the plumbing freezes.
- Insurers cannot cover the land on which the policy owner's dwelling sits.
- Inflation guard, also called the automatic increase endorsement, has to be added by endorsement to a DP policy.
- Insurers would only cover a loss from dust or rain if an opening in the dwelling's walls or the roof was first created by wind or another covered cause of loss.
- When a dwelling is insured by more than one policy, losses are shared pro rata under the other insurance clause. This clause may also be called the pro rata liability clause.
- The Basic dwelling form DP-1 is a specified or named peril policy.
- The DP-1 Basic Form does not cover additional living expenses under Coverage D; only fair rental value is covered.
- On the DP-1 form, the Extended Coverage Endorsement is added to the Standard Fire Policy.
- A DP-2 Broad Form is a named peril policy on the dwelling and its contents.
- On the dwelling broad form DP-2 (Coverages A and B), building structures are issued with an 80% coinsurance requirement.
- On a DP-2 Broad Form, Coverage B (Other Structures) exceeds other coverage limits.
- The DP-3 policy provides identical coverage as the DP-2 (Contents Broad) policy for personal property coverage.
- Although the DP-1 Basic Form does not provide coverage for lawns, plants, shrubs, and trees, the DP-2 and DP-3 forms offer this coverage.
- When a dwelling policy is referred to as DP-2 ('02), it relates to the Dwelling Property Broad Form. The ('02) designates that it is the ISO policy form introduced in 2002.

Homeowners Policy

- Every HO policy is a package policy combining property and liability coverages.
- The limit of liability is the most a policy will pay under the liability section.
- An insured includes residents of a household who are relatives or any other individual under age 21 who is in the care of the insured.
- All HO policies exclude coverage for mudslides, landslides, or floods.
- The homeowners policy does not cover the theft of fish, birds, or animals.
- Personal injury liability for defamation, slander, libel, false arrest, and invasion of privacy is not automatically covered by a HO policy. It can be added by endorsement for an added premium.
- Insurers cannot cover the land on which a house is located on HO policies.

- Section II (Liability) will pay for damage to the property of others up to $1,000 per occurrence.
- The HO policy will not cover the property of a renter or boarder; it will protect the property of a residence employee or guest.
- The HO policy will cover contents worldwide, including theft.
- The HO policy written on a dwelling during construction will not cover theft.
- Medical coverage will pay for charges related to medical, hospital, nursing, ambulance, x-ray, surgical, dental, prosthetic devices, and funeral services.
- Medical payments do not apply to regular household members.
- The bankruptcy of a policyholder does not relieve the insurance provider of their duties under the policy.
- Most property policies do not cover claims resulting from the enforcement of a law or ordinance. However, limited coverage can be provided as additional coverage.
- The insurance provider's responsibility to defend a lawsuit is stated in the insuring agreement.
- Additional coverages (such as for plants, shrubs, and trees) are over and above the policy limit.
- HO liability pays for bodily injury to a third party.
- If an insurance provider cancels the HO policy, they must send advance written notice to the named insured and the mortgage company.
- The HO policy will not cover the cost of defense on an excluded claim.
- The HO policy covers contents in total while in transit for up to 30 days.
- Coverage C will not pay for the property of a tenant, roomer, or boarder unless they are related to the policy owner.
- Most property policies do not cover claims resulting from the enforcement of a law or ordinance. However, limited coverage can be provided as additional coverage.
- Damage resulting from rain is not covered on a property policy unless the wall or roof was first damaged by hail or wind, allowing the rain to enter.
- Property policies will not pay for damage to motorized vehicles other than those used to maintain the premises (e.g., riding lawn mowers).
- Personal liability and medical coverage will pay for the policyholder's activities on and off the premises.
- Loss of use pays for only additional living expenses.
- The insurance provider's responsibility to defend a lawsuit ends when the amount paid out for damages equals the limit of liability.
- A person hired to maintain the premises is called a residence employee.
- At the policy owner's option, recovered property will be returned to the policy owner or retained by the insurance provider. If the property is returned, the insurer must adjust the loss payment.
- After a loss, if the cost of reconstruction for a home exceeds its market value, the insurance provider will consider it a constructive total loss.
- The HO-2 protects against losses caused by named perils on the dwelling and its contents.
- The HO-3 protects the dwelling and other structures on an open peril basis, and personal property is covered only for broad perils.
- The HO-3 special form policy covers the theft of a resident employee's personal property.
- The HO-4 are property policies issued to tenants to insure against losses caused by a covered peril to alterations, improvements, and additions made to the described location at the tenant's expense.
- Under the HO-6 policy, contents coverage protects against losses caused by named perils.
- The HO-6 (condominium unit owners) form does not insure common area buildings.
- The HO-8 form was created specifically for older homes.

Auto Insurance

Liability

- Liability covers PD and BI to others for which a policy owner is negligent.
- The Auto Assigned Risk Plan provides a method for individuals rejected in the normal market to obtain insurance coverage.
- All authorized insurance companies selling auto insurance must participate in the Auto Assigned Risk Plan.
- Supplementary payments under a personal automobile policy (PAP) do not cover the policy owner's loss of earnings except when they attend a trial or hearing at the insurer's request. The policy owner's injuries are not covered.
- The Personal Auto Coverage Form insures tape decks and radios if they are permanently installed in the dash.
- The medical payment section of the PAP will pay necessary medical and funeral expenses resulting from an accident sustained by a policy owner.
- The medical payments coverage listed in the PAP will not pay for lost wages.
- Auto medical in a PAP covers the policy owner and any passengers in the car. It is no-fault, optional coverage, and is not a supplementary payment.
- On a PAP, medical coverage pays for an at-fault driver's injuries.

Physical Damage

- Part D on a PAP is called Coverage for Damage to Your Auto and is optional. It is divided into two coverages: Collision and Other Than Collision.
- Part D has a deductible and is written on an ACV basis. Other Than Collision coverage is also called comprehensive coverage.
- Hitting a pole with an insured automobile is an example of a collision.
- In the PAP, hitting a deer is an example of other than collision.
- If a bird were to hit the policyholder's windshield, the windshield is covered under other than collision coverage.
- Collision coverage on the PAP covers colliding with other objects, rollover, and upset. All others would be covered by Other Than Collision coverage.
- Towing and labor coverage is optional on the PAP and will cost extra.
- The optional coverage limit for towing and labor pays per occurrence or event.
- Under a PAP, flood damage is covered but not included in property policies.
- In an accident, the injured policy owner's PAP is always the primary policy. The driver's PAP, if different, is always the excess policy.

Uninsured Motorists

- Policy owners purchase uninsured motorist coverage because of their concern of being in an auto accident with a person who has no insurance and is at fault.
- An uninsured motorist refers to hit-and-run drivers, drivers whose insurer has gone bankrupt, and drivers who do not carry the minimum state-required limits.
- If a person is concerned about being in an auto accident with someone with inadequate liability insurance limits and who is at fault, they may purchase underinsured motorist coverage.

Exclusions

- A PAP does not offer coverage in Mexico.
- A PAP does not cover a policy owner's property in transit.
- Auto medical covers the policy owner and passengers but does not cover injured pedestrians.
- A personal automobile policy will cover small pick-up trucks, even if they are used for ranching or farming. It will not cover dump trucks, farm implements, or motorcycles driven on the highway.
- On the PAP, exclusions for the Other than Collision coverage include freezing, wear and tear, and mechanical breakdown.
- The PAP does not cover autos used as livery or taxis, but carpools are covered.

Business Auto

- In a business auto policy, insurers would cover damage to an insured vehicle resulting from a falling object under comprehensive coverage.
- The business auto coverage form does not cover an injured employee driving a company car.
- In a business auto policy, if the employer's partner uses their car during company business, the partner must add owned auto coverage.
- In a business auto policy, if the employer wants to cover their employees while driving their own cars on company business, the employer needs to add hired and non-owned auto coverage.
- In garage insurance, car dealers with fluctuating inventories are encouraged to use reporting forms.
- Garage liability covers a product's liability but does not cover the cost of a product recall.
- The garage coverage form was established for repair shops, auto dealers, parking garages, service stations, and similar risks.
- In a garage form, the garagekeepers coverage insures property in the policy owner's control, custody, and care.

Commercial Lines

Commercial Package Policy (CPP)

- The common conditions section of a CPP allows either the policy owner or the insurance provider to cancel the policy.
- CPPs are subject to a premium audit for three years after a policy's expiration.
- Business income insurance is considered a type of time-element coverage.

Commercial Property

- On a commercial property, ordinance or law coverage and replacement cost coverage value reporting forms are all optional endorsements. Valuation is a loss condition in the insurance policy.
- Commercial property insurance covers the building's unattached signs as business personal property.
- The leasehold interest coverage form protects a policy owner for the value of their lease if it is canceled due to loss or damage from a covered cause of loss.
- The causes of loss forms in commercial property are the basic, broad, and special forms.
- The coverage territory on a commercial property policy includes the U.S., Puerto Rico, and Canada.
- The legal actions clause on a commercial property policy states that the policy owner has a maximum of two years to file a lawsuit against the insurance company.
- Commercial fire policies only cover plants, shrubs, and trees up to $500 each.

Inland Marine

- A list of risks eligible for inland marine coverage published by the National Association of Insurance Commissioners (NAIC) is called the Nationwide Definition.
- On equipment breakdown coverage, the insurance provider may inspect the policy owner's equipment. However, they are not required to do so.
- The scheduled personal property endorsement covers personal property with high values, such as jewelry, antiques, and furs.

Personal Article Floaters

- To properly insure computer equipment, a person would purchase a data processing floater.
- A fine arts floater provides automatic coverage for 90 days for newly acquired fine art.
- A scheduled personal property floater will provide coverage on an ACV basis.
- For losses to a pair or set, insurers can pay the difference in value before and after the loss. The insurer may also replace or repair the set to its original value. To calculate the difference, insurers will subtract the remaining value from the value of the full set.

CGL Coverage

- In a commercial general liability (CGL) policy, the occurrence limits are applied separately for each claim. The aggregate limit applies to each claim submitted during the policy period.
- The CGL policy includes three coverage sections: Part A – Liability, Part B – Personal Injury and Advertising Injury, and Part C – Medical Payments to others. These coverages do not have a deductible.
- A CGL policy will provide liability protection anywhere in the world, provided the product was made within the policy territory, and the lawsuit is filed there.
- The CGL policy territory includes the United States, Puerto Rico, and Canada.
- In a CGL policy, the Medical to Others coverage is applied per person.
- In a CGL policy, Fire coverage is applied per occurrence.

Exposures

- Products liability is applied only after the product is out of the policy owner's control.
- Products liability does not cover the cost of a product recall or the resulting lost income.

Occurrence vs. Claims-Made

- An occurrence basis liability policy covers claims that occur in the policy period, even if a claim is submitted after the expiration date.
- The retroactive date on a claims-made CGL policy only applies to Coverage A (BI and PD).
- All claims-made CGL policies include a basic extended reporting period (ERP) that allows an insured with a pending claim an additional 60 days after expiration to notify their insurer.
- If the claimant notifies the insurance provider within 60 days of the pending claim, they have up to five years to complete the claim. The basic ERP is free.
- The CGL policy does not include coverage for pollution liability. This coverage can be added by optional endorsement for an additional premium.
- A claims-made liability policy requires that the claim occurs after the retroactive date and is submitted during the policy period or within the extended reporting period.

Other Coverages

- The minimum deductible listed in an earthquake policy is $250. The deductible on earthquake insurance is a percentage of the policy limit.
- When a boatowners policy owner has both a liability and a personal umbrella policy, the liability limits on the boatowners policy would be the primary coverage.
- Farm policies do not insure growing crops or autos driven on the highway.
- In a farm policy, the definition of a dwelling excludes a building used for agricultural purposes.
- Farm risks are not covered under DP or HO forms.

National Flood Insurance Program (NFIP)

- The Federal Insurance Administration (FIA) establishes flood insurance rates. A community is required to cooperate with the FIA to qualify for NFIP.
- Flood refers to the temporary inundation of normally dry land.
- Flood insurance will not cover docks, piers, or wharves.
- NFIP flood insurance does not insure seepage or sewer backup through walls.
- Flood insurance is sold by the government and participating private insurance companies, but the federal government pays claims.
- The maximum insurance allowed under the regular NFIP program is $250,000 for a single-family home.
- To qualify for federal flood insurance, the community must participate in the NFIP.

Umbrella and Excess Liability

- Personal umbrella liability policies will pay on an excess basis only after the primary policy has already been paid.
- An excess limits policy, such as an umbrella policy, is written in addition to the primary liability policy's limits of insurance.
- Umbrella policies include a retention requirement that is like a deductible and must be paid by the policy owner in case of a claim.
- An umbrella policy is not written on a standardized industry form.
- In a personal umbrella policy, the retained limit refers to the policy limits of the primary policies.

Professional Liability

- Lawyers errors and omissions (E&O) does not cover PD and BI, only claims for financial damages.
- Malpractice liability provides medical professionals with bodily injury liability.
- A directors and officers (D&O) policy will cover a lawsuit brought by a shareholder against a director who unintentionally falsified the company's financial reports.
- Directors and officers liability policies cover the management mistakes of board members and corporate officers.
- An Employment Practices Liability policy covers harassment, discrimination, and unlawful termination. This coverage is not included in a workers compensation policy.

Businessowners Policy

- A businessowners policy (BOP) covers property damage (PD), bodily injury (BI), and personal injury liability, but it does not cover employer liability.
- In a BOP, if the building has been unoccupied for longer than 60 consecutive days, there is no coverage for glass breakage, sprinkler leakage, vandalism, water damage, or theft.
- Auto liability is not covered by an unendorsed BOP, including liability for the operation of a non-owned auto.
- In a BOP, loss of business income is insured without a dollar limit for a maximum of one year.
- Under a businessowners policy, the optional endorsement designed to cover an employee's personal property does not cover theft.
- According to the common conditions section of a BOP, an insurance provider can cancel a policy if the building has been unoccupied or vacant for 60 or more consecutive days.
- Manufacturing companies are not insurable under a BOP.
- A BOP cannot insure a bank or credit union.
- If a policyholder purchases a special policy to cover their printing presses in addition to a BOP, a claim will be pro-rated.
- In a BOP, the protective safeguards warranty allows the insurance provider to deny a claim if systems are not adequately maintained.
- Unendorsed businessowners policies will pay claims on an all-risk basis.
- A BOP written for a tenant will automatically cover betterments and improvements.
- In the BOP, the inflation guard endorsement automatically raises policy limits by 8% on each anniversary date.
- The BOP protects on an all-risk basis for the building and its contents and contains an 80% coinsurance clause. It is issued on a replacement cost basis, and the policy covers theft.
- The BOP automatically covers business liability for PD, BI, personal injury and advertising injury, medical, and fire legal liability.
- When attached to a BOP, the protective safeguard endorsement requires the policy owner to maintain the alarm system or the sprinkler system in good working order.
- The aggregate limit of liability contained in the CGL policy and the BOP is the most the insurance provider will pay for all occurrences during the policy period.

Workers Compensation

- When workers compensation must be purchased from a state fund, it is known as monopolistic.
- When workers compensation can be purchased from either the state fund or any other authorized insurer, it is known as competitive.
- The state establishes workers compensation statutory coverages.
- Workers compensation covers both disease and occupational injury.
- Workers compensation coverage cannot be added to a package policy. It is always a stand-alone policy.
- Under workers compensation, permanent partial disability means the inability to perform job-related functions due to disease or injury.

- If the employee cannot fulfill their job duties but will be able to do so after recovering from a disease or injury, the employee is considered to have a temporary disability.
- Workers compensation covers medical expenses on an unlimited basis.
- An employee who cannot return to work due to a disability is classified as totally disabled.
- If an insurance company issues a workers compensation policy that does not comply with a state's requirements, they must pay the required coverages in case of a claim.
- Upon work-related death, workers compensation will pay income benefits to surviving spouses and children.
- Payroll determines workers compensation premiums and will not be known until after the policy period concludes.
- Under workers compensation insurance, Other States coverage only applies to those states listed in the policy's Declarations.

GLOSSARY

Abandonment – The relinquishment of insured property into the hands of another or into possession of no one in particular.

Absolute Liability – A liability that occurs due to hazardous operations, such as working at extreme heights or using explosives.

Accident – An unforeseen, unplanned event occurring suddenly and at a specific place.

Actual Cash Value (ACV) – The required amount for property loss or to pay damages is determined based on the property's current replacement value minus depreciation.

Additional Coverage – A provision in an insurance policy that allows for more coverage for specific loss expenses without a premium increase.

Additional Insureds – Individuals or businesses that are not named insureds on the declarations page but are protected by the policy, typically regarding a specific interest.

Adhesion – An insurance provider offers a contract on a "take-it-or-leave-it" basis. The policy owner's only option is to accept or reject the contract. Any contract ambiguities will be settled in favor of the policy owner.

Admitted Insurer – An insurance company licensed and authorized to transact business in a particular state.

Adverse Selection – The tendency of risks with a higher probability of loss to buy and maintain insurance coverage more often than those with a lower probability.

Agent – An individual licensed to negotiate, sell, or effect insurance contracts on behalf of an insurance provider.

Aggregate Limit – The maximum coverage limit available under a liability policy during a policy year irrespective of the number of accidents that may occur or the number of claims that may be made.

Agreed Value – A property policy with a provision agreed upon by the insurance provider and policy owner regarding the amount of insurance representing a fair valuation for the property when the coverage is written.

Aleatory – A contract where the participating parties agree to an exchange of unequal amounts. Insurance contracts are aleatory in that the amount the insurance provider will pay in the event of a loss is unequal to the amount the policy owner will pay in premiums.

Alien Insurer – An insurance company that is incorporated outside the United States.

Apparent Authority – The appearance or assumption of authority based on the principal's words, actions, or deeds or because of circumstances the principal created.

Appraisal – An assessment of the property to determine the correct amount of insurance to be written or the amount of loss to be paid.

Arbitration – Method of claim settlement used when the policy owner and insurance provider cannot agree upon the amount of the loss.

Assignment – The transfer of an interest in an insurance policy or a legal right. In property and casualty insurance, assignments of policies are generally valid only with the prior written consent of the insurance provider.

Authorized Insurer – An insurer that has qualified and received a Certificate of Authority from the Department of Insurance to transact insurance business in the state.

Auto – Any land motor vehicle, trailer, or semi-trailer intended for use on public roads, including attached equipment or machinery; auto does not include mobile equipment.

Avoidance – A method to deal with risk by deliberately avoiding it. For instance, if an individual wanted to avoid the risk of dying in a helicopter crash, they might choose never to fly in a helicopter.

Bailee – A person or entity that has possession of personal property entrusted to them by the owner. For example, a computer repair person possessing a customer's computer would be a bailee.

Beneficiary – The individual who receives the proceeds from an insurance policy.

Binder – A temporary contract that puts an insurance policy into force before the premium is paid.

Blanket Bond – A bond that covers losses caused by dishonest employees.

Blanket Insurance – A single property policy that offers insurance for multiple classes of property at a single location or provides insurance for one or more classes of property at multiple locations.

Bodily Injury Liability – Legal liability arising from physical trauma or death to an individual due to a purposeful or negligent act and omissions by an insured.

Boycott – An unfair trade practice where one person refuses to do business with another until they agree to certain conditions.

Builder's Risk Coverage Form – A commercial property form that insures buildings under construction.

Building and Personal Property Coverage Form – A particular commercial property form that insures buildings and their contents.

Burglary – The forced entry into another person's premises with felonious intent.

Cancellation – Terminating an in-force policy before the expiration date by the insurer or insured.

Casualty Insurance – A type of insurance that insures against losses caused by injury to individuals or damage to the property of others.

Cease and Desist Order – A demand to stop committing an act violating a provision.

Certificate of Authority – A document that authorizes a company to start transacting business and specifies the kind(s) of insurance a company can transact. It is illegal for an insurer to transact insurance business without this certificate.

Certificate of Insurance – A legal document stating that an insurance policy has been issued and indicating the types and amounts of insurance provided.

Claim – A demand made by the insured to cover a loss protected by the insurance policy.

Class Rating – The practice of calculating a price per unit of insurance that applies to all applicants possessing a given set of characteristics.

Coercion – An unfair trade practice where an insurance company uses mental or physical force to persuade an applicant to purchase insurance.

Coinsurance – An agreement between an insurance provider and policy owner in which both parties are expected to pay a portion of the potential loss and other expenses.

Combined Single – A single dollar limit of liability applies to the total damages for property damage and bodily injury combined, resulting from one accident or occurrence.

Commercial Lines – Insurance coverage for business, manufacturing, or mercantile establishments.

Commissioner (Superintendent, Director) – The administrative officer and chief executive of a state insurance department.

Common Law – An unwritten body of law based on past judicial decisions, customs, and usages.

Complaint – A written statement of a liability claim provided by the claimant; a reason for a lawsuit.

Components – Factors that determine rates, including loss adjusting expenses, loss reserves, operating expenses, and profits.

Comprehensive Coverage – Also known as Other Than Collision coverage, it insures against losses by fire, falling objects, vandalism, theft, etc.

Concealment – The intentional withholding of known facts that, if material, could void a contract.

Conditional Contract – An agreement in which both parties must perform specific duties and follow rules of conduct to make it enforceable.

Conditions – The section of an insurance policy stating the general rules or procedures that the insurance provider and insured agree to follow under the terms of the policy.

Consideration – The binding force in any contract that involves something of value to be exchanged for the transfer of risk. The consideration on the policy owner's part is the representations made in the application and the premium payment. The consideration on the insurer's part is the promise to pay in the event of a loss.

Consultant – An individual who, for a fee, offers any counsel, advice, opinion, or service regarding the advantages, disadvantages, or benefits promised under a policy of insurance.

Consumer Reports – Written or oral statements regarding a consumer's credit, reputation, character, or habits collected by a reporting agency from credit reports, employment records, and other public sources.

Contract – An agreement or arrangement between two or more parties that is enforceable by law.

Controlled Business – An entity that obtains and possesses a license to write business on the owner, relatives, immediate family, employees, and employer.

Concurrent Causation – Multiple events leading to a loss

Death Benefit – The amount payable upon the death of the individual whose life is insured.

Declarations – The section of an insurance policy that contains the basic underwriting information, such as the policy owner's name, address, amount of coverage and premiums, and a description of insured locations, as well as any supplemental representations by the policy owner.

Deductible – The portion of the loss to be paid by the policy owner before the insurance provider may pay any claim benefits.

Defamation – An unfair trade practice where an insurer or agent makes a defamatory statement about another intending to harm the reputation of a person or company.

Deposit Premium Audit – A condition allowing the insurer to audit the policy owner's records or books at the end of the policy term to ensure sufficient premium is collected for the exposure.

Depreciation – The reduction of the value of real and personal property because of wear and tear and age.

Direct Losses – Physical damage to buildings or personal property caused by a direct consequence of a particular peril.

Director (Superintendent, Commissioner) – The head of the state insurance department.

Disability – A mental or physical impairment, either congenital or resulting from a sickness or injury.

Disclosure – An act of identifying the name of the representative, firm or producer, limited representative, or temporary producer on any policy solicitation.

Domestic Insurer – An insurance company incorporated in the state.

Domicile of Insurer – An insurer's location of incorporation and the legal ability to transact business in a state.

Economic Loss – An accident's projected cost (insured and uninsured).

Endorsement – A printed addendum to the contract that changes the insurance policy's original coverages, terms, or conditions.

Estoppel – A legal obstruction to denying a fact or restoring a right that has been previously waived.

Excess Policy – A policy that pays for a loss only after the primary policy has paid its limit.

Exclusions – Causes of exposures, loss, conditions, etc., listed in the policy for which insurance benefits will not be paid.

Exclusive or Captive Agent – An agent who represents only one insurance company and is compensated by commissions.

Experience Rating – The method of determining the premium based on the policy owner's previous loss experience.

Exposure – A unit of measure used to calculate rates charged for insurance coverage.

Express Authority – The authority granted to an agent through the agent's written contract.

Extensions of Coverage – A provision in certain insurance policies that allows the extension of a major coverage to include specific types of loss or damage to property that is not specifically insured.

Fiduciary – An agent or broker handling an insurer's funds in a trust capacity.

First Named Insured – The individual whose name appears first on the policy's declarations page.

Flood – A temporary and general condition of complete or partial inundation of usually dry land areas from overflow of inland or tidal waters or the rapid and unusual accumulation or runoff of surface waters from any source.

Foreign Insurer – An insurance company incorporated in another state.

Fraternal Benefit Society – A life or health insurance company formed to provide insurance for members of an affiliated lodge, fraternal, or religious organization with a representative form of government.

Fraud – Intentional deceit or misrepresentation with the intent to induce a person to part with something of value.

Functional Replacement Cost – The cost of replacing damaged property with less expensive and more modern equipment or construction.

Gross Negligence – Irresponsible behavior that shows disregard for the lives or safety of others.

Hazard – A circumstance that increases the probability of a loss.

Hazard, Moral – The effect of a person's character, reputation, living habits, etc., on their insurability.

Hazard, Morale – The effect a person's indifference toward loss has on the risk to be insured.

Hazard, Physical – A type of hazard that arises from a person's physical characteristics, such as a physical disability because of either current circumstance or a condition present at birth.

Implied Authority – Authority that is not written into the contract or expressed. The agent is assumed to have implied authority to conduct the insurance business on the principal's behalf.

Indemnity – Compensation to the policy owner that restores them to the same financial position they held before the loss.

Independent Agents – Agents that sell the products of several insurance companies and work for themselves or other agents.

Indirect Losses – Losses caused by a peril but not directly resulting from it. Indirect losses may include extra expenses, business disruption, renters insurance, and other consequences that occur over time.

Inflation Guard – A coverage extension that annually automatically increases the amounts of insurance on buildings by an agreed-upon percentage.

Insurable Interest – Any interest an insured might have in the property that is the subject of insurance coverage so that damage or destruction of that property would cause the policy owner financial loss.

Insurance – The transfer of the possibility of a loss (risk) to an insurance carrier that spreads the costs of unexpected losses to many individuals.

Insurance Policy – A contract between an insured and an insurance provider which agrees to pay the policy owner for loss caused by specific events.

Insured – The individual or organization that is protected by insurance; the party to be indemnified (can also be the "policy owner" or "policyholder").

Insured Contract – A definition of liability forms that explains the types of contracts where liability is assumed by the insured and included for coverage in the policy. Several examples of insured contracts are elevator maintenance agreements, leases of premises, easement agreements, and other agreements about the insured's business.

Insurer – An entity that indemnifies against losses, provides benefits, or renders services (can also be the "company" or "insurance company" or "carrier" or "insurance carrier" or "provider" or "insurance provider").

Insuring Agreement – The section of an insurance policy containing the perils insured against, the description of coverage provided, and the insurance provider's promise to pay.

Intentional Tort – A deliberate act that results in harm to another person.

Interline Endorsement – A written amendment intended to minimize the number of endorsements in the policy and eliminate redundancy.

Judgment Rating – An approach used when no credible statistics are available, or exposure units are so varied that it is challenging to construct a class.

Law of Large Numbers – A principle stating that the larger the number of similar units of exposure, the more closely the reported losses will equal the probability of loss.

Legal Liability – A liability under the law occurs when an individual is responsible for damages or injuries to another because of negligence.

Liability – An individual's responsibility under the law.

Liberalization – A property insurance clause that expands broader regulated or legislated coverage to current policies, as long as it does not cause a premium to increase.

Lien – A security, charge, or encumbrance on a property.

Limit of Liability – The maximum amount for which an insurer is liable.

Lloyd's Associations – Organizations that support underwriters or groups that accept insurance risk.

Loss – The decrease, disappearance, or reduction of value of the property or person insured in a policy by a covered peril.

Loss Payable Clause – A property insurance provision used to protect a secured lender's interest in personal property.

Loss Ratio – A calculation insurance carriers use to relate income from loss expenses: loss ratio = (loss adjusting expense + incurred losses) / earned premium.

Loss Valuation – A factor in calculating the charged premium and the amount of required insurance.

Market Value – A rarely used method of valuing a loss based on the amount a buyer would pay to a seller for the property before the loss.

Misrepresentation – A lie or false statement that can void a contract.

Monoline Policy – A separate policy written as a single coverage.

Mutual Assessment Insurer – A mutual insurer with the right to charge additional premium amounts to meet operational needs.

Mutual Companies – Insurance companies with no capital stock that their policyholders own.

Mysterious Disappearance – The disappearance of any property where the time, location, or manner of the loss cannot be explained.

Named Insured – The individual(s) whose name appears on the policy's declarations page.

Named Peril – A cause of loss covered explicitly by the policy. No coverage is provided for perils not listed in the policy.

Negligence – Failing to use the care that a prudent, reasonable individual would use under the same or similar circumstances.

No Benefit to the Bailee – A provision excluding any assignment or granting of any policy provision to any organization or person moving, repairing, storing, or holding insured property for a fee.

Non-admitted Insurer – An insurance provider that has not applied or has applied and been denied a Certificate of Authority and cannot transact insurance.

Nonconcurrency – A situation where other insurance is written on the same risk but not on the same coverage basis.

Nonrenewal – A policy termination by an insurance provider on the renewal or anniversary date.

Notice of Claim – A provision that details an insured's responsibility to provide the insurer with reasonable notice in the event of a loss.

Occurrence – A broader definition of loss, which differs from an accident. It encompasses losses caused by repeated or continuous exposure to conditions resulting in damage to property or injury to individuals that is neither expected nor intended.

Open Peril – A term used in property insurance to describe the scope of coverage provided under an insurance policy form that covers "any risk of loss" that is not explicitly excluded.

Pair and Set Clause – In many inland marine and property policies, the insurance provider is not required to pay for the total value of a set of items if only one thing has been destroyed, damaged, or lost.

Partnership – A legal entity in which two or more individuals agree to share the profits and losses of the business.

Passive – A description of an anti-theft system or device for autos that automatically activates when the driver turns the ignition key to the off position and removes the key.

Peril – The cause behind a possible loss.

Personal Injury Liability – Legal responsibility for an injury to another individual's character caused by slander, libel, invasion of privacy, false arrest, and other acts.

Personal Lines Insurance – A type of insurance coverage available to families and individuals for non-business risks.

Policy Limits – The maximum amount a policy owner can collect or for which a policy owner is protected under the terms of the policy.

Policy Period – The period or "term" when a policy is effective.

Policyholder – The individual possessing an insurance policy. This person may or may not be the policy owner or the insured.

Policy Owner – The individual entitled to exercise the privileges and rights in the policy. This person may or may not be the insured.

Premium – A periodic payment to the insurance provider keeping the policy in force.

Primary Policy – A fundamental, basic policy that pays first concerning any other outstanding policies.

Pro Rata – Proportional distribution of loss shares for every insurance policy written on a piece of property.

Producer – An individual who acts on behalf of the insurance provider to negotiate, sell, or effect insurance contracts. This person is also called an agent.

Proof of Loss – A sworn statement typically provided by the insured to an insurance carrier before any loss under a policy is paid.

Property Damage Liability – Legal liability stemming from physical damage to the tangible property of others caused by the negligence of a policy owner.

Proximate Cause – An event or act that is the actual or immediate cause of a loss.

Pure Risk – Situations that can only result in no change or a loss; a gain is never possible. Pure risk is the only type of risk that insurance carriers are willing to accept.

Rebating – Any enticement or kickback offered in the sale of insurance products not specified in the policy.

Reciprocal – Insurance resulting from an interchange of reciprocal indemnity agreements among individuals known as subscribers.

Reduction – Lessening or reducing the probability or severity of a loss.

Reinsurance – A form of insurance where one insurer (the reinsurer), in consideration of a premium, agrees to indemnify another insurer (the ceding company) for part or all of its liabilities from any policies it has issued.

Replacement Cost – The cost to replace damaged property with a similar kind and quality at the current price, without any depreciation deduction.

Representations – A statement made by the applicant for insurance that is believed to be true but is not guaranteed to be true.

Retention – A way of dealing with risk by intentionally or unintentionally retaining a portion of it for the policy owner's account. It is the amount of responsibility assumed but not reinsured by the insurer.

Retrospective Rating – A self-rating plan under which the policy period's actual losses determine the final premium (contingent upon a minimum and maximum premium).

Right of Salvage – A policy provision in property insurance requiring that after payment of a total loss to insured property, the policy owner must transfer the property's title (or ownership) to the insurance provider.

Risk – Uncertainty regarding the outcome of an event when two or more possibilities exist.

Risk, Pure – The chance of a loss occurring in a situation that can only result in no change or a loss.

Risk, Speculative – The chance or uncertainty of a loss occurring in a situation involving the opportunity for a gain or a loss.

Robbery – The theft of property from another through the use of violence or the threat of violence.

Salvage – The amount of money realized from selling damaged property or merchandise. A salvage clause is included in ocean marine insurance and typically states that the rescuers of a ship are entitled to the salvage of the vessel and cargo.

Settlement – The process through which agreements are reached and claims are resolved in liability insurance.

Severability of Interests – A provision in which insurance is applied separately to each insured in a policy, treating each person as the only insured.

Sharing – A way to handle risk for a group of businesses or individuals with the same or similar exposure to loss who share the losses within that group.

Specific Insurance – A property insurance policy insures a specific unit or property for a particular amount of insurance.

Speculative Risk – The chance or uncertainty of a loss taking place in a situation that involves the opportunity for either a gain or loss.

Split – Separately stated limits of liability for different coverages, which can be stated on a per occurrence, per person, or per policy period basis, or divided between property damage and bodily injury.

Stated Amount – An amount of scheduled insurance in a property policy that is not contingent upon any coinsurance requirements if a covered loss occurs.

Statute Law – The written law as enacted by a legislative body (e.g., the laws of the state), which usually takes precedence in cases where both statute law and common law apply.

Stock Companies – Companies owned by their stockholders whose investments provide the necessary capital to establish and operate the insurance company.

Strict Liability – A liability that refers to damages resulting from defective products even though the manufacturer's negligence or fault cannot be proven.

Subrogation – The acquisition by an insurance provider of an insured's rights against any third party for indemnification of a loss or other payment to the extent that the insurance provider pays the loss.

Superintendent (Commissioner, Director) – The head of a state's insurance department.

Surety Bond – An assurance that debts and obligations will be fulfilled, and the benefits will be paid for losses resulting from nonperformance.

Surplus Lines – A type of insurance for which there is no readily available, admitted market.

Theft – Any act of removing or stealing property from its rightful owner. Theft embodies both burglary and robbery.

Third-Party Provisions – A set of insurance provisions that address the rights of another person besides the insured to have a secured financial interest in the covered property.

Tort – A wrongful act or violating another person's rights that leads to legal liability. Torts are identified as intentional or unintentional (also referred to as negligence).

Transfer – A basic concept of insurance under which the risk of financial loss is transferred to another party.

Twisting – A misrepresentation in which an agent or producer persuades an insured or policy owner to cancel, switch, or lapse policies, even when it is not to the advantage of the insured.

Umbrella Liability Policy – Coverage that includes extra protection against liability and an excess amount of insurance over and above the primary policy.

Unauthorized Insurer – An insurer that has not applied or has applied and been denied a Certificate of Authority to transact insurance business.

Underwriter – An individual who evaluates and classifies risks to accept or reject them on behalf of the insurance company.

Underwriting – The process of reviewing, accepting, or rejecting insurance applications.

Unilateral Contract – A contract that binds only one party to contractual obligations once the premium is paid.

Underinsured Motorist Coverage – Coverage in an auto policy under which the insurance provider will pay for costs up to specified limits for bodily injury if the liable driver's policy limits are depleted and they cannot pay the total amount for which they are liable.

Uninsured Motorist Coverage – Coverage that permits the named insured, passengers, and resident relative(s) in a covered auto to collect sums another driver would be legally liable to pay for bodily injury caused by an auto accident. The accident must be caused by an uninsured motorist, a hit-and-run driver, or a driver whose insurance provider is insolvent.

Unintentional Tort – The result of acting without care, usually referred to as negligence.

Unoccupied – A property with furnishings or contents but is not being lived in or used

Utmost Good Faith – The equal and fair bargaining by both parties in forming the contract, where the applicant must disclose risk to the insurer fully, and the insurer must be fair in underwriting the risk.

Vacant – A property that has no occupants, furnishings, or contents.

Valued Policy – A policy used when it is hard to determine the actual cash value of the insured property following a loss because of its uniqueness or rarity. This policy provides for payment of the entire policy amount if a total loss occurs without regard to depreciation or actual value.

Vicarious Liability – A liability in which one individual is responsible for the acts of another individual. For instance, parents can be held accountable for negligent acts of their children, and employers can be vicariously liable for the actions of their employees.

Waiting Period – The time between the start of a disability and the beginning of disability insurance benefits.

Waiver – The voluntary abandonment of a legal or known advantage or right.

Warranty – The material stipulation in a policy that, if breached, can void coverage.

Workers Compensation – Benefits required by state law to be paid by an employer to an employee in the case of disability, injury, or death due to an on-the-job hazard.

PRACTICE EXAM:

1

Test your readiness

You are about to take a California Property and Casualty Practice Exam. This exam consists of *150 Questions (plus five to ten non-scored experimental questions)* and is *3 hours and 15 minutes* long. If you do not have enough time to complete this exam right now, it is better to wait until you can fully devote your attention to completing it in the allotted time. Any skipped questions will be graded as incorrect. The following chart breaks down the number of questions in each chapter and by topic.

CHAPTER	# OF QUESTIONS
Basic Insurance Concepts and Principles	7
Contract Law	6
The Insurance Marketplace	8
Basic Legal Concepts – Tort Law	6
Property and Casualty Basics	7
Property and Casualty Policies – General	7
Dwelling Policy	14
Homeowners Policy	12
Homeowners – Section I: Property Coverage	8
Homeowners – Section II: Liability Coverage	8
Personal Auto	14
Other Personal Lines Policies	13
Commercial Coverages	5
Commercial General Liability (CGL)	5
Commercial Auto	5
Other Commercial Coverages	4
Farm	5
Businessowners	4
Ocean Marine	4
Surety Bonds and General Bond Concepts	4
Workers Compensation – General Concepts	4
Total	**150**

To calculate your score, subtract the number of incorrectly answered questions from 150. Take this number and divide it by 150. For example, if you incorrectly answered 60 questions, your score would be 60%, the minimum score needed to pass the exam.

#1. The insured's father-in-law broke his leg, falling down the front steps of the insured's premises. The insured's homeowners medical payments coverage will

a) Only pay if the father-in-law has no health insurance.
b) Share equally in the cost with the father-in-law's health insurance.
c) Apply to injuries of any visitors or guests.
d) Pay as excess over the father-in-law's health insurance.

#2. Under the standard mortgage clause, who can bring a lawsuit in their own name to recover damages, pay policy premiums, and submit proof of loss?

a) Insurer
b) Governor
c) Policyholder
d) Mortgagee

#3. Which of the following will likely be the same in a personal auto policy and a motorcycle endorsement?

a) Usage
b) Driving experience
c) Liability coverage
d) Medical coverage

#4. Which statement is true regarding a bonded contractor who defaults on a construction performance contract?

a) The obligee can engage another contractor and seek reimbursement from the surety
b) The surety can cancel the bond and avoid paying any losses or expenses
c) The contractor will lose their license to operate in the state
d) The principal has no obligation to complete any remaining work or to pay for the expenses

#5. Which of the following would cover the loss of income when an insured rental dwelling is rendered uninhabitable due to a covered loss?

a) Coverage C
b) Coverage D
c) Coverage A
d) Coverage B

#6. Which of the following selections correctly describes the California State Compensation Insurance Fund?

a) A state entity that exists to provide compensation if an employee is injured while working for an uninsured employer, and the employer fails to pay or post a bond to pay compensation owed to the employee
b) A state entity that exists exclusively to transact workers compensation insurance on a nonprofit basis
c) A state entity that exists to protect policy owners against failure in the performance of workers compensation policies due to the impairment or insolvency of a member insurer that issued the policy
d) None of these correctly describe the California State Compensation Insurance Fund

#7. Transportation expenses are covered under a personal auto policy (PAP) for

a) $50 per day, for a maximum of $500.
b) $50 per day, for a maximum of $750.
c) $20 per day, for a maximum of $600.
d) $25 per day, for a maximum of $500.

#8. A premium discount describes when a policy owner owes a total standard premium greater than

a) $15,000.
b) $1,000.
c) $5,000.
d) $10,000.

#9. When an insurance provider cancels an auto policy for a reason other than the nonpayment of premium, the insurance provider is required to meet all of the following requirements EXCEPT

a) Explain the reason for policy cancellation.
b) Offer the insured to renew the policy at a different rate.
c) Send a 20-day notice.
d) Notify the policy owner about the automobile liability assigned risk plan.

#10. The rate charged for a Good Driver Discount policy should be at least what percent below the rate the insured would have been charged for the same coverage?

a) 10%
b) 15%
c) 20%
d) 30%

#11. What is the term used to describe a sales campaign conducted through the mail?

a) Advertising
b) Direct response
c) Direct mail
d) Mass marketing

#12. A property with which of the following deficiencies would be eligible for the California FAIR Plan?

a) Faulty wiring
b) Windows poorly installed
c) Heating system in poor condition
d) Located in a designated hazardous brush area

#13. The risk of loss can be classified as

a) Pure risk and speculative risk.
b) Certain risk and uncertain risk.
c) Named risk and un-named risk.
d) High risk and low risk.

#14. Which of the following best describes policy nonrenewal?

a) Discontinuing an insurance policy by the insured on the policy anniversary date
b) Returning the policy after a 10-day free look
c) Voiding of a policy because of a misrepresentation on the application
d) Revocation of one's insurance policy by the insurance provider

#15. Vandals damaged a grave marker. It would cost $3,000 to have the damage repaired. Under these circumstances, how much would a homeowners policy cover?

a) $3,000
b) $0
c) $500
d) $1,000

#16. How long must an insurance provider keep records of electronic transmission to customers?

a) 5 years
b) 6 years
c) 1 year
d) 3 years

#17. Under a homeowners policy, Coverage F (Medical Payments) would cover

a) A residence employee who is injured on the job.
b) A tenant who is injured while on the premises.
c) An injured family member while residing in the insured premises.
d) The insured for injuries suffered while working at home.

#18. Which of the following is true concerning dwelling policy coverage?

a) There are no exclusions in basic forms
b) Special forms only have special exclusions
c) Exclusions apply to all three policy forms
d) Exclusions apply only to broad policy forms

#19. Which of the following would not be considered a flood?

a) Overflow of tidal waters
b) Mudslides
c) Runoff of surface waters
d) Sewer backup

#20. Which of the following terms describes a shaking or trembling of the earth that is seismic or volcanic?

a) Geotectonic inversion
b) Earthquake
c) Tectonic shifting
d) Tsunami

#21. Under the additional living expenses coverage, if a civil authority prohibits the policy owner from using the dwelling due to direct damage to a neighboring location from a peril covered in the policy, the loss would be covered for up to

a) 2 weeks.
b) 1 month.
c) 90 days.
d) 1 week.

#22. If a person is called upon to handle a deceased's estate, the court will require that individual to post which type of bond?

a) Administer
b) Executor
c) Fiduciary
d) Guardian

#23. The commercial general liability coverage form excludes property damage or bodily injury that the insured has assumed under any agreement or contract. However, the exclusion does not apply to certain types of contracts, provided the injury or damage takes place

a) After the contract expires.
b) Before the execution of the contract.
c) Before the contract expires.
d) After the execution of the contract.

#24. The insured's house is located two miles from the county's new landfill and across the road from the entrance of a rock quarry. The cost to rebuild the home if something happened to it would be $150,000, but when the insured tried to sell it, the best offer she received was $90,000. The insurance company will insure the house for only $90,000. What method of valuation is used to insure this property?

a) Functional replacement cost
b) Market value
c) Actual cost value
d) Replacement cost

#25. When must an application for coverage be submitted for Federal Crop Insurance?

a) All applications need to be submitted by April 15 of each calendar year
b) At any time before the crop is harvested
c) At or before a date set forth by the Federal Crop Insurance Corporation
d) At any time before a loss has taken place

#26. Insurable interest is defined as an individual's or entity's right to property, meaning that such a loss to that property would result in a direct monetary loss to the individual or entity. Which statement is TRUE concerning insurable interest in property and casualty insurance?

a) Only the owner of the property has an insurable interest
b) Insurable interest also includes an indirect monetary loss to the individual or entity
c) The contract is void if the insured has no insurable interest
d) The insurable interest needs to exist only at the time of the insurance application

#27. In a homeowners policy, first aid costs for others injured on the insured's premises

a) Are paid in addition to the liability limit.
b) Only apply if the insured is legally liable.
c) Also covers injuries to the insured's family members.
d) Are deducted from the liability limit.

#28. Following a career change, an insured no longer has to perform many physical activities, so she has implemented a program where she walks and jogs for 45 minutes every morning. The insured has also eliminated most fatty foods from her diet. This scenario describes which method of dealing with risk?

a) Reduction
b) Transfer
c) Avoidance
d) Retention

#29. If a liability policy had split limits of 50/100/30, what is the maximum amount that would be payable in the event of injury to a single individual?

a) $30,000
b) $50,000
c) $100,000
d) $180,000

#30. An insured obtained a National Flood Insurance policy ten days after his community entered an emergency program. When would his coverage be effective?

a) 12:01 p.m. on the 5th day after the endorsement request has been mailed
b) 5 days after the application and premium payment are mailed
c) 12:01 a.m. the day after the application and premium payment are mailed
d) 30 days after the application has been accepted

#31. Under Coverage C of a homeowners policy, the amount of insurance provided to cover the insured's personal property is

a) 50% of the amount provided as Coverage B.
b) 50% of the amount provided as Coverage A.
c) Equal to the amount provided as Coverage B.
d) Equal to the amount provided as Coverage A.

#32. A trucking company owns a large fleet of trucks transporting oil across state lines. According to the financial responsibility requirements established by the Motor Carrier Act of 1980, what is the minimum amount of insurance the trucking company must carry on vehicles transporting oil?

a) $500,000
b) $750,000
c) $1 million
d) $5 million

#33. A vehicle that is owned by a nontraditional household, not comprised of a husband and wife, can be insured under a personal auto policy if

a) An extended ownership endorsement is attached.
b) Separate policies are written for each person involved.
c) A joint ownership coverage endorsement is attached.
d) A miscellaneous-type vehicle endorsement is attached.

#34. Robbery is defined as

a) Taking property without resulting in property damage or bodily harm.
b) Any act of stealing.
c) Taking property from within the premises, leaving visible signs of forced entry.
d) Taking property by use of force, violence, or fear.

#35. If more than one individual has an insurable interest in the covered property insured under a dwelling policy,

a) All involved insurance providers must decide who will be liable for the loss.
b) All insureds must decide which one will be liable for the loss.
c) The insurance provider will be liable for only the insured's interest in the damaged property.
d) Liability will be split evenly among everyone with an insurable interest.

#36. In a commercial package policy, who can cancel the policy in writing and make changes to the policy with the consent of the insurance provider?

a) Insurance provider
b) First named insured
c) Last named insured
d) Beneficiary

#37. While an insured mows their yard with their brother's borrowed lawnmower, the fuel line ruptures, and the lawnmower is destroyed in the fire. How will the insured's HO liability react?

a) It will not cover the damage because the insured is not liable
b) It will pay the insured's brother's property insurance deductible
c) The insured's HO liability and their brother's property coverage will share on a prorated basis
d) It will cover the damage

#38. Which of the following would be considered the most important factor in calculating the premiums and rates for an applicant for an auto policy?

a) The number of miles driven yearly
b) The number of years of driving experience
c) The applicant's zip code
d) The applicant's driving safety record

#39. All of the following are eligibility criteria for applicants in the CAARP EXCEPT

a) Anyone who can state that they tried to obtain insurance through the voluntary market and were denied coverage.
b) The vehicle to be insured must be registered in the state of California.
c) Anyone who has a valid driver's license.
d) Anyone who does not owe money on any automobile insurance policy within the last 18 months.

#40. According to the California Insurance Code, what can be considered an insurable event?

a) Extreme levels of loss
b) Pure risks
c) Unpredictable losses
d) Speculative risks

#41. Under the HO property additional coverages, how much is covered for debris removal?

a) Everything after a $200 deductible
b) Nothing, unless attached by an endorsement
c) All reasonable costs
d) 90% of the total cost of clean-up

#42. In which of the following scenarios is it lawful to limit coverage based on marital status?

a) Divorce within the last six months of applying for insurance
b) It is illegal to limit coverage based on marital status
c) An excessive number of divorces, as specified by the Insurance Code
d) Legal separation during the application process

#43. The removal coverage found in the broad form dwelling policy will insure property that is temporarily removed from the premises to protect it from damage for how long?

a) 5 days
b) 15 days
c) 30 days
d) 60 days

#44. In California, the liability for damage to property is limited to

a) $15,000.
b) $20,000.
c) $30,000.
d) $5,000.

#45. Which of the following endorsements is used to insure Coverage C (personal property) for values beyond the limitations of the homeowners policy?

a) Personal property replacement cost endorsement
b) Blue skies endorsement
c) Personal property injury endorsement
d) Scheduled personal property endorsement

#46. According to the loss payment condition in the HO policy, losses must be paid within how many days of the insurance provider receiving proof of loss?

a) 30 days
b) 60 days
c) 90 days
d) 120 days

#47. A couple bought tickets to a college baseball tournament. At the game, a foul ball flies into the stands hitting the wife in the face and breaking her nose. Which legal defense can bar her from recovering damages for the injury she sustained at the baseball game?

a) Comparative negligence
b) Contributory negligence
c) Defense against negligence
d) Assumption of risk

#48. During a pre-selection interview, a producer is allowed to do all of the following EXCEPT

a) Ask questions that are not on the application but that are important for underwriting.
b) Provide the applicants with negative information concerning their risk.
c) Inquire about specific details of the applicant's health history.
d) Terminate the interview and reject the applicant.

#49. Elaborate homes and those with detailed designs or decorative architecture with replacement costs greater than market value or ACV are insured on a

a) HO-3 with a HO-15 endorsement.
b) HO-8.
c) HO-8 with an inflation guard endorsement.
d) HO-3.

#50. A $100,000 building insured on a policy with an 80% coinsurance requirement has a fire that caused $40,000 of damage; the owner has a policy with $60,000 in coverage. How much can the owner collect for the loss?

a) $20,000
b) $30,000
c) $40,000
d) $60,000

#51. Which services are associated with AM Best and Standard & Poor's?

a) Investigating violations of The Fair Credit Reporting Act
b) Providing employment histories for investigative consumer reports
c) Storing medical information collected by insurers
d) Rating the financial strength of insurers

#52. In the personal auto policy, a newly acquired auto for replacement vehicles are automatically covered for

a) Comprehensive (other-than-collision) coverage.
b) Collision coverage.
c) Uninsured motorist coverage.
d) Towing coverage.

#53. The failure to disclose known facts is called

a) Fraud.
b) Warranty.
c) Misstatement.
d) Concealment.

#54. The regular National Flood Insurance Program would insure an eligible single-family dwelling for up to

a) $200,000.
b) $250,000.
c) $100,000.
d) $150,000.

#55. Umbrella policies provide what type of coverage?

a) Excess coverage over an underlying or primary policy
b) Property coverage for those who do not qualify for homeowners insurance
c) Property coverage for the basic perils of wind, fire, and hail
d) Primary coverage for risks that are difficult to insure

#56. In property insurance policies, what is the intent of the coinsurance clause?

a) Prevent insureds from profiting from a loss
b) Encourage the insured to insure the property closer to its full value
c) Encourage higher standards of care by requiring insureds to pay a portion of every loss
d) Ensure that insureds do not over-insure their property

#57. If an insured has an umbrella liability policy in addition to their personal auto policy, which would be the underlying policy?

a) Excess policy
b) General liability policy
c) Auto policy
d) Umbrella policy

#58. A nail salon burns to the ground. What type of loss is this to the owner of the salon?

a) Specific
b) Consecutive
c) Direct
d) Consequential

#59. In the liability section of a homeowners policy, additional coverages will pay for all of the following EXCEPT

a) Damage to a third-party property for which the insured is legally liable.
b) Claims expense.
c) Expenses the insured incurs providing first aid for bodily injury to third parties.
d) Damage to the property of others.

#60. A type of risk analysis used in commercial insurance in which the underwriter can give credits and debits for specific actions that an insured takes during the normal course of business that either increase the probability of loss or decrease the likelihood of loss is known as the

a) Good credit rating method.
b) Discount rating method.
c) Preferred status method.
d) Schedule rating method.

#61. What describes a situation when poor risks are balanced with preferred risks, with average risks in the middle?

a) Adverse selection
b) Equitable spread of risk
c) Ideally insurable risk
d) Profitable distribution of exposures

#62. A used car dealer takes a car in the trade as partial payment for a vehicle on its car lot. The customer promises to bring in the car's title but does not. Another customer takes the trade-in for a test drive and gets into an accident. Which of these is true regarding the dealership's business auto physical damage coverage?

a) Liability coverage is provided
b) Full coverage is provided
c) Damage to the trade-in is covered
d) There is no coverage

#63. The HO-3 policy provides

a) Open peril coverage on the dwelling and basic form coverage on personal property.
b) Basic coverage for the dwelling and broad form coverage for personal property.
c) All-risk coverage for both the dwelling and personal property.
d) Open peril coverage on the dwelling and broad form coverage on personal property.

#64. The transfer of an insured's right to seek damages from a negligent party to the insurance provider is found in which of the following clauses?

a) Salvage
b) Appraisal
c) Subrogation
d) Arbitration

#65. When applying for a life insurance policy, an applicant states that she went to the doctor for nausea but did not mention that she also had severe chest pains. This scenario is an example of

a) Concealment.
b) Misrepresentation.
c) Fraud.
d) Warranty.

#66. What is the basic limit provided by the towing and labor costs endorsement for costs incurred at the location a vehicle is disabled?

a) $25
b) $50
c) $75
d) $100

#67. Which of the following is a statutory defense?

a) Intervening cause
b) Contributory negligence
c) Comparative negligence
d) Assumption of risk

#68. An insured decided to sue his neighbor for damage to his yard. He was instructed to get a bond that guarantees he can pay court costs and resulting damages if he loses the case. What kind of bond does this insured have?

a) A license and permit bond
b) A bail bond
c) A cost bond
d) An appeal bond

#69. According to the commercial package policy's common policy conditions, if the insured dies, the policy rights and duties

a) Die with the insured.
b) Are suspended until probate is completed.
c) Automatically transfer to a legal representative.
d) Transfer to a legal representative following a court appointment.

#70. Which of the following is eligible for a businessowners policy?

a) A convenience store with gas pumps with 60% of gross sales from gasoline sales
b) A mercantile risk with gross sales of $4 million
c) A 6-story office building with less than 100,000 square feet of total area
d) An 8-story office building

#71. In which of the following situations would off-premises coverage in a broad theft endorsement of the insured's dwelling policy apply?

a) The insured's live-in maid's quarters are burglarized
b) The insured's china set is stolen from their home while traveling on business
c) The insured's vacuum cleaner was stolen from their apartment
d) The insured's camera is stolen from their suitcase while on vacation

#72. Directors and officers liability insurance will defend actions against a corporation or its directors and officers alleging wrongful acts. Regarding the coverage provided, wrongful acts include any of the following EXCEPT

a) Embezzlement.
b) Misstatements.
c) Neglect.
d) Breach of duty.

#73. Business liability insurance will NOT cover which of the following watercraft?

a) Owned watercraft 53 feet long
b) An auto parked at the insured's premises
c) Watercraft while on shore at a premises owned by the insured
d) Non-owned watercraft 50 feet long used for transporting personal property of the insured

#74. Which one of the following symbols used in business auto coverage is correctly described?

a) Symbol 7 – hired autos only
b) Symbol 9 – non-owned autos only
c) Symbol 1 – owned auto only
d) Symbol 2 – owned autos subject to no-fault

#75. In California, the liability for bodily injury or death to one individual has a financial responsibility liability limit of

a) $30,000.
b) $20,000.
c) $15,000.
d) $5,000.

#76. A non-admitted insurer who provides unique insurance coverage that is not available from an admitted insurer is known as a/an

a) Assessment mutual insurer.
b) Capital stock insurer.
c) Reciprocal insurer.
d) Surplus lines insurer.

#77. Which of the following must be TRUE for a Protection and Indemnity policy to pay for a loss?

a) The insurer has to investigate the loss
b) The loss must total
c) The insured has to be legally liable for the loss
d) The insured must have been the individual operating the vessel

#78. An insured has a personal property replacement cost endorsement under their homeowners policy. If an antique chair and an expensive painting are stolen from the insured's home, what will the insured receive on the claim under that endorsement?

a) 70% of the replacement cost
b) 80% of the replacement cost
c) 100% of the actual cash value
d) Nothing

#79. The type of insurance used to cover goods for one specific trip is called

a) Bailee policy.
b) Motor truck cargo policy.
c) Trip transit.
d) Commercial property.

#80. Under a business auto coverage form, which of the following would be considered an insured?

a) A partner of the named insured for any covered auto owned by that individual or a member of their household
b) Anyone while using, with permission, a covered auto owned by the named insured
c) The owner or anyone else from whom the named insured borrows or hires a covered auto
d) Anyone using a covered auto while working in a business selling, repairing, servicing, or parking autos if it is not the named insured's business

#81. An unincorporated, nonprofit association representing all insurance providers in the State of California licensed to transact workers compensation insurance is known as the

a) California Workers Compensation Rating Association (WCRA).
b) Rating Bureau of California.
c) California Workers Comp Inspection Rating Bureau (WCIRB).
d) Inspection Bureau of California Workers Compensation (IBCWC).

#82. The contents coverage on a homeowners policy would pay how much after the loss of one of a pair of golden candlesticks?

a) The replacement cost of the pair
b) The actual cash value of the pair
c) Nothing
d) The difference in the actual cash value as a pair and as a single

#83. An employee of the local grocery store suspects a person of shoplifting. The employee escorts the person through the crowded store to the back office and calls the local police. It is later determined that the person has not stolen any merchandise. The employee is guilty of

a) Assault.
b) Battery.
c) False Arrest.
d) Invasion of Privacy.

#84. Using an air-cooled engine, a proposed insured has developed a new, experimental aircraft. If the inventor applies for liability insurance, what rating type will the insurance provider most likely use?

a) Judgment
b) Class
c) Schedule
d) Merit

#85. If an insurance provider makes a change to broaden coverage in a dwelling policy while it is in force, the changes will apply

a) Within 60 days.
b) Automatically.
c) When the new policy is written.
d) When the policy is up for renewal.

#86. Which of the following risks is eligible for coverage under a businessowners policy?

a) Automobile dealers
b) Bars or taverns
c) Condominiums
d) Banks

#87. All of the following are additional liability coverages automatically provided in a homeowners policy EXCEPT

a) Personal injury.
b) Claims expenses.
c) Damage to the property of others.
d) Loss assessment coverage.

#88. A form of insurance between insurers is called

a) Excess and surplus insurance.
b) Treaty insurance.
c) Concurrent insurance.
d) Reinsurance.

#89. The procedure that allows Certified Producers to submit applications to the California Automobile Assigned Risk Plan (CAARP) and obtain immediate coverage is called

a) Effective Procedure for Certified Producers (EPCP).
b) Eligible Electronic Effective Date (EEED).
c) Electronic Effective Date Procedure (EEDP).
d) Electronic Producer Data Procedure (EPDP).

#90. An optional coverage endorsement to the HO policy that covers scheduled residential structures on the insured's premises that are rented to others is known as

a) Modified residence provision.
b) Residential endorsements.
c) Additional residence rental provision.
d) Other structures – increased limits.

#91. An insurance agent fails to obtain auto insurance for a client after agreeing to do so. The client is involved in an auto accident after running a red light and is found to be at fault. The damage to the other vehicle totals $5,000. Which statement regarding the producer's errors and omissions liability policy is true?

a) It will provide coverage since the damage to the client resulted from the producer's negligence
b) It will not provide coverage; such physical damage to property is not covered
c) It will not provide coverage since the property damage resulted from the client breaking the law
d) It will provide coverage since punitive damages have been awarded

#92. In what type of plan would the employer pay all of the claims?

a) Nondistributed
b) Employer Service Only
c) Noncontributory
d) Self-funded

#93. Under the liability coverage section of a homeowners policy, which of the following describes the amount of loss assessment coverage?

a) Up to $5,000 aggregate for the policy period
b) Up to $1,000 per occurrence
c) Up to $2,500 per occurrence
d) Up to $10,000 aggregate for the policy period

#94. According to the HO policy's appraisal condition, what procedure can be followed if the insurance provider and insured disagree on the size of a loss?

a) The parties must pursue a lawsuit
b) The policyholder is permitted to hire an appraiser, and the insurance provider will pay the amount determined
c) Either party can make a written request for an appraisal
d) The insured must accept what the insurance provider is willing to pay

#95. Under a homeowners policy, how much coverage is provided for theft or unauthorized credit card use?

a) $100
b) $500
c) $1,000
d) $5,000

#96. An insured who plans to cancel their claims-made insurance policy can protect themselves against potential claims that can arise from an occurrence that took place during the policy period but is reported after the cancellation by purchasing

a) A Laser Beam endorsement.
b) Mini-Tail coverage.
c) Midi-Tail coverage.
d) A Supplemental Extended Reporting Period.

#97. The additional living expense coverage in homeowners policies

a) Is automatically paid after any loss to the covered house.
b) Only starts to pay once the family has been out of the house for at least seven days.
c) Is designed to allow the family to stay in the least expensive accommodations available.
d) Is designed to allow the family to maintain its normal standard of living.

#98. Which of the following would be included in the farm liability coverage forms?

a) Bodily injury to a residence employee
b) Any obligation of the insured under a workers compensation law
c) Bodily injury to any individual who is an insured
d) Bodily injury to an employed farmhand

#99. An insured must live in which of the following communities to be eligible for coverage under the National Flood Insurance Program?

a) One that is surrounded by water
b) One that has met the minimum population requirements
c) One that gets flooded at least yearly
d) One that has met the minimum floodplain management guidelines

#100. The owner of a parking garage completed major renovations to the parking garage just before selling it to another company. Four months later, overhead concrete fell onto vehicles parked on the second-floor level. Under the garage coverage policy conditions, which of the following is true?

a) The damage took place when the concrete fell
b) The renovation contractor is liable
c) The first owner is responsible for the damage
d) The damage took place when the renovations were done

#101. An insured's 8-year-old threw a rock, accidentally breaking a neighbor's plate glass window. The insured was determined to be legally liable for the cost of replacing the window. This situation is an example of

a) Intervening cause.
b) Juvenile delinquency.
c) Absolute liability.
d) Vicarious liability.

#102. Concerning the insurance business, a hazard is

a) The risk taken when performing something dangerous.
b) The propensity of poorer risks to seek insurance more often than better risks.
c) The basic reason for an insured to obtain insurance.
d) Any condition or exposure that increases the possibility of loss.

#103. How do surety bonds differ from insurance?

a) Insurance guarantees certain duties or obligations will be fulfilled; surety bonds pay for losses
b) Surety bonds guarantee losses will be paid; insurance pays for obligations to be fulfilled
c) The government issues surety bonds; private insurers issue insurance
d) Surety bonds guarantee certain duties or obligations will be fulfilled; insurance pays for losses

#104. All of the following statements describe the concept of strict liability EXCEPT

a) It is imposed on defendants involved in hazardous activities.
b) Claimants might need to provide proof that a product defect resulted in an injury.
c) It is imposed regardless of fault.
d) It is applied in product liability cases.

#105. In a personal auto policy, the medical payments coverage will pay reasonable medical expenses for all of the following EXCEPT

a) A friend is injured while driving the insured's car with permission.
b) The insured is injured while exiting a friend's mobile home.
c) The insured is injured by a motor vehicle while walking across the street.
d) The insured's child suffers injuries when the car they are in accidentally rolls down a hill.

#106. Which of the following homeowners endorsements increases its limits yearly by a selected percentage?

a) Scheduled personal property
b) Inflation guard
c) Permitted incidental occupancies
d) Personal property replacement cost

#107. Under the businessowners policy, all of these statements are true concerning the fire department service charge additional coverage EXCEPT

a) This coverage is not subject to any deductible.
b) This coverage provides an additional $2,500 of insurance.
c) This coverage limit pays in place of the limit of insurance specified in the Declarations.
d) This coverage limit is payable in addition to the limit of insurance specified in the Declarations.

#108. In addition to the usual notice requirements of insurance policies, if a loss from theft occurs, the insured is required to

a) Hire a competent attorney.
b) Post a surety bond.
c) Take a complete inventory.
d) Inform the proper law enforcement agency.

#109. Under the standard workers compensation and employer liability policy form, a state should be listed in Part Three – Other States' Insurance of the workers compensation and employers liability policy when

a) The state has a monopolistic workers compensation fund.
b) The insured anticipates extending operations to that state.
c) The insured operates in the state where the policy is issued.
d) The insurance provider is not licensed to write workers compensation in that state.

#110. A farmer applying for crop-hail insurance has completed the application and signed it. His agent signed it as well and accepted the first premium. Assuming all this was performed correctly, the application now serves as what?

a) A rider
b) A life insurance policy
c) A binder
d) Nothing

#111. What type of property does a Personal Floaters policy cover?

a) Movable personal property located in the insured's home, only
b) Movable personal property, wherever it might be located
c) Permanently attached property located on the insured's premises
d) None of these

#112. In terms of parties to a contract, which of the following does NOT describe a competent party?

a) The individual must not be under the influence of drugs or alcohol
b) The individual must be of legal age
c) The individual must be mentally competent to understand the contract
d) The individual must have at least completed secondary education

#113. When an umbrella policy is broader than underlying insurance, and it pays a loss that is not covered by the underlying policy, it typically only pays

a) The excess over the self-insured retention.
b) The amount stated in the policy under the additional coverage provisions.
c) The amount over and above the underlying policy deductible.
d) A percentage of the loss as described on the declarations page.

#114. Which of the following is true concerning free insurance issued in this state?

a) It is allowed as a rider
b) It is illegal
c) It is illegal except for health insurance
d) It is permitted if issued by a government insurance provider

#115. What legal defense can be used in most states where proportionate damages can be awarded when both the plaintiff and defendant were negligent?

a) Contributory negligence
b) Proximate cause
c) Comparative negligence
d) Relative degree of damage statute

#116. The endorsement that covers losses resulting from the sudden collapse of earth caused by underground limestone created by the action of water on rock formations is a/an

a) Mine subsidence endorsement.
b) Earthquake endorsement.
c) Earth subsidence endorsement.
d) Sinkhole collapse endorsement.

#117. More than one insured has become liable due to a single loss. How will the personal auto policy's limit of liability be affected?

a) A personal auto policy can have no more than one insured
b) The full limit applies to each insured individually
c) No more than the per occurrence limit applies, regardless of how many insureds are involved
d) Pro rata liability applies

#118. Under a standard fire policy, removal coverage remains in effect for

a) 5 days.
b) 10 days.
c) 15 days.
d) 30 days.

#119. When an applicant makes truthful statements on the insurance application and pays the necessary premium, it is known as which of the following?

a) Consideration
b) Legal purpose
c) Contract of adhesion
d) Acceptance

#120. On the dwelling form, the broad theft coverage endorsement specifies all of the following limitations EXCEPT

a) $1,500 on jewelry.
b) $1,000 on silverware.
c) $200 on money.
d) $1,500 on securities.

#121. The Declarations of the homeowners policy will provide all of the following information EXCEPT

a) What deductible amount will apply to each loss covered by the policy.
b) A statement confirming that earthquake damage is not covered.
c) The premium amount charged for each coverage.
d) The insured's address.

#122. The personal injury liability endorsement to a homeowners policy applies to all the following EXCEPT

a) Invasion of privacy.
b) False arrest.
c) A third party breaks an arm when the insured knocks them down.
d) Slander.

#123. A neighbor's tree has fallen into the insured's yard. The insured's HO policy will only pay to remove the tree if

a) The damage is more than $1,000.
b) The neighbor has no HO insurance.
c) The tree has caused damage to the insured's vehicle.
d) The tree is blocking the driveway.

#124. Which of the following best defines an insurance policy?

a) An agreement between an insurance provider and the Department of Insurance
b) A written request to an insurer for insurance coverage
c) A contract between an insured and an insurance provider that guarantees payment for loss caused by a specific event
d) An endorsement or a modifying provision

#125. The Commissioner of Insurance supervises and regulates the insurance affairs in the State of California and is selected by

a) Admitted insurers.
b) The Governor.
c) The State Senate.
d) The people.

#126. Another individual has alleged that an insured is responsible for damage to their property. The insured notifies their homeowners insurer. The insurance provider will

a) Either pay or defend as it decides.
b) Pay the alleged damages.
c) Proceed according to the insured's request.
d) Defend the allegation with the hopes of not paying damages.

#127. Under the dwelling policy, if an insurance company chooses to repair or replace lost or damaged property, it must inform the insured within how many days of receiving proof of loss?

a) 10 days
b) 30 days
c) 45 days
d) 60 days

#128. An insurer's primary goal is to collect sufficient premiums to cover the insured losses, pay for the costs of expenses, and generate a reasonable profit. The insurance provider predicts the incurred costs while allowing for a margin of error. The final premium charged will be reduced by which of the following?

a) Return of unearned premiums
b) Dividends
c) Investment income
d) Earned premiums

#129. Which of these is known as a marine policy's "amount insured hereunder?"

a) The duration of risk
b) The limit of insurance
c) The deductible
d) The agreed value

#130. Under a homeowners policy, personal property coverage would cover

a) A pet that the insured is temporarily keeping for a friend.
b) The insured's camera if it is stolen while the insured is on vacation.
c) A neighbor's fence if it is damaged by the insured.
d) Property moved to a newly acquired residence after 60 days.

#131. Which of these statements is an example of a product liability claim?

a) The insured's product must be recalled due to an expiration date
b) The faulty packaging of a cereal caused spoilage, resulting in a customer getting sick
c) An insured, while delivering the product to a customer, hits another vehicle with the delivery truck resulting in bodily injury and property damage
d) Someone tampers with the insured's product causing the insured to have to recall every product on the shelf

#132. The standard crop-hail policy does not pay for losses or damage from wind, flood, rain, or frost. What perils are covered under the standard crop-hail policy?

a) Fire
b) Lightning
c) Hail
d) All of the above

#133. Which of these losses would NOT be covered by the dwelling policy if the dwelling is vacant for over 60 days?

a) Windstorm
b) Internal explosion
c) Vandalism
d) Fire

#134. Under Coverage E – Scheduled Farm Personal Property, which of the following is NOT covered?

a) Turkeys while out in the open
b) Portable structures
c) Livestock
d) Farm machinery

#135. The standard fire policy that only covers those perils stated in the policy for that specific reason is known as a/an

a) Broad peril policy.
b) All-inclusive policy.
c) Named peril policy.
d) Open peril policy.

#136. Which one of the following statements relating to coverage for the flood and earthquake perils is true?

a) Flood insurance is typically provided in property policies; earthquake insurance is available by endorsement only
b) Both are excluded perils in every property policy
c) Flood and earthquake coverage will be available in every policy
d) Flood and earthquake coverage will only be available through the government

#137. The main portion of the premium for an equipment breakdown policy will pay

a) For coverage for the bodily injury and property damage of others.
b) For replacement parts.
c) For examinations and inspections.
d) For repairs following a loss.

#138. What is the purpose of the increased value and excess liability (IVEL) clauses?

a) To protect the master and crew of a vessel from being sued
b) To provide additional coverage for the same losses covered by an underlining policy
c) To protect an assured from the errors and omissions of their insurance agent
d) To protect the insurance provider from inflation

#139. Under additional coverages for HO policies, what is the maximum amount that can be charged to the insured for fire department services?

a) $500
b) $1,000
c) $5,000
d) Fire department service charges are not allowed

#140. An insured owns a large dog. The first day she must leave the dog home alone to go to work, the insured returns to find her $400 sofa torn apart, her $100 coffee table chewed up, her $50 tablecloth shredded, and a $200 window pane shattered where her dog jumped through. Suppose the insured has personal property coverage under a special form dwelling policy. How much of this loss will the policy pay?

a) $0
b) $200
c) $250
d) $750

#141. On a DP-3 Dwelling Property Special Form policy, the coverage provided for personal property is

a) All-risk.
b) Open peril.
c) The same as coverage provided on the DP-1 Basic Form.
d) The same as coverage provided on the DP-2 Broad Form.

#142. Workers compensation statutes require employers to meet capital reserves requirements sufficient to cover any claims that could arise. Employers can meet such requirements through all of the following EXCEPT

a) Assigned risk plans.
b) Competitive state funds.
c) Second injury funds programs.
d) Self-insurance plans.

#143. A type of policy that is used to provide a specific amount of replacement cost for a given risk after an insured property has been destroyed is known as a/an

a) Valued policy.
b) Pro-forma appraisal policy.
c) Equitable sum policy.
d) Specific risk policy.

#144. How long is the waiting period after the application has been accepted before flood coverage goes into effect?

a) 5 days
b) 30 days
c) 6 months
d) 12:01 am the next day

#145. The California low-cost auto insurance program can cover how many vehicles per person?

a) Unlimited amount
b) Only one
c) No more than two
d) All the vehicles in the household

#146. The American Institute of Marine Underwriters' cargo clause covers

a) Ordinary leakage, ordinary loss in weight or volume, or ordinary wear and tear.
b) Insolvency or financial default of the owners or operators of the vessel.
c) Windstorm, lightning, hail.
d) Insufficiency or unsuitability of packing.

#147. Who is responsible for equitably evaluating insurable risks and selecting and distributing to the insurance provider those that are profitable to the insurer?

a) Underwriter
b) Insured
c) Insurance Commissioner
d) Governor

#148. Under the dwelling policy form, what is the maximum time limit during which multiple volcanic activities would be considered part of one occurrence?

a) 24 hours
b) 36 hours
c) 48 hours
d) 72 hours

#149. Which of the following policy provisions would automatically broaden coverage under a policy without having to pay an added premium?

a) Assignment
b) Liberalization
c) Other insurance
d) Subrogation

#150. When an auto insurance policy is canceled due to nonpayment of premium, how many days' notice must the insurance provider give to the policy owner?

a) 10 days
b) 15 days
c) 20 days
d) 30 days

Practice Exam 1 Answers

#1. c) Apply to injuries of any visitors or guests.

Homeowners medical payments coverage applies to the injury of any visitors or guests of the insured who are on the insured's premises with the insured's permission. (p. 138)

#2. d) Mortgagee

The standard mortgage clause ensures that mortgagees have the right to receive prior notice if a policy is to be canceled. (p. 87)

#3. d) Medical coverage

While there can be additional limitations placed on coverage for medical payments and uninsured motorists in a motorcycle endorsement, they will more than likely be similar to those in a personal auto policy. (p. 159)

#4. a) The obligee can engage another contractor and seek reimbursement from the surety

When a bonded contractor defaults on a contract, the surety bond financially compensates the obligee. The surety guarantees that an outcome will occur as contracted. The bond will pay the financial consequences to the claimant or obligee if it does not. (p. 308)

#5. b) Coverage D

Coverage D provides fair rental value coverage when insured rental dwellings sustain a loss covered by Coverage A, B, or C. (pp. 99-100)

#6. b) A state entity that exists exclusively to transact workers compensation insurance on a nonprofit basis

The California State Compensation Insurance Fund is a state entity that exists exclusively to transact workers compensation insurance on a nonprofit basis. It actively competes with private insurance providers for business. Also, it operates as the assigned risk pool for workers compensation insurance. (pp. 321-322)

#7. c) $20 per day, for a maximum of $600.

Other-than-collision coverage provides $20 per day for up to 30 days after the theft of the entire auto, provided the auto is not recovered within 48 hours. (p. 154)

#8. c) $5,000.

A premium discount is when an insured owes a total standard premium over $5,000. (p. 321)

#9. b) Offer the insured to renew the policy at a different rate.

Notice of policy cancellation can be effective only if mailed or delivered by the insurance provider to the policy owner at least 20 days before the effective date of cancellation, accompanied by the reason for cancellation. The insurance provider must also inform the insured about the existence of the automobile liability assigned risk plan. (p. 87)

#10. c) 20%

The rate charged for a Good Driver Discount policy will be at least 20% lower than the rate the insured would have been charged for the same coverage. (p. 147)

#11. **b) Direct response**

Solicitation conducted through the mail is one method of direct-response marketing. (p. 22)

#12. **d) Located in a designated hazardous brush area**

Property submitted to the California FAIR Plan needs to be insurable property for which coverage is unavailable in the regular market due to its geographic location. (p. 177)

#13. **a) Pure risk and speculative risk.**

Pure and speculative are the two types of risks. Only pure risk is insurable. (p. 2)

#14. **a) Discontinuing an insurance policy by the insured on the policy anniversary date**

Nonrenewal is a policy termination by an insurer on the renewal or anniversary date. (p. 18)

#15. **a) $3,000**

With additional coverage in a homeowners policy, grave markers will pay up to $5,000 for grave markers, including mausoleums, for loss resulting from a peril insured against, on, or off the residence premises. (p. 136)

#16. **a) 5 years**

Each insurance provider must maintain records of electronic transmissions to customers for five years. (p. 58)

#17. **a) A residence employee who is injured on the job.**

Under a homeowners policy, Coverage F (Medical Payments) would pay for bodily injury to a residence employee if it arises during employment. (p. 138)

#18. **c) Exclusions apply to all three policy forms**

Dwelling policy forms contain several general exclusions that define the actual extent of the coverage provided. These exclusions are found in all three dwelling forms: broad, basic, and special. (p. 102)

#19. **d) Sewer backup**

The National Flood Insurance Program establishes the definition of flood. It does not include sewer backup. (p. 175)

#20. **b) Earthquake**

Most standard property forms exclude earthquakes. Still, coverage can be attached by endorsement to most property policies. It can also be written in a Difference in Conditions policy. (pp. 85, 172)

#21. **a) 2 weeks.**

Suppose the order of a civil authority causes the loss of use. In that circumstance, the additional living expenses and fair rental value payments are limited to two weeks. (pp. 100, 133)

#22. **c) Fiduciary**

A fiduciary bond guarantees the fiduciary will faithfully perform the duties and act in the best interests of the individual being represented. (p. 310)

#23. **d) After the execution of the contract.**

The CGL coverage form excludes property damage or bodily injury that the insured has assumed under any contract or agreement. The exclusion does not apply to particular contracts, provided the damage or injury occurs after the contract's execution. (p. 216)

#24. **b) Market value**

When insured for market value, it is insured for what a willing buyer would pay before a loss. This valuation is different from replacement cost or actual cash value. (p. 86)

#25. **c) At or before a date set forth by the Federal Crop Insurance Corporation**

Dates are set forth by the Federal Crop Insurance Corporation for various crops in various regions of the country. Applications for coverage or reports and requests to continue coverage must be submitted by those dates. (p. 279)

#26. **c) The contract is void if the insured has no insurable interest**

The individual or entity making a claim for the damaged property must have an insurable interest in the property. In most property insurance losses, the insured owns the property. (pp. 6, 81)

#27. **a) Are paid in addition to the liability limit.**

The policy will pay expenses the insured incurs to render first aid for bodily injury to third parties injured on the insured's premises. (p. 139)

#28. **a) Reduction**

This scenario describes reduction, a method of dealing with risk that involves reducing the severity or possibility of a loss. (p. 5)

#29. **b) $50,000**

The first limit shown ($50,000 in this case) is the most the policy will pay for bodily injury to any one person. (pp. 148, 149-150)

#30. **c) 12:01 a.m. the day after the application and premium payment are mailed**

During the first 30 days after a community enters the emergency or normal programs, coverage on a flood policy starts at 12:01 a.m. the day after the application and premium payment are mailed off. (p. 176)

#31. **b) 50% of the amount provided as Coverage A.**

Under the HO forms, Coverage C is provided automatically and is equal to 50% of the amount provided in Coverage A. (p. 131)

#32. **c) $1 million**

The minimum requirement for haulers of oil and specific categories of hazardous waste in interstate commerce is $1 million. (p. 248)

#33. **c) A joint ownership coverage endorsement is attached.**

This endorsement gives coverage to those other than the husband, wife, or family members not living in the same household. (p. 155)

#34. **d) Taking of property by use of force, violence, or fear.**

Robbery is when someone takes another person's property through force, violence, or fear. (p. 253)

#35. **c) The insurance provider will be liable for only the insured's interest in the damaged property.**

If more than one individual has an insurable interest in a property, the insurance provider will be liable only for the insured's interest in the loss. (pp. 103-104)

#36. **b) First named insured**

Some commercial policies can have more than one named insured. Complications and confusion over contractual duties are reduced by making the insurance provider and the first named insured the primary parties for carrying out responsibilities. (p. 188)

#37. **d) It will cover the damage**

The insured's HO liability will pay for damage to the property of others even if the insured is not liable. (p. 139)

#38. **d) The applicant's driving safety record**

The insured's driving safety record is the most important factor in calculating rates and premiums for an auto insurance policy. (p. 147)

#39. **d) Anyone who does not owe money on any automobile insurance policy within the last 18 months.**

Anyone with a valid driver's license who does not owe money on any auto insurance policy within the last 12 months and can state that they were denied coverage through the voluntary market is eligible. (p. 161)

#40. **b) Pure risks**

Any past or future event that can cause damage or loss to an individual having an insurable interest, or create a liability against them, can be insured. The higher the predictability of a loss, the more insurable it becomes. Only pure risks can be insured; speculative losses cannot be insured. (p. 2)

#41. **c) All reasonable costs**

When the debris is the result of a peril insured against, the insurance provider pays the reasonable cost of debris removal. (pp. 133-134)

#42. **b) It is illegal to limit coverage based on marital status**

Insurance benefits or coverage availability cannot be denied based on marital status or sex. Insurers can consider marital status to define eligible individuals for dependent benefits. (p. 60)

#43. **c) 30 days**

Removal coverage is provided for 30 days in the broad and special form as long as endangerment by a covered peril made the removal necessary. (p. 101)

#44. **d) $5,000.**

$5,000 is the coverage based on the California Financial Responsibility Liability Limits for damage to property unless higher limits are mandated by law. (p. 157)

#45. **d) Scheduled personal property endorsement**

Under a scheduled personal property endorsement, scheduled and insured items are covered on a valued basis. (pp. 122-123, 170)

#46. **b) 60 days**

All losses are required to be paid within 60 days of receiving the proof of loss. (p. 119)

#47. **d) Assumption of risk**

When an individual recognizes and understands the danger involved in an activity and voluntarily decides to encounter it, this assumption of risk can bar recovery for injury caused by negligence. (p. 71)

#48. **a) Ask questions that are not on the application but that are important for underwriting.**

The producer is not permitted to collect information not asked for on the application but can seek details for those items that do appear. These items can include the extent of involvement in hazardous activities, the dosages and frequency of use of medications, the specifics relating to employment duties, etc. (p. 46)

#49. **b) HO-8.**

The HO-8 form covers houses with replacement cost more than market value and those houses built with irreplaceable materials. It is a modified HO-1 form and provides ACV coverage for Coverage A. (p. 115)

#50. **b) $30,000**

For insurers to pay the total amount of partial losses, a building must be insured for at least 80% of its value on the date of loss. In this scenario, since the building is insured for only $60,000 (75% of the minimum requirement), the policy will only cover 75% of the loss. (p. 198)

#51. **d) Rating the financial strength of insurers**

Reports generated by these organizations help prospective consumers judge various insurers' financial security. (p. 76)

#52. **c) Uninsured motorist coverage.**

Uninsured motorist coverage, medical payments, and liability will be extended to a newly acquired auto for replacement vehicles. (p. 145)

#53. **d) Concealment.**

According to Cal. Ins. Code Sections 333 and 339, concealment is the act of neglecting to communicate what one party knows and should communicate. (p. 17)

#54. **b) $250,000.**

The regular National Flood Insurance Program is written for the value of the dwelling up to $250,000 on a replacement cost basis. (p. 175)

#55. **a) Excess coverage over an underlying or primary policy**

Umbrella or excess policies are used when an insured is required or chooses to purchase limits higher than what is offered in the primary or underlying policy. (p. 179)

#56. **b) Encourage the insured to insure the property closer to its full value**

In return for the insured's promise to cover the property to some certain percentage of its value, the insurer agrees to provide the insured a reduced rate on the coverage and pay partial losses in full. (pp. 198-199)

#57. **c) Auto policy**

The underlying policy is the primary liability policy. In this scenario, it is the insured's personal auto policy. (p. 179)

#58. **c) Direct**

Damage caused by a peril insured against is classified as a direct loss. (p. 77)

#59. **a) Damage to a third-party property for which the insured is legally liable.**

Additional coverages in the liability section of a homeowners policy will cover up to $1,000 per occurrence on a replacement cost basis for damage the insured causes to the property of others. In Section I, this coverage does not apply to the extent a loss is covered for intentional damage to property rented to or owned by a tenant of the insured or arising from a business owned by the insured. (pp. 138-139)

#60. **d) Schedule rating method.**

Under the schedule rating method, the underwriter can give credits and debits for specific actions that an insured takes in the ordinary course of business that either increase or decrease the chance of loss. (p. 80)

#61. **d) Profitable distribution of exposures**

The profitable distribution of exposures occurs when poor risks are balanced with preferred risks, with average risks in the middle. (p. 6)

#62. **d) There is no coverage**

The dealership does not have legal title to the trade-in vehicle. Therefore, no coverage is provided under the business auto physical damage coverage because of the false pretense clause. (pp. 235-236)

#63. **d) Open peril coverage on the dwelling and broad form coverage on personal property.**

The open peril coverage is applied to insured property under Coverages A and B only. (pp. 113-114)

#64. **c) Subrogation**

After an insured accepts payment from the insurance provider, they have been indemnified. Insurance policies require the insured to transfer any right to recovery to the insurance provider so that it can seek recovery up to the amount paid as a loss. (p. 81)

#65. **a) Concealment.**

Concealment is the withholding of known facts that, if material, can void a contract. (p. 17)

#66. **a) $25**

The towing and labor costs endorsement provides a $25 basic limit for towing and labor costs incurred at the location a vehicle is disabled. Higher limits are available for an extra premium. (p. 155)

#67. **c) Comparative negligence**

Many states, by statute, mandate that damages be apportioned based on the degree of negligence of each party involved in an accident. (p. 72)

#68. **c) A cost bond**

Cost bonds guarantee that the individual (plaintiff) who brings legal action against another person (defendant) will be able to cover court costs and any resulting damages if they lose the case. (p. 309)

#69. **c) Automatically transfer to a legal representative.**

The Insurance Services Office (ISO) common policy conditions for the commercial package policy specify that in the event of the insured's death, rights and duties are automatically transferred to the insured's legal representative. (pp. 188-189)

#70. **c) A 6-story office building with less than 100,000 square feet of total area**

The maximum eligibility requirements for a BOP are six stories high, 100,000 square feet for the office building, 25,000 square feet of mercantile space in the apartment building, and at least $3 million in gross sales. (pp. 282-283)

#71. **d) The insured's camera was stolen from their suitcase while on vacation**

A broad theft endorsement on the off-premises coverage insures property that is either used or owned by the insured when the property is away from the insured premises. (p. 106)

#72. **a) Embezzlement.**

Wrongful acts trigger directors and officers liability coverage as opposed to being triggered on an accident or occurrence basis. Wrongful acts include misstatements made by the directors and officers and breach of duty and neglect. (p. 226)

#73. **a) Owned watercraft 53 feet long**

Non-owned watercraft less than 51 feet long and not used to carry individuals or property for a fee will be covered by business liability insurance. (p. 291)

#74. **b) Symbol 9 – non-owned autos only**

Symbol 1 is used for any auto, Symbol 2 is used only for owned autos, and Symbol 7 is used only for specifically described autos. (p. 233)

#75. **c) $15,000.**

The program provides coverage based on the California Financial Responsibility Liability Limits of $15,000 for liability for bodily injury or death to one individual, subject to a cumulative limit of $30,000 for all individuals, and $5,000 for liability for damage to property unless higher limits are required by law. (p. 161)

#76. **d) Surplus lines insurer.**

Surplus lines insurers are those insurance providers that do not have a certificate of authority to transact business in the state. They are on the Commissioner's approved list to conduct business under the state's surplus lines laws. (pp. 28, 34, 44, 65-66)

#77. **c) The insured has to be legally liable for the loss**

For the P&I policy to pay for a loss, the insured must be legally liable for the loss. The vessel owner can be held liable for the actions of the ship's master, officers, and crew. (p. 305)

#78. **d) Nothing**

The personal property replacement cost endorsement excludes property like antiques and art. (p. 124)

#79. **c) Trip transit.**

Trip transit policies insure a single shipment of goods for a specific trip. (p. 267)

#80. **b) Anyone while using, with permission, a covered auto owned by the named insured**

The business auto coverage form provides coverage on covered autos while they are used by the insured or the insured's employees (or others using the covered auto with the insured's permission) but does not cover the exposure of other autos not hired, owned, or leased by the named insured. (p. 234)

#81. **c) California Workers Comp Inspection Rating Bureau (WCIRB).**

The California Workers Comp Inspection Rating Bureau (WCIRB) is an unincorporated, nonprofit association with over 400 member companies licensed to transact workers compensation insurance in California. (p. 76)

#82. **d) The difference in the actual cash value as a pair and as a single**

According to the pair or set clause, the insurance provider can choose to restore the set to its value before the loss or pay the difference between the property's actual cash value before and after the loss. (pp. 104, 120)

#83. **c) False Arrest.**

False arrest is the unlawful physical restraint of another person's freedom. False arrest causes embarrassment and inconvenience to the customer. (p. 70)

#84. **a) Judgment**

A judgment rating is an approach that insurance providers use when credible statistics are lacking or when the exposure units are so different that it is impossible to construct a class. (p. 80)

#85. **b) Automatically.**

Changes made to broaden coverage in a dwelling policy will automatically apply and will not have to be endorsed to the policy if made while the policy is effective or 60 days before it goes into effect. (p. 105)

#86. **c) Condominiums**

The Insurance Services Office (ISO) manages a list of risks not eligible for consideration for a BOP. Bars and grills, auto dealers, and financial institutions are expressly excluded from coverage. (pp. 282-283)

#87. **a) Personal injury.**

The liability section of the HO policy contains a few additional coverages that are paid in addition to the limit of liability. Additional coverages include damage to the property of others, first aid to others, claims expense, and loss assessment coverage. (pp. 138-139)

#88. **d) Reinsurance.**

Reinsurance is a form of insurance between insurers. It occurs when an insurance provider (the reinsurer) agrees to accept all or a portion of a risk covered by another insurer (the ceding company). (p. 8)

#89. **c) Electronic Effective Date Procedure (EEDP).**

Only Certified Producers can submit applications to the assigned risk plan and obtain immediate coverage through CAARP's Electronic Effective Date Procedure (EEDP). (p. 161)

#90. **c) Additional residence rental provision.**

The additional residence rental provision is an optional coverage endorsement to the HO policy that insures scheduled residential structures on the insured's premises that are rented to others. (p. 124)

#91. **a) It will provide coverage since the damage to the client resulted from the producer's negligence**

Errors and Omissions insurance is written for professionals to protect against actions charging that the professional did not render reasonable services or duties. (pp. 38-39, 225-226)

#92. **d) Self-funded**

The employer pays all claims in the case of a self-funded plan. It is the responsibility of the employer to hire a claims administrator and handle all procedural issues. (p. 7)

#93. **b) Up to $1,000 per occurrence**

Section II – Loss Assessment Coverage applies to assessments against the insured by a condominium association or other cooperative body of property owners. Coverage is limited to $1,000, but a higher limit of coverage is available by endorsement. (p. 139)

#94. **c) Either party can make a written request for an appraisal**

When the insurance provider and the insured cannot agree regarding the value of the damaged property, either party can make a written request for appraisal. (p. 119)

#95. **b) $500**

$500 is automatically provided and can be increased by endorsement. (p. 134)

#96. **d) A Supplemental Extended Reporting Period.**

The Supplemental Extended Reporting Period is an optional reporting period of unlimited duration. It will pay claims arising from occurrences after the retroactive date and before the end of the policy period, contingent upon the policy aggregate limit for the entire term. (p. 224)

#97. **d) Is designed to allow the family to maintain its normal standard of living.**

The family is permitted to maintain its normal standard of living while waiting for its house to be repaired after a covered loss. (p. 100)

#98. **a) Bodily injury to a residence employee**

The farm liability coverage forms include bodily injury to a residence employee. (p. 272)

#99. **d) One that has met the minimum floodplain management guidelines**

An insured must live in a community that has satisfied the minimum floodplain management guidelines to qualify for the flood program. (p. 175)

#100. **a) The damage took place when the concrete fell**

Under the Work Performed exclusion in the Garage Coverage form, no liability coverage is provided for property damage to work performed by the policy owner if the damage results from the work or the materials or parts used. The loss takes place at the time of the incident. (p. 241)

#101. **d) Vicarious liability.**

Under vicarious liability, an insured can be held responsible for the acts of other family members or independent contractors. (p. 71)

#102. **d) Any condition or exposure that increases the possibility of loss.**

A hazard is any condition or exposure that increases the chance of a loss occurring. (pp. 2-3)

#103. **d) Surety bonds guarantee certain duties or obligations will be fulfilled; insurance pays for losses**

Unlike insurance, surety bonds do not pay for losses. Instead, they guarantee specific obligations or duties will be fulfilled. (p. 308)

#104. **a) It is imposed on defendants involved in hazardous activities.**

Strict liability is generally applied in product liability cases. When the product results in an injury and the claimant can prove the defect, the defendant will be held strictly liable for the damage. (p. 71)

#105. **b) The insured is injured while exiting a friend's mobile home.**

Medical payments only cover the insured and any passengers in their vehicle. (pp. 150-151)

#106. **b) Inflation guard**

With the inflation guard endorsement, the limit of insurance automatically increases by a selected percentage every year. (p. 124)

#107. **c) This coverage limit pays in place of the limit of insurance specified in the Declarations.**

The fire department service charge pays for charges up to $2,500. It is payable in addition to the limit of insurance listed in the Declarations. (p. 285)

#108. **d) Inform the proper law enforcement agency.**

In addition to the usual notice requirements of insurance policies, the insured must inform the proper law enforcement agency in the event of a loss. (p. 118)

#109. **b) The insured anticipates extending operations to that state.**

An employer contends that it can conduct company operations in that state by designating a state in Part Three of a workers compensation and employers liability policy. (p. 319)

#110. **c) A binder**

When properly completed, signed, dated, and accompanied by the premium, the application serves as a binder. (pp. 277, 278)

#111. **b) Movable personal property, wherever it might be located**

A personal floater inland marine policy insures movable personal property, wherever it might be located. (p. 169)

#112. **d) The individual must have at least completed secondary education**

Under the law, the parties to a contract must be capable of entering into a contract. Usually, this requires that both parties be mentally competent to understand the contract, of legal age, and not under the influence of alcohol or drugs. (p. 14)

#113. **a) The excess over the self-insured retention.**

Once a liability claim is filed for recovery of damage or injury, the primary policy pays up to the policy limits, after which the umbrella policy will apply. If there is no primary underlying insurance, the excess policy will apply after the insured pays the self-insured retention. (pp. 179-181)

#114. **b) It is illegal**

It is illegal for any insurance licensee to offer free insurance as an incentive to conduct some other type of business. (p. 35)

#115. **c) Comparative negligence**

Comparative negligence is the allotment of damages when both the plaintiff and the defendant are at fault. Recovery by the plaintiff is reduced or increased depending upon the degree of each party's negligence. (p. 72)

#116. **d) Sinkhole collapse endorsement.**

The sinkhole collapse endorsement will provide coverage for sinkhole collapse, which means a sudden collapse or settlement of the earth. (pp. 107, 200)

#117. **c) No more than the per occurrence limit applies, regardless of how many insureds are involved**

The insurance applies separately to each insured. This condition does not increase the insurance provider's liability for any one occurrence. (pp. 147-148)

#118. **a) 5 days.**

The Standard Fire Policy (SFP) is a named perils contract. It only covers those perils stated in the policy, like the removal of property from the premises endangered by the insured against perils (fire and lightning). Removal coverage automatically applies for five days. (p. 167)

#119. **a) Consideration**

In a contract, consideration is the binding force that requires something of value to be exchanged for the transfer of risk. (p. 14)

#120. **b) $1,000 on silverware.**

For a Dwelling Policy, the coverage limit on silverware is $2,500. (p. 106)

#121. **b) A statement that earthquake damage is not covered.**

The Declarations section includes information on who is insured, the insured's location, how much coverage, the amount of deductible applied to a loss, and when the policy provides coverage. The statement that earthquake damage is not covered is located in the policy's exclusions. (pp. 84, 172)

#122. **c) A third party breaks an arm when the insured knocks them down.**

The personal injury endorsement covers an invasion of privacy, defamation of character, libel, slander, and false arrest. The policy's personal liability coverage will cover the broken arm. (p. 124)

#123. **d) The tree is blocking the driveway.**

An insured's HO policy will pay up to $1,000 to remove the tree from the premises if a neighbor's tree fell by a covered peril. The policy will also pay if the tree blocks a handicapped ramp or driveway, even if no damage to a covered structure has occurred. (pp. 133-134)

#124. **c) A contract between an insured and an insurance provider that guarantees payment for loss caused by a specific event**

A policy is a contract between an insurer and an insured agreeing to pay the insured for losses caused by specific events. (pp. 2, 14)

#125. **d) The people.**

The Commissioner of Insurance is elected at the same time that other California officials are chosen. (p. 49)

#126. **a) Either pay or defend as it decides.**

The insurance provider will decide whether to defend the claim or pay the loss. They will typically decide on the option that is the least expensive. (p. 228)

#127. **b) 30 days**

The insurance company has 30 days to inform the insured that it has chosen to repair or replace the covered property. (p. 105)

#128. **c) Investment income**

The additional charge added to the premium is reduced by any investment income earned on the funds being held for future claim payments. (p. 81)

#129. **b) The limit of insurance**

The limit of insurance is known as the amount insured hereunder. (p. 299)

#130. **b) The insured's camera if it is stolen while the insured is on vacation.**

Coverage C – Personal Property in homeowners policies extends coverage to anywhere in the world. (pp. 131-133)

#131. **b) The faulty packaging of a cereal caused spoilage, resulting in a customer getting sick**

Strict liability is usually applied in product liability cases. Product liability covers damage caused by the product, not damage to the product. (p. 71)

#132. **d) All of the above**

The perils covered under the standard crop-hail policy are fire, hail, and lightning. (p. 278)

#133. **c) Vandalism**

There is no vandalism and malicious mischief (VMM) coverage if the insured's location has been vacant for more than 60 consecutive days. (p. 95)

#134. **a) Turkeys while out in the open**

Covered property includes farm personal property insured on a scheduled basis. It can include property like poultry while out in the open or in any building designated for poultry in the Declarations (excluding turkeys, unless expressly stated). (p. 271)

#135. **c) Named peril policy.**

The standard fire policy is a named perils contract and only covers the perils stated in the policy. (p. 167)

#136. **b) Both are excluded perils in every property policy**

Flood and earthquake are both excluded perils in all property policies. However, coverage for both or either peril can typically be obtained separately for an additional premium or by endorsement. (pp. 102, 118, 172, 174-176)

#137. **c) For examinations and inspections.**

Inspecting the machinery to be insured is critical to underwriting equipment breakdown coverage. The intention is to identify flaws that could lead to losses and require corrective action. (p. 259)

#138. **b) To provide additional coverage for the same losses covered by an underlining policy**

These clauses offer excess coverage for the same losses insured by an underlining policy. (p. 302)

#139. **a) $500**

Fire department service charges will cover up to $500 for liability assumed by an agreement for fire department charges to protect insured property. (p. 134)

#140. **a) $0**

Under the special form dwelling policy, damage that domestic animals cause is excluded. (p. 99)

#141. **d) The same as coverage provided on the DP-2 Broad Form.**

Coverages A and B on a DP-3 form are written on an all-risk or open peril basis. The coverage for personal property is written on a specified or named peril basis. (p. 97)

#142. **c) Second injury funds programs.**

Second injury funds are a method by which employers manage the risks associated with hiring potential employees that were previously injured. (pp. 317-318)

#143. **a) Valued policy.**

Valued policies are used when it is difficult to establish the value of the insured property after a loss or when it is desirable to agree on a specific value in advance. A valued policy allows for payment of the full policy amount in the event of a total loss without regard to depreciation or actual value. (p. 87)

#144. **b) 30 days**

Upon purchasing a flood policy, a 30-day waiting period begins from the time of application and premium payment. (p. 175)

#145.   **c) No more than two**

All qualified consumers are allowed up to two low-cost policies under the program guidelines. When the household has two qualified consumers, each can have up to two policies for a total of up to four per household. (p. 162)

#146.   **c) Windstorm, lightning, hail**

Answers A, B, and D are excluded perils not covered by the American Institute of Marine Underwriters' Cargo Clauses. (p. 304)

#147.   **a) Underwriter**

An underwriter is an individual who evaluates and classifies risks to accept or reject them on behalf of the insurance provider. (p. 6)

#148.   **d) 72 hours**

All volcanic eruptions will be considered one occurrence if they occur within one 72-hour period. (p. 105)

#149.   **b) Liberalization**

The liberalization clause specifies that if an insurer changes a policy form to the policy owner's benefit, all policies issued within a certain time before the change will be interpreted as if they had been changed. This change must not require an additional premium. (p. 86)

#150.   **a) 10 days**

In most states, the insurer must provide ten days' notice if cancellation is for nonpayment of premium or if the policy is canceled within the first 60 days of initial coverage. Insurers must provide 20 days' notice for every other reason. (p. 156)

PRACTICE EXAM:
2

Your preparation is paying off

You are about to take another California Property and Casualty Practice Exam. This exam consists of *150 Questions (plus five to ten non-scored experimental questions)* and is *3 hours and 15 minutes* long. If you do not have enough time to complete this exam right now, it is better to wait until you can fully devote your attention to completing it in the allotted time. Any skipped questions will be graded as incorrect. The following chart breaks down the number of questions in each chapter and by topic.

CHAPTER	# OF QUESTIONS
Basic Insurance Concepts and Principles	7
Contract Law	6
The Insurance Marketplace	8
Basic Legal Concepts – Tort Law	6
Property and Casualty Basics	7
Property and Casualty Policies – General	7
Dwelling Policy	14
Homeowners Policy	12
Homeowners – Section I: Property Coverage	8
Homeowners – Section II: Liability Coverage	8
Personal Auto	14
Other Personal Lines Policies	13
Commercial Coverages	5
Commercial General Liability (CGL)	5
Commercial Auto	5
Other Commercial Coverages	4
Farm	5
Businessowners	4
Ocean Marine	4
Surety Bonds and General Bond Concepts	4
Workers Compensation – General Concepts	4
Total	**150**

To calculate your score, subtract the number of incorrectly answered questions from 150. Take this number and divide it by 150. For example, if you incorrectly answered 60 questions, your score would be 60%, the minimum score needed to pass the exam.

#1. Insurance shares which of the following among the members of a large, homogeneous group with similar exposure to loss?

a) Risk
b) Hazards
c) Perils
d) Loss

#2. What is the primary distinction between a hired auto and a non-owned auto?

a) Who owns the auto
b) The length of time the insured uses the auto
c) The amount of premium
d) Whether a payment is made for the use of the auto

#3. A statement made by an applicant for an insurance policy that must be true in every regard is deemed to be a

a) Misrepresentation.
b) Warranty.
c) Concealment.
d) Representation.

#4. Upon payment for a loss, the insured is required to surrender to the insurance provider the right to sue a negligent third party. This is known as

a) Entirety.
b) Subrogation.
c) Indemnity.
d) Insurable interest.

#5. Which of the following perils is NOT covered by the DP-2 form?

a) Damage caused by falling objects
b) Damage to birds, fish, or pets
c) Damage caused by burglars
d) Damage caused by the weight of snow and ice

#6. The limited theft endorsement intended for a landlord excludes all of the following EXCEPT

a) Silverware stolen from the landlord's china cabinet.
b) A lawnmower the landlord owns and stores at the rented premises.
c) Jewelry stolen from the landlord's home.
d) Money stolen from the tenant's apartment.

#7. Financially restoring an insured following a claim is called

a) Indemnity.
b) Adhesion.
c) Restoration.
d) Reasonable expectations.

#8. In the businessowners liability coverage form, which of the following is the other major coverage provided?

a) Medical payments
b) Personal liability
c) Auto liability
d) Employers liability

#9. HO policies limit the amount of property and liability coverage available for Boatowners. How much coverage is provided in the HO policy for damage to watercraft, equipment, accessories, and trailers?

a) $2,000
b) $2,500
c) $1,000
d) $1,500

#10. Which of the following is the consideration on the part of an insurance provider?

a) Underwriting
b) Paying a claim
c) Decreasing premium amounts
d) Paying the premium

#11. An insured rents a bedroom in their residence to a tenant for $50 per week. A fire badly damages the home. During the three weeks needed to repair the fire damage, the insured pays $900 in rent for a short-term apartment. The renter is forced to find other accommodations. Ignoring any extra meal expenses, how much would the HO-3 pay under Coverage D?

a) $150
b) $300
c) $900
d) $1,050

#12. Under a building and personal property form, coverage for loss by some perils is suspended if

a) The insured fails to meet the coinsurance provision.
b) An uninsured peril causes a partial loss.
c) The insured building has been vacant for over 60 days.
d) A loss happens when a hazard beyond the insured's control is increased.

#13. Which of these following statements is true concerning a workers compensation and employers liability policy?

a) Insurers will not cover claims of surviving children
b) Insurers will not cover claims of a surviving spouse
c) Insurers will cover punitive or exemplary damages
d) Insurers will cover exposures in states listed on the information page

#14. In a standard fire policy, all of the following are covered perils EXCEPT

a) Friendly fire.
b) Hostile fire.
c) Removal from premises.
d) Lightning.

#15. The Dwelling Policy form DP-3 provides what kind of coverage?

a) Open peril
b) Basic peril
c) Named peril
d) Broad peril

#16. After a covered loss on a homeowners policy, the insured must do all of the following EXCEPT

a) Allow the insurance provider to inspect the property as often as reasonably necessary.
b) Submit to an examination under oath, if requested.
c) Prepare an inventory of damaged and undamaged property, including receipts, bills, and related documentation.
d) Abandon the property involved to the insurance provider.

#17. An insured has an auto policy with limits of 100/300/50 and a deductible of $1,000. They are involved in an auto accident and crash into another driver's vehicle. The other driver is awarded $125,000 for their injuries and $25,000 for the damage to their car. The insured's vehicle has $1,200 in damage. The total payment made under the insured's policy is

a) $125,200.
b) $126,200.
c) $100,200.
d) $150,200.

#18. Under the flood insurance program, which of the following could be insured with replacement cost coverage?

a) An apartment building
b) A shed
c) A single-family home
d) A garage

#19. A scheduled personal property endorsement will be used to insure

a) Personal vehicles used by travelers anywhere in the world.
b) Personal items at their actual cash value.
c) Higher limits of coverage for fine arts items.
d) High-value items only within the United States.

#20. In homeowners policy forms, Coverage C offers all of the following EXCEPT

a) Coverage for the property that is located at another residence premises.
b) Coverage for loss of use.
c) Worldwide coverage.
d) Coverage for the property of others.

#21. Insurance contracts are unilateral in nature. This concept means that

a) Each party to the contract exchanges something of value.
b) A promise is made only at the time of policy application.
c) Only one party makes a promise.
d) The insured is required to make a promise to pay the premium.

#22. When does the federal emergency flood insurance program go into effect?

a) Yearly for the flood season
b) When mandated by the U.S. president
c) When a community applies for the program
d) As soon as the flooding takes place

#23. The livestock coverage form provides coverage for livestock. Livestock refers to any of the following EXCEPT

a) Turkeys and chickens.
b) Cattle and swine.
c) Sheep and goats.
d) Horses and mules.

#24. Which of the following statements is true regarding newly acquired autos when Symbol 7 is provided?

a) They are only covered until the end of the policy term
b) They are covered once the insurance provider is notified
c) They are automatically covered only for 30 days
d) They are covered if they are used to replace previously owned autos with that coverage

#25. XYZ Construction Company has the best safety record of any construction firm in the country. It has been recognized by OSHA for its record and received an award for having no accidents in the past five years. XYZ has suffered economically because of increased insurance, lumber, and labor costs. One method by which XYZ could lower its insurance costs for its commercial policy is through the use of

a) Decreased deductibles on the current commercial policy that will result in a decreased level of self-insurance.
b) A schedule rating risk assessment that allows the insured to receive credits and debits for business practices that increase or decrease the risk of loss.
c) Premium financing plans that allow XYZ to pay lower premiums when needed and make up the difference when profits increase.
d) A reinsurance contract that is purchased from a direct reinsurer, ultimately bypassing the agent commissions.

#26. At the expiration (or cancellation) of a claims-made policy, the insured is guaranteed to have the option to obtain a/an

a) Basic extended reporting period.
b) Extended Hold harmless insurance endorsement.
c) Extended supplemental limits of insurance.
d) Supplemental extended reporting period.

#27. Homeowners personal property coverage does NOT cover

a) The personal property of roomers not related to the insured.
b) The personal property of the spouse.
c) The personal property of the insured in another country.
d) The personal property of the resident's daughter.

#28. Under the property and casualty conditions of a homeowners policy, what can happen if it is discovered that the policy owner committed fraud or concealment?

a) The policy will only be voided if the fraud was committed before a loss
b) The policy can be voided
c) The insurance provider can void the policy only if it gives the insured ten days' notice
d) The insured can have the opportunity to reapply for the policy

#29. While engaged in a pick-up basketball game in the neighborhood park, the insured collides with another player, breaking his nose. Would the medical payments coverage under the insured's homeowners policy pay for the injury?

a) No, because even though it was a pick-up game, it was an organized event
b) No, personal liability applies only on-premises
c) No, the insured was not negligent
d) Yes, medical payments coverage is also applied off the insured premises

#30. In the agent's contract, which type of authority is found?

a) Express
b) Apparent
c) Implied
d) Assumed

#31. According to Coverage A in the homeowners policy, how much of a house's value must be insured to qualify for replacement coverage?

a) 50%
b) 75%
c) 80%
d) 85%

#32. The amount of loss the insured is willing to absorb without insurance protection is called

a) Self-insured retention.
b) Maximum deductible.
c) Stop loss.
d) Limit of liability.

#33. The extended coverages written on the basic form dwelling policy would cover which of the following for an additional premium?

a) Vandalism
b) Glass breakage
c) Fire
d) Riot

#34. Which is NOT true of workers compensation coverage?

a) It offers death benefits
b) It offers rehabilitation benefits
c) Medical payment benefits are limited
d) Medical payment benefits are unlimited

#35. The cost bond guarantees

a) The plaintiff will cover court costs and damages to the defendant if the plaintiff loses the court case.
b) A contractor's cost overruns will be paid.
c) An individual will appear in court when required.
d) Damages will be paid when an injunction should not have been issued but was.

#36. All of the following statements about mutual insurers are correct EXCEPT

a) Policy dividends issued by mutual insurers are guaranteed and not taxable.
b) Dividends allow policy owners to share in a mutual insurer's divisible surplus.
c) Dividends are a return of unused premiums.
d) Mutual insurers issue policies referred to as participating.

#37. All of the following statements relating to personal property coverage in the HO program are correct EXCEPT

a) The HO-3 policy covers the mysterious disappearance of personal property.
b) Coverage on money is limited to $200.
c) Personal property coverage is typically 50% of the Coverage A limit.
d) Earthquake coverage can be added by endorsement.

#38. Which of the following is an endorsement that changes the actual cash value settlement on personal property to a replacement cost basis?

a) Preservation of property
b) Permanent total compensation
c) Personal property replacement cost
d) Actual cash loss

#39. Which bonds guarantee that a supplier will provide materials, supplies, products, and equipment as stated in the written contract?

a) Supply bonds
b) Labor and materials bonds
c) Performance bonds
d) Bid bonds

#40. How does the equipment breakdown coverage form value a loss?

a) On a valued basis
b) On a stated amount basis
c) On an actual cash value basis
d) On a replacement cost basis

#41. Each of the following can be insured under the HO-3 homeowners policy EXCEPT

a) A dwelling's occupant under a life estate arrangement when dwelling coverage is at least 80% of the current replacement cost.
b) One co-owner when co-owners occupy each distinct section of a two-family dwelling.
c) The intended owner-occupant of a dwelling that is under construction.
d) The owner-occupant of a condo unit.

#42. Under a dwelling policy form, which of the following risks would be eligible for coverage?

a) A duplex that two families occupy, each of which has a bedroom rented to a boarder
b) A single-family dwelling occupied by a single individual operating a business that buys and sells firearms in the basement
c) A single-family dwelling containing a beauty shop that employs three full-time operators
d) A single-family dwelling that is located on farm premises

#43. The equipment breakdown coverage form provides coverage for all of the following EXCEPT

a) Bodily injury liability.
b) Expediting expenses after a covered loss.
c) Damage to the insured's property.
d) Damage to the property of others in the insured's custody and care.

#44. During an ocean marine adventure, a person must jettison a piece of cargo to save the rest of the cargo and the ship. This action is considered

a) A salvage loss.
b) Sue and labor.
c) A particular average.
d) A general average.

#45. The owner of a rental dwelling, insured under a DP-2 form, turns off the heat in the insured dwelling during the winter since the dwelling is not occupied. The building's water pipes freeze and break, causing damage. How will the policy react to this particular loss?

a) The DP policy will cover the pipes but not the labor
b) The DP policy will cover the labor but not the pipes
c) This loss is excluded from coverage
d) This loss is covered

#46. A personal umbrella policy can act as excess over any of the following insurance coverage policies EXCEPT

a) Auto liability coverage.
b) Comprehensive personal liability.
c) Auto collision coverage.
d) Homeowners Section II coverage.

#47. Which of the following is NOT one of the independent rating services that publish guides regarding the financial integrity of insurance companies?

a) Moody's
b) NAIC
c) Fitch
d) AM Best

#48. An insured was building a new home. While digging the foundation's footings, the excavator struck a solid rock formation and determined that it was necessary to blast the formation to remove the rocks. The force of the explosion broke several windows and some chinaware in a neighbor's home several blocks away. Who will pay for this damage?

a) The insured's insurance provider, regardless of negligence
b) The contractor
c) The neighbor's insurance provider
d) The insured's insurance provider if the neighbor proves that the insured was negligent

#49. What type of insurer uses a formal sharing agreement?

a) Mutual insurers
b) Fraternal Benefit Societies
c) Reciprocal insurers
d) Stock insurers

#50. Coverage E (Personal Liability) and Coverage F (Medical Payments to Others) would respond to a claim resulting from all of the following scenarios EXCEPT

a) While sweeping the floors, an insured's resident maid trips and falls down the stairs, breaking her arm.
b) An insured's boat stored in the garage that slips off of its supports and injures a visitor.
c) An insured's dog left in the care of a friend bites a delivery person.
d) An insured's 13-year-old grandson threw rocks at the neighbor's house and broke several windows.

#51. Which valuation method will consider what a potential buyer would pay for an insured property?

a) Actual cost value
b) Functional replacement value
c) Market value
d) Replacement value

#52. An insurer that the policyholders own is known as a

a) Mutual insurer.
b) Fraternal insurer.
c) Stock insurer.
d) Reciprocal insurer.

#53. In addition to the common policy conditions, which condition is NOT included for farm liability?

a) Arbitration
b) Bankruptcy of the insured
c) Duties in the event of an occurrence, claim, or suit
d) Liberalization

#54. A golfer slices a shot off the tee. The ball crashes through the window of a house right beside the fairway. The broken window is paid for by

a) The golf course's property coverage.
b) The golfer's HO liability coverage.
c) The homeowner's property coverage on the house.
d) The liability policy of the golf course.

#55. An insurance provider incorporated under the laws of another state but doing business in California is considered

a) Alien.
b) Domestic.
c) Foreign.
d) Multi-national.

#56. An insured's friend's dog that they are pet sitting while the friend is out of town attacked and bit a visitor in their home. Does the insured's homeowners liability coverage apply?

a) Yes, if the visitor does not have health coverage
b) No, because the dog is not owned by the insured
c) No, because injury to others by animals is not covered
d) Yes, the coverage would apply for any animal in the insured's care

#57. A homeowner has misplaced some insured personal property and needs to know what might have happened to the items. Which of the following homeowners policy forms would cover such a loss?

a) HO-2
b) HO-3
c) HO-4
d) HO-5

#58. An insured has a personal umbrella with a $2,000 self-insured retention (SIR). If no other policy is involved, the umbrella would be over by how much after a $12,000 personal injury liability claim?

a) $2,000
b) $1,000
c) $10,000
d) $12,000

#59. Under a personal auto policy, which of the following would NOT be eligible for coverage?

a) A trailer owned by the insured
b) A vehicle purchased 90 days ago
c) A vehicle listed on the Declarations page
d) A non-owned temporary substitute vehicle

#60. A homeowner sets a fire in a fireplace, but a log rolls out, causing fire damage to the living room. Under the Standard Fire Policy, how would this be classified?

a) Second-tier fire
b) Friendly fire
c) Hostile fire
d) Indirect fire

#61. Which homeowners form provides open peril coverage for dwelling (Coverage A) and contents (Coverage C)?

a) HO-2
b) HO-3
c) HO-5
d) HO-8

#62. Under the Business Personal Property Limit – Seasonal Increase provision, if no percentage is stated on the declarations page, seasonal fluctuations will automatically increase the business personal property limit by

a) 10%.
b) 15%.
c) 25%.
d) 50%.

#63. Section III of the business auto policy provides physical damage coverage. All of the following are physical damages that can be selected coverages EXCEPT

a) Comprehensive coverage.
b) Collision coverage.
c) Limited peril coverage.
d) Specified causes of loss coverage.

#64. All of the following are optional endorsements that can be added to the standard equipment breakdown coverage form EXCEPT

a) Debris removal.
b) Utility interruption.
c) Extra expense.
d) Business interruption.

#65. An audit revealed the administrator for a pension plan had made investments that were not consistent with the risk tolerance established in the plan for its members. The earnings for the past year are substantially below the average for comparable funds. The governing board wants to act against the administrator. What type of commercial liability would the board have to provide for this risk?

a) An employee dishonesty bond
b) Personal injury liability
c) Fiduciary liability owned by the administrator
d) A fiduciary liability policy paid by the pension fund

#66. Vehicle owners can meet mandatory automobile financial responsibility laws in all of the following ways, EXCEPT

a) A certificate of passing a safe driver's education course.
b) Posting a bond with the motor vehicle department.
c) The purchase of insurance from an insurance company.
d) A Certificate of self-insurance.

#67. According to the principles of ocean marine insurance, a total loss can occur in which of the following ways?

a) Collision
b) Actual
c) Labor
d) Sue

#68. Under a homeowners policy, all of the following are additional coverages EXCEPT

a) Outbuildings.
b) The fire department service charge.
c) Coverage for shrubs, trees, and other plants.
d) Payment for reasonable repairs and debris removal after a covered loss.

#69. An insured was judged at fault in an auto accident. She has 100/300 bodily injury liability coverage. Three other people were also injured in the vehicle hit by the insured. They were awarded damages of $150,000, $75,000, and $75,000. What amount, if any, was not covered by her policy?

a) $150,000
b) All of the damages were covered by her policy
c) $50,000
d) $100,000

#70. What sublimit in a liability policy sets the maximum amount insurers will pay for all claims resulting from a single accident?

a) Combined single
b) Aggregate
c) Per occurrence
d) Per person

#71. Which commercial property form is used to insure buildings while under construction?

a) Builders risk
b) Legal liability
c) Building and personal property
d) Business income

#72. Under the Coverage C – Personal Property section in a dwelling policy, which property type would be covered?

a) Any personal watercraft
b) Motor vehicles
c) Rowboats
d) 2-passenger aircraft

#73. Which endorsement, when added to the personal auto policy, alters the definition of a covered auto to include golf carts, motor homes, or motorcycles?

a) Nonhighway vehicle endorsement
b) Miscellaneous type vehicle endorsement
c) Recreational vehicle endorsement
d) Extended coverage endorsement

#74. The California FAIR Plan offers a basic property insurance policy that can include all of the following features EXCEPT

a) Extended coverage for the structure and personal property; perils include damage from hail, wind, aircraft damage, vehicle damage, riot, explosion, and smoke.
b) Vandalism and Malicious Mischief (VMM) for the structure and personal property.
c) Automobile and farm coverage.
d) Fire coverage for the personal property or personal property of others.

#75. A tornado blows a house insured with a homeowners policy off its foundation. It must be demolished and removed so a replacement house can be built. Which of the following is true about debris removal?

a) HO policies do not pay for debris removal
b) An additional 5% of the policy limit can be paid for debris removal
c) Since the full policy limit must be paid for the house, there is no coverage for debris removal
d) It will be paid if the debris removal endorsement has been attached

#76. Besides perils, the difference between the three DP forms is in the coverage. Which of the following coverage options is covered by the DP-2 and DP-3 but not the DP-1?

a) Coverage D – Fair Rental Value
b) Coverage E – Additional Living Expense
c) Coverage A – Dwelling
d) Coverage B – Other Structures

#77. A combined ratio is the percentage of each premium dollar a property or casualty insurance provider spends on claims and expenses. Which of these statements is TRUE concerning the combined ratio?

a) An increase in the combined ratio signifies that profitability is improving
b) When the ratio is over 100, the insurance provider has an underwriting profit
c) A decrease in the combined ratio signifies financial profitability is improving
d) A decrease in the combined ratio signifies financial profitability is decreasing

#78. A person skilled in the process of choosing risks that will not create an adverse selection for an insurer is called a/an

a) Actuary.
b) Underwriter.
c) Adjuster.
d) General agent.

#79. All of the following are eligibility criteria for the low-cost automobile program EXCEPT

a) The vehicle's value.
b) Any felony convictions.
c) Income level.
d) The insured driver's age.

#80. Wagering on a sporting event is referred to as what type of risk?

a) Simple
b) Pure
c) Speculative
d) Calculated

#81. Concerning surety bonds, which of the following statements is true?

a) The principal is the designated beneficiary of the surety bond's holder
b) The individual who promises to fulfill the obligation of the bond is called the obligee
c) The purpose of the surety bond is to guarantee that specific obligations or duties will be fulfilled
d) A surety bond is also called third-party guarantee insurance because it always involves three parties

#82. The workers compensation rating is established by applying a rating bureau job classification rate to which of the following?

a) Noncash compensation
b) Minimum wage
c) Job title
d) Payroll

#83. Which hull policy clause states that if the insured does not take immediate steps to minimize the loss and protect the property from additional loss, the coverage can be invalidated?

a) Protection and indemnity
b) Sue and labor
c) Pilotage and towage
d) War and strikes

#84. Regarding the homeowners policy, which of the following does NOT satisfy the definition of insured location?

a) A plot of farmland rented or owned by the insured
b) A meeting hall rented to the insured to hold a party for his son's birthday
c) A cabin rented to the insured for a family vacation
d) A secondary residence obtained by the insured during the policy period

#85. The statistical probability of loss for a particular class of insureds is best predicted when the insured group is

a) Older.
b) Smaller.
c) Larger.
d) Diverse.

#86. An insured goes to an expensive five-star restaurant one night and parks their car using the restaurant's valet parking services. The restaurant hires a third-party company to perform the valet services that rents parking spaces in a private parking garage nearby. While the valet was parking the insured's car, they had an accident. Whose insurance coverage will be primary in this scenario?

a) The parking garage insurance
b) The valet service's insurance
c) The insured's personal auto policy
d) The restaurant's liability insurance

#87. What coverage form in the farm policy insures farming equipment on an open peril basis?

a) Farm property
b) Farm liability
c) Mobile agriculture machinery and equipment
d) Livestock

#88. A provision found in most claims-made liability forms that will cover the insured for claims resulting from events that took place during the policy period but was not reported until after the policy expiration is called

a) Extended warranty agreement.
b) Extended reporting period (ERP).
c) Extended period of indemnity.
d) Extended coverages.

#89. Which of the following types of property would be insured under Coverage B (Other Structures) when insurance is written on a dwelling form?

a) A garage separated from the dwelling
b) Supplies and materials used for the repair or construction of the dwelling
c) A laundry room attached to the dwelling
d) Outdoor equipment and building equipment

#90. Which property is covered for loss by the perils of flood or earthquake under the livestock coverage form?

a) Farm machinery
b) Attacks by the insured's dogs
c) Household contents
d) Sheep, goats, and swine

#91. In a homeowners policy, which of the following exposures is NOT covered?

a) Personal liability
b) Medical payments to an insured
c) Unscheduled personal property damage
d) Bodily injury to others

#92. Under a building and personal property coverage form, which of the following would be covered?

a) Personal property while airborne
b) Underground pipes
c) Outdoor sign
d) Building foundations

#93. A property insurance applicant owns a building in which combustible materials are stored in the furnace room. From an underwriting perspective, this risk would more than likely be considered a

a) Morale hazard.
b) Speculative risk.
c) Moral hazard.
d) Physical hazard.

#94. The purpose of obtaining an umbrella liability policy is to provide

a) Coverage that is not readily available through an authorized insurance provider in the state.
b) Coverage that typically can only be added by endorsement.
c) Excess insurance over the primary liability policy.
d) Coverage to those who cannot purchase it on a regular market.

#95. Which of the following is NOT true regarding the automatic increase in the insurance endorsement in dwelling policies?

a) It raises the amount of coverage by an annual percentage
b) It is optional
c) It protects against inflation
d) It does not require an extra premium

#96. What risk management technique is the insured exercising if an insured obtains an insurance policy with a large deductible?

a) Sharing
b) Retention
c) Transfer only
d) Avoidance

#97. Which of the following defines the unfair trade practice known as rebating?

a) Charging premium amounts over and above the amount specified in the policy
b) Making false statements that are maliciously critical and intended to injure another individual in the insurance business
c) Offering an inducement of something of value not stated in the policy
d) Making statements that misrepresent an insurance policy to induce an insured to replace the policy

#98. In an insurance contract, a representation qualifies as a/an

a) Express warranty.
b) Policy provision.
c) Opinion.
d) Implied warranty.

#99. Under the directors and officers liability coverage, which of the following would NOT be covered?

a) Illegal acts while directors and officers are acting in an official capacity
b) Breach of duty and neglect
c) Misstatements made by the directors and officers
d) Reimbursement for penalties and fines

#100. When an insured's gardener was spraying weeds in the backyard, he failed to notice that the wind was blowing the spray into the neighbor's yard, where he damaged their flower bed. The insured was found to be legally liable for this damage. This scenario is an example of

a) Gross negligence.
b) Vicarious liability.
c) Intervening cause.
d) Comparative negligence.

#101. Which of the following scenarios would be covered by workers compensation insurance?

a) A construction worker who refused to wear a hard hat gets hit on the head at a construction site
b) A professional chef burns themselves on their stove at home while preparing for a private dinner party
c) A publisher gets their hand crushed in a printing press at work
d) An administrative assistant secretary chokes on an apple during a break in the break room

#102. The dwelling form personal property off-premises extension provides limits of coverage up to

a) 10% of Coverage A anywhere in the United States or Canada.
b) 10% of Coverage A anywhere in the world.
c) 10% of Coverage C anywhere in the United States or Canada.
d) 10% of Coverage C anywhere in the world.

#103. Unless the Commissioner denies a rate-change application, it will be assumed to be approved after

a) 30 days.
b) 60 days.
c) 90 days.
d) 180 days.

#104. A trucking company's truck is out of service for repairs. While making the delivery in a borrowed truck, the driver is responsible for an accident that results in $55,000 in property damage to other vehicles and injuries to two individuals. Which policy pays for this loss under the commercial auto liability policy conditions?

a) The insurers will share in the settlement based on the other insurance condition
b) Only the insurer for the borrower of the truck will pay for damages and injuries
c) The policy for the titled owner of the truck will be the primary coverage, and the borrower's insurance will be the excess coverage
d) The policy for the company that borrowed the truck will be the primary coverage, and the titled owner of the truck will be the excess coverage

#105. HO policies consider all of the following insured locations EXCEPT

a) A blueberry patch owned by the insured.
b) The insured's land on which their new home is under construction.
c) An individual cemetery plot.
d) The hotel ballroom rented by the insured for a family reunion.

#106. Which of the following is FALSE regarding liability coverage of a business auto policy?

a) The insurer will pay any interest between the time of judgment and payment
b) The insurer will defend any lawsuit alleging bodily injury or property damage covered by the policy
c) The insurer will reimburse the insured for all loss of earnings
d) The insurer will pay the premium on any appeal bond

#107. The garage coverage form is written to cover the insurance needs of an insured in the business of selling, servicing, repairing, or storing automobiles. Which of the following coverages are not contained in a garage policy?

a) Product liability
b) Physical damage on a customer's auto
c) Auto liability
d) Premises and operations liability

#108. All of the following are TRUE statements regarding cancellation procedures EXCEPT

a) The termination of an insurance contract with the premium charge being adjusted with the exact time the protection has been effective is considered a pro-rata cancellation.
b) Short-rate cancellation lets the insured pay less for each day of coverage than if the policy had remained effective for the full term.
c) Short-rate cancellation is a procedure in which the returned premium is not directly proportional to the number of days left in the policy period.
d) When a policy is canceled upon its effective date, it is considered a flat cancellation, and no premium charge is usually made.

#109. The extended non-owned coverage in a personal auto policy protects

a) The individual named and their spouse only.
b) Anyone who is permitted to drive by the named insured.
c) Only the individual(s) named on the policy.
d) The individual named on the policy and all residence family members.

#110. The part of the policy that clarifies the terms that are used throughout the policy is the

a) Definitions.
b) Conditions.
c) Insuring agreement.
d) Declarations.

#111. All of the following must exist for there to be negligent liability EXCEPT

a) A reasonable expectation that the act can cause damage or injury.
b) A breach of the legal duty that results in damage or injury to another person.
c) A legal duty to act, or not to act, under the circumstances.
d) Proximate cause between the wrong and the damage or injury.

#112. Aleatory contracts are based on what kind of exchange?

a) Equal amounts for pay in and pay out
b) Balanced benefits
c) An exchange of equal obligations
d) Unequal exchange of values

#113. Which of the following is covered by auto other-than-collision (comprehensive) coverage?

a) A portable compact disc player
b) An awning attached to a car for camping
c) Electric equipment needed for the normal operation of the car
d) A radar detector

#114. When a fire erupts in the kitchen and spreads upstairs to the office, causing the destruction of furniture, what type of loss has occurred?

a) Indirect
b) Consequential
c) Proximate
d) Direct

#115. Under a dwelling policy, which of the following is covered?

a) Fire caused by an earthquake
b) Freezing plumbing systems
c) Flood or surface water
d) Structures used for commercial manufacturing

#116. The businessowners liability coverage form responds to a claim from which of the following events?

a) An injury arising out of a customer falling due to a wet floor
b) An injury to an employee while performing their job
c) Damages sought by a third party as a result of an accounting error
d) An injury arising out of the sale of alcoholic beverages

#117. Which action by an insurance provider or its representatives is NOT considered an unfair claims violation?

a) The claims department fails to affirm or deny coverage within a reasonable period after proof of loss has been submitted
b) A producer advises a claimant to obtain the services of an attorney
c) A claims adjustor misrepresents relevant policy provisions to dissuade an insured from filing a claim
d) A producer does not respond to a claimant's communication regarding a claim where a response is required

#118. What are the two types of compensatory damages?

a) Unique and general
b) Special and punitive
c) Special and general
d) Punitive and reward

#119. All of these are factors in determining actual cash value EXCEPT

a) Property type.
b) Insurance premium paid.
c) Age of property.
d) Replacement cost.

#120. What is the limit of the businessowners policy extension coverage form for personal property off-premises?

a) $2,500
b) $5,000
c) $10,000
d) $15,000

#121. The broad cause of loss form in the commercial property policy includes three additional perils above and beyond the basic form perils. Which of these is NOT one of those three perils?

a) Utility services
b) Water damage
c) Weight of snow, ice, or sleet
d) Falling objects

#122. If a vehicle is carjacked and left in a snow bank, resulting in a frozen radiator and heavy damage, is the damage covered by the auto policy?

a) No, freezing is never covered
b) No, theft is never covered
c) Yes, the freezing exclusion is removed if the car is stolen
d) Yes, there is no exclusion for freezing

#123. An insured was involved in an accident resulting from a tire blowing out. The insured was severely injured and incurred $100,000 in medical expenses. The insured brought a recovery action against the manufacturers of the car and the tires. The court determined that the tire was the cause of the accident. Who must pay for this loss?

a) Both manufacturers would share the loss
b) Neither manufacturer would have to pay due to the "buyer beware" doctrine
c) The manufacturer of the auto
d) The manufacturer of the tire

#124. Insurance providers CANNOT transact insurance in California without a

a) Certificate of Authority.
b) Broker's license.
c) Certificate of Insurance.
d) Letter of Clearance.

#125. Which of the following forms insures buildings and personal property on an open peril basis?

a) HO-2
b) HO-3
c) HO-4
d) HO-5

#126. Which of the following best describes how underinsured motorist coverage works?

a) The coverage pays the difference between the insured's underinsured motorist limit and the other driver's property damage coverage limit
b) The coverage pays for the insurer to sue the underinsured motorist and their insurer for full payment
c) The liability for the loss is divided evenly between the underinsured motorist's insurance and the insured's insurance
d) The insured's policy covers the whole amount of the liability

#127. In the past 72 hours, three instances of volcanic eruptions damaged a property insured by a dwelling policy. How many deductibles must the insured pay before the policy covers the damages caused by the eruptions?

a) Zero
b) One
c) Two
d) Three

#128. Insurance rates developed by the underwriter based on their skill and experience instead of an actuarial analysis are called

a) Manual rates.
b) Judgment rates.
c) Merit rates.
d) Experience rates.

#129. In a homeowners policy, the Declarations section provides all of the following information EXCEPT

a) The amount of deductible applied to a loss.
b) Insured locations.
c) Policy exclusions.
d) Basic underwriting information.

#130. The insurance contract section that describes the covered perils and the nature of coverage of the contractual agreement between the insured and the insurance provider is the

a) Insuring agreement
b) Exclusions
c) Declarations
d) Conditions

#131. A performance bond is an example of which of these types of bonds?

a) Injunction bonds
b) Contract bonds
c) Judicial bonds
d) Fiduciary bonds

#132. At the request of an insured, under Coverage C, the personal property of a residence employee or guest is insured

a) While it is in any residence premises occupied by a named insured.
b) Anywhere in the world.
c) Only while on a residence premises.
d) While it is in any residence premises occupied by an insured.

#133. An individual applies for National Flood Insurance. How many days must they wait before coverage becomes effective?

a) 20
b) 30
c) 45
d) 60

#134. In a liability policy with split limits of 25/50/25, which number is the maximum amount that would be payable should damage to an individual's property occur?

a) The amount of the third number, $25,000
b) The amount of all three numbers, $100,000
c) The amount of the first number, $25,000
d) The amount of the second number, $50,000

#135. How would a standard fire policy be described?

a) As a basic perils contract
b) As a broad perils contract
c) As a named perils contract
d) As an all-risk perils contract

#136. What information is contained in the conditions section of an insurance policy?

a) The description of the obligations and duties of the insured
b) The individuals or risks not covered under the policy
c) The named insured's identity
d) The amount of coverage provided by the policy

#137. What is it called when an insurance provider pays for the cost to exchange damaged property with new property of like kind and quality?

a) Market value
b) Stated amount
c) Replacement cost
d) Actual cash value

#138. The home of an insured catches on fire. As a result, the insured's family has to stay in a motel until repairs on the house are completed. The cost of the motel stay would be a

a) Consequential loss.
b) Resulting loss.
c) Direct loss.
d) Negligent loss.

#139. Under Coverage D of a homeowners policy, which of the following would NOT be covered as a loss?

a) After a fire in a building next to the insured's home, the insured could not occupy their home and had to stay at a motel for one week.
b) The home of an insured is damaged by fire. The insured incurs expenses for living in a motel and eating meals in a restaurant while repairs are made.
c) An insured leased a dwelling for five years. Two years later, the property owner died. The new property owners wanted to make the property their primary residence, so the lease was canceled.
d) An insured has an apartment in their home. The tenant's negligence caused a fire, and the apartment was unfit to live in for four months while repairs were being completed.

#140. When a vessel's ownership changes, the premium will be returned on a/an

a) Annual basis.
b) Lump sum basis.
c) Pro rata basis.
d) Monthly basis.

#141. A pair of insureds operate a travel business out of their home. Because of the acts of terrorism recently, the insureds want to obtain a property and liability policy to insure their home-based business. A plan that is appropriate for their needs would be a

a) Home business policy endorsement.
b) Standard homeowners policy.
c) Travel insurance policy.
d) Commercial travel liability policy.

#142. Which of the following individuals would be eligible for Homeowners Coverage F – Medical Payments in the event of an injury at the insured's premises?

a) The named insured's spouse
b) A guest who was injured at the insured's party five years ago
c) An individual regularly residing with the insured
d) A full-time maid

#143. Which of the following statements is CORRECT regarding the replacement cost coverages under the businessowners policy (BOP)?

a) Damage of property belonging to others is indemnified on the same replacement cost basis
b) There are no coinsurance requirements for the businessowners policy
c) An 80% insurance-to-value requirement is in place
d) A coinsurance percentage varies from risk to risk and will be found in the Declarations

#144. In a DP-1 form, if the insured chooses to apply Coverage B to a detached garage, Coverage A will

a) Only be applicable if the insured pays an added premium.
b) Be increased by 10%.
c) Be decreased by 10%.
d) Only be applicable if the insured pays a higher deductible.

#145. Which is NOT considered mobile equipment under a commercial general liability policy?

a) An auto used as a company car by a real estate firm
b) A combine used on a farm
c) The Department of Transportation's resurfacing equipment
d) The backhoe used by an excavating company

#146. The commercial crime coverage that would cover losses resulting from the theft of money, securities, and other property by employees is

a) Inside the premises – theft of money and securities.
b) Employee theft.
c) Funds transfer fraud.
d) Forgery or alteration.

#147. Under the farm property special form, which of these losses would be excluded from coverage?

a) Loss of livestock resulting from an attack by dogs or wild animals
b) Theft of property from the insured's residence
c) Drowning of livestock
d) Fire caused by curing tobacco

#148. If the premiums collected by an insurance provider participating in the WYO flood program are inadequate to cover losses, which of the following would be true?

a) The insurance provider must apply for disaster relief funds
b) The Federal Insurance Administration will remove the insurance provider from the NFIP
c) The insurance provider will be reimbursed for the excess costs by the NFIP
d) The insurance provider must cover the loss out of its surplus

#149. The statutory law defense that reduces injury and awards for damages proportionately when the plaintiff and defendant are both responsible is known as

a) Intervening cause.
b) Contributory negligence.
c) Comparative negligence.
d) Assumption of risk.

#150. What policy would a business owner whose business fills scuba tanks more than likely require to insure compressors and unfired pressure vessels?

a) Contractors equipment floater
b) Equipment breakdown
c) Inland marine scuba floater
d) Commercial general liability

Practice Exam 2 Answers

#1. a) Risk

Insurance involves the transfer of the possibility of a loss (risk) to an insurer, which spreads the costs of unexpected losses to many people. (p. 2)

#2. a) Who owns the auto

The classes of hired auto and non-owned auto are mutually exclusive, and the distinction between the two is who owns the auto. (p. 146)

#3. d) Representation.

A representation of the future is a promise unless it is purely a statement of a belief or an expectation. (p. 16)

#4. b) Subrogation.

Claims should be paid only once and by the liable party. The insurance provider pays policy claims and has the right to try to be repaid by the party who caused the loss. (p. 81)

#5. b) Damage to birds, fish, or pets

Pets, birds, and fish are not covered under Coverage C – Personal Property of the DP-2 broad form. (pp. 97, 99)

#6. b) A lawnmower the landlord owns and stores at the rented premises.

This form excludes coverage for money, bank notes, accounts, deeds, securities, gold and silver, stamps, tickets, watches, jewelry, furs, precious and semi-precious stones, goldware, silverware, and pewterware. (p. 107)

#7. a) Indemnity.

Indemnity (sometimes called reimbursement) is a provision in an insurance policy that specifies that in the event of loss, an insured or a beneficiary is allowed to collect only to the extent of the financial loss. (p. 15)

#8. a) Medical payments

Medical payments coverage of a businessowners policy will pay the medical, hospital, dental, and funeral service costs incurred within one year from the date of an accident to an individual who sustains bodily injury by accident on or next to the insured's premises or due to the insured's operations. (p. 291)

#9. d) $1,500

Only $1,500 of coverage is provided in the HO policy for damage to watercraft, equipment, accessories, and trailers. If additional coverage is required, a separate Boatowners policy can be purchased. (p. 131)

#10. b) Paying a claim

Consideration is the binding force in any contract. The health representations made in the application and the payment of premiums are consideration on the part of the insured. The promise to pay in the event of a loss is a consideration on the part of the insurance provider. (p. 14)

#11. d) $1,050

Coverage D would pay $900 as an additional living expense and $150 as a loss of rent for a total of $1,050. (p. 133)

#12. **c) The insured building has been vacant for over 60 days.**

Suppose a building has been unoccupied for more than 60 consecutive days before the loss. In that circumstance, the insurer will not cover damage caused by glass breakage, sprinkler leakage, water damage, vandalism, theft, or attempted theft. (p. 192)

#13. **d) Insurers will cover exposures in states listed on the information page**

Insurers will provide workers compensation and employers liability coverage in all states named in Part Three of the information page, except those that maintain a monopolistic fund. (p. 319)

#14. **a) Friendly fire.**

In a standard fire policy, friendly fire, a deliberately ignited flame or glow that remains within its intended confines, is not a covered peril. (p. 167)

#15. **a) Open peril**

The special form DP-3 is an open peril form, meaning all perils are insured against except those expressly excluded. (p. 97)

#16. **d) Abandon the property involved to the insurance provider.**

Answers A, B, and C are policy owners' duties following a loss. This condition is similar to the one found in the dwelling policy. The insured cannot abandon property to the insurer for any reason. (pp. 104, 118-119)

#17. **a) $125,200.**

After the $1,000 deductible is paid, the insured's policy pays $200 for the insured's vehicle damage, totaling $125,200. (pp. 148, 149-150)

#18. **c) A single-family home**

A single-family home will be covered with replacement cost coverage if it is insured to at least 80% of its replacement value. Insurers will cover every other building on an actual cash value basis. (p. 176)

#19. **c) Higher limits of coverage for fine arts items.**

Suppose the insured requires higher limits for certain types of property. In that scenario, they can use the scheduled personal property endorsement to schedule individually described items like fine arts, jewelry, coins, cameras, musical instruments, etc. The coverage is provided worldwide. (pp. 122-123)

#20. **b) Coverage for loss of use.**

Coverage D protects against loss of use. The other listed coverages are available through Coverage C. (pp. 131-133)

#21. **c) Only one party makes a promise.**

Only one of the parties to the contract is legally bound to do anything in a unilateral contract. The insured does not make any legally binding promises. However, an insurance provider is legally bound to pay losses covered by an in-force policy. (p. 15)

#22. **c) When a community applies for the program**

The federal emergency flood insurance program goes into effect when a community applies for the program. It ends when all NFIP criteria have been satisfied, and the regular program can start. (p. 174)

#23. **a) Turkeys and chickens.**

Livestock means horses, donkeys, mules, cattle, swine, sheep, and goats. The livestock coverage form is a named peril coverage insuring losses that cause the necessary destruction or death of livestock by the basic causes of loss. (p. 272)

#24. **d) They are covered if they are used to replace previously owned autos with that coverage**

If Symbol 7 is used, coverage for newly acquired vehicles applies if the insurance provider already covers all autos owned by the insured or if the newly acquired vehicle replaces a previously owned auto that had that prior coverage. The insured must notify the insurer that coverage is requested within 30 days of obtaining the vehicle. (pp. 233-234)

#25. **b) A schedule rating risk assessment that allows the insured to receive credits and debits for business practices that increase or decrease the risk of loss.**

A schedule rating risk assessment is a method of credits and debits to standard premiums. It allows an insured to benefit from business practices that reduce the risk potential associated with normal business operations. Such an assessment also penalizes an insured that has poor risk management practices by charging higher than standard premiums for standard coverage. (p. 80)

#26. **d) Supplemental extended reporting period.**

Once the basic extended reporting period goes into effect, the insured is guaranteed the option to obtain supplemental extended reporting period coverage. (p. 224)

#27. **a) The personal property of roomers not related to the insured.**

The property of roomers, boarders, and tenants (not related to the policyholder) will not be covered by homeowners personal property coverage. (p. 132)

#28. **b) The policy can be voided**

Concealment or fraud on the insured's part can result in the policy being immediately voided, whether the fraud was committed before or after the loss. (p. 17)

#29. **d) Yes, medical payments coverage is also applied off the insured premises**

Homeowners medical payments coverage applies as long as the loss happened during the insured's personal activity. (p. 138)

#30. **a) Express**

The authority a principal intends to grant an agent through the agent's contract is called express authority. It is the authority that is written into the contract. (p. 23)

#31. **c) 80%**

A home must be insured for at least 80% of its value on the date of loss to qualify for replacement coverage. (pp. 119, 130-131)

#32. **a) Self-insured retention.**

The primary or underlying policy does not pay for the loss, but the umbrella does. In these instances, the insured will be required to pay a deductible called a self-insured retention or SIR. (pp. 179-180, 229)

#33. **d) Riot**

Coverage for damage by riots is one of the seven perils included in the extended coverages. (pp. 93-95)

#34. **c) Medical payment benefits are limited**

In every state, workers compensation medical payments are unlimited. (p. 317)

#35. **a) The plaintiff will cover court costs and damages to the defendant if the plaintiff loses the court case.**

This bond guarantees that the plaintiff who brings legal action against a defendant will be able to cover the court costs and any resulting damages if the plaintiff loses the case. (p. 309)

#36. **a) Policy dividends issued by mutual insurers are guaranteed and not taxable.**

Policy dividends issued by mutual insurers are not guaranteed and are taxable. (p. 44)

#37. **a) The HO-3 policy covers the mysterious disappearance of personal property.**

The HO-5 form covers the mysterious disappearance of personal property that cannot be explained as to the manner, time, or location of the property loss. (pp. 113-114)

#38. **c) Personal property replacement cost**

The personal property replacement cost endorsement changes the actual cash value settlement on personal property to a replacement cost basis, except for certain types of property, like antiques and fine art. (p. 124)

#39. **a) Supply bonds**

Supply bonds guarantee that a supplier will provide materials, supplies, products, and equipment as stated in the written contract. (p. 309)

#40. **d) On a replacement cost basis**

The property is insured on a replacement cost basis. However, when the damaged property is not repaired or replaced within two years after the accident, settlement is the cost to repair or replace or the actual cash value, whichever is less (p. 257).

#41. **d) The owner-occupant of a condo unit.**

The HO-3 form insures a structure under Coverage A. A condo unit owner does not own the building, only space in the building. The HO-6 form expands coverage for condo unit owners. (pp. 113, 114)

#42. **a) A duplex that two families occupy, each of which has a bedroom rented to a boarder**

A duplex occupied by two families, each with a bedroom rented to a boarder, would be a risk that is eligible for coverage under the dwelling property broad form (DP-2). (pp. 78, 95-97)

#43. **a) Bodily injury liability.**

The equipment breakdown coverage form does not provide coverage for bodily injury liability. (p. 257)

#44. **d) A general average.**

Average in ocean marine language refers to loss or damage. If one piece of cargo is sacrificed to save the rest, it is a general average, and all associated with the voyage help pay. (p. 300)

#45. **c) This loss is excluded from coverage**

The freezing and breaking of pipes are not covered unless the insured maintains heat inside the building. (p. 96)

#46. **c) Auto collision coverage.**

Auto collision is not a liability coverage; therefore, the personal umbrella will not act as excess coverage. (pp. 158, 179-181)

#47. **b) NAIC**

The various independent rating services are Standard and Poor's, AM Best, Moody's, Fitch, and Weiss. NAIC is a regulatory organization comprised of insurance commissioners. (p. 76)

#48. **b) The contractor**

The neighbor would not need to prove negligence, only that the damage occurred. The contractor's negligence was the proximate cause of the damage, and the accident would not have happened without it. (pp. 70-71)

#49. **c) Reciprocal insurers**

When insurance is obtained through a reciprocal insurer, the insureds share the risk of loss with other subscribers. (pp. 4, 45-46)

#50. **d) An insured's 13-year-old grandson threw rocks at the neighbor's house and broke several windows.**

Coverage will apply if the damage results from a minor under age 13 to property owned by a policy owner or resident of the household. Deliberate damage caused by any insured, age 13 years or older, is not covered. (p. 139)

#51. **c) Market value**

A property insured for market value is covered for what a willing buyer would pay before a loss. (p. 86)

#52. **a) Mutual insurer.**

Mutual companies are owned by the policy owners and issue participating policies. (p. 44)

#53. **a) Arbitration**

The farm liability coverage form is identical to the commercial general liability form. The condition of arbitration is not included in the farm liability coverage form. (pp. 272, 275-276)

#54. **b) The golfer's HO liability coverage.**

Liability coverage is included in every HO policy form. Coverage E – Personal Liability of the insured's HO policy will pay for damage to the property of others. (p. 138)

#55. **c) Foreign.**

A foreign insurer is an insurance provider incorporated in another state or territorial possession. (p. 43)

#56. **d) Yes, the coverage would apply to any animal in the insured's care**

Personal liability coverage in Section II will respond to any claim against an insured for damages due to bodily injury or property damage. The insured's liability coverage would apply to damage caused by their animals and any other animals in their care. (p. 138)

#57. **d) HO-5**

The HO-5 form covers losing or misplacing (mysterious disappearance) personal property as a theft loss. (p. 114)

#58. **c) $10,000**

If there is no primary underlying insurance, the excess policy will apply after the insured pays the self-insured retention. (pp. 179-180, 229)

#59. **b) A vehicle purchased 90 days ago**

A covered auto includes autos listed in the Declarations, owned trailers, non-owned temporary substitute vehicles, newly acquired autos (for 30 days), and additional temporary vehicles because of breakdown, servicing, repair, or loss. (pp. 233-234)

#60. **c) Hostile fire**

Under the Standard Fire Policy, a hostile fire is a fire that escapes its intended confines. Although not specified in the Standard Fire Policy, coverage is only provided for loss by hostile fires. (p. 167)

#61. **c) HO-5**

Form HO-2 is named peril (broad form perils) coverage for a dwelling and its contents. Form HO-3 is open peril for a dwelling and named peril for its contents. Form HO-5 is open peril for both a dwelling and its contents. Form HO-8 is named peril (basic perils) coverage for both. (pp. 112-115)

#62. **c) 25%.**

Under Business Personal Property Limit – Seasonal Increase, the business personal property limit will automatically increase by 25% for seasonal fluctuations unless stated in the Declarations. (p. 288)

#63. **c) Limited peril coverage.**

The personal auto policy's comprehensive coverage is the same as other-than-collision coverage. Collision coverage is the same as that coverage in the PAP. Specified causes of loss cover theft, explosion, fire, windstorm, lightning, hail, flood, or earthquake. (pp. 235-236)

#64. **a) Debris removal.**

The equipment breakdown form does not insure bodily injury liability or consequential losses, such as an interruption in business and extra expense. However, the insured may obtain optional coverage for business interruptions. It cannot add an optional debris removal endorsement. (pp. 256-259)

#65. **d) A fiduciary liability policy paid by the pension fund**

Fiduciary liability covers individuals who administer employee benefits or pension plans and have a fiduciary responsibility to manage the funds in the plan participants' best interests. When the fund pays the premiums for fiduciary liability insurance, by law, the policy has to allow for subrogation against the individual trustees involved in the loss. (p. 229)

#66. **a) A certificate of passing a safe driver's education course**

A certificate of passing a safe driver's education course is not a way to meet compulsory automobile financial responsibility laws. (p. 157)

#67. **b) Actual**

According to the principles and practice of ocean marine insurance, a total loss can take place in actual total loss and constructive total loss. (pp. 300, 302)

#68. **a) Outbuildings.**

Under a homeowners policy, outbuildings are not an additional coverage. They are insured under Coverage B – Other Structures in the HO policy. Answers B, C, and D are additional coverages available under HO policy forms. (p. 131)

#69. **c) $50,000**

The number 100 in the 100/300 limits means the most that only one individual will be awarded for bodily injury is $100,000. The $150,000 leaves $50,000 unpaid. (pp. 148, 149-150)

#70. **c) Per occurrence**

Per occurrence is a sublimit that puts a ceiling on the payment for claims that arise from a single accident. (pp. 147-148)

#71. **a) Builders risk**

The builders risk coverage form is used to insure buildings while under construction. (pp. 193-194)

#72. **c) Rowboats**

Aircraft designed for flight and carrying people, motor vehicles, and motor-powered boats are excluded. However, canoes and rowboats would be covered. (p. 99)

#73. **b) Miscellaneous type vehicle endorsement**

The miscellaneous-type vehicle endorsement alters the definition of a covered auto to include motor homes, motorcycles, golf carts, and dune buggies. It also restricts the coverage for non-owned vehicles. (p. 154)

#74. **c) Automobile and farm coverage.**

FAIR plans were created to assist individuals with an insurable interest in real or tangible property. These individuals cannot secure basic property insurance from an admitted provider through standard channels. Farm and automobile coverage are NOT part of the FAIR plan in California. (p. 177)

#75. **b) An additional 5% of the policy limit can be paid for debris removal**

When the amount of loss plus the cost to remove debris exceeds the policy limit, policy owners can pay an additional 5% of the limit for debris removal. (pp. 133-134)

#76. **b) Coverage E – Additional Living Expense**

In a DP-1 policy, insureds must obtain Coverage E – Additional Living Expense through an endorsement. (p. 100)

#77. **c) A decrease in the combined ratio signifies financial profitability is improving**

The combined ratio is the percentage of each premium dollar a property and casualty insurer spends on expenses and claims. A decrease in the combined ratio indicates profitability is improving; an increase means profitability will decrease. When the ratio is over 100, the insurer takes an underwriting loss. (p. 80)

#78. **b) Underwriter.**

An underwriter's function is to review insurance applications and determine who can be insured under which classification and rates. (p. 6)

#79. **b) Any felony convictions.**

Only misdemeanors or felonies related to Vehicle Code violations would be considered an eligibility factor for low-cost auto insurance. (p. 162)

#80. **c) Speculative**

Regarding speculative risk, a chance to win or lose must exist. Speculative risks cannot be insured. (p. 12)

#81. **c) The purpose of the surety bond is to guarantee that specific obligations or duties will be fulfilled**

The principal is the individual who promises to fulfill the obligation of the bond. Surety bonds are not insurance, nor are they known as third-party insurance. The obligee is the individual to whom the promise has been made, and the bond is payable. (p. 308)

#82. **d) Payroll**

The workers compensation rating is developed by applying a rating bureau job classification rate to every $100 of payroll. (pp. 320-321)

#83. **b) Sue and labor**

The master and crew must sue and labor to prevent loss and additional loss. If they do not, the insurance provider can refuse to pay. The insurer will pay expenses incurred while trying to keep the loss as small as possible. (p. 301)

#84. **a) A plot of farmland rented or owned by the insured**

A plot of farmland rented or owned by the insured does not meet the definition of insured location according to the homeowners policy. (p. 116)

#85. **c) Larger.**

As stated by the law of large numbers, the larger the number of individuals with a similar loss exposure, the more predictable actual losses will be. (p. 3)

#86. **b) The valet service's insurance**

Suppose an insured auto is in an accident while in the custody and care of a facility like a parking lot, garage, or valet. In that situation, the PAP covering the vehicle is excess coverage over any coverage belonging to the facility. The valet service's insurance will be the primary coverage. (pp. 146-147)

#87. **c) Mobile agriculture machinery and equipment**

The mobile agriculture machinery and equipment coverage form will cover eligible equipment on an open perils basis, subject to policy limitations and exclusions. (p. 273)

#88. **b) Extended reporting period (ERP).**

The extended reporting period is a limited time (60 days) for the insured under a claims-made form to report claims caused by an occurrence that took place after the retroactive date and before the policy's expiration date. (pp. 223, 224)

#89. **a) A garage separated from the dwelling**

Under Coverage B (Other Structures) on a dwelling form, a garage separated from the dwelling is a type of property that would be insured. (p. 98)

#90. **d) Sheep, goats, and swine**

Under the livestock coverage form, livestock, including cattle, horses, donkeys, mules, sheep, goats, and swine, is covered for loss because of earthquakes or floods. (pp. 272-273)

#91. **b) Medical payments to an insured**

Section II of the HO policy provides medical payments to others. It excludes coverage for the payment of an insured's medical expenses. (p. 138)

#92. **c) Outdoor sign**

Business Personal Property (BPP) coverage insures business personal property located in or on the structure or building. Outdoor signs are insured for up to a specified amount if attached to a building. Answers A, B, and D are expressly excluded. (pp. 189-190)

#93. **a) Morale hazard.**

A morale hazard is an increase in the hazard presented by a risk arising from the insured's indifference to loss due to the existence of insurance. (p. 3)

#94. **c) Excess insurance over the primary liability policy.**

An umbrella policy, also called catastrophe insurance, provides excess coverage over the primary liability policy. Coverage is typically broader than the underlying policies. (p. 179)

#95. **d) It does not require an extra premium**

An automatic increase in insurance is an optional endorsement that can be added to a dwelling policy to increase the insurance amount by an annual percentage to offset inflation. This endorsement requires an extra premium. (p. 105)

#96. **b) Retention**

When an insured obtained a policy with a large deductible, they received a lower premium rate. In return for the lower premium, the insured was required to retain a larger loss amount, should it occur. (p. 5)

#97. **c) Offering an inducement of something of value not stated in the policy**

Rebating refers to offering anything of value not stated in the policy as an inducement to buy insurance. (pp. 59-60)

#98. d) Implied warranty.

A representation is a statement that is believed to be true to the best of the knowledge of the individual making the statement. A warranty refers to a statement that is guaranteed to be true. Representations in insurance contracts qualify as implied warranties. (p. 16)

#99. d) Reimbursement for penalties and fines

Directors and officers (D&O) liability policies generally will not pay for fines, penalties, or punitive damages. (p. 226)

#100. b) Vicarious liability.

Vicarious liability can be imposed on one individual as the result of the acts of another individual acting on their behalf or under their control. (p. 71)

#101. c) A publisher gets their hand crushed in a printing press at work

Workers compensation covers job-related injuries but not willful misconduct, intentional self-injury, or violation of safety. (p. 318)

#102. d) 10% of Coverage C anywhere in the world.

Under all dwelling forms, the insured can apply up to 10% of the Coverage C limit against losses by covered perils to personal property while it is anywhere in the world. Canoes or rowboats are excluded. (p. 101)

#103. d) 180 days.

A rate change application will be considered approved 180 days after the Commissioner receives the rate application unless a final order from the Commissioner has disapproved that application. (p. 56)

#104. d) The policy for the company that borrowed the truck will be the primary coverage, and the titled owner of the truck will be the excess coverage

The additional condition, Other Insurance – Primary and Excess Insurance Provision, specifies that the truckers auto liability coverage will be considered primary when a covered auto is hired or borrowed by the insured for use in business as a trucker and used according to the operating rights granted by a public authority. (p. 247)

#105. a) A blueberry patch owned by the insured.

HO policies exclude land, in this scenario, a blueberry patch, owned by the insured as an insured location. (pp. 116, 117)

#106. c) The insurer will reimburse the insured for all loss of earnings

Only a limited amount of lost earnings per day will be paid, and only on those days when the insurance provider requires the insured to be elsewhere besides at work. (pp. 234-235)

#107. b) Physical damage on a customer's auto

The garage policy has a care, custody, and control exclusion which would eliminate coverage for any damage to a customer's auto. This exposure would have to be covered under a garagekeepers policy. (pp. 241, 242)

#108. b) Short-rate cancellation lets the insured pay less for each day of coverage than if the policy had remained effective for the full term.

Short-rate cancellation is a procedure in which the premium returned to the insured is not directly proportionate to the number of days remaining in the policy period. The insured has paid more for each day of coverage than if the policy remained in force for the full term. (p. 79)

#109. **c) Only the individual(s) named on the policy.**

Only the individual(s) named will be covered. There is no automatic coverage for a spouse or other family members. (p. 154)

#110. **a) Definitions.**

The definitions component of an insurance policy explains the terms used in the policy. Usually, words printed in bold, italics, or quotations have a definition as to their meaning in that contract. (p. 84)

#111. **a) A reasonable expectation that the act can cause damage or injury.**

A reasonable expectation that the act can cause injury or damage does not need to exist for there to be negligence. (pp. 70-71)

#112. **d) Unequal exchange of values**

An aleatory contract is a contract in which the parties exchange unequal values or amounts. The premium the insured pays is small compared to the amount the insurance provider will pay in the event of a loss. (p. 15)

#113. **c) Electric equipment needed for the normal operation of the car**

A personal auto policy's physical damage coverage section excludes loss or damage to radar detectors, electronic equipment not permanently installed, and custom equipment or furnishings. (pp. 152-153)

#114. **d) Direct**

Direct loss means any direct physical damage to buildings and personal property. Since the fire was the initial cause of loss that spread to the bedroom, damages would be considered a direct loss of the fire. (p. 77)

#115. **a) Fire caused by an earthquake**

Under a dwelling policy, earthquakes and land shock waves associated with volcanic activity are not covered. However, any resulting damages caused by the ensuing fire or explosion are covered. (p. 102)

#116. **a) An injury arising out of a customer falling due to a wet floor**

The businessowners liability coverage form would respond to a claim caused by an injury arising from a customer falling due to a wet floor. (pp. 290-293)

#117. **b) A producer advises a claimant to obtain the services of an attorney**

It is an unfair claims practice to encourage a claimant not to obtain an attorney. A claimant always has the right to seek legal counsel. (p. 59)

#118. **c) Special and general**

Special and general damages are two classes of compensatory damages that can be awarded. (pp. 71-72)

#119. **b) Insurance premium paid.**

Actual cash value (ACV) is a method of valuation in which the property's value is determined using the replacement cost for property of like kind and quality, with a deduction for depreciation. The original cost of the property is not a factor. (p. 86)

#120. **c) $10,000**

Under the businessowners policy, the personal property off-premises extension is limited to $10,000. (p. 287)

#121. **a) Utility services**

Utility services are not covered under the broad cause of loss form in the commercial property policy. Answers B, C, and D are covered perils. (pp. 200-201)

#122. **c) Yes, the freezing exclusion is removed if the car is stolen**

The exclusion for damage caused by freezing and mechanical breakdown is not applicable if the entire car has been stolen. (p. 153)

#123. **d) The manufacturer of the tire**

The tire manufacturer made an implied warranty that the product was safe to use; therefore, it would be held strictly liable. (p. 71)

#124. **a) Certificate of Authority.**

Before insurance providers can transact business in California, they must apply for and be granted a license or Certificate of Authority from the state Department of Insurance. They must also satisfy any financial (capital and surplus) requirements established by the state. (p. 42)

#125. **d) HO-5**

Only the HO-5 form insures the buildings and personal property on an open peril basis. (p. 114)

#126. **a) The coverage pays the difference between the insured's underinsured motorist limit and the other driver's property damage coverage limit**

Underinsured motorist coverage typically pays the difference between the other driver's property damage coverage limit and the insured's underinsured motorist property damage limit. (p. 152)

#127. **b) One**

All volcanic eruptions occurring within 72 hours (of the initial eruption) will be deemed one occurrence, with only one deductible. (p. 105)

#128. **b) Judgment rates.**

Underwriters develop insurance rates, known as judgment rates, based on their skill and experience. (p. 80)

#129. **c) Policy exclusions.**

The declarations page details who is insured, the coverage amount, when the policy provides coverage, where they are located, and the deductible amount applied to a loss. The exclusions section is a separate part of the policy. (p. 84)

#130. **a) Insuring agreement**

The insuring agreement is an insurance policy section containing the insurance provider's promise to pay, the description of coverage, and the covered perils. (p. 84)

#131. **b) Contract bonds**

A performance bond is a contract bond that guarantees the principal will complete the contract as agreed. (p. 309)

#132. **d) While it is in any residence premises occupied by an insured.**

At an insured's request, insurers can cover the personal property of a residence employee or guest while it is in any residence occupied by an insured. (p. 99)

#133. **b) 30**

There is a 30-day waiting period before coverage is effective, except during the first 30 days after a community enters the regular or emergency programs. (p. 175)

#134. **a) The amount of the third number, $25,000**

Policy limits expressed as 25/50/25 provide $25,000 in coverage for bodily injury per person, with a maximum of $50,000 for all bodily injuries and $25,000 in property damage coverage per accident. (pp. 148, 149-150)

#135. c) As a named perils contract

The Standard Fire Policy can be described as a named perils contract. (p. 167)

#136. a) The description of the obligations and duties of the insured

The section of an insurance policy specifying the procedures or general rules the insured and insurance provider agree to follow under the terms of the policy is called the Conditions. (pp. 84-85)

#137. c) Replacement cost

The cost to replace damaged property with like kind and quality at today's price without deducting any depreciation is known as replacement cost. (p. 86)

#138. a) Consequential loss.

The most prevalent type of consequential loss for individual homeowners is the extra living expense that can be incurred. (p. 77)

#139. c) An insured leased a dwelling for five years. Two years later, the property owner died. The new property owners wanted to make the property their primary residence, so the lease was canceled.

Under Coverage D – Loss of Use, when a covered loss makes part of the residence premises unfit to live in, the insurer will cover the loss of rent and additional living expenses for the shortest time required to replace or repair the damage. HO policies do not cover loss or expense because of the cancellation of a lease. (p. 133)

#140. c) Pro rata basis.

The premium will be returned on a pro rata basis when the ownership of a vessel changes. (p. 299)

#141. a) Home business policy endorsement.

The home business endorsement provides a broader range of coverages than the standard HO policy that includes property and liability coverage commonly found in a commercial insurance policy. (p. 125)

#142. d) A full-time maid

Medical payments on the HO policy cover costs incurred for up to three years after the accident. Coverage does not apply to any insured or a regular resident of the premises, except residence employees not covered by workers compensation. (p. 138)

#143. c) An 80% insurance-to-value requirement is in place

Many insurers felt that BOP insureds were not carrying adequate insurance amounts, so an insurance-to-value provision was added. To collect full replacement cost, the insured must carry insurance equal to at least 80% of the insurable value of the covered property. The insurance-to-value requirement is nearly the same as the homeowners insurance-to-value requirement. (pp. 124, 289)

#144. c) Be decreased by 10%.

The policy owner may apply up to 10% of the dwelling insurance amount (Coverage A) to protect other structures on the insured premises (Coverage B). In the basic form, this is not an additional amount of insurance and will lower the available amount under Coverage A by 10%. (pp. 98-99, 100)

#145. a) An auto used as a company car by a real estate firm

An automobile used as a company car by a real estate firm is not considered mobile equipment under a commercial general liability policy. (pp. 215-216)

#146. **b) Employee theft.**

Employee theft coverage covers loss by theft if committed by the insured's employees. (p. 254)

#147. **d) Fire caused by curing tobacco**

Fire losses resulting from the curing of tobacco are expressly excluded from coverage. (p. 274)

#148. **c) The insurance provider will be reimbursed for the excess costs by the NFIP**

The federal government will not let a WYO flood insurance provider lose money on flood policies. If the premium is not enough to pay for the losses, the insurance providers will be reimbursed for the excess costs by the NFIP. (p. 175)

#149. **c) Comparative negligence.**

In comparative negligence, the amount awarded to the claimant is based upon the defendant's percentage of fault. (p. 72)

#150. **b) Equipment breakdown**

The equipment breakdown form defines covered objects as covered equipment, including high-pressure systems. (p. 259)

FINAL EXAM

This last test will ensure you are ready to pass the licensing exam

You are about to take a California Property and Casualty Final Practice Exam. This exam consists of *150 Questions (plus five to ten non-scored experimental questions)* and is *3 hours and 15 minutes* long. If you do not have enough time to complete this exam right now, it is better to wait until you can fully devote your attention to completing it in the allotted time.

If you score well answering the Final Exam, you can be reasonably certain that you have the knowledge necessary to perform well on the actual test.

Any skipped questions will be graded as incorrect. The following chart breaks down the number of questions in each chapter and by topic.

CHAPTER	# OF QUESTIONS
Basic Insurance Concepts and Principles	7
Contract Law	6
The Insurance Marketplace	8
Basic Legal Concepts – Tort Law	6
Property and Casualty Basics	7
Property and Casualty Policies – General	7
Dwelling Policy	14
Homeowners Policy	12
Homeowners – Section I: Property Coverage	8
Homeowners – Section II: Liability Coverage	8
Personal Auto	14
Other Personal Lines Policies	13
Commercial Coverages	5
Commercial General Liability (CGL)	5
Commercial Auto	5
Other Commercial Coverages	4
Farm	5
Businessowners	4
Ocean Marine	4
Surety Bonds and General Bond Concepts	4
Workers Compensation – General Concepts	4
Total	**150**

To calculate your score, subtract the number of incorrectly answered questions from 150. Take this number and divide it by 150. For example, if you incorrectly answered 60 questions, your score would be 60%, the minimum score needed to pass the exam.

#1. Under the Broad Form (DP-2) policy's falling object peril, which of the following would be covered?

a) Exterior pavement and patio damage
b) Interior damage to the building if the exterior was damaged first
c) Damage to the building's awnings
d) Damage to outdoor television antennas if there is no interior damage

#2. A deliberate act causing harm to another individual, irrespective of whether the harm is intended, is called a/an

a) Tortfeasor.
b) Vicarious tort.
c) Intentional tort.
d) Absolute liability.

#3. All of the following statements concerning coinsurance are true EXCEPT

a) It is used to help equity and adequacy in rates.
b) The insured agrees to maintain insurance equal to some specified percentage of the property's value.
c) If the insurance carried is less than required, the insurance might not cover the entire loss.
d) The coinsurance formula will apply to total losses.

#4. Under which of the following circumstances would the policy provide all risk of loss coverage on the insured property, even though the Standard Fire Policy is a named peril contract?

a) Never
b) Always
c) When the loss is classified as an act of God
d) When the loss is to insured property that must be removed due to endangerment by a covered peril under the policy

#5. Under the dwelling policy, all of the following are other coverages EXCEPT

a) Debris removal.
b) Improvements, additions, and alterations.
c) Earth movement.
d) Other structures.

#6. Which of the following would be covered by a homeowners policy?

a) Structures used to conduct business
b) Fire or lightning
c) Property of tenants
d) Electronic data and paper records

#7. All of the following are true of Coverage B – Other Structures EXCEPT

a) This coverage does not apply to the HO-4 policy form.
b) The amount of coverage provided by Coverage B is an amount that is equal to 10% of Coverage A.
c) Land, where the other structures are located, is not covered.
d) It must be attached by endorsement to a homeowners policy.

#8. In a commercial package policy, which of the following is NOT a component?

a) General liability
b) Inland Marine
c) Professional liability
d) Commercial auto

#9. Which of these is a cancellation procedure in which the returned premium is NOT directly proportionate to the number of days remaining in the policy period?

a) Flat rate
b) Proportional
c) Short rate
d) Pro rata

#10. Insurance is a contract by which a person seeks to protect another individual from

 a) Exposure.
 b) Uncertainty.
 c) Hazards.
 d) Loss.

#11. Which of these would NOT be considered a flood?

 a) Overflow of tidal waters
 b) Mudslides
 c) Runoff of surface waters
 d) Sewer backup

#12. How does the mobile home endorsement affect the other coverage of law or ordinance in a homeowners policy?

 a) It removes the coverage
 b) It broadens the coverage
 c) It limits the coverage
 d) It does not affect this coverage

#13. Stan and Francine each own a 50% interest in a dwelling insured under a standard fire policy issued to Francine to cover her interest in the structure. The amount of insurance is $40,000. Following a $10,000 fire loss to the structure, Francine will receive

 a) $10,000.
 b) $5,000.
 c) $2,500.
 d) Nothing.

#14. While getting into a friend's car, the passenger is injured. Which of these statements would be applicable if the driver and the passenger had medical payments coverage under a personal auto policy?

 a) The driver's policy will act in excess of the passenger's policy
 b) The passenger's policy would be primary
 c) Both policies will share equally in the loss
 d) The driver's policy would be primary

#15. While an insured's covered auto is in the repair shop after damage caused by a collision, the insured would have coverage for which of the following vehicles under a personal auto policy?

 a) Any vehicle not owned by the insured but provided for use while the covered auto is out of regular use due to repair
 b) Any vehicle used by the insured without reasonable belief that the insured is entitled to use such a vehicle
 c) Any auto provided for the insured's regular use but not named on the policy
 d) Any vehicle located inside a racing facility for racing

#16. A wrongful act or the violation of a person's rights that leads to legal liability is called a

 a) Hazard
 b) Peril
 c) Loss
 d) Tort

#17. The claims-made trigger is based on

 a) The date when the claim is first made orally against an insurance provider for damage or injury that occurred after the policy's retroactive date.
 b) The date when the claim is first made orally against an insured for damage or injury that occurred after the policy's retroactive date.
 c) The date when the claim is first made in writing against an insured for damage or injury that occurred on or after the policy's retroactive date.
 d) The date when the claim is first made in writing against an insurance provider for injury or damage that occurred after the policy's retroactive date.

#18. The primary purpose of a surety bond is to

 a) Ensure obligations are fulfilled.
 b) Eliminate the chance of loss.
 c) Secure a line of credit from a contractor.
 d) Pay employer losses.

#19. An insurance company must be fair in underwriting and pay any insured's covered losses. For the faithful execution of these duties, an insurance company has the right to

a) Implement strict guidelines for the initiation of claims against all policies.
b) Accept the payment of premiums for every policy currently in force.
c) Use flexible underwriting standards to exclude higher-risk insureds.
d) Employ all available resources to avoid paying legitimate claims.

#20. An insured deliberately did not disclose a material fact on an insurance application. This would be considered

a) Misrepresentation.
b) Concealment.
c) Coercion.
d) Avoidance.

#21. A business income coverage form would insure all of the following scenarios EXCEPT

a) A replacement part for needed equipment is ordered with overnight delivery charges.
b) The building next door was damaged during a drug bust, and the area is closed off from the public.
c) A construction workers union strike causes the repair of the insured's building to be delayed for some time.
d) A hurricane damages the insured's building; a temporary relocation to another building is required.

#22. Which of these statements does NOT explain what endorsements are?

a) Endorsements have to be signed by an executive officer
b) Endorsements can only add coverage to a current policy, not remove it
c) Endorsements can be added during the policy term
d) Endorsements are printed addenda to a policy

#23. All of the following are TRUE regarding the California Automobile Assigned Risk Plan (CAARP) EXCEPT

a) CAARP was created to provide auto insurance for motorists who cannot purchase coverage in the conventional market because of their driving records or other extraordinary circumstances.
b) Administers the state's assigned risk insurance plan for drivers who cannot buy insurance and is designated by state law as the California Low-Cost Auto Insurance Program administrator.
c) The Federal government has regulatory oversight over the program because of the pilot California Low-Cost Auto Insurance Program.
d) The Plan assigns drivers to private insurance providers based on each insurer's share of the auto insurance market in the state.

#24. Which of the following limits in a policy's Declarations applies to medical expenses?

a) Per injury
b) Per incident
c) Per person
d) Per occurrence

#25. The mobile home endorsement alters the HO policy to cover a mobile home and other structures on land

a) Leased or owned by the resident of the mobile home.
b) Leased or owned by a landlord who does not reside on the premises.
c) Owned by a landlord who does not use the mobile home located on it.
d) Leased by the owner of the land.

#26. All of the following are conditions usually found in the insurance policy EXCEPT

a) Subrogation.
b) Appraisal.
c) Insuring agreement.
d) Cancellation and nonrenewal.

#27. The farm property coverage form covers

a) Losses caused by off-premises power failure.
b) Intentional loss.
c) Mobile agricultural machinery and equipment.
d) Business property while located on the insured premises.

#28. An insured has a standard HO-4 policy with a $30,000 limit of coverage for personal property. While traveling, a fire in her hotel destroys her clothes and luggage. These items have a replacement value of $10,000. Her jewelry also has a replacement value of $10,000. Overlooking any deductible and assuming a depreciation of 20% has occurred in both properties, what amount is the insurance provider required to pay?

a) $11,000
b) $16,000
c) $20,000
d) $30,000

#29. What fundamental principle in property insurance maintains that when there is an unbroken connection between an occurrence and damage arising out of the occurrence, the resulting damage is all a part of the occurrence?

a) Proximate cause
b) Concurrent causation
c) Indemnity
d) Common cause

#30. Under the dwelling policy, if an insured is in the process of moving to a new location, their personal property coverage will apply on a pro rata basis at both locations for

a) 30 days.
b) 60 days.
c) 90 days.
d) 5 days.

#31. All of the following are TRUE regarding the cancellation condition of a businessowners policy EXCEPT

a) The insured can cancel the policy at any time by mailing a written notice of cancellation to the insurer.
b) The insurance provider can only cancel the policy by mailing a written notice to the first named insured.
c) The insurance provider must give the insured advance notice of its cancellation.
d) The insurance provider must provide proof that the insured received the notice.

#32. In dwelling and homeowners policies, which coverage is for indirect losses?

a) Contents
b) Loss of use
c) Dwelling
d) Structures

#33. Standard Fire Policy limits are the maximum amount an insured can collect or for which an insured is protected under the terms of the

a) Insuring agreement.
b) Conditional receipt.
c) Application.
d) Policy.

#34. A dealership reported $500,000 worth of vehicles on its lot at the end of June to its insurance company. On July 10, $200,000 worth of cars were received. By July 20, the auto dealer sold $100,000 worth of vehicles. A hail storm on July 21 caused the inventory $50,000 worth of damage. How much will the insurance company pay for damages without considering any deductibles? (Rounded to the nearest hundred.)

a) $35,700
b) $40,000
c) $41,700
d) $50,000

#35. The party to a surety or fidelity bond promising to fulfill the obligation is the

a) Obligee.
b) Principal.
c) Custodian.
d) Surety.

#36. In most claims-made liability policy forms, a provision that provides a specified period after the policy expiration, during which claims arising out of occurrences during the policy period can be made against the policy at no extra cost, is called

a) Extension of coverage.
b) Supplemental extended reporting period.
c) Grace period.
d) Basic extended reporting period.

#37. A specific coverage part is shown on the declarations page of a commercial package policy, but there is no premium listed. What does that mean?

a) Coverage is automatic
b) There is no coverage
c) Coverage applies without premium
d) This must be a misprint on the form

#38. The building owned by an insured has an actual cash value of $200,000, and the property is insured for $120,000 with an 80% coinsurance clause. A $40,000 loss takes place. How much will the policy pay?

a) $0
b) $30,000
c) $32,000
d) $40,000

#39. An insured's personal liability supplement establishes the amount for all claims arising from a single incident at $100,000. This policy has which type of limit of liability?

a) Split
b) Per occurrence
c) Per person
d) Aggregate

#40. Any individual who claims that they meet the criteria based on a driver's license and driving experience obtained anywhere other than the United States or Canada is presumed to be eligible to obtain a Good Driver Discount policy if that individual has been licensed to drive in the U.S. or Canada and meets the criteria for that period for at least the previous

a) 24 months.
b) 6 months.
c) 12 months.
d) 18 months.

#41. Which of the following types of property would be covered in any of the homeowners coverage forms?

a) Structures rented to others who are not tenants of the dwelling other than a garage
b) Birds, animals, or fish
c) Landlord furnishings in an on-premises apartment
d) Structures used for business purposes

#42. How long is the waiting period after obtaining flood coverage through the National Flood Insurance Program?

a) 10 days
b) 30 days
c) 60 days
d) There is no waiting period

#43. All of the following are supplementary payments found in a commercial general liability (CGL) policy EXCEPT

a) Limited amounts for bail bonds and other bonds concerning a claim.
b) Costs incurred by the insured in hiring a lawyer.
c) All defense costs and expenses incurred by the insurance provider.
d) Reasonable expenses incurred by the insured.

#44. The two types of compensatory damages are

a) Special and general.
b) Pure and speculative.
c) Tort and general.
d) Normal and punitive.

#45. Which of these refers to the process of post-selection?

a) A producer is conducting a second interview with an applicant
b) A producer is completing and submitting an application
c) An insurance provider is investigating the client's risk profile
d) An applicant is choosing an insurance provider

#46. There are over 200 different crops that can be covered under crop insurance policies; however, the eligibility list varies

a) Seasonally.
b) According to weather patterns.
c) Annually.
d) Geographically.

#47. Which of the following individuals can be covered under a farm policy's Coverage J – Medical Payments?

a) Additional insureds
b) Farm workers
c) Resident employees
d) First named insured

#48. The insurer requires that an insured installs a fire alarm and an automatic sprinkler system as a condition for insurance coverage. This stipulation is an example of

a) A business owner common policy rider.
b) Business liability coverage.
c) A protective safeguards condition.
d) A utility services direct damage condition.

#49. Under the HO-4 and HO-6 policy forms, the homeowner's property is insured against

a) Basic form perils.
b) Special form perils.
c) Comprehensive form perils.
d) Broad form perils.

#50. Which of the following would be covered by contract law?

a) A consumer suing the manufacturer for a defective product
b) Neighbors suing each other for trespassing
c) An employer suing an employee for spreading damaging rumors
d) An insured suing the insurance company for failure to provide promised benefits

#51. In both the broad and special form dwelling policies, replacement cost coverage is provided when

a) The amount of insurance on both the dwelling and personal property is at least 80% of its replacement cost when the policy is written.
b) The amount of insurance is at least 90% of the dwelling's replacement cost when the policy is written.
c) The dwelling is insured for 100% of its replacement cost when a loss occurs.
d) The amount of insurance is at least 80% of the dwelling's replacement cost at the time of loss.

#52. All of these are FALSE regarding eligibility to place business through the CAARP EXCEPT

a) Only CAARP-certified agents who have a place of business in the two pilot counties of Los Angeles and San Francisco are eligible.
b) Low-cost automobile insurance is only available through a surplus lines broker.
c) Only CAARP-certified brokers or CAARP-certified agents are authorized to accept applications.
d) Any licensed agents are authorized to accept applications.

#53. Which method of loss valuation is contrary to the fundamental concept of indemnity?

a) Market value
b) Agreed value
c) Replacement cost
d) Functional replacement cost

#54. What is used by individuals to transfer their risk of loss to a larger group?

a) Indemnity
b) Insurance
c) Insurable interest
d) Exposure

#55. The defendant being released on a surety bail bond is known as the

a) Insured.
b) Principal.
c) Surety.
d) Obligee.

#56. Which policy will help an auto dealership cover most of its liability exposures?

a) Motor carrier coverage form
b) A commercial general liability policy with an attached crime endorsement
c) Businessowners policy
d) Garage liability coverage

#57. An insurance producer has been in a sales slump for the last six months. To compensate, the producer offers free health insurance for the first year on every life insurance policy they sell for the next 12 months. This practice is an example of

a) Free insurance as an inducement to purchase real property. It is prohibited by the Insurance Code.
b) An option in a purchase contract that is allowed.
c) A violation of the Insurance Code.
d) Free insurance as an inducement to purchase real property. It is allowed by the Insurance Code.

#58. Under Coverage A in the dwelling policy, which of the following losses would likely NOT be covered?

a) Supplies used to repair the dwelling
b) Theft of a renter's lawnmower used to service the premises
c) Fire damage to building material located on the premises
d) Outdoor personal property of the insured

#59. In equipment breakdown coverage, all accidents would be deemed a single accident if they take place

a) At the same location within 24 hours
b) At the same location within 48 hours
c) At a single location at the same time and from the same cause
d) At every insured location at the same time and from the same cause

#60. Which of the following is NOT an indicator of a competent party?

a) Comprehension of contract
b) Business profession
c) Legal age
d) Mental proficiency

#61. An applicant makes the premium payment on a new insurance policy. If the insured dies, the insurance provider will pay the death benefit to the beneficiary if the policy is approved. What kind of contract is this?

a) Conditional
b) Adhesion
c) Personal
d) Unilateral

#62. Insurance is the transfer of

a) Loss.
b) Hazard.
c) Peril.
d) Risk.

#63. An insured has an auto liability policy with limits of 25/50/15. The insured caused an accident resulting from her negligence. She is legally liable for bodily injuries of three individuals in the other vehicle as follows: "Person A" $15,000, "Person B" $30,000, and "Person C" $35,000. How much will her insurance provider pay in total for all injuries?

a) $105,000
b) $25,000
c) $30,000
d) $50,000

#64. A public official bond is commonly written for what length of term?

a) Biannual
b) Continuous
c) For the term the principal is elected to serve
d) Annual

#65. Which of the following is true for single-family dwellings that are insured to at least 80% of the replacement value?

a) They are subject to a $1,000 deductible
b) They are automatically provided with replacement cost coverage
c) They qualify for maximum compensation under the flood insurance program
d) They are excluded from the flood insurance policy

#66. An insured is an owner and operator of a commercial business. The owner has added a business income coverage form to their commercial package policy. When the insured's business is badly damaged by fire, the business income coverage will pay for

a) Sales value production minus the cost of raw stock.
b) Annual sales minus the cost of the merchandise.
c) Loss of total annual sales.
d) Net income plus continuing expenses of the business.

#67. When are the limits for uninsured motorist coverage set?

a) The limits vary depending on the accident's severity
b) After the first qualifying accident
c) At the time of the first claim
d) When the coverage is purchased

#68. An insured believes that his insurance company needs to be appropriately fulfilling its obligations regarding his policy. What section of the policy will give the insured more information about the specific duties of the insurance company?

a) Obligations
b) Conditions
c) Endorsements
d) Definitions

#69. What term describes the cost and charges associated with the transfer of goods from one location to another?

a) Shipping
b) Freight
c) Transfer
d) Cargo

#70. Loss of yield resulting from which of the following causes would be covered under a Federal Crop Insurance policy?

a) Flood
b) Drought
c) Insect infestation
d) Any of the above

#71. After the loss of one of a pair of golden candlesticks, the contents coverage on a homeowners policy would pay how much?

a) The replacement cost of the pair
b) The actual cash value of the pair
c) Nothing
d) The difference in the actual cash value as a single and as a pair

#72. Which statement is true regarding a mobile equipment endorsement in commercial auto policies?

a) Liability coverage is not offered on equipment that is being towed
b) Mobile equipment is covered by property insurance
c) The endorsement is available for an added premium
d) The endorsement is automatic

#73. When transacting business in California, an insurance provider formed under the laws of another country is known as a/an

a) Admitted insurer.
b) Alien insurer.
c) Domestic insurer.
d) Foreign insurer.

#74. Regardless of the number of accidents or claims made, an insured has a maximum limit of coverage available under her liability policy during a policy year. Her limits are restored on the policy's anniversary date. This insured has what type of limit?

a) Combined single
b) Per occurrence
c) Aggregate
d) Split

#75. The term "proximate cause" refers to which of the following?

a) Reason for filing a lawsuit
b) Negligence that leads to an injury
c) Injury that leads to monetary compensation
d) Duty of the defendant to act

#76. Which of the following is used in the formula for calculating the actual cash value of a property?

a) Replacement cost
b) Stated value
c) Fair market value
d) Agreed value

#77. Which organization has the primary responsibility forms for the standard market?

a) The Insurance Services Office
b) The Office of Financial Services
c) The National Association of Insurance Commissioners
d) The Governor's Office

#78. According to the HO policy's appraisal condition, what procedure can be followed if the insured and insurance provider disagree on the size of a loss?

a) The policyholder can hire an appraiser, and the insurance provider will pay the amount determined
b) Either party can make a written request for an appraisal
c) The insured must accept what the insurance provider is willing to pay
d) The parties must pursue a lawsuit

#79. While it is executing a seizure order, what are the consequences of a failure to comply with the Commissioner's office?

a) It is a misdemeanor punishable by one-year imprisonment, a fine of $1,000, or both
b) It can become grounds for license revocation and termination of all agency contracts
c) It is a felony and is punishable by a 5-year imprisonment and restitution to victims consistent with damages claimed
d) It would be deemed an obstruction of justice and is subject to a fine of $5,000 per day

#80. A neighbor's tree has fallen into the insured's yard. The insured's homeowners policy will only cover the expense of removing the tree if

a) The damage is more than $1,000.
b) The neighbor has no homeowners insurance.
c) The tree damaged the insured's vehicle.
d) The tree is blocking the driveway.

#81. Which of the following claims does NOT fall under the purview of liability coverage of Section II of a homeowners policy?

a) The named insured borrows a friend's coat which later becomes damaged
b) The named insured's 7-year-old son throws a rock and hits a neighbor's child, breaking her glasses and cutting her face
c) The named insured's dog bites the neighbor, tearing her clothes and causing her to be treated by a doctor
d) A visitor slips on some ice, causing her to be injured when falling down the porch steps

#82. An annual transit policy is written on a/an

a) Automatic basis.
b) Named peril basis.
c) Temporary basis.
d) Open-peril basis.

#83. When a parent must pay for damages caused by their children, this illustrates

a) Vicarious liability.
b) Strict liability.
c) Intervening cause.
d) Assumption of risk.

#84. A structure that is not inhabited and stores no property is considered

a) Empty.
b) Derelict.
c) Vacant.
d) Unoccupied.

#85. All of these are considerations in determining which state's law applies when a worker must travel into another state and is injured while working in the other state EXCEPT

a) The location where the accident took place.
b) The regular place of employment where the employee works.
c) The state where the employee was hired.
d) The insurer's chartered location or domicile.

#86. Which of the following provisions is typically found in homeowners policies and provides a replacement cost settlement to policyholders who carry adequate insurance?

a) Coinsurance
b) Actual cash value
c) Pro rata
d) Insurance to value

#87. A person obtained a personal property insurance policy on their newly purchased dream home. This type of insurance coverage that applies to the insured's own property is called

a) Personal lines coverage.
b) Commercial risk protection.
c) Third-party coverage protection.
d) First-party risk protection.

#88. Following a loss, an insured covered by business property coverage is NOT required to

a) Resume operating the business as soon as possible.
b) Send the insurance provider a sworn proof of loss within 60 days.
c) Take all reasonable steps to protect property from additional damage.
d) Reconstruct a timeline of activities leading up to the loss for the insurance provider to use in an investigation.

#89. A small appliance manufacturer in California provides products around the world. A customer in Sweden is injured using one of its products. When the appliance manufacturer is found liable for the damages, why would its commercial general liability (CGL) policy pay the customer's claim for bodily injury?

a) The appliance manufacturer is negligent
b) The appliance was made in the U.S.
c) The commercial general liability policy extends rights to Sweden
d) The appliance manufacturer did not have a permit to sell internationally

#90. Under a dwelling policy, within the first 60 days of coverage, how much notice is required to cancel a policy?

a) 5 days
b) 10 days
c) 15 days
d) 20 days

#91. When rating workers compensation insurance, all of these are factors EXCEPT

a) Payroll.
b) Loss experience.
c) Job classification.
d) Sales.

#92. When does a binder expire?

a) When an original policy is replaced
b) No later than 30 days
c) As soon as the policy is issued
d) After ten days

#93. If other valid insurance is written on the same risk, which provision defines how the policy will respond?

a) Over-insurance
b) Concurrent coverage
c) Other insurance
d) Coinsurance

#94. An insured works outside the home. The insured's brother lives with her and cares for her four children. When the insured's home is badly damaged by fire, the family moves into an apartment while repairs are being done. The largest apartment available in the area has two bedrooms, so the insured's brother has to stay at a hotel. How much will the HO-3 form cover for these additional living expenses?

a) The expense of renting an apartment, and 50% of the expense of the hotel
b) Nothing
c) All of the cost up to the Coverage D limit
d) The expense of renting an apartment, but not the expense of the hotel room

#95. Which amount is calculated by subtracting depreciation from the replacement cost of a covered item?

a) Pro rata percentage
b) Actual cash value
c) Interest of the insured
d) Repair cost

#96. An apartment occupant's personal property would be insured under which HO form?

a) Broad form (HO-2)
b) Unit-owners form (HO-6)
c) Tenant broad form (HO-4)
d) Comprehensive form (HO-5)

#97. Insureds covered under a mobile home endorsement move their mobile home to prevent it from being damaged by a fire. What is the maximum amount of coverage provided by the policy?

a) $350
b) $500
c) $1,000
d) $5,000

#98. How does insurance allocate the financial consequences of individual losses?

a) It transfers the risk to a small number of insured individuals
b) It transfers the risk to all insured individuals
c) It retains the financial consequences
d) It transfers the risk to the insured's associates

#99. An insured is involved in a car accident in another state. The state has a financial responsibility law that specifies limits of liability higher than those listed in the Declarations. What amount will the insured's policy pay?

a) Higher limits
b) Lower limits
c) The insurance provider will not pay for accidents that occur out-of-state
d) Only the limits stated in the policy

#100. To have an insurable interest in the individual or property covered by a property insurance policy, which potential risk must the policy owner face?

a) Property damage
b) Illness
c) Financial loss
d) Physical injury

#101. Assuming the insurer and insured agree on the amount payable for a loss covered under a dwelling policy, how soon after the insurer has received proof of loss must it make payment?

a) 30 days
b) 45 days
c) 60 days
d) 90 days

#102. The potential client must take the initiative and respond to an advertisement through a mail or telephone contact with the insurance company in which distribution system?

a) Direct response system
b) Managing general agent system
c) Home service system
d) Direct agency system

#103. Bobby's neighbor will not stop parking his motorcycle in Bobby's rose garden after repeated attempts by Bobby to ask his neighbor to quit parking there. Bobby obtains a court order requiring the neighbor to stop parking on his property. It turns out that Bobby was mistaken since it was his neighbor's property all along. What bond did Bobby have to post, guaranteeing that his neighbor would pay damages in this wrongful action?

a) Bail
b) Cost
c) Injunction
d) Attachment

#104. The New York Standard Fire Policy has a "Standard" classification because

a) The rates charged for coverage are identical in each state.
b) The policy conditions are identical in each state.
c) The policy's inception and expiration time are based upon the "standard" time.
d) All of the above.

#105. According to the Nationwide Marine definitions, risks that can be the subject of inland marine insurance include all of the following EXCEPT

a) Large pleasure boats.
b) Property while stored at a warehouse.
c) Shipments made by a freight train.
d) Cargo transported by truck.

#106. The American Institute's Hull Clause for the Return of Premium will be applied if a vessel has been laid up in port, not under repair, and not used for storage. The premium will be returned for

a) Each 30-day period.
b) The first 10 days only.
c) The first 30 days only.
d) Each 10-day period.

#107. Businessowners liability coverage automatically includes all of the following liability coverages EXCEPT

a) Contractual.
b) Host liquor.
c) Product.
d) Pollution.

#108. Before paying a claimant under a professional liability policy, the insurance company must

a) Provide legal counsel to the claimant.
b) Reaffirm the claimant's insurance.
c) Obtain the consent of the insured.
d) Terminate the insured's policy.

#109. In an insurance contract, which of the following individuals would qualify as a competent party?

a) The applicant is drunk at the time of application
b) The applicant is a 13-year-old student
c) The applicant is under the influence of a mind-impairing drug at the time of application
d) The applicant has a prior felony conviction

#110. Which of the following is true concerning inspection and surveys as a common policy condition in a commercial policy?

a) It does not allow findings to be used for establishing premium charges
b) It grants the insurance provider the right to inspect issued insurance
c) It does not allow insurance providers to make recommendations
d) It requires the insurance provider to conduct an inspection at least once during the policy period

#111. Under a homeowners policy, which of these would NOT be considered an insured?

a) Residents of the household who are the insured's blood relatives
b) A person under age 21 in the care of but not related to the insured
c) Individuals named in the policy Declarations
d) A divorced spouse residing in another state

#112. All of the following are special personal property limits under a homeowners policy EXCEPT

a) $500 for business personal property on the insured premises.
b) $1,500 for securities, deeds, accounts, and evidence of debt.
c) $1,500 for trailers not used with watercraft.
d) $2,500 for the theft of firearms.

#113. Which of these is included under the physical damage coverage of a personal auto policy?

a) A cell phone located inside a locked vehicle
b) Custom furnishings or equipment in a van or pickup
c) Sound reproduction equipment permanently installed in the insured auto
d) An insured auto that is seized and destroyed by a government authority

#114. Under a Commercial Crime coverage form, after a covered loss, the insured is required to submit written proof of loss within

a) 60 days.
b) 90 days.
c) 120 days.
d) One year.

#115. A large antenna is damaged when a large tree branch hits an insured farm dwelling during a storm. The Farm Property – Coverage A form would insure damages for this occurrence up to

a) $1,000.
b) $2,000.
c) $3,000.
d) $4,000.

#116. All of the following statements are FALSE concerning garage physical damage coverage EXCEPT

a) Specific causes-of-loss coverage is not available for physical damage coverage.
b) Insurers will not cover any auto stored for more than 45 days at a location not listed in the Declarations.
c) Collision coverage is only provided for dealers.
d) Autos held for sale by a dealer are individually listed in the policy.

#117. When an applicant submits the initial premium with an application, which action demonstrates acceptance?

a) The applicant provides a statement of good health
b) The agent delivers the policy
c) The insurer receives the application and initial premium
d) The underwriters approve the application

#118. A property and casualty producer has been licensed for seven years. How many continuing education hours must the producer complete during this licensing period?

a) 30
b) 24
c) 15
d) 0

#119. An insured with a homeowners policy must be a member of her neighborhood's homeowners association. The association's community house has burned down, and the insured has been assessed $1,200 for her share of the rebuilding cost. How much of the assessment will her HO policy pay?

a) None
b) $500
c) $1,000
d) $1,200

#120. A personal auto policy would be considered excess coverage when an insured

a) Buys a car and is involved in an accident less than 30 days later.
b) Pays more for collision coverage than the car is worth.
c) Has another auto policy, and the car is involved in an accident.
d) Leaves the car in a parking garage, and the car is involved in an accident.

#121. An insured's uninsured motorist coverage would NOT cover which of these?

a) A neighbor borrowed the insured's car and was hit by an uninsured motorist
b) The insured's car is hit by someone with an insolvent auto insurer
c) A hit-and-run driver strikes the insured's daughter
d) The insured causes a collision with an uninsured motorist's car

#122. Which of the following special liability coverages will protect managers of a corporation from claims arising from a wrongful act committed by the manager while serving in an official capacity?

a) Directors and officers liability
b) Employment practices liability
c) Errors and omissions insurance
d) Malpractice insurance

#123. In personal auto policies, the term "you" refers to

a) The named insured.
b) Any individual injured in a covered accident.
c) Any individual reading the policy.
d) The insurance provider.

#124. A commercial property special form covers property in transit up to

a) Full replacement cost.
b) $5,000.
c) ACV.
d) $500.

#125. In the basic form dwelling policy, which of these other coverages is NOT included?

a) Breakage of glass
b) Removal coverage
c) Personal property temporarily away from the insured premises
d) A tenant's improvements, additions, and alterations

#126. Which of the following homeowners forms is intended for individuals that own and live in a condominium?

a) HO-4
b) HO-6
c) HO-2
d) HO-3

#127. Barry invites his coworkers out for an afternoon on the water in his motorboat powered with a 150hp outboard. While docking the boat, his coworker's hand is broken when caught between the boat and the dock. What coverage would apply to the coworker's broken hand?

a) Section II – Personal Liability of Barry's HO policy
b) Barry's Boatowners policy is the primary coverage; if its limits are too low, his HO liability will pay as the excess coverage
c) Barry's Boatowners policy
d) Barry's Outboard Boat and Motor policy

#128. Which of these would NOT be considered personal property for insurance purposes?

a) Equipment
b) Furniture
c) A house
d) A vehicle

#129. A contract in which one party attempts to indemnify another against loss is called

a) Adverse Selection.
b) Risk.
c) Indemnity.
d) Insurance.

#130. How soon does the period of restoration for business income coverage start after the direct loss?

a) Immediately
b) 24 hours
c) 48 hours
d) 72 hours

#131. An individual's construction company leaves construction machinery and mobile equipment on the job site until the project is completed. What could this person use to insure it?

a) Bailee's customers form
b) Builders risk form
c) General property form
d) Contractors equipment floater

#132. An insurance contract requires that both the insurance provider and the insured meet certain conditions for the contract to be enforceable. What characteristic of the contract does this describe?

a) Conditional
b) Contingent
c) Aleatory
d) Unilateral

#133. Which HO policy coverage will respond if a claim is made or a lawsuit is brought against an insured for damages resulting from bodily injury or property damage caused by an event to which the coverage applies?

a) Coverage C – Personal Property
b) Coverage D – Loss of Use
c) Coverage E – Personal Liability
d) Coverage F – Medical Payments to Others

#134. In Section II of an insured's HO policy, which of these would NOT be covered by medical payments to others?

a) An insured is walking their neighbor's dog, and it bites someone
b) An insured allows the neighborhood kids to play flag football in their yard, and one is injured
c) An insured who cuts their leg while whacking weeds in their backyard with their neighbor's weed whacker
d) An insured's nanny falls while walking down the insured's steps

#135. An insured can cancel the policy

a) Only at the time of renewal.
b) By mailing the insurer a written notice of cancellation at any time.
c) At any time with a 10-day advanced written notice to the insurer.
d) Only after the policy has been effective for 120 days.

#136. What is another term that is used to refer to unintentional torts?

a) Hazard
b) Peril
c) Breach of contract
d) Negligence

#137. Under Coverage D (Loss of Use) in a homeowners policy, the amount an insurer will pay depends on

a) The length of time a dwelling has been occupied.
b) If the dwelling is rented out or owner-occupied.
c) How long the dwelling is uninhabitable.
d) The amount of the loss of rent and additional living expenses.

#138. Which of the following is a unit of measurement an underwriter uses when calculating the premium rates for insurance?

a) Hazard
b) Risk
c) Exposure
d) Loss

#139. The insured's car was hit and damaged by a deer. In a personal auto policy, under which of the following coverages would this loss be paid?

a) Liability
b) Uninsured motorist
c) Collision
d) Other-than-collision

#140. Under the Inside the Premises – Robbery or Safe Burglary of Other Property coverage, which would NOT be covered?

a) Two individuals break a window during an attempted robbery
b) Someone breaks in after business hours, pries open a safe, and steals several valuable paintings
c) A jewelry store clerk is forced into the storage room and locked in by an intruder while they steal high-value merchandise
d) An employee is caught stealing from the cash register

#141. Under the dwelling policy special form Coverage A – Dwelling, what type of property would NOT be covered?

a) Outdoor equipment located on the premises and used to service the location
b) Attached structures
c) Land on which the dwelling is located
d) Supplies and materials on the premises used to repair or alter the dwelling

#142. If the insured owns a Rolex watch valued at $10,000, full coverage can be provided on a homeowners policy by obtaining the

a) Scheduled personal property endorsement.
b) Special limits of liability endorsement.
c) Personal property replacement cost endorsement.
d) Blanket personal property endorsement.

#143. An insurer is domiciled in Wyoming and transacts insurance in Montana. Which term best describes the insurance provider's classification in Montana?

a) Unauthorized
b) Foreign
c) Alien
d) Domestic

#144. Workers compensation laws offer all of the following types of benefits EXCEPT

a) Disability benefits.
b) Death benefits.
c) Compensatory benefits.
d) Medical benefits.

#145. All of the following are optional coverages that can be added to a Garage Policy EXCEPT

a) Fire Legal liability.
b) Incidental Medical malpractice.
c) Owned Watercraft liability.
d) Personal and Advertising Injury.

#146. Increased value and excess liability clauses function like which of the following policies?

a) Umbrella
b) Professional liability
c) Cargo
d) Errors and omissions

#147. An insured's business is damaged because of a fire, and she is forced to close the business for repairs temporarily. As a result, the insured lost income. This scenario is considered what type of loss?

a) Special
b) Additional
c) Consequential
d) Direct

#148. Cargo is damaged short of its destination. An insurance company agent at an immediate port sells the damaged cargo at the best price. Settlement is based on the difference between the net sales proceeds and the insured value. This settlement is considered

a) A particular average.
b) A salvage loss.
c) Sue and labor.
d) A general average.

#149. Employment practices liability insurance (EPLI) will NOT cover claims arising from

a) Discrimination.
b) Deliberate law violation.
c) Sexual harassment.
d) Wrongful termination.

#150. Which contract element best describes insurance written in support of public policy?

a) Consideration
b) Offer and acceptance
c) Competent parties
d) Legal purpose

Final Exam Answers

#1. **b) Interior damage to the building if the exterior was damaged first**

Damage to the interior of the building is only covered if the exterior has been damaged first. (p. 95)

#2. **c) Intentional tort.**

An intentional tort refers to a deliberate (or intentional) act that causes harm to another individual. (p. 14)

#3. **d) The coinsurance formula will apply to total losses.**

In the event of a total loss, the coinsurance clause is not applicable, and the face amount of the policy is paid. (pp. 198-199)

#4. **d) When the loss is to insured property that must be removed due to endangerment by a covered peril under the policy**

Property removed to protect against a possible loss resulting from a peril covered by the policy is insured for five days at another location for practically any type of loss. (p. 166)

#5. **c) Earth movement.**

In the other coverages of the dwelling policy, earth movement is excluded. (pp. 85, 100-101, 102)

#6. **b) Fire or lightning**

Fire and lightning are included in the basic perils of almost all HO policies. (pp. 116, 117)

#7. **d) It must be attached by endorsement to a homeowners policy.**

HO policies automatically provide an insurance amount in Coverage B equal to 10% of the amount written in Coverage A. This amount of coverage can be increased by endorsement. (p. 131)

#8. **c) Professional liability**

Professional liability is not a component of a commercial package policy. Answers A, B, and D are components of a Commercial Package Policy (CPP). (p. 187)

#9. **c) Short rate**

Short-rate cancellation is a cancellation procedure where the premium returned to the insured is not directly proportionate to the number of days remaining in the policy period. (p. 79)

#10. **d) Loss.**

Insurance will protect an individual, entity, or business from loss. (pp. 2, 3)

#11. **d) Sewer backup**

As defined by the National Flood Insurance Program, a flood does not include sewer backup. (p. 175)

#12. **a) It removes the coverage**

The mobile home endorsement alters the homeowners policy to cover a mobile home and other structures on land leased or owned by the mobile home resident. The additional coverage of law or ordinance is removed. (p. 122)

#13. **b) $5,000.**

Since Francine's interest in the property is 50%, she will receive an amount equal to 50% of the loss. (pp. 167-168)

#14. **d) The driver's policy would be primary**

Under a PAP, medical payments coverage would pay all essential medical and funeral expenses incurred and services rendered to the insured or the insured's passengers, regardless of fault. (pp. 146-147, 150-151)

#15. **a) Any vehicle not owned by the insured but provided for use while the covered auto is out of regular use due to repair**

The personal auto policy covers any auto or trailer not owned by an insured while used as a temporary substitute for any other vehicle listed in the policy that is out of regular use due to breakdown, destruction, loss, servicing, or repair. (pp. 144-145)

#16. **d) Tort**

A tort is a wrongful act or the violation of a person's rights that leads to legal liability. (p. 14)

#17. **c) The date when the claim is first made in writing against an insured for damage or injury that occurred on or after the policy's retroactive date.**

A claims-made trigger is based on the date the claim was made in writing for damage or injury that occurred on or after the policy's retroactive date. (pp. 222-225)

#18. **a) Ensure obligations are fulfilled.**

A surety bond guarantees that the principal will carry out all debts and obligations. (p. 308)

#19. **b) Accept the payment of premiums for every policy currently in force.**

An insurer can accept premiums for policies that have been underwritten fairly and for which covered losses are paid. (p. 14)

#20. **b) Concealment.**

Concealment is intentionally withholding information about a material fact that is important to make a decision. In insurance, concealment refers to withholding information that will result in an imprecise underwriting decision. (p. 17)

#21. **c) A construction workers union strike causes the repair of the insured's building to be delayed for some time.**

The business income form excludes coverage for the following: finished stock exclusion, off-premises services interruption, delay caused by the interference of strikers, antenna exclusion, and loss of privilege. (pp. 194-196)

#22. **b) Endorsements can only add coverage to a current policy, not remove it**

Policy owners can use endorsements to add or delete coverage from an existing policy and make corrections to items. (pp. 18, 85)

#23. **c) The Federal government has regulatory oversight over the program because of the pilot California Low-Cost Auto Insurance Program.**

CDI maintains regulatory oversight over the California Automobile Assigned Risk Plan (CAARP). (pp. 160-161)

#24. **c) Per person**

A combined single limit of insurance applies for all property damage and bodily injury losses that arise from a single occurrence. Medical expenses are limited to the per person-limit listed in the Declarations. (pp. 147-148)

#25. **a) Leased or owned by the resident of the mobile home.**

The mobile home endorsement alters the HO policy to cover a mobile home and other structures on land leased or owned by the mobile home's resident. (p. 122)

#26. **c) Insuring agreement.**

The insuring agreement furnishes information on the policy's coverages. Conditions specify the legal obligations and duties of the parties to the contract. (pp. 84, 103)

#27. **d) Business property while located on the insured premises.**

The farm coverage form (Coverage C – Household Personal Property) applies to personal property owned by an insured when the property is located on the covered premises. It includes $2,500 for loss of business property while on the premises. (pp. 270-271)

#28. **b) $16,000**

This loss would be settled on an ACV basis: $20,000 total for the loss minus $4,000 for depreciation. The limitation on the loss of jewelry only applies to the peril of theft. (p. 119)

#29. **a) Proximate cause**

Proximate cause is an act or event deemed a natural and reasonably foreseeable cause of the damage or occurrence that occurs and damages property or injures a plaintiff. (pp. 70-71)

#30. **a) 30 days.**

Property moved to a newly acquired residence will be covered for 30 days. The limit specified in the Declarations will apply proportionally to each residence. Coverage will not extend beyond the policy's expiration date. (p. 99)

#31. **d) The insurance provider must provide proof that the insured received the notice.**

In a businessowners policy, the insurance provider only has to prove that the notice was mailed to the address on file, not that the insured received the notice. (pp. 293-294)

#32. **b) Loss of use**

Loss of use coverage only applies after an indirect loss caused by a covered peril has occurred. (pp. 100, 130, 133)

#33. **d) Policy.**

Standard Fire Policy limits are the maximum amount an insured can collect or for which an insured is protected under the policy's terms. (pp. 167-168)

#34. **c) $41,700**

Inventory at the time of the damage was greater than the reported inventory at the end of the prior month. The insurance provider will pay only a portion of the total damages. Reported inventory = $500,000 + $200,000 = $700,000. $700,000 - $100,000 worth of cars sold = $600,000. Therefore, the insurance provider will pay $50,000 X 5/6 = $41,667 (or $41,700 rounded up). (pp. 243-244)

#35. **b) Principal.**

The principal obtains the bond and promises to perform. (p. 308)

#36. **d) Basic extended reporting period.**

The ISO commercial general liability claims-made form provides an additional 60 days to report claims at no extra cost. (p. 224)

#37. **b) There is no coverage**

In the Declarations of a commercial package policy, if no premium amount is listed, there is no coverage for that component. (p. 188)

#38. **b) $30,000**

The insured only carried $120,000 of the agreed $160,000 (75% of the insurance amount they agreed to carry), so the insurance provider will pay only 75% of the loss, or $30,000. (p. 198)

#39. **b) Per occurrence**

Policy owners can add the personal liability supplement to the dwelling policy. A basic limit of $100,000 per occurrence applies to personal liability coverage. (p. 108)

#40. **d) 18 months.**

Along with meeting the criteria, insureds must have been licensed to drive in the U.S. or Canada for at least the prior 18 months. (p. 147)

#41. **c) Landlord furnishings in an on-premises apartment**

On the HO-5 form, landlord furnishings in an on-premises apartment are insured for up to $2,500. (p. 114)

#42. **b) 30 days**

Upon purchasing a flood policy, a 30-day waiting period is in place starting from the time of application and premium payment. (p. 175)

#43. **b) Costs incurred by the insured in hiring a lawyer.**

Supplemental payments are the amounts the insurer will pay in addition to the stated policy limits. A CGL policy will pay for court costs taxed against the policy owner, except attorney's fees or expenses. (p. 219)

#44. **a) Special and general.**

Special and general damages are two classes of compensatory damages that can be awarded. (pp. 71-72)

#45. **c) An insurance provider is investigating the client's risk profile**

The process of post-selection involves investigating the client's risk profile. After reviewing the legally available information, the underwriters will evaluate and rate the risks. (pp. 46-47)

#46. **d) Geographically.**

Under crop insurance policies, insurers can cover over 200 different crops; however, the eligibility list varies based on geography. (p. 277)

#47. **c) Resident employees**

Farm employees are excluded from this coverage. However, resident employees are included. Also, this coverage applies only to individuals who are not insureds. (p. 272)

#48. **c) A protective safeguards condition.**

The protective safeguards endorsement adds a policy condition requiring the insured to maintain protective safeguards (fire alarm, automatic sprinkler system, etc.) as a condition for coverage. (p. 263)

#49. **d) Broad form perils.**

The HO-4 and HO-6 forms provide the same level of coverage as Coverage C in the HO-2 and HO-3 forms. (p. 117)

#50. **d) An insured suing the insurance company for failure to provide promised benefits**

The insurance provider's failure to deliver the benefits promised to the insured would be in breach of contract and covered by contract law. (p. 14)

#51. **d) The amount of insurance is at least 80% of the dwelling's replacement cost at the time of loss.**

It is always a requirement on property forms that provide replacement cost coverage that insurance on the dwelling be at least 80% of its replacement cost when the time of loss occurred. (pp. 86, 104)

#52. **c) Only CAARP-certified brokers or CAARP-certified agents are authorized to accept applications.**

Only CAARP-certified brokers or CAARP-certified agents are authorized to accept applications for the low-cost auto insurance policy. (p. 161)

#53. **c) Replacement cost**

Contrary to the basic concept of indemnity is the replacement cost method of loss valuation. After a loss, it can provide the insured with a settlement exceeding the actual cash value of the property. (p. 86)

#54. **b) Insurance**

Insurance is the mechanism through which an insured is protected against loss by peril or specified future contingency in return for the current premium payment. (p. 2)

#55. **b) Principal.**

The defendant promised to show up in court at the designated time. The principal makes a promise to perform. (p. 309)

#56. **d) Garage liability coverage**

The garage liability coverage form protects the insured's autos, premises, products, and work performed. (pp. 240-241)

#57. **c) A violation of the Insurance Code.**

It is illegal for any insurance licensee to offer free insurance as an incentive to transact some other type of business. (p. 35)

#58. **b) Theft of a renter's lawnmower used to service the premises**

Coverage A on the dwelling insures all attached structures and outdoor personal property or equipment used to service or maintain the premises if not covered elsewhere. (p. 98)

#59. **c) At a single location at the same time and from the same cause**

If an accident results in other accidents, all related accidents will be treated as one accident. All accidents taking place at a single location at the same time having the same cause will be considered one accident. (p. 259)

#60. **b) Business profession**

Competent parties to a contract must be mentally competent, of legal age, clearly understand the contract, and not be under the influence of alcohol or drugs. (p. 14)

#61. **a) Conditional**

A conditional contract requires that certain conditions be met by the insured and the insurer for the contract to be executed and before each party fulfills its obligations. (p. 15)

#62. **d) Risk.**

Insurance transfers the financial responsibility associated with a potential loss (risk) to an insurer. (pp. 2, 4)

#63. **d) $50,000**

The first limit shown is the most the policy will cover for injuries to any individual. The second limit is the most the policy will cover for all injuries if more than one individual is injured in a single accident. The third limit is the most the policy will cover for property damage caused by a single accident. (pp. 148, 149-150)

#64. **c) For the term the principal is elected to serve**

A public official bond is commonly written for the term of public office the principal is elected to serve. (p. 309)

#65. **b) They are automatically provided with replacement cost coverage**

Single-family dwellings are automatically provided with replacement cost coverage if they are insured to at least 80% of the replacement value or the maximum allowed under the regular flood insurance program. (p. 176)

#66. **d) Net income plus continuing expenses of the business.**

If a covered loss occurs, the business income coverage will pay those profits that would have been earned if no loss had occurred. It also pays the business's expenses, even though it is not operating. (pp. 194-196)

#67. **d) When the coverage is purchased**

The limits for uninsured motorist coverage are established at the purchase of the policy. (p. 152)

#68. **b) Conditions**

The conditions section of an insurance policy explains the obligations of the insured and the insurance provider concerning the policy. (pp. 84-85)

#69. **b) Freight**

The term freight describes the cost and charges associated with shipping cargo from place to place. The term freight insurance describes the indirect loss that an insured would sustain if insured cargo is damaged or lost. (p. 305)

#70. **d) Any of the above**

Under Federal Crop Insurance, nearly every unavoidable cause of loss for most field crops is insured. (p. 279)

#71. **d) The difference in the actual cash value as a single and as a pair**

Under the pair or set clause, insurers can restore the set to its value before the loss. It could also pay the difference between the property's actual cash value before and after the loss. (pp. 104, 120)

#72. **c) The endorsement is available for an added premium**

The mobile equipment endorsement will provide auto coverage to mobile equipment after paying an additional premium. (pp. 232, 238)

#73. **b) Alien insurer.**

An alien insurer is an insurance company formed under the laws of another country. (p. 43)

#74. **c) Aggregate**

The maximum limit of coverage available under a liability policy during a policy year, regardless of the number of accidents that occur or the number of claims made, is known as the aggregate limit. (p. 148)

#75. **b) Negligence that leads to an injury**

Proximate cause is the reasonably foreseeable event or act that causes injury or damage. Negligence can often be the proximate cause of the damage; without it, the accident would not have occurred. This concept is also called direct liability. (pp. 70-71)

#76. **a) Replacement cost**

Replacement cost refers to replacing the damaged property with like kind and quality at today's current price, without deducting any depreciation. (p. 86)

#77. **a) The Insurance Services Office**

The advisory organization that develops forms for the standard market is called the Insurance Services Office (ISO). (p. 76)

#78. **b) Either party can make a written request for an appraisal**

Either party can make a written request for an appraisal if the insured and the insurer cannot reach an agreement. (p. 119)

#79. **a) It is a misdemeanor punishable by one-year imprisonment, a fine of $1,000, or both**

Such a misdemeanor could be punishable by a maximum fine of $1,000, imprisonment for no longer than one year, or both. (p. 51)

#80. **d) The tree is blocking the driveway.**

An insured's HO policy will pay up to $1,000 to remove a tree from the premises if a neighbor's tree falls due to a covered peril or the fallen tree blocks a handicapped ramp or driveway. (pp. 133-134)

#81. **a) The named insured borrows a friend's coat which later becomes damaged**

Damage to the property of others in the custody, care, or control of the insured does not fall under the scope of liability coverage in Section II of a homeowners policy. It is additional coverage that can be added for an extra premium. (p. 139)

#82. **b) Named peril basis.**

Annual transit policies are used by businesses that ship goods regularly. Coverage can be issued for various types of shipments. These policies are written on a named peril basis. (p. 169)

#83. **a) Vicarious liability.**

In some jurisdictions, parents may be held vicariously liable for their children's negligent acts, and employers can be held liable for their employees' actions. (p. 71)

#84. **c) Vacant.**

For insurance coverage purposes, a structure is considered vacant if no person uses the building for the storage of property or personal or work-related reasons. (p. 78)

#85. **d) The insurer's chartered location or domicile.**

The insurance provider's location is irrelevant to processing workers compensation claims. (pp. 317, 319)

#86. **d) Insurance to value**

The Insurance to Value provision in a homeowners policy provides a replacement cost settlement, provided the policyholder carries adequate insurance. (p. 198)

#87. **d) First-party risk protection.**

First-party risk protection refers to insurance coverage that applies to the insured's own property or person. (p. 80)

#88. **d) Reconstruct a timeline of activities leading up to the loss for the insurance provider to use in an investigation.**

The insured must describe when, how, and where the loss or damage occurred. There is no demand for a timeline leading up to the loss. (pp. 288-289)

#89. **b) The appliance was made in the U.S.**

Coverage territory refers to anywhere in the world if injury or damage results from goods manufactured in a coverage territory. (pp. 214, 215)

#90. **b) 10 days**

Regardless of the reason, if a policy is canceled within the first 60 days, only ten days' advance notice is required. (p. 105)

#91. **d) Sales.**

The amount of payroll, the hazard of the work, and the employer's prior loss experience are all rating factors. (p. 314)

#92. **c) As soon as the policy is issued**

Binders expire when the policy is issued. The period for a binder varies from insurer to insurer. (p. 37)

#93. **c) Other insurance**

In an insurance policy, other insurance is a provision that defines how the policy will respond if there is other valid insurance written on the same risk. (pp. 104, 119)

#94. **c) All of the cost up to the Coverage D limit**

Coverage D pays the expenses to maintain the same lifestyle as before the loss. (p. 133)

#95. **b) Actual cash value**

A property's actual cash value is the replacement cost of that property minus depreciation. (p. 86)

#96. **c) Tenant broad form (HO-4)**

An apartment dweller uses the HO-4 form (tenant broad form). It insures the policyholder's property and does not cover the apartment. (p. 114)

#97. **b) $500**

A mobile home endorsement will cover up to $500 if the insured moves the mobile home to a safer area to protect it from loss by a covered peril. (p. 122)

#98. **b) It transfers the risk to all insured individuals**

Insurance is defined as transferring the possibility of loss (risk) to an insurer, which spreads the costs of unexpected losses to many individuals. In most cases, only a small number of insureds will suffer a loss. Insurance redistributes the financial consequences of individual losses to every insured person. (pp. 2, 4)

#99. **a) Higher limits**

If the state has a financial responsibility law specifying limits of liability that are higher than the limits shown in the Declarations, the insured's policy will provide the higher specified limits. (p. 150)

#100. **c) Financial loss**

To obtain insurance, the policy owner must face the possibility of financial loss in the event of a loss. This concept is known as insurable interest. In property and casualty insurance, insurable interest has to exist at the time of loss. (p. 6)

#101. **c) 60 days**

Losses will be paid within 60 days of receiving a signed, sworn proof of loss and reaching an agreement with the policy owner regarding the amount payable. (p. 105)

#102. **a) Direct response system**

The term direct response refers to the necessity of the potential client to take the initiative and respond to the advertisement through a mail or telephone contact with the insurance provider as directed in the ad. (p. 22)

#103. **c) Injunction**

Injunction bonds guarantee that if the injunction should not have been issued, damages will be paid to the injured party. (p. 309)

#104. **b) The policy conditions are identical in each state.**

The New York Standard Fire Policy includes the same 165 lines of policy conditions irrespective of the state of issuance. Every state will add endorsements to the contract to conform to that state's requirements. (p. 166)

#105. **a) Large pleasure boats.**

Inland Marine coverage can be issued for almost any type of moveable property. A large pleasure boat, like a yacht, would be insured under a Yacht policy. (pp. 168, 172)

#106. **a) Each 30-day period.**

Premiums will be returned on a pro rata basis for each 30 consecutive day period laid up in port not under repair and not being used for lighting or storage. (p. 299)

#107. **d) Pollution.**

The businessowners liability coverage form explicitly excludes claims resulting from pollution. (p. 291)

#108. **c) Obtain the consent of the insured.**

Under a professional liability policy, after a claim is filed, the insurance provider must obtain the insured's consent before paying a claimant and settling the claim. (p. 229)

#109. **d) The applicant has a prior felony conviction**

A contract's competent parties must be mentally competent to comprehend the contract, of legal age, and not under the influence of alcohol or drugs. It is legal for a person convicted of a felony to purchase an insurance contract. (p. 14)

#110. **b) It grants the insurance provider the right to inspect issued insurance**

A common policy condition allows the insurance provider to inspect the insured's premises and make recommendations based on what is found. (p. 188)

#111. **d) A divorced spouse residing in another state**

Insureds are the named insured and their spouse if they reside in the same household. Insureds also include individuals related to the named insured by blood or marriage. (p. 115)

#112. **a) $500 for business personal property on the insured premises.**

A special limit covered under a homeowners policy is $2,500 for business personal property on the insured premises. (p. 132)

#113. **c) Sound reproduction equipment permanently installed in the insured auto**

Sound reproduction equipment is covered if the manufacturer installed it. (p. 153)

#114. **c) 120 days.**

In the Common Conditions of a commercial crime coverage section, in the event of a loss, written proof of loss has to be submitted to the insurance provider within 120 days of request. (p. 255)

#115. **a) $1,000.**

Towers, antennas, and satellite dishes attached to the dwelling are covered under Coverage A but have a special limit of insurance of $1,000 in any one occurrence. (p. 270)

#116. **b) Insurers will not cover any auto stored for more than 45 days at a location not listed in the Declarations.**

Collision coverage is not for any specific risk. Autos held for sale are covered when Symbol 31 is listed in the Declarations. The specific causes of loss coverage will be available for physical damage coverage. (pp. 243-244)

#117. **d) The underwriters approve the application**

Acceptance occurs when an insurance provider's underwriter approves the application and issues a policy. (p. 14)

#118. **b) 24**

All brokers and agents must complete 24 hours of continuing education (CE), including three hours of ethics for every 2-year license term. (p.)

#119. **c) $1,000**

As an additional coverage, homeowners policies will cover up to $1,000 of a loss assessment. (p. 134)

#120. **d) Leaves the car in a parking garage, and the car is involved in an accident.**

The personal auto policy is excess coverage when the insured's car is left at a facility, such as a parking garage, and the vehicle is involved in an accident. (pp. 146-147)

#121. **d) The insured causes a collision with an uninsured motorist's car**

Uninsured motorist coverage applies to the insured, resident relatives, and those occupying the covered auto. (pp. 151-152)

#122. **a) Directors and officers liability**

Directors and officers liability coverage will protect directors and officers of an organization from any claims for losses resulting from a wrongful act made while serving in an official capacity. (p. 226)

#123. **a) The named insured.**

The terms "you" and "your" used throughout the personal auto policy (PAP) refer to the named insured listed in the Declarations. (p. 144)

#124. **b) $5,000.**

A commercial property special form insures property in transit up to $5,000. This extension of coverage can be attached to the special form. It is additional insurance (in addition to the coverage limit), and coinsurance is not applied. (p. 203)

#125. **a) Breakage of glass**

In the basic form dwelling policy, breakage of glass is not a peril or cause of loss that is covered. However, it is insured under the broad form. (pp. 93-95, 95, 96)

#126. **b) HO-6**

The HO-6 condominium unit-owners form is designed for the owner-occupant of a condo. (pp. 114-115)

#127. **c) Barry's Boatowners policy**

Boatowners policies include property, liability, and medical payments coverage. (pp. 170-172)

#128. **c) A house**

Personal property refers to moveable property; real property is non-moveable. (p. 87)

#129. **d) Insurance.**

Insurance is a contract in which one individual seeks to indemnify another individual against damage, loss, or liability resulting from a contingent or unknown event. (p. 2)

#130. **d) 72 hours**

The period of restoration for business income coverage starts 72 hours after the direct loss or immediately for extra expense coverage. (p. 195)

#131. **d) Contractors equipment floater**

The contractors equipment floater insures equipment that is left unattended on a job site until the project is completed. (p. 262)

#132. **a) Conditional**

A conditional contract requires that certain conditions be met by the policy owner and the insurance provider for the contract to be executed and before each party fulfills its obligations. (p. 15)

#133. **c) Coverage E – Personal Liability**

Coverage E – Personal liability in a homeowners policy will respond if a claim is made or a lawsuit is brought against an insured for damages due to property damage or bodily injury caused by a covered occurrence. (p. 138)

#134. **c) An insured who cuts their leg while whacking weeds in their backyard with their neighbor's weed whacker**

Medical payments to others will cover invitees, residence employees, and injury to others caused by animals in the insured's control. If the insured is injured, separate insurance would be needed for their injuries. (p. 138)

#135. **b) By mailing the insurer a written notice of cancellation at any time.**

The insured can cancel the policy at any time by mailing the insurer a written notice of cancellation. (p. 85)

#136. **d) Negligence**

An unintentional tort is a result of acting without proper care. This concept is commonly referred to as negligence. (p. 14)

#137. **d) The amount of the loss of rent and additional living expenses.**

Loss of use is typically limited to a percentage of the overall dwelling or personal property coverage (when dealing with HO-4 and HO-6 forms). (pp. 115, 133)

#138. **c) Exposure**

Exposure is a unit of measurement used to calculate premium rates charged for insurance coverage. (p. 3)

#139. **d) Other-than-collision**

Insurers would cover damage from contact with birds or animals or damage from a falling object under other-than-collision coverage. (p. 145)

#140. **d) An employee is caught stealing from the cash register**

Dishonest or criminal acts of any representative or employee are expressly excluded. (p. 254)

#141. c) Land on which the dwelling is located

The insurance provider will not cover any land, including land on which the dwelling described in the Declarations is located. (p. 98)

#142. a) Scheduled personal property endorsement.

The scheduled personal property endorsement covers personal property with high values, such as jewelry, antiques, and furs. (pp. 122-123)

#143. b) Foreign

A foreign insurance provider is domiciled in one state and transacts insurance in another. A domestic insurance provider transacts insurance in the domicile state (in this case, Wyoming). An alien insurance provider is domiciled in one country and transacts insurance in another. (p. 43)

#144. c) Compensatory benefits.

Under workers compensation, awards for pain and suffering are not compensated. (p. 316)

#145. c) Owned Watercraft liability.

The additional coverages include Fire Legal liability, Personal and Advertising Injury, Limited Non-owned Watercraft liability, Incidental Medical malpractice, and Broader Host Liquor liability. (p. 238)

#146. a) Umbrella

Umbrella liability policies offer coverage that provides extra protection against liability and an excess amount of insurance above the primary policy. (p. 302)

#147. c) Consequential

Consequential loss, also called indirect loss, is a second financial loss caused by a covered direct loss. (p. 77)

#148. b) A salvage loss.

Suppose the cargo is damaged short of the destination port. In that situation, an agent of the insurance provider at an intermediate port can agree to sell it at the best price. The settlement will be based on the difference between the net proceeds of the sale and the insured value. This settlement is referred to as a salvage loss. (p. 303)

#149. b) Deliberate law violation.

Claims arising due to intentional acts of the insured are not covered. (pp. 226-227)

#150. d) Legal purpose

Insurance contracts must be written for a lawful reason. They cannot go against public policy. This requirement is known as legal purpose. (p. 15)

INDEX

A NOTE FROM LELAND

What did you think of *California Property and Casualty Insurance License Exam Prep*?

First of all, thank you for purchasing this study guide. I know you could have picked any resource to help prepare for your Property and Casualty exam, but you chose this book, and I am incredibly grateful.

I hope that it added value and provided the confidence to pass the exam on your first attempt. If you feel this book adequately prepared you and helped you pass the exam, I'd like to hear from you. I hope you can take some time to post a review on Amazon and include a screenshot of your passing score. Your feedback and support will help this author improve this book and his writing craft for future projects.

Thank you again, and I wish you all the best in your future success!

Leland Chant

Made in the USA
Las Vegas, NV
30 April 2024

89358380R00254